The LEAGUE of EXTRAORDINARY GENTLEMEN

Volume II

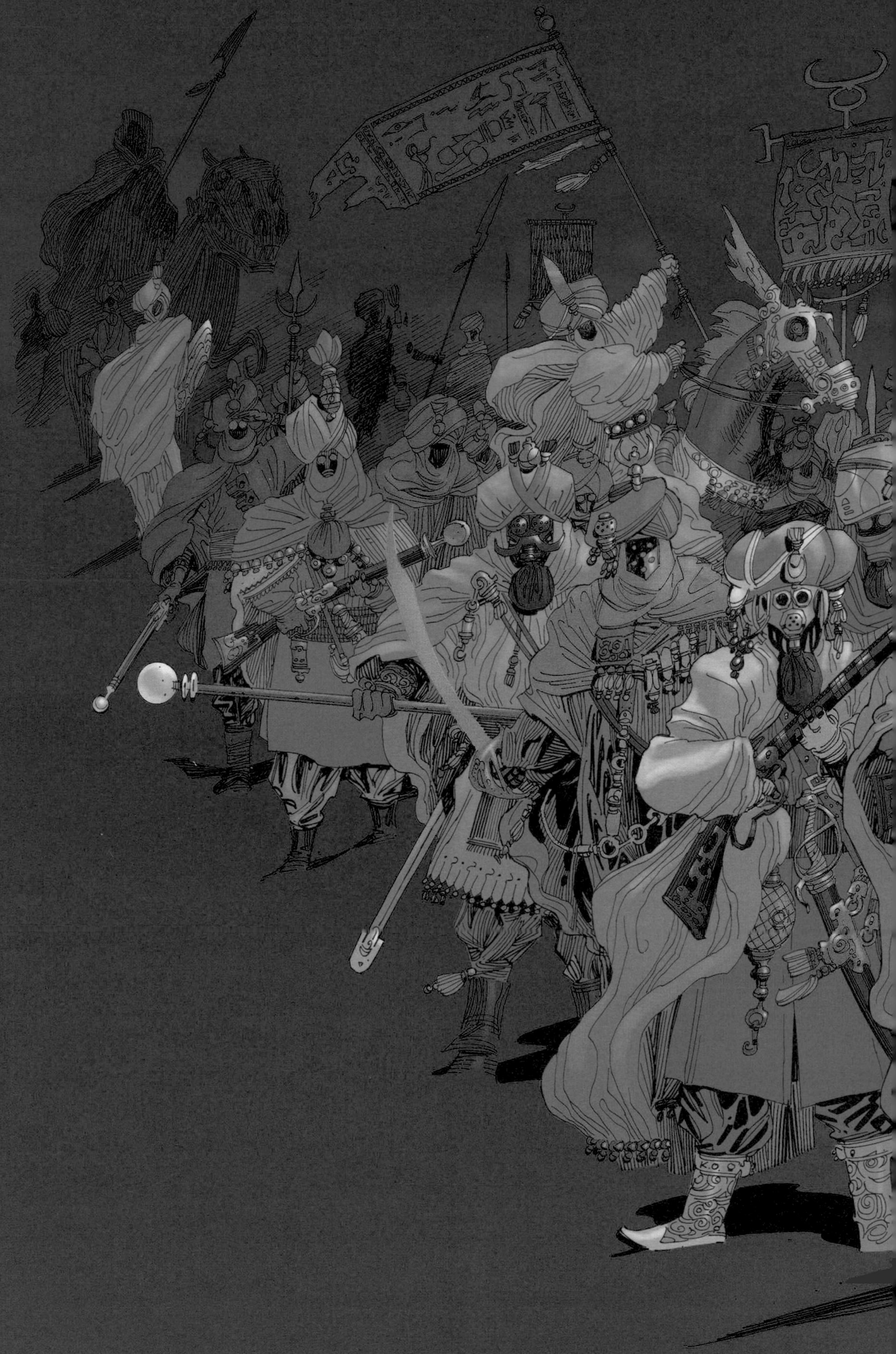
K.O.

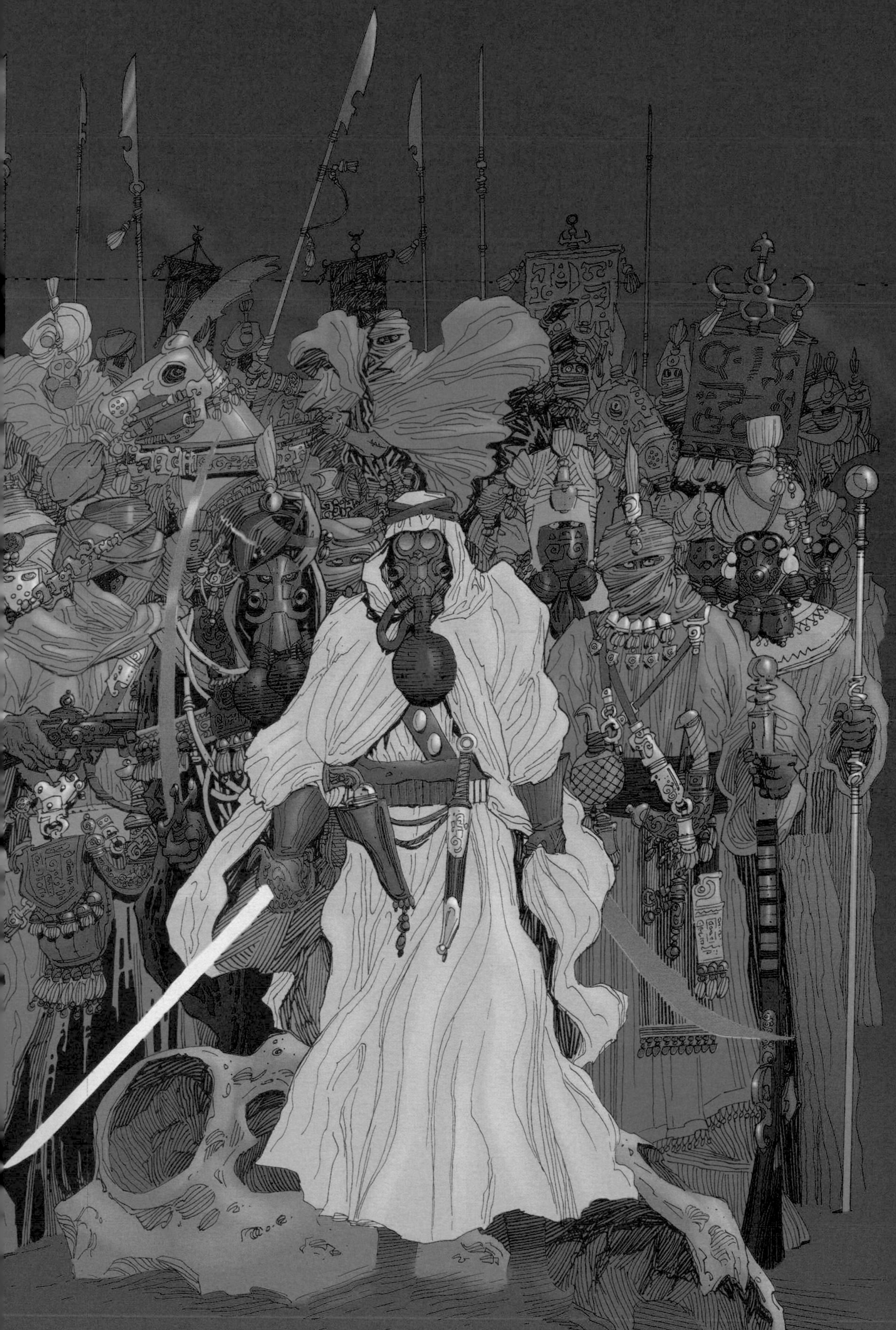

THE LEAGUE OF EXTRAORDINARY GENTLEMEN

VOLUME TWO

PRESENTED BY CO-CREATORS

MR. ALAN MOORE
— WRITER —

MR. KEVIN O'NEILL
— ARTIST —

WITH THE ASSISTANCE OF

MR. BEN DIMAGMALIW
— COLORIST —

MR. WILLIAM OAKLEY
— LETTERER —

MR. TODD KLEIN
— DESIGNER —

MISS KRISTY QUINN
— ASST. EDITOR —

MR. SCOTT DUNBIER
— GROUP EDITOR —

MR. JAMES LEE
EDITORIAL DIRECTOR

MR. JOHN NEE
VP & GENERAL MANAGER

THE LEAGUE OF EXTRAORDINARY GENTLEMEN Volume 2, published by Titan Books, a division of Titan Publishing Group Ltd., 144 Southwark Street, London SE1 0UP. THE LEAGUE OF EXTRAORDINARY GENTLEMEN is ™ and © 2003 Alan Moore and Kevin O'Neill. Cover, design pages and compilation © Alan Moore and Kevin O'Neill. Originally published in single magazine form as The League of Extraordinary Gentlemen Vol. 2 #1-6 © 2002, 2003. All rights reserved. The stories, characters and incidents mentioned in this magazine are entirely fictional. A CIP catalogue record for this book is available from the British Library. Printed in Spain. ISBN: 9781840238488 First published: October 2004.
10 9 8 7 6 5 4 3

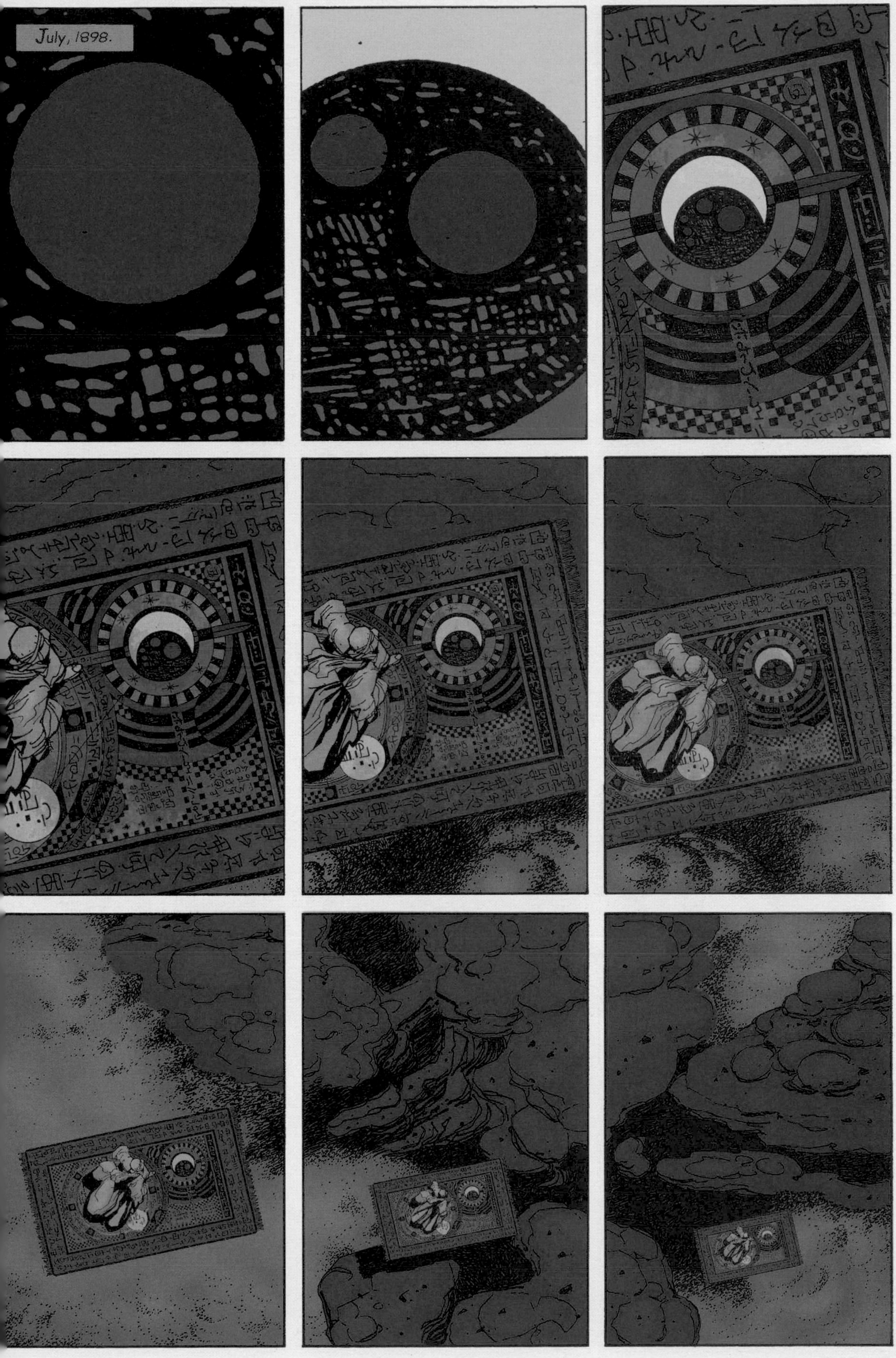
July, 1898.

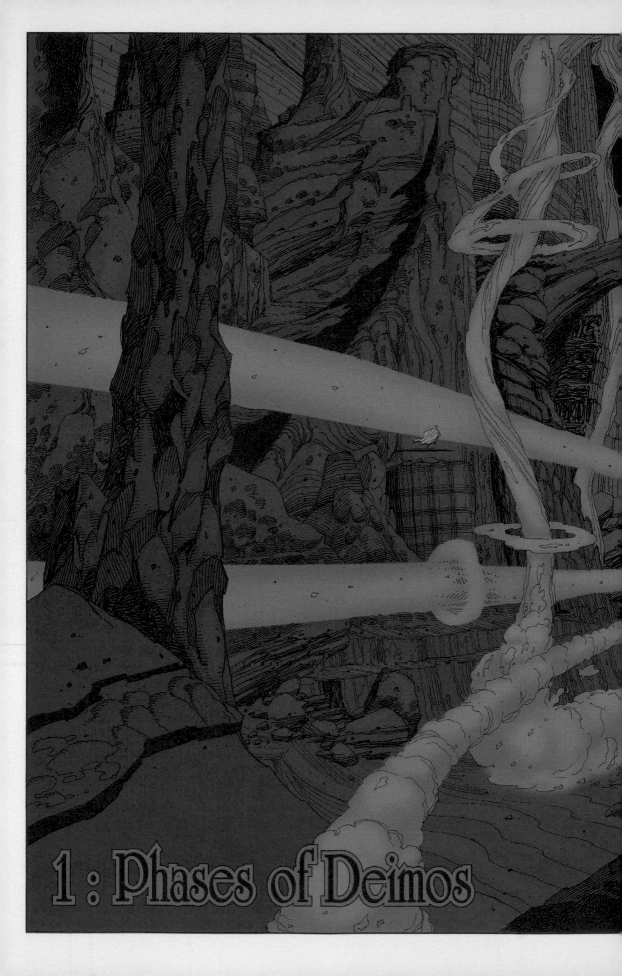

1 : Phases of Deimos

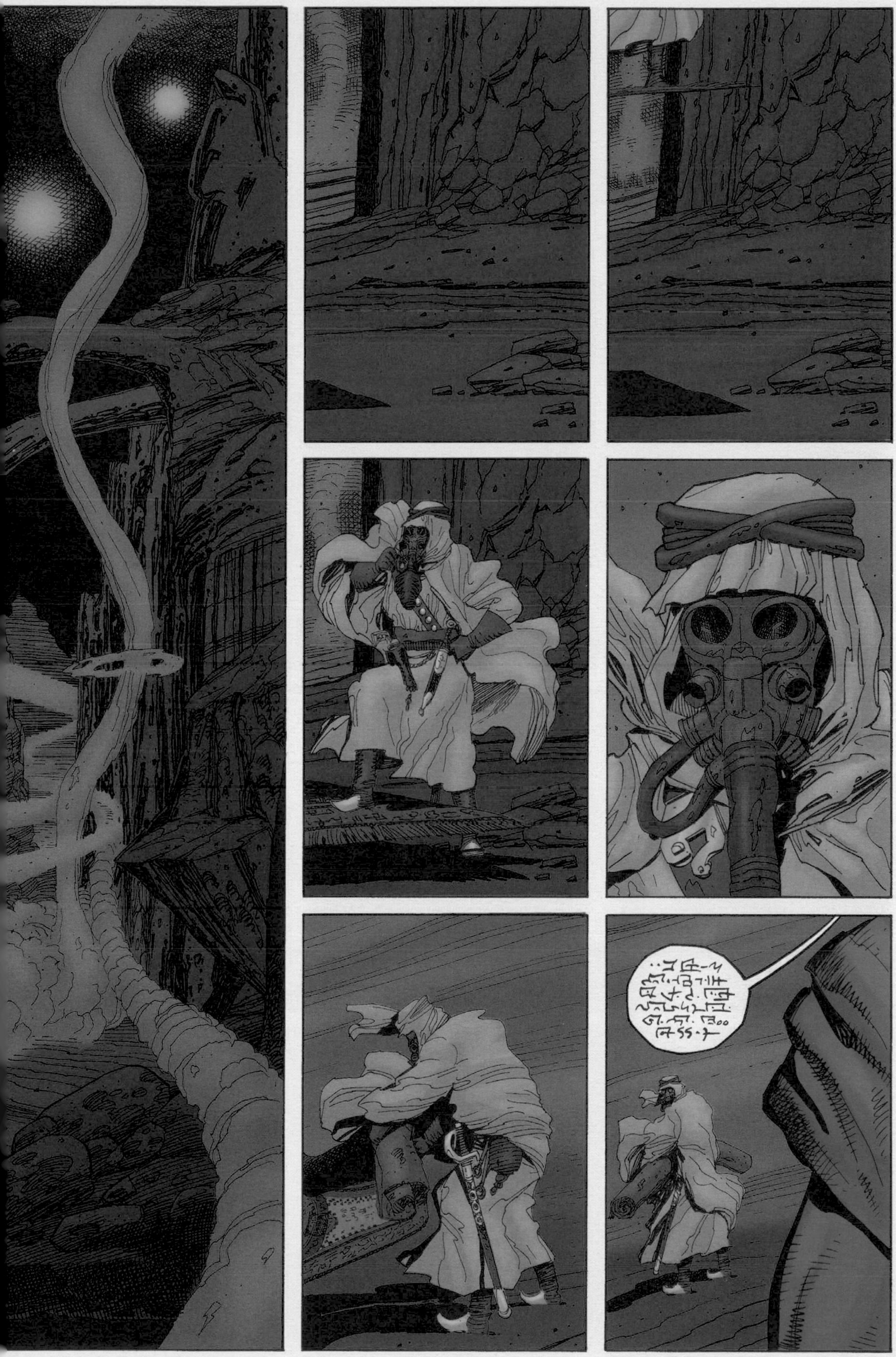

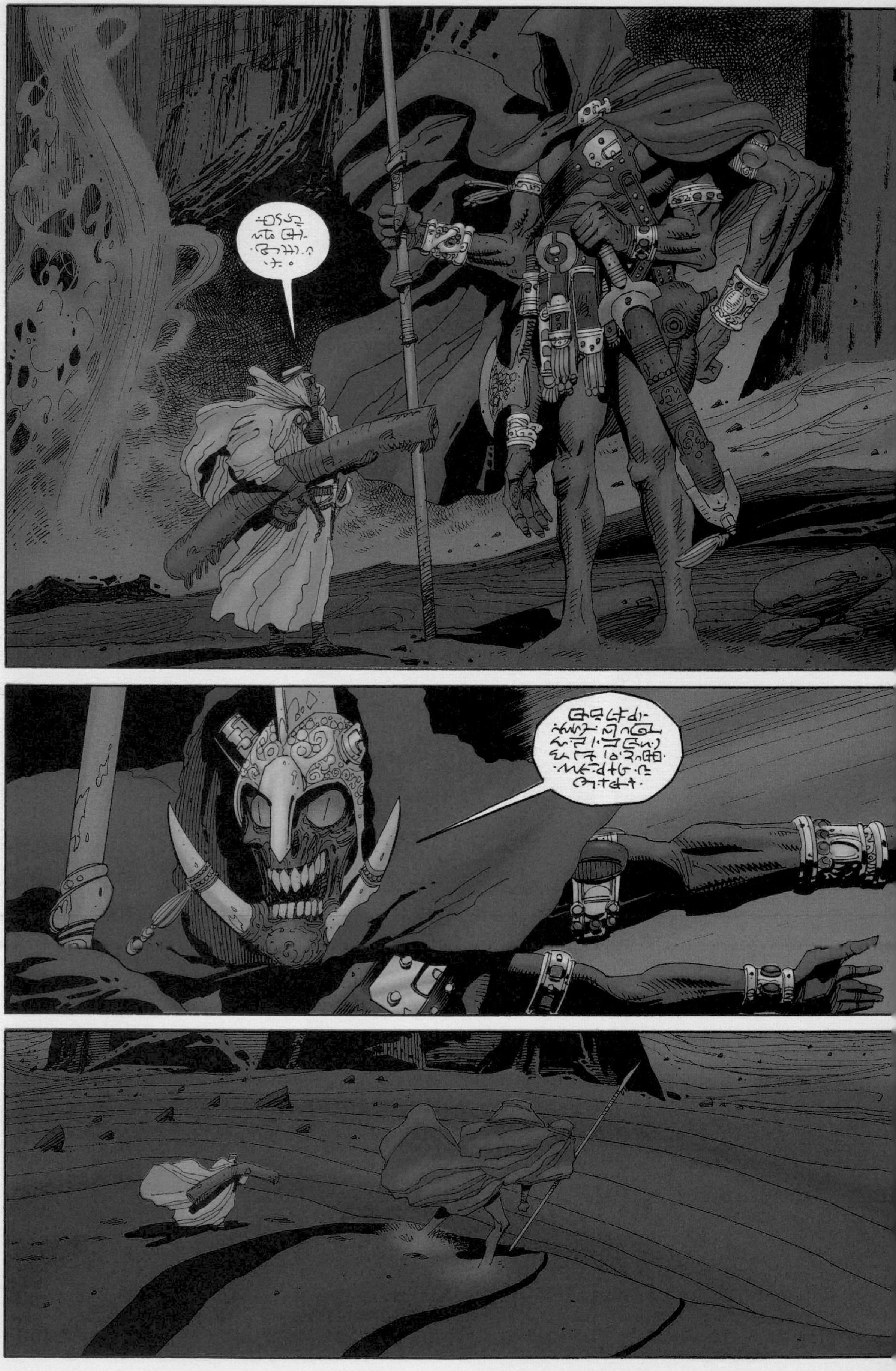

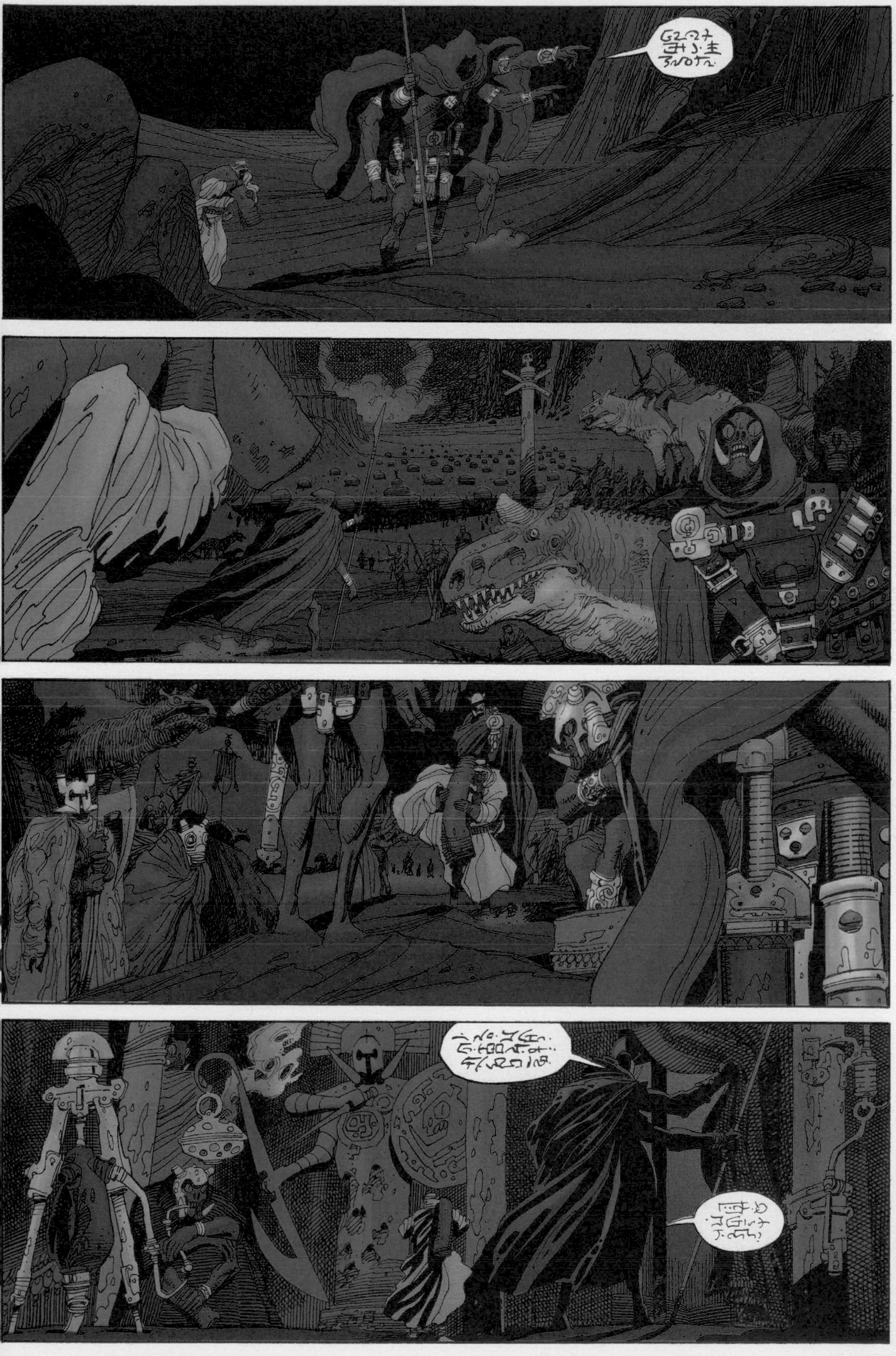

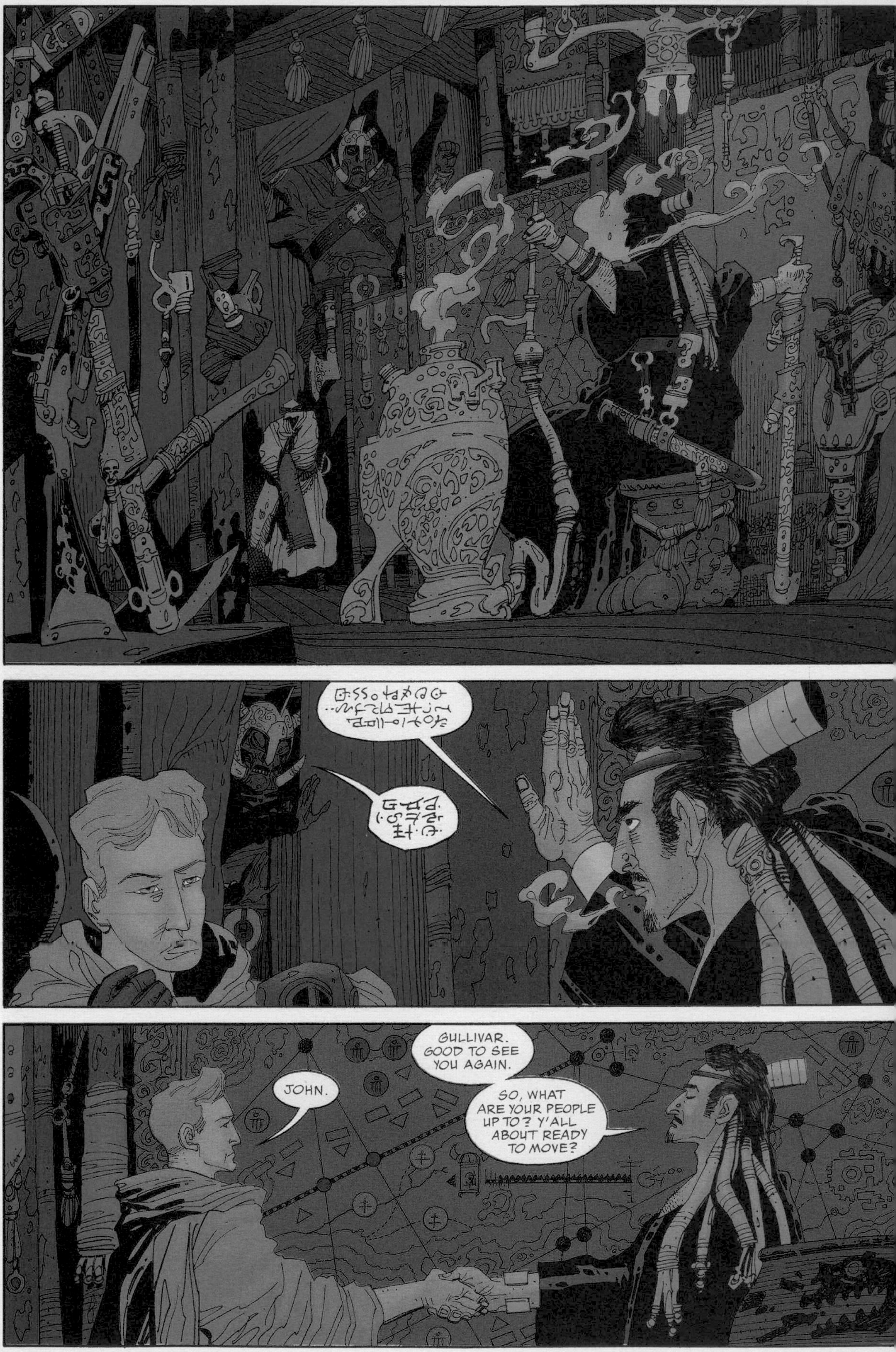
GULLIVAR. GOOD TO SEE YOU AGAIN.
JOHN.
SO, WHAT ARE YOUR PEOPLE UP TO? Y'ALL ABOUT READY TO MOVE?

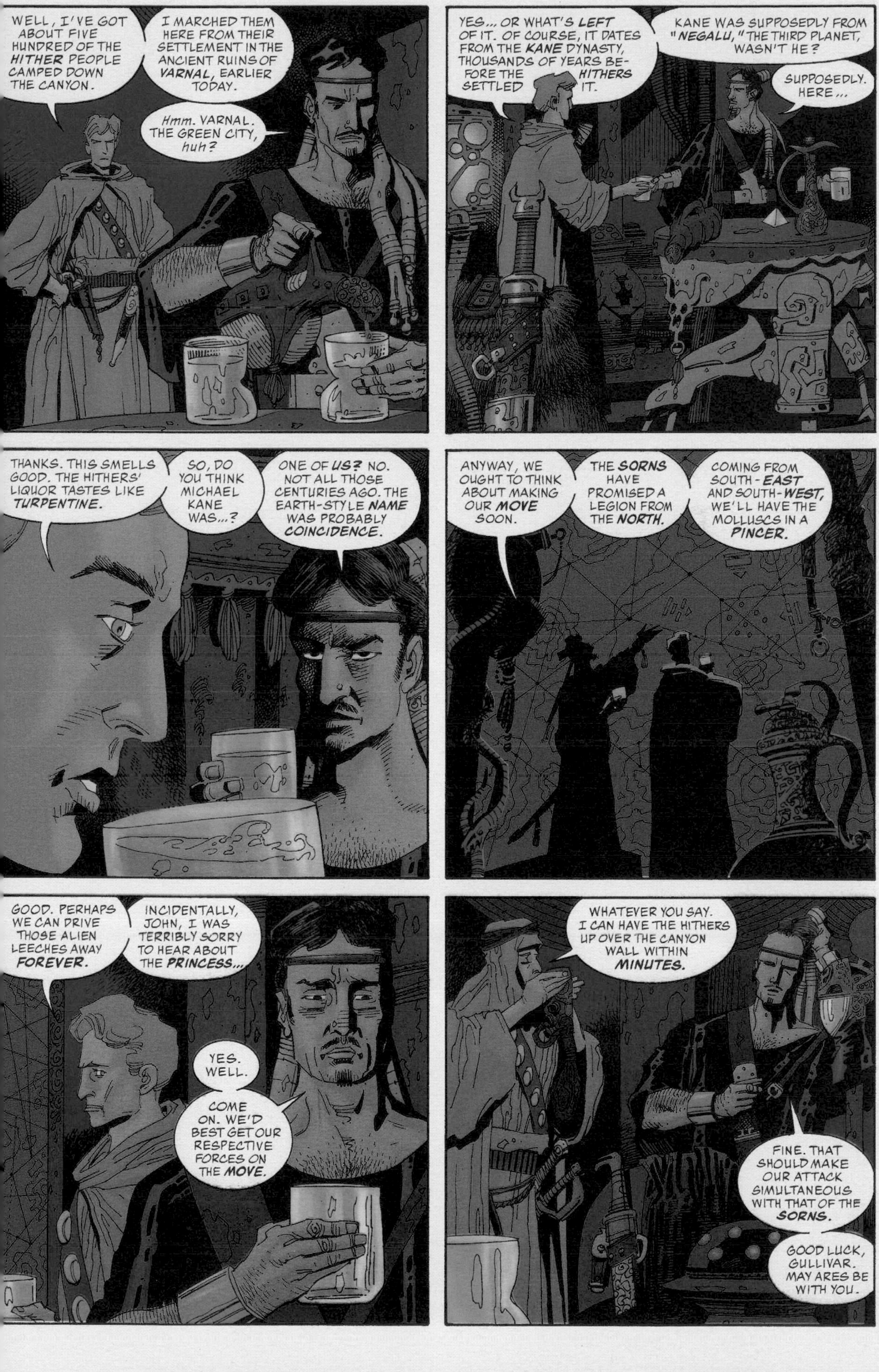

WELL, I'VE GOT ABOUT FIVE HUNDRED OF THE HITHER PEOPLE CAMPED DOWN THE CANYON.
I MARCHED THEM HERE FROM THEIR SETTLEMENT IN THE ANCIENT RUINS OF VARNAL, EARLIER TODAY.
Hmm. VARNAL. THE GREEN CITY, huh?
YES... OR WHAT'S LEFT OF IT. OF COURSE, IT DATES FROM THE KANE DYNASTY, THOUSANDS OF YEARS BEFORE THE HITHERS SETTLED IT.
KANE WAS SUPPOSEDLY FROM "NEGALU," THE THIRD PLANET, WASN'T HE?
SUPPOSEDLY. HERE...
THANKS. THIS SMELLS GOOD. THE HITHERS' LIQUOR TASTES LIKE TURPENTINE.
SO, DO YOU THINK MICHAEL KANE WAS...?
ONE OF US? NO. NOT ALL THOSE CENTURIES AGO. THE EARTH-STYLE NAME WAS PROBABLY COINCIDENCE.
ANYWAY, WE OUGHT TO THINK ABOUT MAKING OUR MOVE SOON.
THE SORNS HAVE PROMISED A LEGION FROM THE NORTH.
COMING FROM SOUTH-EAST AND SOUTH-WEST, WE'LL HAVE THE MOLLUSCS IN A PINCER.
GOOD. PERHAPS WE CAN DRIVE THOSE ALIEN LEECHES AWAY FOREVER.
INCIDENTALLY, JOHN, I WAS TERRIBLY SORRY TO HEAR ABOUT THE PRINCESS...
YES. WELL.
COME ON. WE'D BEST GET OUR RESPECTIVE FORCES ON THE MOVE.
WHATEVER YOU SAY. I CAN HAVE THE HITHERS UP OVER THE CANYON WALL WITHIN MINUTES.
FINE. THAT SHOULD MAKE OUR ATTACK SIMULTANEOUS WITH THAT OF THE SORNS.
GOOD LUCK, GULLIVAR. MAY ARES BE WITH YOU.

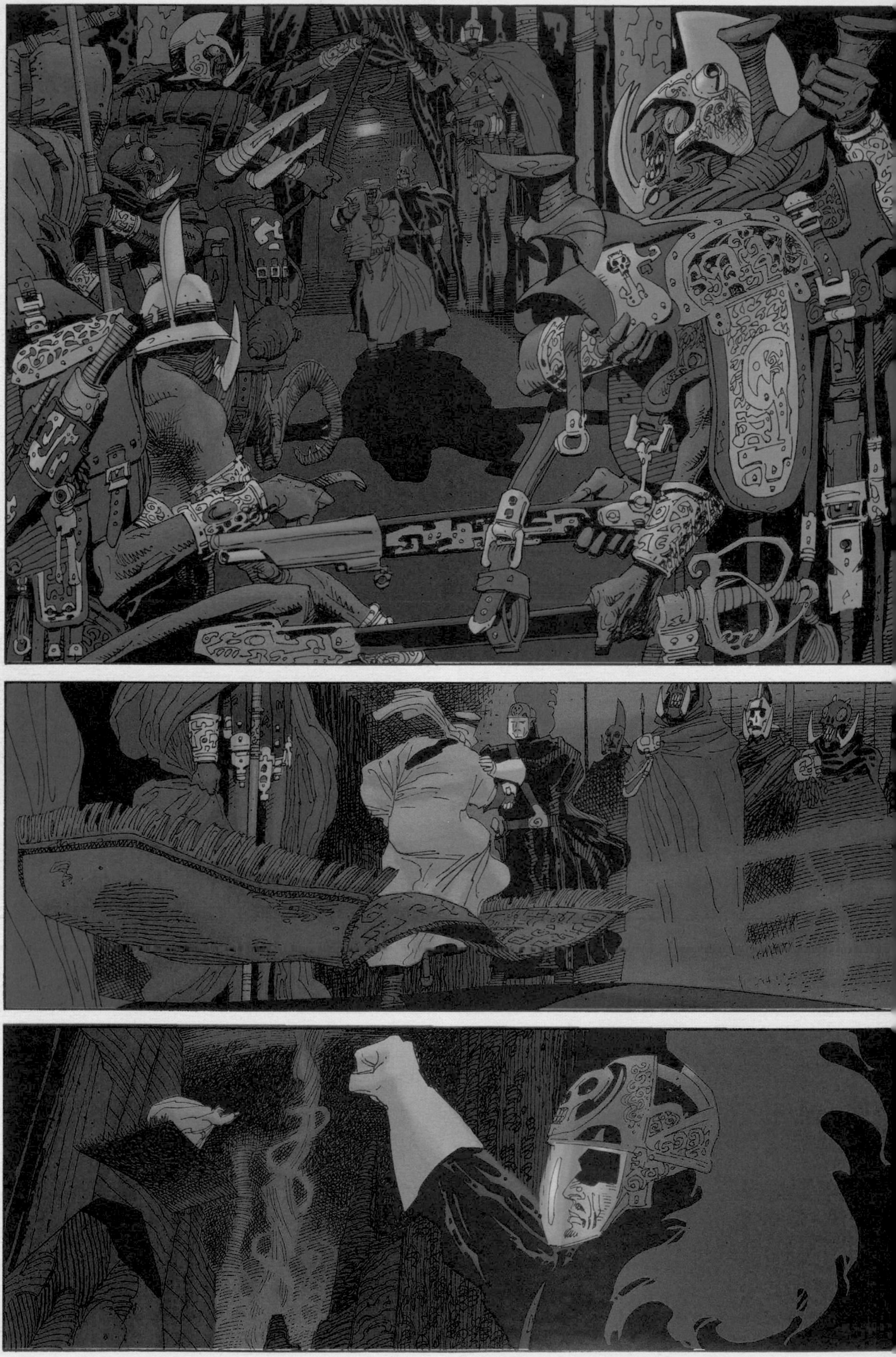

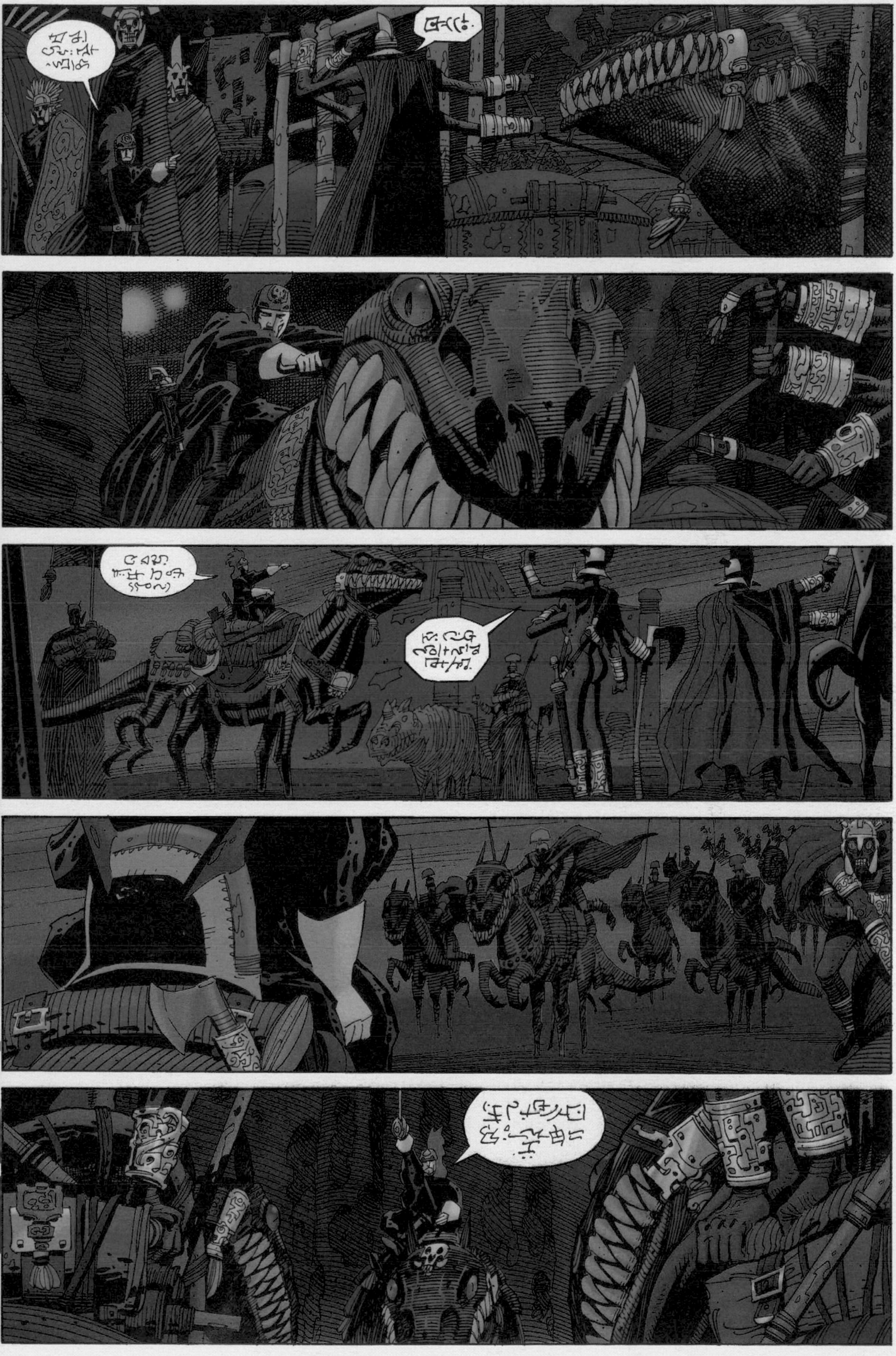

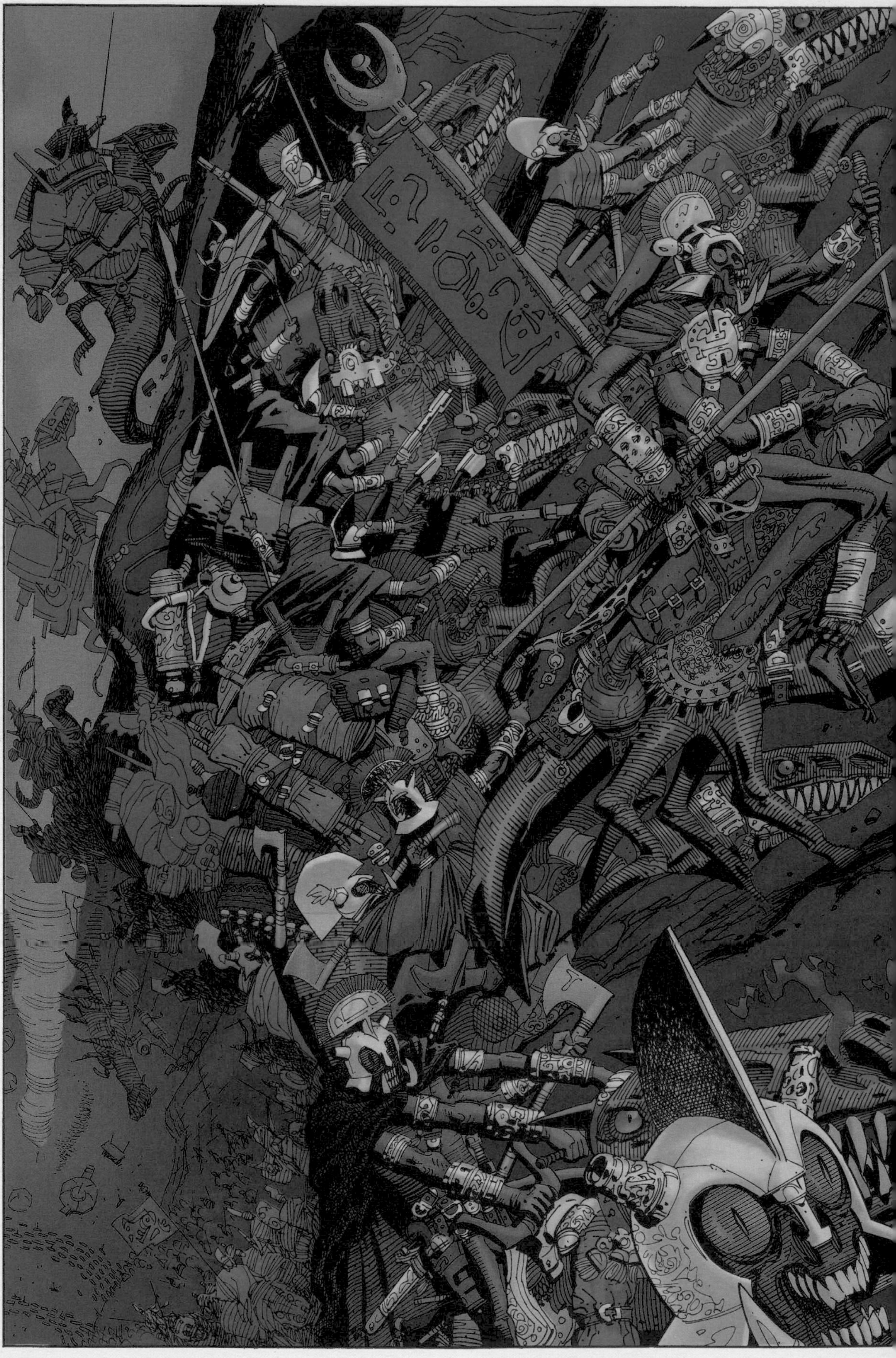

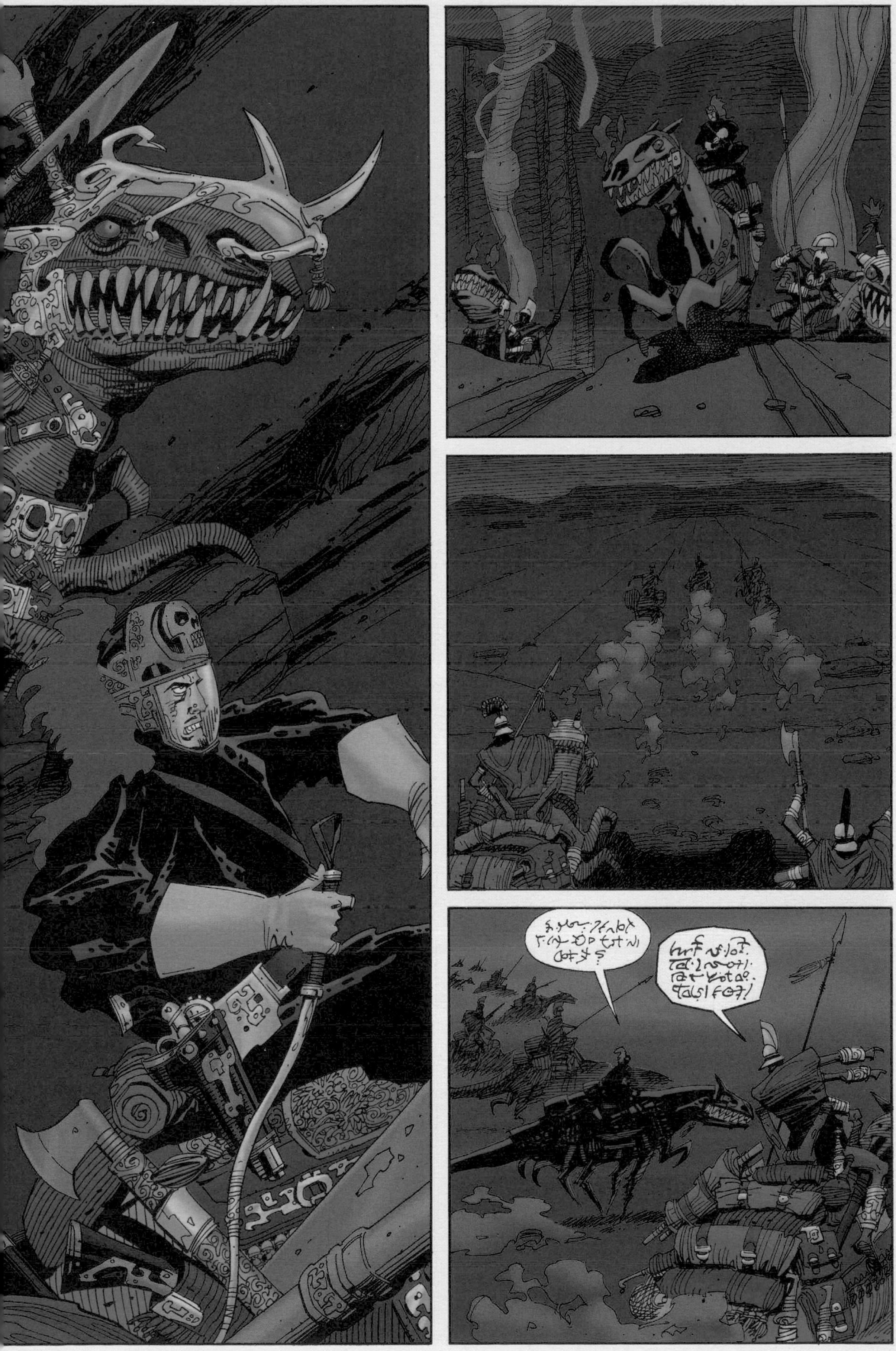

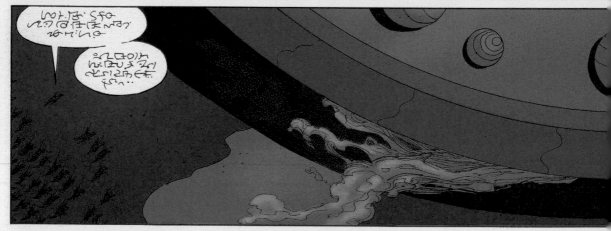

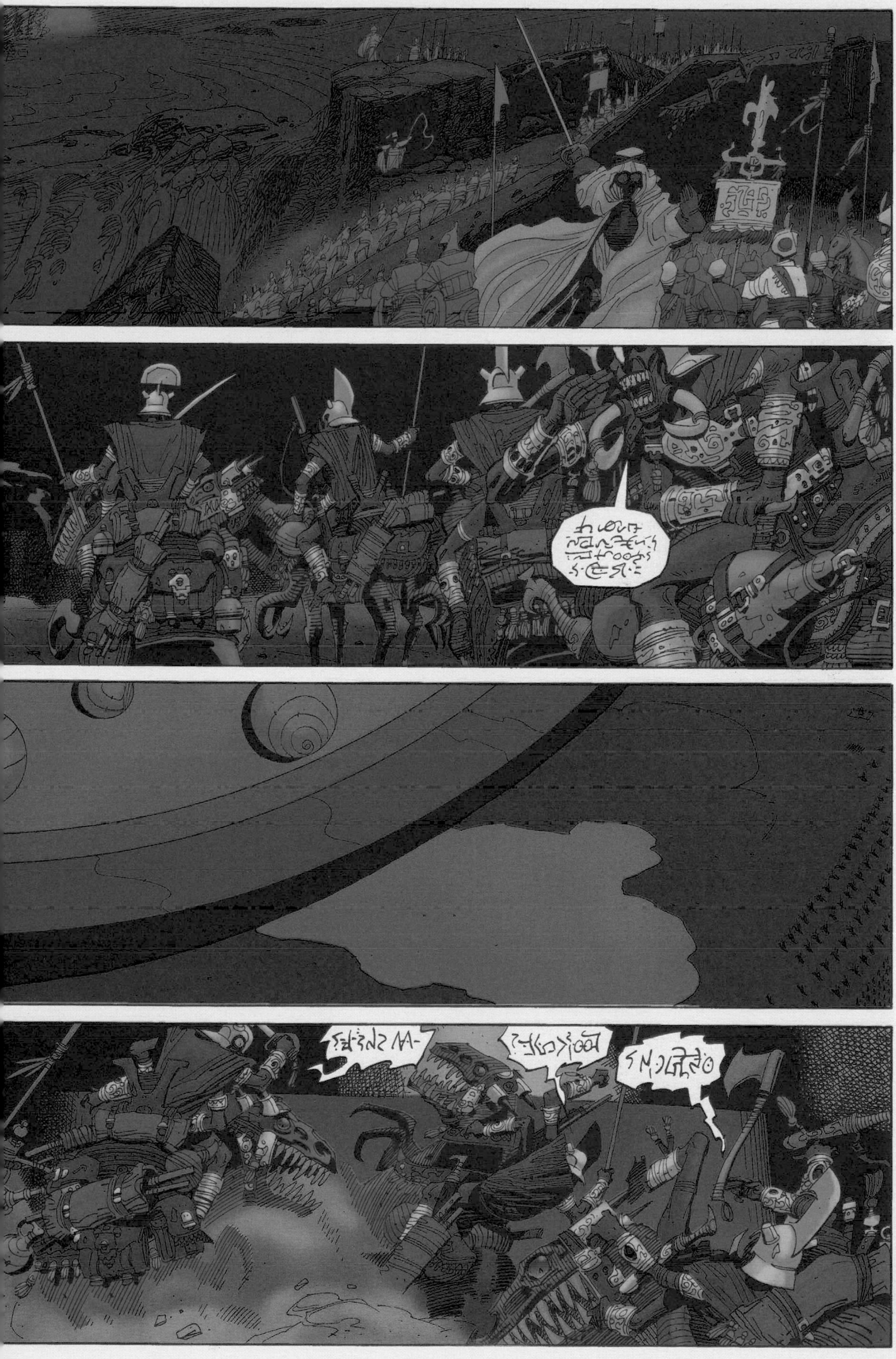

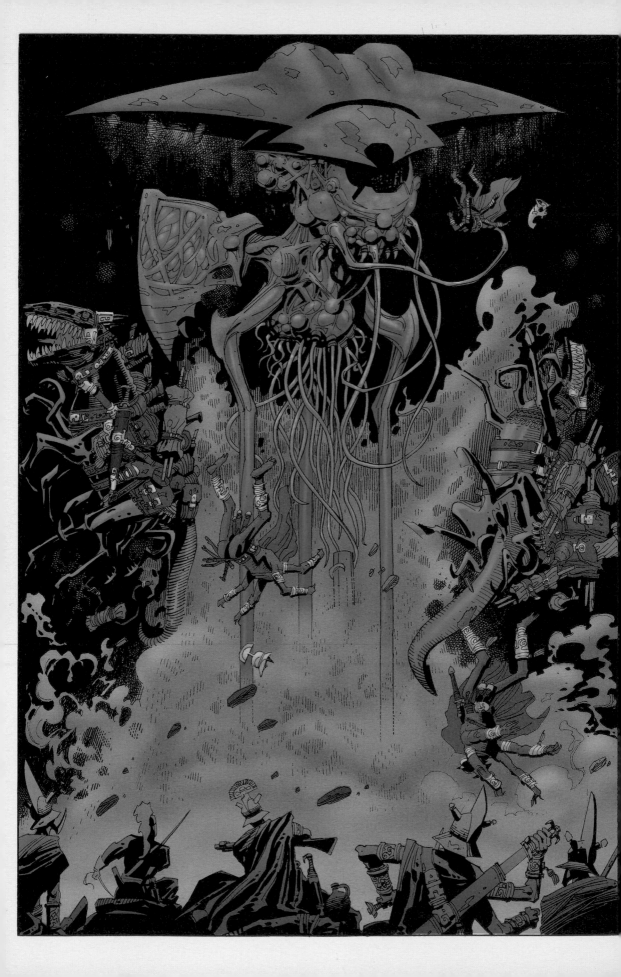

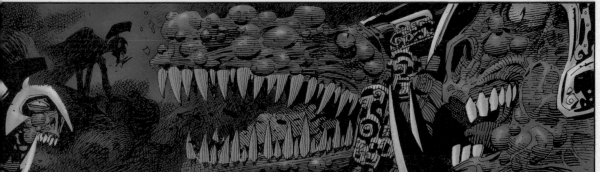

JOHN!

JOHN, DOWN TO THE *SOUTH-EAST*, THEY HAD A *TRIPOD* WAITING! THEY...

O-OH GOD. HERE *TOO?*

I'M AFRAID SO. THE MOLLUSCS ARE USING THEIR *BLACK SMOKE.*

WHAT ABOUT THE HITHERS' *RAY-CANNON?* CAN'T WE AT LEAST *CRIPPLE* THEM?

THE TRIPOD WAS *ON* US BEFORE WE COULD REMOVE ITS *DUST-TARPAULIN.*

JOHN, WE HAVE TO FALL *BACK...*

WAIT A MINUTE.

MAYBE *NOT...*

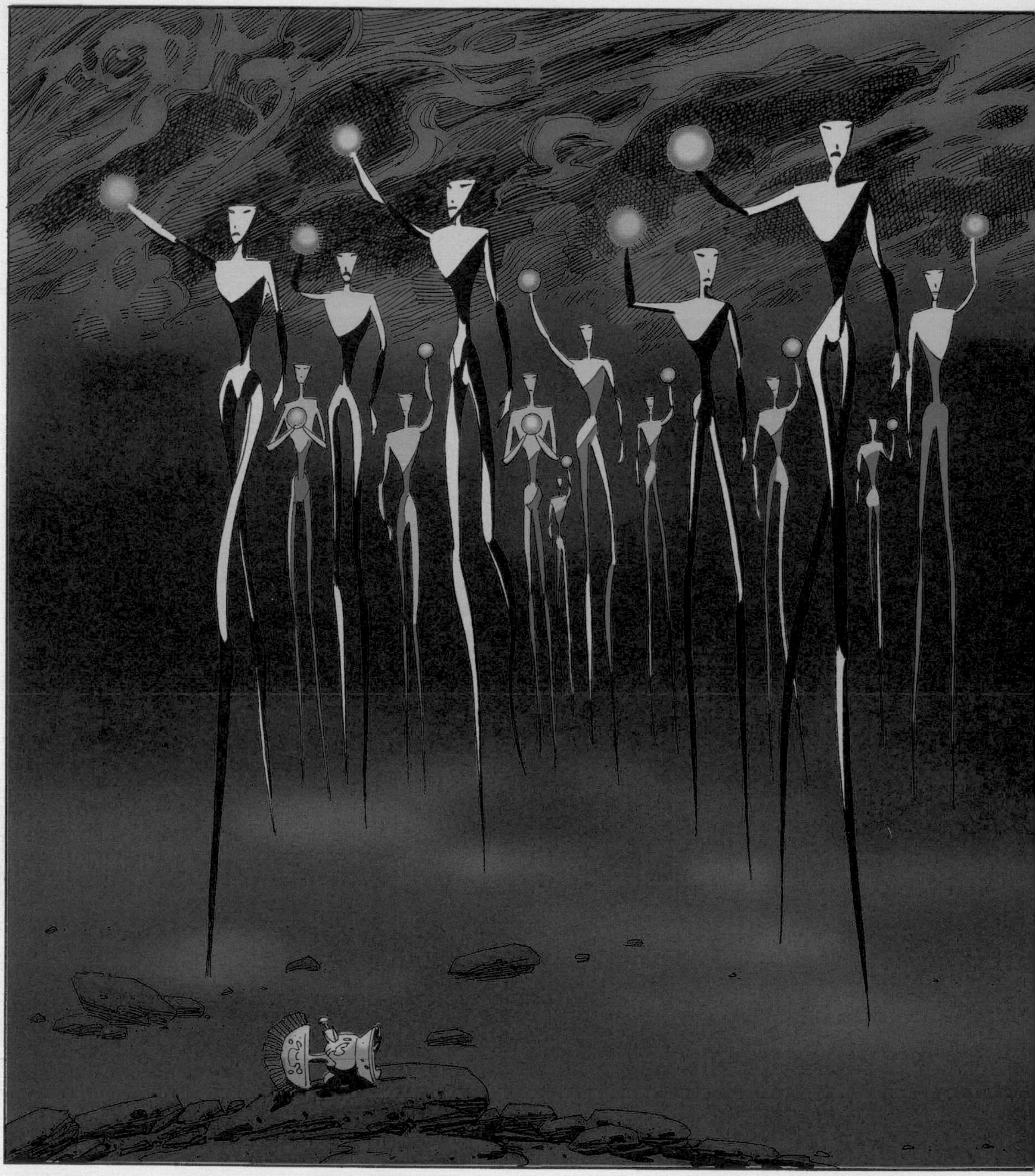

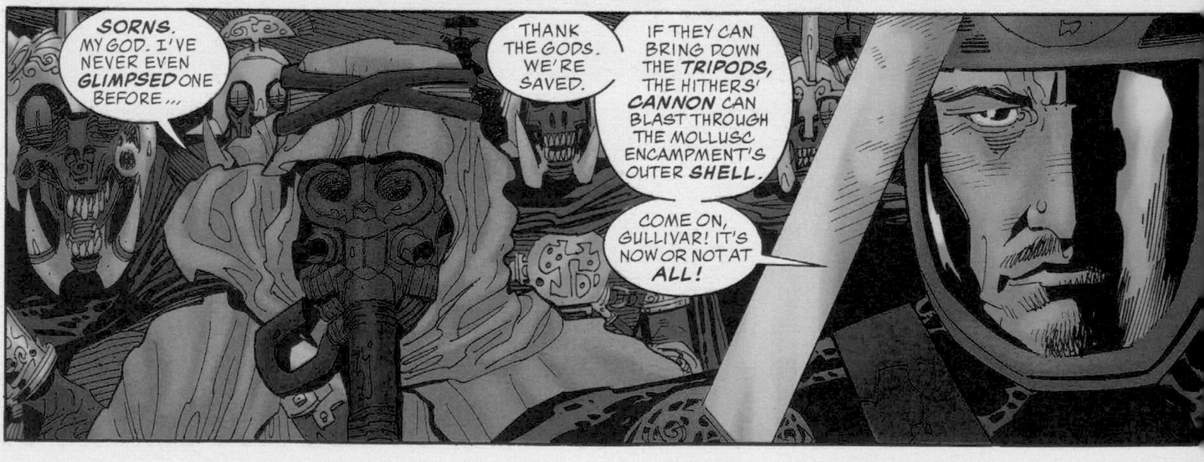
SORNS. MY GOD. I'VE NEVER EVEN GLIMPSED ONE BEFORE...
THANK THE GODS. WE'RE SAVED.
IF THEY CAN BRING DOWN THE TRIPODS, THE HITHERS' CANNON CAN BLAST THROUGH THE MOLLUSC ENCAMPMENT'S OUTER SHELL.
COME ON, GULLIVAR! IT'S NOW OR NOT AT ALL!

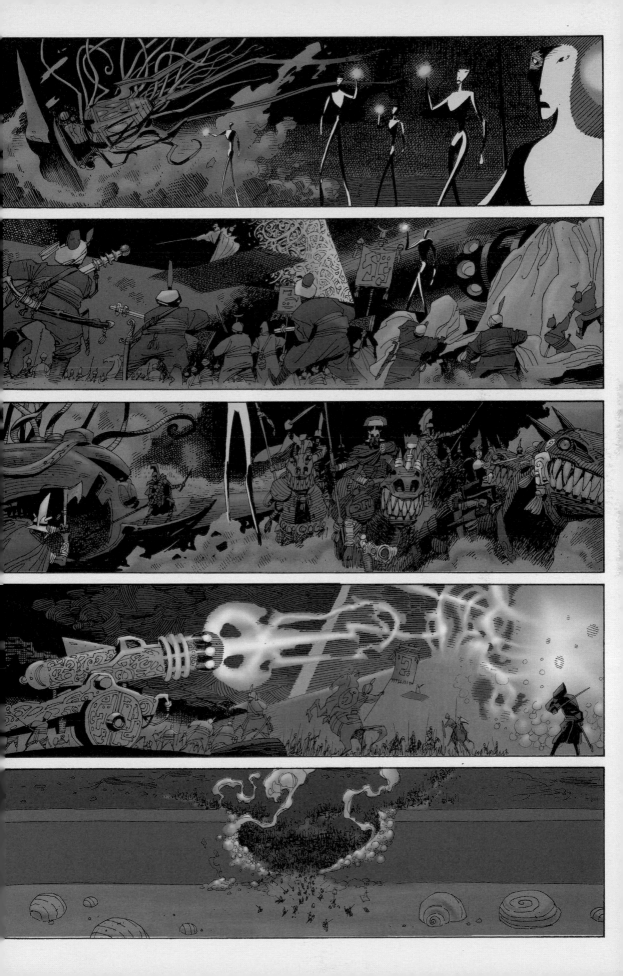

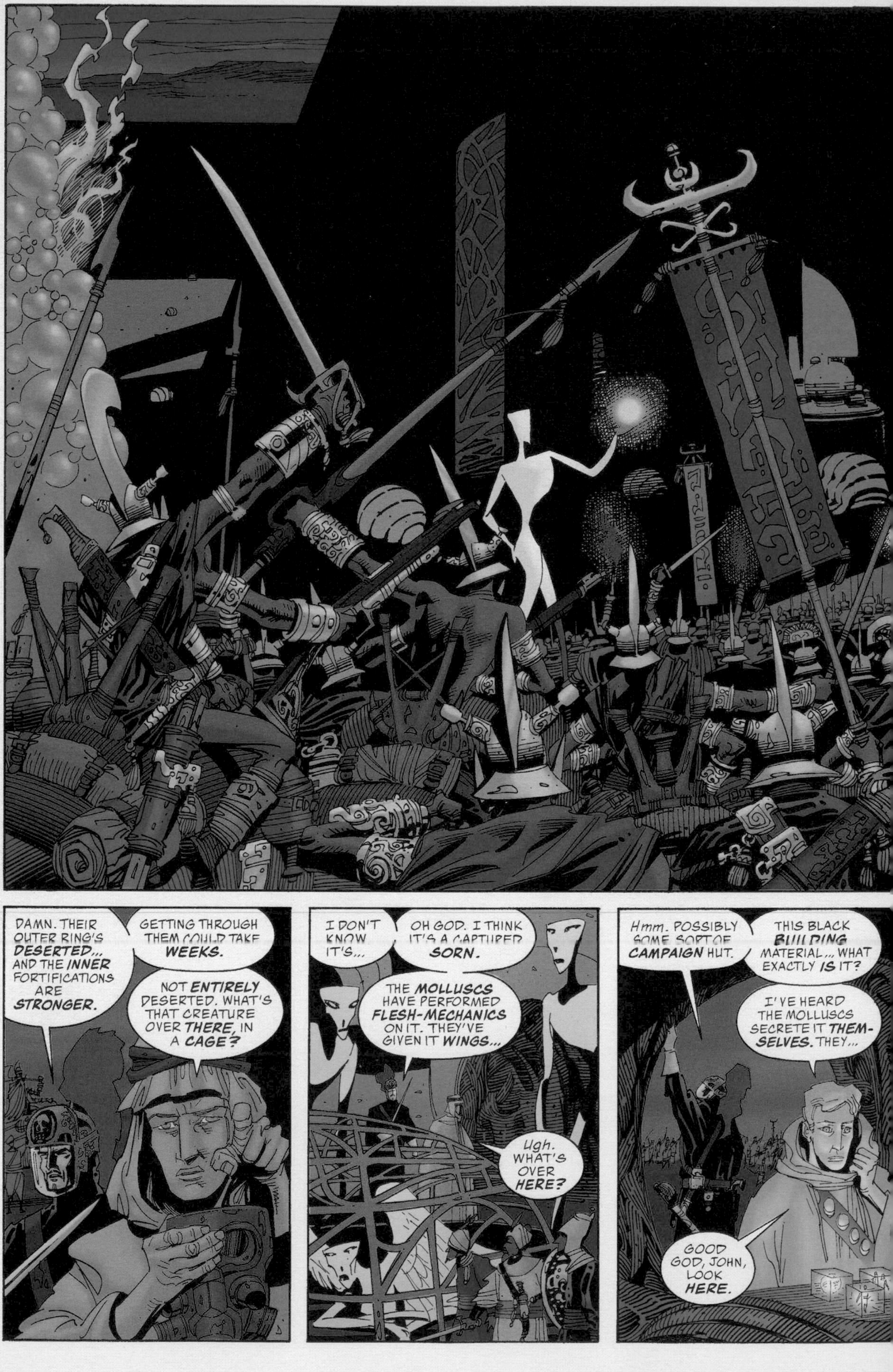
DAMN. THEIR OUTER RING'S **DESERTED...** AND THE **INNER** FORTIFICATIONS ARE **STRONGER.**
GETTING THROUGH THEM COULD TAKE **WEEKS.**
NOT **ENTIRELY** DESERTED. WHAT'S THAT CREATURE OVER **THERE,** IN A **CAGE?**
I DON'T KNOW IT'S...
OH GOD. I THINK IT'S A CAPTURED **SORN.**
THE **MOLLUSCS** HAVE PERFORMED **FLESH-MECHANICS** ON IT. THEY'VE GIVEN IT **WINGS...**
Ugh. WHAT'S OVER **HERE?**
Hmm. POSSIBLY SOME SORT OF **CAMPAIGN** HUT.
THIS BLACK **BUILDING** MATERIAL... WHAT EXACTLY **IS** IT?
I'VE HEARD THE MOLLUSCS SECRETE IT **THEMSELVES.** THEY...
GOOD GOD, JOHN, LOOK **HERE.**

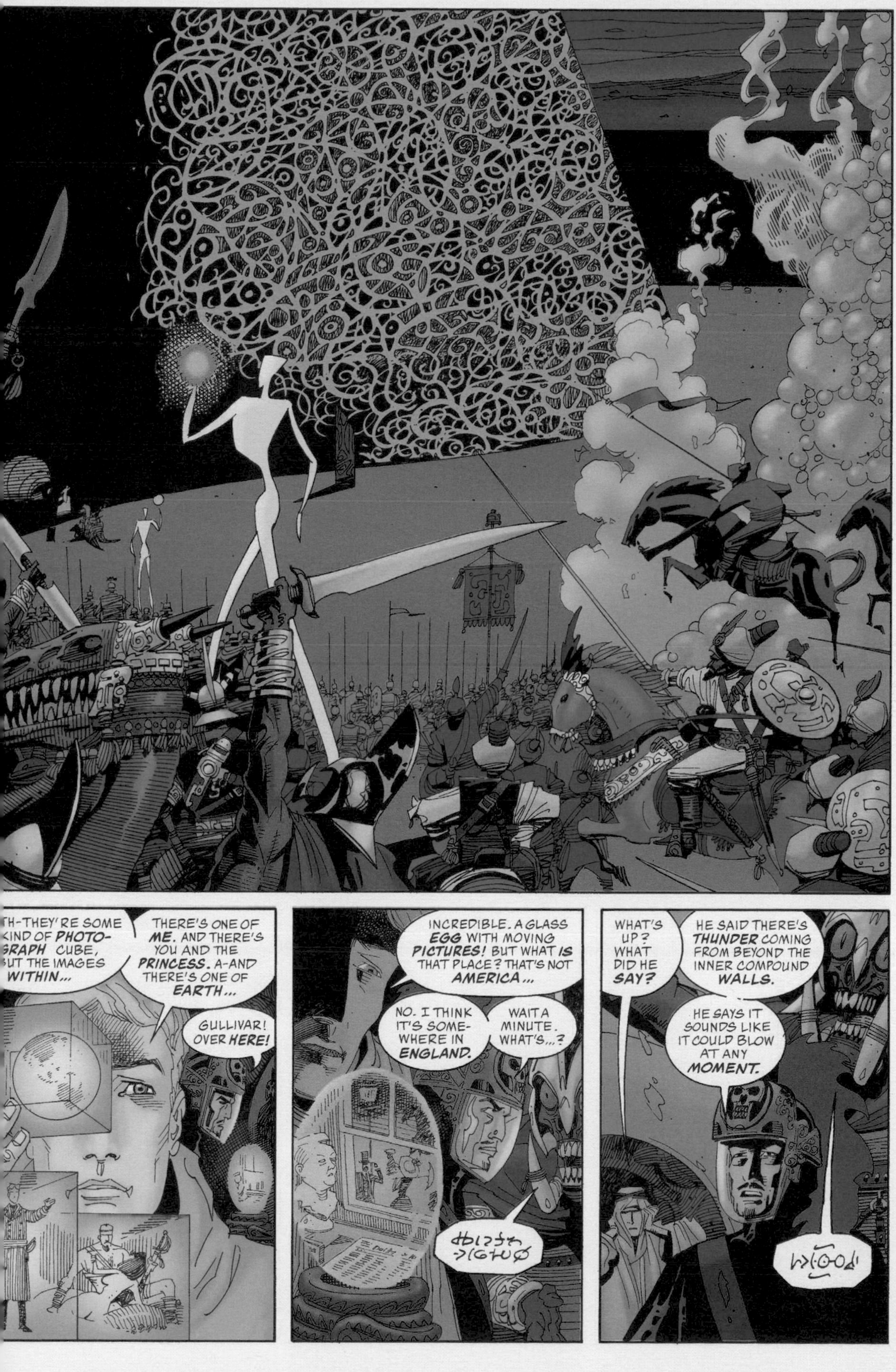

TH-THEY'RE SOME KIND OF PHOTO-GRAPH CUBE, BUT THE IMAGES WITHIN...
THERE'S ONE OF ME. AND THERE'S YOU AND THE PRINCESS. A-AND THERE'S ONE OF EARTH...
GULLIVAR! OVER HERE!
INCREDIBLE. A GLASS EGG WITH MOVING PICTURES! BUT WHAT IS THAT PLACE? THAT'S NOT AMERICA...
NO. I THINK IT'S SOME-WHERE IN ENGLAND.
WAIT A MINUTE. WHAT'S...?
WHAT'S UP? WHAT DID HE SAY?
HE SAID THERE'S THUNDER COMING FROM BEYOND THE INNER COMPOUND WALLS.
HE SAYS IT SOUNDS LIKE IT COULD BLOW AT ANY MOMENT.

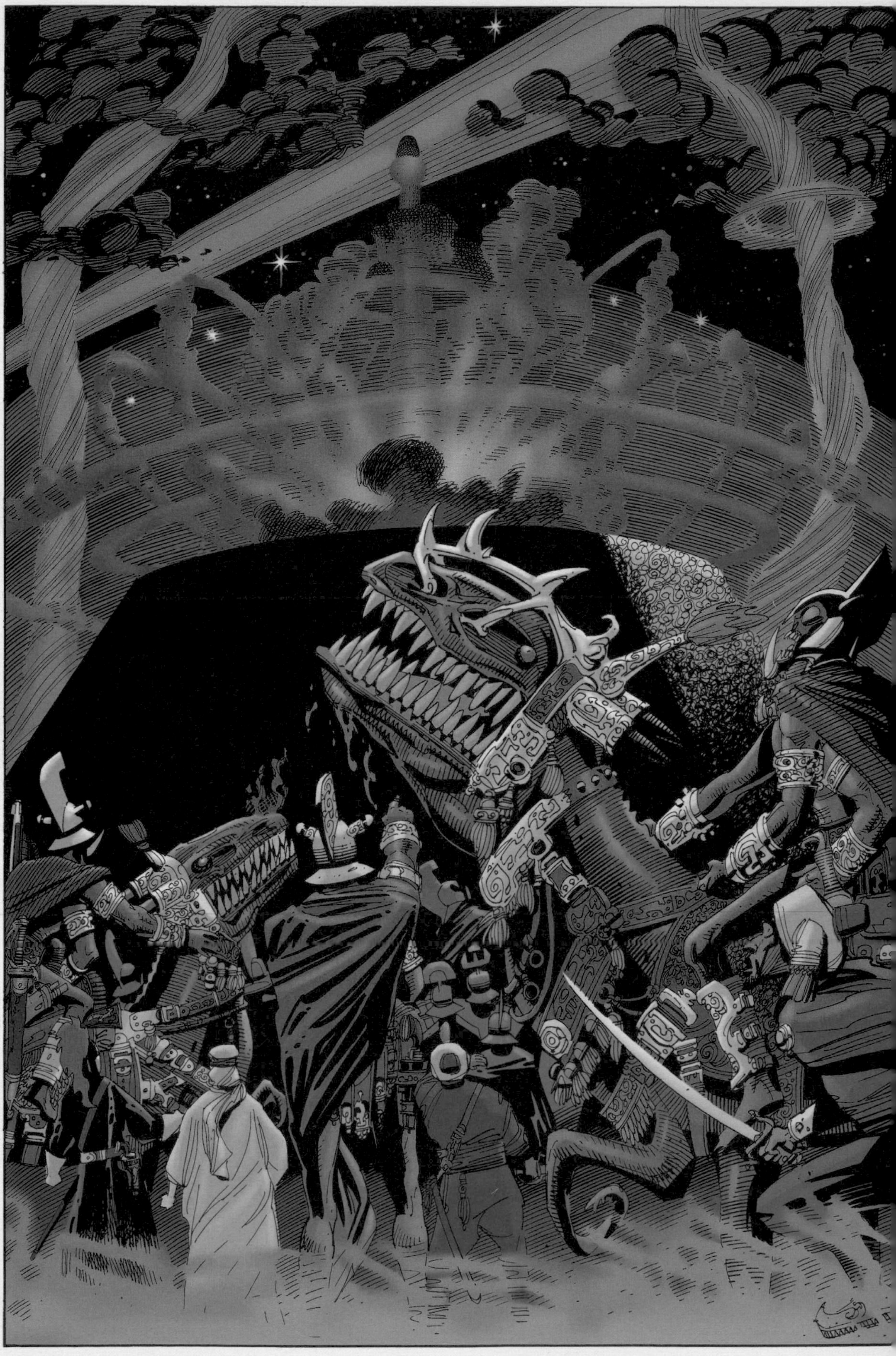

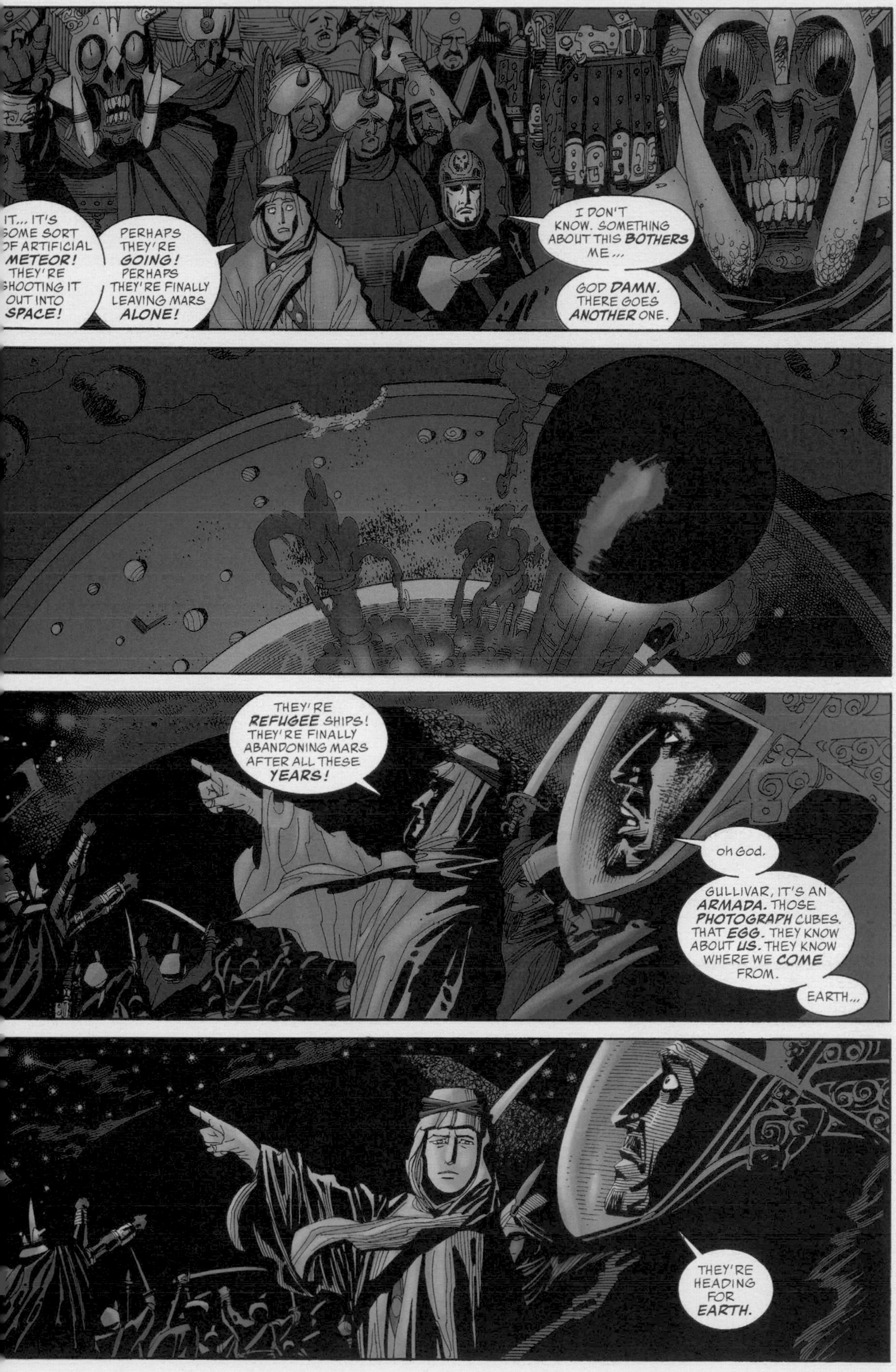
IT... IT'S SOME SORT OF ARTIFICIAL METEOR! THEY'RE SHOOTING IT OUT INTO SPACE!
PERHAPS THEY'RE GOING! PERHAPS THEY'RE FINALLY LEAVING MARS ALONE!
I DON'T KNOW. SOMETHING ABOUT THIS BOTHERS ME...
GOD DAMN. THERE GOES ANOTHER ONE.
THEY'RE REFUGEE SHIPS! THEY'RE FINALLY ABANDONING MARS AFTER ALL THESE YEARS!
oh God.
GULLIVAR, IT'S AN ARMADA. THOSE PHOTOGRAPH CUBES. THAT EGG. THEY KNOW ABOUT US. THEY KNOW WHERE WE COME FROM.
EARTH...
THEY'RE HEADING FOR EARTH.

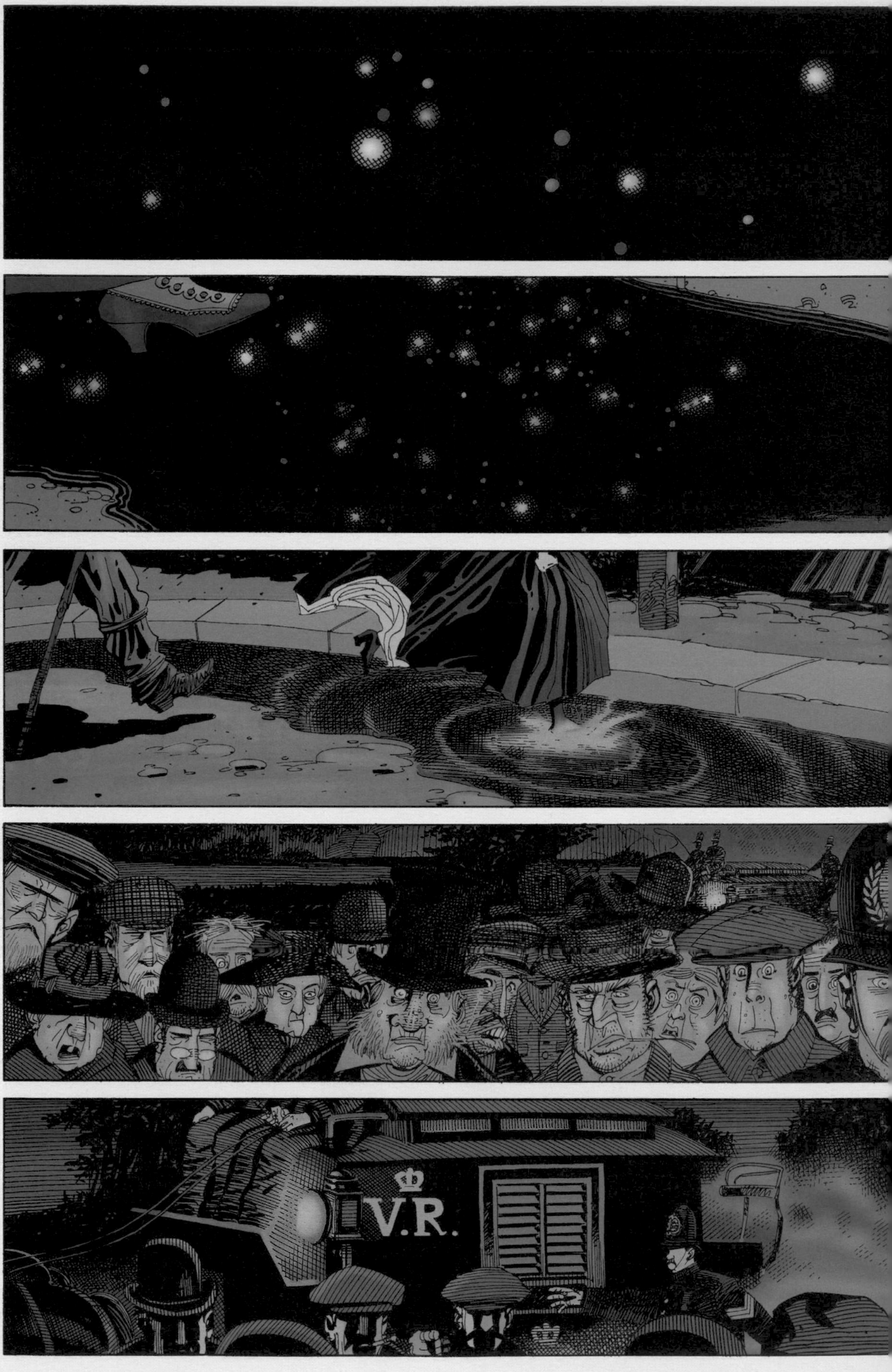
V.R.

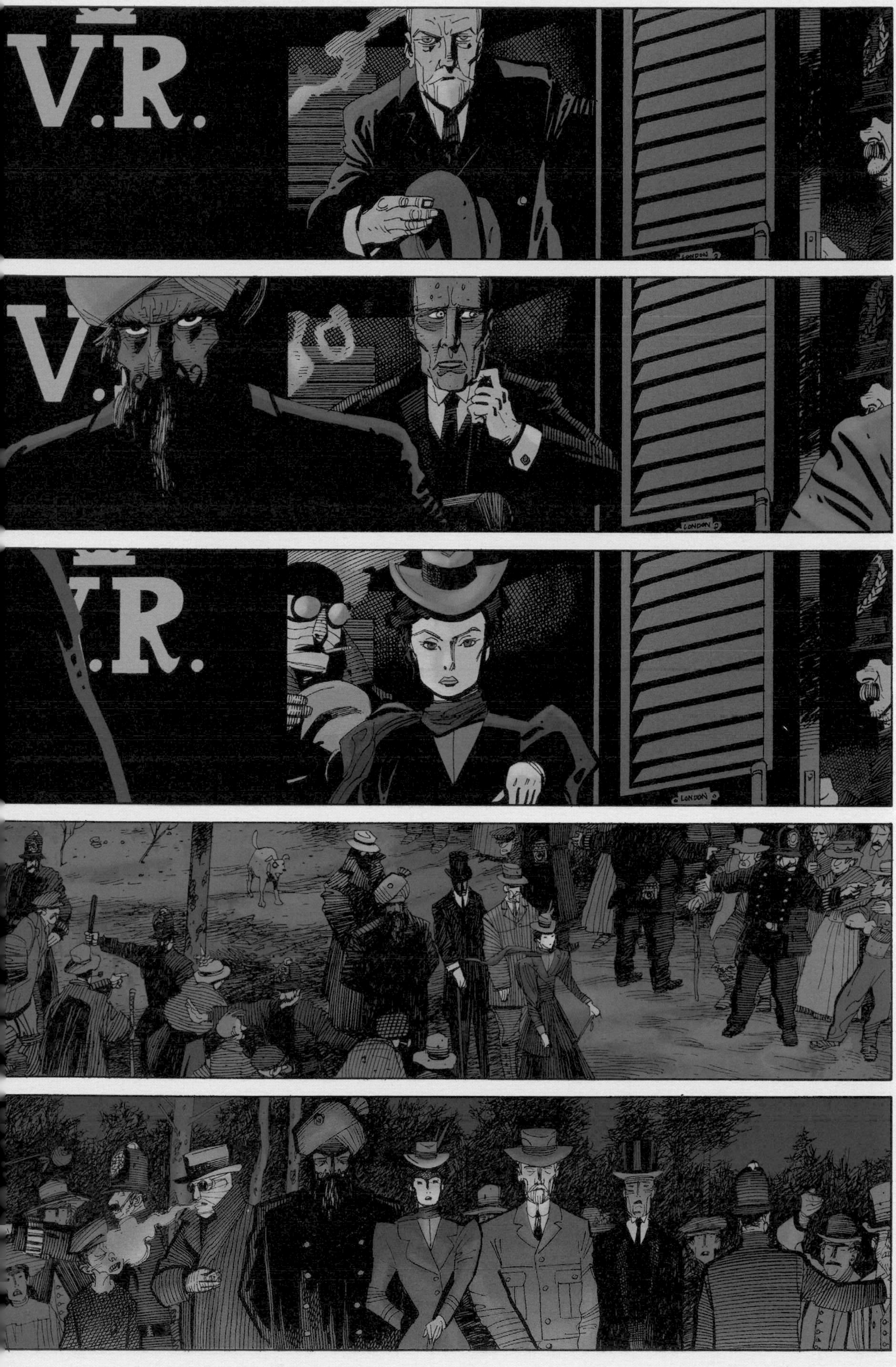
V.R.
LONDON
V.
LONDON
V.R.
LONDON

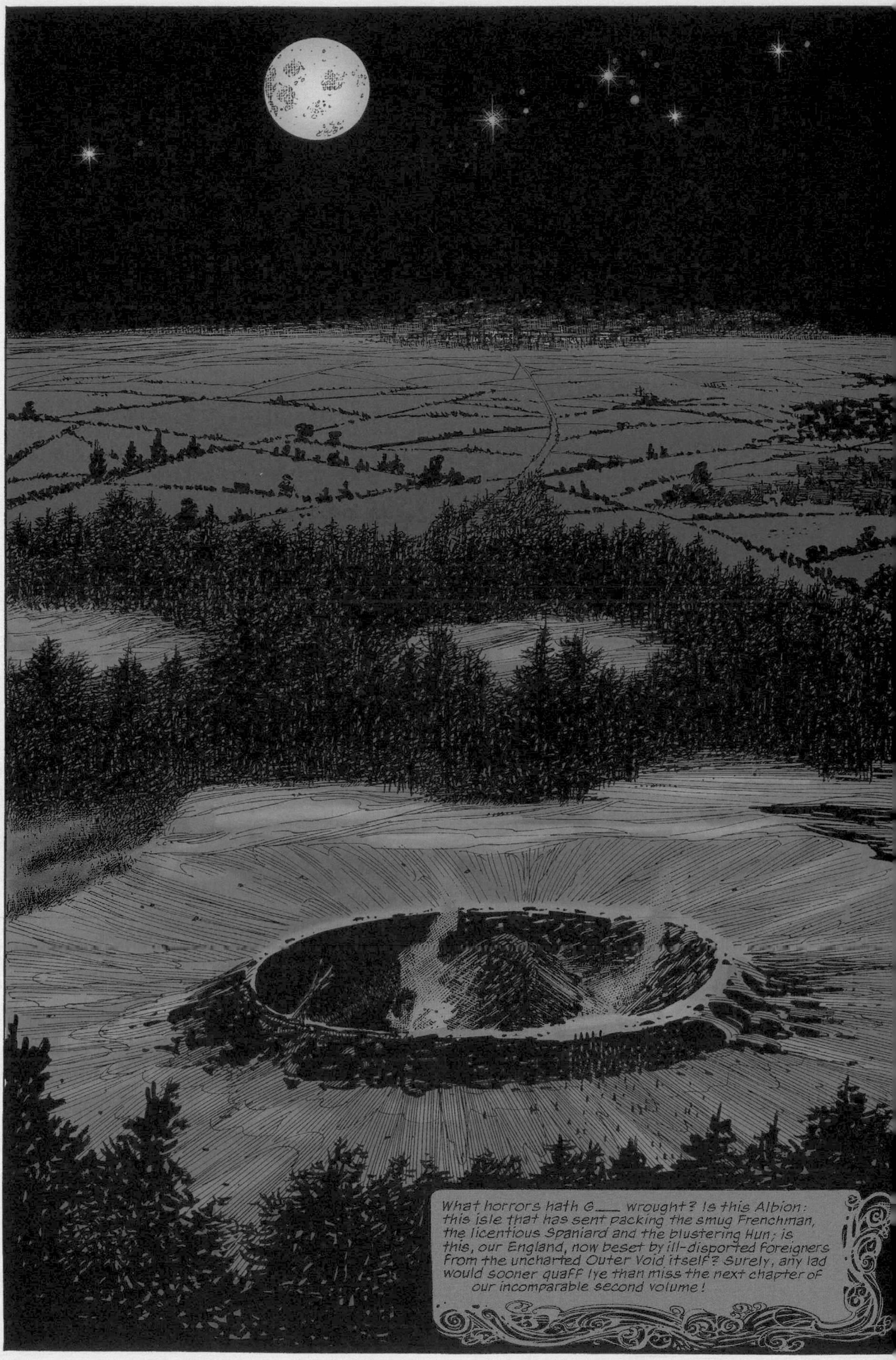
What horrors hath G___ wrought? Is this Albion: this isle that has sent packing the smug Frenchman, the licentious Spaniard and the blustering Hun; is this, our England, now beset by ill-disported foreigners from the uncharted Outer Void itself? Surely, any lad would sooner quaff lye than miss the next chapter of our incomparable second volume!

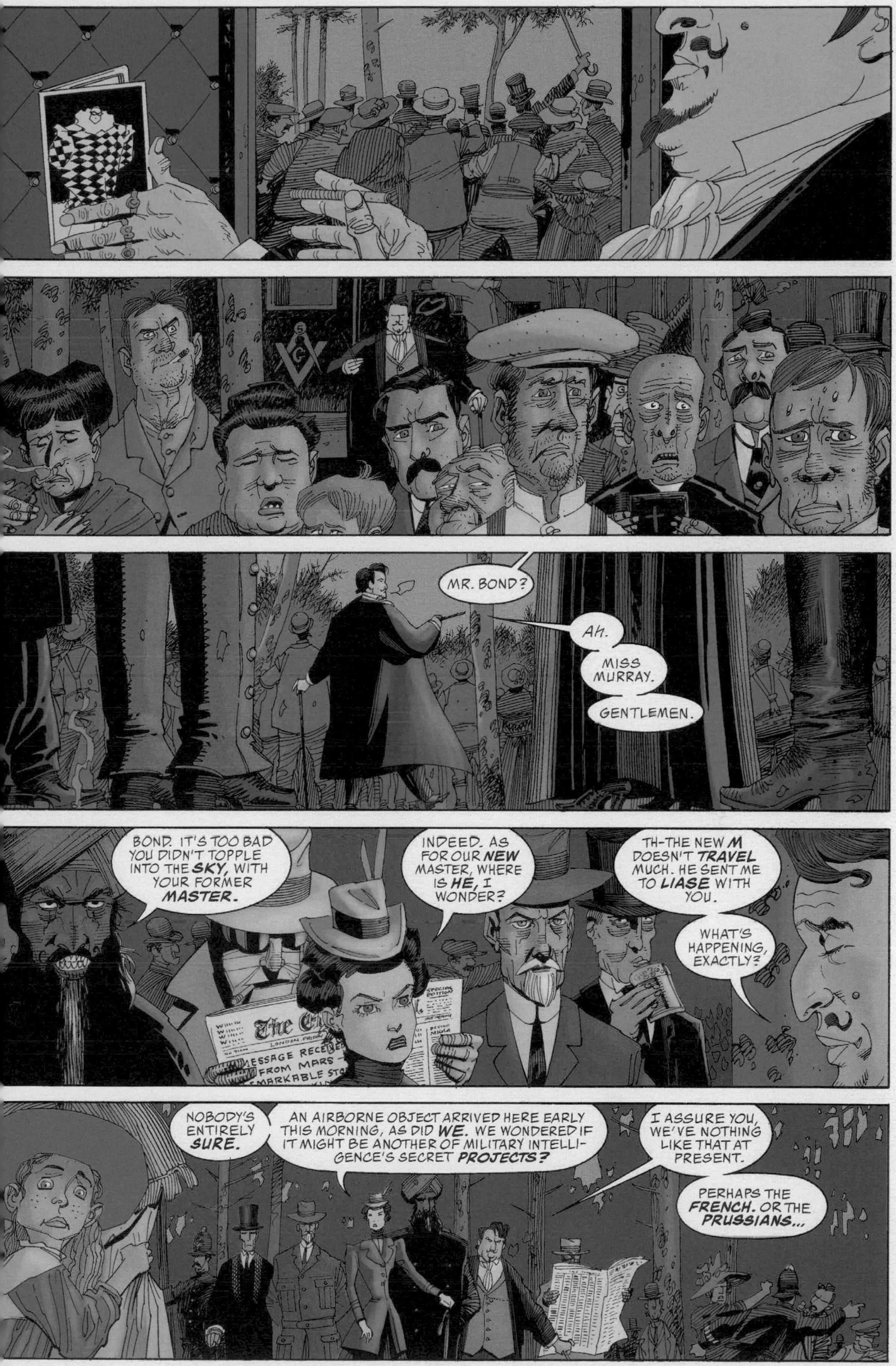
MR. BOND?
Ah.
MISS MURRAY.
GENTLEMEN.
BOND. IT'S TOO BAD YOU DIDN'T TOPPLE INTO THE **SKY,** WITH YOUR FORMER **MASTER.**
INDEED. AS FOR OUR **NEW** MASTER, WHERE IS **HE,** I WONDER?
TH-THE NEW **M** DOESN'T **TRAVEL** MUCH. HE SENT ME TO **LIASE** WITH YOU.
WHAT'S HAPPENING, EXACTLY?
NOBODY'S ENTIRELY **SURE.**
AN AIRBORNE OBJECT ARRIVED HERE EARLY THIS MORNING, AS DID **WE.** WE WONDERED IF IT MIGHT BE ANOTHER OF MILITARY INTELLIGENCE'S SECRET **PROJECTS?**
I ASSURE YOU, WE'VE NOTHING LIKE THAT AT PRESENT.
PERHAPS THE **FRENCH.** OR THE **PRUSSIANS...**

2: People of Other Lands

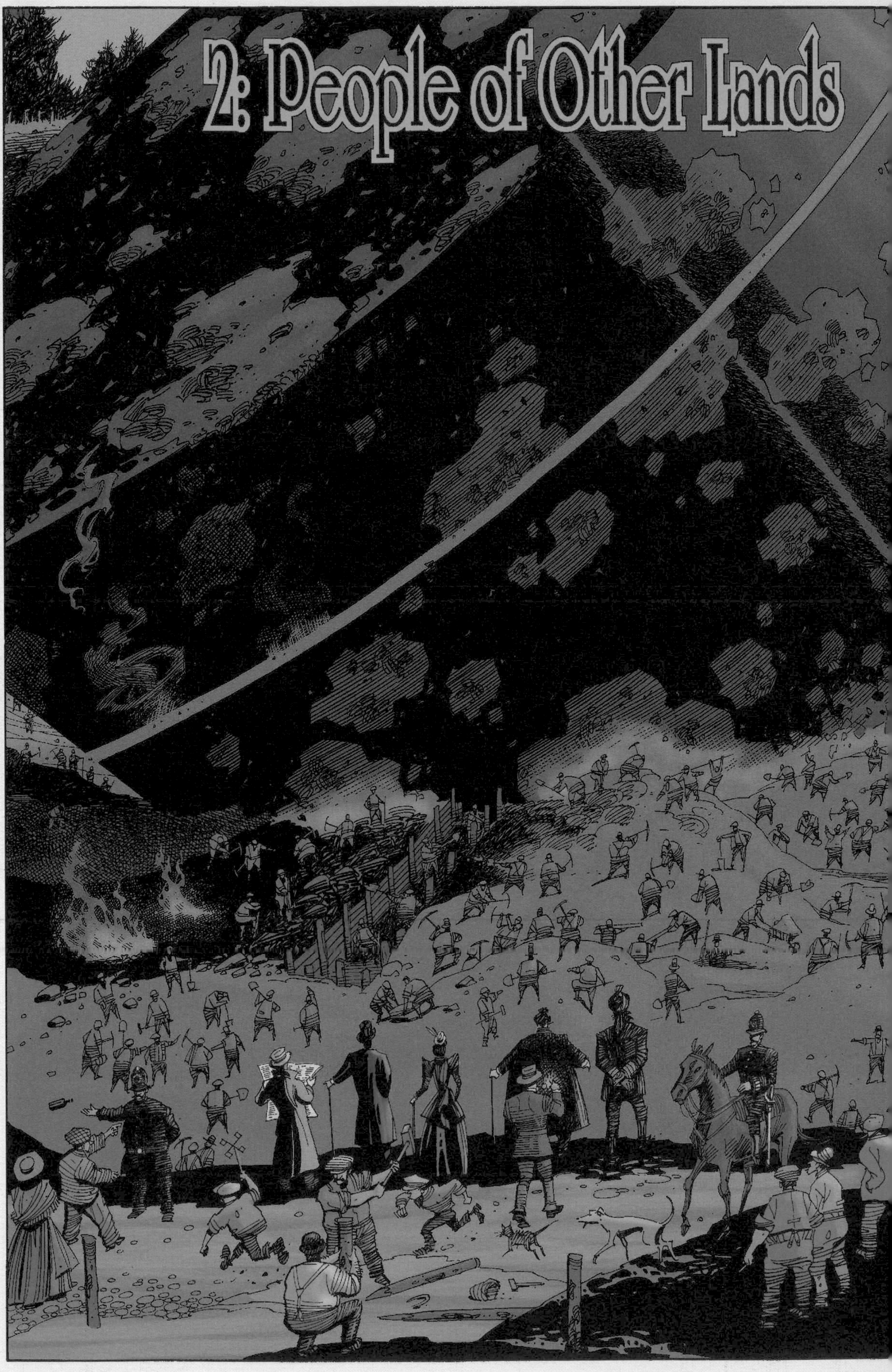

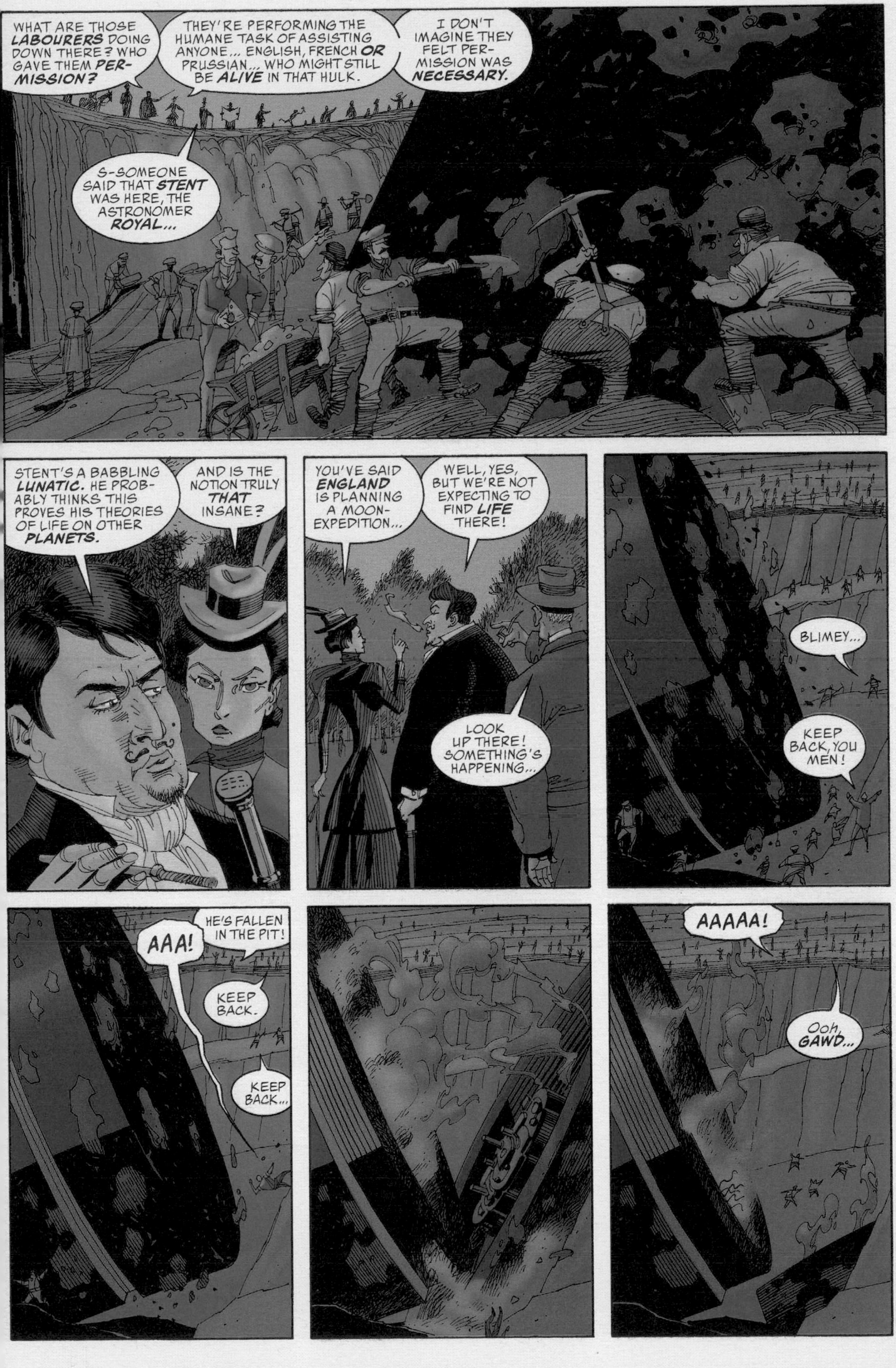
WHAT ARE THOSE LABOURERS DOING DOWN THERE? WHO GAVE THEM PER-MISSION?
THEY'RE PERFORMING THE HUMANE TASK OF ASSISTING ANYONE... ENGLISH, FRENCH OR PRUSSIAN... WHO MIGHT STILL BE ALIVE IN THAT HULK.
I DON'T IMAGINE THEY FELT PER-MISSION WAS NECESSARY.
S-SOMEONE SAID THAT STENT WAS HERE, THE ASTRONOMER ROYAL...
STENT'S A BABBLING LUNATIC. HE PROB-ABLY THINKS THIS PROVES HIS THEORIES OF LIFE ON OTHER PLANETS.
AND IS THE NOTION TRULY THAT INSANE?
YOU'VE SAID ENGLAND IS PLANNING A MOON-EXPEDITION...
WELL, YES, BUT WE'RE NOT EXPECTING TO FIND LIFE THERE!
LOOK UP THERE! SOMETHING'S HAPPENING...
BLIMEY...
KEEP BACK, YOU MEN!
HE'S FALLEN IN THE PIT!
AAA!
KEEP BACK.
KEEP BACK...
AAAAA!
Ooh, GAWD...

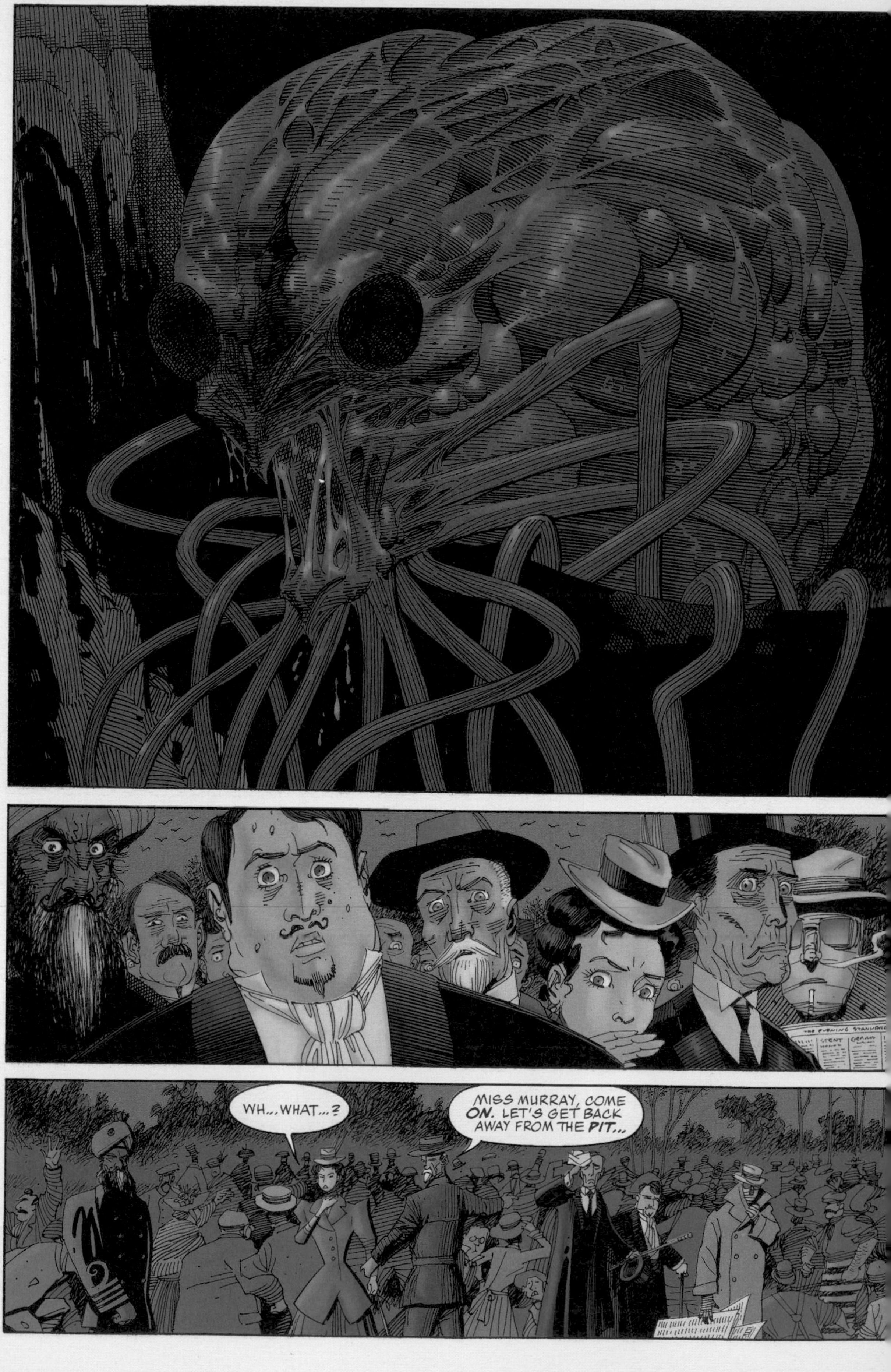
WH... WHAT...?
MISS MURRAY, COME ON. LET'S GET BACK AWAY FROM THE PIT...

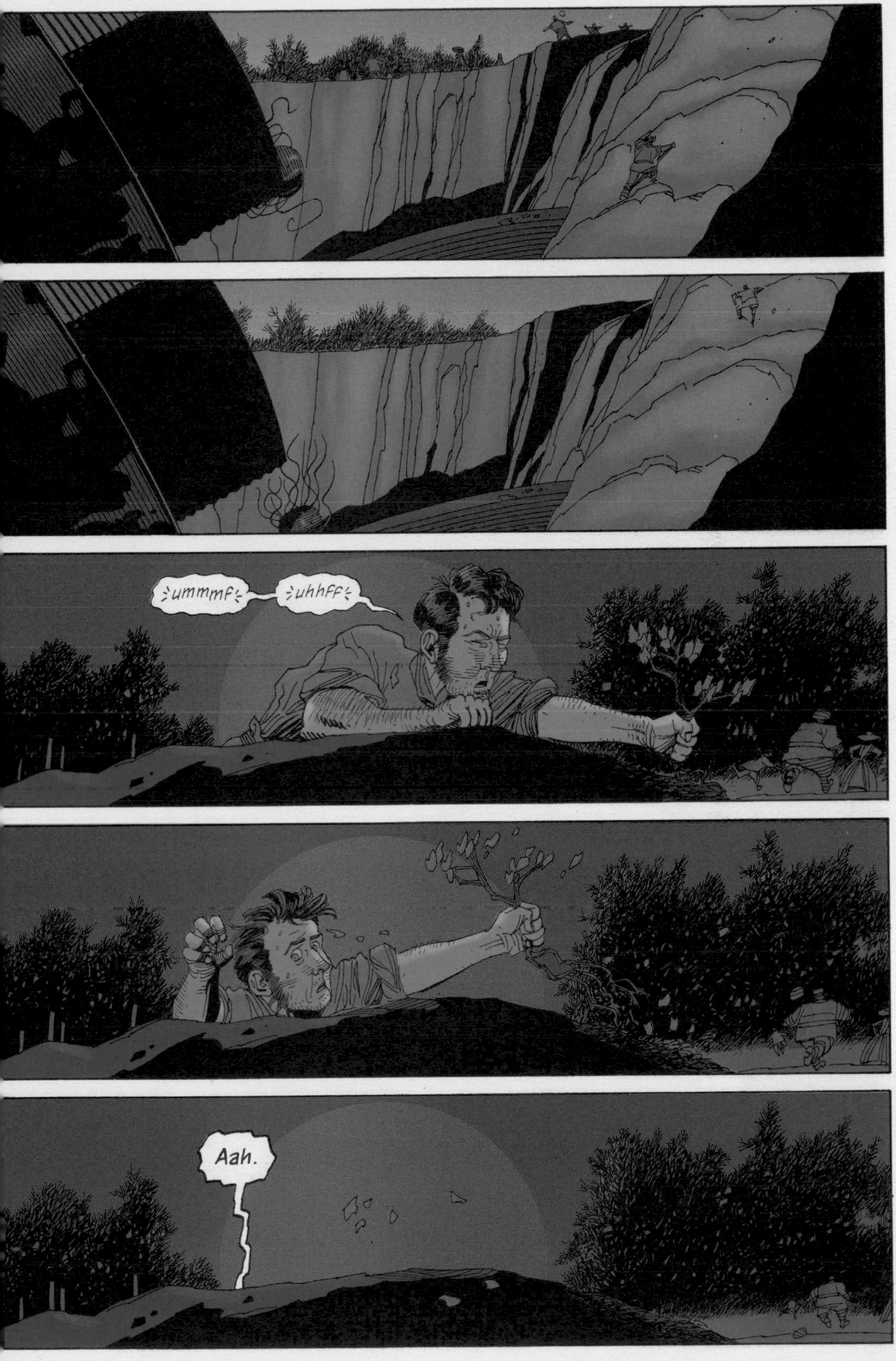
ummmf
uhhff
Aah.

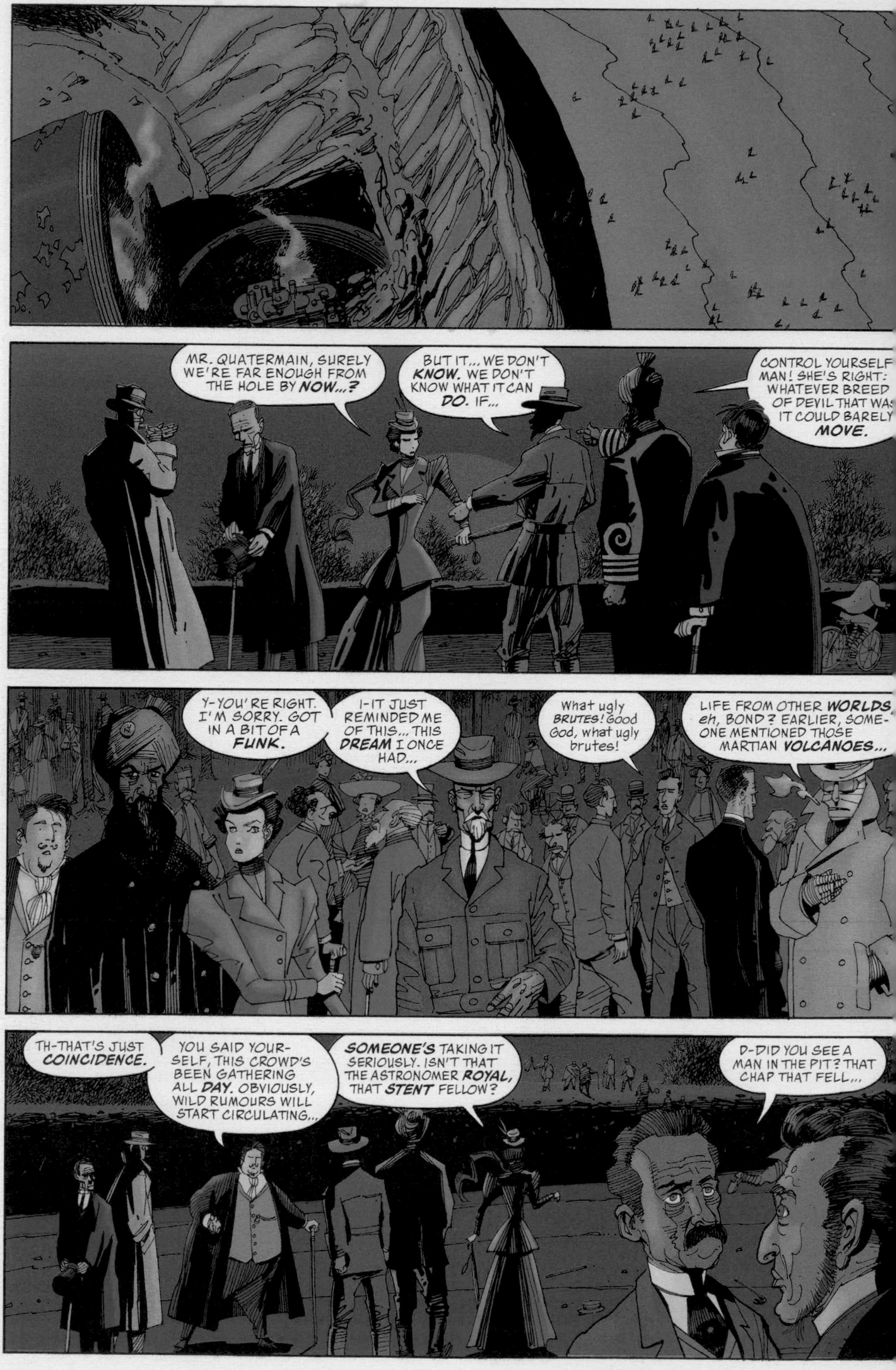
MR. QUATERMAIN, SURELY WE'RE FAR ENOUGH FROM THE HOLE BY NOW...?
BUT IT... WE DON'T KNOW. WE DON'T KNOW WHAT IT CAN DO. IF...
CONTROL YOURSELF MAN! SHE'S RIGHT: WHATEVER BREED OF DEVIL THAT WAS IT COULD BARELY MOVE.
Y-YOU'RE RIGHT. I'M SORRY. GOT IN A BIT OF A FUNK.
I-IT JUST REMINDED ME OF THIS... THIS DREAM I ONCE HAD...
What ugly BRUTES! Good God, what ugly brutes!
LIFE FROM OTHER WORLDS, eh, BOND? EARLIER, SOME-ONE MENTIONED THOSE MARTIAN VOLCANOES...
TH-THAT'S JUST COINCIDENCE.
YOU SAID YOUR-SELF, THIS CROWD'S BEEN GATHERING ALL DAY. OBVIOUSLY, WILD RUMOURS WILL START CIRCULATING...
SOMEONE'S TAKING IT SERIOUSLY. ISN'T THAT THE ASTRONOMER ROYAL, THAT STENT FELLOW?
D-DID YOU SEE A MAN IN THE PIT? THAT CHAP THAT FELL...

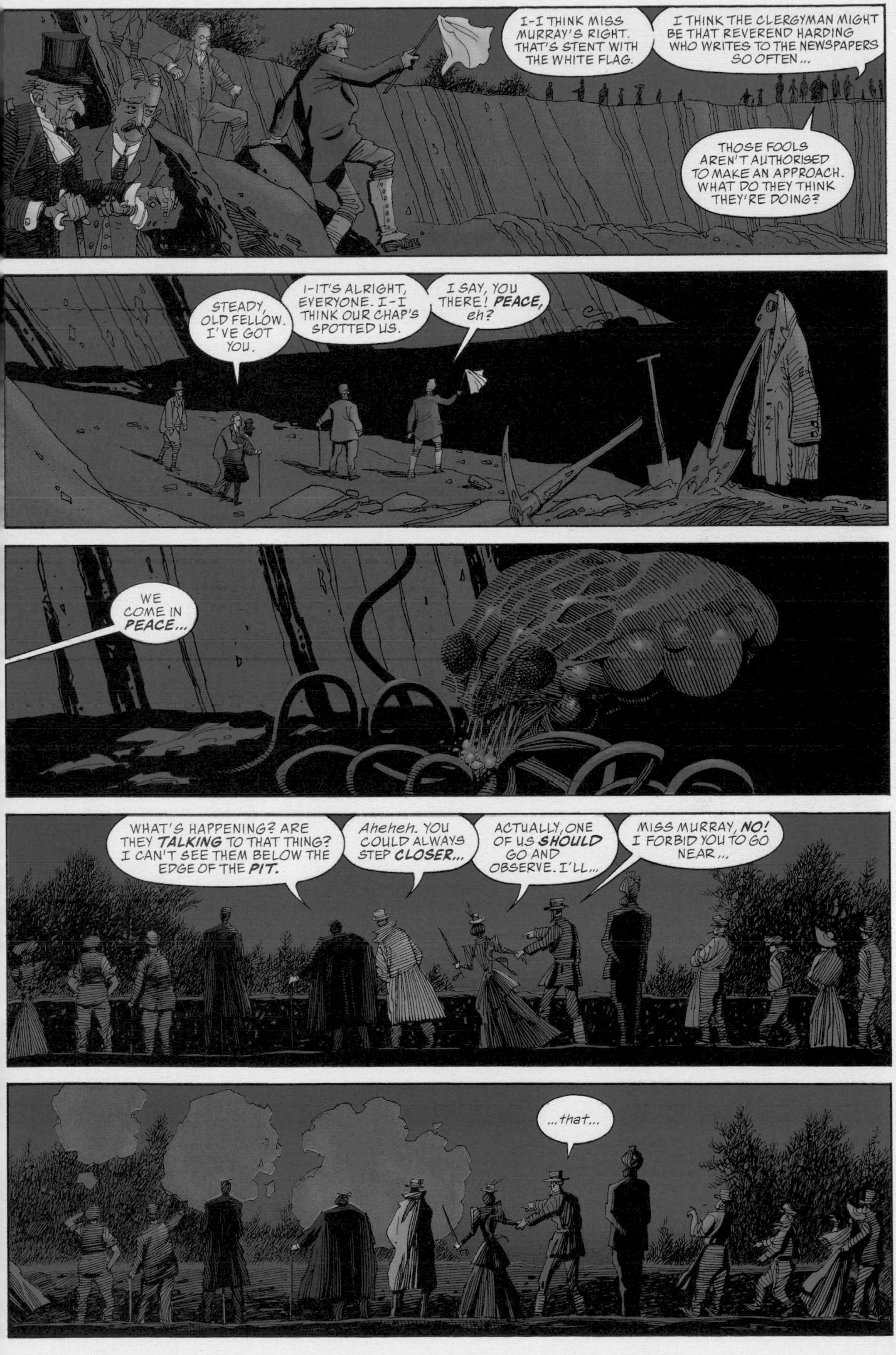
I-I THINK MISS MURRAY'S RIGHT. THAT'S STENT WITH THE WHITE FLAG.
I THINK THE CLERGYMAN MIGHT BE THAT REVEREND HARDING WHO WRITES TO THE NEWSPAPERS SO OFTEN...
THOSE FOOLS AREN'T AUTHORISED TO MAKE AN APPROACH. WHAT DO THEY THINK THEY'RE DOING?
STEADY, OLD FELLOW. I'VE GOT YOU.
I-IT'S ALRIGHT, EVERYONE. I-I THINK OUR CHAP'S SPOTTED US.
I SAY, YOU THERE! PEACE, eh?
WE COME IN PEACE...
WHAT'S HAPPENING? ARE THEY TALKING TO THAT THING? I CAN'T SEE THEM BELOW THE EDGE OF THE PIT.
Aheheh. YOU COULD ALWAYS STEP CLOSER...
ACTUALLY, ONE OF US SHOULD GO AND OBSERVE. I'LL...
MISS MURRAY, NO! I FORBID YOU TO GO NEAR...
...that...

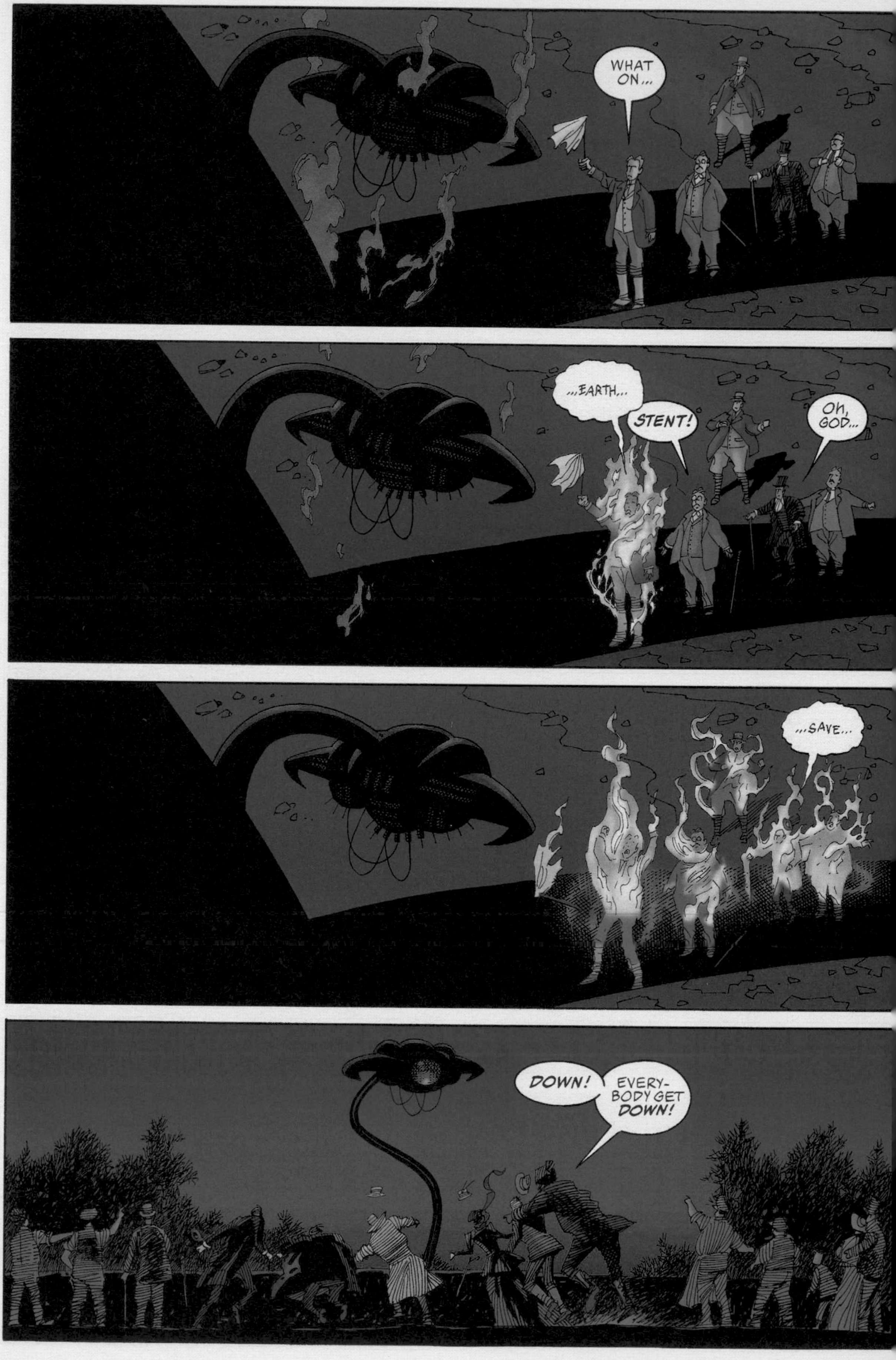
WHAT ON...
...EARTH...
STENT!
OH, GOD...
...SAVE...
DOWN!
EVERY-BODY GET DOWN!

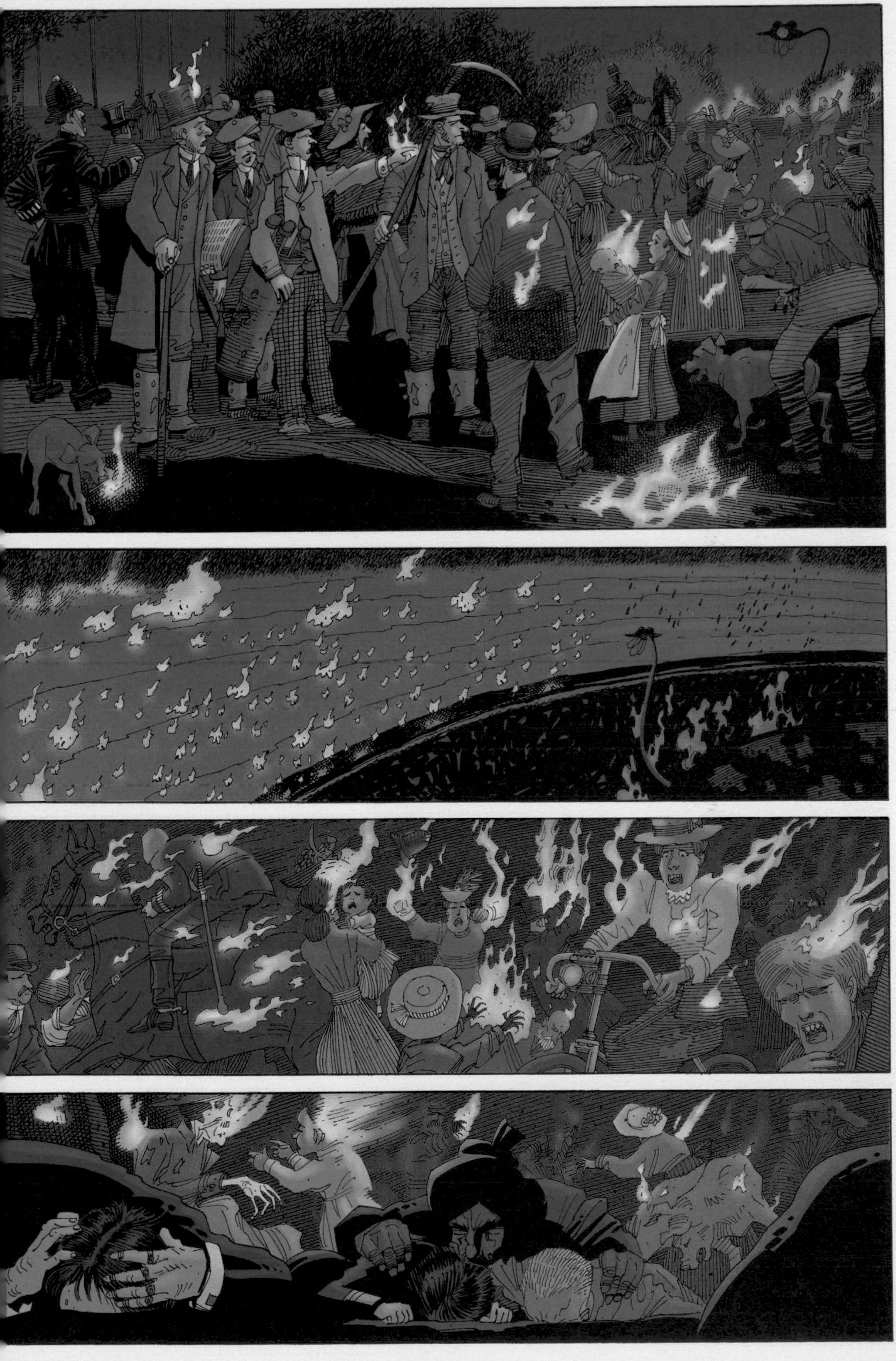

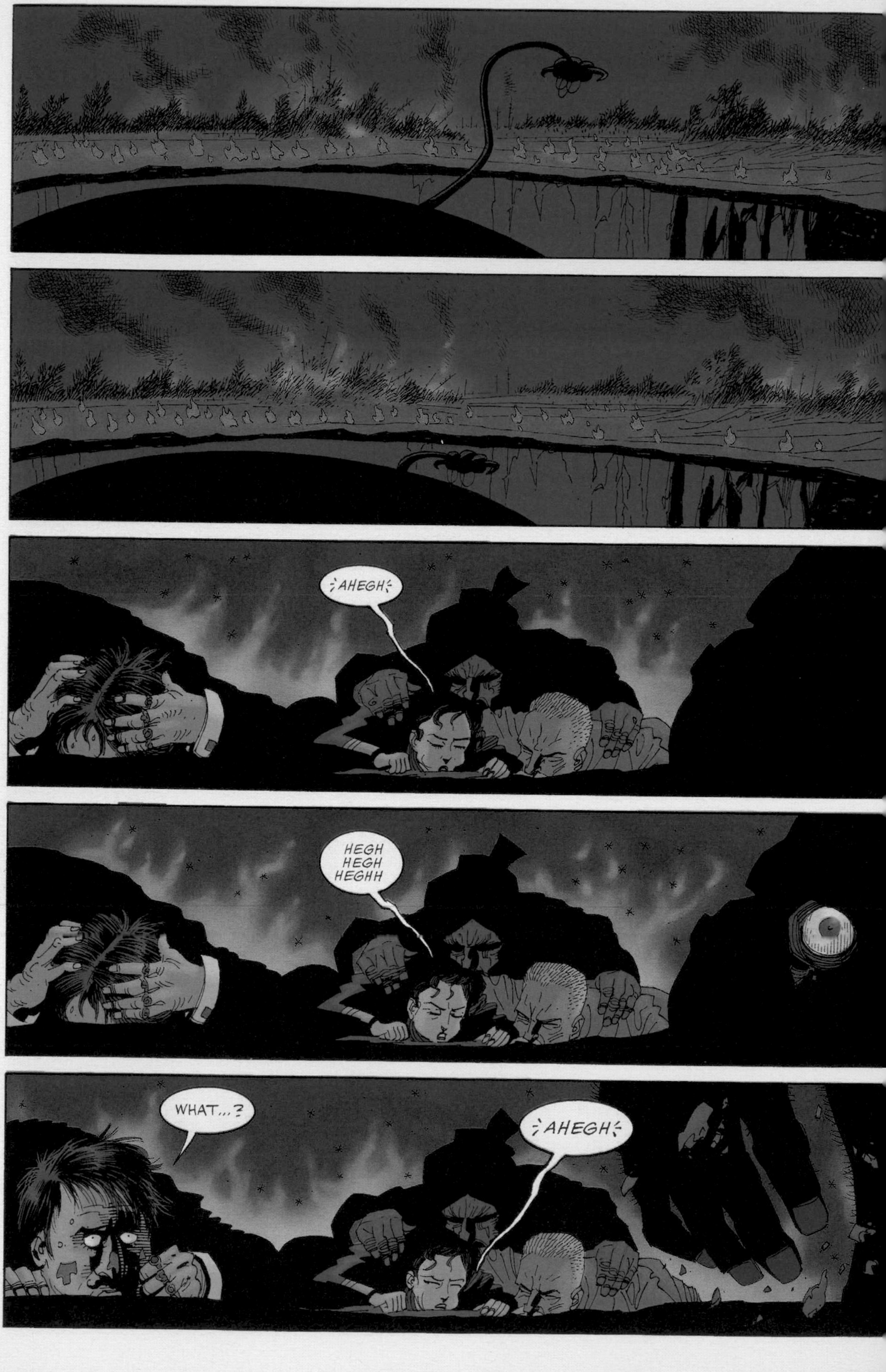
AHEGH
HEGH HEGH HEGHH
WHAT...?
AHEGH

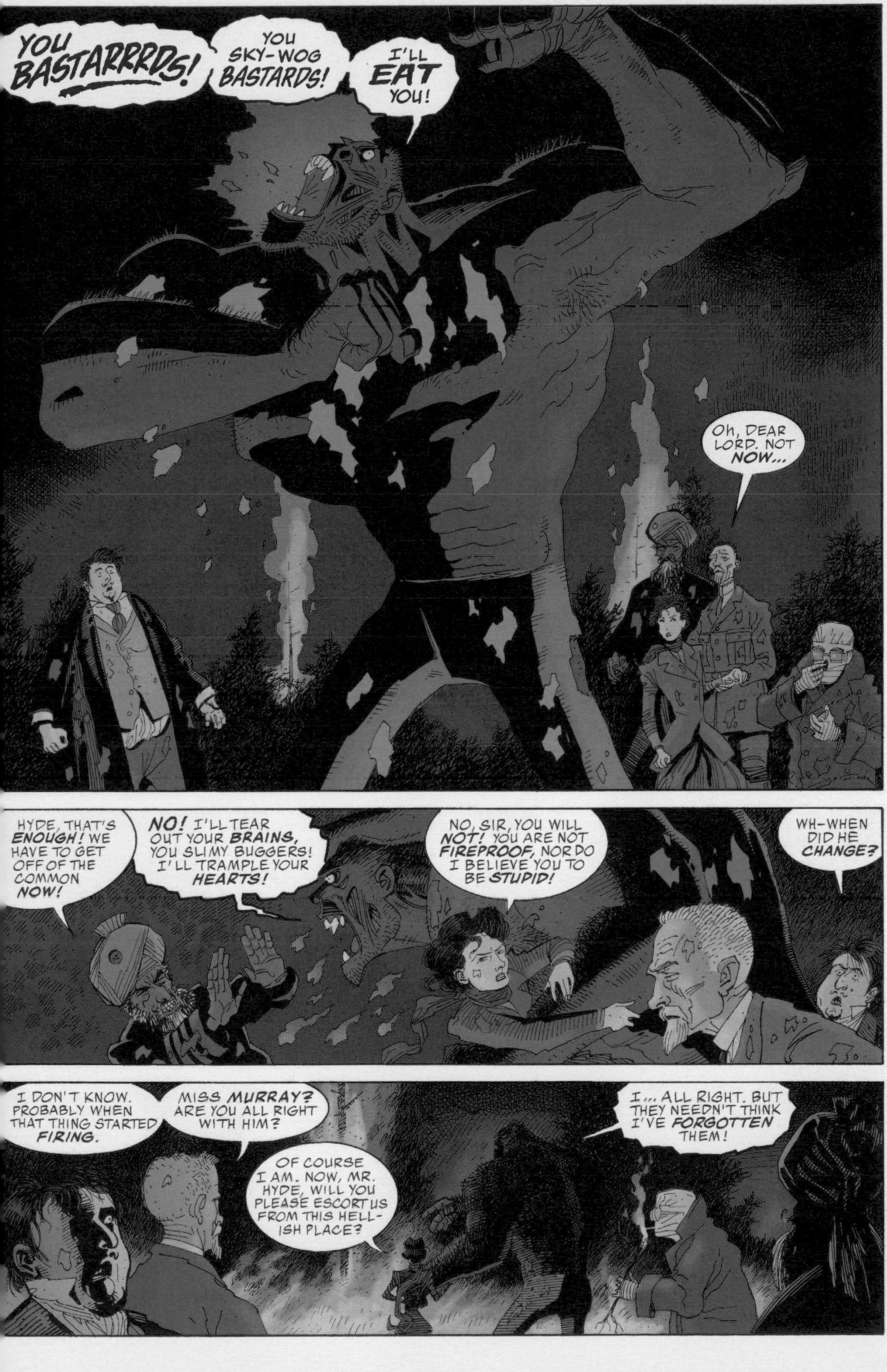
YOU BASTARRRRDS!
YOU SKY-WOG BASTARDS!
I'LL EAT YOU!
Oh, DEAR LORD. NOT NOW...
HYDE, THAT'S ENOUGH! WE HAVE TO GET OFF OF THE COMMON NOW!
NO! I'LL TEAR OUT YOUR BRAINS, YOU SLIMY BUGGERS! I'LL TRAMPLE YOUR HEARTS!
NO, SIR, YOU WILL NOT! YOU ARE NOT FIREPROOF, NOR DO I BELIEVE YOU TO BE STUPID!
WH-WHEN DID HE CHANGE?
I DON'T KNOW. PROBABLY WHEN THAT THING STARTED FIRING.
MISS MURRAY? ARE YOU ALL RIGHT WITH HIM?
OF COURSE I AM. NOW, MR. HYDE, WILL YOU PLEASE ESCORT US FROM THIS HELL-ISH PLACE?
I... ALL RIGHT. BUT THEY NEEDN'T THINK I'VE FORGOTTEN THEM!

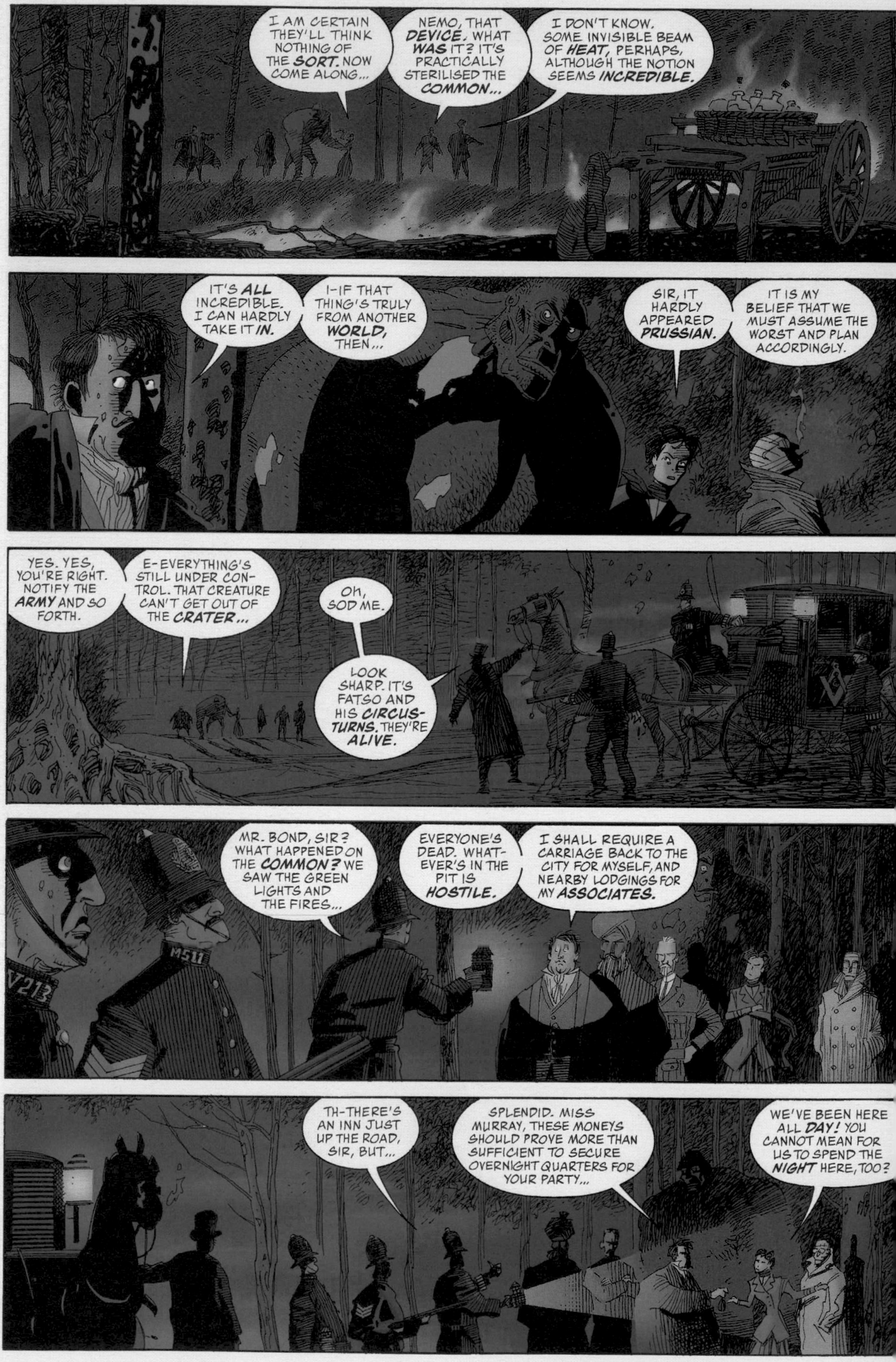

I AM CERTAIN THEY'LL THINK NOTHING OF THE SORT. NOW COME ALONG...
NEMO, THAT DEVICE. WHAT WAS IT? IT'S PRACTICALLY STERILISED THE COMMON...
I DON'T KNOW. SOME INVISIBLE BEAM OF HEAT, PERHAPS, ALTHOUGH THE NOTION SEEMS INCREDIBLE.
IT'S ALL INCREDIBLE. I CAN HARDLY TAKE IT IN.
I-IF THAT THING'S TRULY FROM ANOTHER WORLD, THEN...
SIR, IT HARDLY APPEARED PRUSSIAN.
IT IS MY BELIEF THAT WE MUST ASSUME THE WORST AND PLAN ACCORDINGLY.
YES. YES, YOU'RE RIGHT. NOTIFY THE ARMY AND SO FORTH.
E-EVERYTHING'S STILL UNDER CONTROL. THAT CREATURE CAN'T GET OUT OF THE CRATER...
OH, SOD ME.
LOOK SHARP. IT'S FATSO AND HIS CIRCUS-TURNS. THEY'RE ALIVE.
M511
V213
MR. BOND, SIR? WHAT HAPPENED ON THE COMMON? WE SAW THE GREEN LIGHTS AND THE FIRES...
EVERYONE'S DEAD. WHATEVER'S IN THE PIT IS HOSTILE.
I SHALL REQUIRE A CARRIAGE BACK TO THE CITY FOR MYSELF, AND NEARBY LODGINGS FOR MY ASSOCIATES.
TH-THERE'S AN INN JUST UP THE ROAD, SIR, BUT...
SPLENDID. MISS MURRAY, THESE MONEYS SHOULD PROVE MORE THAN SUFFICIENT TO SECURE OVERNIGHT QUARTERS FOR YOUR PARTY...
WE'VE BEEN HERE ALL DAY! YOU CANNOT MEAN FOR US TO SPEND THE NIGHT HERE, TOO?

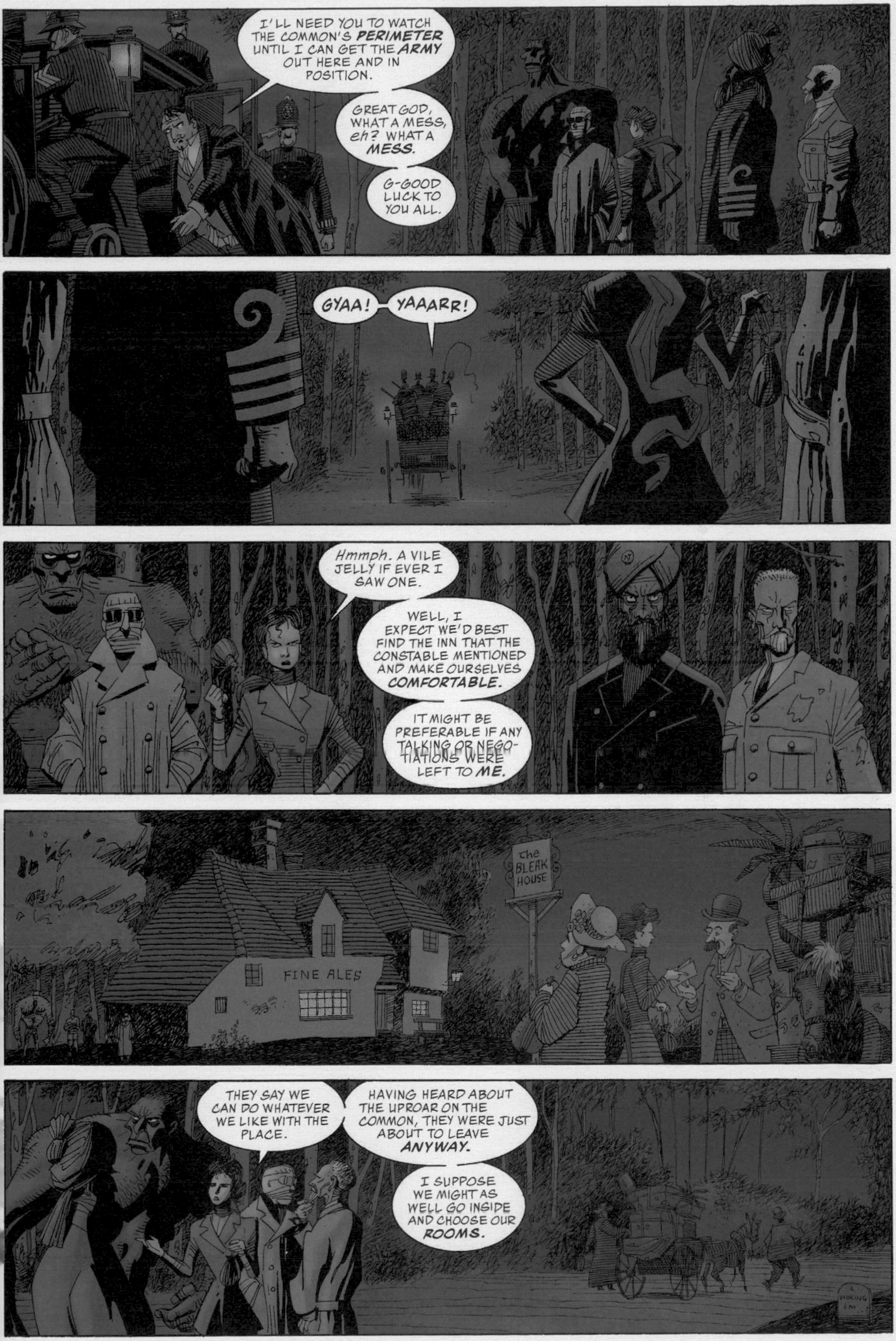

I'LL NEED YOU TO WATCH THE COMMON'S PERIMETER UNTIL I CAN GET THE ARMY OUT HERE AND IN POSITION.
GREAT GOD, WHAT A MESS, eh? WHAT A MESS.
G-GOOD LUCK TO YOU ALL.
GYAA!
YAAARR!
Hmmph. A VILE JELLY IF EVER I SAW ONE.
WELL, I EXPECT WE'D BEST FIND THE INN THAT THE CONSTABLE MENTIONED AND MAKE OURSELVES COMFORTABLE.
IT MIGHT BE PREFERABLE IF ANY TALKING OR NEGOTIATIONS WERE LEFT TO ME.
The BLEAK HOUSE
FINE ALES
THEY SAY WE CAN DO WHATEVER WE LIKE WITH THE PLACE.
HAVING HEARD ABOUT THE UPROAR ON THE COMMON, THEY WERE JUST ABOUT TO LEAVE ANYWAY.
I SUPPOSE WE MIGHT AS WELL GO INSIDE AND CHOOSE OUR ROOMS.

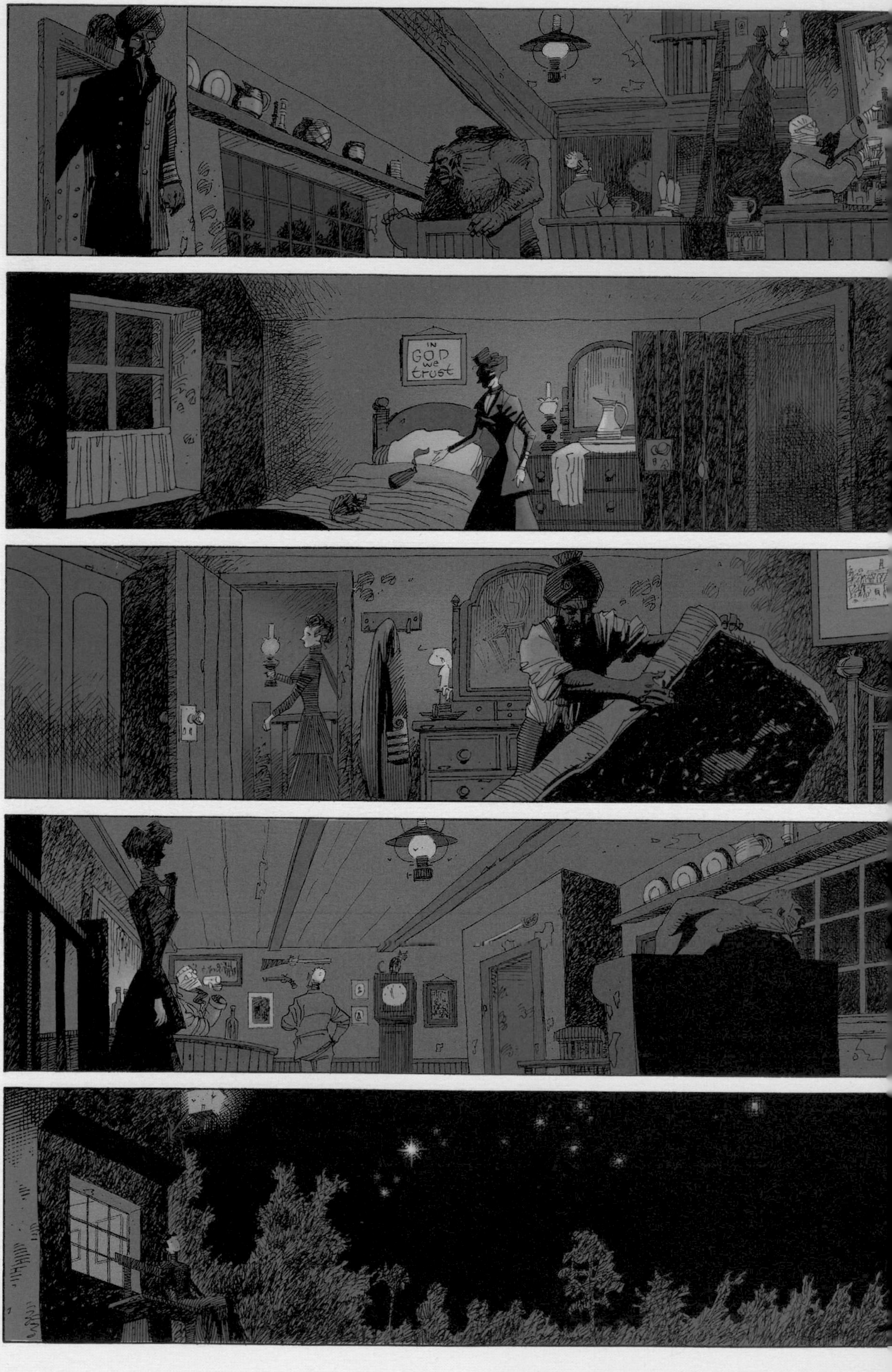
IN
GOD
we
trust

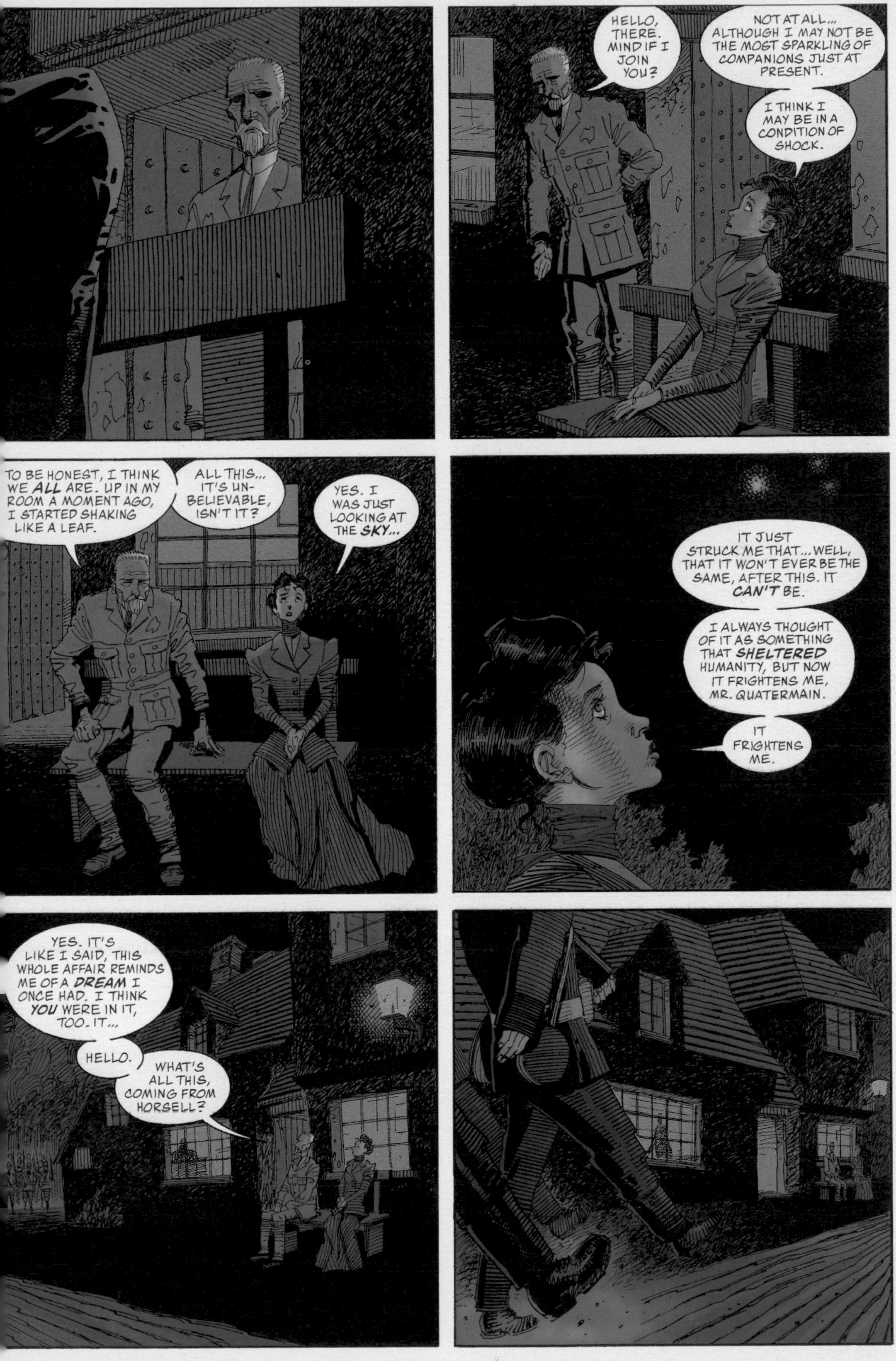
HELLO, THERE. MIND IF I JOIN YOU?
NOT AT ALL... ALTHOUGH I MAY NOT BE THE MOST SPARKLING OF COMPANIONS JUST AT PRESENT.
I THINK I MAY BE IN A CONDITION OF SHOCK.
TO BE HONEST, I THINK WE ALL ARE. UP IN MY ROOM A MOMENT AGO, I STARTED SHAKING LIKE A LEAF.
ALL THIS... IT'S UN-BELIEVABLE, ISN'T IT?
YES. I WAS JUST LOOKING AT THE SKY...
IT JUST STRUCK ME THAT... WELL, THAT IT WON'T EVER BE THE SAME, AFTER THIS. IT CAN'T BE.
I ALWAYS THOUGHT OF IT AS SOMETHING THAT SHELTERED HUMANITY, BUT NOW IT FRIGHTENS ME, MR. QUATERMAIN.
IT FRIGHTENS ME.
YES. IT'S LIKE I SAID, THIS WHOLE AFFAIR REMINDS ME OF A DREAM I ONCE HAD. I THINK YOU WERE IN IT, TOO. IT...
HELLO.
WHAT'S ALL THIS, COMING FROM HORSELL?

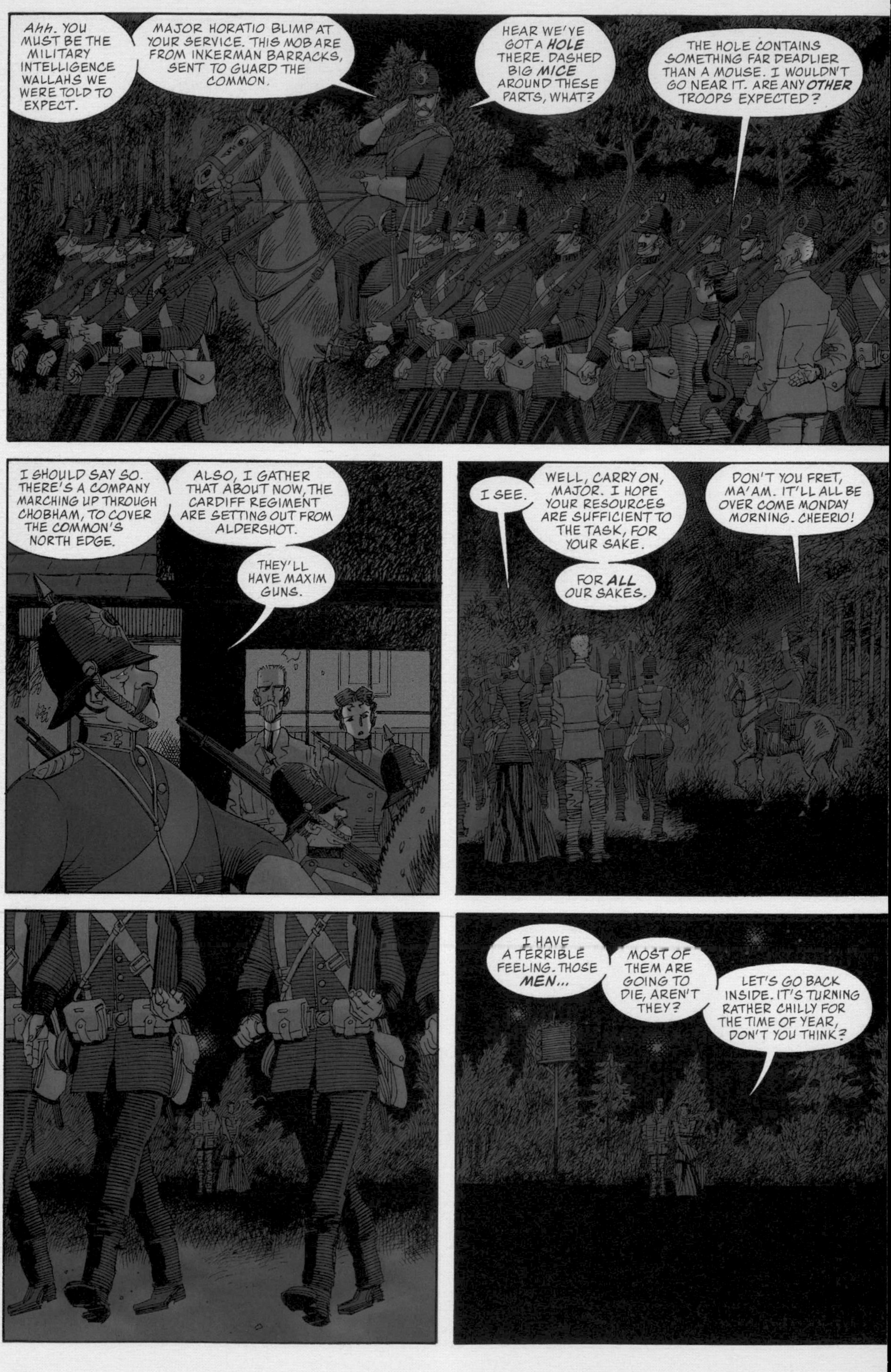

AHH. YOU MUST BE THE MILITARY INTELLIGENCE WALLAHS WE WERE TOLD TO EXPECT.
MAJOR HORATIO BLIMP AT YOUR SERVICE. THIS MOB ARE FROM INKERMAN BARRACKS, SENT TO GUARD THE COMMON.
HEAR WE'VE GOT A HOLE THERE. DASHED BIG MICE AROUND THESE PARTS, WHAT?
THE HOLE CONTAINS SOMETHING FAR DEADLIER THAN A MOUSE. I WOULDN'T GO NEAR IT. ARE ANY OTHER TROOPS EXPECTED?
I SHOULD SAY SO. THERE'S A COMPANY MARCHING UP THROUGH CHOBHAM, TO COVER THE COMMON'S NORTH EDGE.
ALSO, I GATHER THAT ABOUT NOW, THE CARDIFF REGIMENT ARE SETTING OUT FROM ALDERSHOT.
THEY'LL HAVE MAXIM GUNS.
I SEE.
WELL, CARRY ON, MAJOR. I HOPE YOUR RESOURCES ARE SUFFICIENT TO THE TASK, FOR YOUR SAKE.
FOR ALL OUR SAKES.
DON'T YOU FRET, MA'AM. IT'LL ALL BE OVER COME MONDAY MORNING. CHEERIO!
I HAVE A TERRIBLE FEELING. THOSE MEN...
MOST OF THEM ARE GOING TO DIE, AREN'T THEY?
LET'S GO BACK INSIDE. IT'S TURNING RATHER CHILLY FOR THE TIME OF YEAR, DON'T YOU THINK?

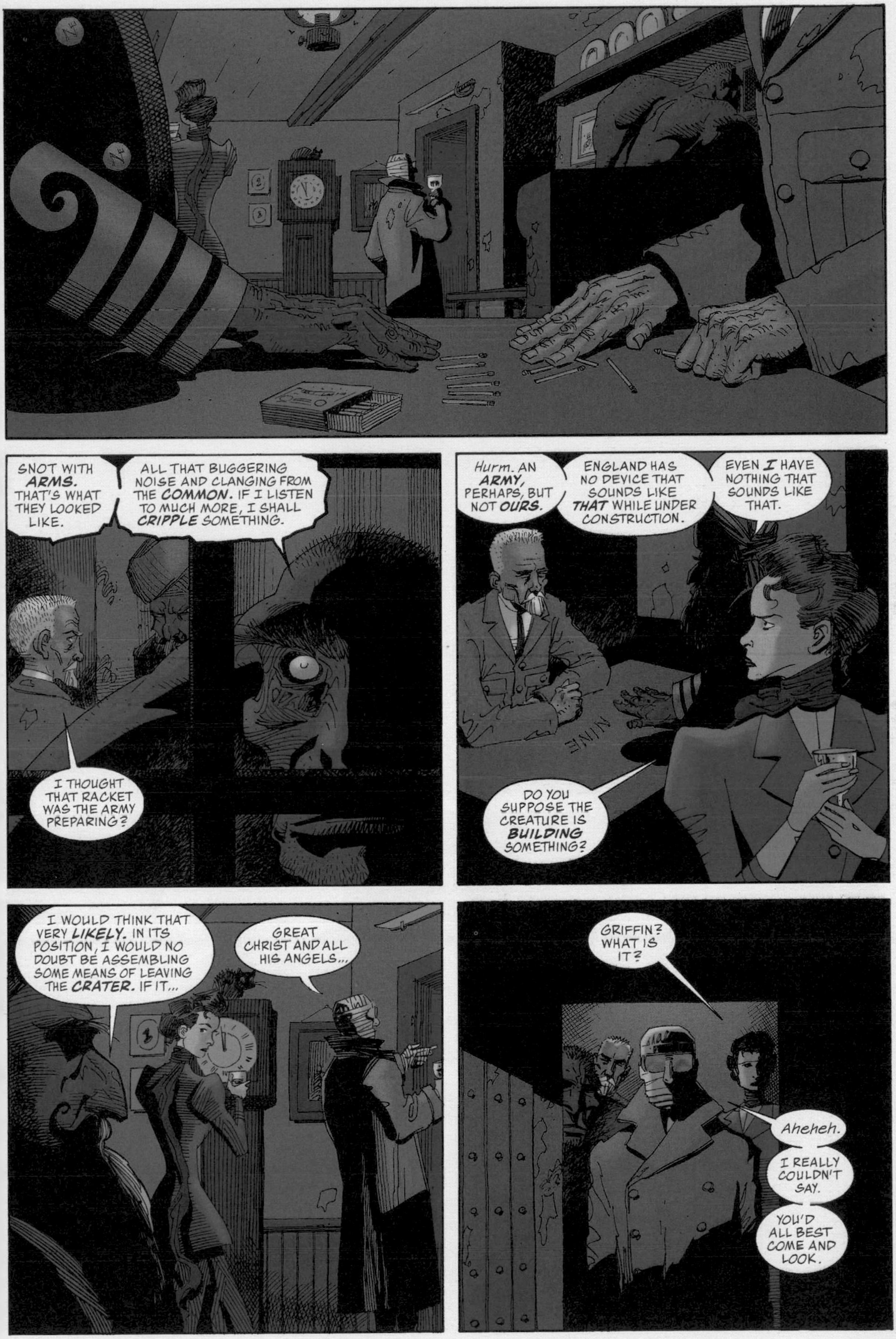
SNOT WITH ARMS. THAT'S WHAT THEY LOOKED LIKE.
ALL THAT BUGGERING NOISE AND CLANGING FROM THE COMMON. IF I LISTEN TO MUCH MORE, I SHALL CRIPPLE SOMETHING.
I THOUGHT THAT RACKET WAS THE ARMY PREPARING?
Hurm. AN ARMY, PERHAPS, BUT NOT OURS.
ENGLAND HAS NO DEVICE THAT SOUNDS LIKE THAT WHILE UNDER CONSTRUCTION.
EVEN I HAVE NOTHING THAT SOUNDS LIKE THAT.
DO YOU SUPPOSE THE CREATURE IS BUILDING SOMETHING?
I WOULD THINK THAT VERY LIKELY. IN ITS POSITION, I WOULD NO DOUBT BE ASSEMBLING SOME MEANS OF LEAVING THE CRATER. IF IT...
GREAT CHRIST AND ALL HIS ANGELS...
GRIFFIN? WHAT IS IT?
Aheheh.
I REALLY COULDN'T SAY.
YOU'D ALL BEST COME AND LOOK.

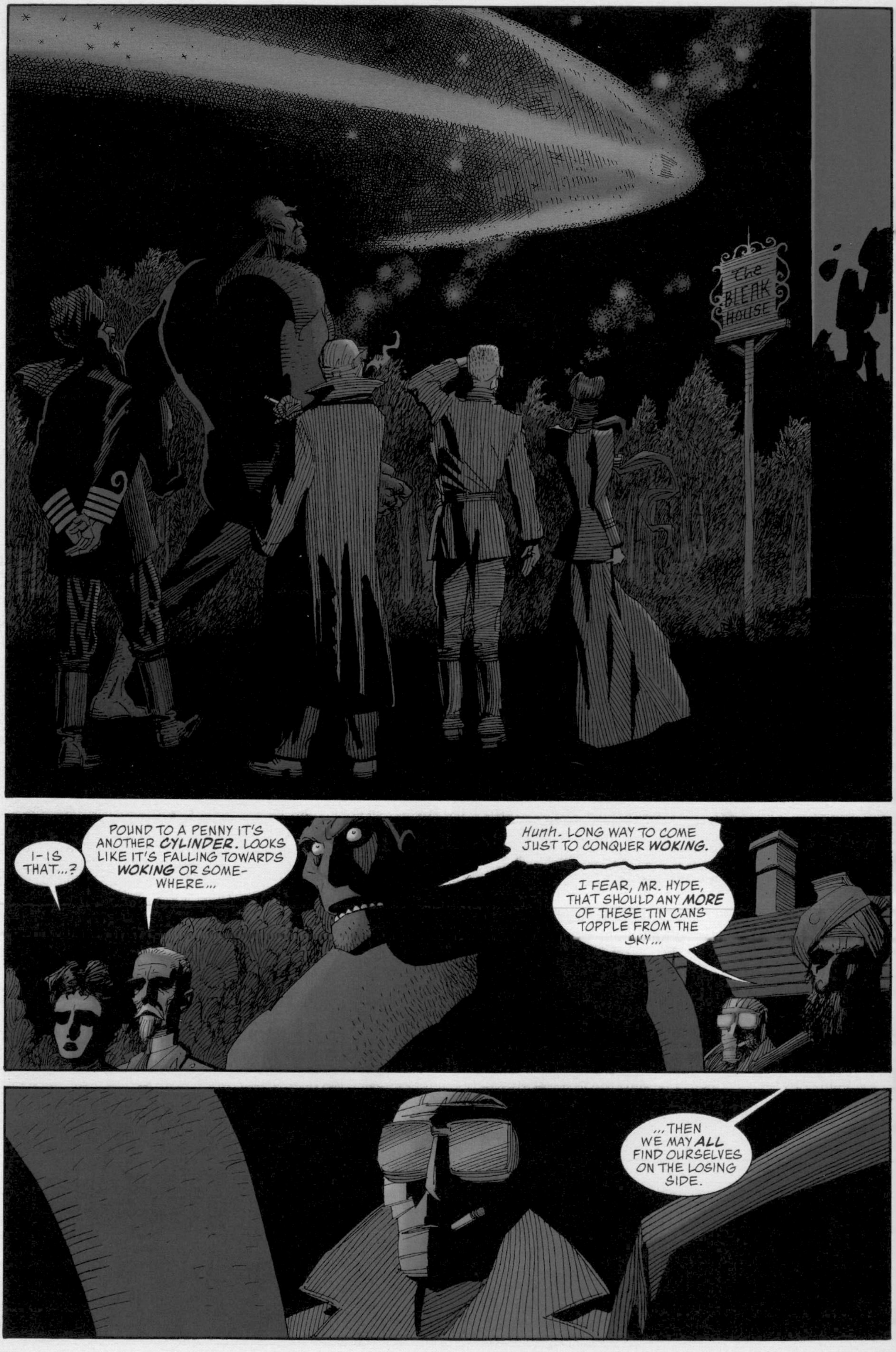

The BLEAK House
I-IS THAT...?
POUND TO A PENNY IT'S ANOTHER CYLINDER. LOOKS LIKE IT'S FALLING TOWARDS WOKING OR SOMEWHERE...
Hunh. LONG WAY TO COME JUST TO CONQUER WOKING.
I FEAR, MR. HYDE, THAT SHOULD ANY MORE OF THESE TIN CANS TOPPLE FROM THE SKY...
...THEN WE MAY ALL FIND OURSELVES ON THE LOSING SIDE.

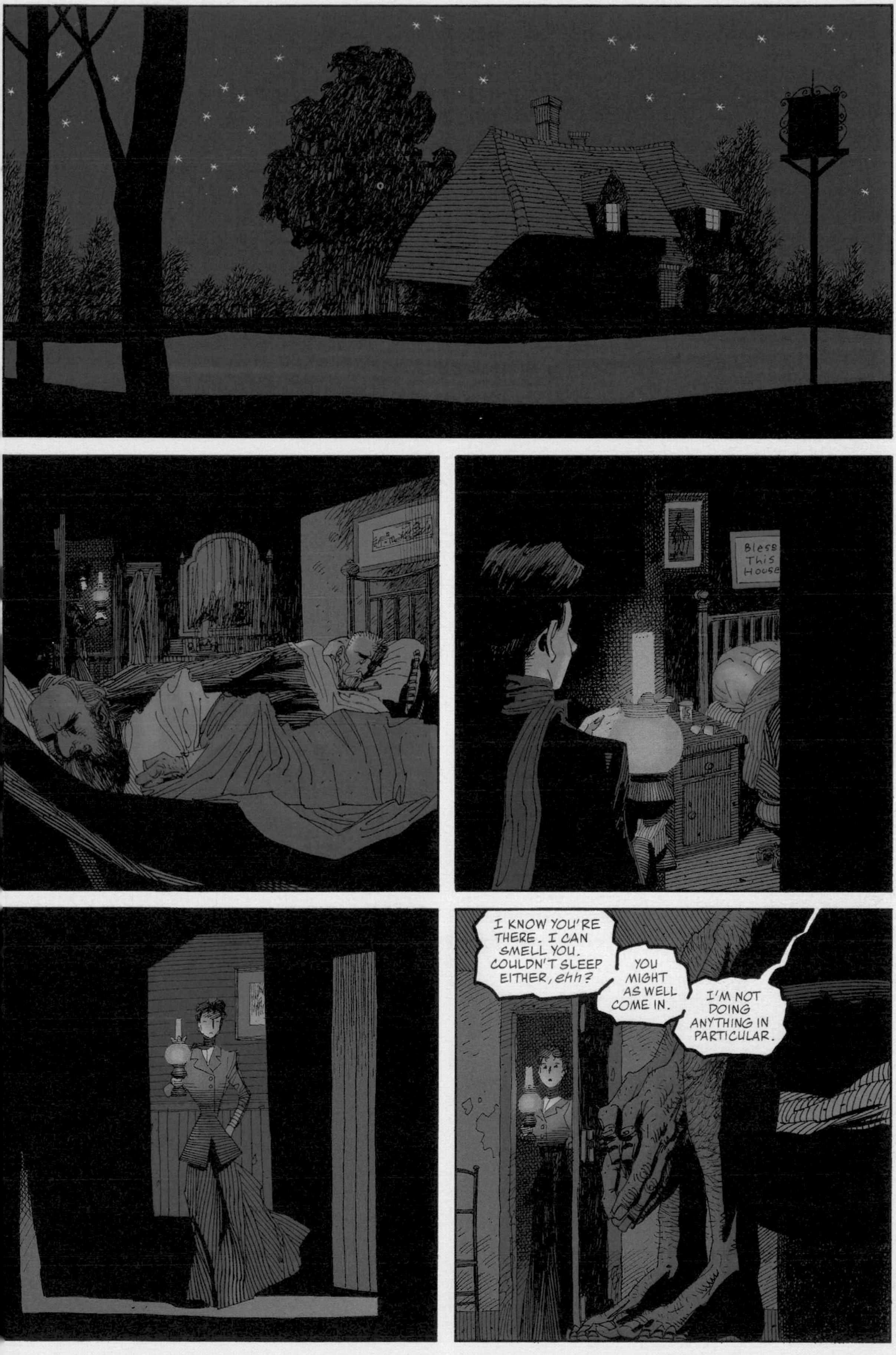
Bless This House
I KNOW YOU'RE THERE. I CAN SMELL YOU. COULDN'T SLEEP EITHER, *ehh*?
YOU MIGHT AS WELL COME IN.
I'M NOT DOING ANYTHING IN PARTICULAR.

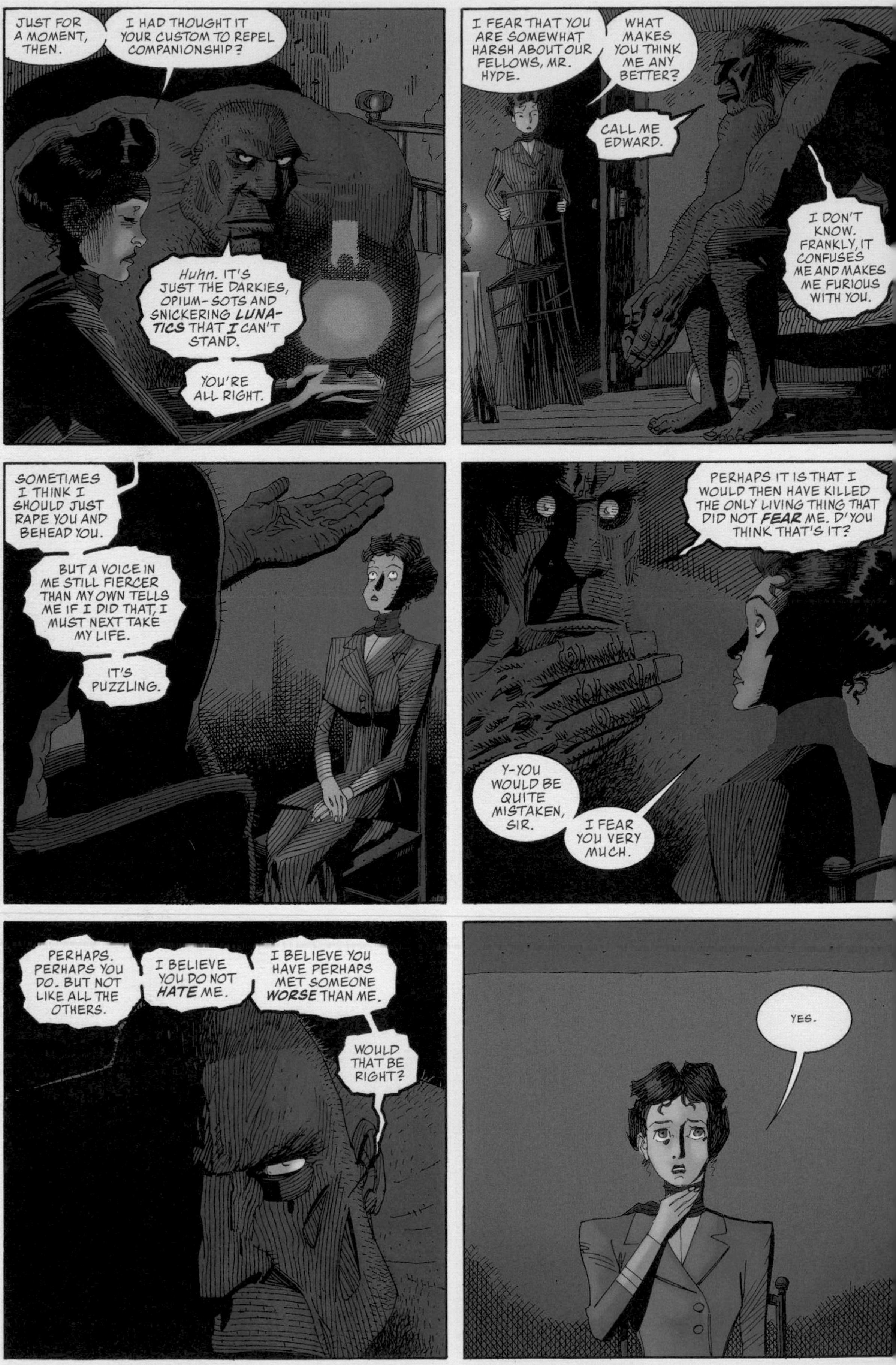
JUST FOR A MOMENT, THEN.
I HAD THOUGHT IT YOUR CUSTOM TO REPEL COMPANIONSHIP?
Huhn. IT'S JUST THE DARKIES, OPIUM-SOTS AND SNICKERING LUNATICS THAT I CAN'T STAND.
YOU'RE ALL RIGHT.
I FEAR THAT YOU ARE SOMEWHAT HARSH ABOUT OUR FELLOWS, MR. HYDE.
WHAT MAKES YOU THINK ME ANY BETTER?
CALL ME EDWARD.
I DON'T KNOW. FRANKLY, IT CONFUSES ME AND MAKES ME FURIOUS WITH YOU.
SOMETIMES I THINK I SHOULD JUST RAPE YOU AND BEHEAD YOU.
BUT A VOICE IN ME STILL FIERCER THAN MY OWN TELLS ME IF I DID THAT, I MUST NEXT TAKE MY LIFE.
IT'S PUZZLING.
PERHAPS IT IS THAT I WOULD THEN HAVE KILLED THE ONLY LIVING THING THAT DID NOT FEAR ME. D'YOU THINK THAT'S IT?
Y-YOU WOULD BE QUITE MISTAKEN, SIR.
I FEAR YOU VERY MUCH.
PERHAPS. PERHAPS YOU DO. BUT NOT LIKE ALL THE OTHERS.
I BELIEVE YOU DO NOT HATE ME.
I BELIEVE YOU HAVE PERHAPS MET SOMEONE WORSE THAN ME.
WOULD THAT BE RIGHT?
YES.

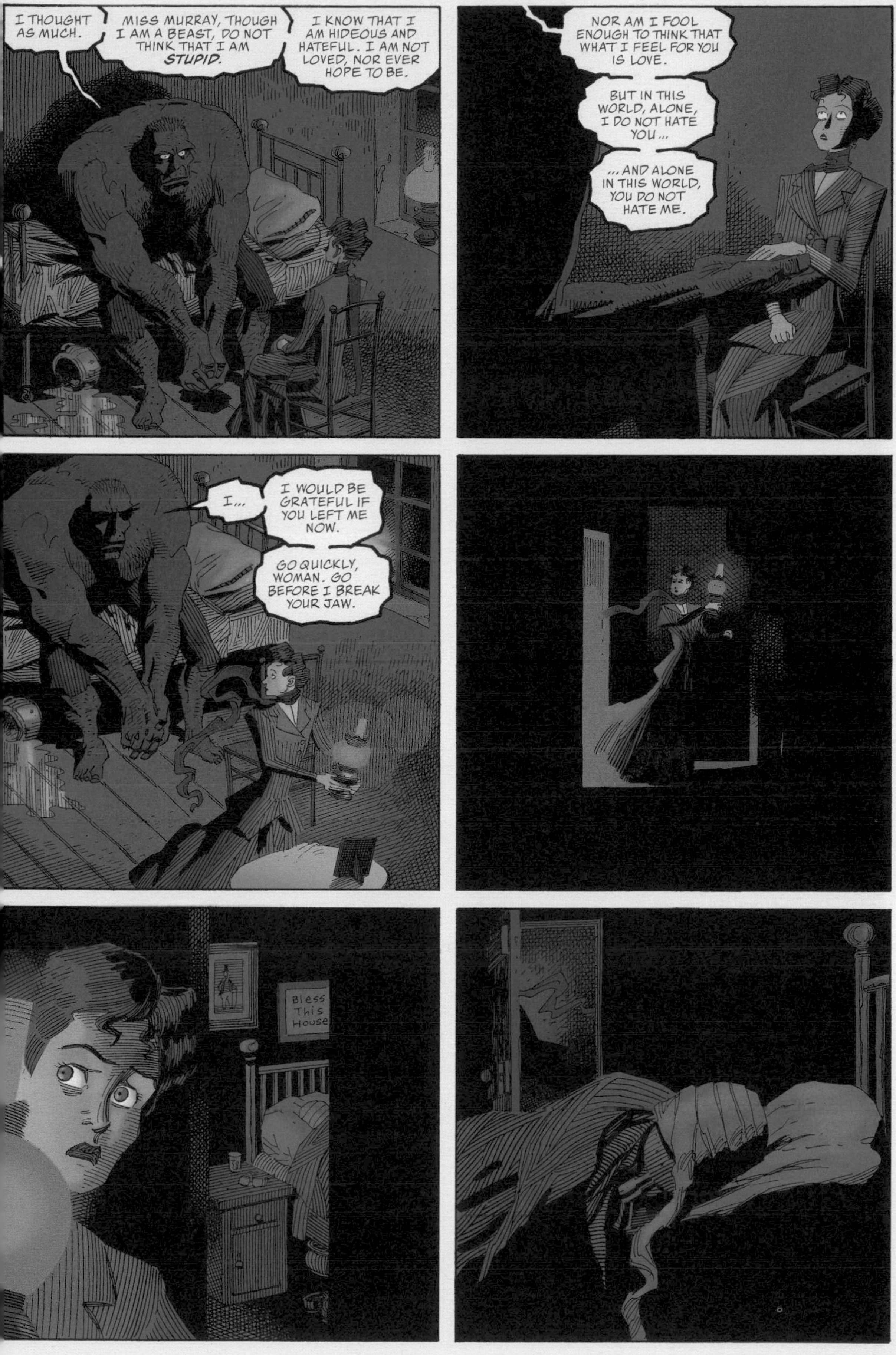
I THOUGHT AS MUCH.
MISS MURRAY, THOUGH I AM A BEAST, DO NOT THINK THAT I AM STUPID.
I KNOW THAT I AM HIDEOUS AND HATEFUL. I AM NOT LOVED, NOR EVER HOPE TO BE.
NOR AM I FOOL ENOUGH TO THINK THAT WHAT I FEEL FOR YOU IS LOVE.
BUT IN THIS WORLD, ALONE, I DO NOT HATE YOU...
...AND ALONE IN THIS WORLD, YOU DO NOT HATE ME.
I...
I WOULD BE GRATEFUL IF YOU LEFT ME NOW.
GO QUICKLY, WOMAN. GO BEFORE I BREAK YOUR JAW.
Bless This House

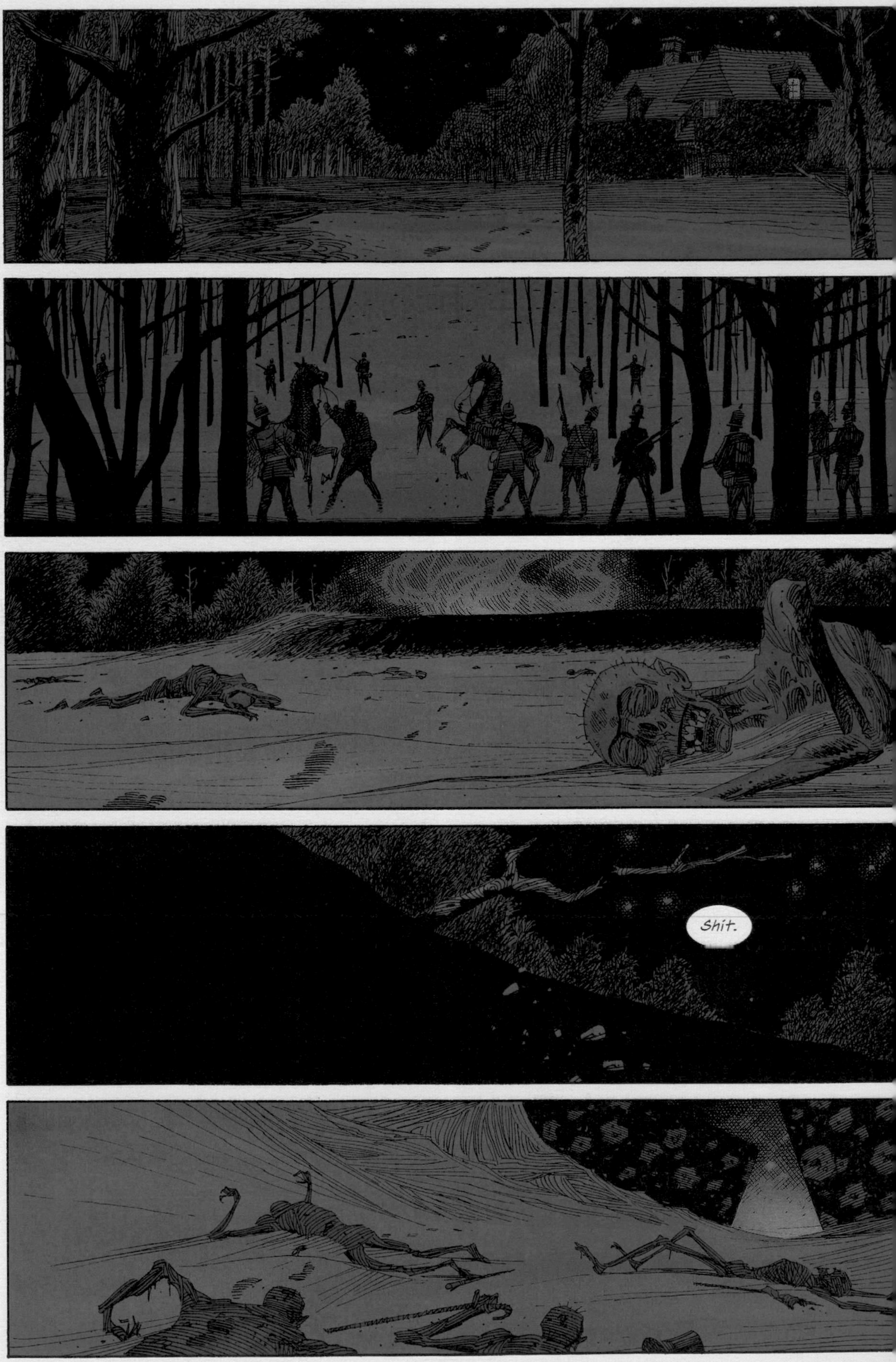
Shit.

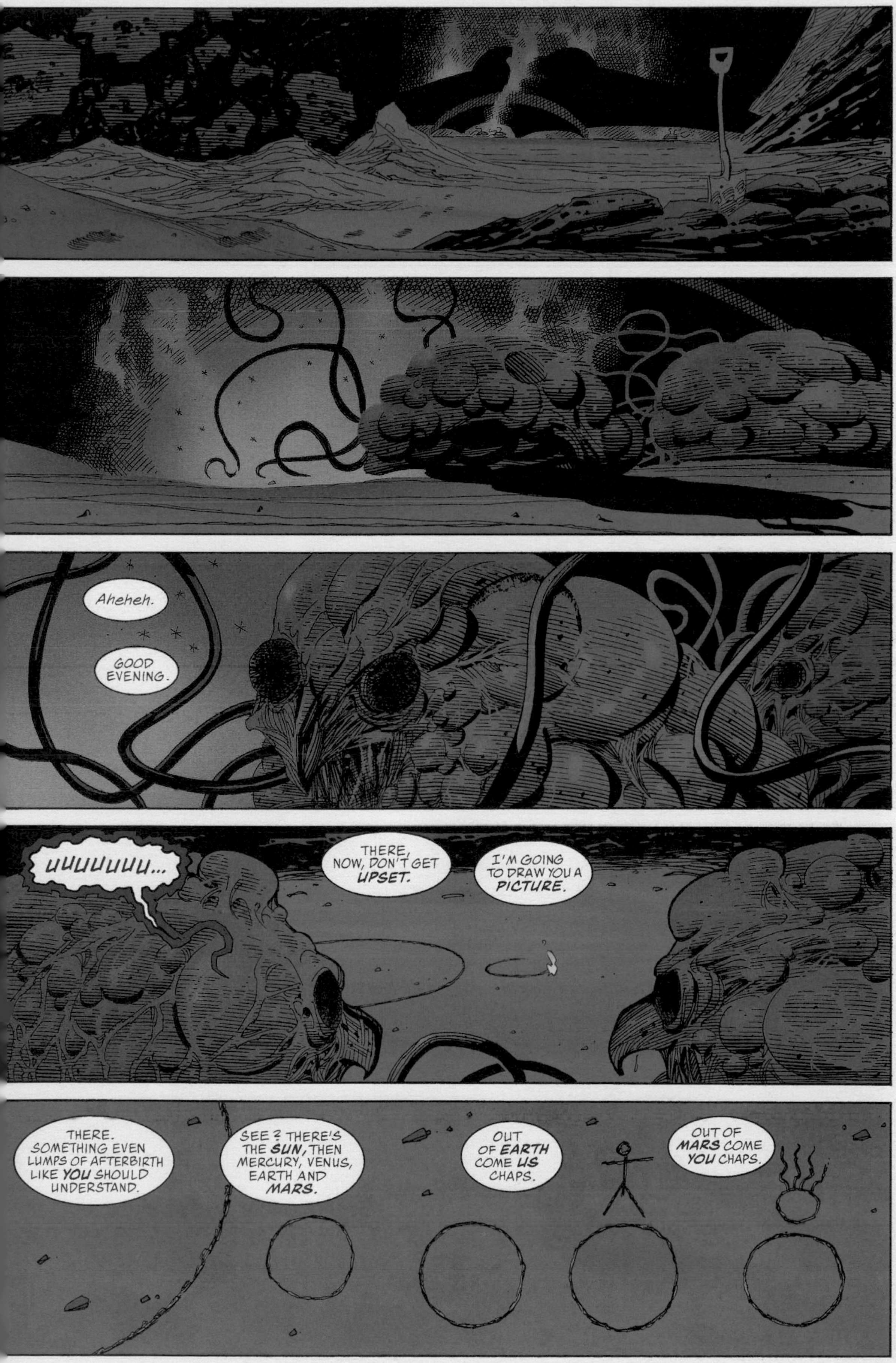
Aheheh.
GOOD EVENING.
UUUUUUU...
THERE, NOW, DON'T GET UPSET.
I'M GOING TO DRAW YOU A PICTURE.
THERE. SOMETHING EVEN LUMPS OF AFTERBIRTH LIKE YOU SHOULD UNDERSTAND.
SEE? THERE'S THE SUN, THEN MERCURY, VENUS, EARTH AND MARS.
OUT OF EARTH COME US CHAPS.
OUT OF MARS COME YOU CHAPS.

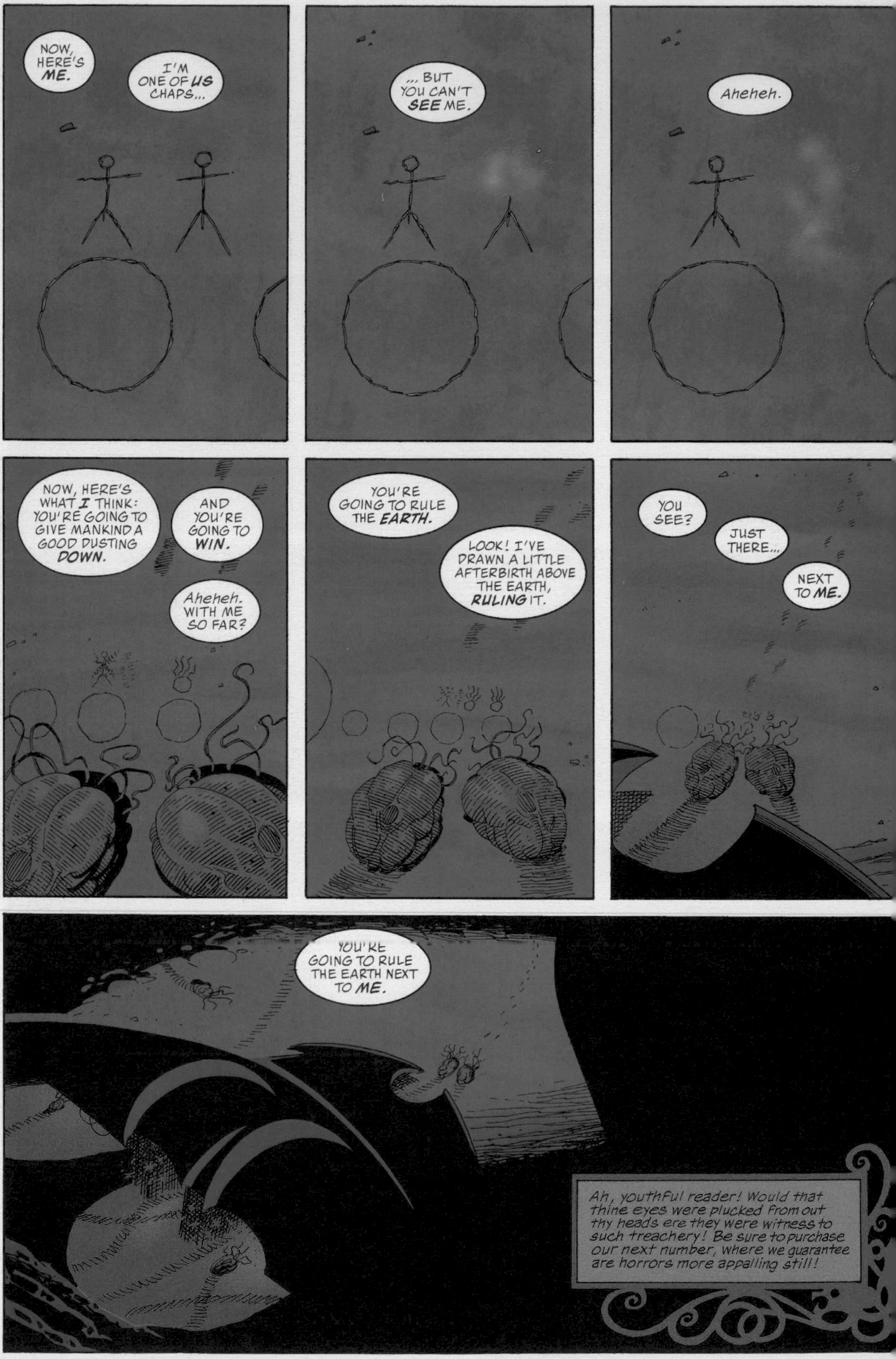
NOW, HERE'S ME.
I'M ONE OF US CHAPS...
... BUT YOU CAN'T SEE ME.
Aheheh.
NOW, HERE'S WHAT I THINK: YOU'RE GOING TO GIVE MANKIND A GOOD DUSTING DOWN.
AND YOU'RE GOING TO WIN.
Aheheh. WITH ME SO FAR?
YOU'RE GOING TO RULE THE EARTH.
LOOK! I'VE DRAWN A LITTLE AFTERBIRTH ABOVE THE EARTH, RULING IT.
YOU SEE?
JUST THERE...
NEXT TO ME.
YOU'RE GOING TO RULE THE EARTH NEXT TO ME.
Ah, youthful reader! Would that thine eyes were plucked from out thy heads ere they were witness to such treachery! Be sure to purchase our next number, where we guarantee are horrors more appalling still!

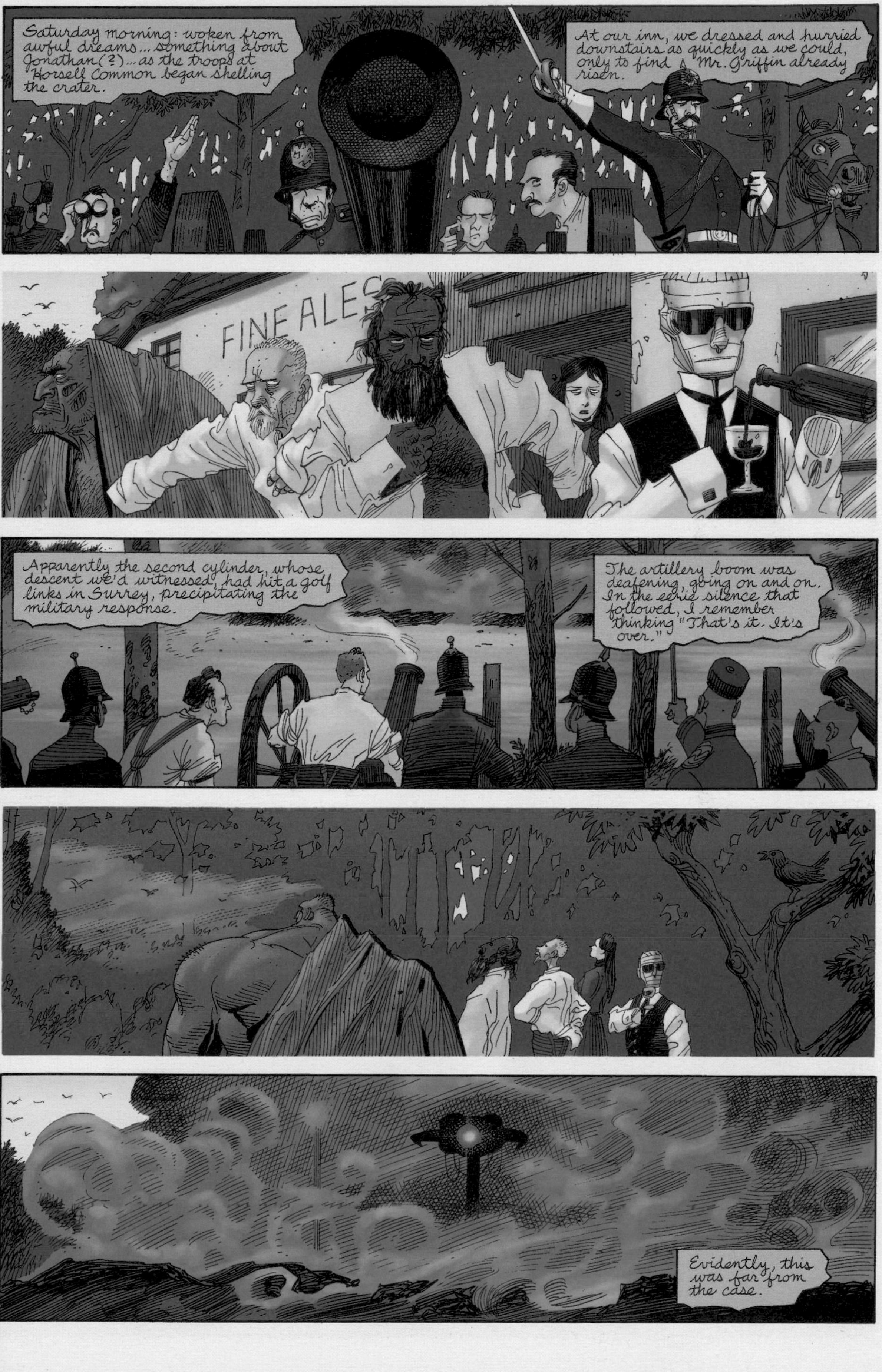
Saturday morning: woken from awful dreams... something about Jonathan(?)... as the troops at Horsell Common began shelling the crater.
At our inn, we dressed and hurried downstairs as quickly as we could, only to find Mr. Griffin already risen.
FINE ALES
Apparently the second cylinder, whose descent we'd witnessed, had hit a golf links in Surrey, precipitating the military response.
The artillery boom was deafening, going on and on. In the eerie silence that followed, I remember thinking "That's it. It's over."
Evidently, this was far from the case.

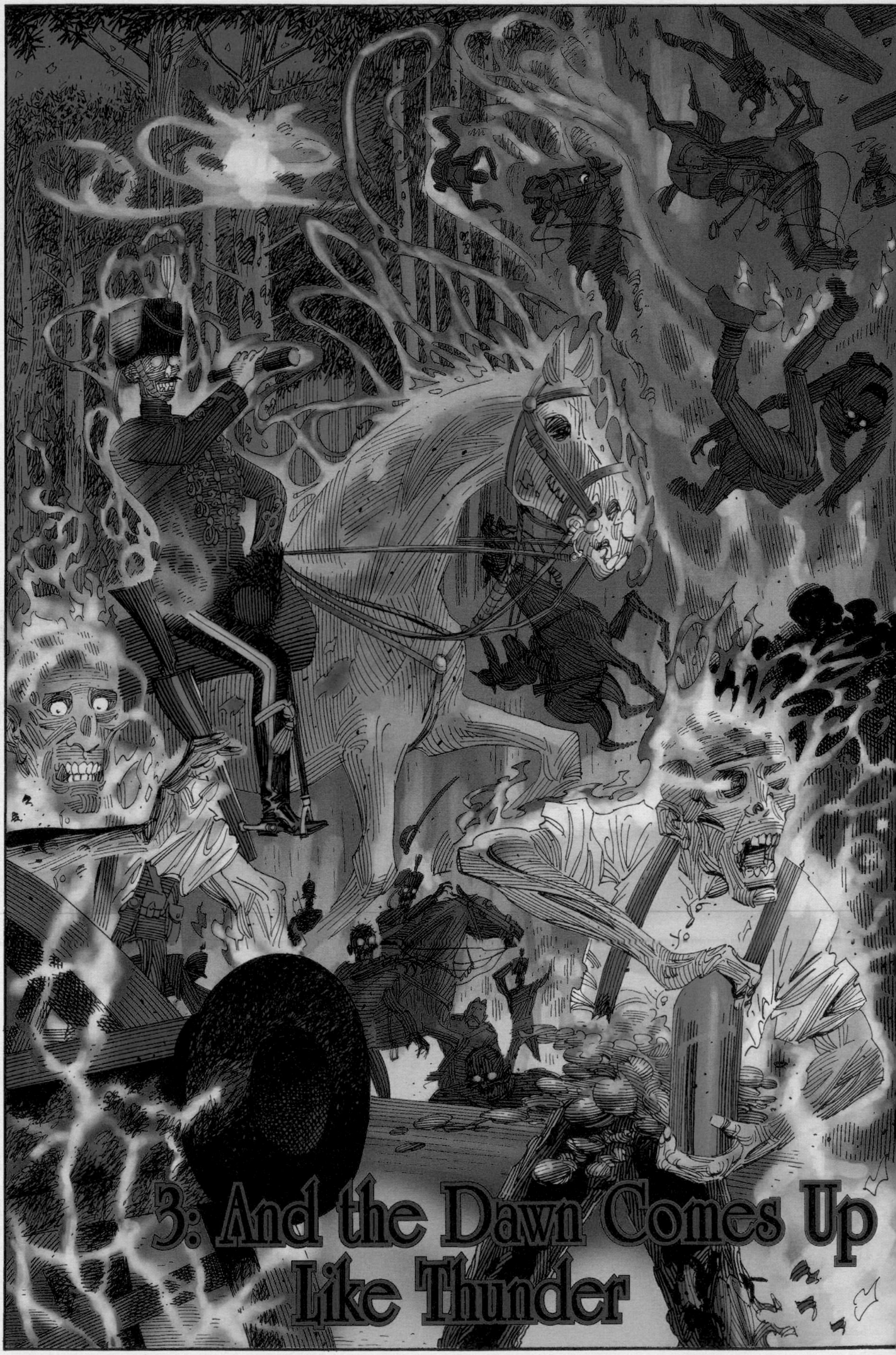
3: And the Dawn Comes Up
Like Thunder

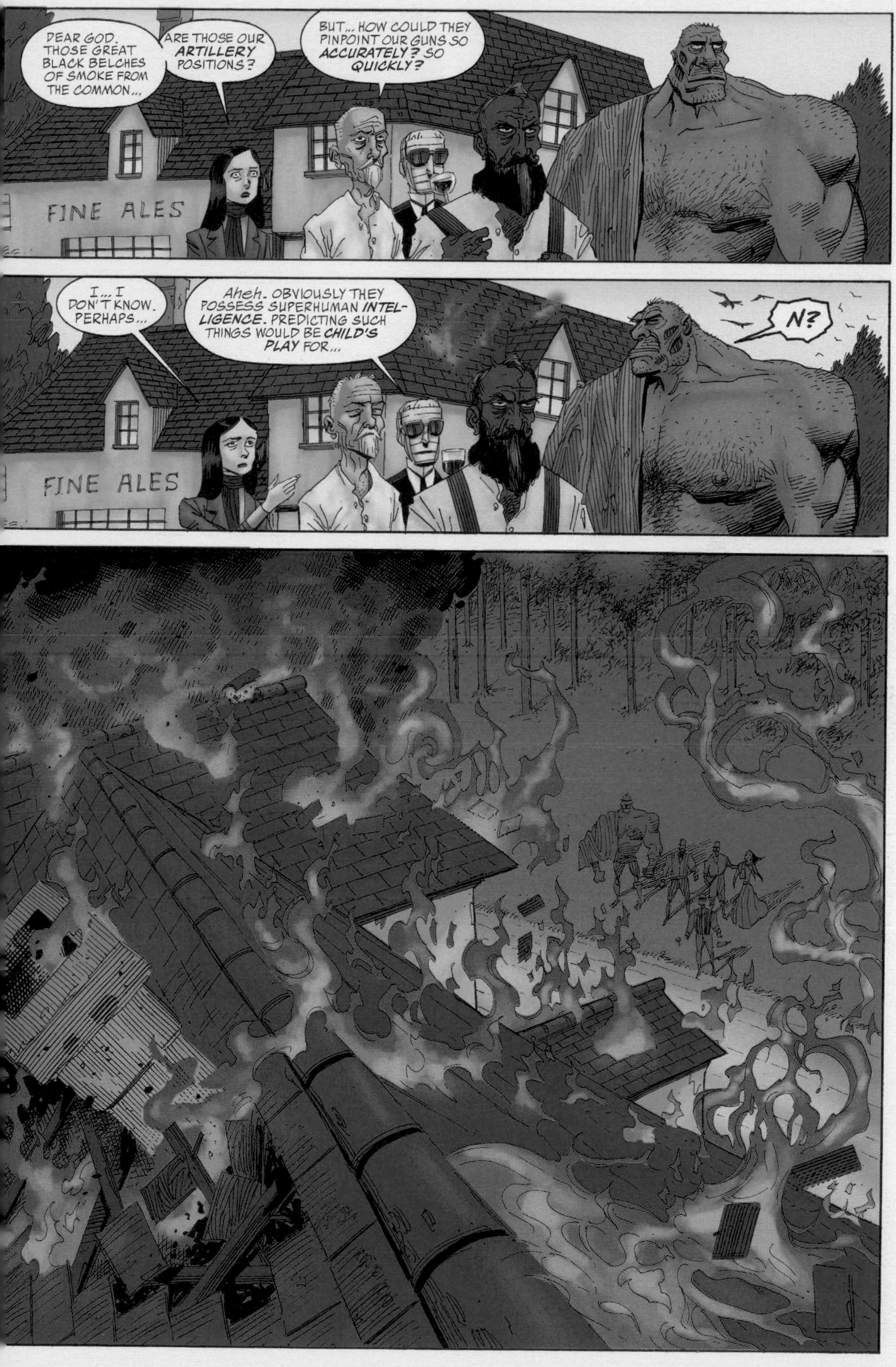
DEAR GOD. THOSE GREAT BLACK BELCHES OF SMOKE FROM THE COMMON...
ARE THOSE OUR ARTILLERY POSITIONS?
BUT... HOW COULD THEY PINPOINT OUR GUNS SO ACCURATELY? SO QUICKLY?
FINE ALES
I... I DON'T KNOW. PERHAPS...
Aheh. OBVIOUSLY THEY POSSESS SUPERHUMAN INTEL-LIGENCE. PREDICTING SUCH THINGS WOULD BE CHILD'S PLAY FOR...
N?
FINE ALES

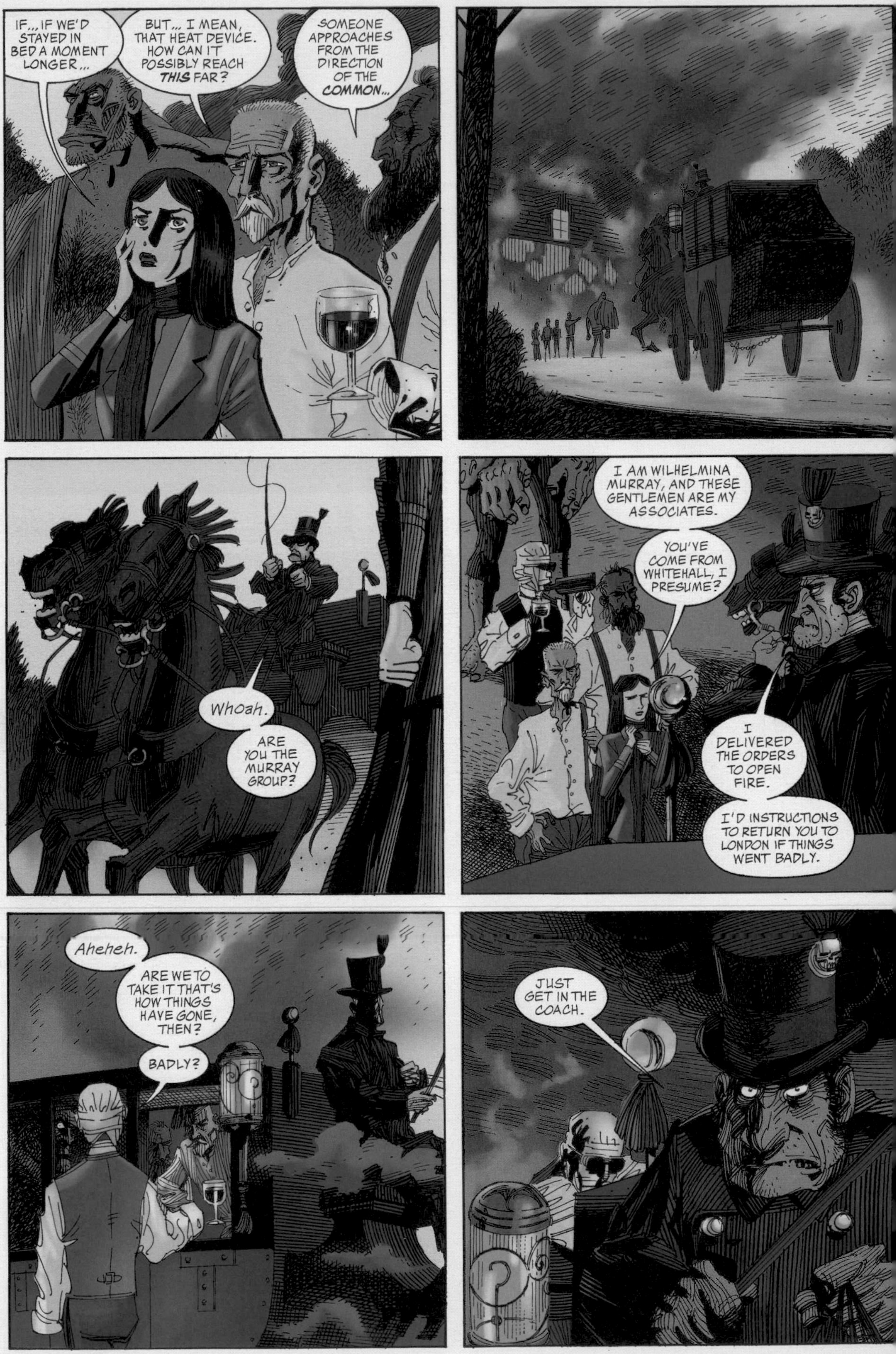
IF... IF WE'D STAYED IN BED A MOMENT LONGER...
BUT... I MEAN, THAT HEAT DEVICE. HOW CAN IT POSSIBLY REACH THIS FAR?
SOMEONE APPROACHES FROM THE DIRECTION OF THE COMMON...
Whoah.
ARE YOU THE MURRAY GROUP?
I AM WILHELMINA MURRAY, AND THESE GENTLEMEN ARE MY ASSOCIATES.
YOU'VE COME FROM WHITEHALL, I PRESUME?
I DELIVERED THE ORDERS TO OPEN FIRE.
I'D INSTRUCTIONS TO RETURN YOU TO LONDON IF THINGS WENT BADLY.
Aheheh.
ARE WE TO TAKE IT THAT'S HOW THINGS HAVE GONE, THEN?
BADLY?
JUST GET IN THE COACH.

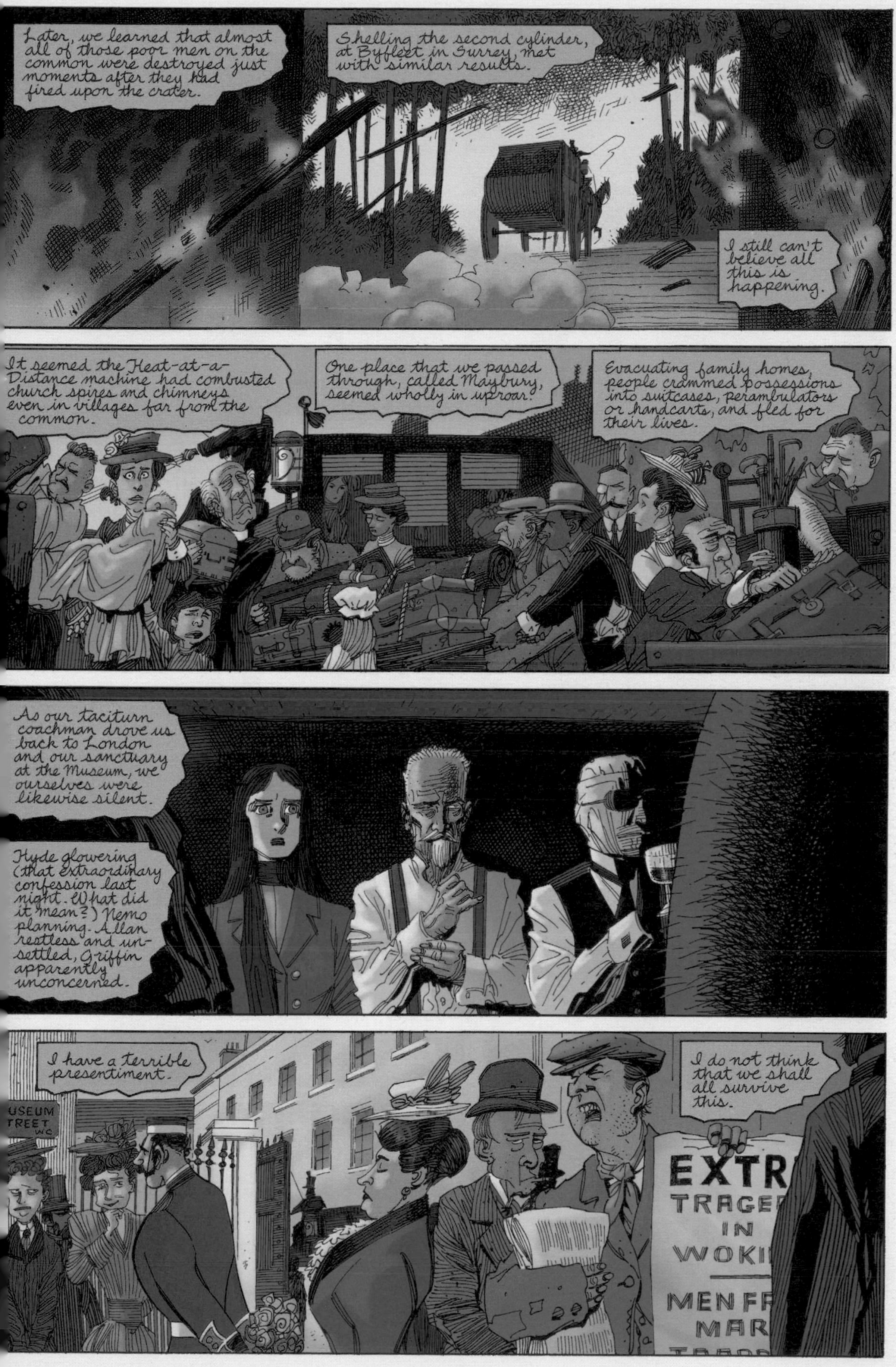
Later, we learned that almost all of those poor men on the common were destroyed just moments after they had fired upon the crater.
Shelling the second cylinder, at Byfleet in Surrey, met with similar results.
I still can't believe all this is happening.
It seemed the Heat-at-a-Distance machine had combusted church spires and chimneys even in villages far from the common.
One place that we passed through, called Maybury, seemed wholly in uproar.
Evacuating family homes, people crammed possessions into suitcases, perambulators or handcarts, and fled for their lives.
As our taciturn coachman drove us back to London and our sanctuary at the Museum, we ourselves were likewise silent.
Hyde glowering (that extraordinary confession last night. What did it mean?) Nemo planning. Allan restless and unsettled, Griffin apparently unconcerned.
I have a terrible presentiment.
USEUM TREET WC
I do not think that we shall all survive this.
EXTR
TRAGE
IN
WOKI
MEN FR
MAR

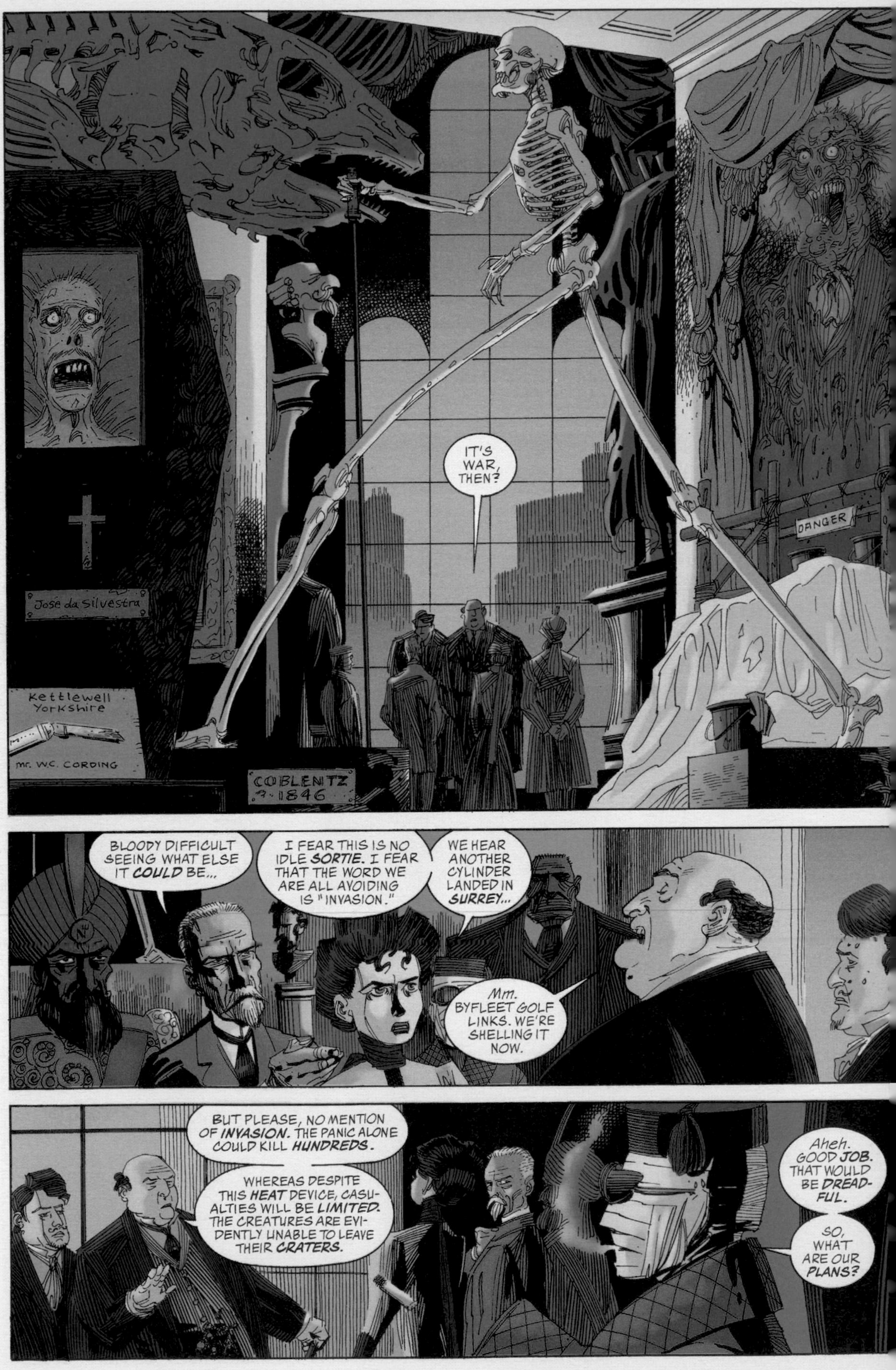
José da Silvestra
Kettlewell Yorkshire
mr. W.C. CORDING
COBLENTZ 1846
DANGER
IT'S WAR, THEN?
BLOODY DIFFICULT SEEING WHAT ELSE IT COULD BE...
I FEAR THIS IS NO IDLE SORTIE. I FEAR THAT THE WORD WE ARE ALL AVOIDING IS "INVASION."
WE HEAR ANOTHER CYLINDER LANDED IN SURREY...
Mm. BYFLEET GOLF LINKS. WE'RE SHELLING IT NOW.
BUT PLEASE, NO MENTION OF INVASION. THE PANIC ALONE COULD KILL HUNDREDS.
WHEREAS DESPITE THIS HEAT DEVICE, CASUALTIES WILL BE LIMITED. THE CREATURES ARE EVIDENTLY UNABLE TO LEAVE THEIR CRATERS.
Aheh. GOOD JOB. THAT WOULD BE DREADFUL.
SO, WHAT ARE OUR PLANS?

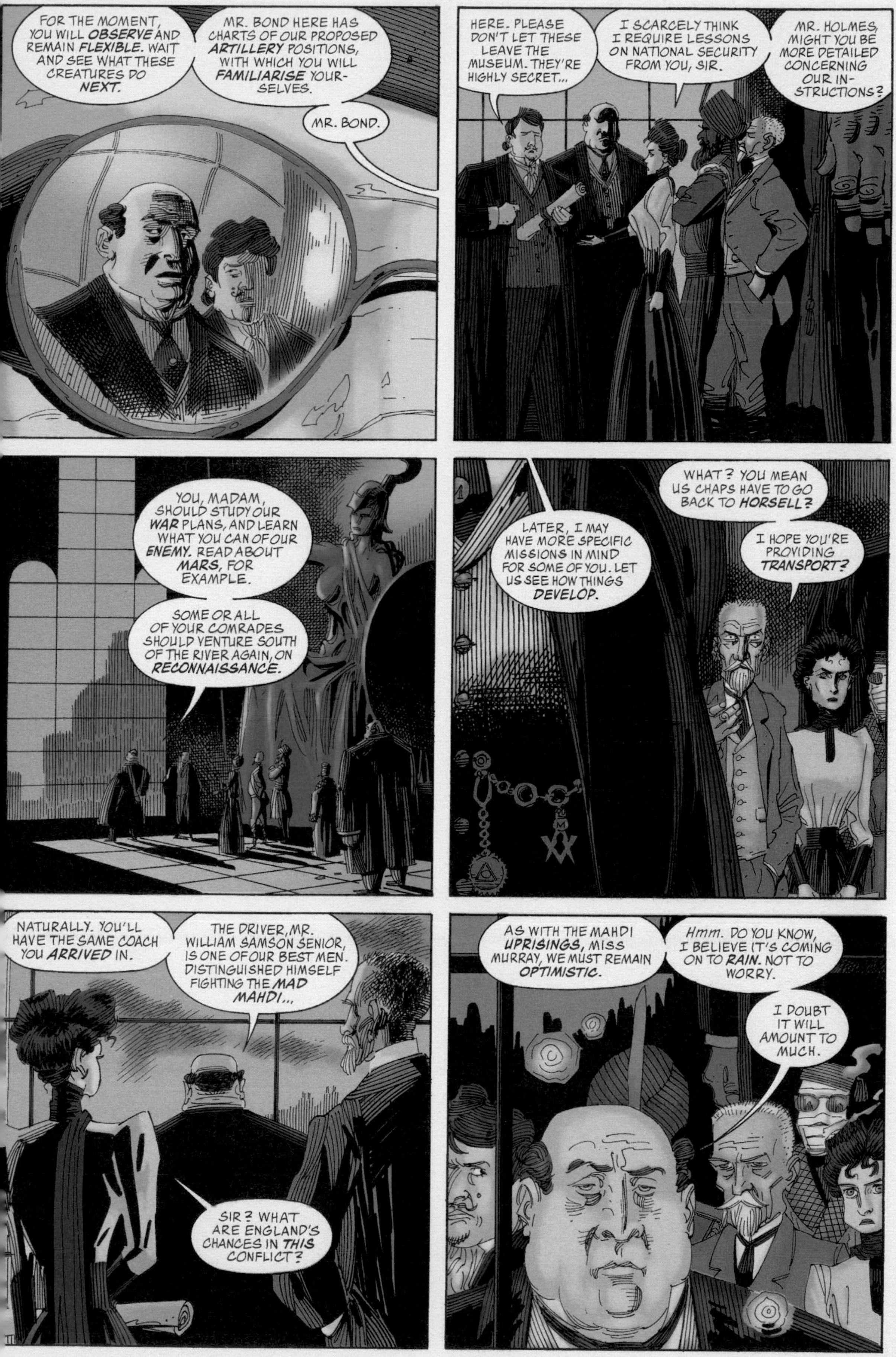
FOR THE MOMENT, YOU WILL OBSERVE AND REMAIN FLEXIBLE. WAIT AND SEE WHAT THESE CREATURES DO NEXT.
MR. BOND HERE HAS CHARTS OF OUR PROPOSED ARTILLERY POSITIONS, WITH WHICH YOU WILL FAMILIARISE YOURSELVES.
MR. BOND.
HERE. PLEASE DON'T LET THESE LEAVE THE MUSEUM. THEY'RE HIGHLY SECRET...
I SCARCELY THINK I REQUIRE LESSONS ON NATIONAL SECURITY FROM YOU, SIR.
MR. HOLMES, MIGHT YOU BE MORE DETAILED CONCERNING OUR INSTRUCTIONS?
YOU, MADAM, SHOULD STUDY OUR WAR PLANS, AND LEARN WHAT YOU CAN OF OUR ENEMY. READ ABOUT MARS, FOR EXAMPLE.
SOME OR ALL OF YOUR COMRADES SHOULD VENTURE SOUTH OF THE RIVER AGAIN, ON RECONNAISSANCE.
LATER, I MAY HAVE MORE SPECIFIC MISSIONS IN MIND FOR SOME OF YOU. LET US SEE HOW THINGS DEVELOP.
WHAT? YOU MEAN US CHAPS HAVE TO GO BACK TO HORSELL?
I HOPE YOU'RE PROVIDING TRANSPORT?
NATURALLY. YOU'LL HAVE THE SAME COACH YOU ARRIVED IN.
THE DRIVER, MR. WILLIAM SAMSON SENIOR, IS ONE OF OUR BEST MEN. DISTINGUISHED HIMSELF FIGHTING THE MAD MAHDI...
SIR? WHAT ARE ENGLAND'S CHANCES IN THIS CONFLICT?
AS WITH THE MAHDI UPRISINGS, MISS MURRAY, WE MUST REMAIN OPTIMISTIC.
Hmm. DO YOU KNOW, I BELIEVE IT'S COMING ON TO RAIN. NOT TO WORRY.
I DOUBT IT WILL AMOUNT TO MUCH.

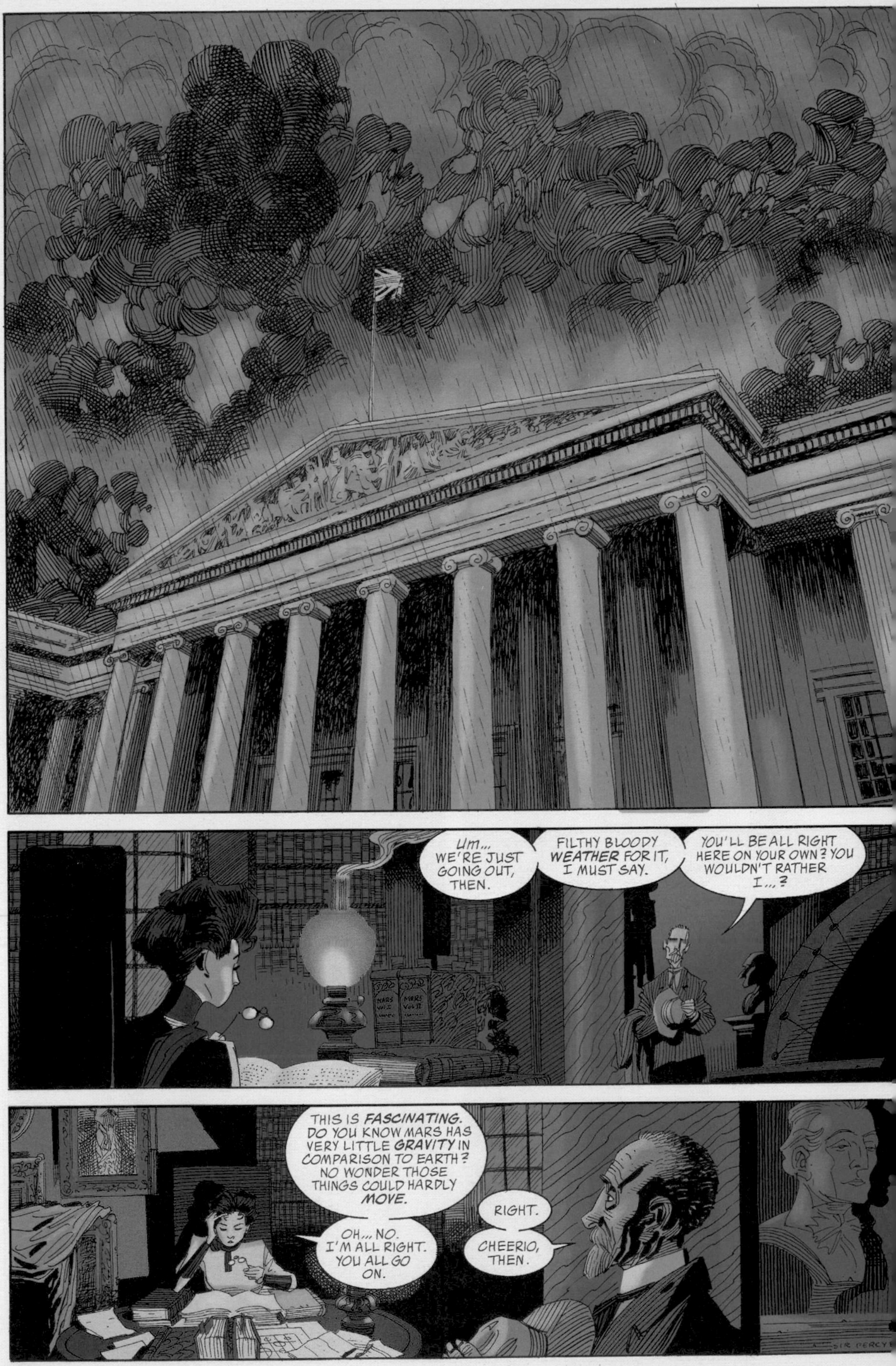
UM... WE'RE JUST GOING OUT, THEN.
FILTHY BLOODY *WEATHER* FOR IT, I MUST SAY.
YOU'LL BE ALL RIGHT HERE ON YOUR OWN? YOU WOULDN'T RATHER I...?
THIS IS *FASCINATING*. DO YOU KNOW MARS HAS VERY LITTLE *GRAVITY* IN COMPARISON TO EARTH? NO WONDER THOSE THINGS COULD HARDLY *MOVE*.
OH... NO. I'M ALL RIGHT. YOU ALL GO ON.
RIGHT.
CHEERIO, THEN.

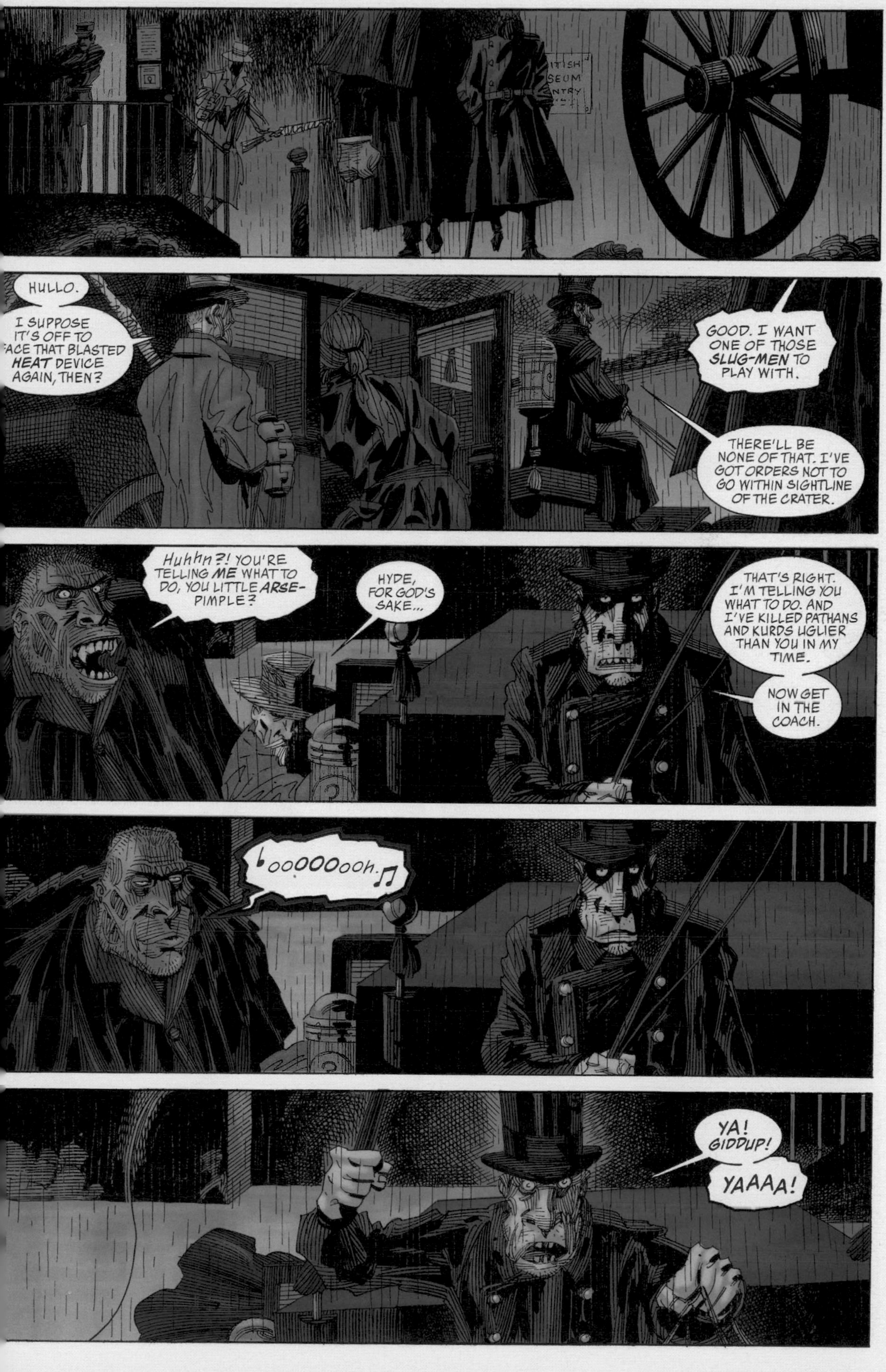
ITISH
SEUM
NTRY
HULLO.
I SUPPOSE IT'S OFF TO FACE THAT BLASTED HEAT DEVICE AGAIN, THEN?
GOOD. I WANT ONE OF THOSE SLUG-MEN TO PLAY WITH.
THERE'LL BE NONE OF THAT. I'VE GOT ORDERS NOT TO GO WITHIN SIGHTLINE OF THE CRATER.
Huhhn?! YOU'RE TELLING ME WHAT TO DO, YOU LITTLE ARSE-PIMPLE?
HYDE, FOR GOD'S SAKE...
THAT'S RIGHT. I'M TELLING YOU WHAT TO DO. AND I'VE KILLED PATHANS AND KURDS UGLIER THAN YOU IN MY TIME.
NOW GET IN THE COACH.
booOOOooh.
YA! GIDDUP!
YAAAA!

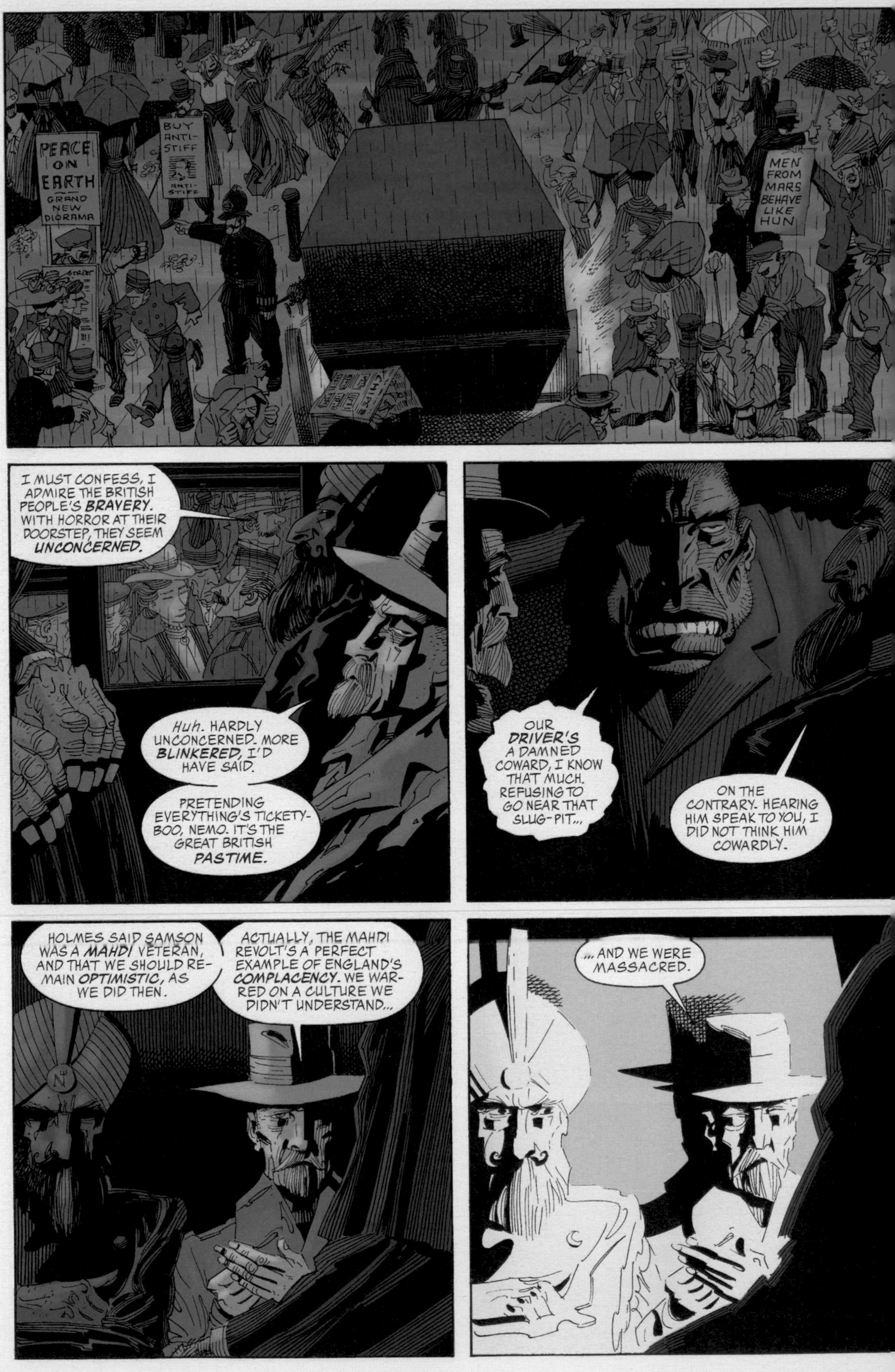
PEACE ON EARTH GRAND NEW DIORAMA
BUY ANTI-STIFF
MEN FROM MARS BEHAVE LIKE HUN
I MUST CONFESS, I ADMIRE THE BRITISH PEOPLE'S BRAVERY. WITH HORROR AT THEIR DOORSTEP, THEY SEEM UNCONCERNED.
Huh. HARDLY UNCONCERNED. MORE BLINKERED, I'D HAVE SAID.
PRETENDING EVERYTHING'S TICKETY-BOO, NEMO. IT'S THE GREAT BRITISH PASTIME.
OUR DRIVER'S A DAMNED COWARD, I KNOW THAT MUCH. REFUSING TO GO NEAR THAT SLUG-PIT...
ON THE CONTRARY. HEARING HIM SPEAK TO YOU, I DID NOT THINK HIM COWARDLY.
HOLMES SAID SAMSON WAS A MAHDI VETERAN, AND THAT WE SHOULD REMAIN OPTIMISTIC, AS WE DID THEN.
ACTUALLY, THE MAHDI REVOLT'S A PERFECT EXAMPLE OF ENGLAND'S COMPLACENCY. WE WARRED ON A CULTURE WE DIDN'T UNDERSTAND...
...AND WE WERE MASSACRED.

MEN FROM MARS— FRESH ATTEM HAVE BEEN TO SIG WITH

1898

Hunngh. WHAT'S THE POINT OF ALL THIS, IF WE'RE NOT GOING NEAR THAT DAMN CRATER?

PRESUMABLY, WE ARE OBSERVING CONDITIONS HERE. THE HAMLET OF MAYBURY, FOR EXAMPLE, IS QUITE DESERTED...

WAIT A MINUTE. WHERE'S GRIFFIN?

I'D ASSUMED HE'D STAYED AT THE MUSEUM. HOLMES DIDN'T SPECIFY THAT WE SHOULD ALL ACCOMPANY THIS RECONNAISSANCE.

I-- I SUPPOSE NOT.

THIS PISSING STORM'S GETTING WORSE. LET'S HOPE THAT LITTLE BASTARD'S HORSES DON'T--

What...?

ARRRR!

DRIVER, WHAT ARE YOU DOING? YOU ALMOST TURNED US OVER!

THAT LAST LIGHTNING FLASH. I THOUGHT I SAW SOMETHING!

WH-WHAT'S THAT NOISE, BENEATH THE THUNDER? IT'S ALMOST AS IF--

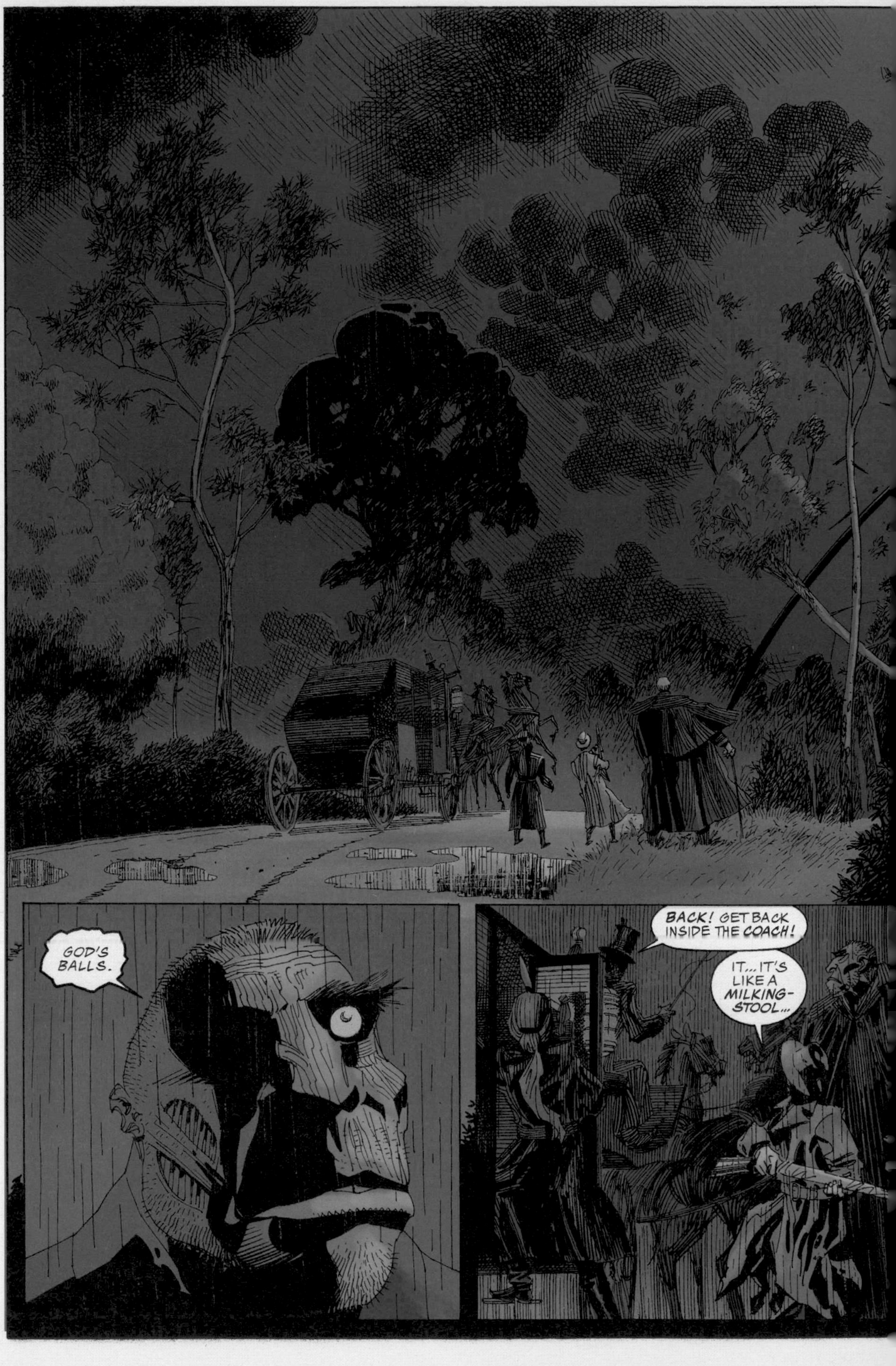
GOD'S BALLS.
BACK! GET BACK INSIDE THE COACH!
IT... IT'S LIKE A MILKING-STOOL...

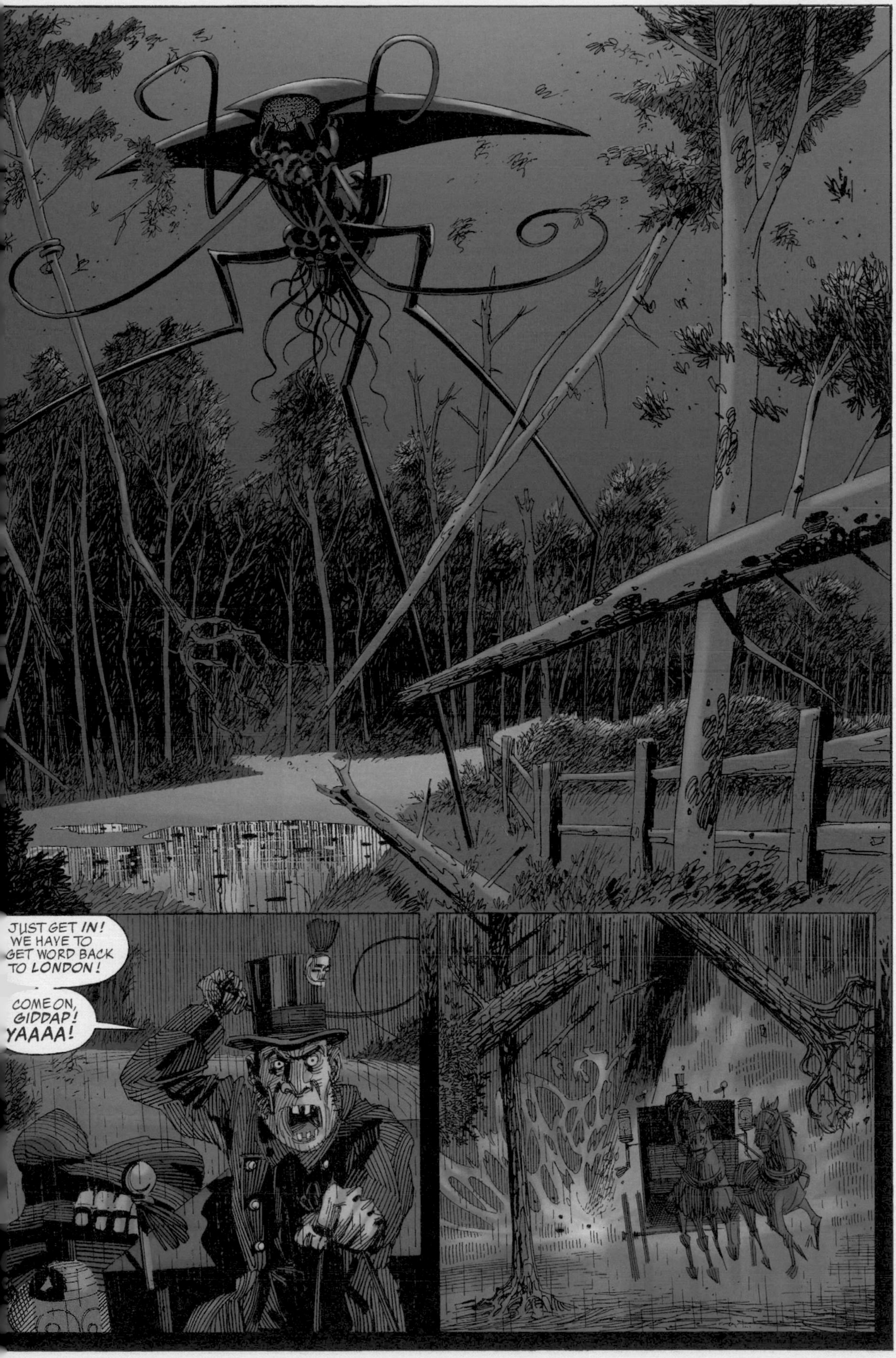
JUST GET IN! WE HAVE TO GET WORD BACK TO LONDON!
COME ON, GIDDAP! YAAAA!

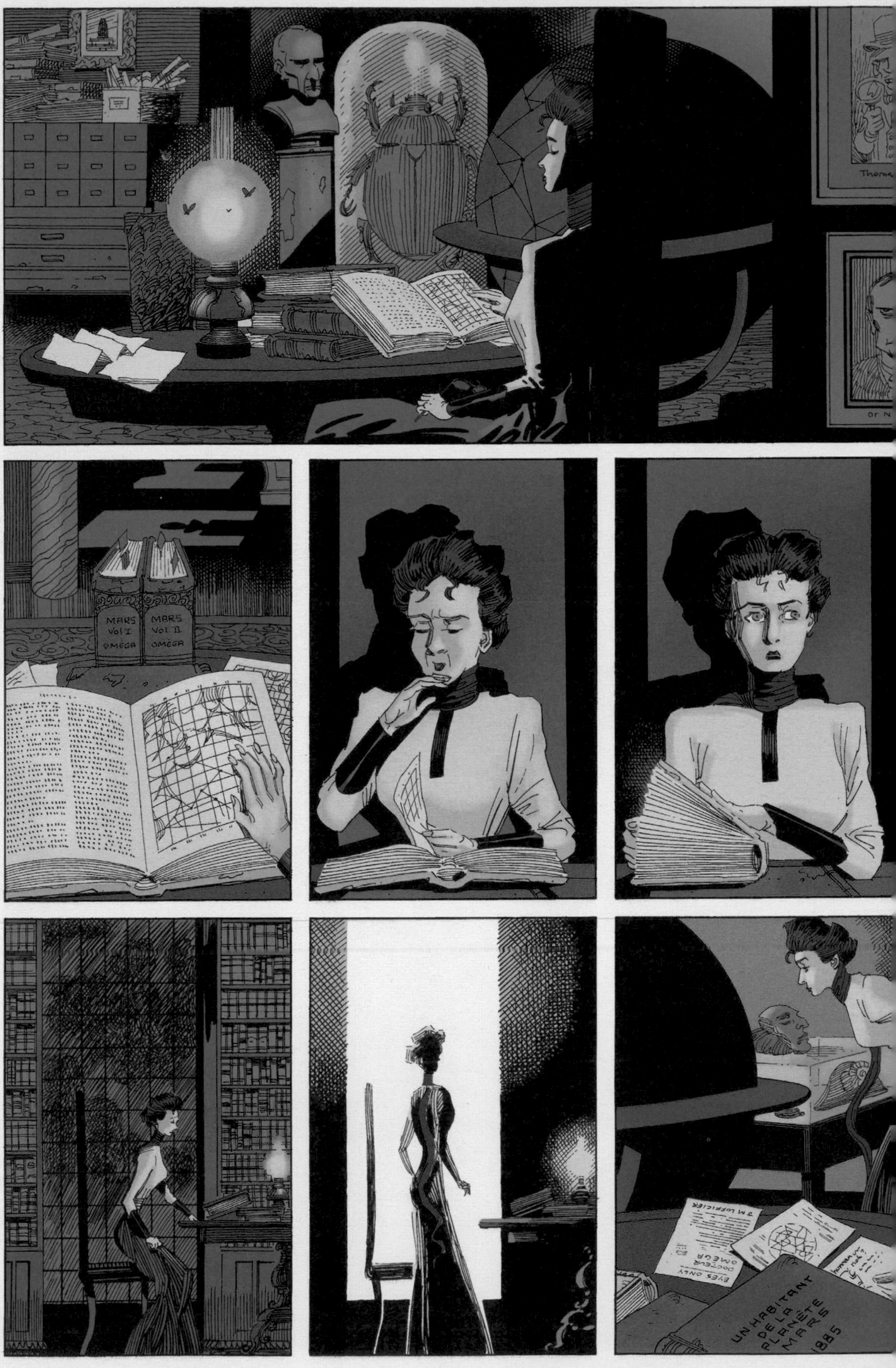
MARS Vol I OMÉGA
MARS Vol II OMÉGA
J M LUFFICIER
EYES ONLY
DOCTEUR OMEGA
UN HABITANT DE LA PLANÈTE MARS 1885

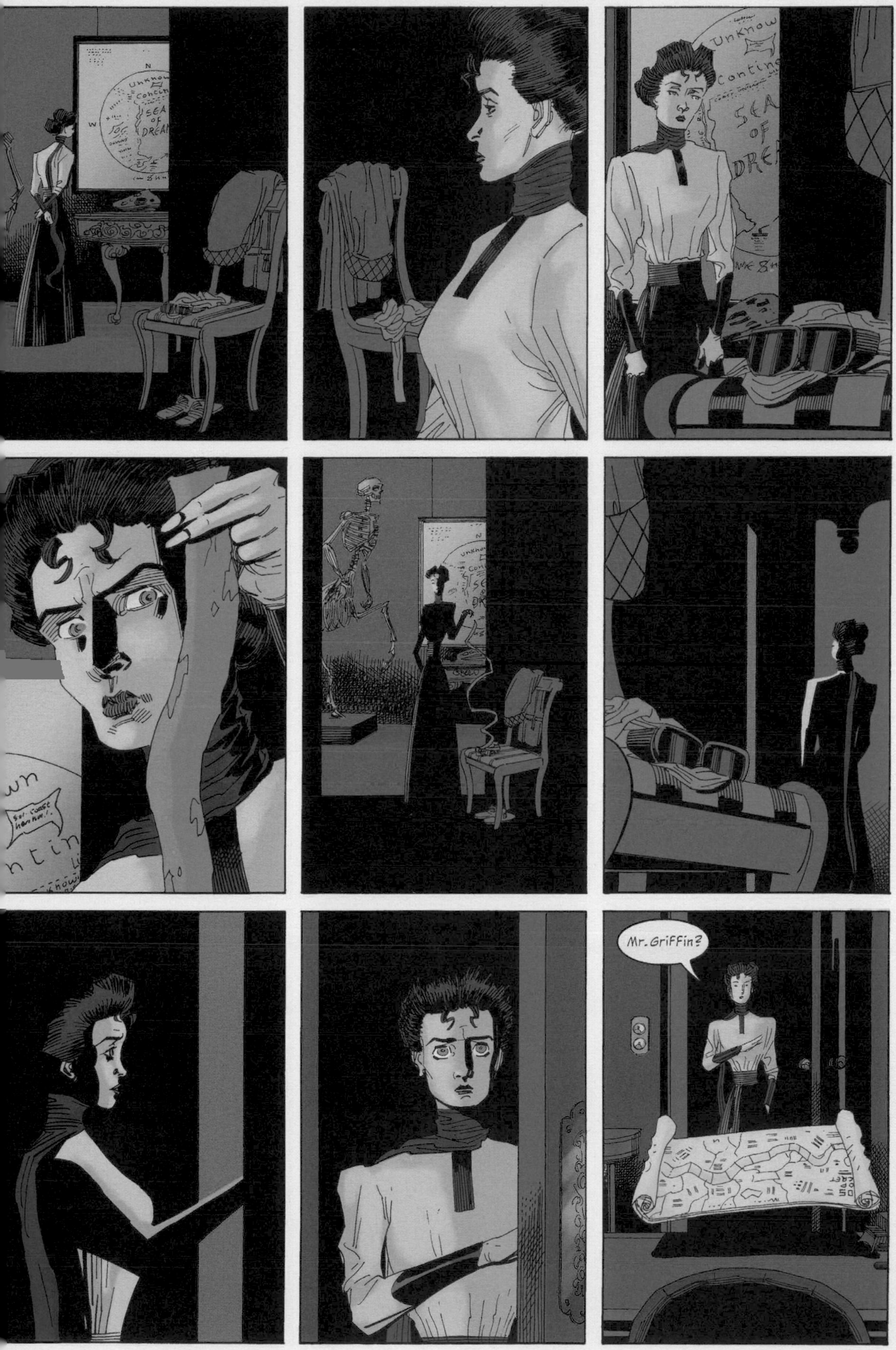
Mr. Griffin?

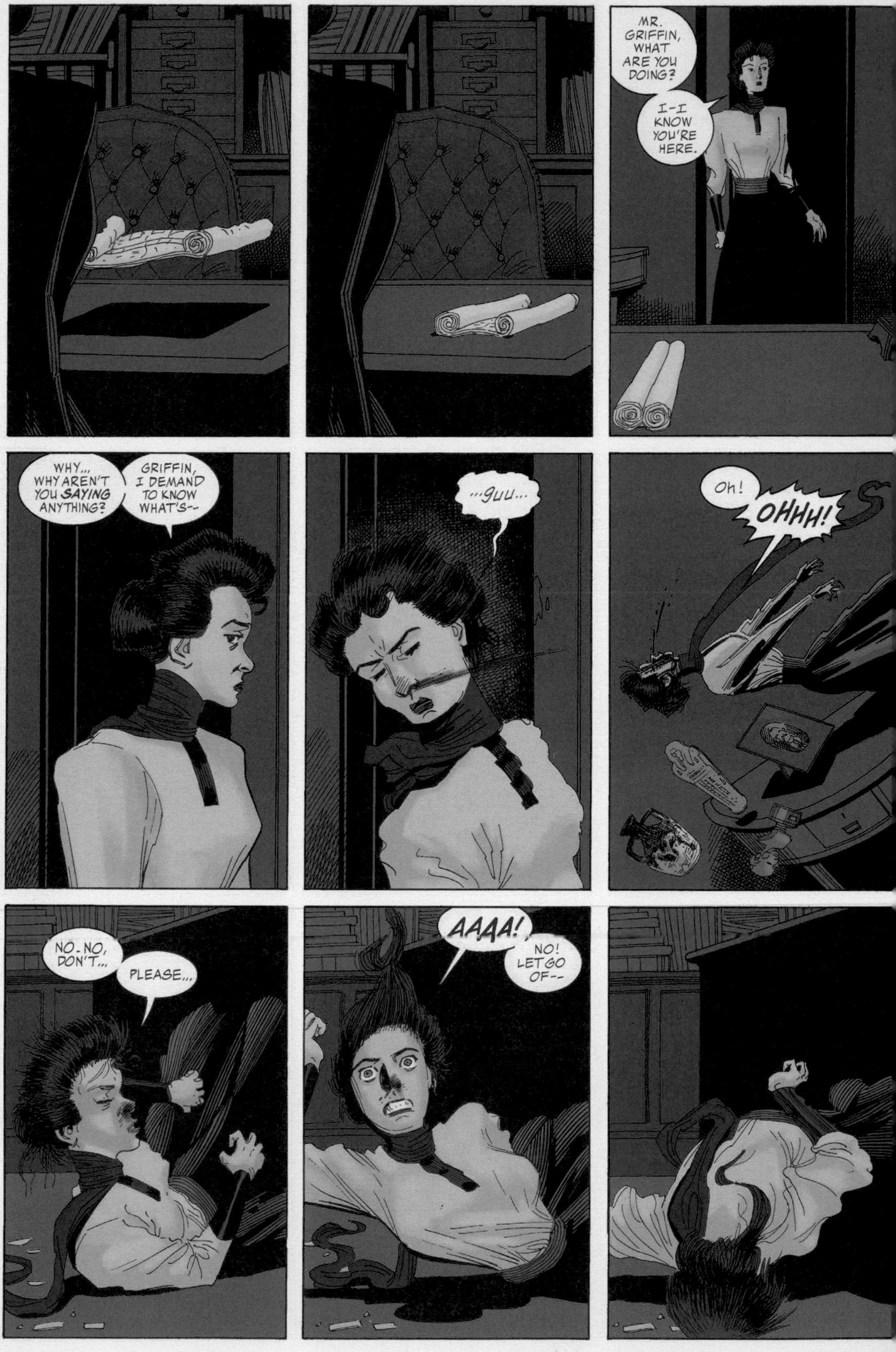
MR. GRIFFIN, WHAT ARE YOU DOING?
I-I KNOW YOU'RE HERE.
WHY... WHY AREN'T YOU SAYING ANYTHING?
GRIFFIN, I DEMAND TO KNOW WHAT'S--
...guu...
Oh!
OHHH!
NO-NO, DON'T...
PLEASE...
AAAA!
NO! LET GO OF--

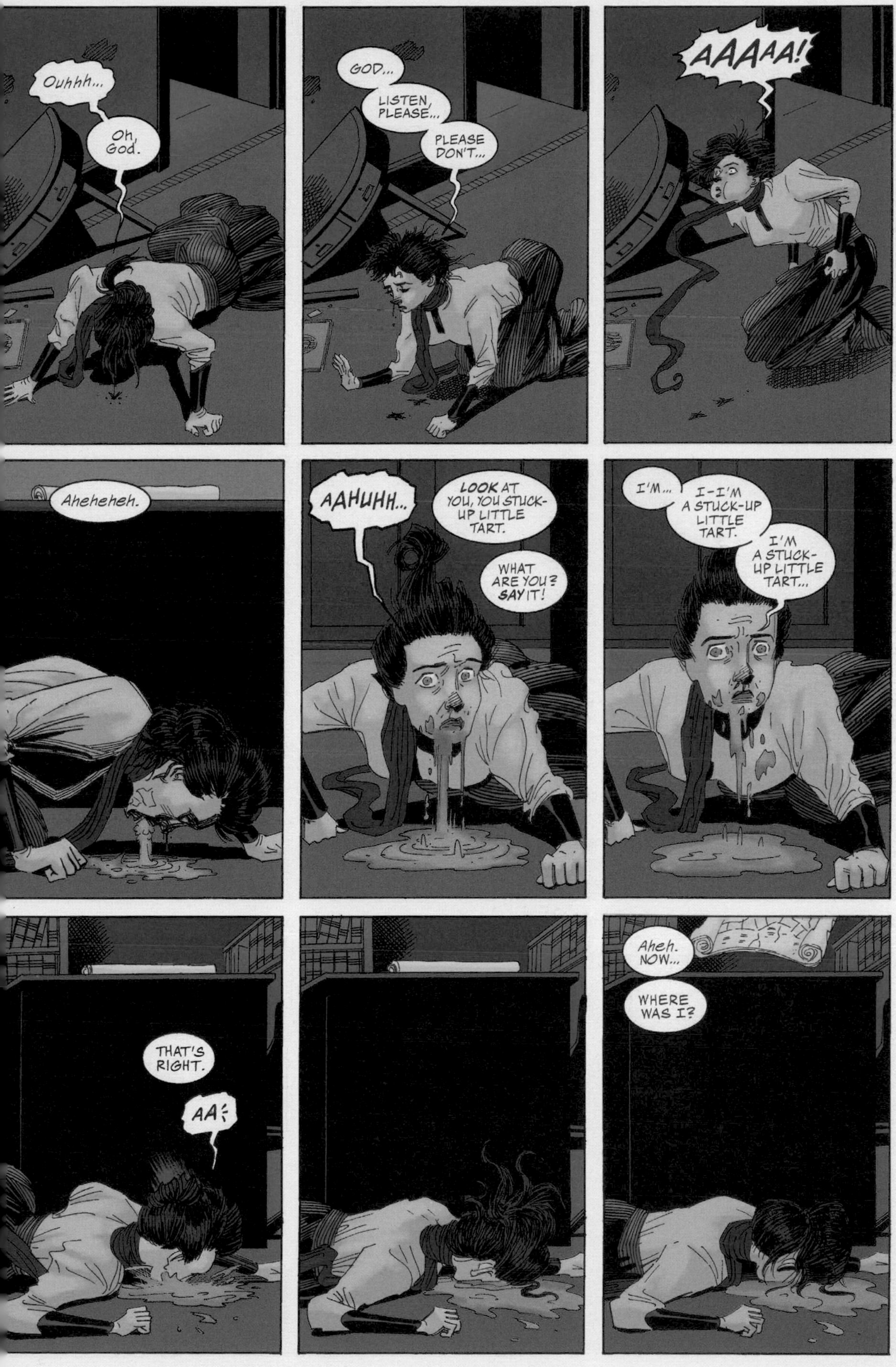
Ouhhh...
Oh, God.
GOD...
LISTEN, PLEASE...
PLEASE DON'T...
AAAAA!
Aheheheh.
AAHUHH...
LOOK AT YOU, YOU STUCK-UP LITTLE TART.
WHAT ARE YOU? SAY IT!
I'M...
I-I'M A STUCK-UP LITTLE TART.
I'M A STUCK-UP LITTLE TART...
THAT'S RIGHT.
AA;
Aheh. NOW...
WHERE WAS I?

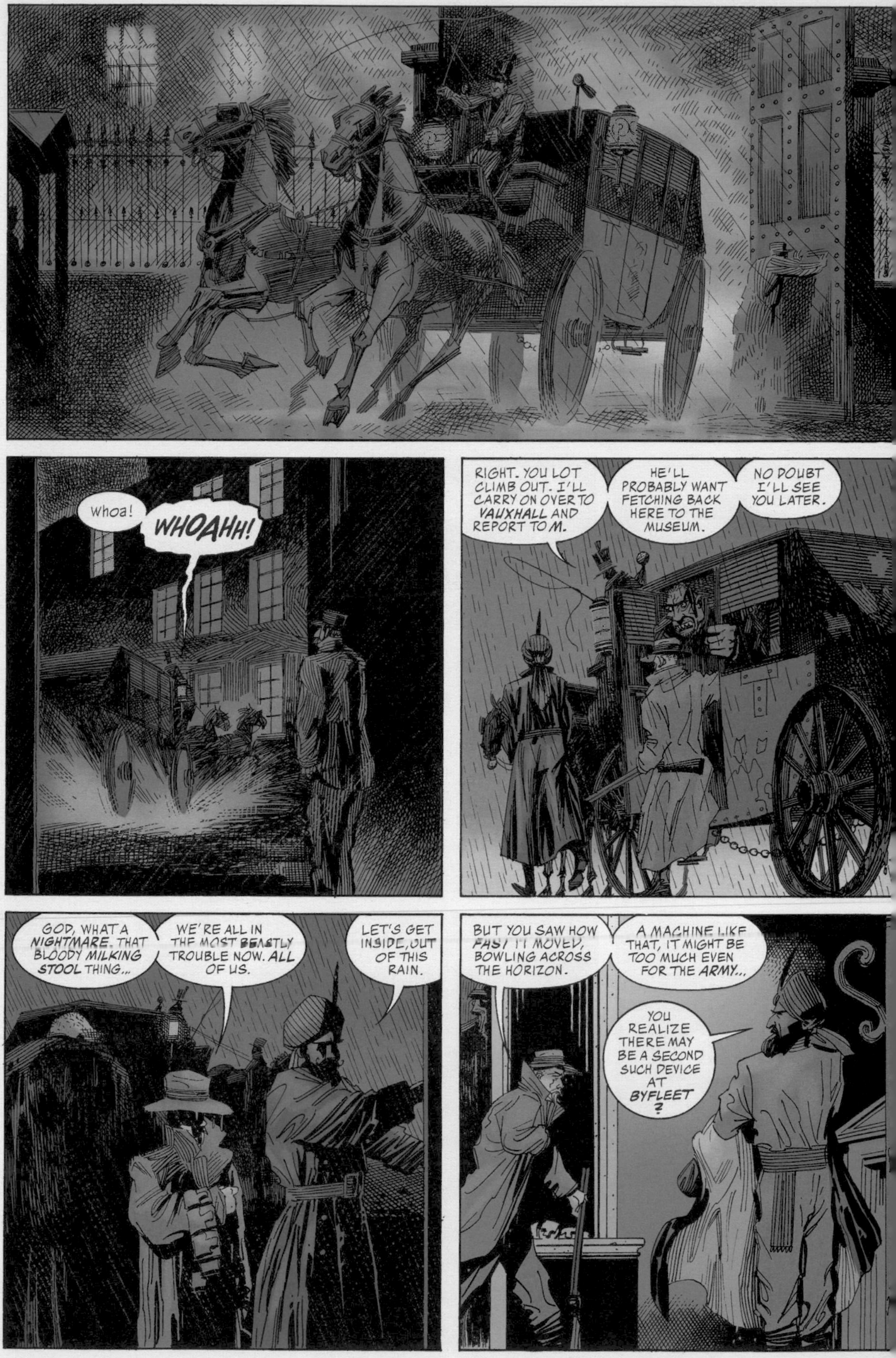
Whoa!
WHOAHH!
RIGHT. YOU LOT CLIMB OUT. I'LL CARRY ON OVER TO VAUXHALL AND REPORT TO M.
HE'LL PROBABLY WANT FETCHING BACK HERE TO THE MUSEUM.
NO DOUBT I'LL SEE YOU LATER.
GOD, WHAT A NIGHTMARE. THAT BLOODY MILKING STOOL THING...
WE'RE ALL IN THE MOST BEASTLY TROUBLE NOW. ALL OF US.
LET'S GET INSIDE, OUT OF THIS RAIN.
BUT YOU SAW HOW FAST IT MOVED, BOWLING ACROSS THE HORIZON.
A MACHINE LIKE THAT, IT MIGHT BE TOO MUCH EVEN FOR THE ARMY...
YOU REALIZE THERE MAY BE A SECOND SUCH DEVICE AT BYFLEET ?

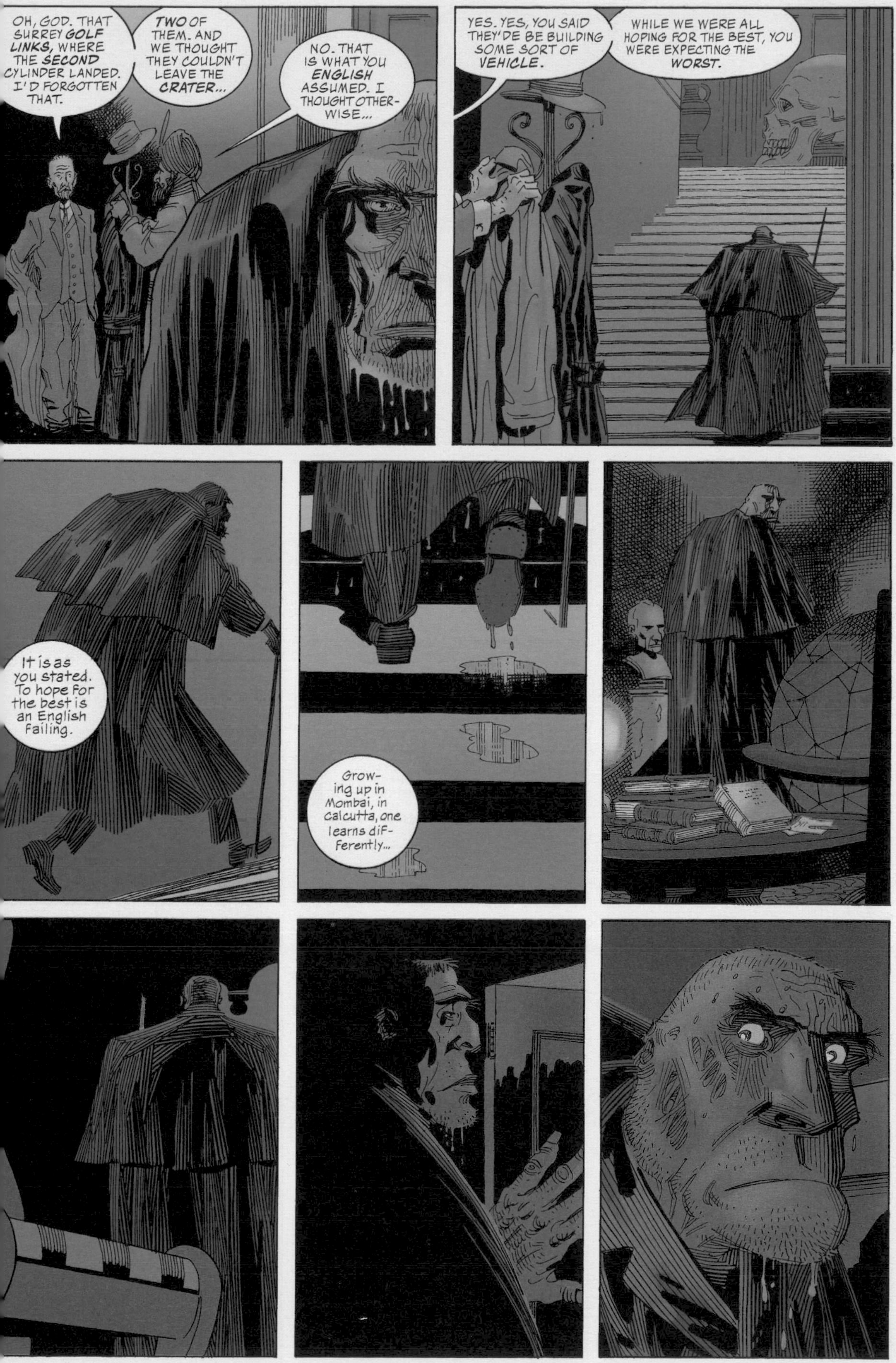
OH, GOD. THAT SURREY GOLF LINKS, WHERE THE SECOND CYLINDER LANDED. I'D FORGOTTEN THAT.
TWO OF THEM. AND WE THOUGHT THEY COULDN'T LEAVE THE CRATER...
NO. THAT IS WHAT YOU ENGLISH ASSUMED. I THOUGHT OTHER-WISE...
YES. YES, YOU SAID THEY'DE BE BUILDING SOME SORT OF VEHICLE.
WHILE WE WERE ALL HOPING FOR THE BEST, YOU WERE EXPECTING THE WORST.
It is as you stated. To hope for the best is an English failing.
Grow-ing up in Mombai, in Calcutta, one learns dif-ferently...

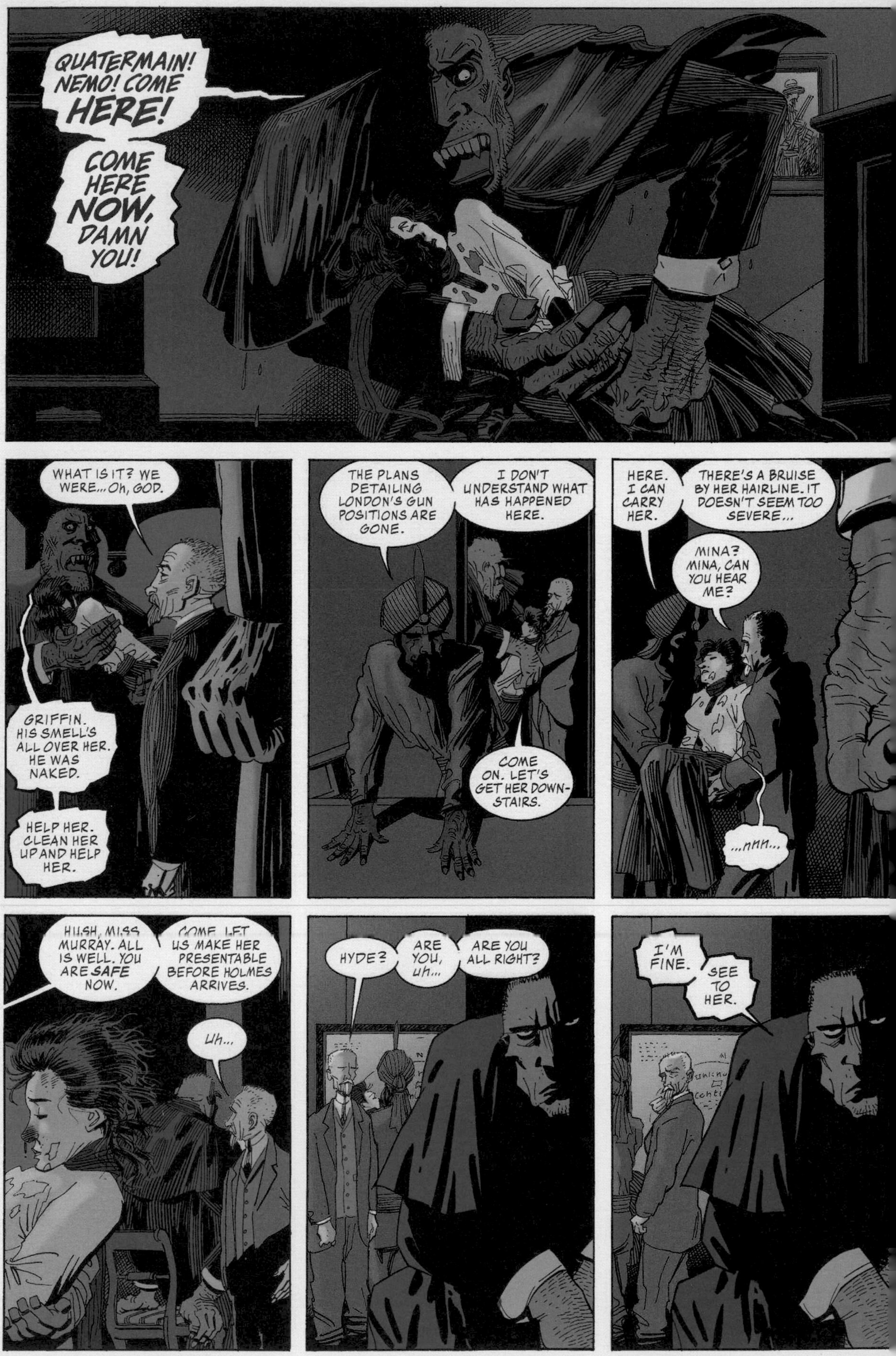
QUATERMAIN! NEMO! COME HERE!
COME HERE NOW, DAMN YOU!
WHAT IS IT? WE WERE... Oh, GOD.
GRIFFIN. HIS SMELL'S ALL OVER HER. HE WAS NAKED.
HELP HER. CLEAN HER UP AND HELP HER.
THE PLANS DETAILING LONDON'S GUN POSITIONS ARE GONE.
I DON'T UNDERSTAND WHAT HAS HAPPENED HERE.
COME ON. LET'S GET HER DOWN-STAIRS.
HERE. I CAN CARRY HER.
THERE'S A BRUISE BY HER HAIRLINE. IT DOESN'T SEEM TOO SEVERE...
MINA? MINA, CAN YOU HEAR ME?
...nnn...
HUSH, MISS MURRAY. ALL IS WELL. YOU ARE SAFE NOW.
COME. LET US MAKE HER PRESENTABLE BEFORE HOLMES ARRIVES.
Uh...
HYDE?
ARE YOU, uh...
ARE YOU ALL RIGHT?
I'M FINE.
SEE TO HER.

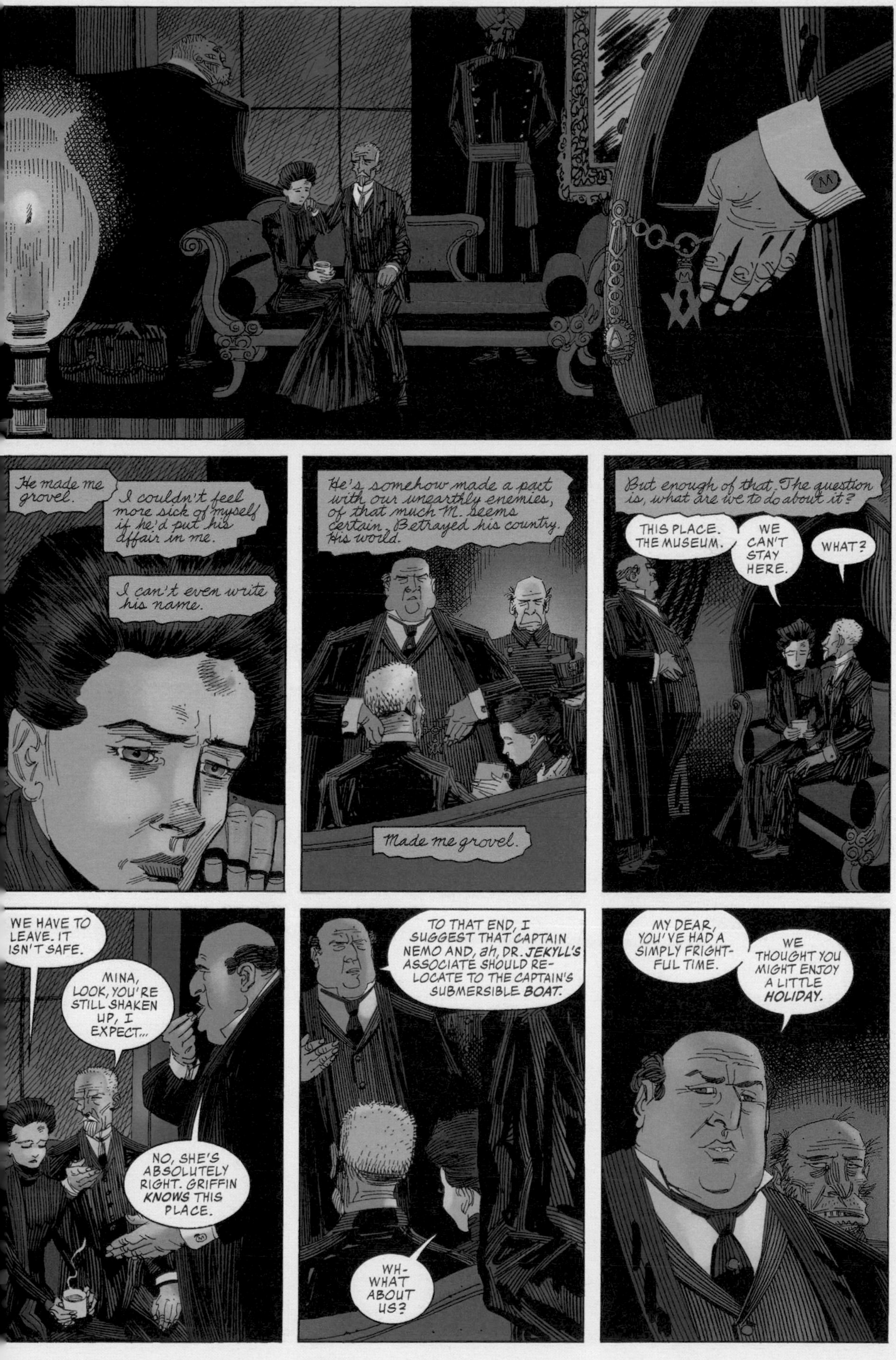
He made me grovel.
I couldn't feel more sick of myself if he'd put his affair in me.
I can't even write his name.
He's somehow made a pact with our unearthly enemies, of that much M. seems certain. Betrayed his country. His world.
Made me grovel.
But enough of that. The question is, what are we to do about it?
THIS PLACE. THE MUSEUM.
WE CAN'T STAY HERE.
WHAT?
WE HAVE TO LEAVE. IT ISN'T SAFE.
MINA, LOOK, YOU'RE STILL SHAKEN UP, I EXPECT...
NO, SHE'S ABSOLUTELY RIGHT. GRIFFIN KNOWS THIS PLACE.
TO THAT END, I SUGGEST THAT CAPTAIN NEMO AND, ah, DR. JEKYLL'S ASSOCIATE SHOULD RELOCATE TO THE CAPTAIN'S SUBMERSIBLE BOAT.
WH-WHAT ABOUT US?
MY DEAR, YOU'VE HAD A SIMPLY FRIGHTFUL TIME.
WE THOUGHT YOU MIGHT ENJOY A LITTLE HOLIDAY.

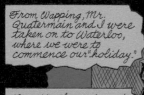
We saw Nemo and Hyde aboard the Nautilus. M. wants them to defend the Thames against that milking-stool they and Allan saw.

It's hoped they can contain the battle in South London.

Mr. Hyde seemed rather quiet. Almost ominously so, I thought.

From Wapping, Mr. Quatermain and I were taken on to Waterloo, where we were to commence our "holiday."

Despite the rain and lateness of the hour, there were some families with their belongings in the streets.

The panic has begun. It will no doubt be worse by morning.

We were put on our train by Mr. Samson, our coachman, who wished us luck.

As M. explained it, we're to visit the South Downs, there to locate a scientist engaged in highly secret Government endeavours.

So secret, in fact, that we were told neither his name nor whereabouts.

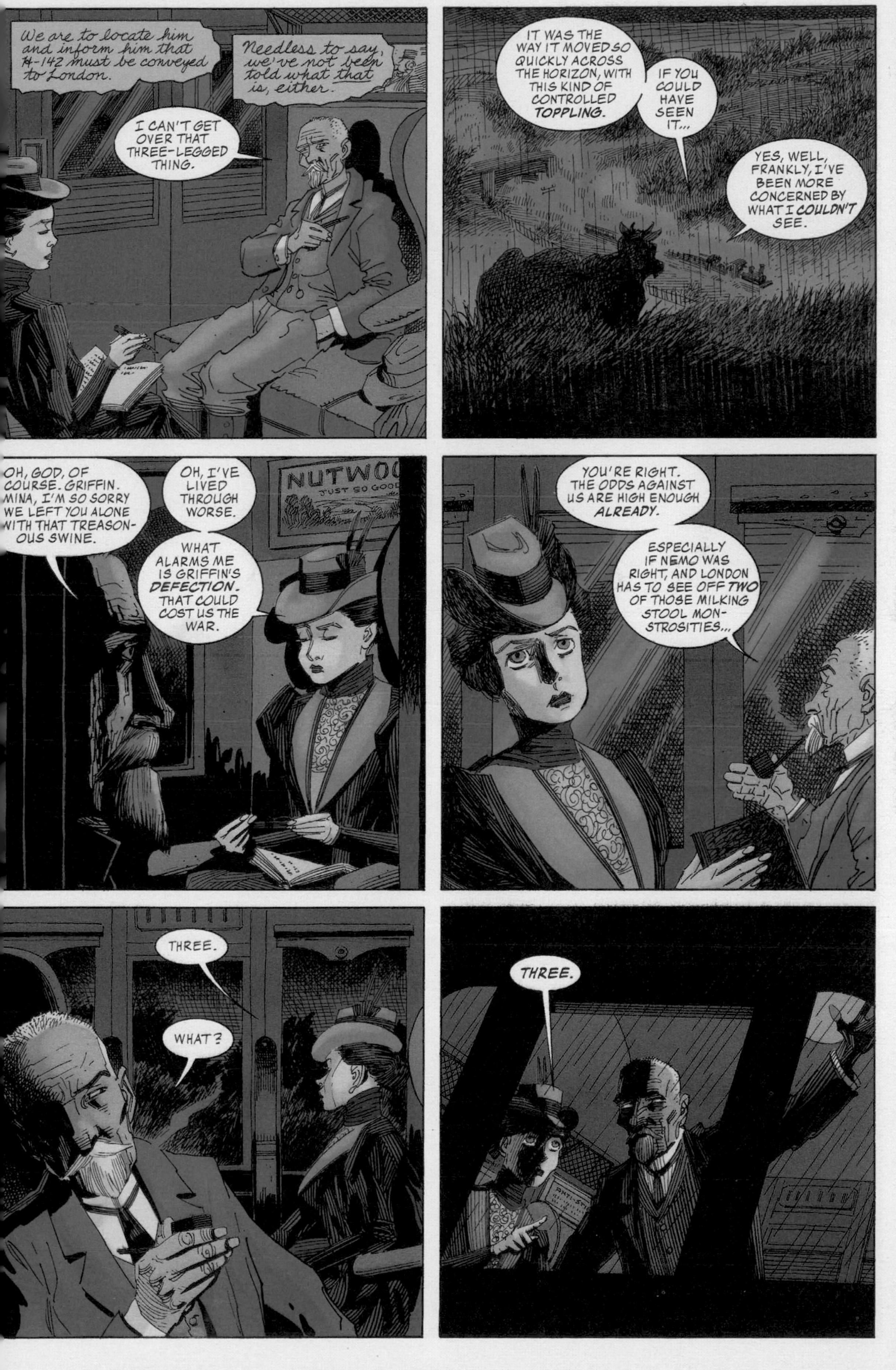
We are to locate him and inform him that H-142 must be conveyed to London.
Needless to say, we've not been told what that is, either.
I CAN'T GET OVER THAT THREE-LEGGED THING.
IT WAS THE WAY IT MOVED SO QUICKLY ACROSS THE HORIZON, WITH THIS KIND OF CONTROLLED TOPPLING.
IF YOU COULD HAVE SEEN IT...
YES, WELL, FRANKLY, I'VE BEEN MORE CONCERNED BY WHAT I COULDN'T SEE.
OH, GOD, OF COURSE. GRIFFIN. MINA, I'M SO SORRY WE LEFT YOU ALONE WITH THAT TREASON-OUS SWINE.
OH, I'VE LIVED THROUGH WORSE.
WHAT ALARMS ME IS GRIFFIN'S DEFECTION. THAT COULD COST US THE WAR.
NUTWOO
JUST SO GOOD
YOU'RE RIGHT. THE ODDS AGAINST US ARE HIGH ENOUGH ALREADY.
ESPECIALLY IF NEMO WAS RIGHT, AND LONDON HAS TO SEE OFF TWO OF THOSE MILKING STOOL MON-STROSITIES...
THREE.
WHAT?
THREE.

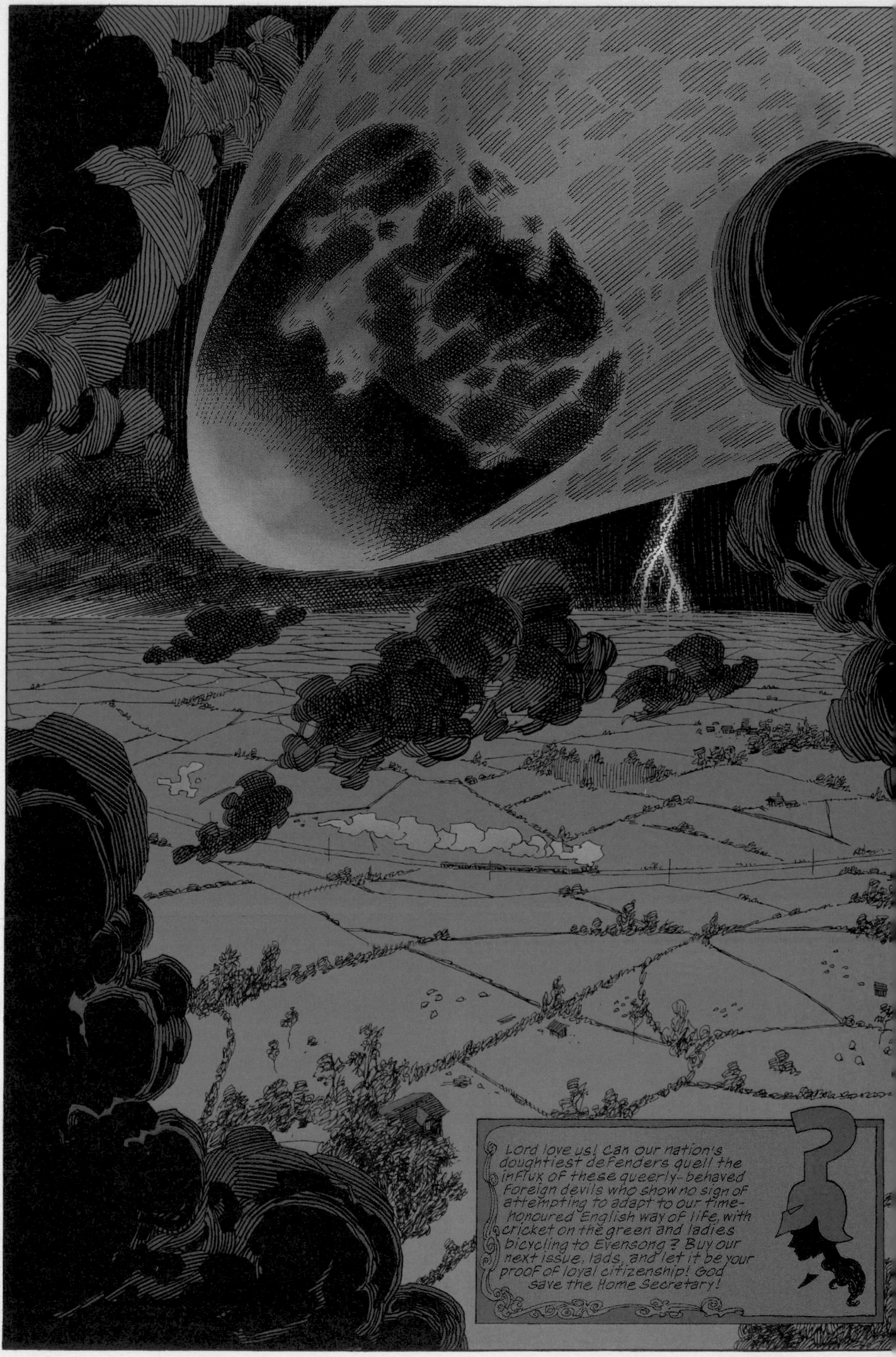
Lord love us! Can our nation's doughtiest defenders quell the influx of these queerly-behaved foreign devils who show no sign of attempting to adapt to our time-honoured English way of life, with cricket on the green and ladies bicycling to Evensong? Buy our next issue, lads, and let it be your proof of loyal citizenship! God save the Home Secretary!

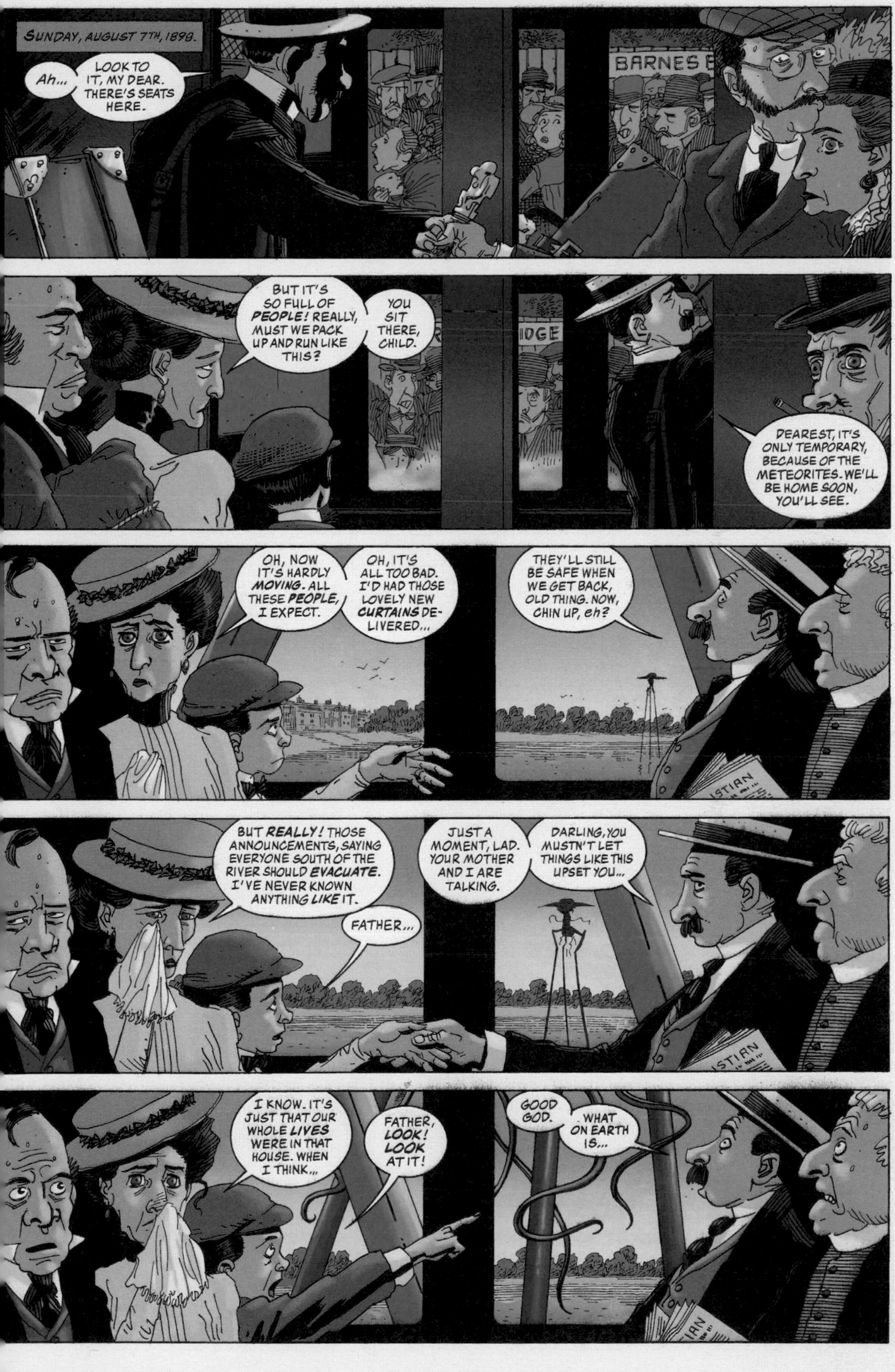
SUNDAY, AUGUST 7TH, 1898.
Ah...
LOOK TO IT, MY DEAR. THERE'S SEATS HERE.
BARNES B
BUT IT'S SO FULL OF PEOPLE! REALLY, MUST WE PACK UP AND RUN LIKE THIS?
YOU SIT THERE, CHILD.
IDGE
DEAREST, IT'S ONLY TEMPORARY, BECAUSE OF THE METEORITES. WE'LL BE HOME SOON, YOU'LL SEE.
OH, NOW IT'S HARDLY MOVING. ALL THESE PEOPLE, I EXPECT.
OH, IT'S ALL TOO BAD. I'D HAD THOSE LOVELY NEW CURTAINS DELIVERED...
THEY'LL STILL BE SAFE WHEN WE GET BACK, OLD THING. NOW, CHIN UP, eh?
BUT REALLY! THOSE ANNOUNCEMENTS, SAYING EVERYONE SOUTH OF THE RIVER SHOULD EVACUATE. I'VE NEVER KNOWN ANYTHING LIKE IT.
FATHER...
JUST A MOMENT, LAD. YOUR MOTHER AND I ARE TALKING.
DARLING, YOU MUSTN'T LET THINGS LIKE THIS UPSET YOU...
I KNOW. IT'S JUST THAT OUR WHOLE LIVES WERE IN THAT HOUSE. WHEN I THINK...
FATHER, LOOK! LOOK AT IT!
GOOD GOD.
WHAT ON EARTH IS...

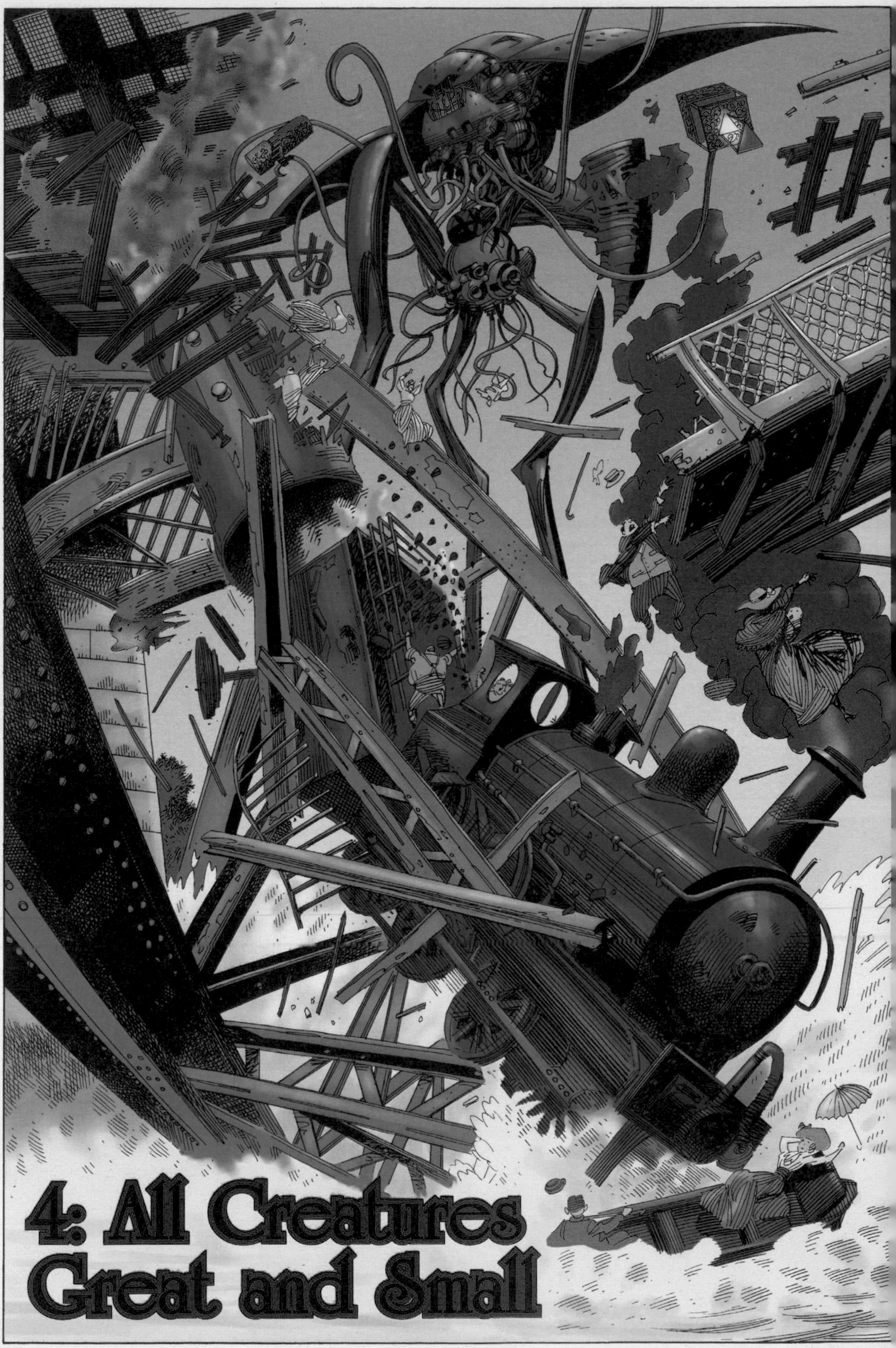

4: All Creatures Great and Small

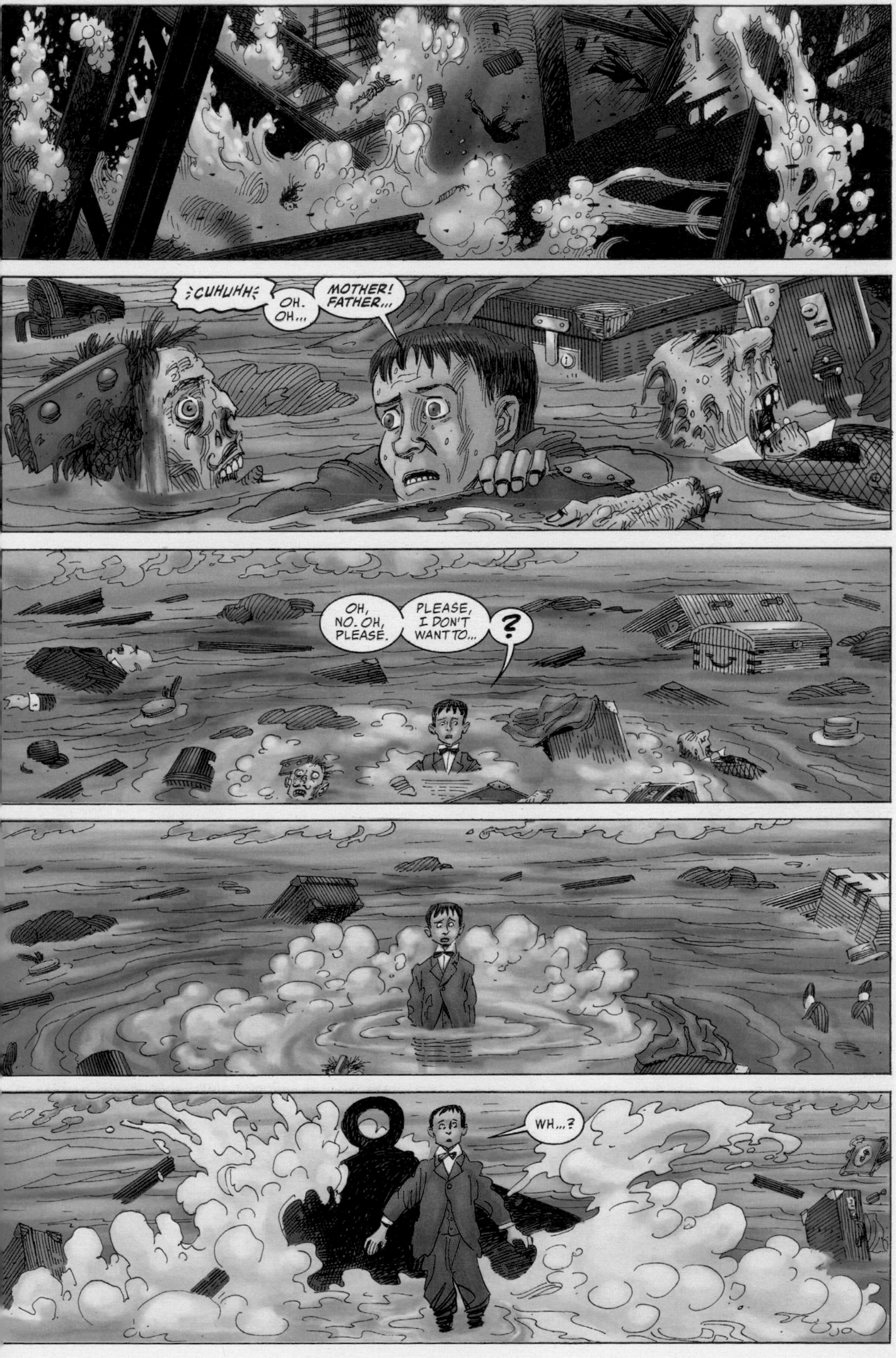
CUHUHH
OH. OH...
MOTHER! FATHER...
OH, NO. OH, PLEASE.
PLEASE, I DON'T WANT TO...
?
WH...?

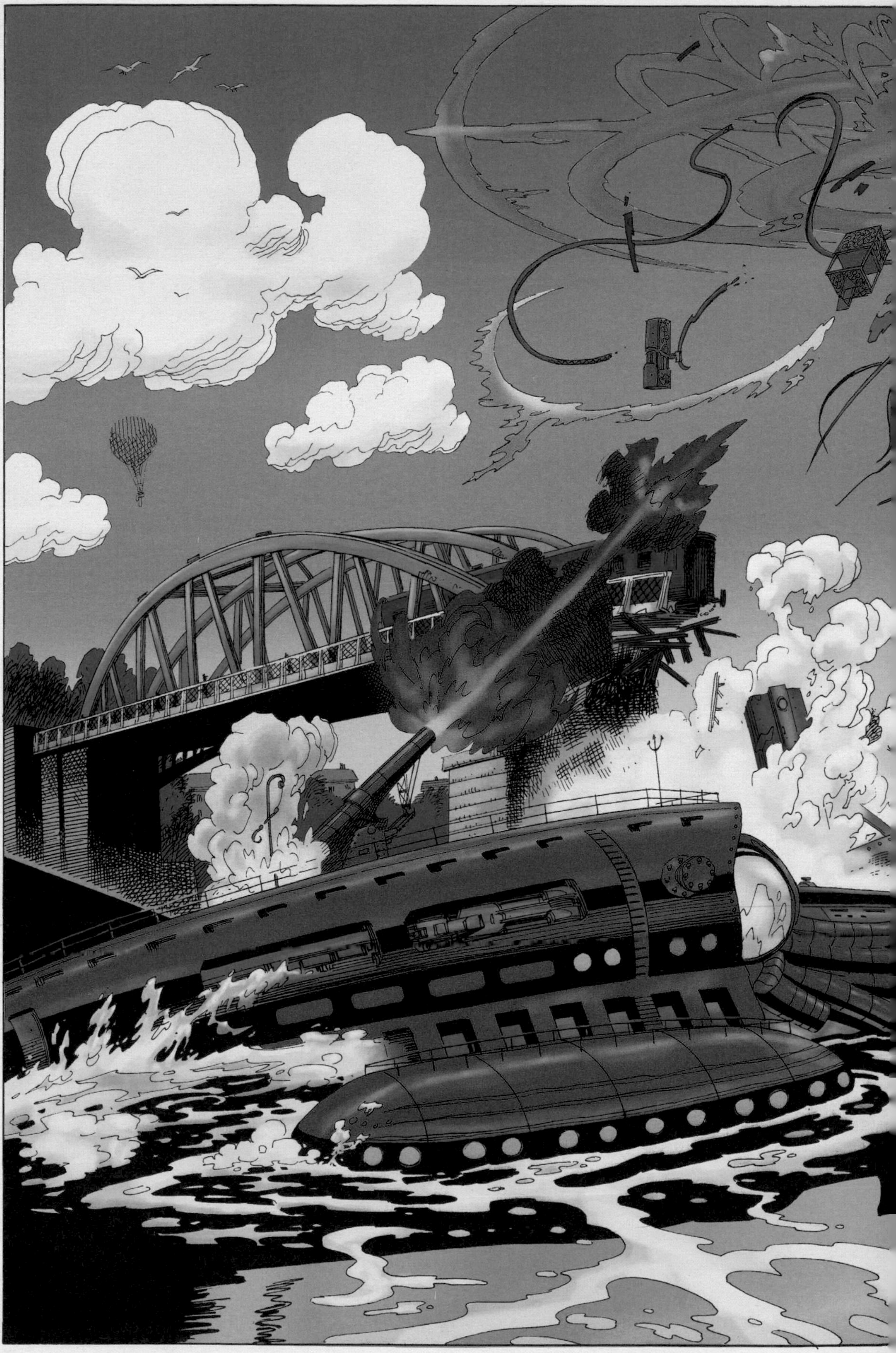

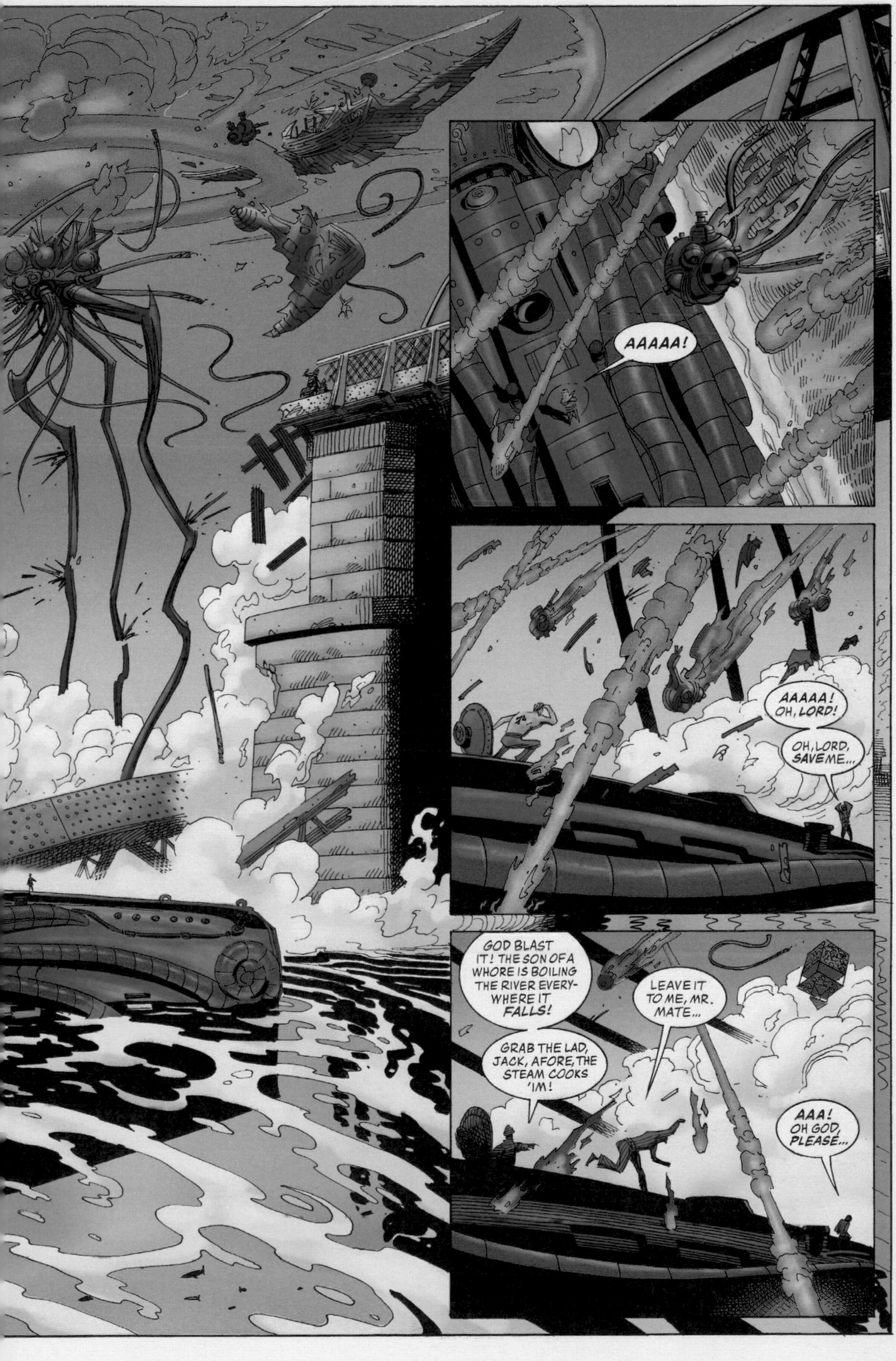
AAAAA!
AAAAA! OH, LORD!
OH, LORD, SAVE ME...
GOD BLAST IT! THE SON OF A WHORE IS BOILING THE RIVER EVERY-WHERE IT FALLS!
GRAB THE LAD, JACK, AFORE, THE STEAM COOKS 'IM!
LEAVE IT TO ME, MR. MATE...
AAA! OH GOD, PLEASE...

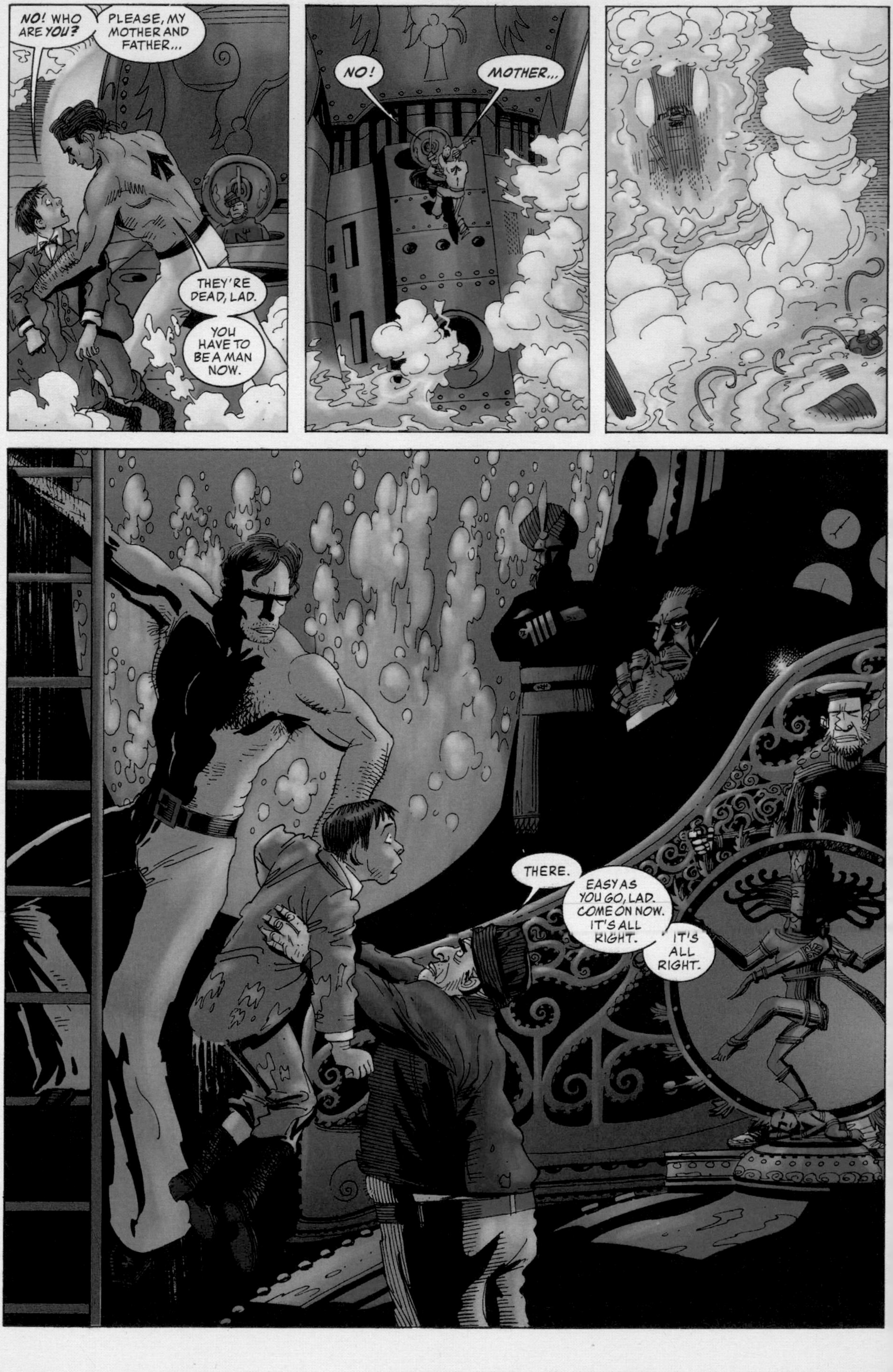
NO! WHO ARE YOU?
PLEASE, MY MOTHER AND FATHER...
THEY'RE DEAD, LAD.
YOU HAVE TO BE A MAN NOW.
NO!
MOTHER...
THERE.
EASY AS YOU GO, LAD. COME ON NOW. IT'S ALL RIGHT.
IT'S ALL RIGHT.

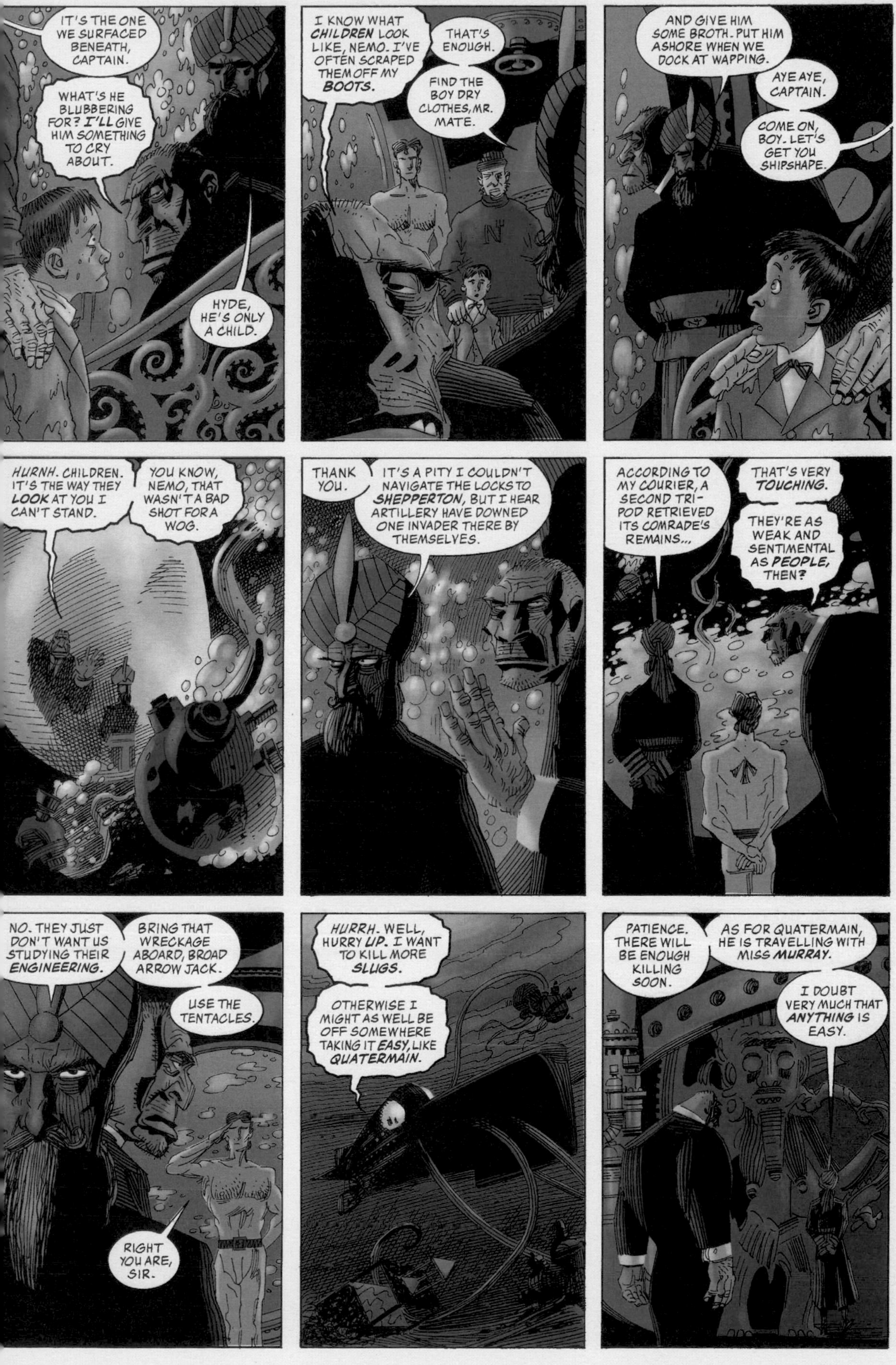
IT'S THE ONE WE SURFACED BENEATH, CAPTAIN.
WHAT'S HE BLUBBERING FOR? I'LL GIVE HIM SOMETHING TO CRY ABOUT.
HYDE, HE'S ONLY A CHILD.
I KNOW WHAT CHILDREN LOOK LIKE, NEMO. I'VE OFTEN SCRAPED THEM OFF MY BOOTS.
THAT'S ENOUGH.
FIND THE BOY DRY CLOTHES, MR. MATE.
AND GIVE HIM SOME BROTH. PUT HIM ASHORE WHEN WE DOCK AT WAPPING.
AYE AYE, CAPTAIN.
COME ON, BOY. LET'S GET YOU SHIPSHAPE.
HURNH. CHILDREN. IT'S THE WAY THEY LOOK AT YOU I CAN'T STAND.
YOU KNOW, NEMO, THAT WASN'T A BAD SHOT FOR A WOG.
THANK YOU.
IT'S A PITY I COULDN'T NAVIGATE THE LOCKS TO SHEPPERTON, BUT I HEAR ARTILLERY HAVE DOWNED ONE INVADER THERE BY THEMSELVES.
ACCORDING TO MY COURIER, A SECOND TRIPOD RETRIEVED ITS COMRADE'S REMAINS...
THAT'S VERY TOUCHING.
THEY'RE AS WEAK AND SENTIMENTAL AS PEOPLE, THEN?
NO. THEY JUST DON'T WANT US STUDYING THEIR ENGINEERING.
BRING THAT WRECKAGE ABOARD, BROAD ARROW JACK.
USE THE TENTACLES.
RIGHT YOU ARE, SIR.
HURRH. WELL, HURRY UP. I WANT TO KILL MORE SLUGS.
OTHERWISE I MIGHT AS WELL BE OFF SOMEWHERE TAKING IT EASY, LIKE QUATERMAIN.
PATIENCE. THERE WILL BE ENOUGH KILLING SOON.
AS FOR QUATERMAIN, HE IS TRAVELLING WITH MISS MURRAY.
I DOUBT VERY MUCH THAT ANYTHING IS EASY.

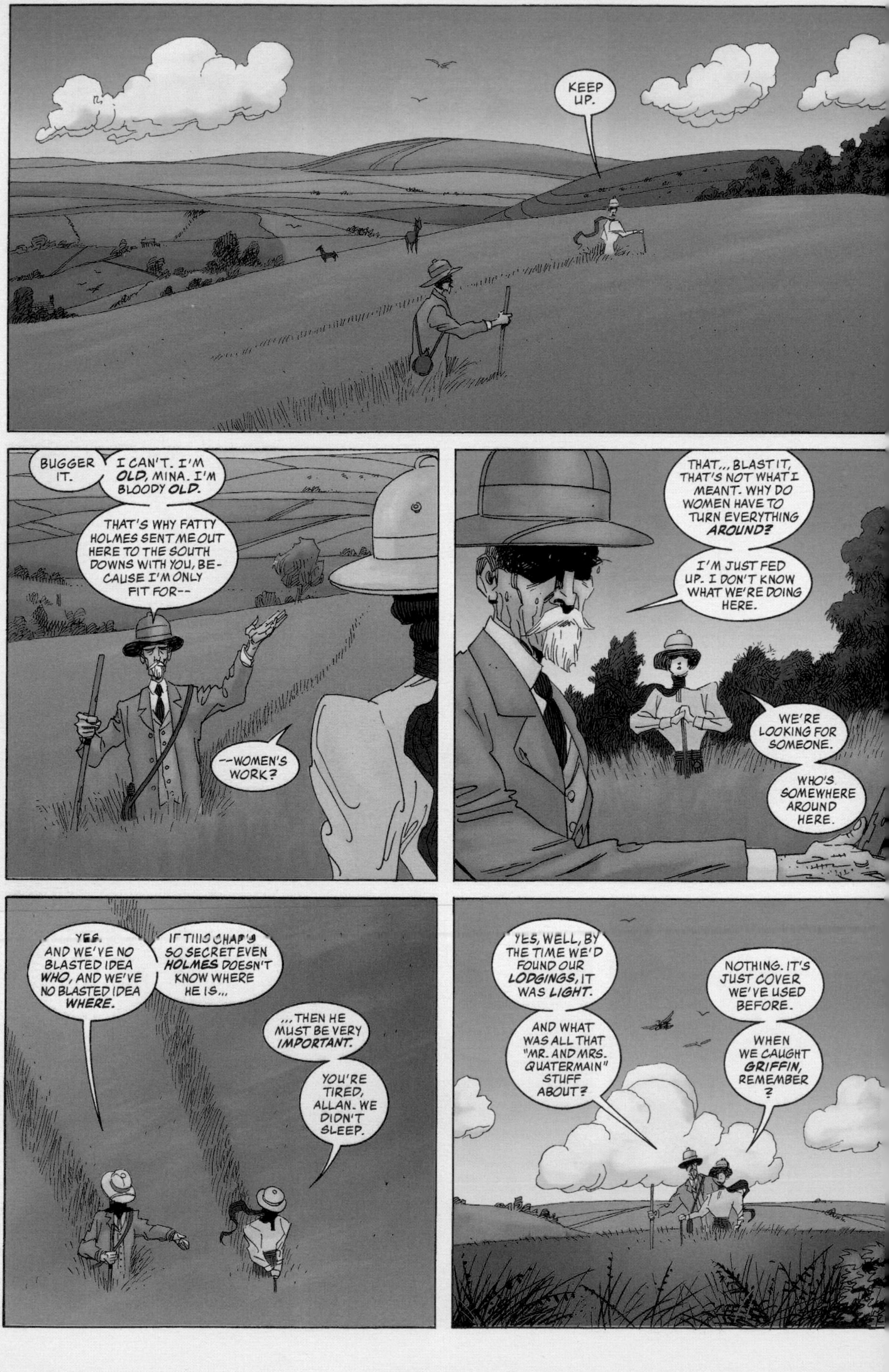
KEEP UP.
BUGGER IT.
I CAN'T. I'M OLD, MINA. I'M BLOODY OLD.
THAT'S WHY FATTY HOLMES SENT ME OUT HERE TO THE SOUTH DOWNS WITH YOU, BECAUSE I'M ONLY FIT FOR--
--WOMEN'S WORK?
THAT... BLAST IT, THAT'S NOT WHAT I MEANT. WHY DO WOMEN HAVE TO TURN EVERYTHING AROUND?
I'M JUST FED UP. I DON'T KNOW WHAT WE'RE DOING HERE.
WE'RE LOOKING FOR SOMEONE.
WHO'S SOMEWHERE AROUND HERE.
YES. AND WE'VE NO BLASTED IDEA WHO, AND WE'VE NO BLASTED IDEA WHERE.
IF THIS CHAP'S SO SECRET EVEN HOLMES DOESN'T KNOW WHERE HE IS...
...THEN HE MUST BE VERY IMPORTANT.
YOU'RE TIRED, ALLAN. WE DIDN'T SLEEP.
YES, WELL, BY THE TIME WE'D FOUND OUR LODGINGS, IT WAS LIGHT.
AND WHAT WAS ALL THAT "MR. AND MRS. QUATERMAIN" STUFF ABOUT?
NOTHING. IT'S JUST COVER WE'VE USED BEFORE.
WHEN WE CAUGHT GRIFFIN, REMEMBER?

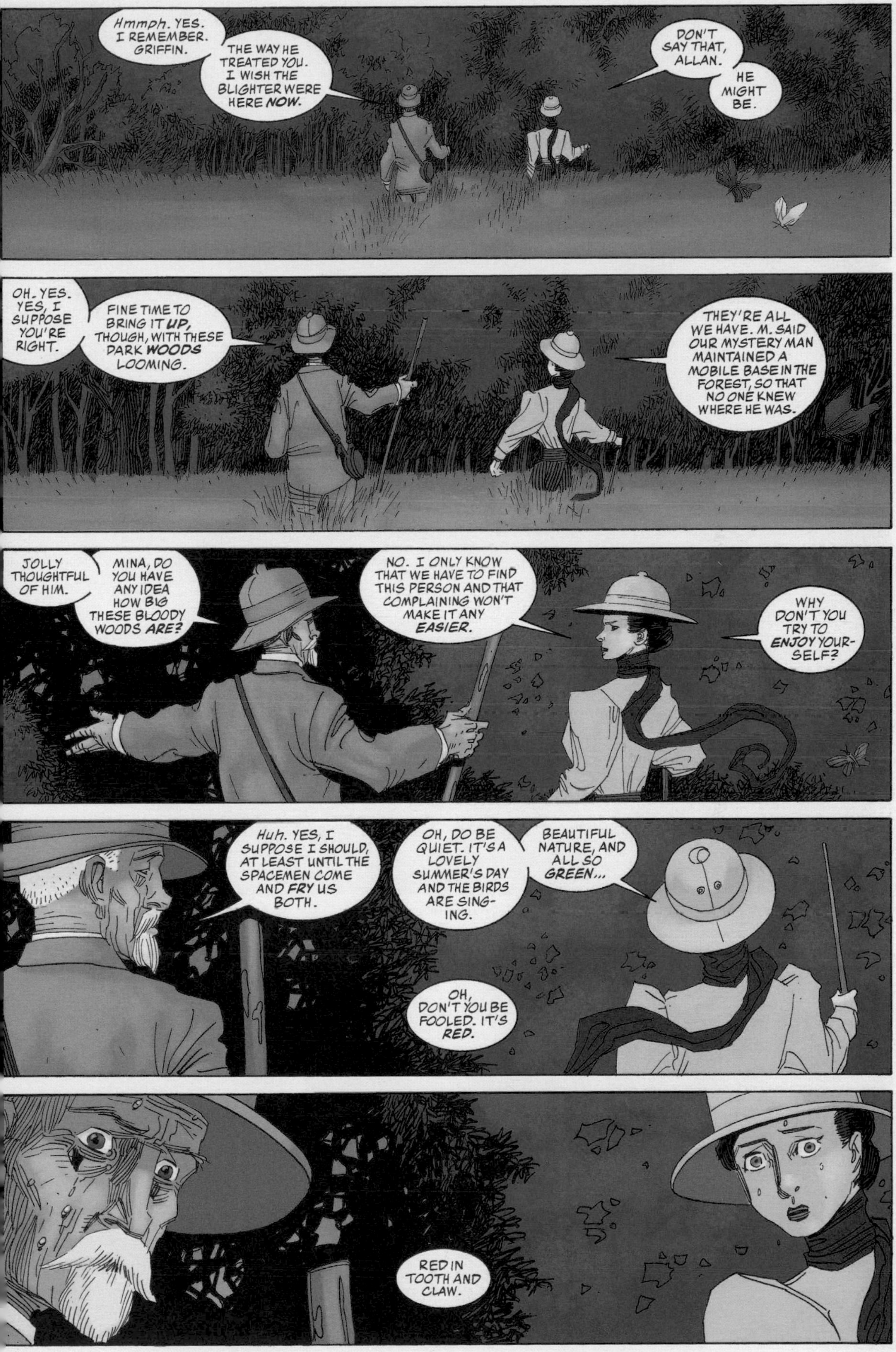
Hmmph. YES. I REMEMBER. GRIFFIN.
THE WAY HE TREATED YOU. I WISH THE BLIGHTER WERE HERE NOW.
DON'T SAY THAT, ALLAN.
HE MIGHT BE.
OH. YES. YES, I SUPPOSE YOU'RE RIGHT.
FINE TIME TO BRING IT UP, THOUGH, WITH THESE DARK WOODS LOOMING.
THEY'RE ALL WE HAVE. M. SAID OUR MYSTERY MAN MAINTAINED A MOBILE BASE IN THE FOREST, SO THAT NO ONE KNEW WHERE HE WAS.
JOLLY THOUGHTFUL OF HIM.
MINA, DO YOU HAVE ANY IDEA HOW BIG THESE BLOODY WOODS ARE?
NO. I ONLY KNOW THAT WE HAVE TO FIND THIS PERSON AND THAT COMPLAINING WON'T MAKE IT ANY EASIER.
WHY DON'T YOU TRY TO ENJOY YOUR-SELF?
Huh. YES, I SUPPOSE I SHOULD, AT LEAST UNTIL THE SPACEMEN COME AND FRY US BOTH.
OH, DO BE QUIET. IT'S A LOVELY SUMMER'S DAY AND THE BIRDS ARE SING-ING.
BEAUTIFUL NATURE, AND ALL SO GREEN...
OH, DON'T YOU BE FOOLED. IT'S RED.
RED IN TOOTH AND CLAW.

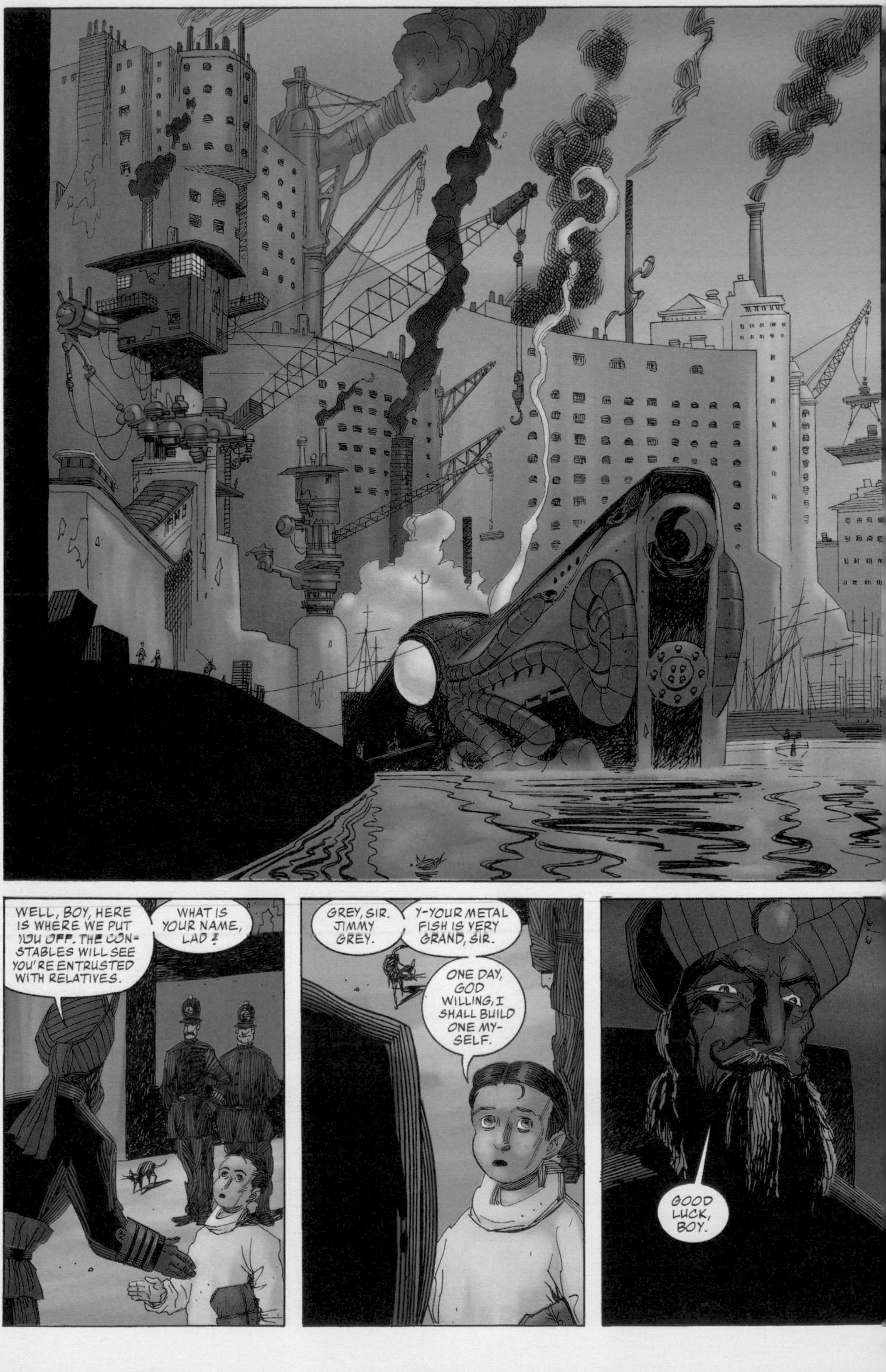
WELL, BOY, HERE IS WHERE WE PUT YOU OFF. THE CONSTABLES WILL SEE YOU'RE ENTRUSTED WITH RELATIVES.
WHAT IS YOUR NAME, LAD?
GREY, SIR. JIMMY GREY.
Y-YOUR METAL FISH IS VERY GRAND, SIR.
ONE DAY, GOD WILLING, I SHALL BUILD ONE MYSELF.
GOOD LUCK, BOY.

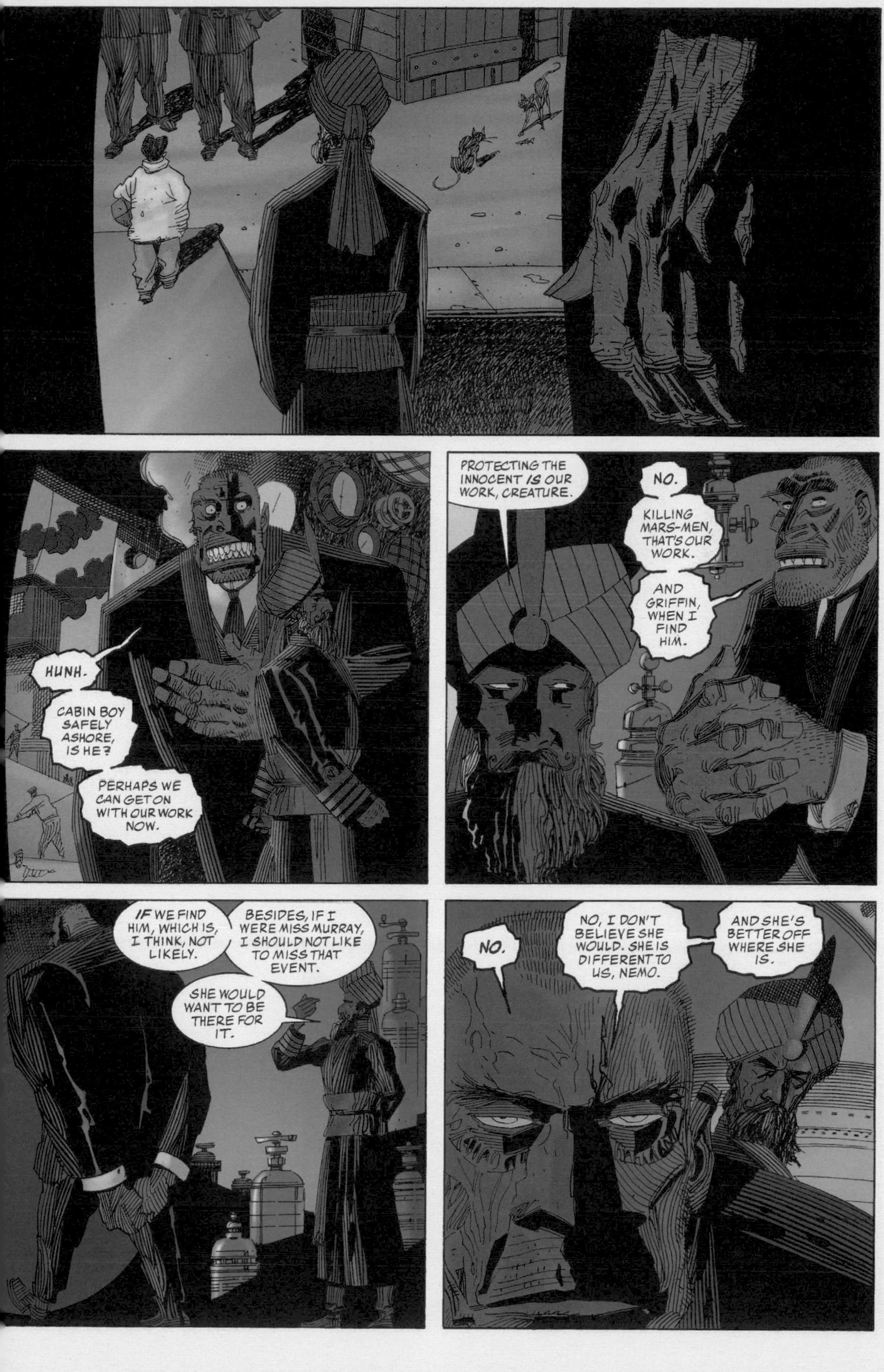
HUNH.
CABIN BOY SAFELY ASHORE, IS HE?
PERHAPS WE CAN GET ON WITH OUR WORK NOW.
PROTECTING THE INNOCENT IS OUR WORK, CREATURE.
NO.
KILLING MARS-MEN, THAT'S OUR WORK.
AND GRIFFIN, WHEN I FIND HIM.
IF WE FIND HIM, WHICH IS, I THINK, NOT LIKELY.
BESIDES, IF I WERE MISS MURRAY, I SHOULD NOT LIKE TO MISS THAT EVENT.
SHE WOULD WANT TO BE THERE FOR IT.
NO.
NO, I DON'T BELIEVE SHE WOULD. SHE IS DIFFERENT TO US, NEMO.
AND SHE'S BETTER OFF WHERE SHE IS.

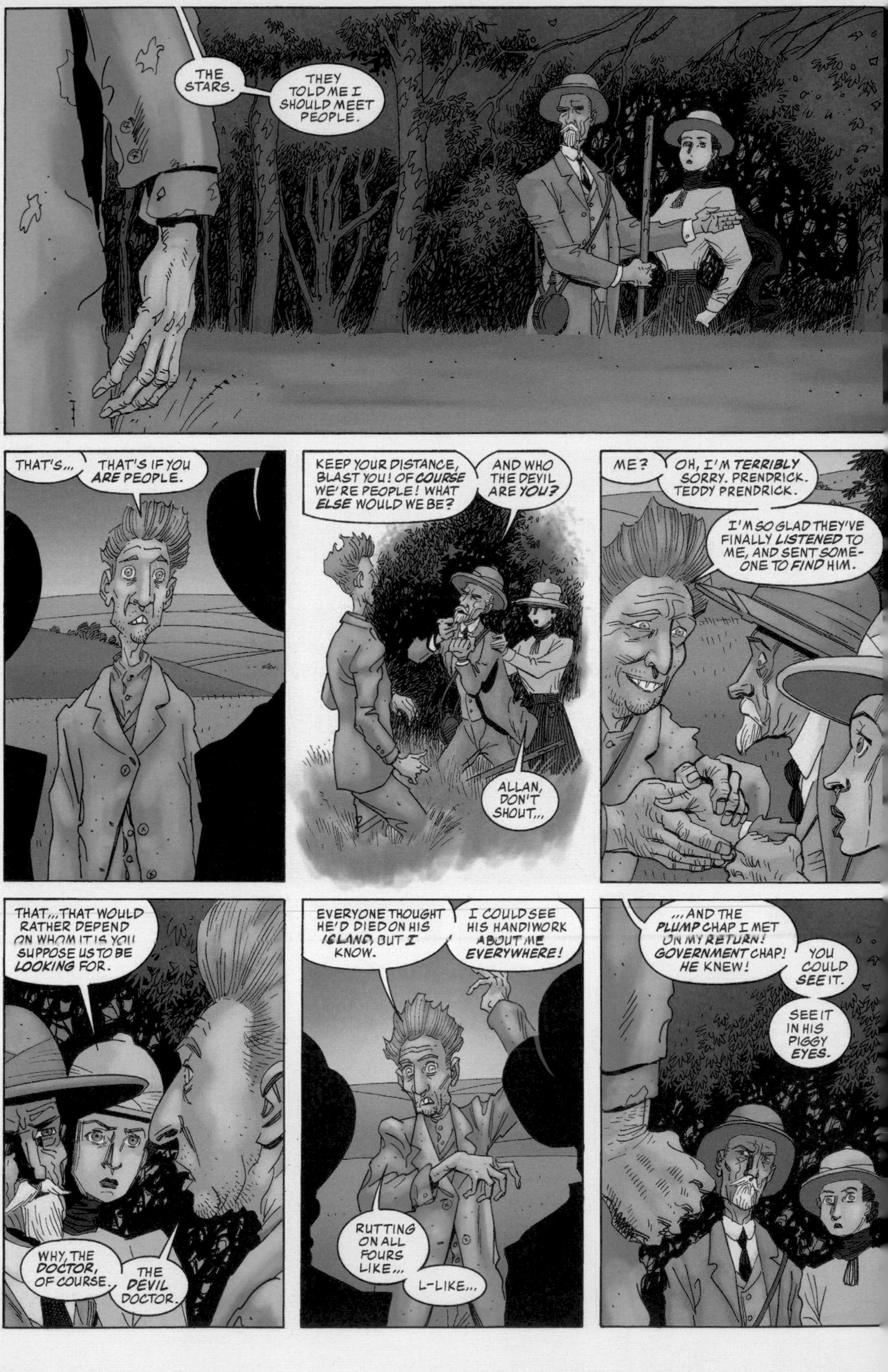
THE STARS.
THEY TOLD ME I SHOULD MEET PEOPLE.
THAT'S...
THAT'S IF YOU ARE PEOPLE.
KEEP YOUR DISTANCE, BLAST YOU! OF COURSE WE'RE PEOPLE! WHAT ELSE WOULD WE BE?
AND WHO THE DEVIL ARE YOU?
ALLAN, DON'T SHOUT...
ME?
OH, I'M TERRIBLY SORRY. PRENDRICK. TEDDY PRENDRICK.
I'M SO GLAD THEY'VE FINALLY LISTENED TO ME, AND SENT SOMEONE TO FIND HIM.
THAT... THAT WOULD RATHER DEPEND ON WHOM IT IS YOU SUPPOSE US TO BE LOOKING FOR.
WHY, THE DOCTOR, OF COURSE.
THE DEVIL DOCTOR.
EVERYONE THOUGHT HE'D DIED ON HIS ISLAND, BUT I KNOW.
I COULD SEE HIS HANDIWORK ABOUT ME EVERYWHERE!
RUTTING ON ALL FOURS LIKE...
L-LIKE...
...AND THE PLUMP CHAP I MET ON MY RETURN! GOVERNMENT CHAP! HE KNEW!
YOU COULD SEE IT.
SEE IT IN HIS PIGGY EYES.

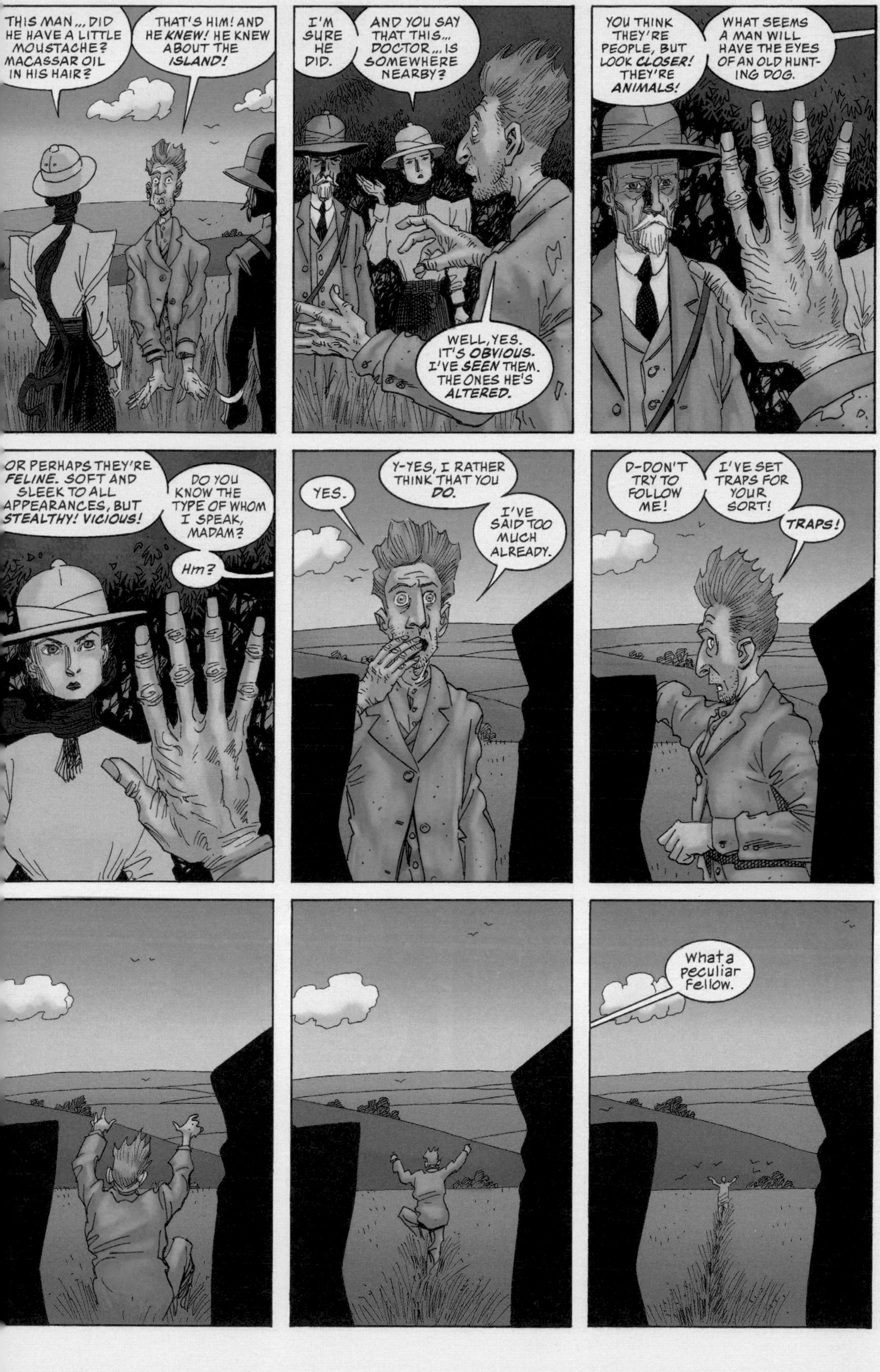
THIS MAN... DID HE HAVE A LITTLE MOUSTACHE? MACASSAR OIL IN HIS HAIR?
THAT'S HIM! AND HE KNEW! HE KNEW ABOUT THE ISLAND!
I'M SURE HE DID.
AND YOU SAY THAT THIS... DOCTOR... IS SOMEWHERE NEARBY?
WELL, YES. IT'S OBVIOUS. I'VE SEEN THEM. THE ONES HE'S ALTERED.
YOU THINK THEY'RE PEOPLE, BUT LOOK CLOSER! THEY'RE ANIMALS!
WHAT SEEMS A MAN WILL HAVE THE EYES OF AN OLD HUNTING DOG.
OR PERHAPS THEY'RE FELINE. SOFT AND SLEEK TO ALL APPEARANCES, BUT STEALTHY! VICIOUS!
DO YOU KNOW THE TYPE OF WHOM I SPEAK, MADAM?
Hm?
YES.
Y-YES, I RATHER THINK THAT YOU DO.
I'VE SAID TOO MUCH ALREADY.
D-DON'T TRY TO FOLLOW ME!
I'VE SET TRAPS FOR YOUR SORT!
TRAPS!
What a peculiar Fellow.

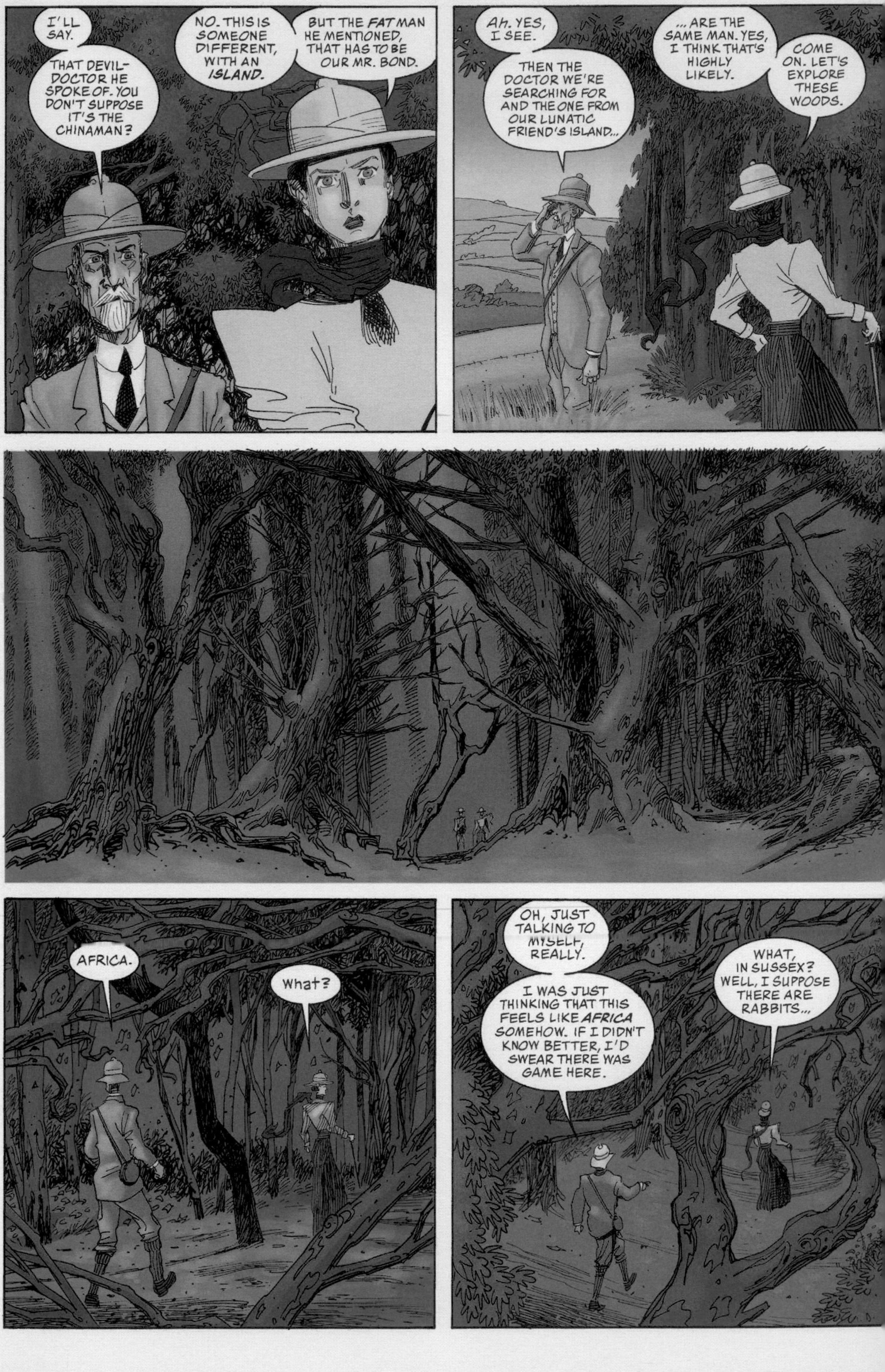
I'LL SAY.
THAT DEVIL-DOCTOR HE SPOKE OF. YOU DON'T SUPPOSE IT'S THE CHINAMAN?
NO. THIS IS SOMEONE DIFFERENT, WITH AN *ISLAND*.
BUT THE *FAT* MAN HE MENTIONED, THAT HAS TO BE OUR MR. BOND.
Ah. YES, I SEE.
THEN THE DOCTOR WE'RE SEARCHING FOR AND THE ONE FROM OUR LUNATIC FRIEND'S ISLAND...
... ARE THE SAME MAN. YES, I THINK THAT'S HIGHLY LIKELY.
COME ON. LET'S EXPLORE THESE WOODS.
AFRICA.
What?
OH, JUST TALKING TO MYSELF, REALLY.
I WAS JUST THINKING THAT THIS FEELS LIKE *AFRICA* SOMEHOW. IF I DIDN'T KNOW BETTER, I'D SWEAR THERE WAS GAME HERE.
WHAT, IN SUSSEX? WELL, I SUPPOSE THERE ARE RABBITS...

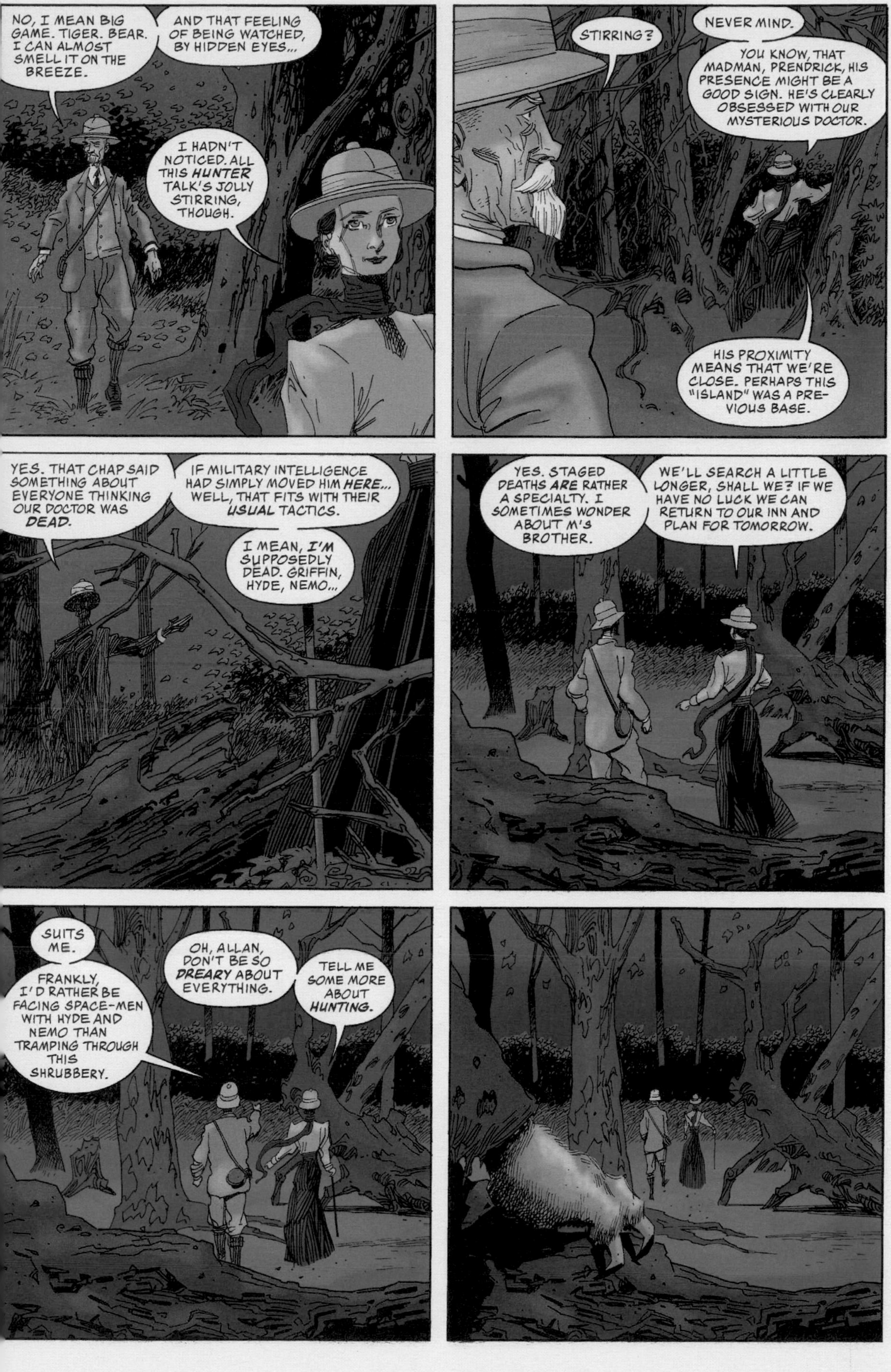
NO, I MEAN BIG GAME. TIGER. BEAR. I CAN ALMOST SMELL IT ON THE BREEZE.
AND THAT FEELING OF BEING WATCHED, BY HIDDEN EYES...
I HADN'T NOTICED. ALL THIS **HUNTER** TALK'S JOLLY STIRRING, THOUGH.
STIRRING?
NEVER MIND.
YOU KNOW, THAT MADMAN, PRENDRICK, HIS PRESENCE MIGHT BE A GOOD SIGN. HE'S CLEARLY OBSESSED WITH OUR MYSTERIOUS DOCTOR.
HIS PROXIMITY MEANS THAT WE'RE CLOSE. PERHAPS THIS "ISLAND" WAS A PREVIOUS BASE.
YES. THAT CHAP SAID SOMETHING ABOUT EVERYONE THINKING OUR DOCTOR WAS **DEAD**.
IF MILITARY INTELLIGENCE HAD SIMPLY MOVED HIM **HERE**... WELL, THAT FITS WITH THEIR **USUAL** TACTICS.
I MEAN, **I'M** SUPPOSEDLY DEAD. GRIFFIN, HYDE, NEMO...
YES. STAGED DEATHS **ARE** RATHER A SPECIALTY. I SOMETIMES WONDER ABOUT M'S BROTHER.
WE'LL SEARCH A LITTLE LONGER, SHALL WE? IF WE HAVE NO LUCK WE CAN RETURN TO OUR INN AND PLAN FOR TOMORROW.
SUITS ME.
FRANKLY, I'D RATHER BE FACING SPACE-MEN WITH HYDE AND NEMO THAN TRAMPING THROUGH THIS SHRUBBERY.
OH, ALLAN, DON'T BE SO **DREARY** ABOUT EVERYTHING.
TELL ME SOME MORE ABOUT **HUNTING**.

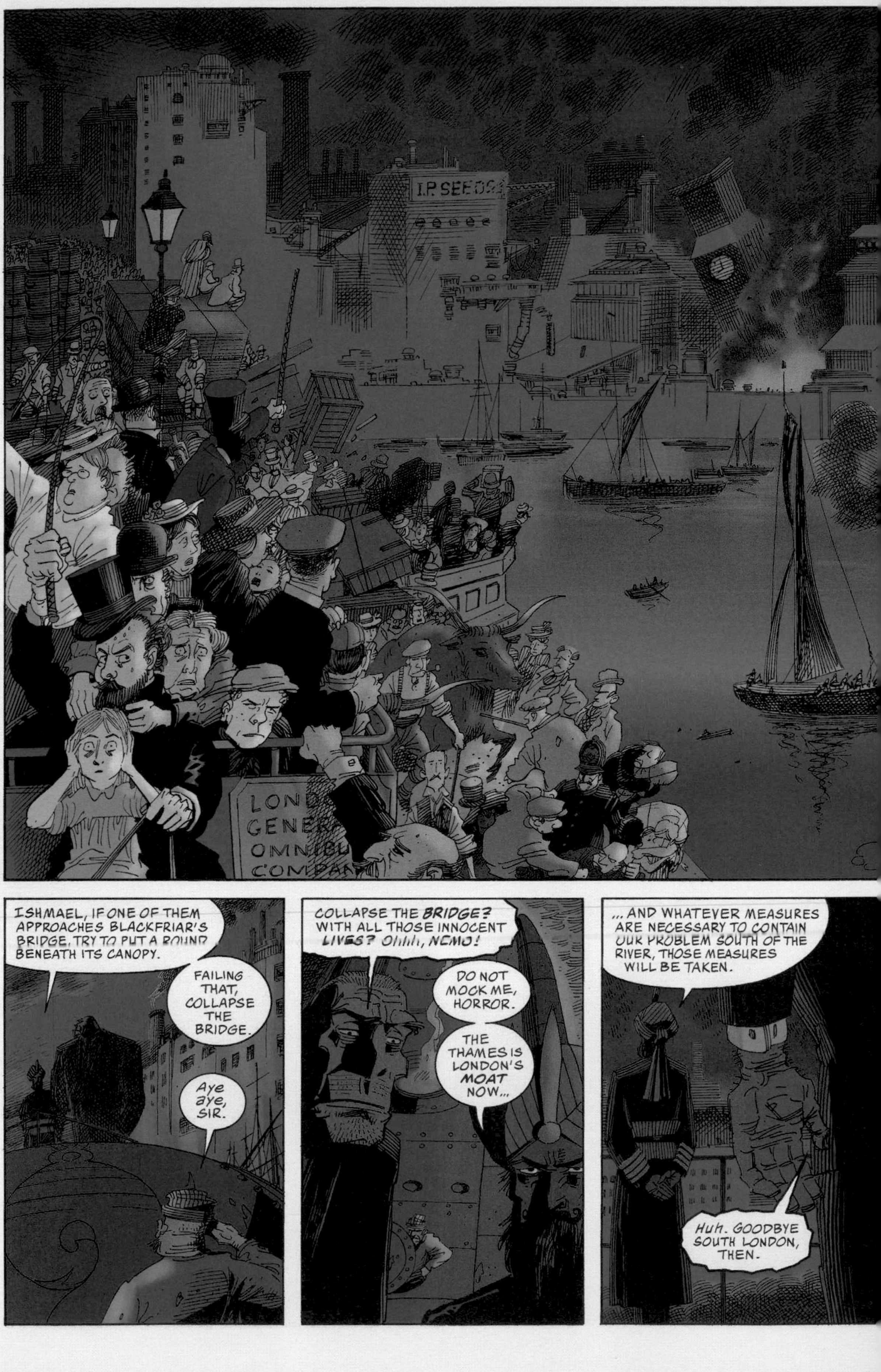
I.P. SEEDS
ISHMAEL, IF ONE OF THEM APPROACHES BLACKFRIAR'S BRIDGE, TRY TO PUT A ROUND BENEATH ITS CANOPY.
FAILING THAT, COLLAPSE THE BRIDGE.
Aye aye, SIR.
COLLAPSE THE BRIDGE? WITH ALL THOSE INNOCENT LIVES? Ohhh, NEMO!
DO NOT MOCK ME, HORROR.
THE THAMES IS LONDON'S MOAT NOW...
... AND WHATEVER MEASURES ARE NECESSARY TO CONTAIN OUR PROBLEM SOUTH OF THE RIVER, THOSE MEASURES WILL BE TAKEN.
Huh. GOODBYE SOUTH LONDON, THEN.

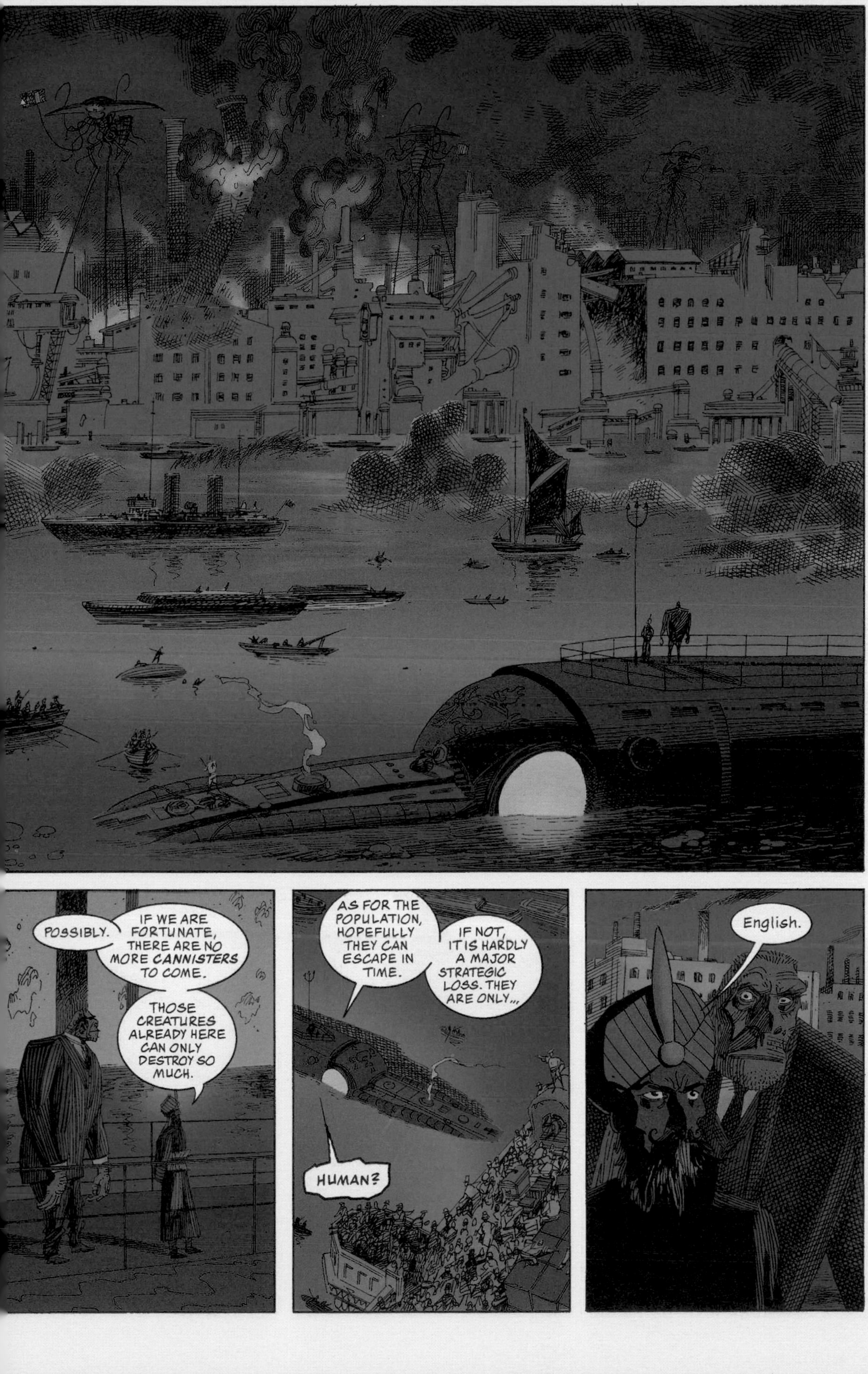

POSSIBLY.
IF WE ARE FORTUNATE, THERE ARE NO MORE CANNISTERS TO COME.
THOSE CREATURES ALREADY HERE CAN ONLY DESTROY SO MUCH.
AS FOR THE POPULATION, HOPEFULLY THEY CAN ESCAPE IN TIME.
IF NOT, IT IS HARDLY A MAJOR STRATEGIC LOSS. THEY ARE ONLY...
HUMAN?
English.

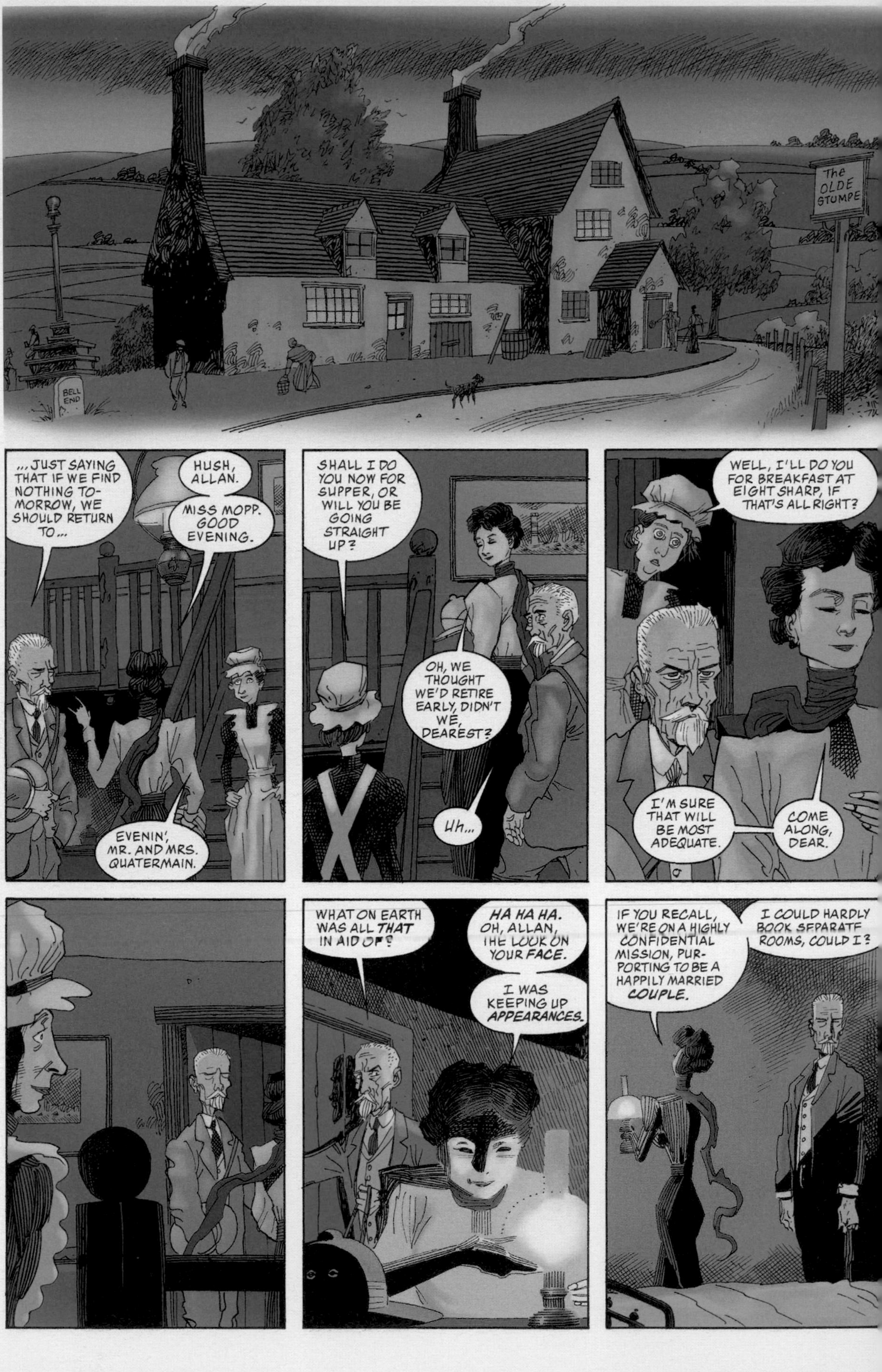
The OLDE STUMPE
BELL END
...JUST SAYING THAT IF WE FIND NOTHING TO-MORROW, WE SHOULD RETURN TO...
HUSH, ALLAN.
MISS MOPP. GOOD EVENING.
EVENIN', MR. AND MRS. QUATERMAIN.
SHALL I DO YOU NOW FOR SUPPER, OR WILL YOU BE GOING STRAIGHT UP?
OH, WE THOUGHT WE'D RETIRE EARLY, DIDN'T WE, DEAREST?
Uh...
WELL, I'LL DO YOU FOR BREAKFAST AT EIGHT SHARP, IF THAT'S ALL RIGHT?
I'M SURE THAT WILL BE MOST ADEQUATE.
COME ALONG, DEAR.
WHAT ON EARTH WAS ALL THAT IN AID OF?
HA HA HA. OH, ALLAN, THE LOOK ON YOUR FACE.
I WAS KEEPING UP APPEARANCES.
IF YOU RECALL, WE'RE ON A HIGHLY CONFIDENTIAL MISSION, PURPORTING TO BE A HAPPILY MARRIED COUPLE.
I COULD HARDLY BOOK SEPARATE ROOMS, COULD I?

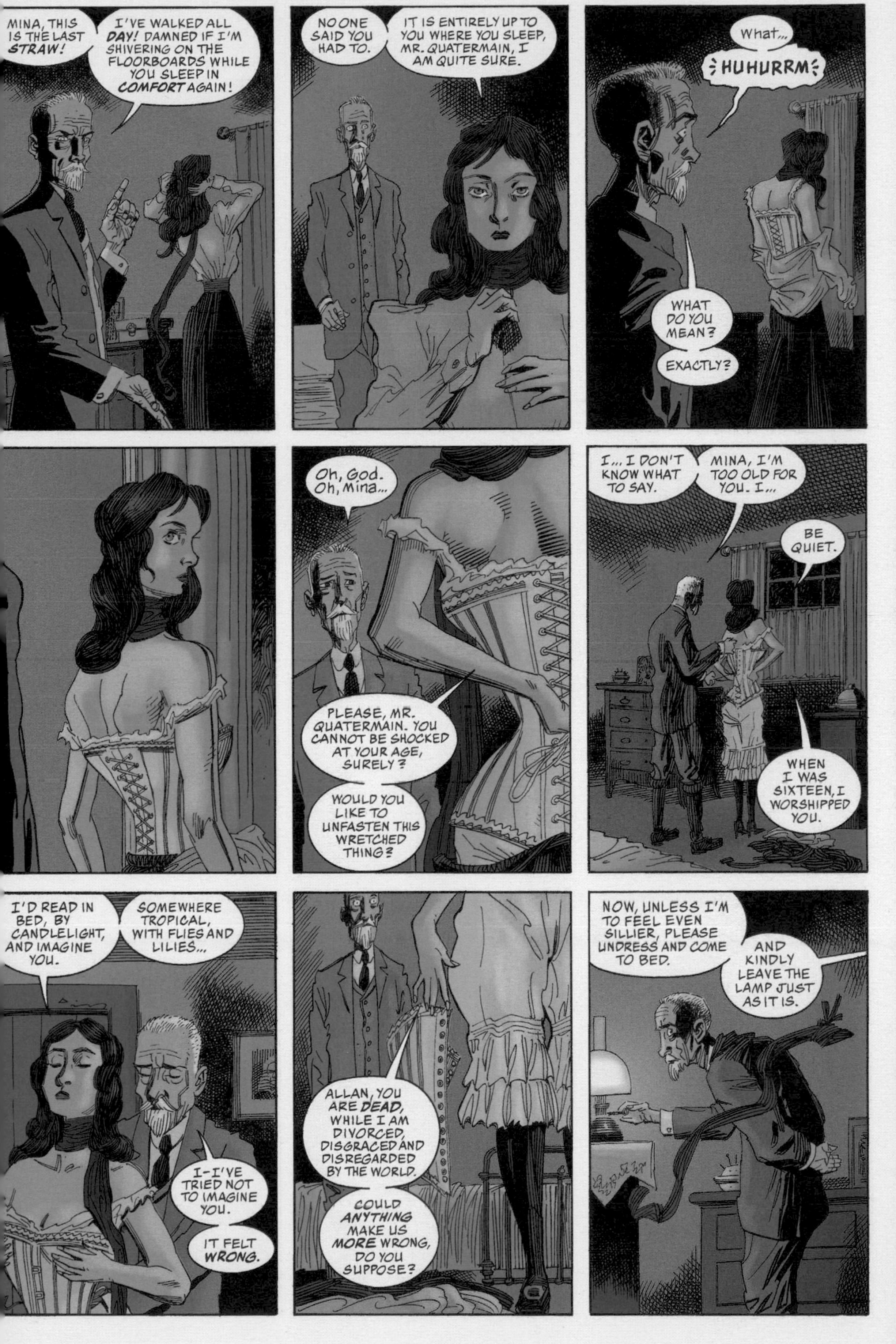
MINA, THIS IS THE LAST STRAW!
I'VE WALKED ALL DAY! DAMNED IF I'M SHIVERING ON THE FLOORBOARDS WHILE YOU SLEEP IN COMFORT AGAIN!
NO ONE SAID YOU HAD TO.
IT IS ENTIRELY UP TO YOU WHERE YOU SLEEP, MR. QUATERMAIN, I AM QUITE SURE.
What...
HUHURRM
WHAT DO YOU MEAN?
EXACTLY?
Oh, God. Oh, Mina...
PLEASE, MR. QUATERMAIN. YOU CANNOT BE SHOCKED AT YOUR AGE, SURELY?
WOULD YOU LIKE TO UNFASTEN THIS WRETCHED THING?
I... I DON'T KNOW WHAT TO SAY.
MINA, I'M TOO OLD FOR YOU. I...
BE QUIET.
WHEN I WAS SIXTEEN, I WORSHIPPED YOU.
I'D READ IN BED, BY CANDLELIGHT, AND IMAGINE YOU.
SOMEWHERE TROPICAL, WITH FLIES AND LILIES...
I-I'VE TRIED NOT TO IMAGINE YOU.
IT FELT WRONG.
ALLAN, YOU ARE DEAD, WHILE I AM DIVORCED, DISGRACED AND DISREGARDED BY THE WORLD.
COULD ANYTHING MAKE US MORE WRONG, DO YOU SUPPOSE?
NOW, UNLESS I'M TO FEEL EVEN SILLIER, PLEASE UNDRESS AND COME TO BED.
AND KINDLY LEAVE THE LAMP JUST AS IT IS.

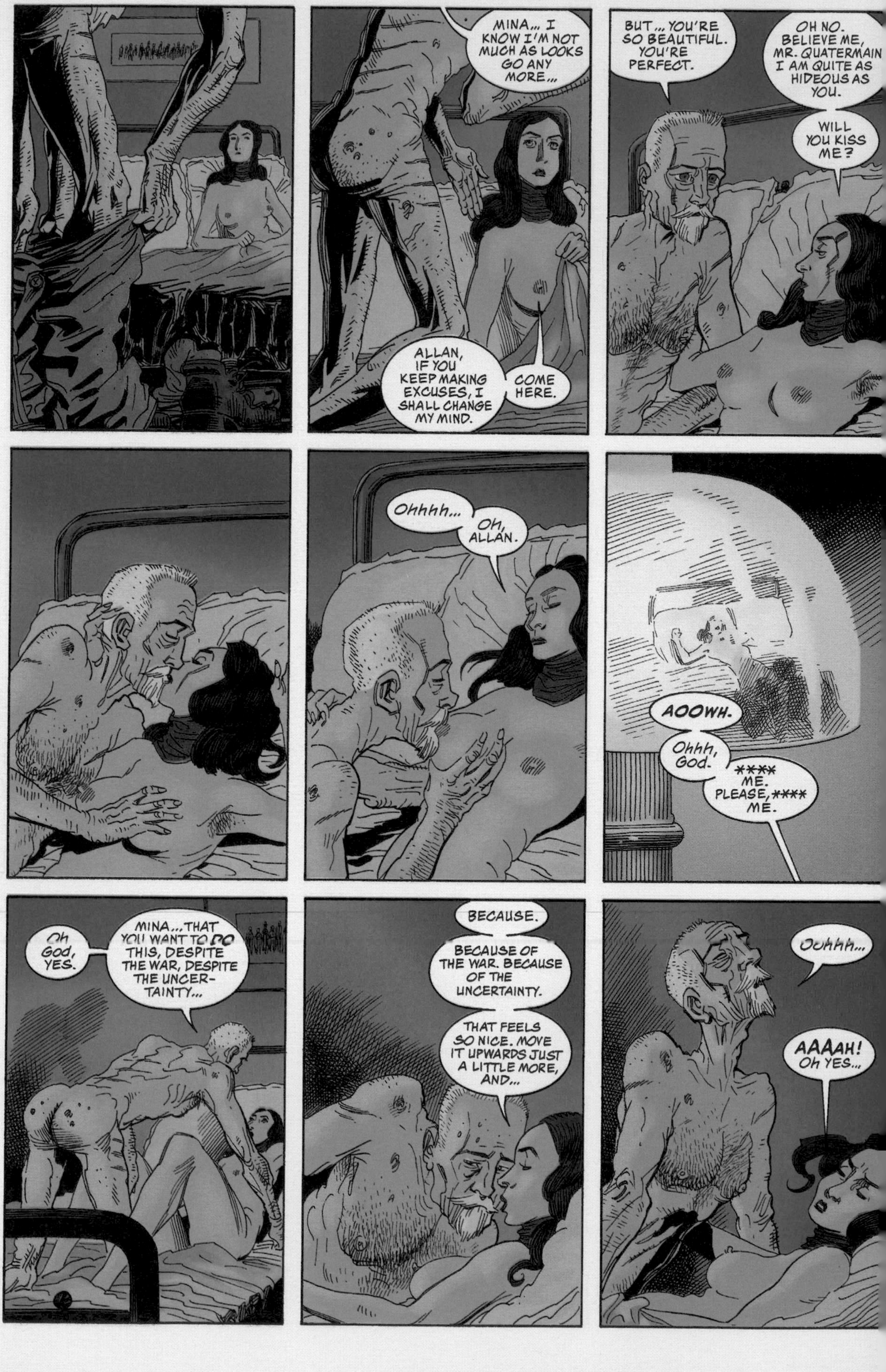
MINA... I KNOW I'M NOT MUCH AS LOOKS GO ANY MORE...
ALLAN, IF YOU KEEP MAKING EXCUSES, I SHALL CHANGE MY MIND.
COME HERE.
BUT... YOU'RE SO BEAUTIFUL. YOU'RE PERFECT.
OH NO. BELIEVE ME, MR. QUATERMAIN I AM QUITE AS HIDEOUS AS YOU.
WILL YOU KISS ME?
Ohhhh...
Oh, ALLAN.
AOOWH.
Ohhh, God.
**** ME. PLEASE, **** ME.
MINA... THAT YOU WANT TO DO THIS, DESPITE THE WAR, DESPITE THE UNCERTAINTY...
Oh God, YES.
BECAUSE.
BECAUSE OF THE WAR. BECAUSE OF THE UNCERTAINTY.
THAT FEELS SO NICE. MOVE IT UPWARDS JUST A LITTLE MORE, AND...
Oohhh...
AAAAH! Oh YES...

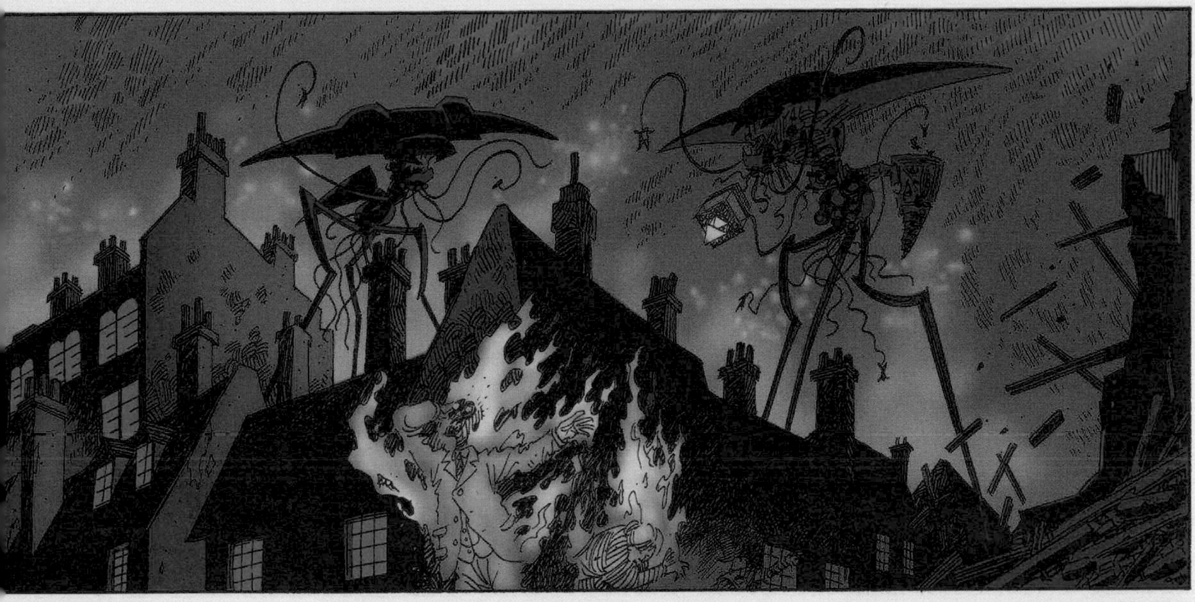

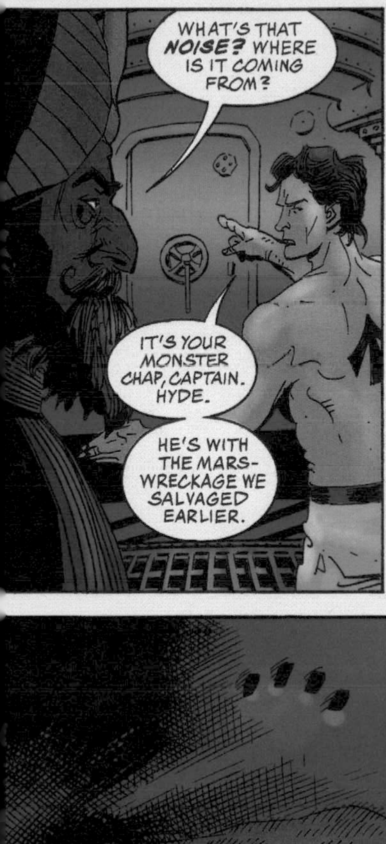
WHAT'S THAT NOISE? WHERE IS IT COMING FROM?
IT'S YOUR MONSTER CHAP, CAPTAIN. HYDE.
HE'S WITH THE MARS-WRECKAGE WE SALVAGED EARLIER.

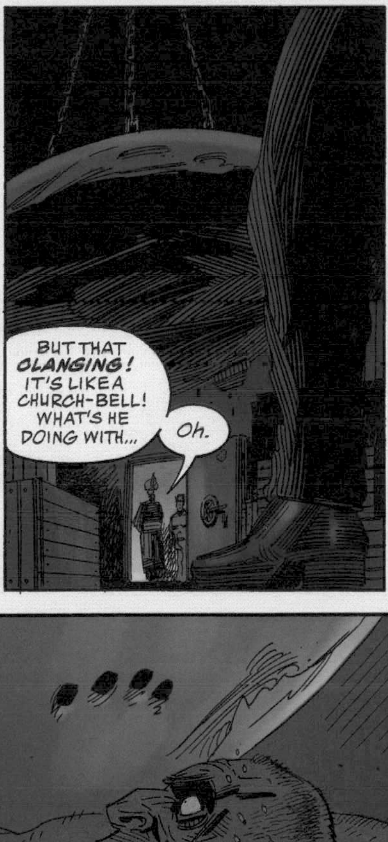
BUT THAT CLANGING! IT'S LIKE A CHURCH-BELL! WHAT'S HE DOING WITH...
Oh.

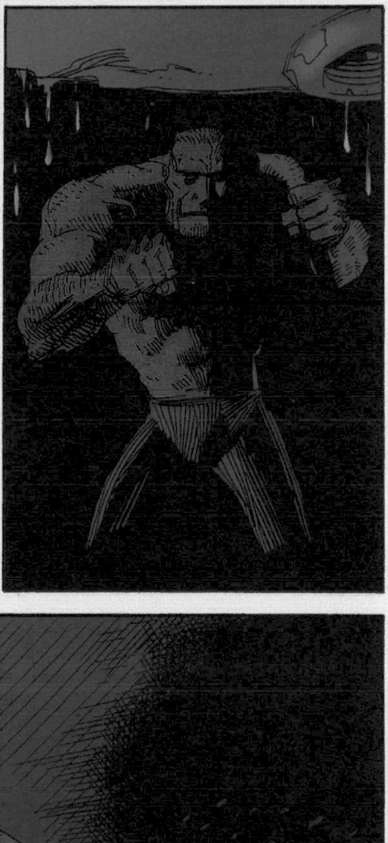

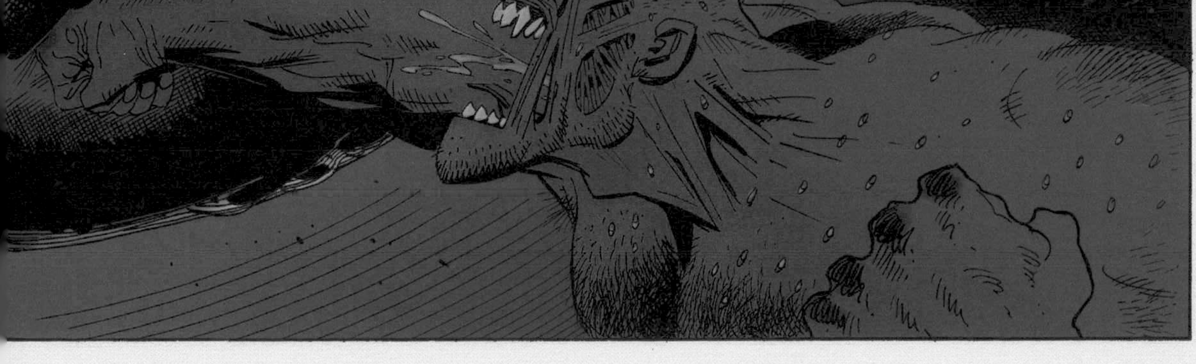

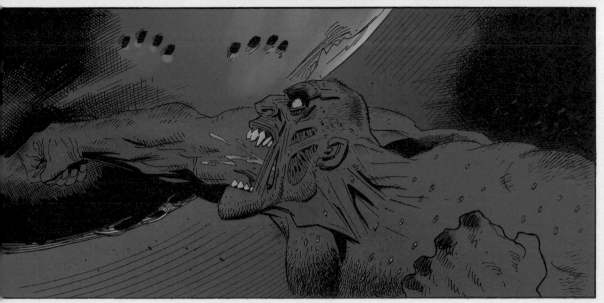

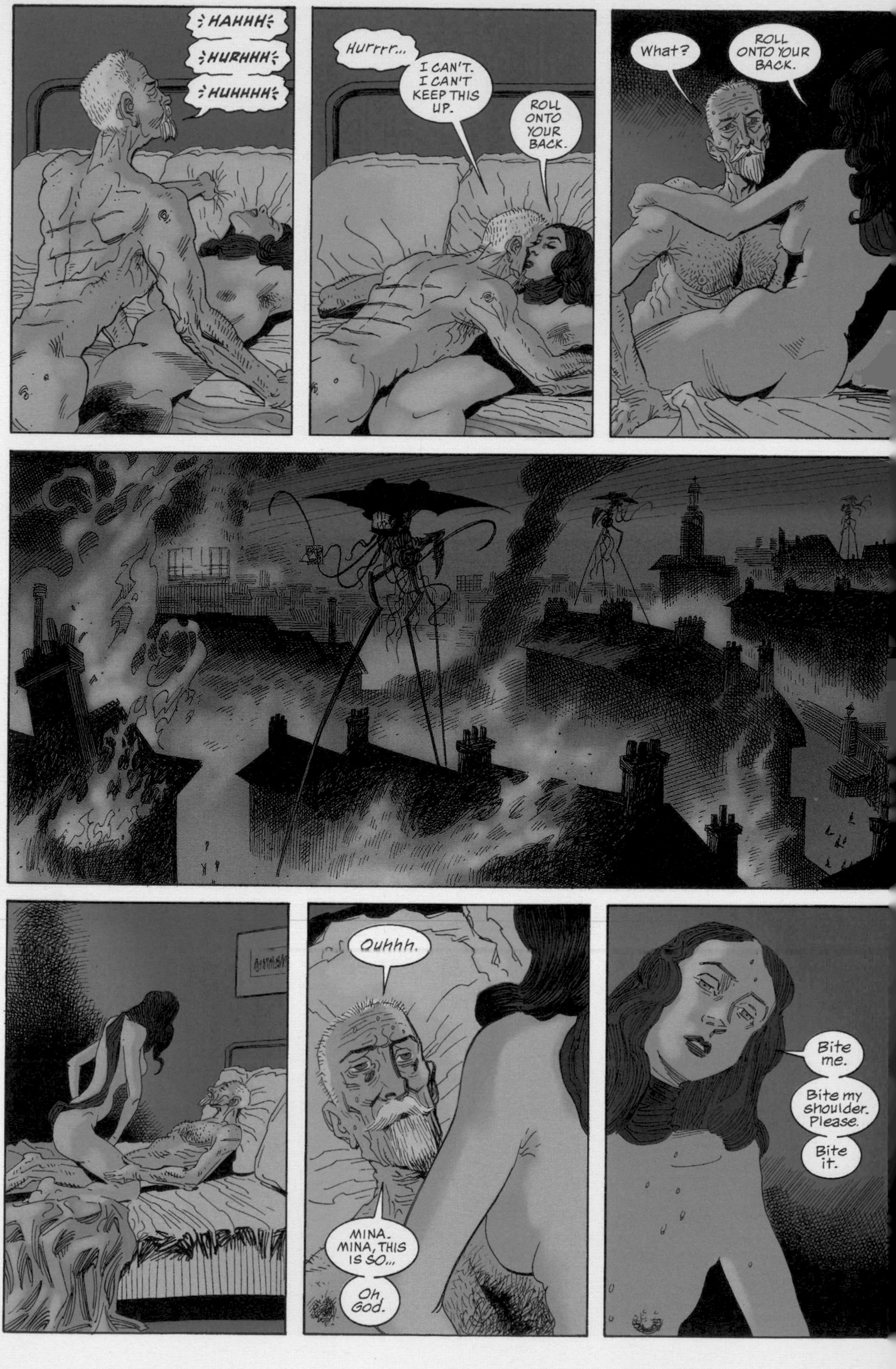
HAHHH
HURHHH
HUHHHH
Hurrrr...
I CAN'T. I CAN'T KEEP THIS UP.
ROLL ONTO YOUR BACK.
What?
ROLL ONTO YOUR BACK.
Ouhhh.
MINA. MINA, THIS IS SO...
Oh, God.
Bite me.
Bite my shoulder. Please.
Bite it.

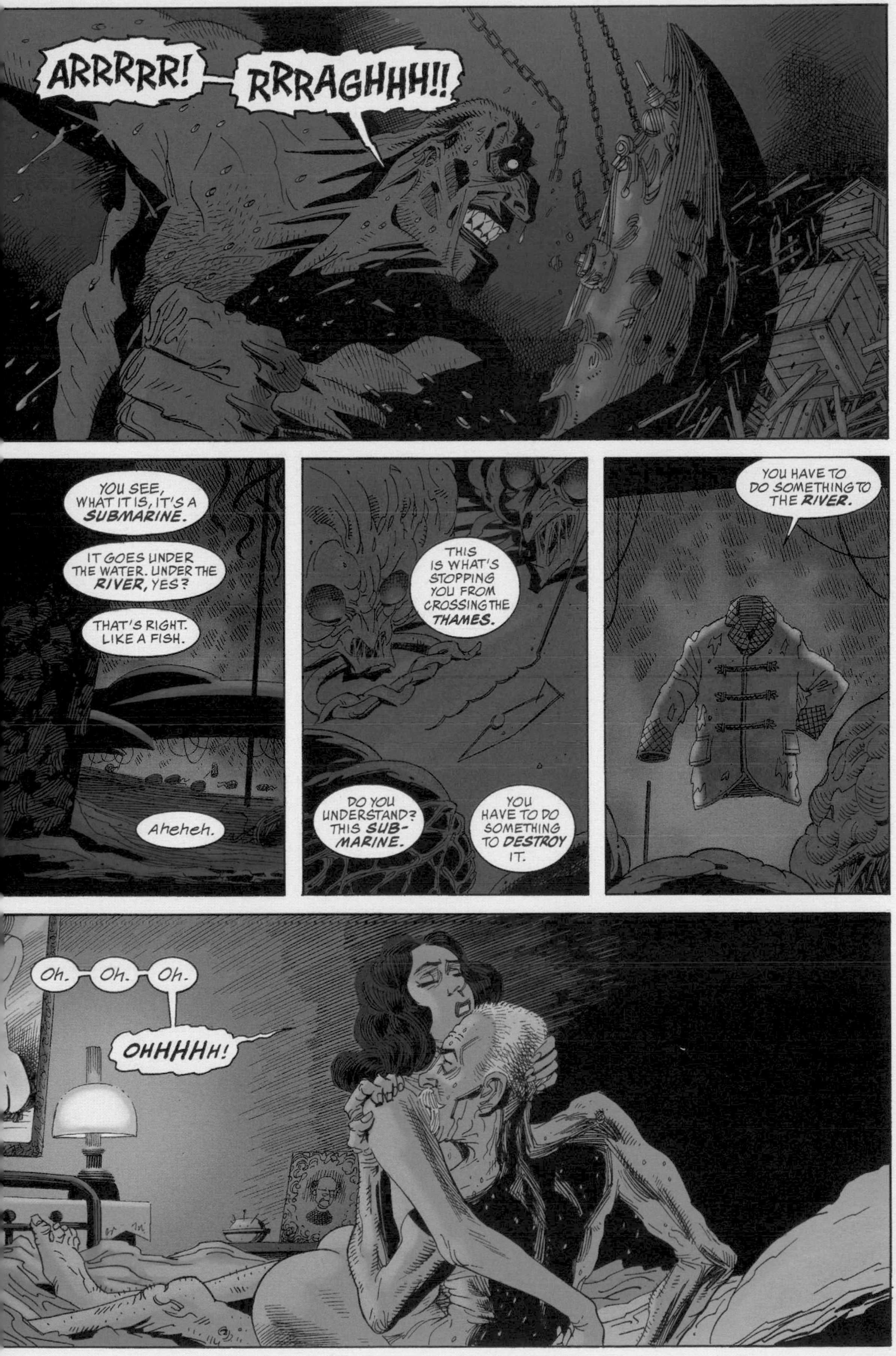
ARRRRR!
RRRAGHHH!!
YOU SEE, WHAT IT IS, IT'S A SUBMARINE.
IT GOES UNDER THE WATER. UNDER THE RIVER, YES?
THAT'S RIGHT. LIKE A FISH.
Aheheh.
THIS IS WHAT'S STOPPING YOU FROM CROSSING THE THAMES.
DO YOU UNDERSTAND? THIS SUB-MARINE.
YOU HAVE TO DO SOMETHING TO DESTROY IT.
YOU HAVE TO DO SOMETHING TO THE RIVER.
Oh. Oh. Oh.
OHHHHh!

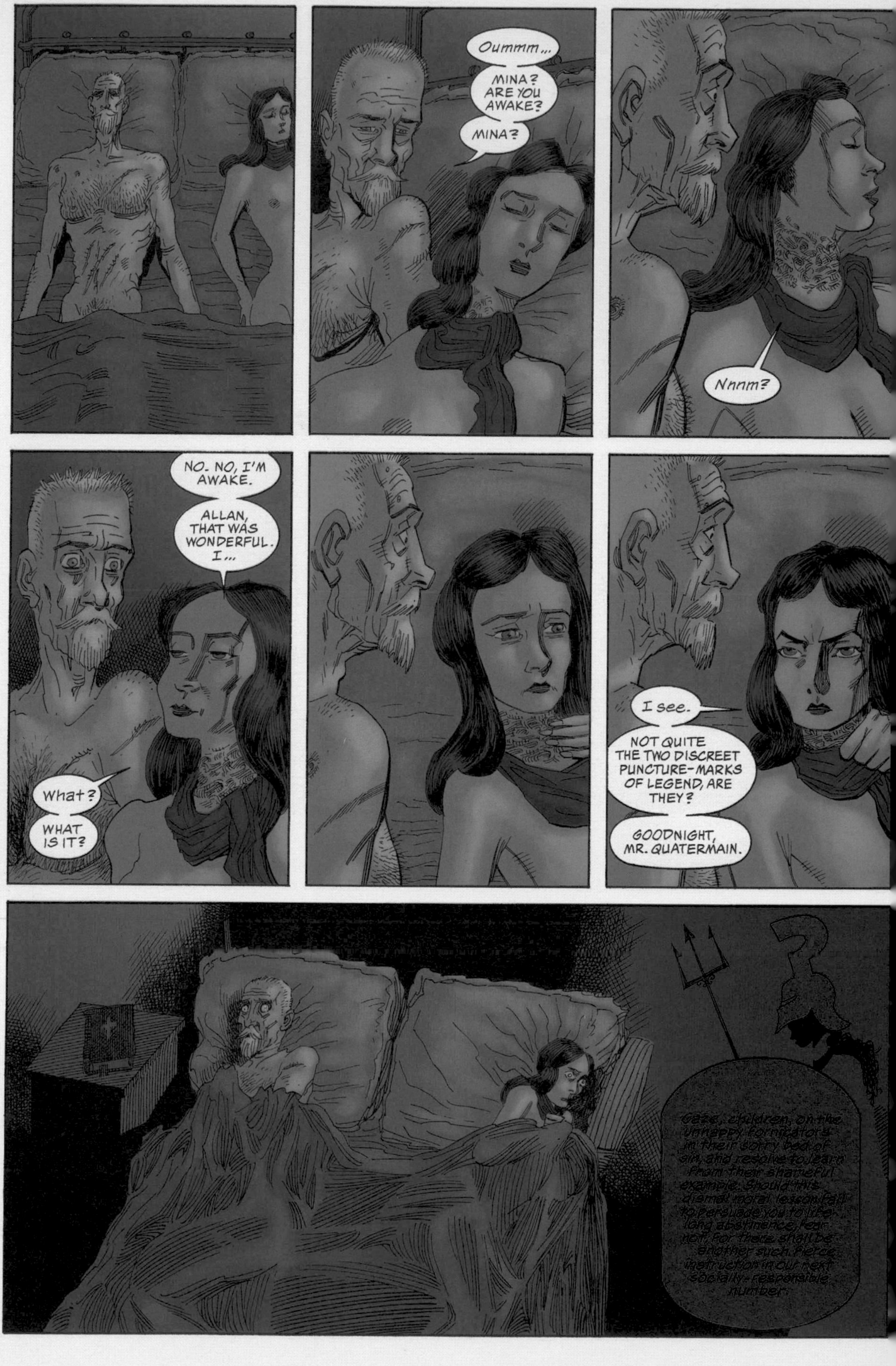
Oummm...
MINA? ARE YOU AWAKE?
MINA?
Nnnm?
NO. NO, I'M AWAKE.
ALLAN, THAT WAS WONDERFUL. I...
What?
WHAT IS IT?
I see.
NOT QUITE THE TWO DISCREET PUNCTURE-MARKS OF LEGEND, ARE THEY?
GOODNIGHT, MR. QUATERMAIN.
Gaze, children, on the unhappy fornicators in their sorry bed of sin, and resolve to learn from their shameful example. Should this dismal moral lesson fail to persuade you to life-long abstinence, fear not, for there shall be another such fierce instruction in our next socially-responsible number.

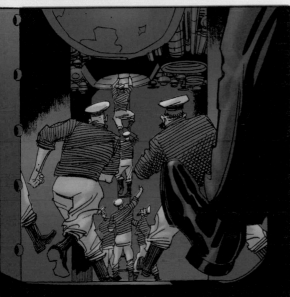

≷HHHUAHH!

Huh. RIVER SUPPOSED TO BE LIKE THAT, IS IT?

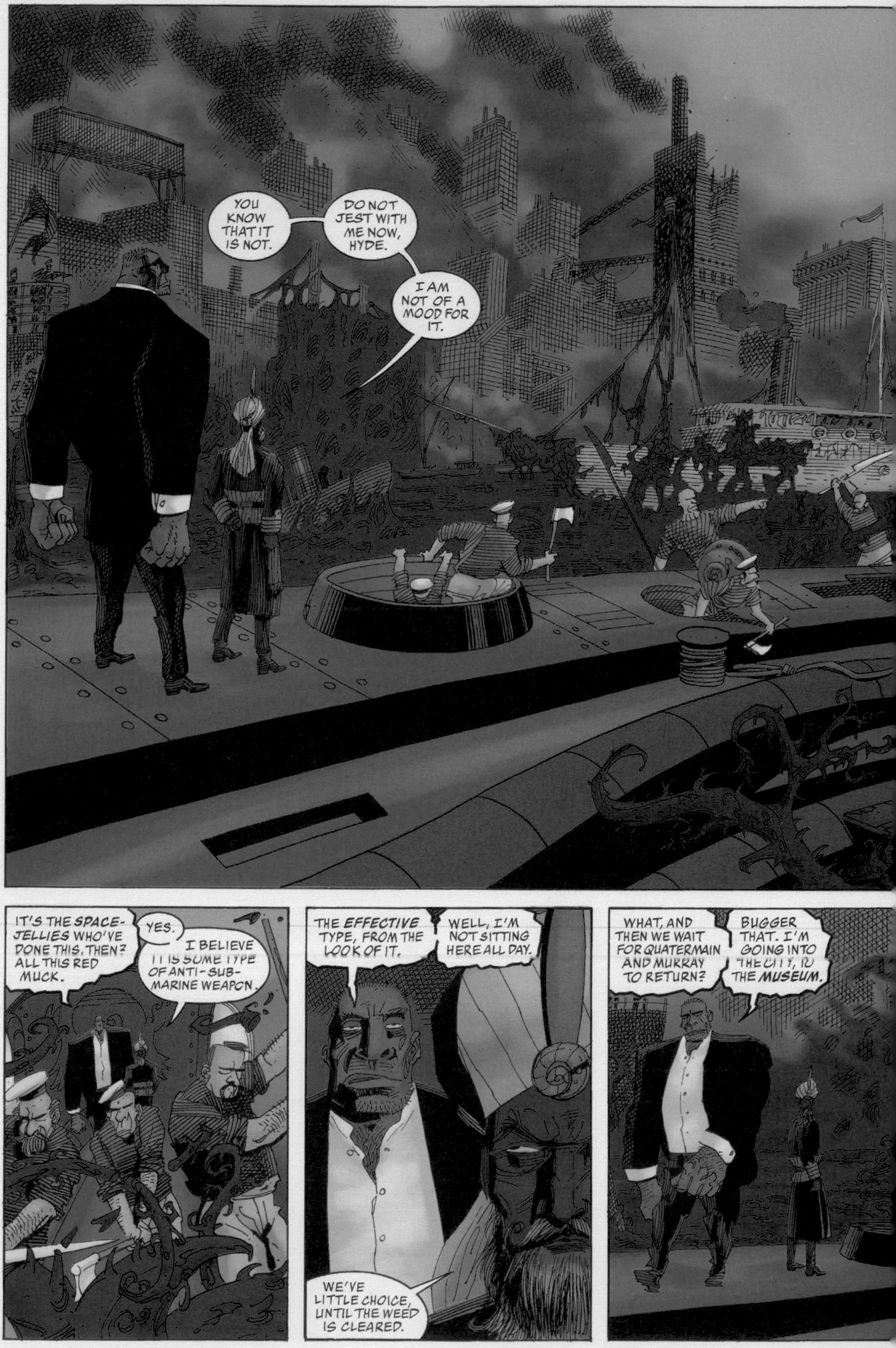
YOU KNOW THAT IT IS NOT.
DO NOT JEST WITH ME NOW, HYDE.
I AM NOT OF A MOOD FOR IT.
IT'S THE *SPACE-JELLIES* WHO'VE DONE THIS, THEN? ALL THIS RED MUCK.
YES.
I BELIEVE IT IS SOME TYPE OF ANTI-SUB-MARINE WEAPON.
THE *EFFECTIVE* TYPE, FROM THE LOOK OF IT.
WELL, I'M NOT SITTING HERE ALL DAY.
WE'VE LITTLE CHOICE, UNTIL THE WEED IS CLEARED.
WHAT, AND THEN WE WAIT FOR QUATERMAIN AND MURRAY TO RETURN?
BUGGER THAT. I'M GOING INTO THE CITY, TO THE *MUSEUM*.

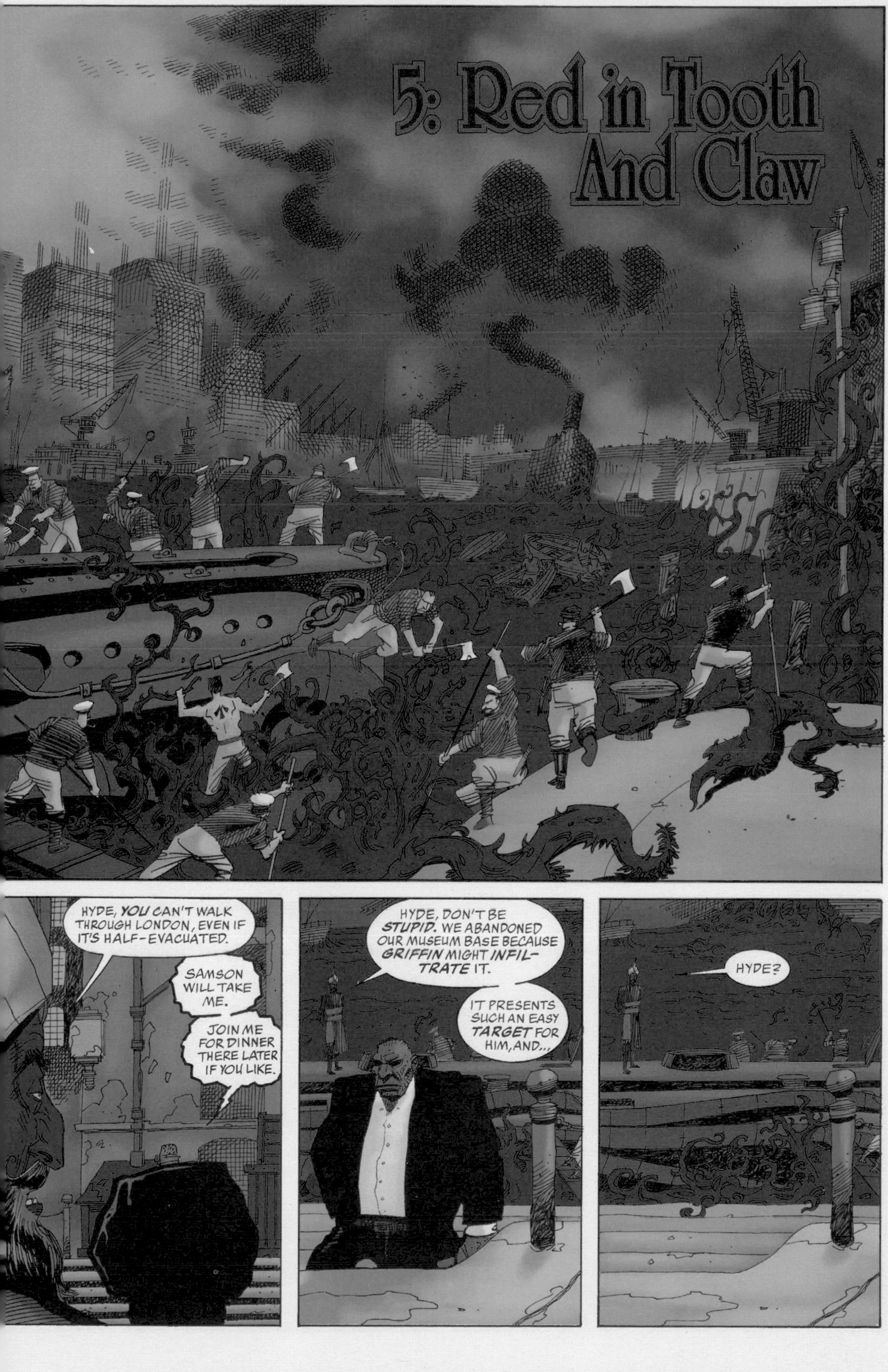
5: Red in Tooth And Claw
HYDE, YOU CAN'T WALK THROUGH LONDON, EVEN IF IT'S HALF-EVACUATED.
SAMSON WILL TAKE ME.
JOIN ME FOR DINNER THERE LATER IF YOU LIKE.
HYDE, DON'T BE STUPID. WE ABANDONED OUR MUSEUM BASE BECAUSE GRIFFIN MIGHT INFIL-TRATE IT.
IT PRESENTS SUCH AN EASY TARGET FOR HIM, AND...
HYDE?

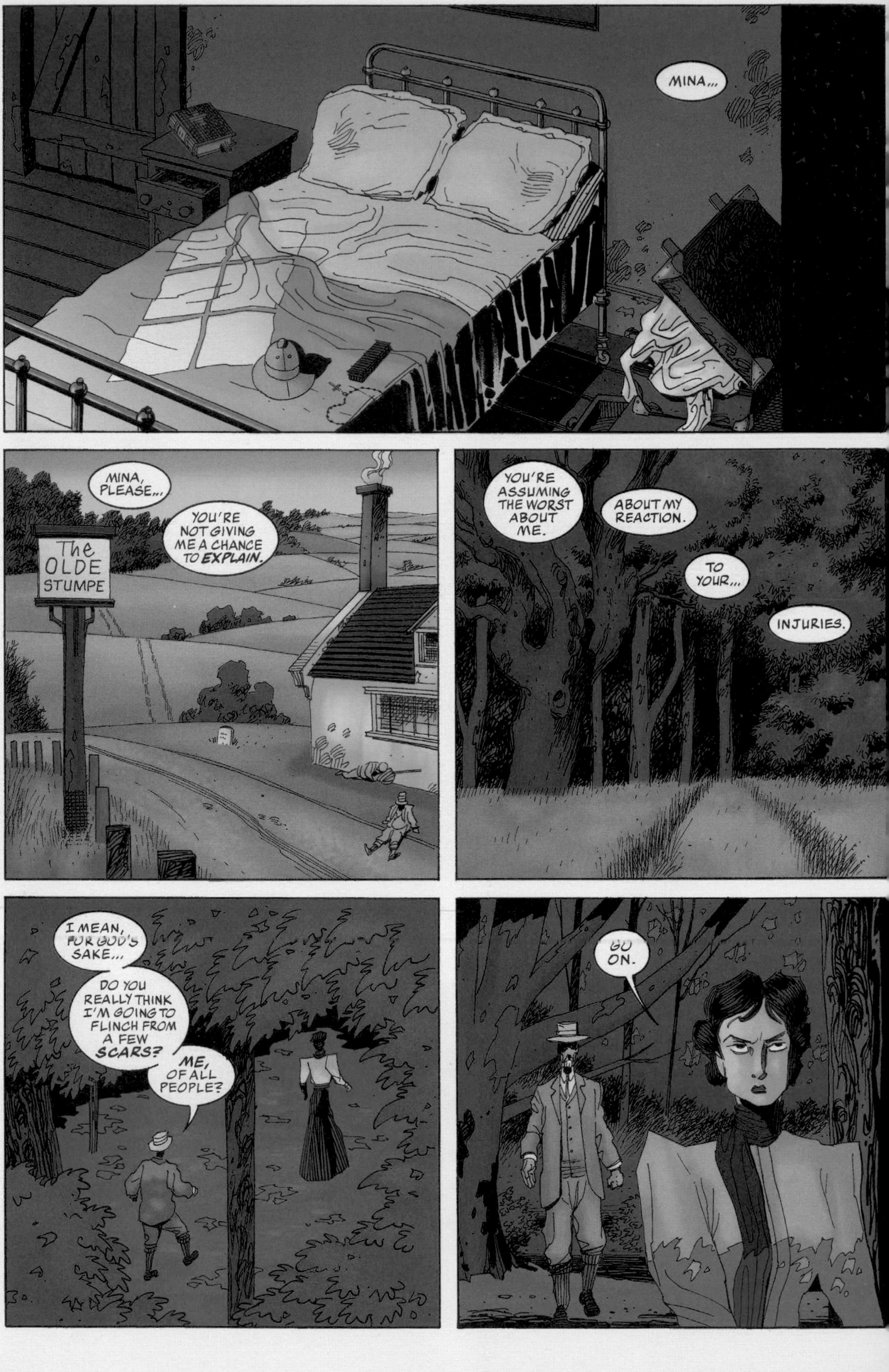
MINA...
MINA, PLEASE...
YOU'RE NOT GIVING ME A CHANCE TO EXPLAIN.
The OLDE STUMPE
YOU'RE ASSUMING THE WORST ABOUT ME.
ABOUT MY REACTION.
TO YOUR...
INJURIES.
I MEAN, FOR GOD'S SAKE...
DO YOU REALLY THINK I'M GOING TO FLINCH FROM A FEW SCARS?
ME, OF ALL PEOPLE?
GO ON.

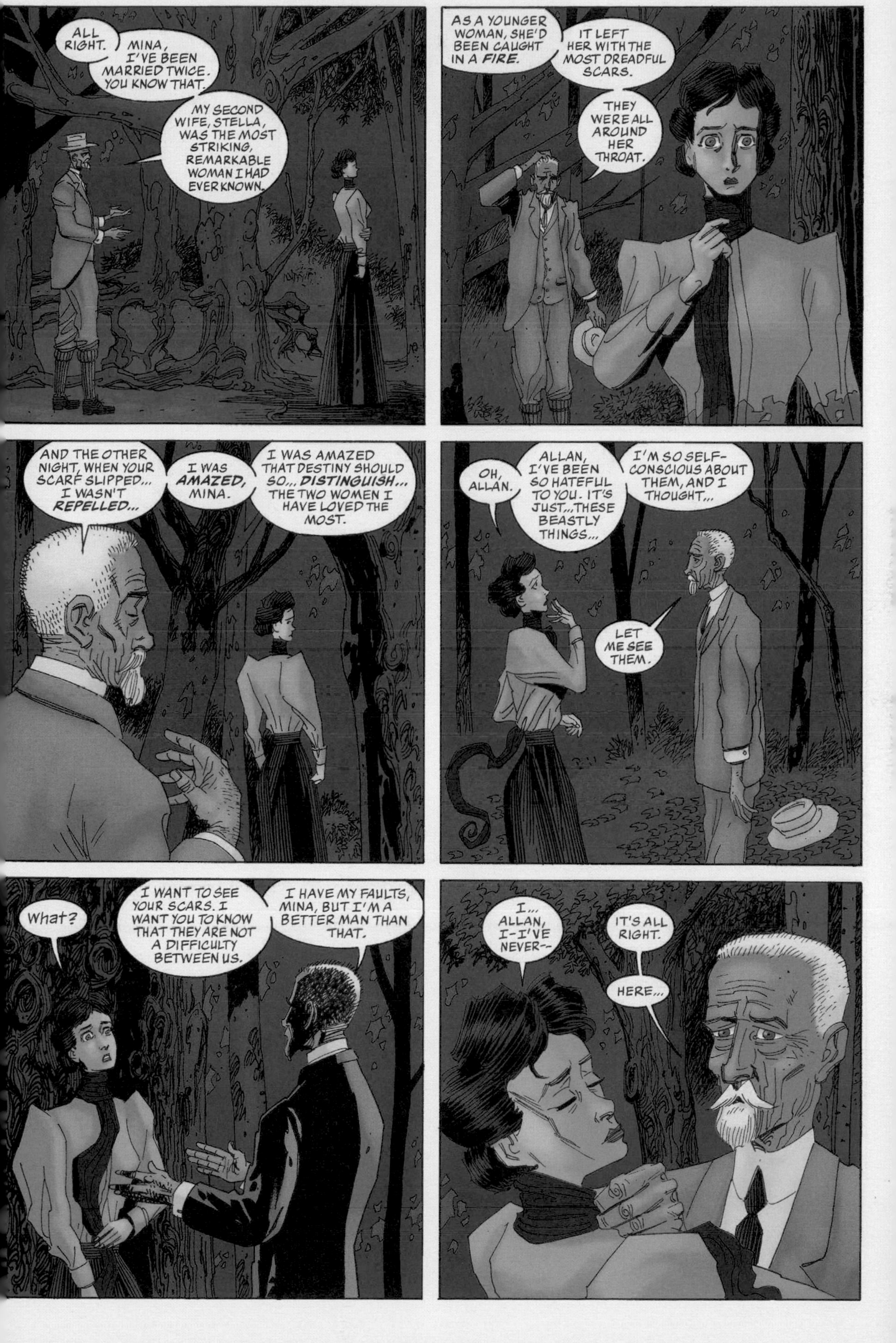
ALL RIGHT.
MINA, I'VE BEEN MARRIED TWICE. YOU KNOW THAT.
MY SECOND WIFE, STELLA, WAS THE MOST STRIKING, REMARKABLE WOMAN I HAD EVER KNOWN.
AS A YOUNGER WOMAN, SHE'D BEEN CAUGHT IN A FIRE.
IT LEFT HER WITH THE MOST DREADFUL SCARS.
THEY WERE ALL AROUND HER THROAT.
AND THE OTHER NIGHT, WHEN YOUR SCARF SLIPPED... I WASN'T REPELLED...
I WAS AMAZED, MINA.
I WAS AMAZED THAT DESTINY SHOULD SO... DISTINGUISH... THE TWO WOMEN I HAVE LOVED THE MOST.
OH, ALLAN.
ALLAN, I'VE BEEN SO HATEFUL TO YOU. IT'S JUST... THESE BEASTLY THINGS...
I'M SO SELF-CONSCIOUS ABOUT THEM, AND I THOUGHT...
LET ME SEE THEM.
What?
I WANT TO SEE YOUR SCARS. I WANT YOU TO KNOW THAT THEY ARE NOT A DIFFICULTY BETWEEN US.
I HAVE MY FAULTS, MINA, BUT I'M A BETTER MAN THAN THAT.
I... ALLAN, I-I'VE NEVER--
IT'S ALL RIGHT.
HERE...

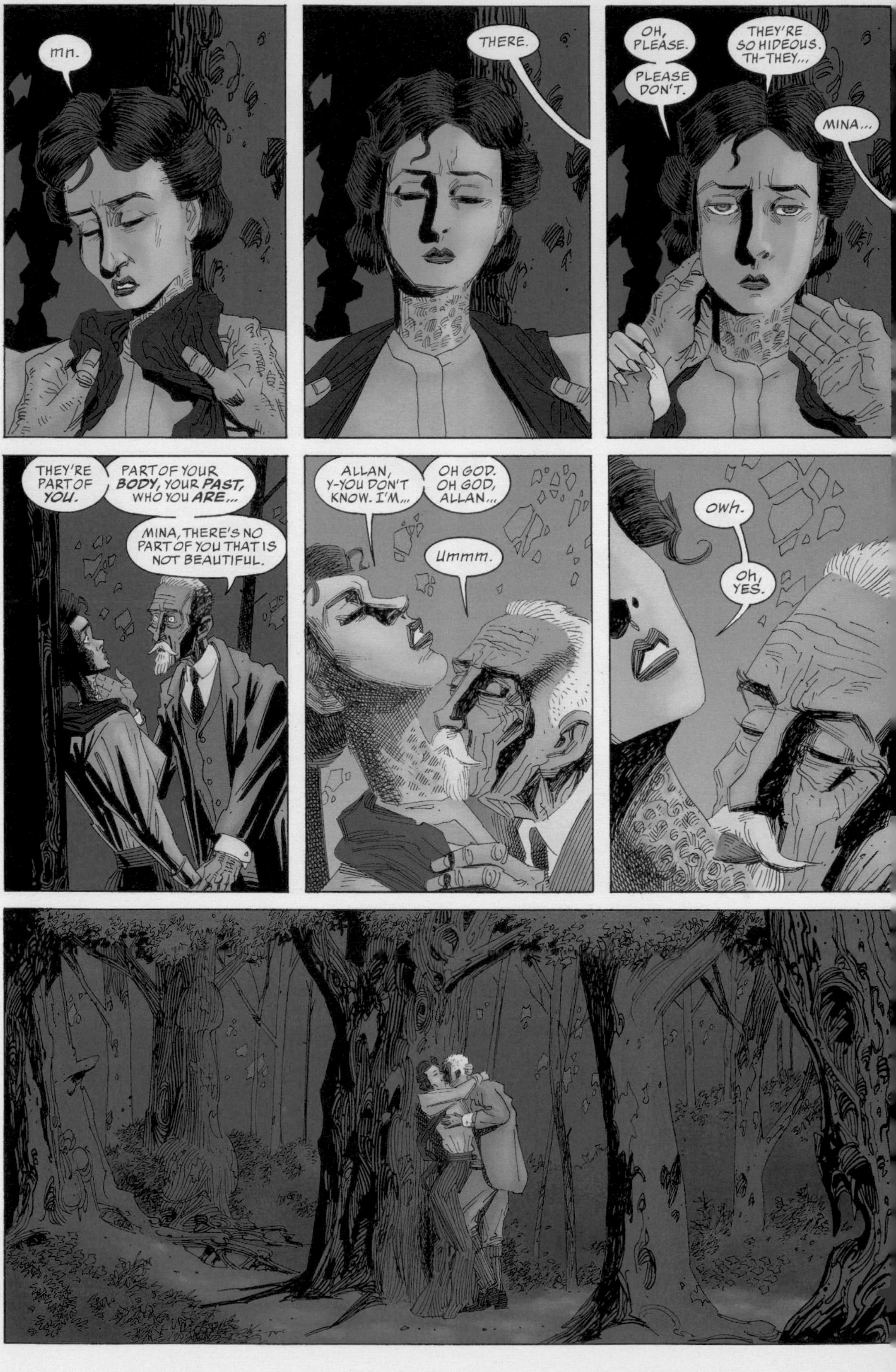
MN.
THERE.
OH, PLEASE.
PLEASE DON'T.
THEY'RE SO HIDEOUS. TH-THEY...
MINA...
THEY'RE PART OF YOU.
PART OF YOUR BODY, YOUR PAST, WHO YOU ARE...
MINA, THERE'S NO PART OF YOU THAT IS NOT BEAUTIFUL.
ALLAN, Y-YOU DON'T KNOW. I'M...
OH GOD. OH GOD, ALLAN...
Ummm.
Owh.
Oh, YES.

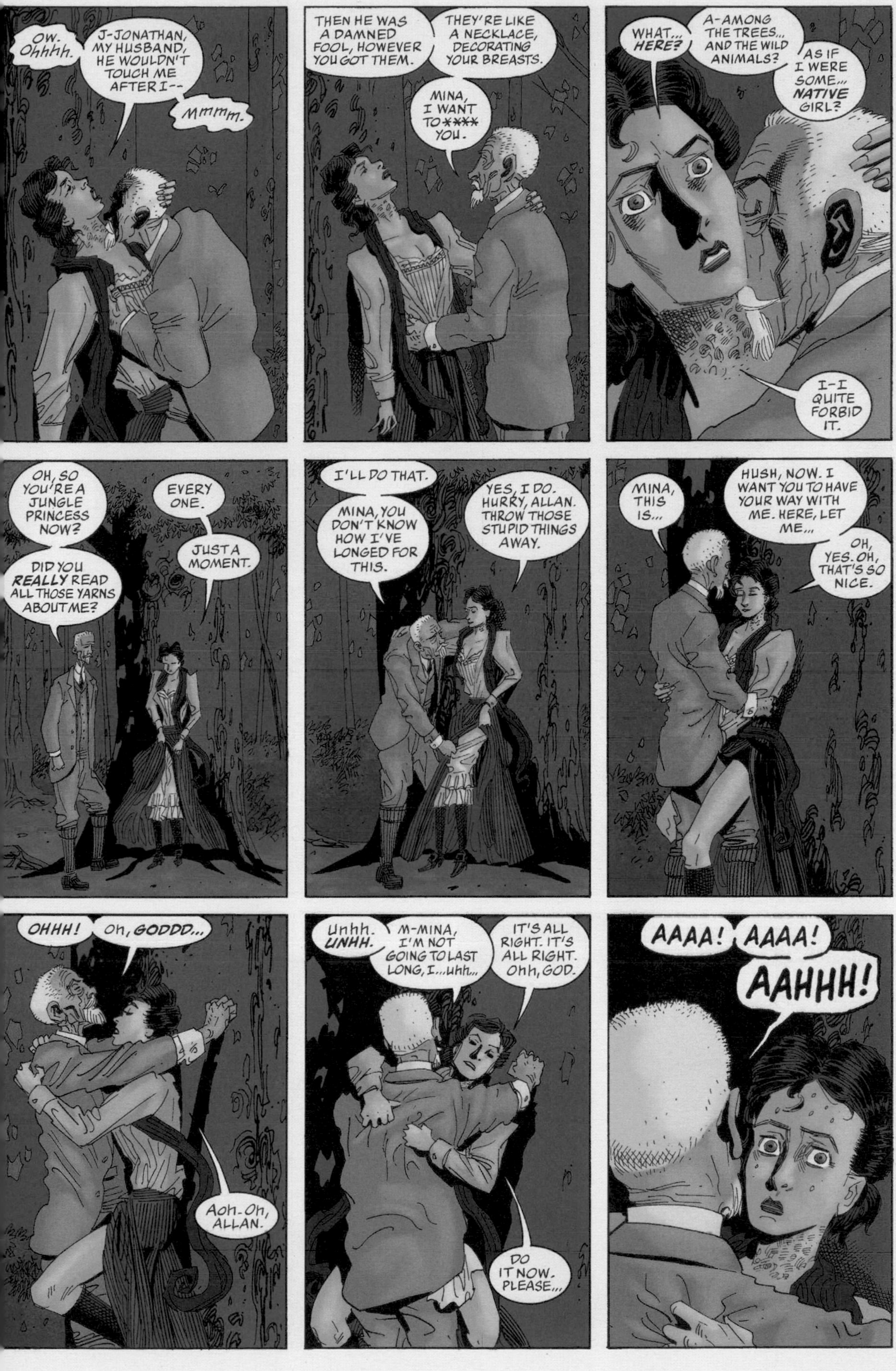
Ow. Ohhhh.
J-JONATHAN, MY HUSBAND, HE WOULDN'T TOUCH ME AFTER I--
Mmmm.
THEN HE WAS A DAMNED FOOL, HOWEVER YOU GOT THEM.
THEY'RE LIKE A NECKLACE, DECORATING YOUR BREASTS.
MINA, I WANT TO **** YOU.
WHAT... HERE?
A-AMONG THE TREES... AND THE WILD ANIMALS?
AS IF I WERE SOME... NATIVE GIRL?
I-I QUITE FORBID IT.
OH, SO YOU'RE A JUNGLE PRINCESS NOW?
EVERY ONE.
JUST A MOMENT.
DID YOU REALLY READ ALL THOSE YARNS ABOUT ME?
I'LL DO THAT.
MINA, YOU DON'T KNOW HOW I'VE LONGED FOR THIS.
YES, I DO. HURRY, ALLAN. THROW THOSE STUPID THINGS AWAY.
MINA, THIS IS...
HUSH, NOW. I WANT YOU TO HAVE YOUR WAY WITH ME. HERE, LET ME...
OH, YES. OH, THAT'S SO NICE.
OHHH!
Oh, GODDD...
Aoh-Oh, ALLAN.
Unhh. UNHH.
M-MINA, I'M NOT GOING TO LAST LONG, I...uhh...
IT'S ALL RIGHT. IT'S ALL RIGHT. Ohh, GOD.
DO IT NOW. PLEASE...
AAAA! AAAA!
AAHHH!

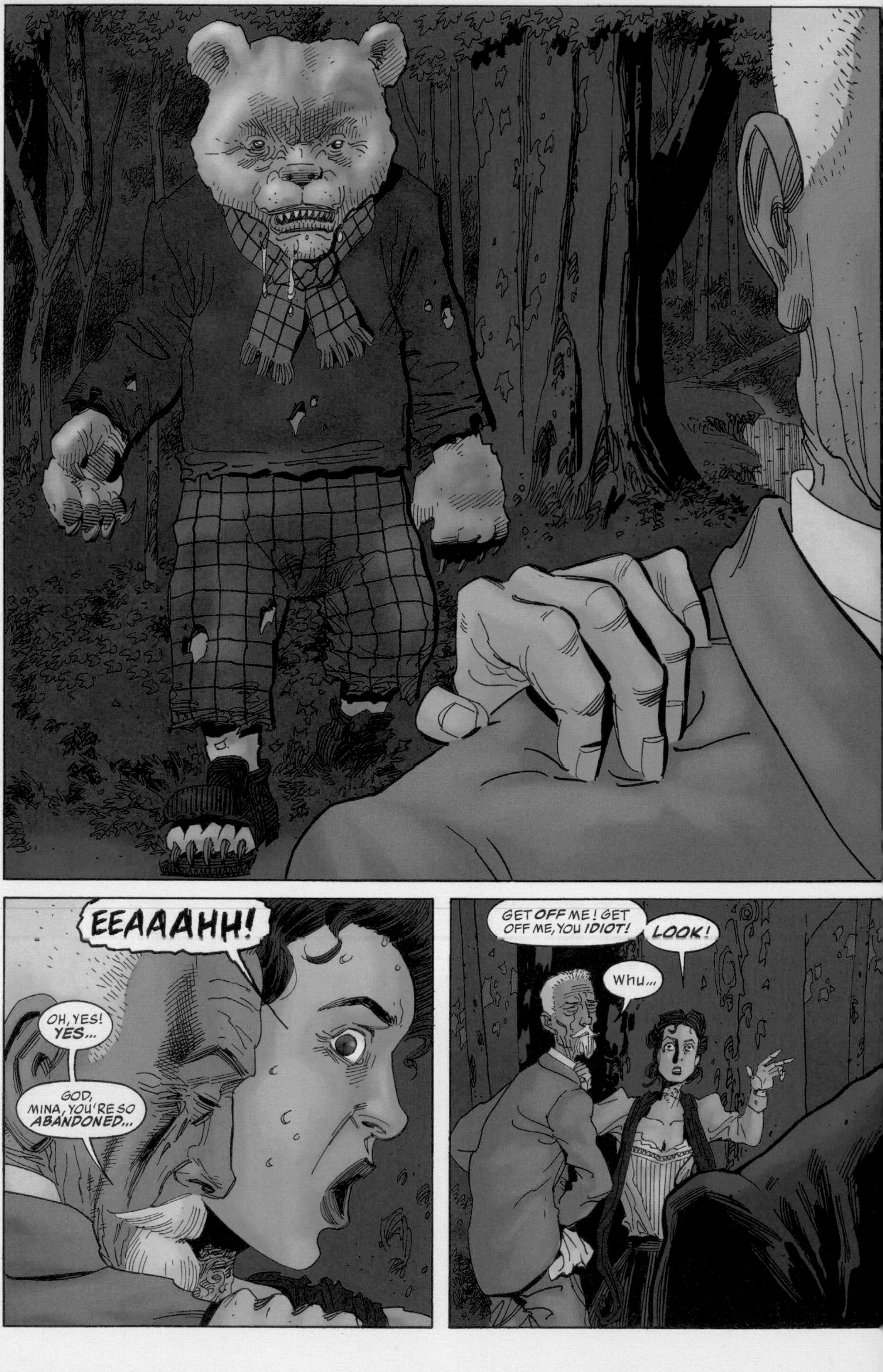
EEAAAHH!
OH, YES! YES...
GOD, MINA, YOU'RE SO ABANDONED...
GET OFF ME! GET OFF ME, YOU IDIOT!
LOOK!
Whu...

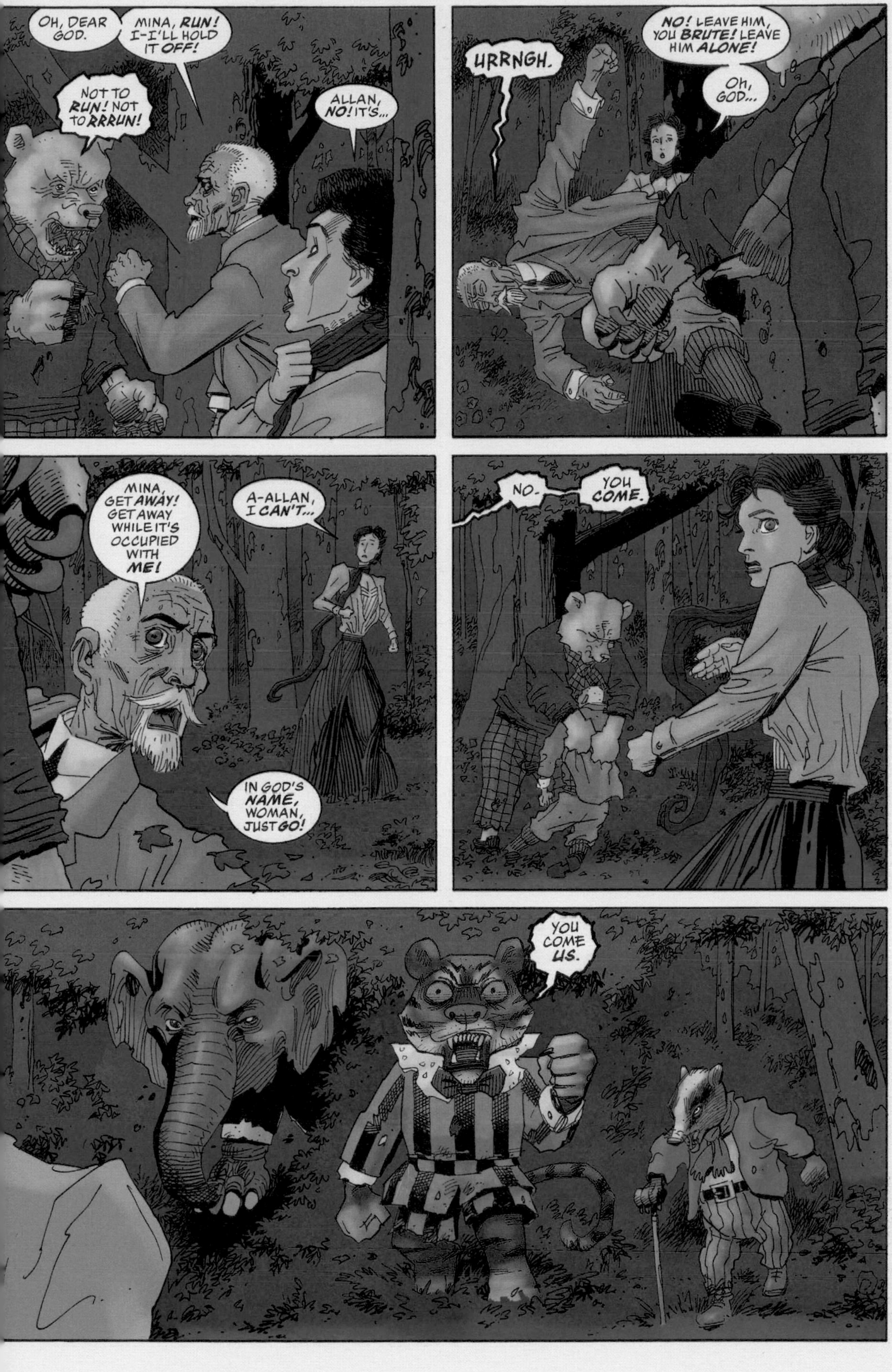
OH, DEAR GOD.
MINA, RUN! I-I'LL HOLD IT OFF!
NOT TO RUN! NOT TO RRRUN!
ALLAN, NO! IT'S...
URRNGH.
NO! LEAVE HIM, YOU BRUTE! LEAVE HIM ALONE!
Oh, GOD...
MINA, GET AWAY! GET AWAY WHILE IT'S OCCUPIED WITH ME!
A-ALLAN, I CAN'T...
IN GOD'S NAME, WOMAN, JUST GO!
NO.
YOU COME.
YOU COME US.

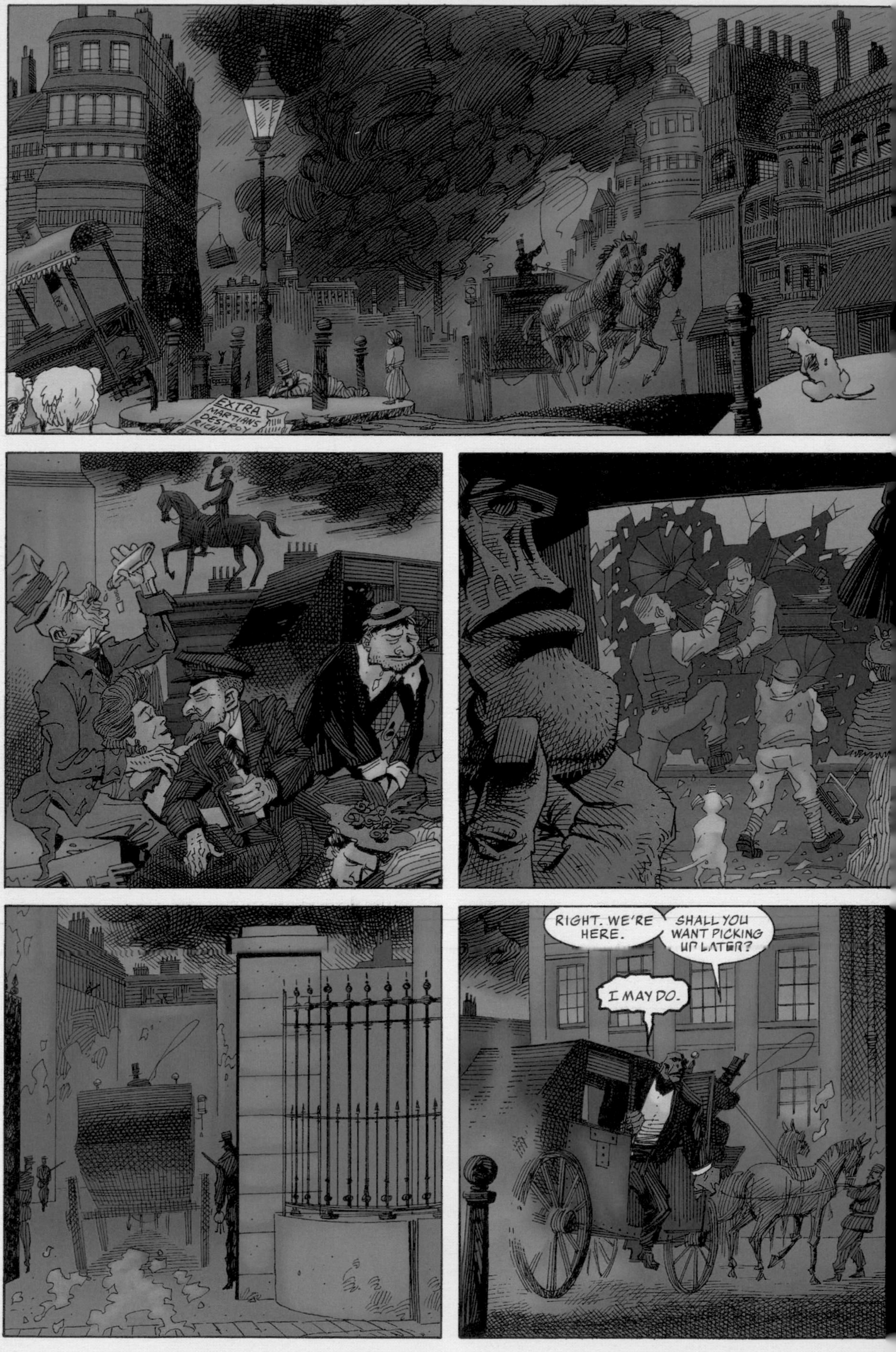
EXTRA
MARTIANS
DESTROY
RIGHT. WE'RE HERE.
SHALL YOU WANT PICKING UP LATER?
I MAY DO.

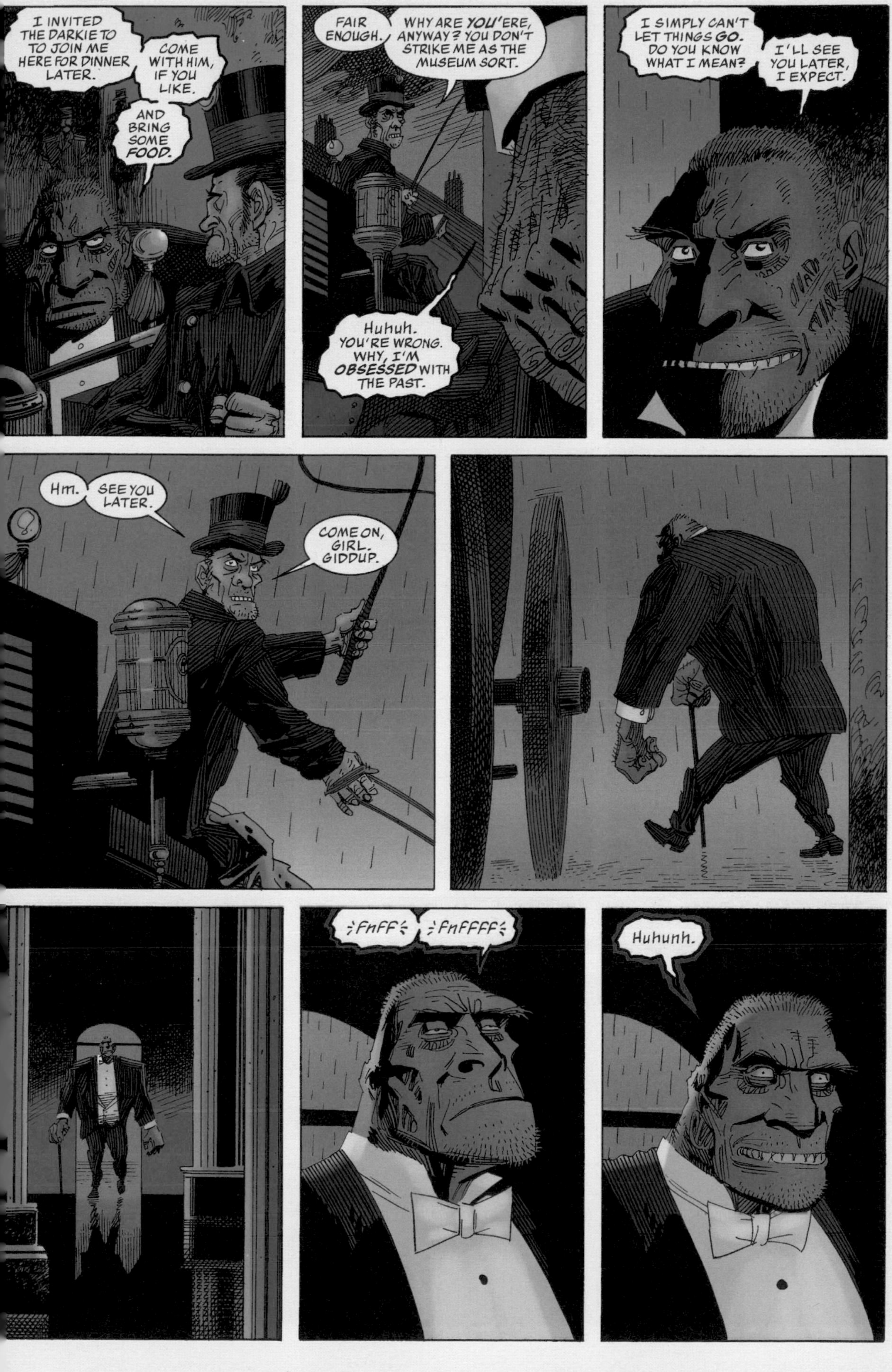
I INVITED THE DARKIE TO TO JOIN ME HERE FOR DINNER LATER.
COME WITH HIM, IF YOU LIKE.
AND BRING SOME FOOD.
FAIR ENOUGH.
WHY ARE YOU'ERE, ANYWAY? YOU DON'T STRIKE ME AS THE MUSEUM SORT.
Huhuh. YOU'RE WRONG. WHY, I'M OBSESSED WITH THE PAST.
I SIMPLY CAN'T LET THINGS GO. DO YOU KNOW WHAT I MEAN?
I'LL SEE YOU LATER, I EXPECT.
Hm.
SEE YOU LATER.
COME ON, GIRL. GIDDUP.
Fnff
Fnffff
Huhunh.

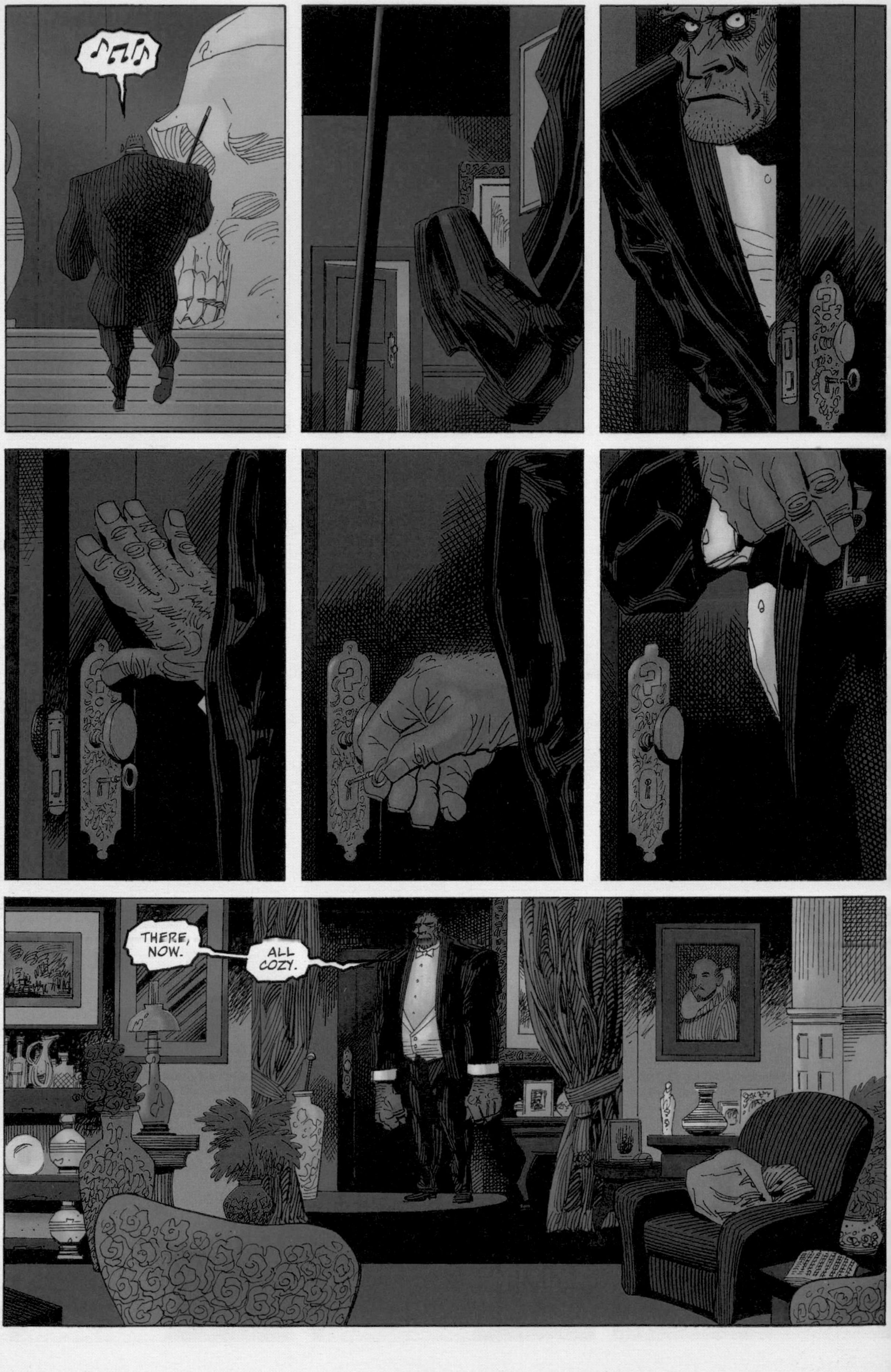
♪♫♪
THERE, NOW.
ALL COZY.

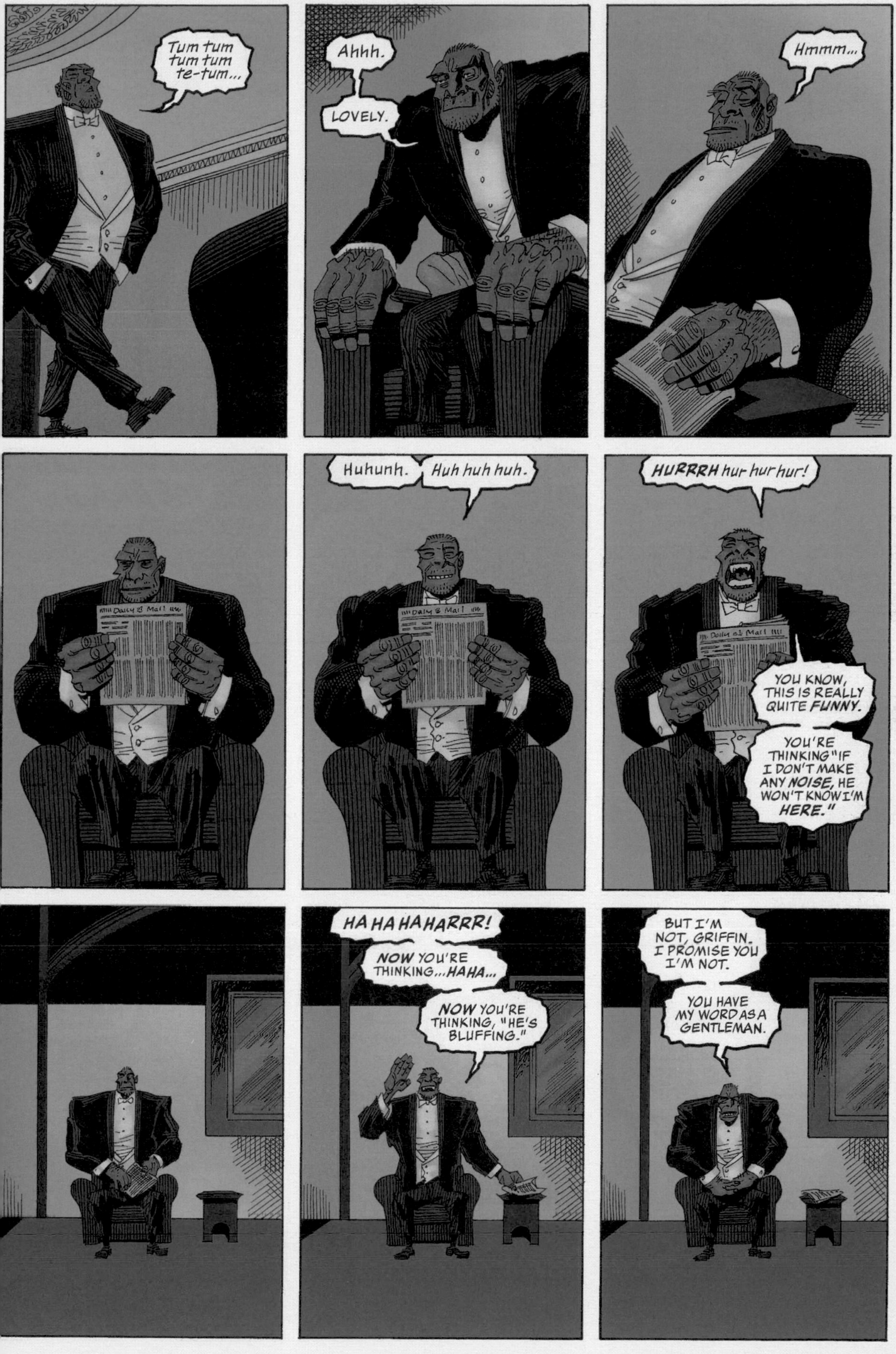
Tum tum tum tum te-tum...
Ahhh.
LOVELY.
Hmmm...
Huhunh.
Huh huh huh.
HURRRH hur hur hur!
Daily Mail
YOU KNOW, THIS IS REALLY QUITE FUNNY.
YOU'RE THINKING "IF I DON'T MAKE ANY NOISE, HE WON'T KNOW I'M HERE."
HA HA HA HARRR!
NOW YOU'RE THINKING... HAHA...
NOW YOU'RE THINKING, "HE'S BLUFFING."
BUT I'M NOT, GRIFFIN. I PROMISE YOU I'M NOT.
YOU HAVE MY WORD AS A GENTLEMAN.

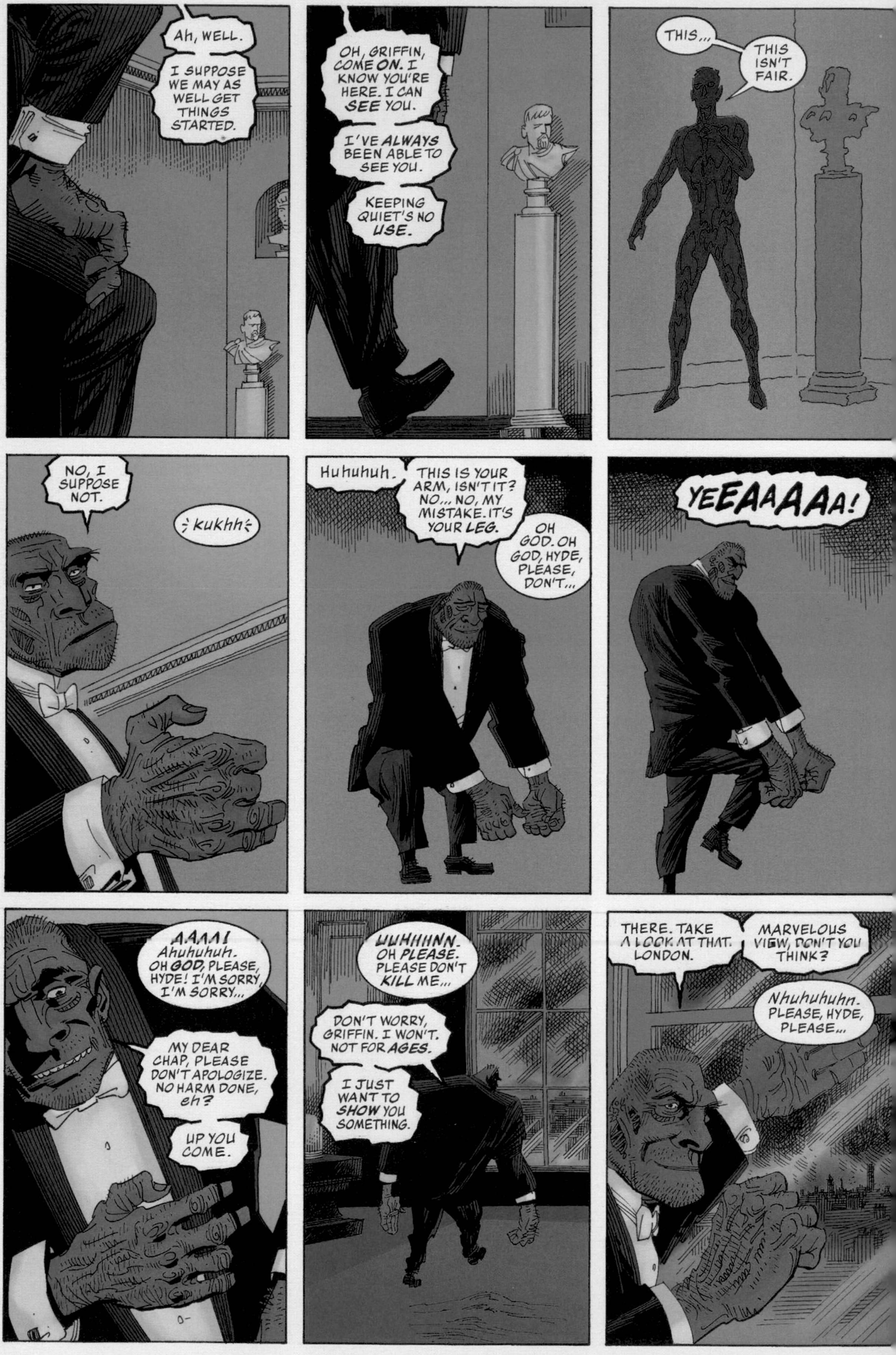
Ah, WELL.
I SUPPOSE WE MAY AS WELL GET THINGS STARTED.
OH, GRIFFIN, COME ON. I KNOW YOU'RE HERE. I CAN SEE YOU.
I'VE ALWAYS BEEN ABLE TO SEE YOU.
KEEPING QUIET'S NO USE.
THIS...
THIS ISN'T FAIR.
NO, I SUPPOSE NOT.
kukhh
Huhuhuh.
THIS IS YOUR ARM, ISN'T IT? NO... NO, MY MISTAKE. IT'S YOUR LEG.
OH GOD. OH GOD, HYDE, PLEASE, DON'T...
YEEAAAAAA!
AAAA! Ahuhuhuh. OH GOD, PLEASE, HYDE! I'M SORRY, I'M SORRY...
MY DEAR CHAP, PLEASE DON'T APOLOGIZE. NO HARM DONE, eh?
UP YOU COME.
UUHHHNN. OH PLEASE. PLEASE DON'T KILL ME...
DON'T WORRY, GRIFFIN. I WON'T. NOT FOR AGES.
I JUST WANT TO SHOW YOU SOMETHING.
THERE. TAKE A LOOK AT THAT. LONDON.
MARVELOUS VIEW, DON'T YOU THINK?
Nhuhuhuhn. PLEASE, HYDE, PLEASE...

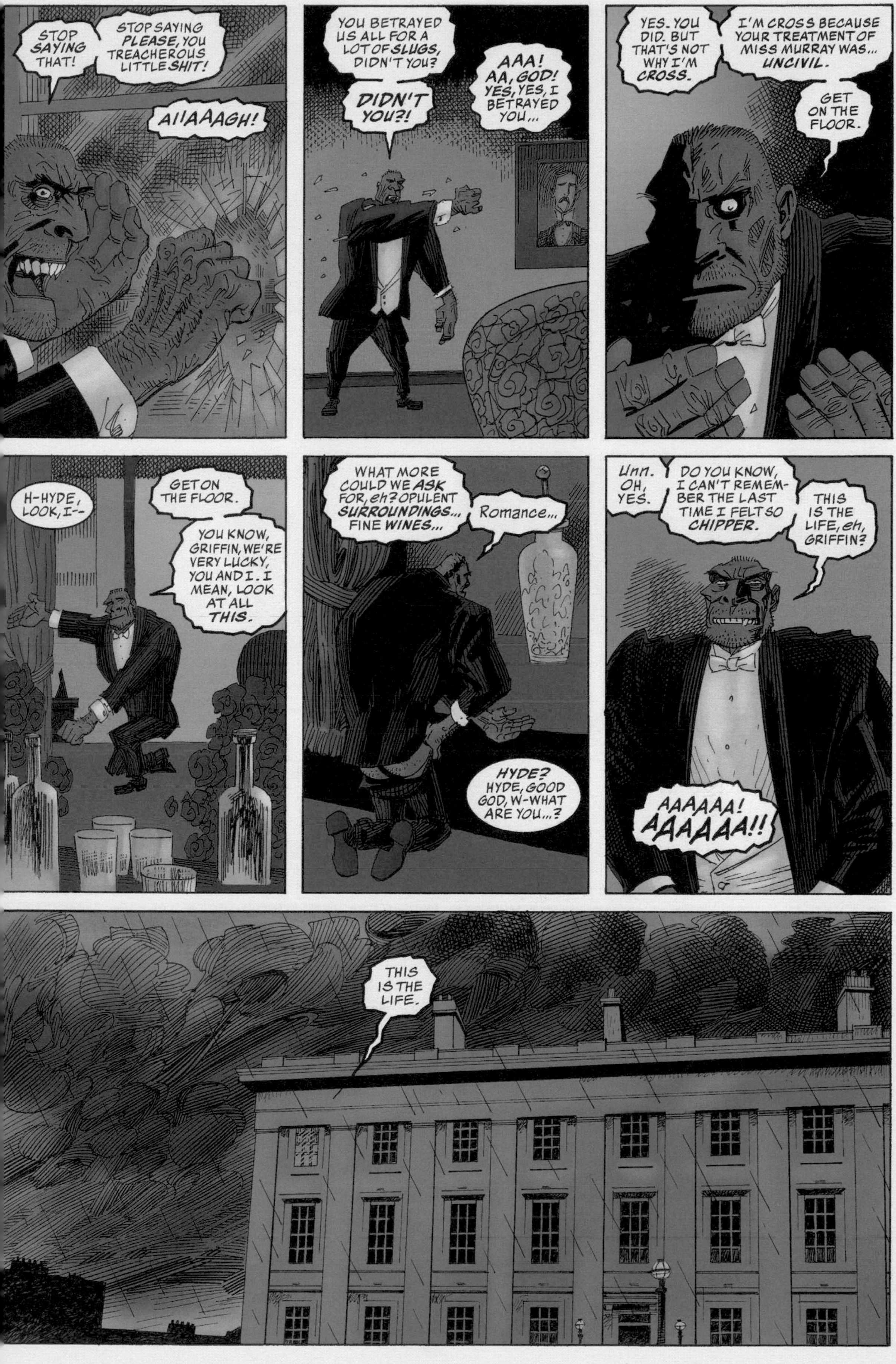
STOP SAYING THAT!
STOP SAYING PLEASE, YOU TREACHEROUS LITTLE SHIT!
AI!AAAGH!
YOU BETRAYED US ALL FOR A LOT OF SLUGS, DIDN'T YOU?
DIDN'T YOU?!
AAA! AA, GOD! YES, YES, I BETRAYED YOU...
YES. YOU DID. BUT THAT'S NOT WHY I'M CROSS.
I'M CROSS BECAUSE YOUR TREATMENT OF MISS MURRAY WAS... UNCIVIL.
GET ON THE FLOOR.
H-HYDE, LOOK, I--
GET ON THE FLOOR.
YOU KNOW, GRIFFIN, WE'RE VERY LUCKY, YOU AND I. I MEAN, LOOK AT ALL THIS.
WHAT MORE COULD WE ASK FOR, eh? OPULENT SURROUNDINGS... FINE WINES...
Romance...
HYDE? HYDE, GOOD GOD, W-WHAT ARE YOU...?
Unn. OH, YES.
DO YOU KNOW, I CAN'T REMEMBER THE LAST TIME I FELT SO CHIPPER.
THIS IS THE LIFE, eh, GRIFFIN?
AAAAAA! AAAAAA!!
THIS IS THE LIFE.

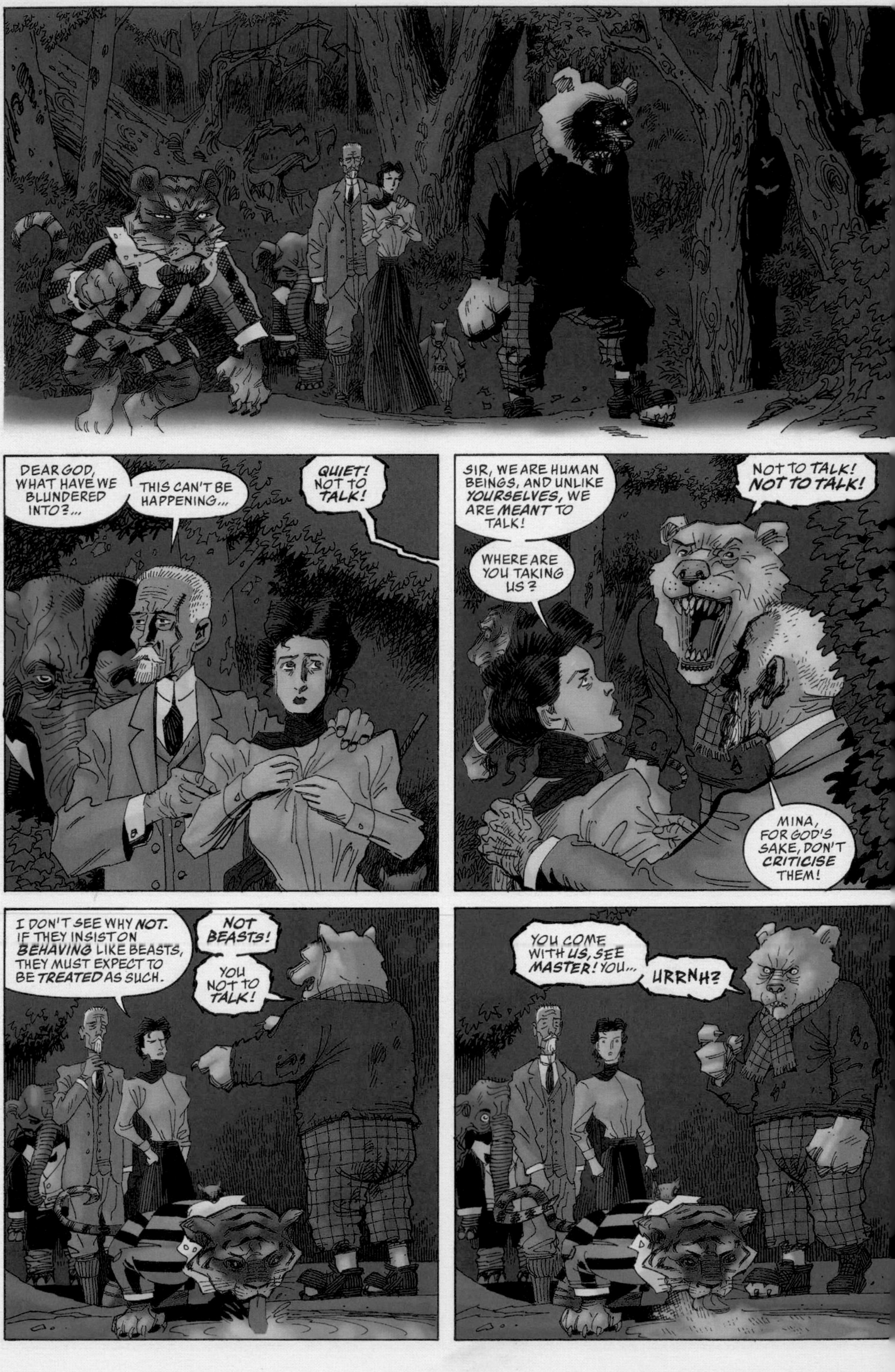
DEAR GOD, WHAT HAVE WE BLUNDERED INTO?...
THIS CAN'T BE HAPPENING...
QUIET! NOT TO TALK!
SIR, WE ARE HUMAN BEINGS, AND UNLIKE YOURSELVES, WE ARE MEANT TO TALK!
NOT TO TALK! NOT TO TALK!
WHERE ARE YOU TAKING US?
MINA, FOR GOD'S SAKE, DON'T CRITICISE THEM!
I DON'T SEE WHY NOT. IF THEY INSIST ON BEHAVING LIKE BEASTS, THEY MUST EXPECT TO BE TREATED AS SUCH.
NOT BEASTS!
YOU NOT TO TALK!
YOU COME WITH US, SEE MASTER! YOU...
URRNH?

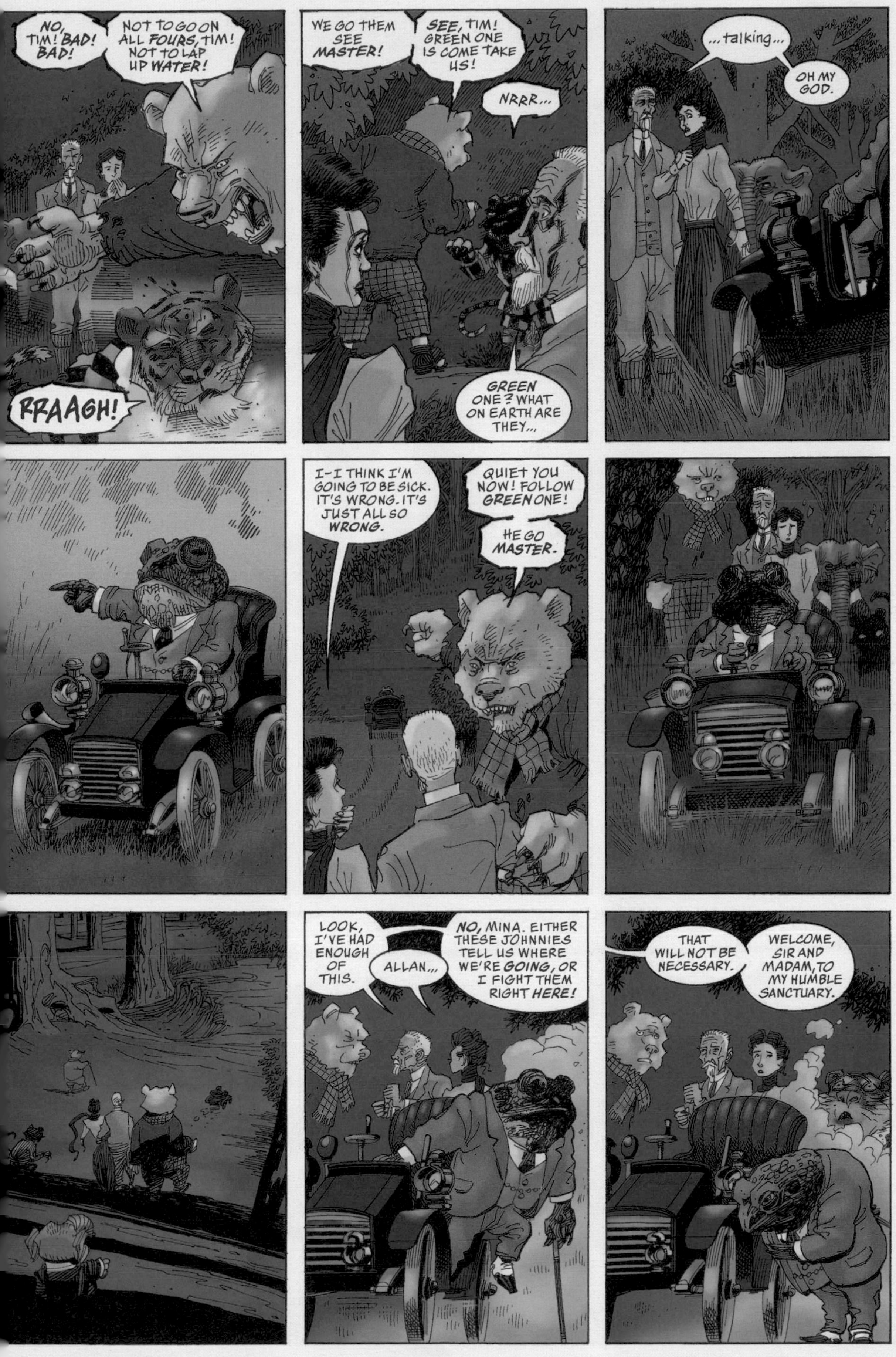
NO, TIM! BAD! BAD!
NOT TO GO ON ALL FOURS, TIM! NOT TO LAP UP WATER!
RRAAGH!
WE GO THEM SEE MASTER!
SEE, TIM! GREEN ONE IS COME TAKE US!
NRRR...
GREEN ONE? WHAT ON EARTH ARE THEY...
...talking...
OH MY GOD.
I-I THINK I'M GOING TO BE SICK. IT'S WRONG. IT'S JUST ALL SO WRONG.
QUIET YOU NOW! FOLLOW GREEN ONE!
HE GO MASTER.
LOOK, I'VE HAD ENOUGH OF THIS.
ALLAN...
NO, MINA. EITHER THESE JOHNNIES TELL US WHERE WE'RE GOING, OR I FIGHT THEM RIGHT HERE!
THAT WILL NOT BE NECESSARY.
WELCOME, SIR AND MADAM, TO MY HUMBLE SANCTUARY.

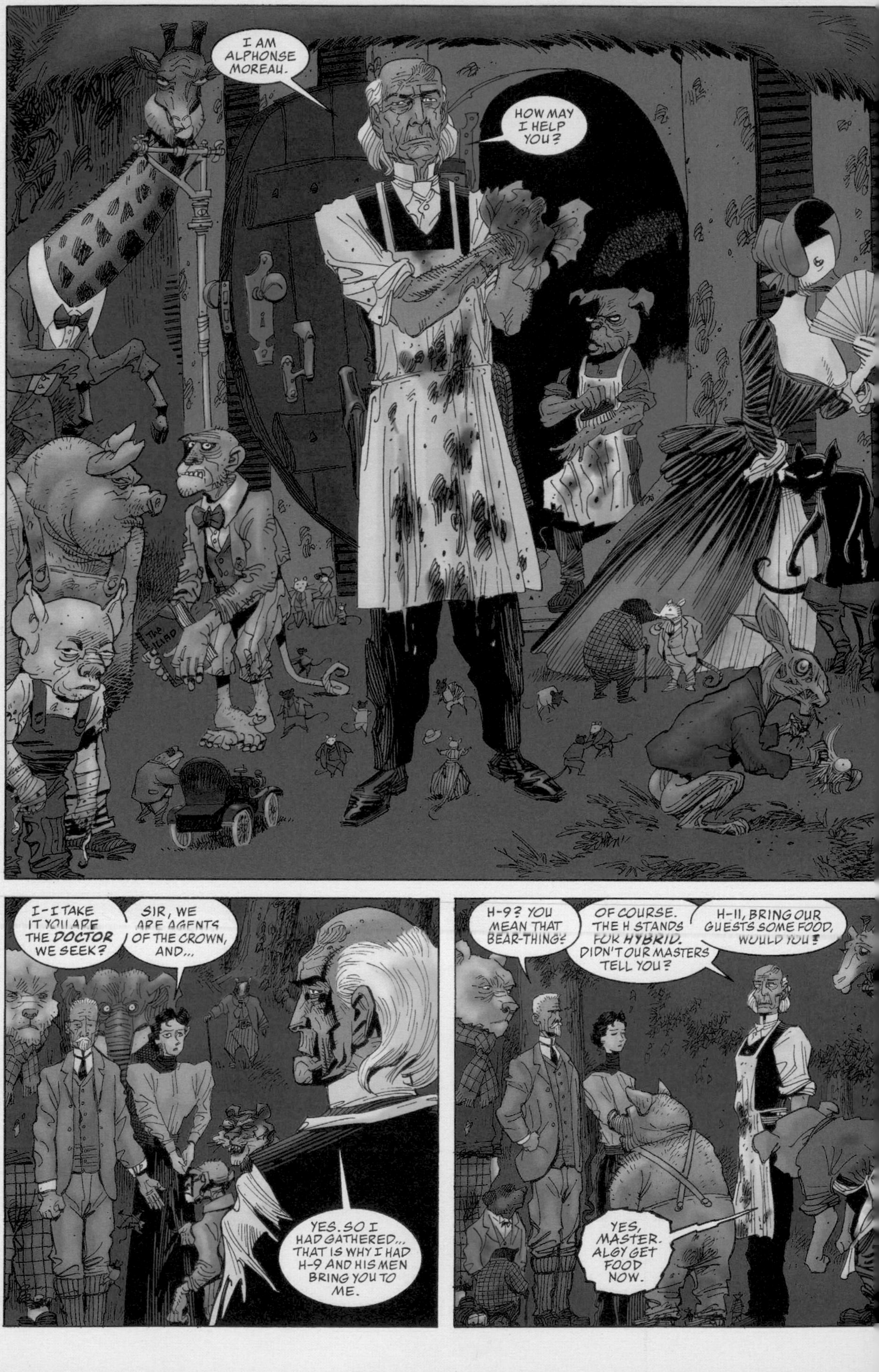
I AM ALPHONSE MOREAU.
HOW MAY I HELP YOU?
I-I TAKE IT YOU ARE THE DOCTOR WE SEEK?
SIR, WE ARE AGENTS OF THE CROWN, AND...
YES. SO I HAD GATHERED... THAT IS WHY I HAD H-9 AND HIS MEN BRING YOU TO ME.
H-9? YOU MEAN THAT BEAR-THING?
OF COURSE. THE H STANDS FOR HYBRID. DIDN'T OUR MASTERS TELL YOU?
H-11, BRING OUR GUESTS SOME FOOD, WOULD YOU?
YES, MASTER. ALGY GET FOOD NOW.

A PUG-DOG. INCREDIBLE.

LOOK, MOREAU OR WHATEVER YOUR NAME IS, HOW DID YOU KNOW WE'D BEEN SENT BY THE GOVERNMENT TO FIND YOU?

H-9 OVERHEARD YOU TALKING ABOUT ME. HIS ENGLISH IS QUITE GOOD.

AS FOR THE GOVERNMENT, WHO ELSE KNOWS I *EXIST*? THEY REPOSITIONED ME HERE WHEN THERE WERE... DIFFICULTIES ...AT MY PREVIOUS ESTABLISHMENT.

PLEASE COME THROUGH.

H-9 TELLS ME THAT YOU MET WITH PRENDRICK YESTERDAY.

YES. HE SEEMS OBSESSED WITH YOU.

HE IS A FORMER ACQUAINTANCE WHO HAS, UNFORTUNATELY, GONE MAD.

MY CREATIONS KEEP HIM UNDER DISCREET OBSERVATION. HE POSES NO THREAT.

GOOD *LORD*. WHAT ON EARTH'S *THIS*?

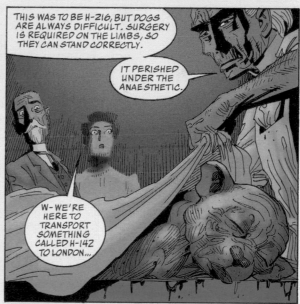

THIS WAS TO BE H-216, BUT DOGS ARE ALWAYS DIFFICULT. SURGERY IS REQUIRED ON THE LIMBS, SO THEY CAN STAND CORRECTLY.

IT PERISHED UNDER THE ANAESTHETIC.

W-WE'RE HERE TO TRANSPORT SOMETHING CALLED H-142 TO LONDON...

H-142? YOU ARE SURE OF THIS?

THEN I TAKE IT THAT LONDON IS IN GRAVE DANGER.

IT'S BEEN INVADED BY... THINGS. FROM ANOTHER WORLD. PERHAPS MARS...

LOOK, WHOEVER YOU ARE, YOU'VE GOT TO *HELP* US!

I SEE. THEN WE MUST DISCUSS THIS OVER *DINNER*, YES...?

LIKE CIVILISED BEINGS...

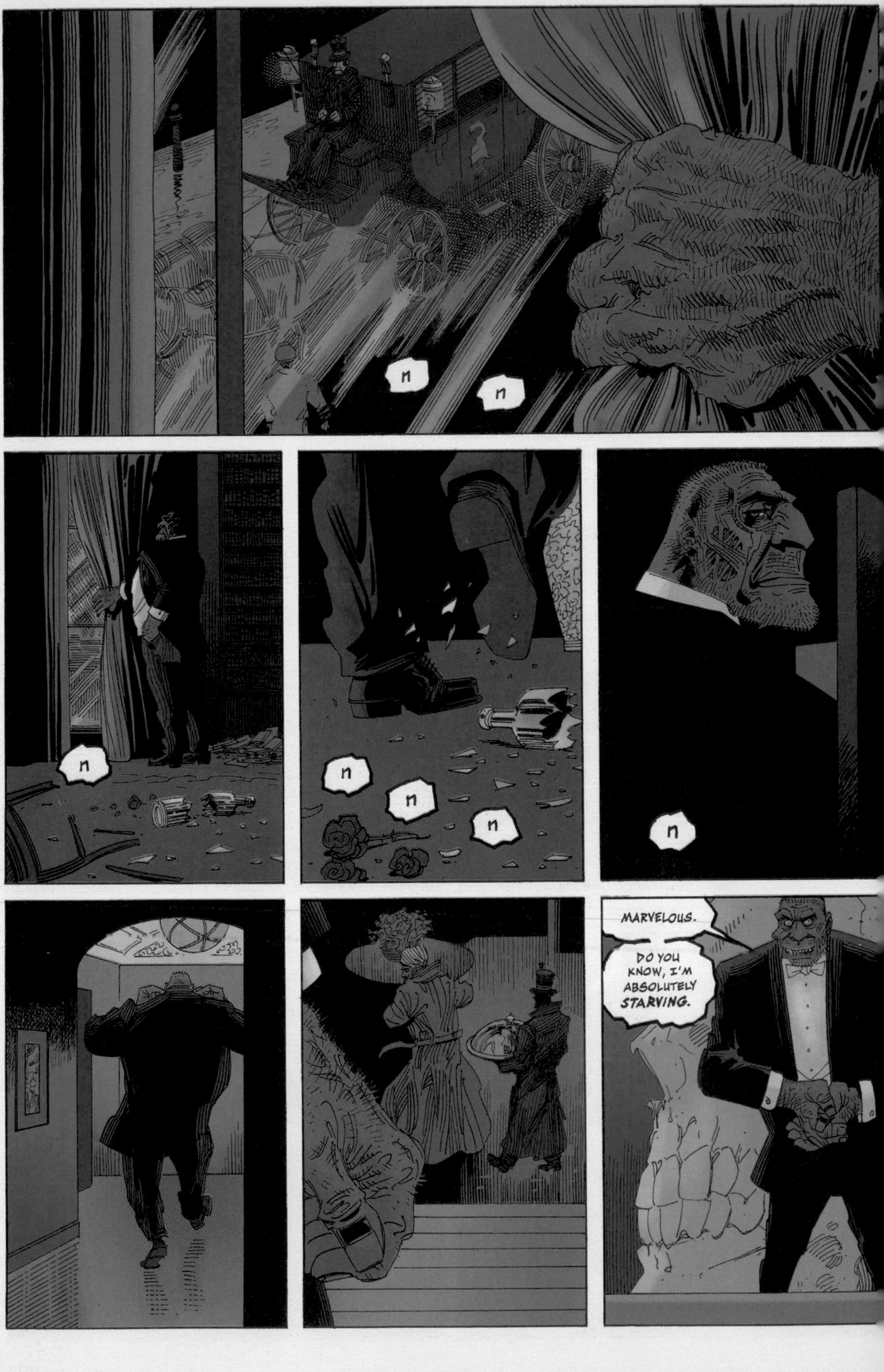
n
n
n
n
n
n
n
MARVELOUS.
DO YOU KNOW, I'M ABSOLUTELY **STARVING.**

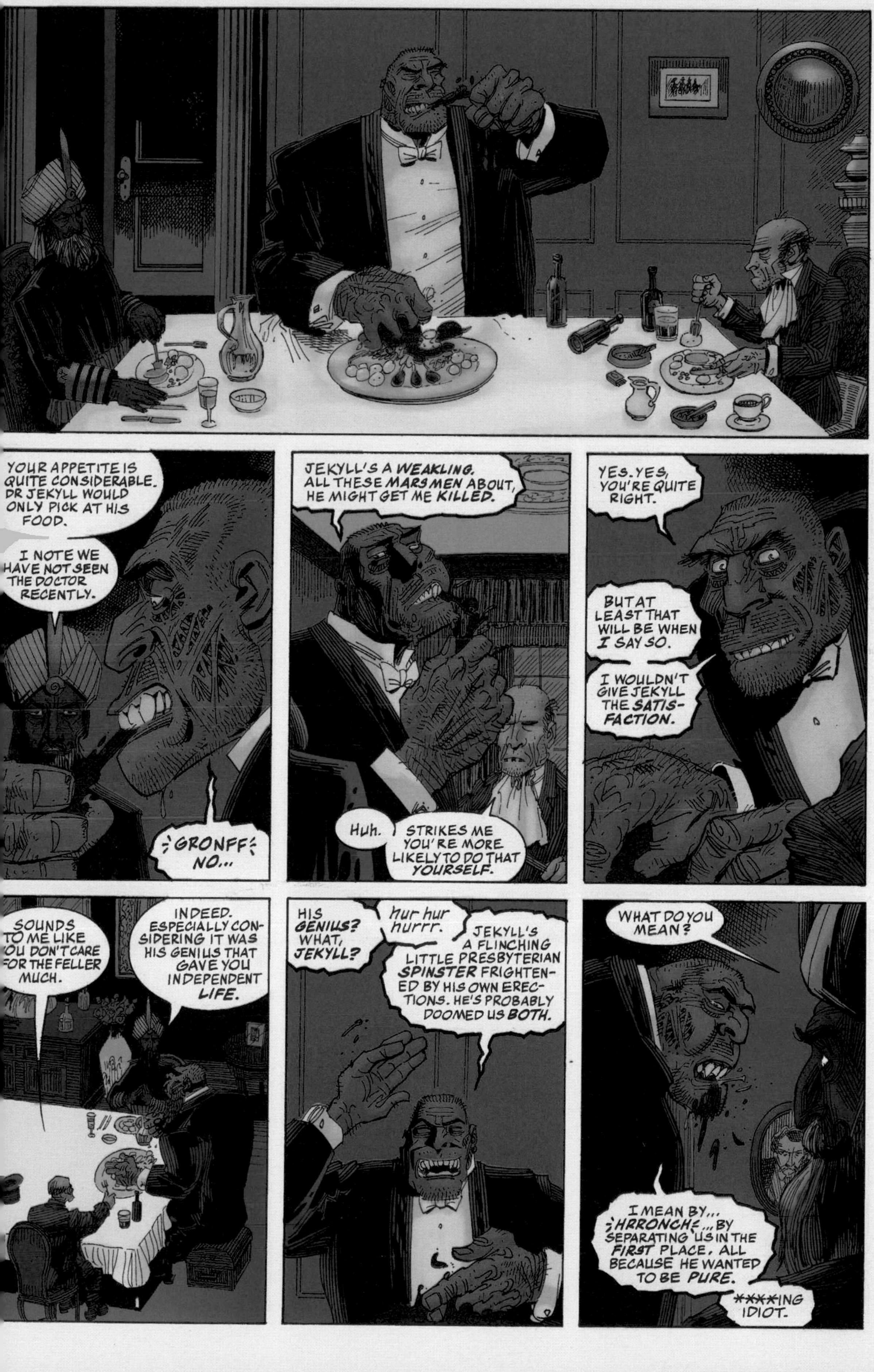
YOUR APPETITE IS QUITE CONSIDERABLE. DR JEKYLL WOULD ONLY PICK AT HIS FOOD.
I NOTE WE HAVE NOT SEEN THE DOCTOR RECENTLY.
GRONFF NO...
JEKYLL'S A WEAKLING. ALL THESE MARS MEN ABOUT, HE MIGHT GET ME KILLED.
Huh.
STRIKES ME YOU'RE MORE LIKELY TO DO THAT YOURSELF.
YES. YES, YOU'RE QUITE RIGHT.
BUT AT LEAST THAT WILL BE WHEN I SAY SO.
I WOULDN'T GIVE JEKYLL THE SATIS-FACTION.
SOUNDS TO ME LIKE YOU DON'T CARE FOR THE FELLER MUCH.
INDEED. ESPECIALLY CON-SIDERING IT WAS HIS GENIUS THAT GAVE YOU INDEPENDENT LIFE.
HIS GENIUS? WHAT, JEKYLL?
hur hur hurrr.
JEKYLL'S A FLINCHING LITTLE PRESBYTERIAN SPINSTER FRIGHTEN-ED BY HIS OWN EREC-TIONS. HE'S PROBABLY DOOMED US BOTH.
WHAT DO YOU MEAN?
I MEAN BY... HRRONCH ... BY SEPARATING US IN THE FIRST PLACE. ALL BECAUSE HE WANTED TO BE PURE.
****ING IDIOT.

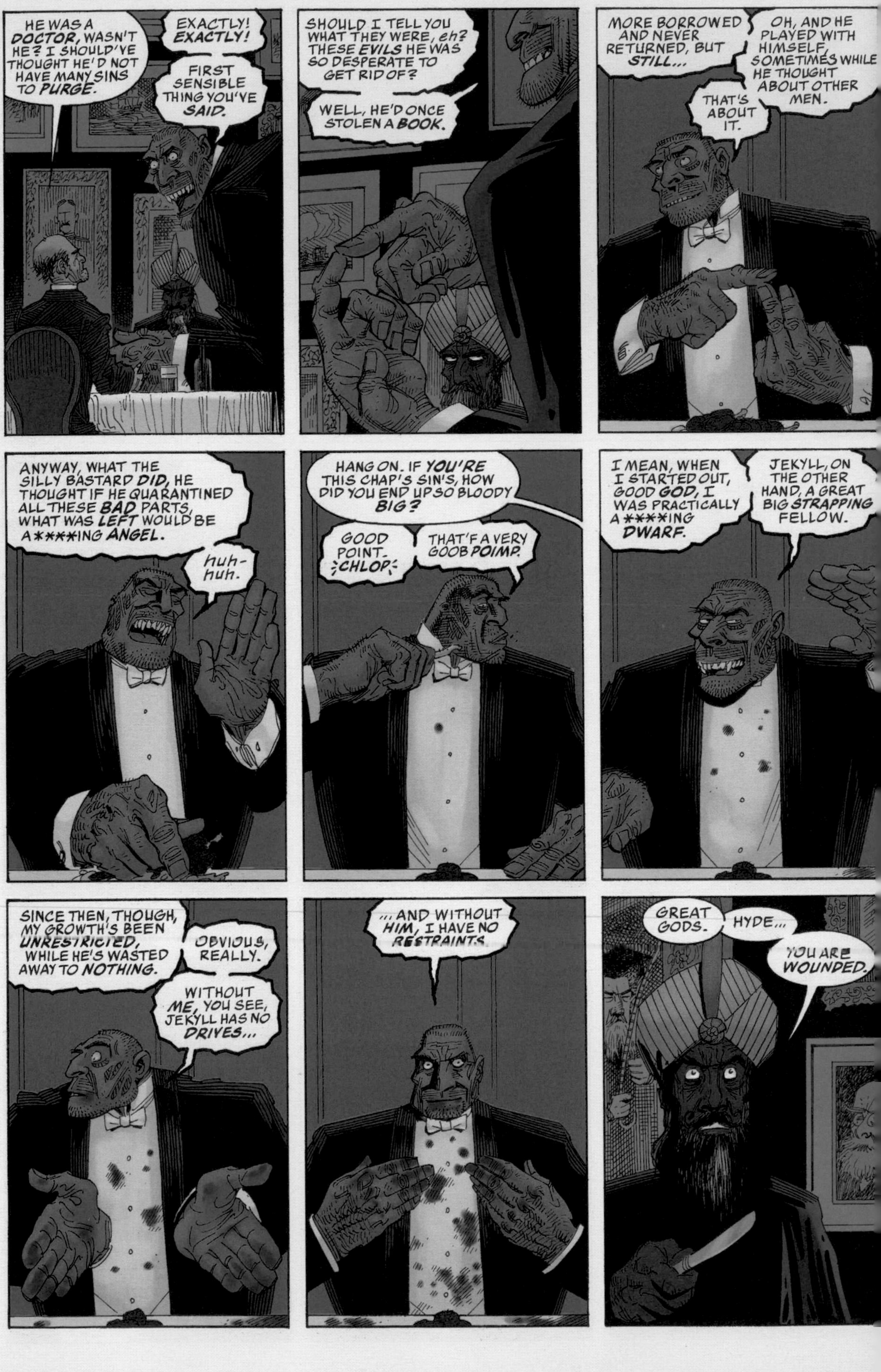
HE WAS A DOCTOR, WASN'T HE? I SHOULD'VE THOUGHT HE'D NOT HAVE MANY SINS TO PURGE.
EXACTLY! EXACTLY!
FIRST SENSIBLE THING YOU'VE SAID.
SHOULD I TELL YOU WHAT THEY WERE, eh? THESE EVILS HE WAS SO DESPERATE TO GET RID OF?
WELL, HE'D ONCE STOLEN A BOOK.
MORE BORROWED AND NEVER RETURNED, BUT STILL...
OH, AND HE PLAYED WITH HIMSELF, SOMETIMES WHILE HE THOUGHT ABOUT OTHER MEN.
THAT'S ABOUT IT.
ANYWAY, WHAT THE SILLY BASTARD DID, HE THOUGHT IF HE QUARANTINED ALL THESE BAD PARTS, WHAT WAS LEFT WOULD BE A****ING ANGEL.
huh-huh.
HANG ON. IF YOU'RE THIS CHAP'S SIN'S, HOW DID YOU END UP SO BLOODY BIG?
GOOD POINT. CHLOP
THAT'F A VERY GOOB POIMP.
I MEAN, WHEN I STARTED OUT, GOOD GOD, I WAS PRACTICALLY A****ING DWARF.
JEKYLL, ON THE OTHER HAND, A GREAT BIG STRAPPING FELLOW.
SINCE THEN, THOUGH, MY GROWTH'S BEEN UNRESTRICTED, WHILE HE'S WASTED AWAY TO NOTHING.
OBVIOUS, REALLY.
WITHOUT ME, YOU SEE, JEKYLL HAS NO DRIVES...
...AND WITHOUT HIM, I HAVE NO RESTRAINTS.
GREAT GODS.
HYDE...
YOU ARE WOUNDED.

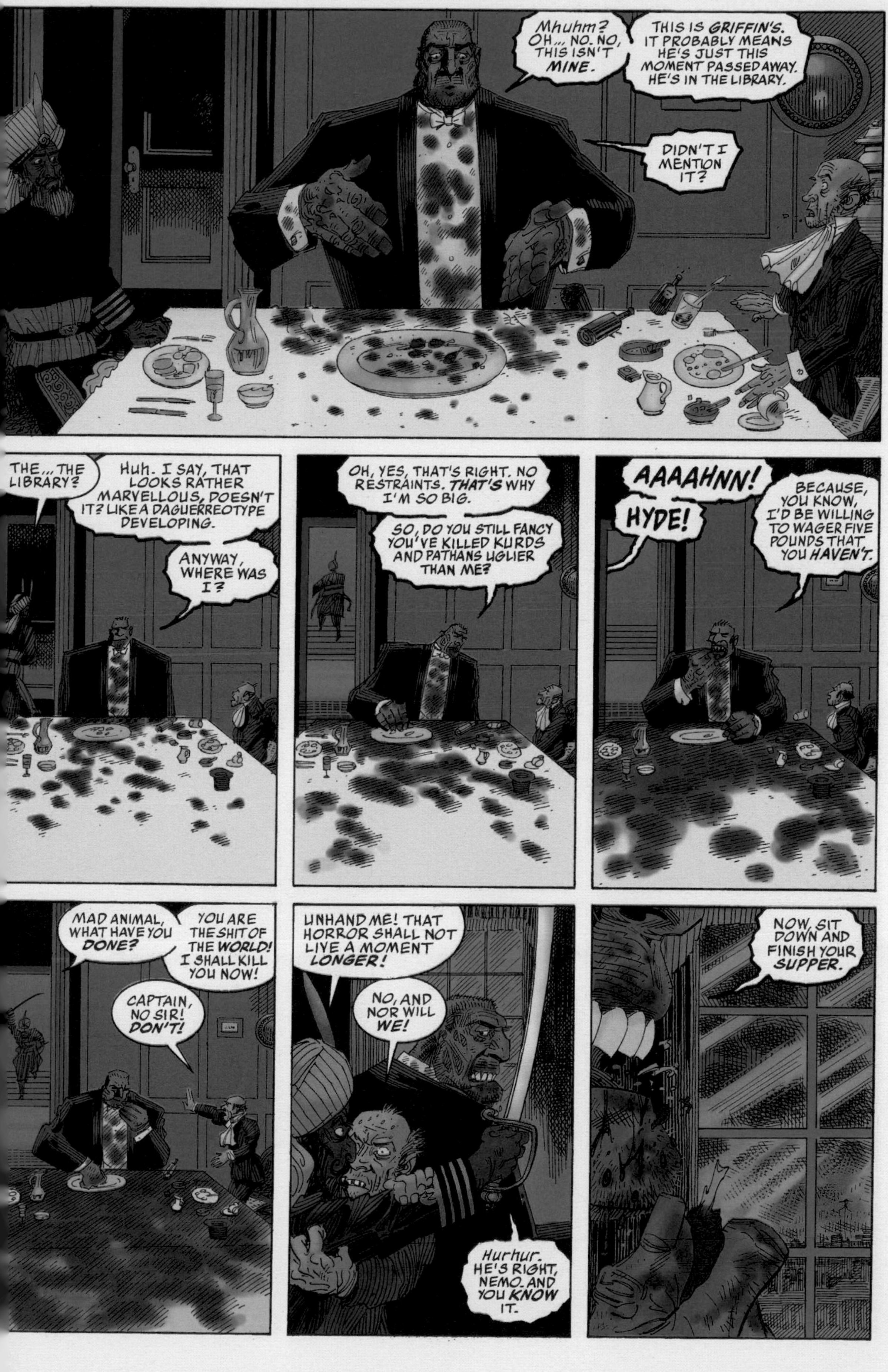
Mhuhm? Oh... no. No, this isn't *mine*.
THIS IS *GRIFFIN'S*. IT PROBABLY MEANS HE'S JUST THIS MOMENT PASSED AWAY. HE'S IN THE LIBRARY.
DIDN'T I MENTION IT?
THE... THE LIBRARY?
Huh. I SAY, THAT LOOKS RATHER MARVELLOUS, DOESN'T IT? LIKE A DAGUERREOTYPE DEVELOPING.
ANYWAY, WHERE WAS I?
OH, YES, THAT'S RIGHT. NO RESTRAINTS. *THAT'S* WHY I'M SO BIG.
SO, DO YOU STILL FANCY YOU'VE KILLED KURDS AND PATHANS UGLIER THAN ME?
AAAAHNN!
HYDE!
BECAUSE, YOU KNOW, I'D BE WILLING TO WAGER FIVE POUNDS THAT YOU *HAVEN'T*.
MAD ANIMAL, WHAT HAVE YOU *DONE*?
YOU ARE THE SHIT OF THE *WORLD*! I SHALL KILL YOU NOW!
CAPTAIN, NO SIR! *DON'T!*
UNHAND ME! THAT HORROR SHALL NOT LIVE A MOMENT *LONGER*!
NO, AND NOR WILL *WE*!
Hurhur. HE'S RIGHT, NEMO. AND YOU *KNOW* IT.
NOW, SIT DOWN AND FINISH YOUR *SUPPER*.

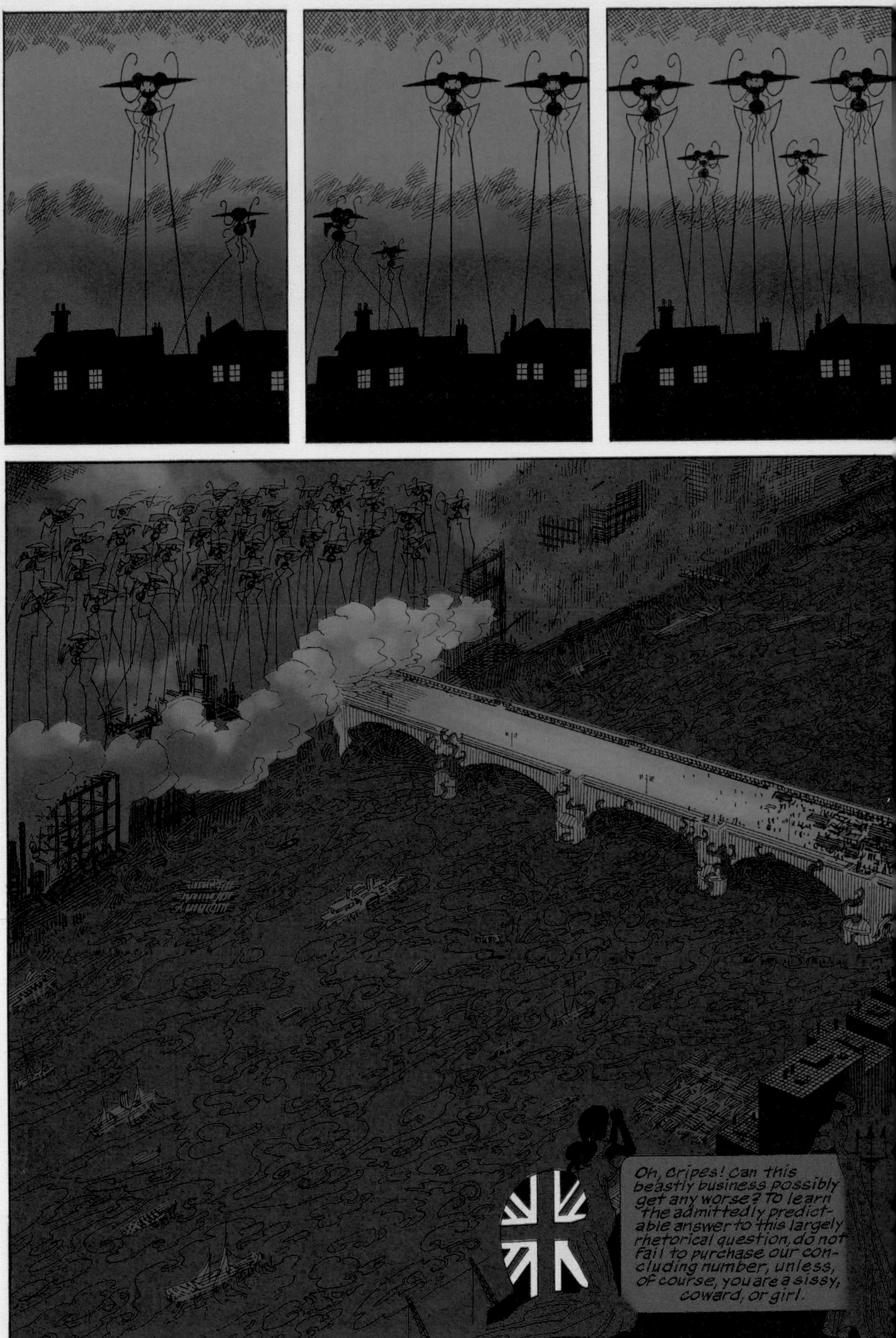
Oh, cripes! Can this beastly business possibly get any worse? To learn the admittedly predictable answer to this largely rhetorical question, do not fail to purchase our concluding number, unless, of course, you are a sissy, coward, or girl.

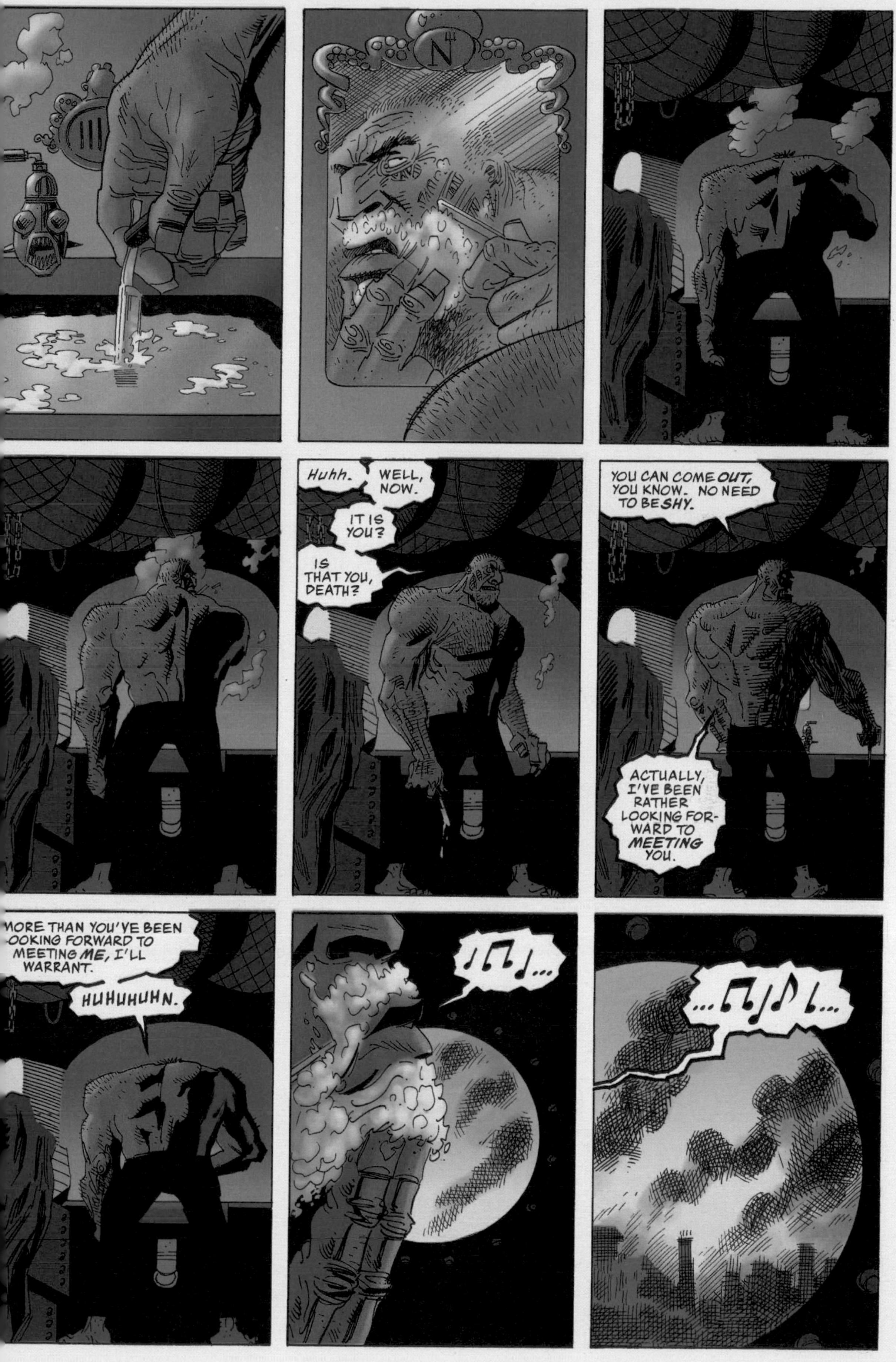
N
Huhh.
WELL, NOW.
IT IS YOU?
IS THAT YOU, DEATH?
YOU CAN COME OUT, YOU KNOW. NO NEED TO BE SHY.
ACTUALLY, I'VE BEEN RATHER LOOKING FOR-WARD TO MEETING YOU.
MORE THAN YOU'VE BEEN LOOKING FORWARD TO MEETING ME, I'LL WARRANT.
HUHUHUHN.
...
...

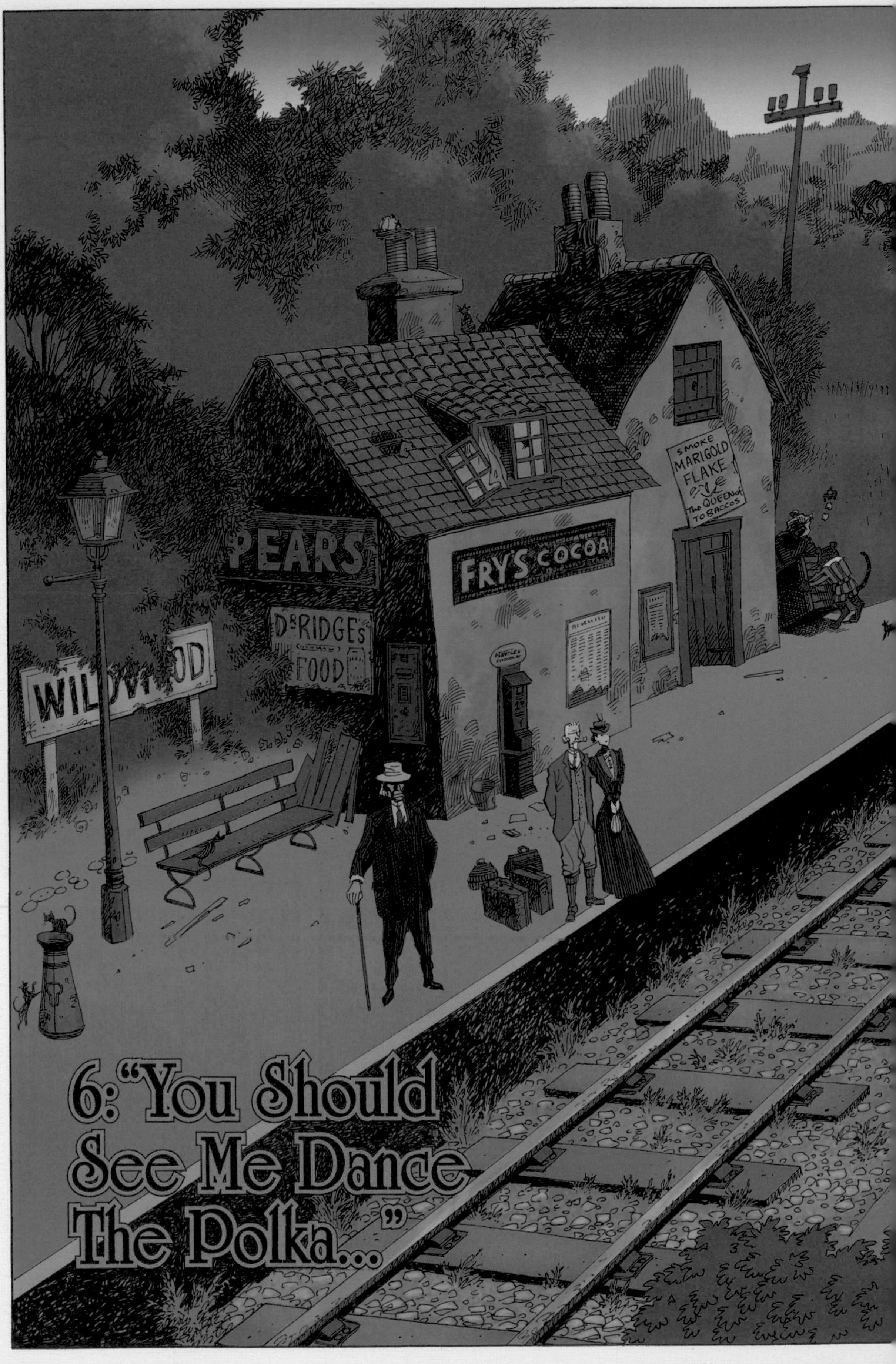
PEARS
DR RIDGE'S FOOD
FRY'S COCOA
SMOKE
MARIGOLD
FLAKE
The QUEEN of TOBACCOS

6: "You Should See Me Dance The Polka..."

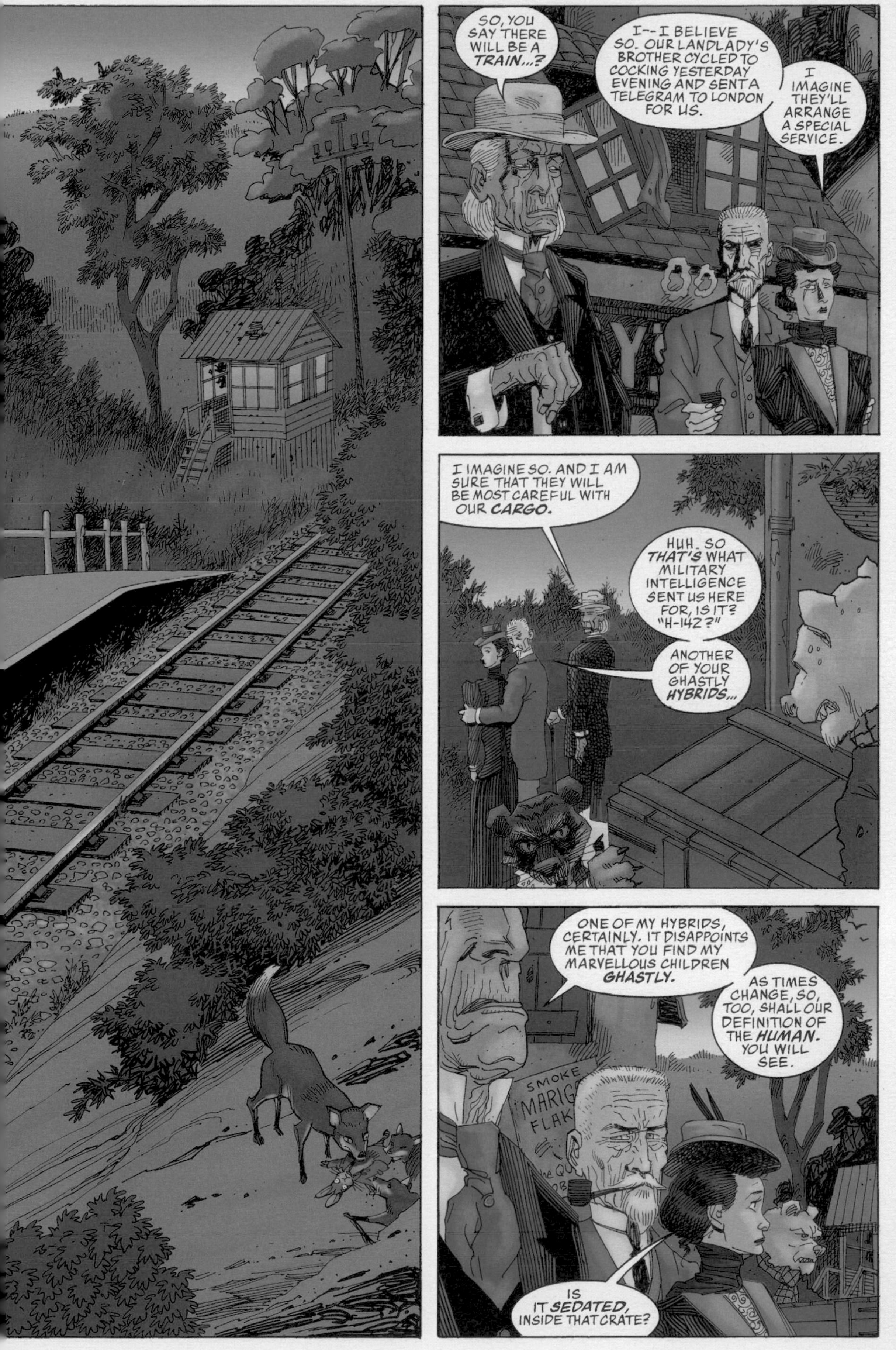
SO, YOU SAY THERE WILL BE A TRAIN...?
I-- I BELIEVE SO. OUR LANDLADY'S BROTHER CYCLED TO COCKING YESTERDAY EVENING AND SENT A TELEGRAM TO LONDON FOR US.
I IMAGINE THEY'LL ARRANGE A SPECIAL SERVICE.
I IMAGINE SO. AND I AM SURE THAT THEY WILL BE MOST CAREFUL WITH OUR CARGO.
HUH. SO THAT'S WHAT MILITARY INTELLIGENCE SENT US HERE FOR, IS IT? "H-142?"
ANOTHER OF YOUR GHASTLY HYBRIDS...
ONE OF MY HYBRIDS, CERTAINLY. IT DISAPPOINTS ME THAT YOU FIND MY MARVELLOUS CHILDREN GHASTLY.
AS TIMES CHANGE, SO, TOO, SHALL OUR DEFINITION OF THE HUMAN. YOU WILL SEE.
SMOKE
IS IT SEDATED, INSIDE THAT CRATE?

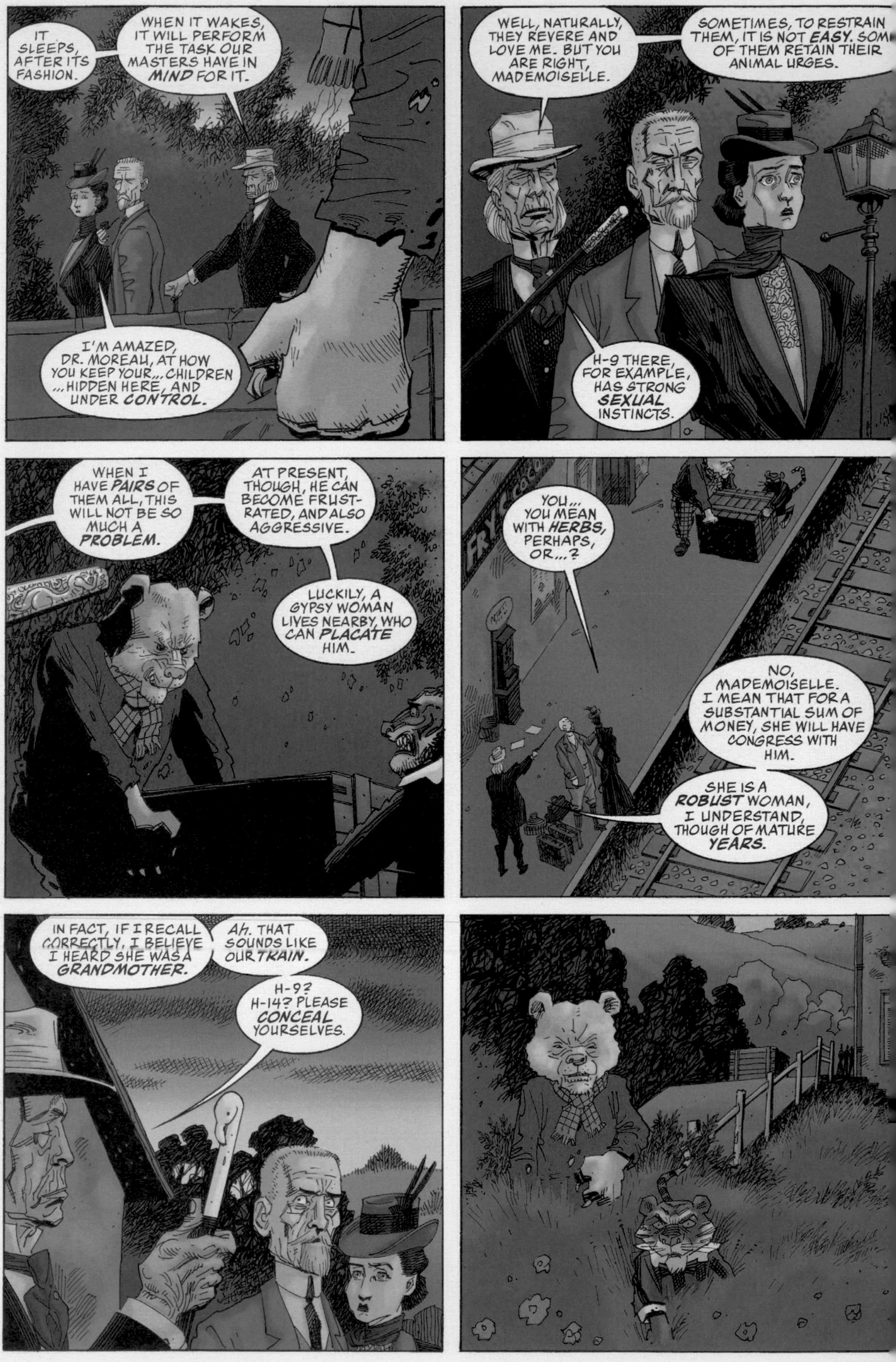
IT SLEEPS, AFTER ITS FASHION.
WHEN IT WAKES, IT WILL PERFORM THE TASK OUR MASTERS HAVE IN MIND FOR IT.
I'M AMAZED, DR. MOREAU, AT HOW YOU KEEP YOUR... CHILDREN ...HIDDEN HERE, AND UNDER CONTROL.
WELL, NATURALLY, THEY REVERE AND LOVE ME. BUT YOU ARE RIGHT, MADEMOISELLE.
SOMETIMES, TO RESTRAIN THEM, IT IS NOT EASY. SOM OF THEM RETAIN THEIR ANIMAL URGES.
H-9 THERE, FOR EXAMPLE, HAS STRONG SEXUAL INSTINCTS.
WHEN I HAVE PAIRS OF THEM ALL, THIS WILL NOT BE SO MUCH A PROBLEM.
AT PRESENT, THOUGH, HE CAN BECOME FRUST-RATED, AND ALSO AGGRESSIVE.
LUCKILY, A GYPSY WOMAN LIVES NEARBY, WHO CAN PLACATE HIM.
YOU... YOU MEAN WITH HERBS, PERHAPS, OR...?
NO, MADEMOISELLE. I MEAN THAT FOR A SUBSTANTIAL SUM OF MONEY, SHE WILL HAVE CONGRESS WITH HIM.
SHE IS A ROBUST WOMAN, I UNDERSTAND, THOUGH OF MATURE YEARS.
IN FACT, IF I RECALL CORRECTLY, I BELIEVE I HEARD SHE WAS A GRANDMOTHER.
Ah. THAT SOUNDS LIKE OUR TRAIN.
H-9? H-14? PLEASE CONCEAL YOURSELVES.

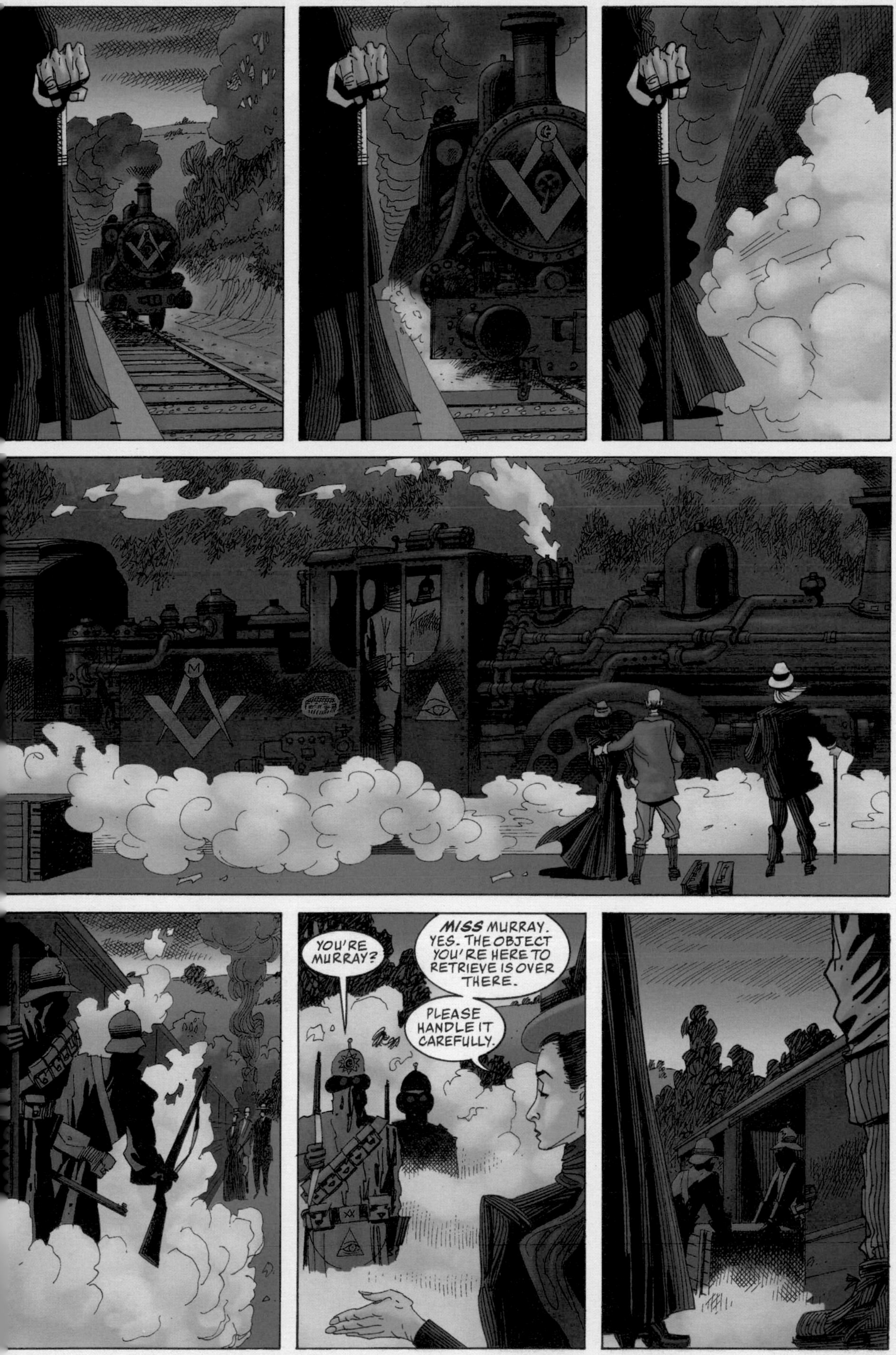
YOU'RE MURRAY?
MISS MURRAY. YES. THE OBJECT YOU'RE HERE TO RETRIEVE IS OVER THERE.
PLEASE HANDLE IT CAREFULLY.

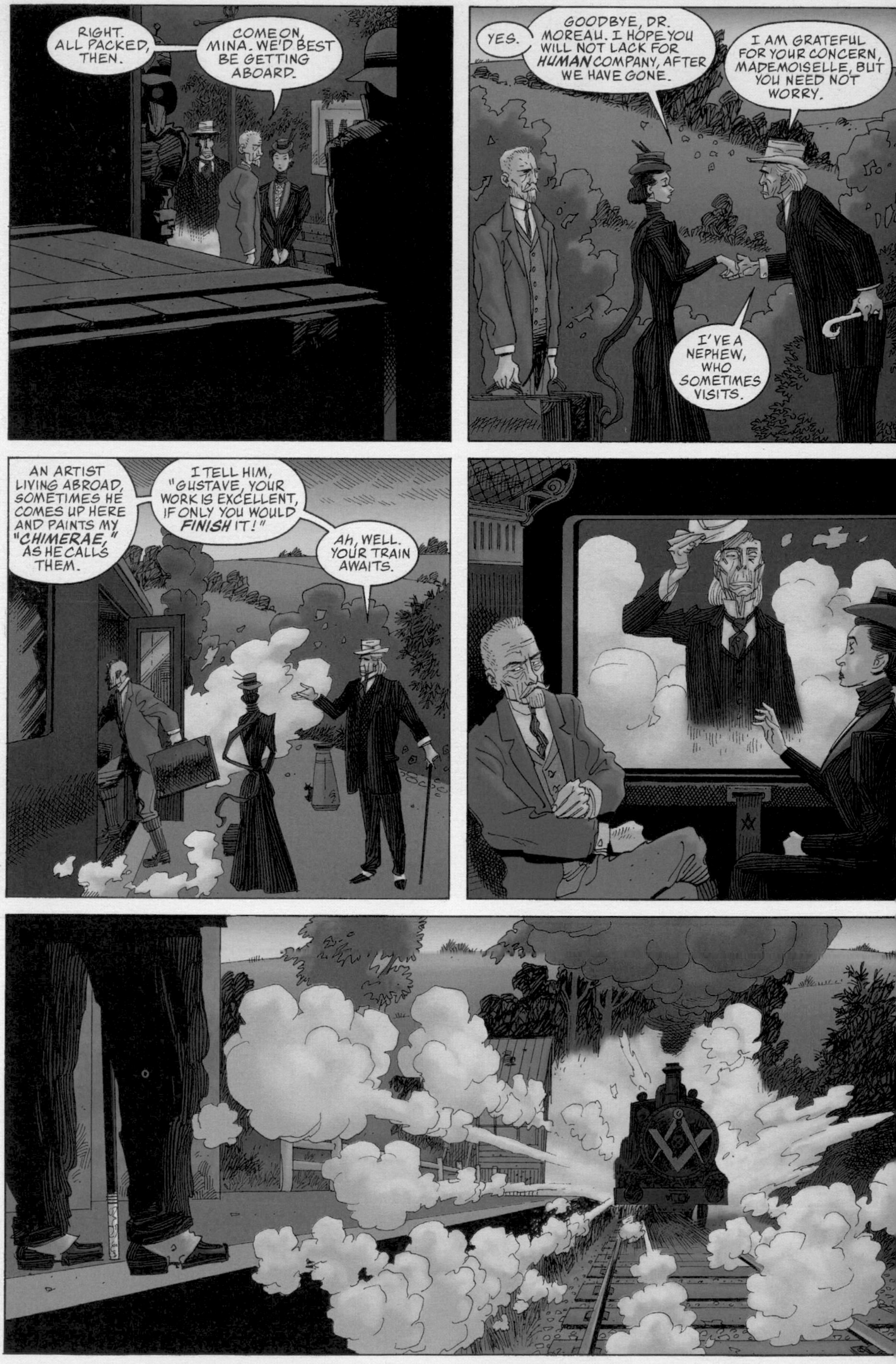
RIGHT. ALL PACKED, THEN.
COME ON, MINA. WE'D BEST BE GETTING ABOARD.
YES.
GOODBYE, DR. MOREAU. I HOPE YOU WILL NOT LACK FOR HUMAN COMPANY, AFTER WE HAVE GONE.
I AM GRATEFUL FOR YOUR CONCERN, MADEMOISELLE, BUT YOU NEED NOT WORRY.
I'VE A NEPHEW, WHO SOMETIMES VISITS.
AN ARTIST LIVING ABROAD, SOMETIMES HE COMES UP HERE AND PAINTS MY "CHIMERAE," AS HE CALLS THEM.
I TELL HIM, "GUSTAVE, YOUR WORK IS EXCELLENT, IF ONLY YOU WOULD FINISH IT!"
Ah, WELL. YOUR TRAIN AWAITS.

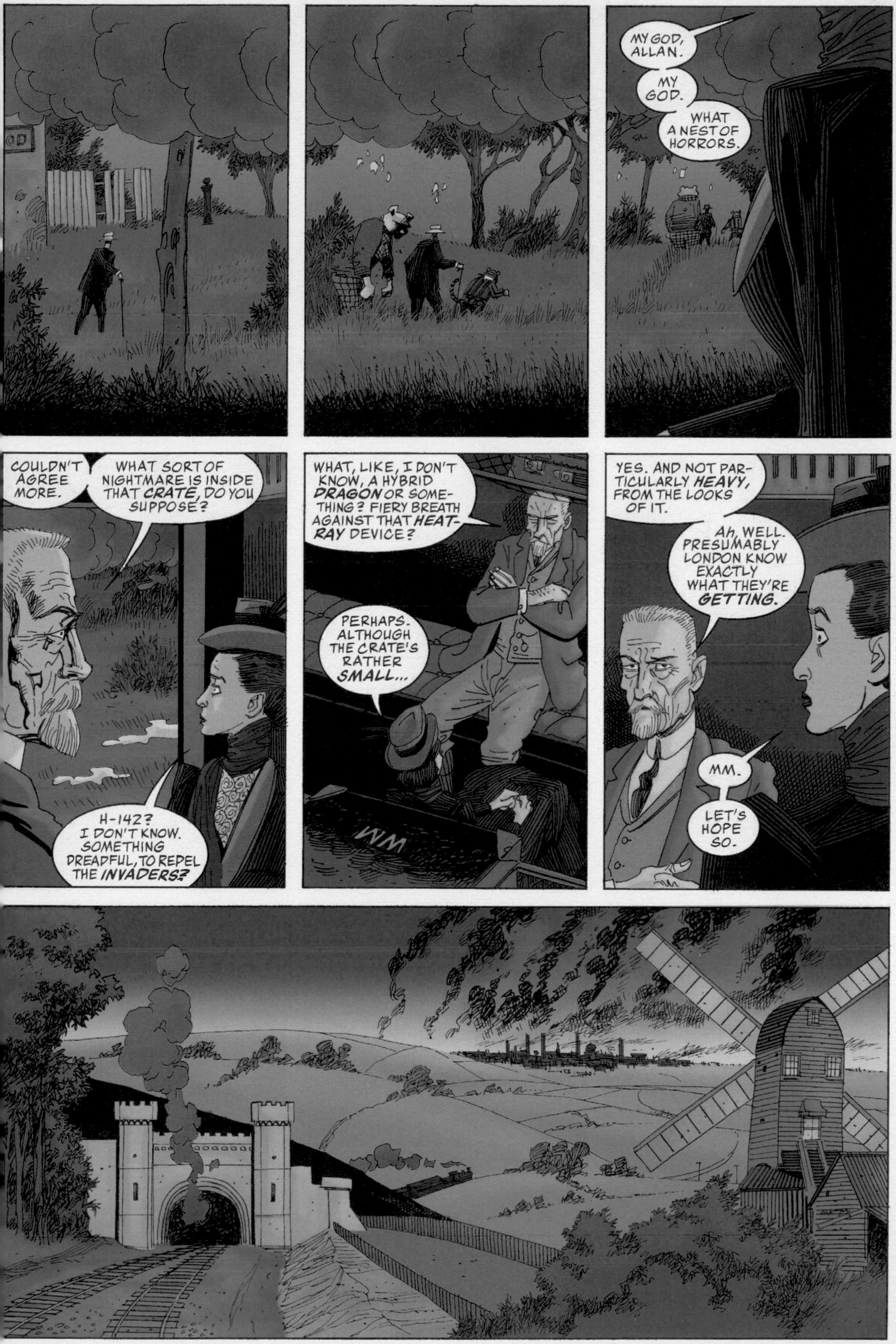
MY GOD, ALLAN.
MY GOD.
WHAT A NEST OF HORRORS.
COULDN'T AGREE MORE.
WHAT SORT OF NIGHTMARE IS INSIDE THAT CRATE, DO YOU SUPPOSE?
H-142? I DON'T KNOW. SOMETHING DREADFUL, TO REPEL THE INVADERS?
WHAT, LIKE, I DON'T KNOW, A HYBRID DRAGON OR SOMETHING? FIERY BREATH AGAINST THAT HEAT-RAY DEVICE?
PERHAPS. ALTHOUGH THE CRATE'S RATHER SMALL...
YES. AND NOT PARTICULARLY HEAVY, FROM THE LOOKS OF IT.
Ah, WELL. PRESUMABLY LONDON KNOW EXACTLY WHAT THEY'RE GETTING.
MM.
LET'S HOPE SO.

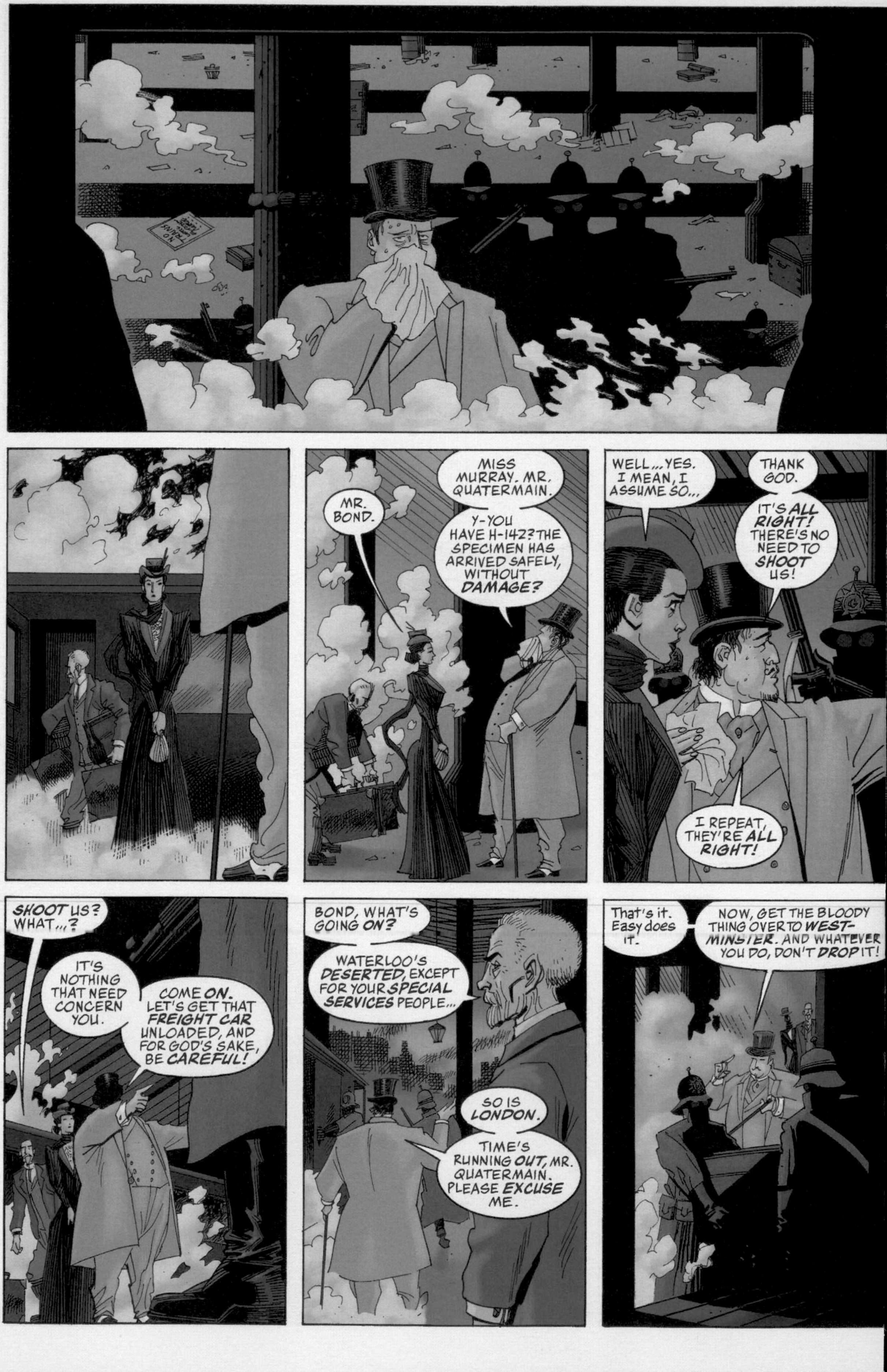
MR. BOND.
MISS MURRAY. MR. QUATERMAIN.
Y-YOU HAVE H-142? THE SPECIMEN HAS ARRIVED SAFELY, WITHOUT DAMAGE?
WELL... YES. I MEAN, I ASSUME SO...
THANK GOD.
IT'S ALL RIGHT! THERE'S NO NEED TO SHOOT US!
I REPEAT, THEY'RE ALL RIGHT!
SHOOT US? WHAT...?
IT'S NOTHING THAT NEED CONCERN YOU.
COME ON. LET'S GET THAT FREIGHT CAR UNLOADED, AND FOR GOD'S SAKE, BE CAREFUL!
BOND, WHAT'S GOING ON?
WATERLOO'S DESERTED, EXCEPT FOR YOUR SPECIAL SERVICES PEOPLE...
SO IS LONDON.
TIME'S RUNNING OUT, MR. QUATERMAIN. PLEASE EXCUSE ME.
That's it. Easy does it.
NOW, GET THE BLOODY THING OVER TO WEST-MINSTER. AND WHATEVER YOU DO, DON'T DROP IT!

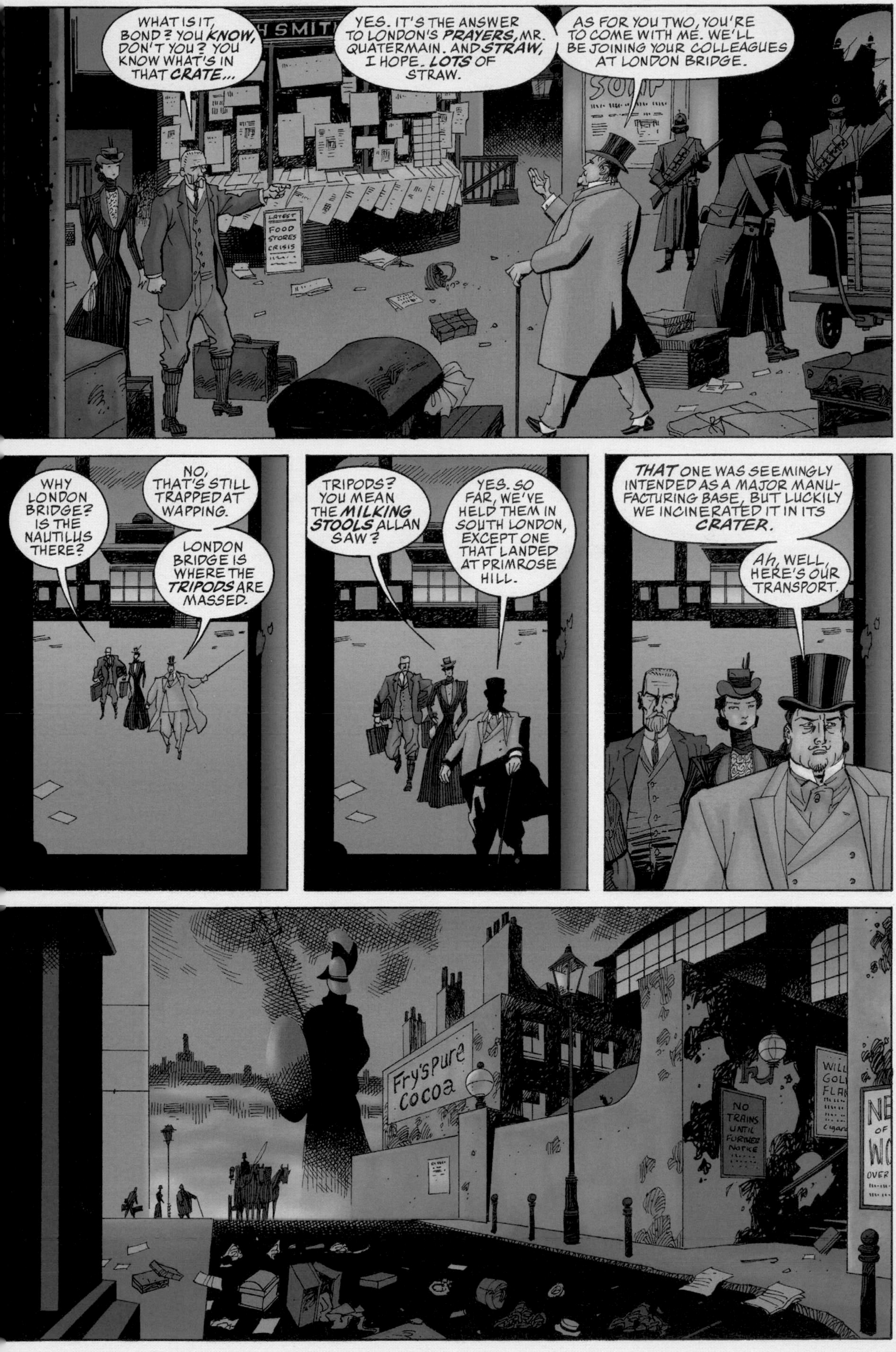
WHAT IS IT, BOND? YOU KNOW, DON'T YOU? YOU KNOW WHAT'S IN THAT CRATE...
YES. IT'S THE ANSWER TO LONDON'S PRAYERS, MR. QUATERMAIN. AND STRAW, I HOPE. LOTS OF STRAW.
AS FOR YOU TWO, YOU'RE TO COME WITH ME. WE'LL BE JOINING YOUR COLLEAGUES AT LONDON BRIDGE.
LATEST FOOD STORES CRISIS
WHY LONDON BRIDGE? IS THE NAUTILUS THERE?
NO, THAT'S STILL TRAPPED AT WAPPING.
LONDON BRIDGE IS WHERE THE TRIPODS ARE MASSED.
TRIPODS? YOU MEAN THE MILKING STOOLS ALLAN SAW?
YES. SO FAR, WE'VE HELD THEM IN SOUTH LONDON, EXCEPT ONE THAT LANDED AT PRIMROSE HILL.
THAT ONE WAS SEEMINGLY INTENDED AS A MAJOR MANU-FACTURING BASE, BUT LUCKILY WE INCINERATED IT IN ITS CRATER.
Ah, WELL, HERE'S OUR TRANSPORT.
Fry's pure Cocoa
NO TRAINS UNTIL FURTHER NOTICE

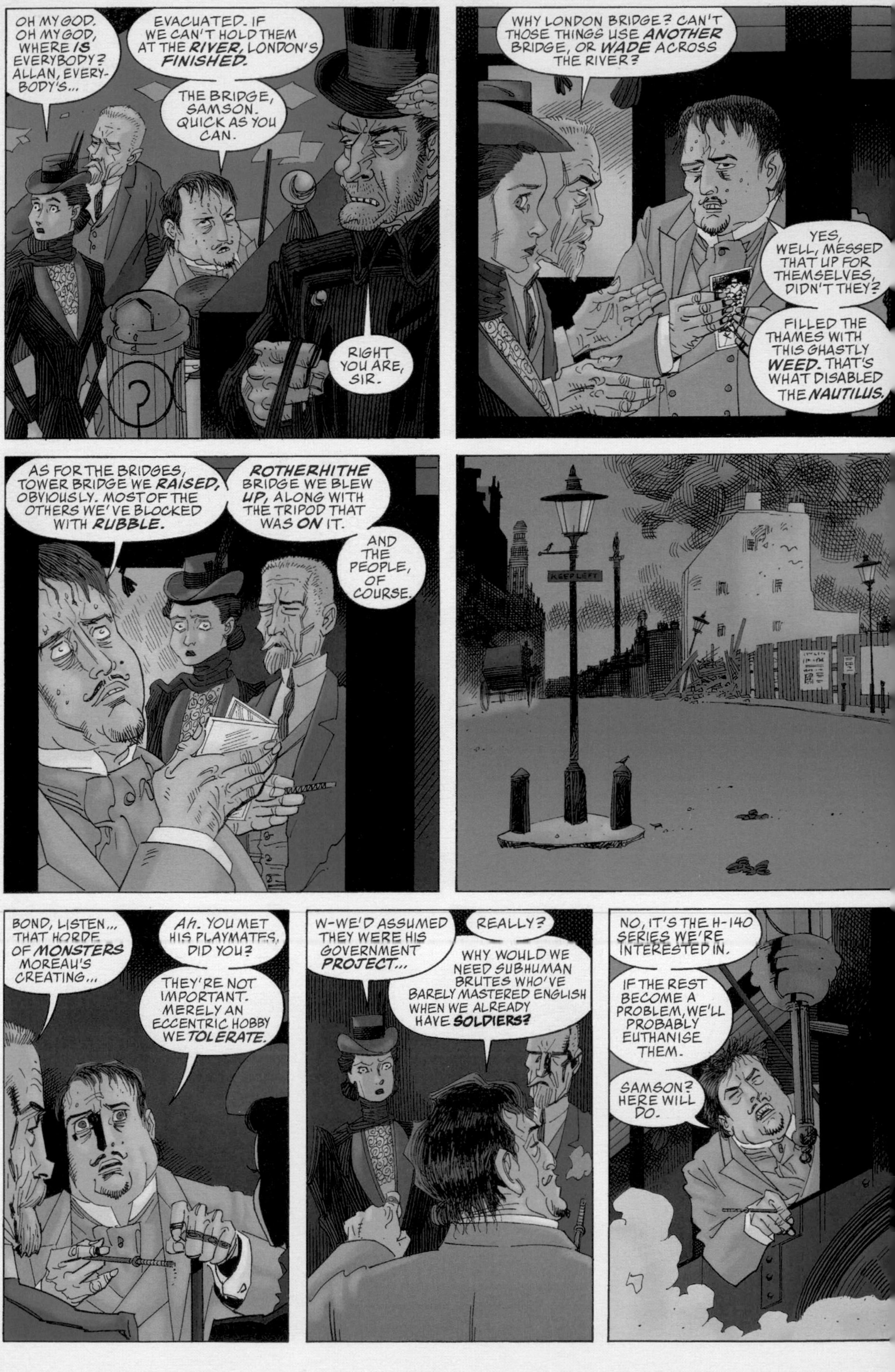

OH MY GOD. OH MY GOD, WHERE *IS* EVERYBODY? ALLAN, EVERY-BODY'S...
EVACUATED. IF WE CAN'T HOLD THEM AT THE *RIVER,* LONDON'S *FINISHED.*
THE BRIDGE, SAMSON. QUICK AS YOU CAN.
RIGHT YOU ARE, SIR.
WHY LONDON BRIDGE? CAN'T THOSE THINGS USE *ANOTHER* BRIDGE, OR *WADE* ACROSS THE RIVER?
YES, WELL, MESSED THAT UP FOR THEMSELVES, DIDN'T THEY?
FILLED THE THAMES WITH THIS GHASTLY *WEED.* THAT'S WHAT DISABLED THE *NAUTILUS.*
AS FOR THE BRIDGES, TOWER BRIDGE WE *RAISED,* OBVIOUSLY. MOST OF THE OTHERS WE'VE BLOCKED WITH *RUBBLE.*
ROTHERHITHE BRIDGE WE BLEW *UP,* ALONG WITH THE TRIPOD THAT WAS *ON* IT.
AND THE PEOPLE, OF COURSE.
KEEP LEFT
BOND, LISTEN... THAT HORDE OF *MONSTERS* MOREAU'S CREATING...
Ah. YOU MET HIS PLAYMATES, DID YOU?
THEY'RE NOT IMPORTANT. MERELY AN ECCENTRIC HOBBY WE *TOLERATE.*
W-WE'D ASSUMED THEY WERE HIS GOVERNMENT *PROJECT...*
REALLY?
WHY WOULD WE NEED SUBHUMAN BRUTES WHO'VE BARELY MASTERED ENGLISH WHEN WE ALREADY HAVE *SOLDIERS?*
NO, IT'S THE H-140 SERIES WE'RE INTERESTED IN.
IF THE REST BECOME A PROBLEM, WE'LL PROBABLY EUTHANISE THEM.
SAMSON? HERE WILL DO.

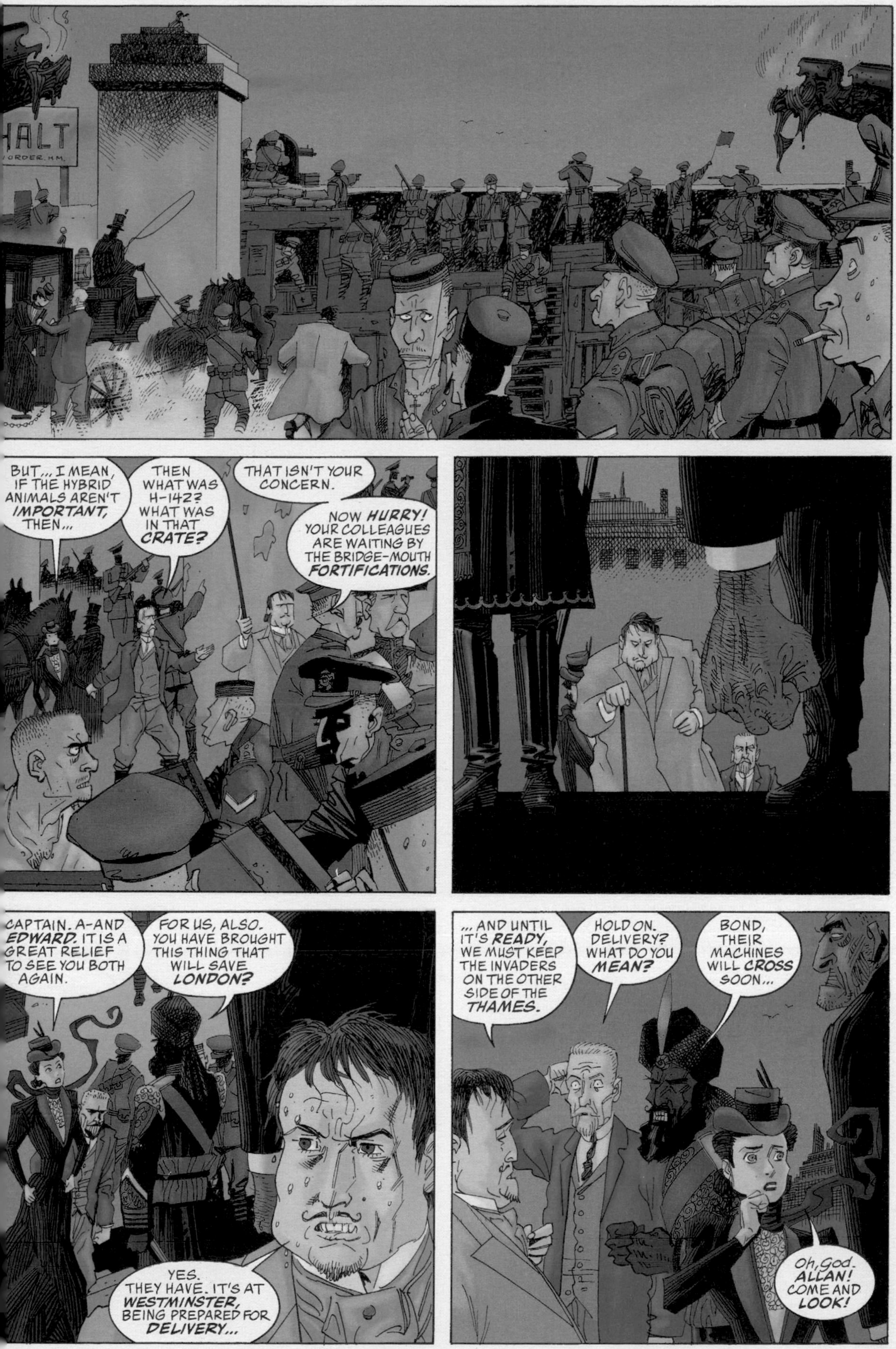
HALT
BUT... I MEAN, IF THE HYBRID ANIMALS AREN'T IMPORTANT, THEN...
THEN WHAT WAS H-142? WHAT WAS IN THAT CRATE?
THAT ISN'T YOUR CONCERN.
NOW HURRY! YOUR COLLEAGUES ARE WAITING BY THE BRIDGE-MOUTH FORTIFICATIONS.
CAPTAIN. A-AND EDWARD. IT IS A GREAT RELIEF TO SEE YOU BOTH AGAIN.
FOR US, ALSO. YOU HAVE BROUGHT THIS THING THAT WILL SAVE LONDON?
YES. THEY HAVE. IT'S AT WESTMINSTER, BEING PREPARED FOR DELIVERY...
...AND UNTIL IT'S READY, WE MUST KEEP THE INVADERS ON THE OTHER SIDE OF THE THAMES.
HOLD ON. DELIVERY? WHAT DO YOU MEAN?
BOND, THEIR MACHINES WILL CROSS SOON...
Oh, God. ALLAN! COME AND LOOK!

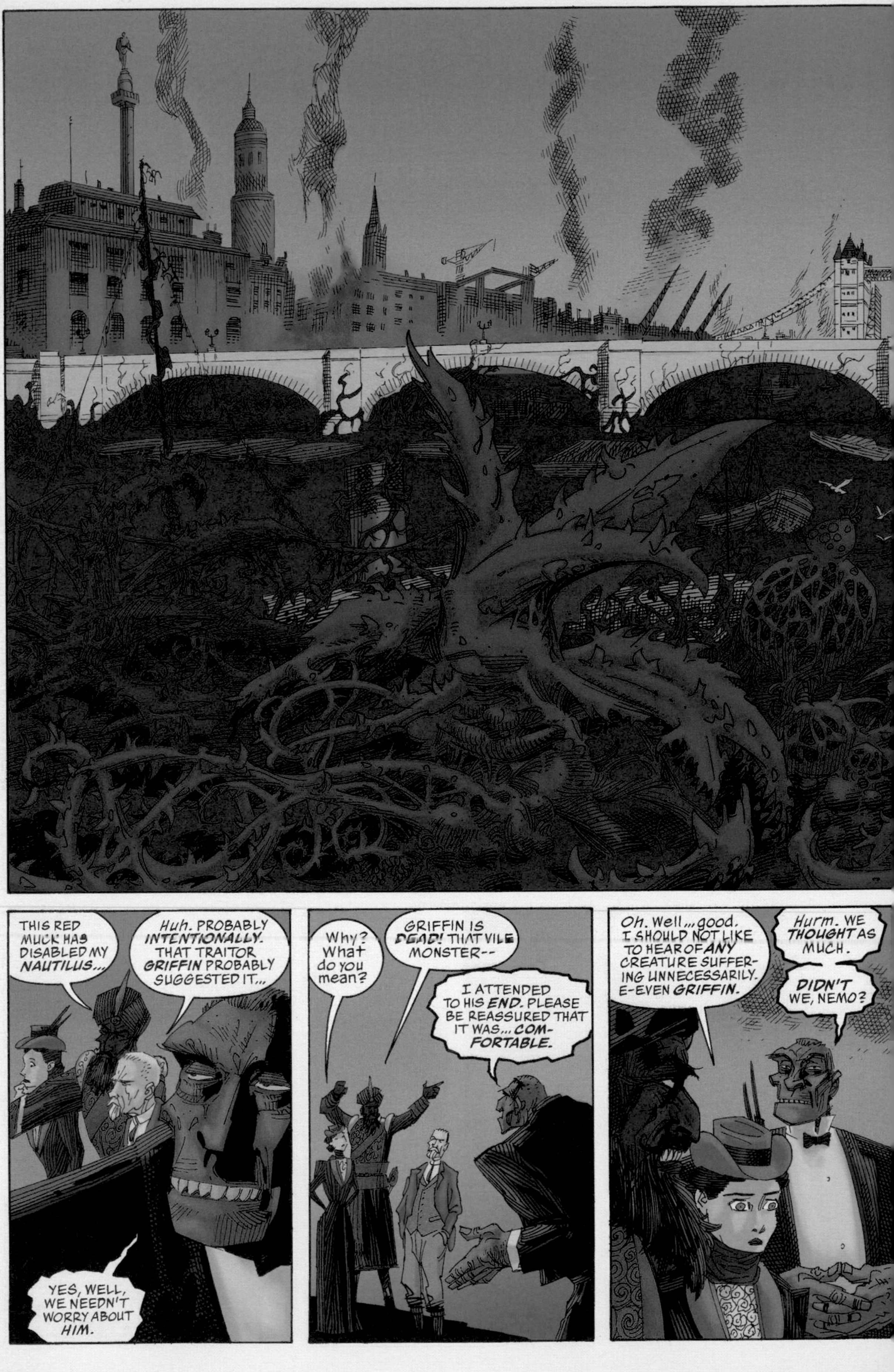
THIS RED MUCK HAS DISABLED MY NAUTILUS...
Huh. PROBABLY INTENTIONALLY. THAT TRAITOR GRIFFIN PROBABLY SUGGESTED IT...
YES, WELL, WE NEEDN'T WORRY ABOUT HIM.
Why? What do you mean?
GRIFFIN IS DEAD! THAT VILE MONSTER--
I ATTENDED TO HIS END. PLEASE BE REASSURED THAT IT WAS... COMFORTABLE.
Oh. Well... good. I SHOULD NOT LIKE TO HEAR OF ANY CREATURE SUFFERING UNNECESSARILY. E-EVEN GRIFFIN.
Hurm. WE THOUGHT AS MUCH.
DIDN'T WE, NEMO?

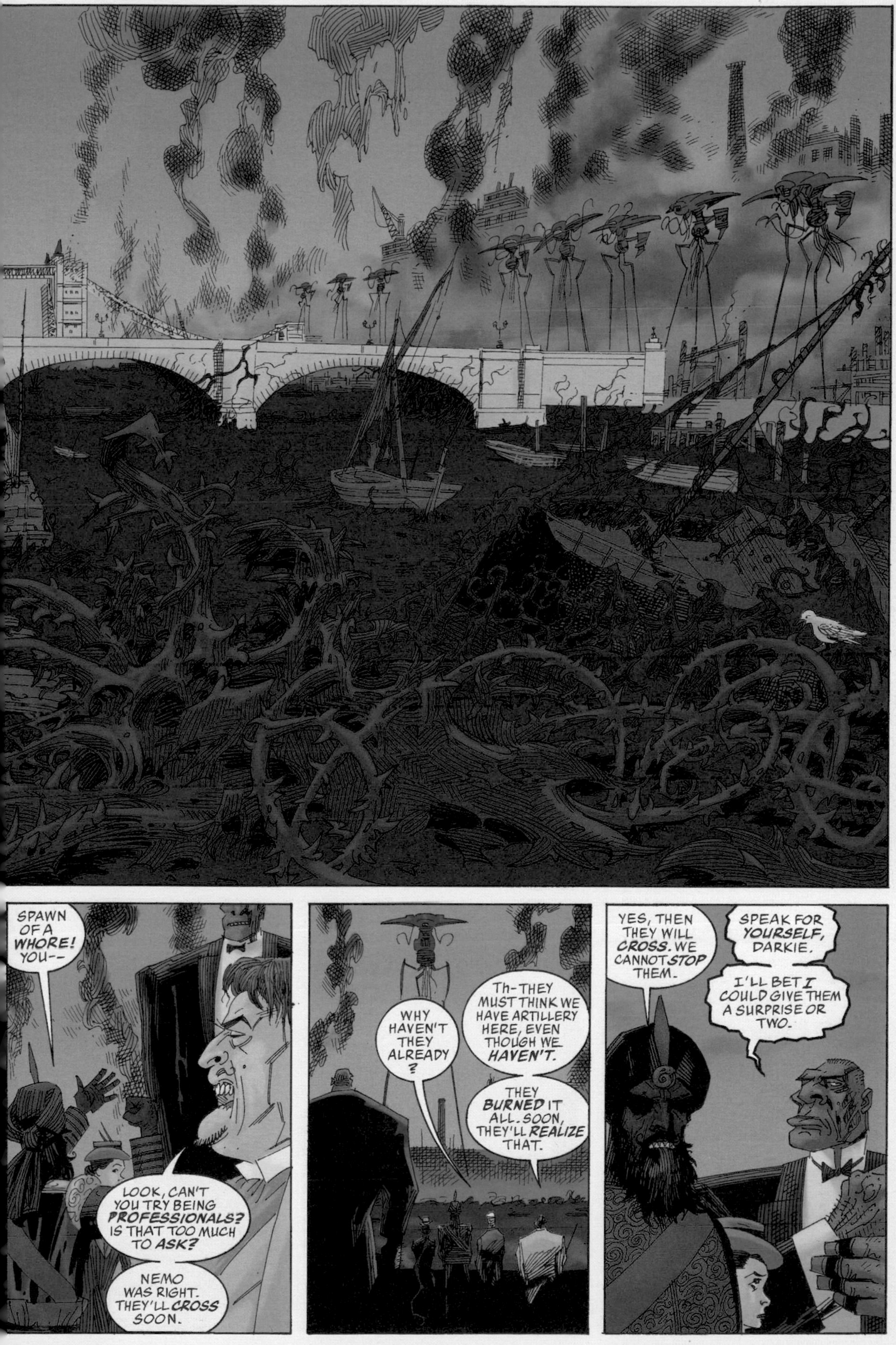
SPAWN OF A WHORE! YOU--
LOOK, CAN'T YOU TRY BEING PROFESSIONALS? IS THAT TOO MUCH TO ASK?
NEMO WAS RIGHT. THEY'LL CROSS SOON.
WHY HAVEN'T THEY ALREADY?
Th-THEY MUST THINK WE HAVE ARTILLERY HERE, EVEN THOUGH WE HAVEN'T.
THEY BURNED IT ALL. SOON, THEY'LL REALIZE THAT.
YES, THEN THEY WILL CROSS. WE CANNOT STOP THEM.
SPEAK FOR YOURSELF, DARKIE.
I'LL BET I COULD GIVE THEM A SURPRISE OR TWO.

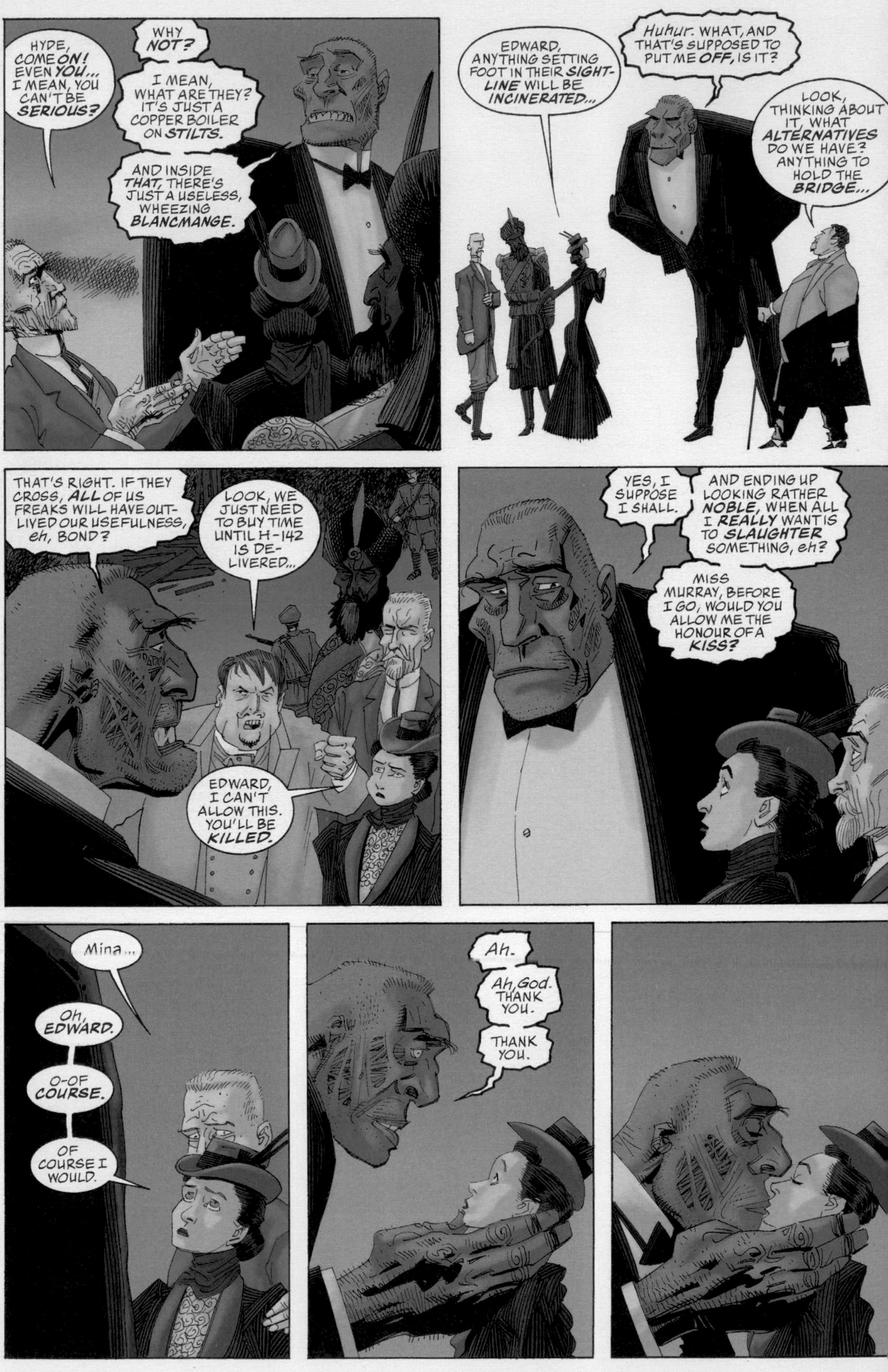

HYDE, COME ON! EVEN YOU... I MEAN, YOU CAN'T BE SERIOUS?
WHY NOT?
I MEAN, WHAT ARE THEY? IT'S JUST A COPPER BOILER ON STILTS.
AND INSIDE THAT, THERE'S JUST A USELESS, WHEEZING BLANCMANGE.
EDWARD, ANYTHING SETTING FOOT IN THEIR SIGHT-LINE WILL BE INCINERATED...
Huhur. WHAT, AND THAT'S SUPPOSED TO PUT ME OFF, IS IT?
LOOK, THINKING ABOUT IT, WHAT ALTERNATIVES DO WE HAVE? ANYTHING TO HOLD THE BRIDGE...
THAT'S RIGHT. IF THEY CROSS, ALL OF US FREAKS WILL HAVE OUT-LIVED OUR USEFULNESS, eh, BOND?
LOOK, WE JUST NEED TO BUY TIME UNTIL H-142 IS DE-LIVERED...
EDWARD, I CAN'T ALLOW THIS. YOU'LL BE KILLED.
YES, I SUPPOSE I SHALL.
AND ENDING UP LOOKING RATHER NOBLE, WHEN ALL I REALLY WANT IS TO SLAUGHTER SOMETHING, eh?
MISS MURRAY, BEFORE I GO, WOULD YOU ALLOW ME THE HONOUR OF A KISS?
Mina...
Oh, EDWARD.
O-OF COURSE.
OF COURSE I WOULD.
Ah.
Ah, God. THANK YOU.
THANK YOU.

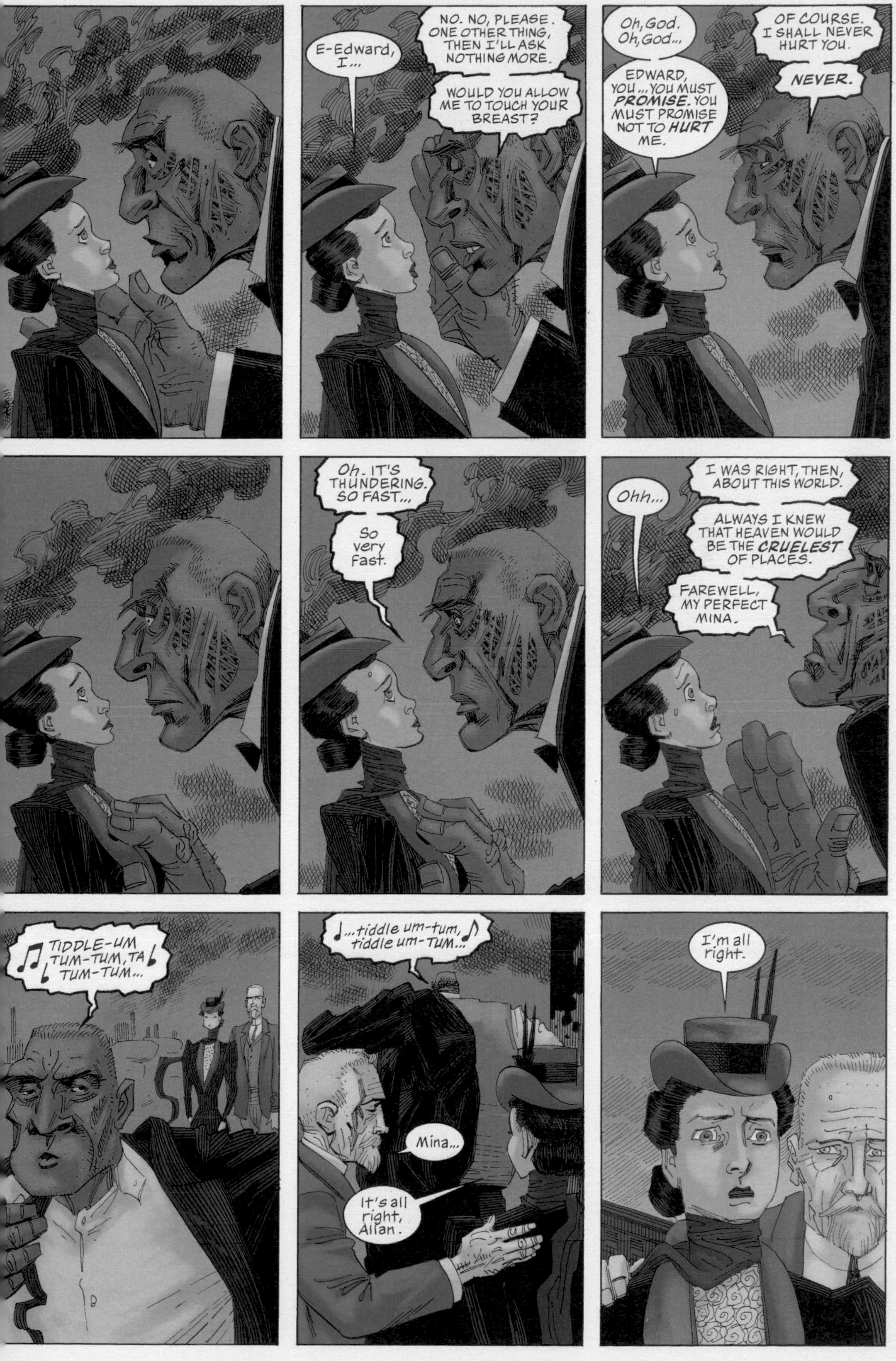
E-Edward, I...
NO. NO, PLEASE. ONE OTHER THING, THEN I'LL ASK NOTHING MORE.
WOULD YOU ALLOW ME TO TOUCH YOUR BREAST?
Oh, God. Oh, God...
EDWARD, YOU... YOU MUST PROMISE. YOU MUST PROMISE NOT TO HURT ME.
OF COURSE. I SHALL NEVER HURT YOU.
NEVER.
Oh. IT'S THUNDERING. SO FAST...
So very Fast.
Ohh...
I WAS RIGHT, THEN, ABOUT THIS WORLD.
ALWAYS I KNEW THAT HEAVEN WOULD BE THE CRUELEST OF PLACES.
FAREWELL, MY PERFECT MINA.
TIDDLE-UM TUM-TUM, TA TUM-TUM...
...tiddle um-tum, tiddle um-TUM...
Mina...
It's all right, Allan.
I'm all right.

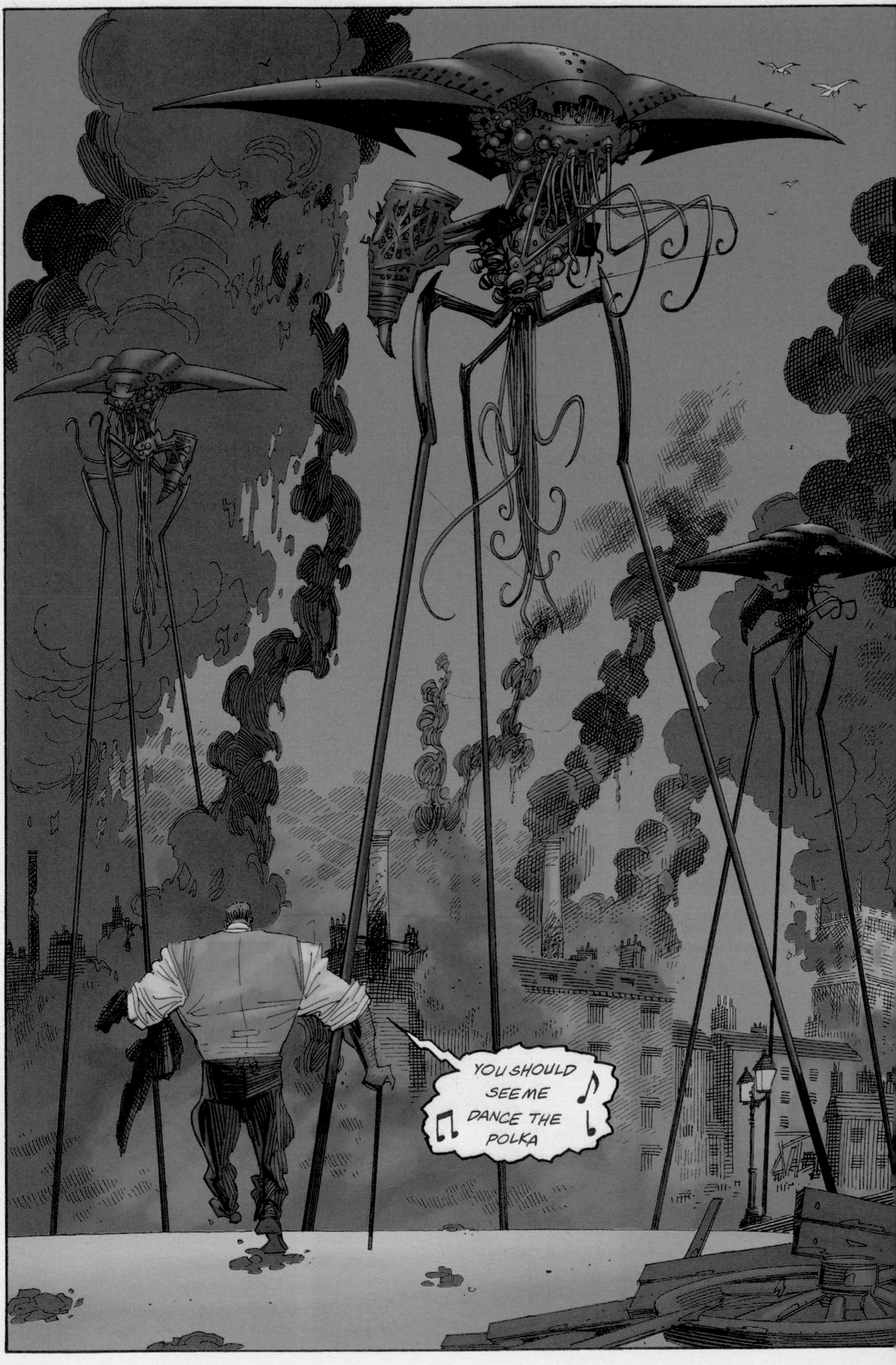
YOU SHOULD SEE ME DANCE THE POLKA

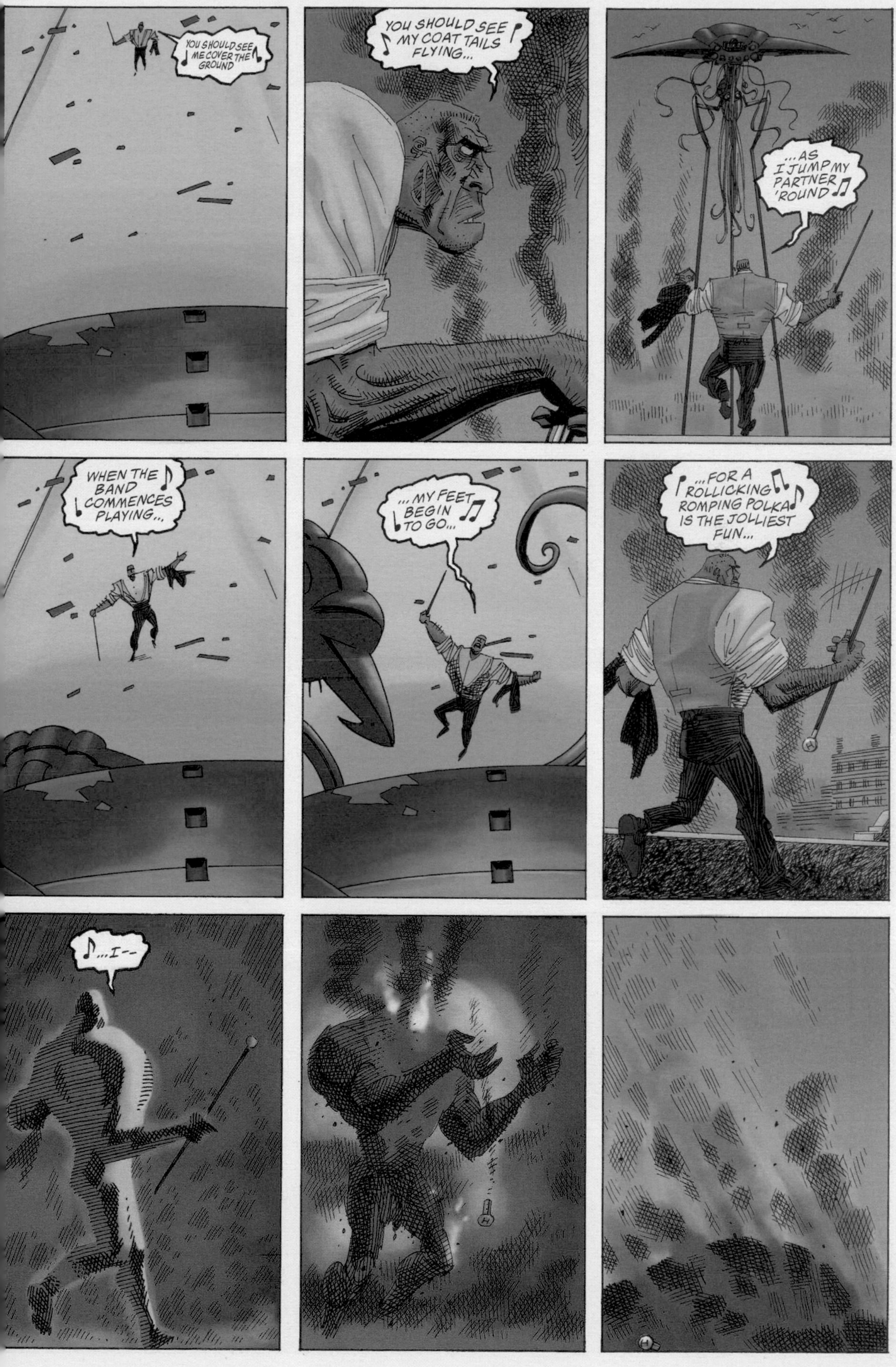
YOU SHOULD SEE ME COVER THE GROUND
YOU SHOULD SEE MY COAT TAILS FLYING...
...AS I JUMP MY PARTNER 'ROUND
WHEN THE BAND COMMENCES PLAYING...
...MY FEET BEGIN TO GO...
...FOR A ROLLICKING ROMPING POLKA IS THE JOLLIEST FUN...
...I--

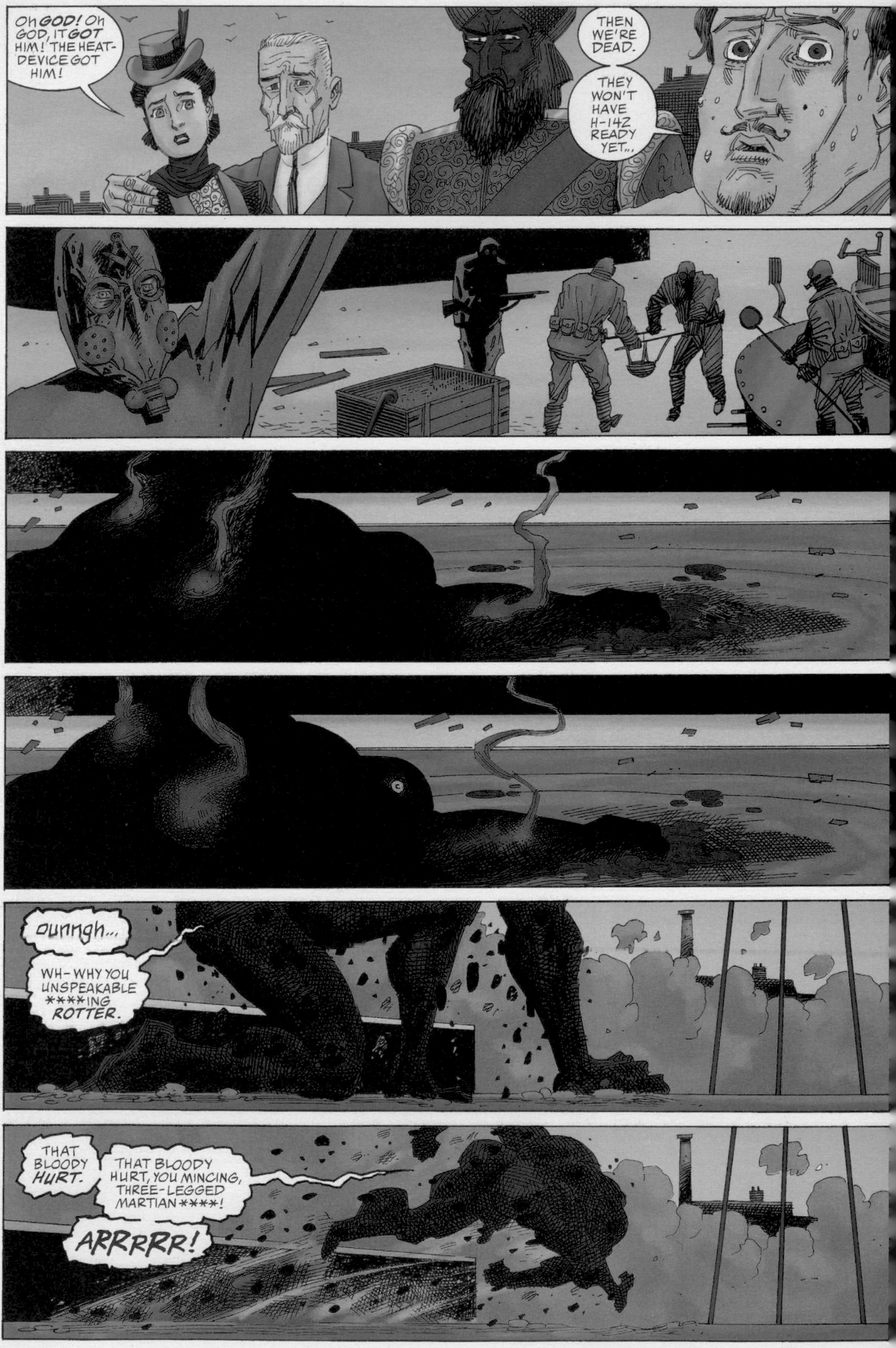

Oh GOD! On GOD, IT GOT HIM! THE HEAT-DEVICE GOT HIM!
THEN WE'RE DEAD.
THEY WON'T HAVE H-142 READY YET...
ounngh...
WH-WHY YOU UNSPEAKABLE ****ING ROTTER.
THAT BLOODY HURT.
THAT BLOODY HURT, YOU MINCING, THREE-LEGGED MARTIAN ****!
ARRRRR!

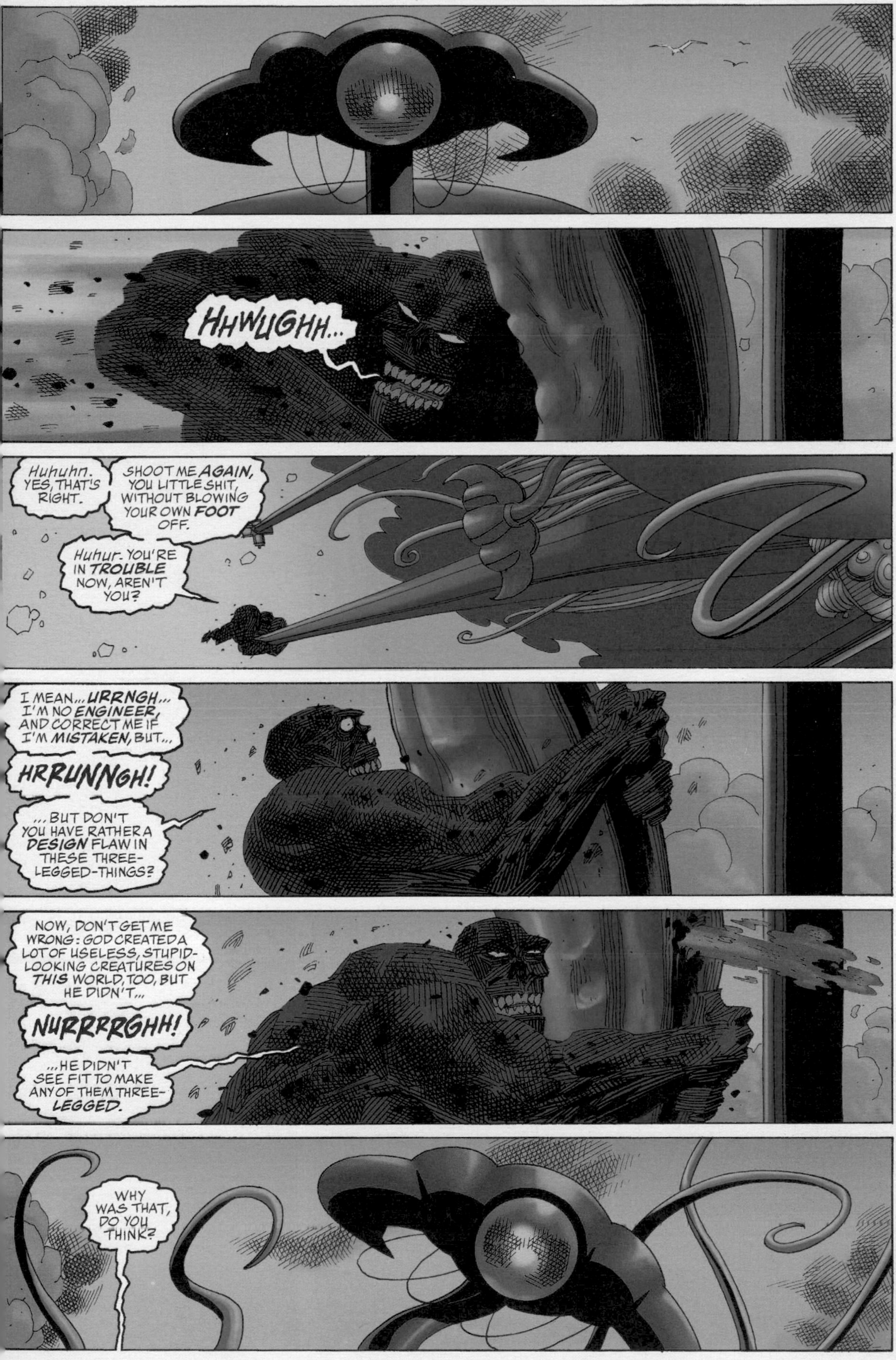
HHWUGHH...
Huhuhn. YES, THAT'S RIGHT.
SHOOT ME AGAIN, YOU LITTLE SHIT, WITHOUT BLOWING YOUR OWN FOOT OFF.
Huhur. YOU'RE IN TROUBLE NOW, AREN'T YOU?
I MEAN... URRNGH... I'M NO ENGINEER, AND CORRECT ME IF I'M MISTAKEN, BUT...
HRRUNNGH!
...BUT DON'T YOU HAVE RATHER A DESIGN FLAW IN THESE THREE-LEGGED-THINGS?
NOW, DON'T GET ME WRONG: GOD CREATED A LOT OF USELESS, STUPID-LOOKING CREATURES ON THIS WORLD, TOO, BUT HE DIDN'T...
NURRRRGHH!
...HE DIDN'T SEE FIT TO MAKE ANY OF THEM THREE-LEGGED.
WHY WAS THAT, DO YOU THINK?

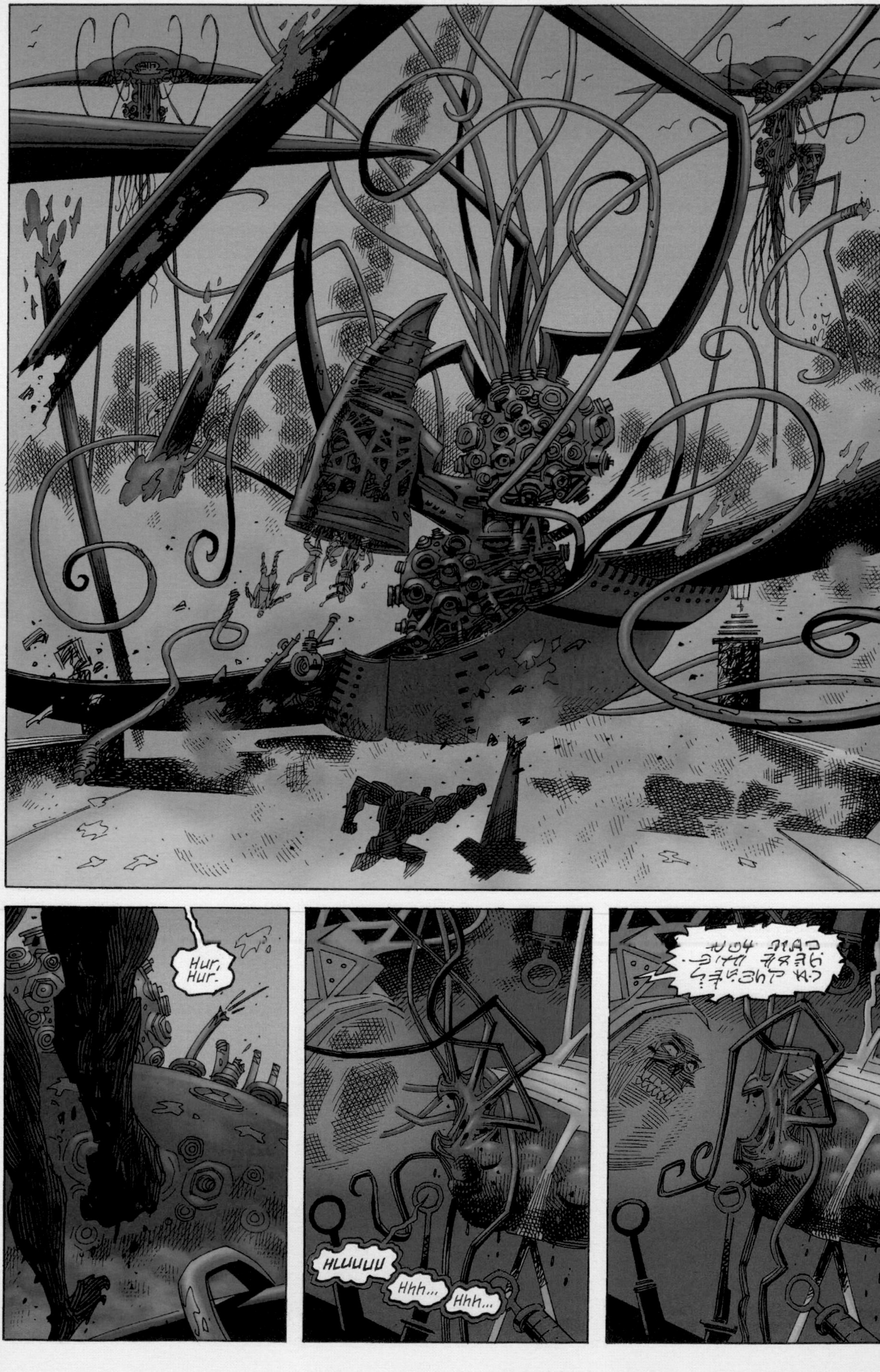
Hur, Hur.
HLUUUUU
Hhh...
Hhh...

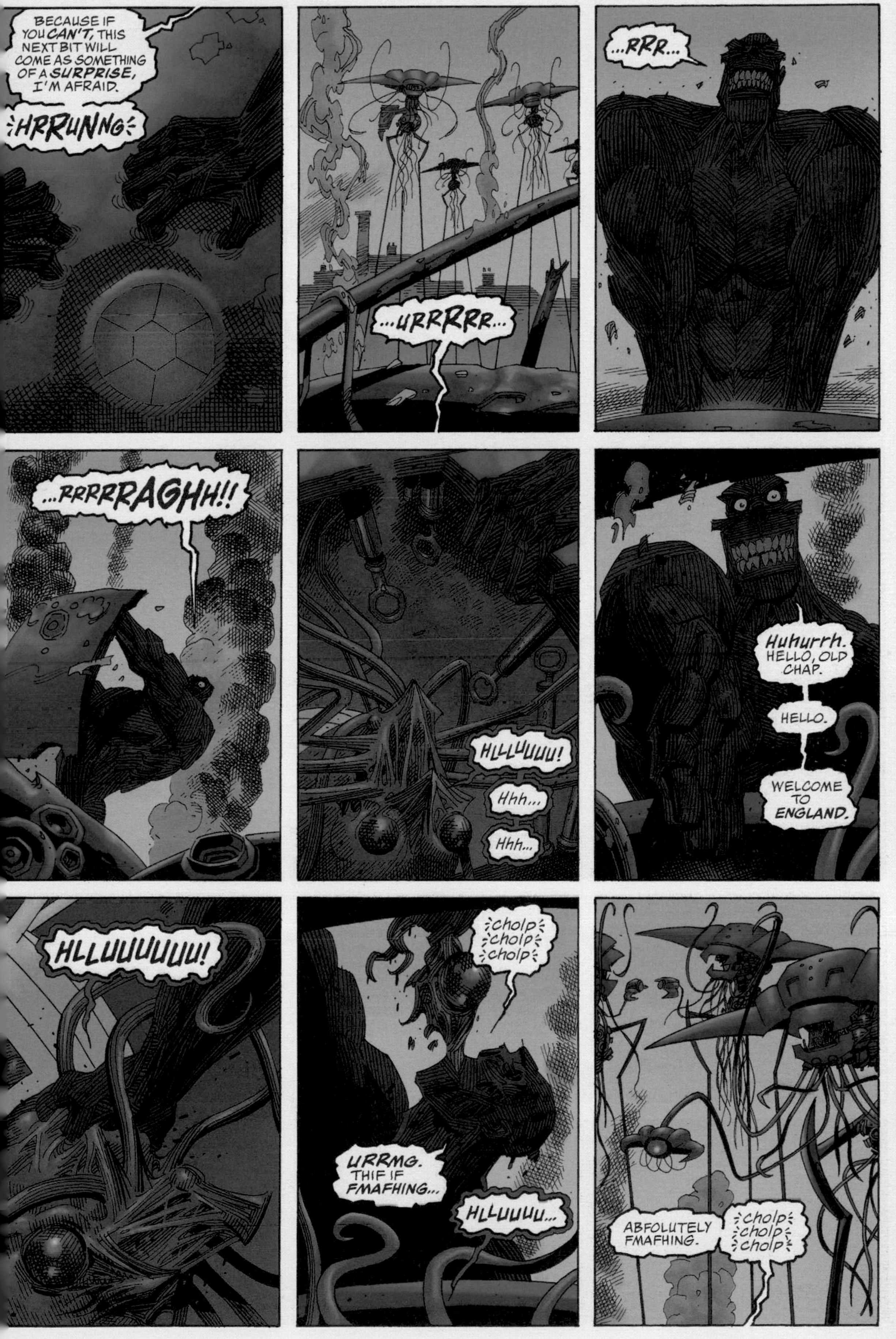
BECAUSE IF YOU CAN'T, THIS NEXT BIT WILL COME AS SOMETHING OF A SURPRISE, I'M AFRAID.
HRRUNNG
...URRRRR...
...RRR...
...RRRRRAGHH!!
HLLLUUUU!
Hhh...
Hhh...
Huhurrh. HELLO, OLD CHAP.
HELLO.
WELCOME TO ENGLAND.
HLLUUUUUUU!
cholp cholp cholp
URRMG. THIF IF FMAFHING...
HLLUUUU...
ABFOLUTELY FMAFHING.
cholp cholp cholp

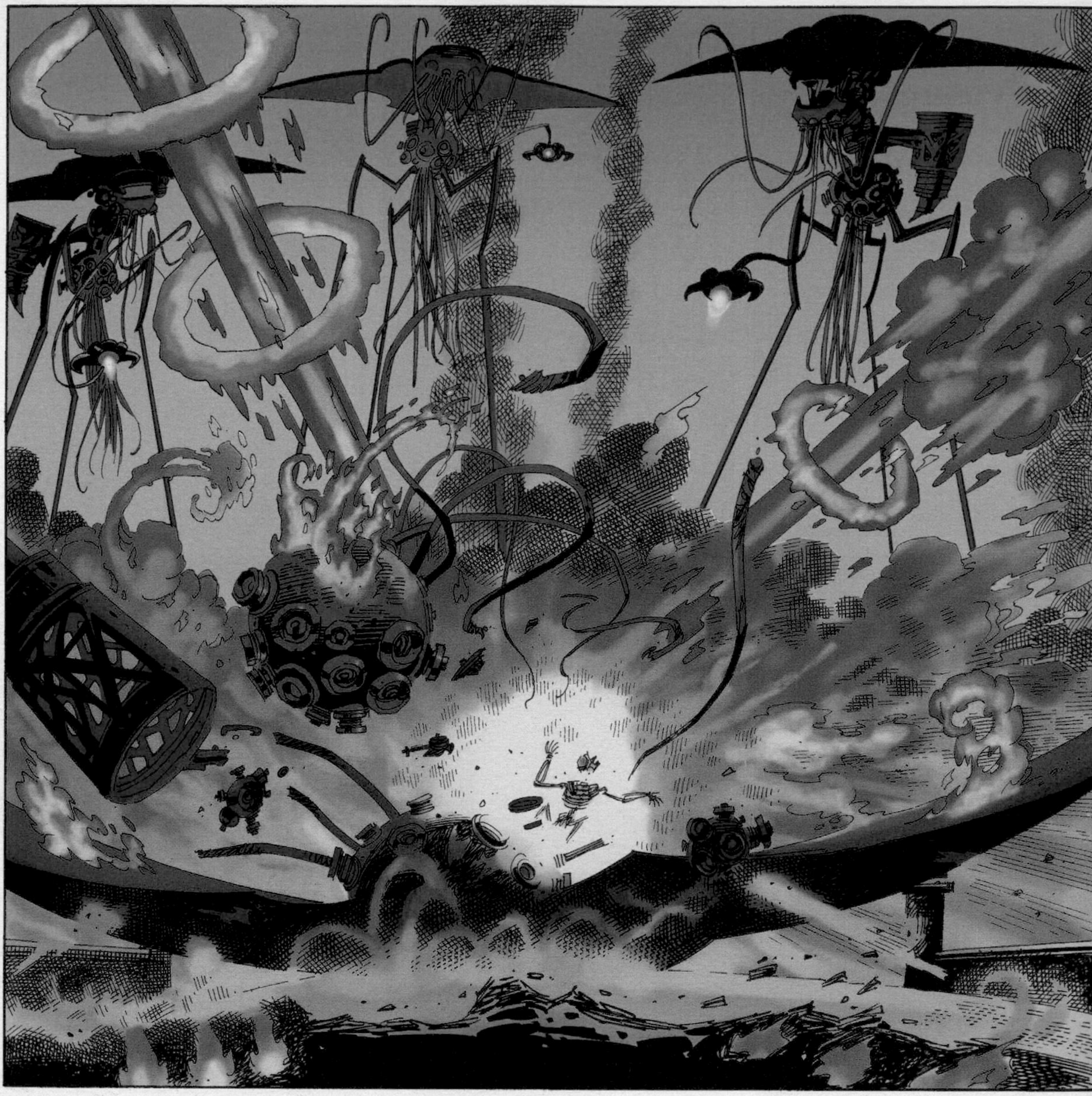
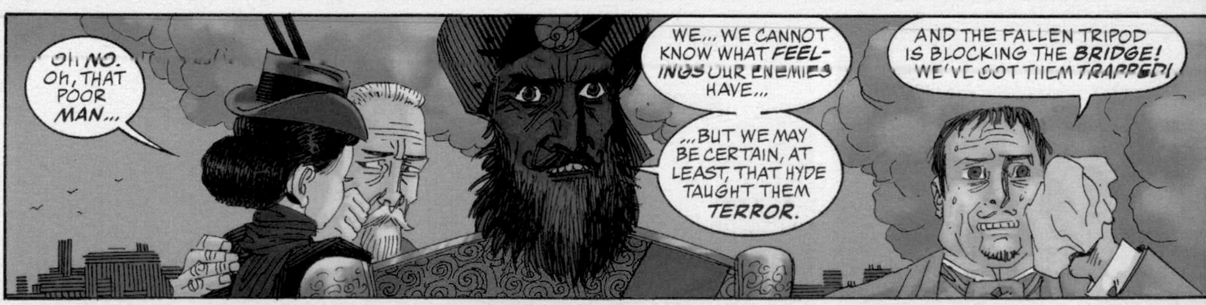
Oh NO. Oh, THAT POOR MAN...
WE... WE CANNOT KNOW WHAT FEEL-INGS OUR ENEMIES HAVE...
...BUT WE MAY BE CERTAIN, AT LEAST, THAT HYDE TAUGHT THEM TERROR.
AND THE FALLEN TRIPOD IS BLOCKING THE BRIDGE! WE'VE GOT THEM TRAPPED!
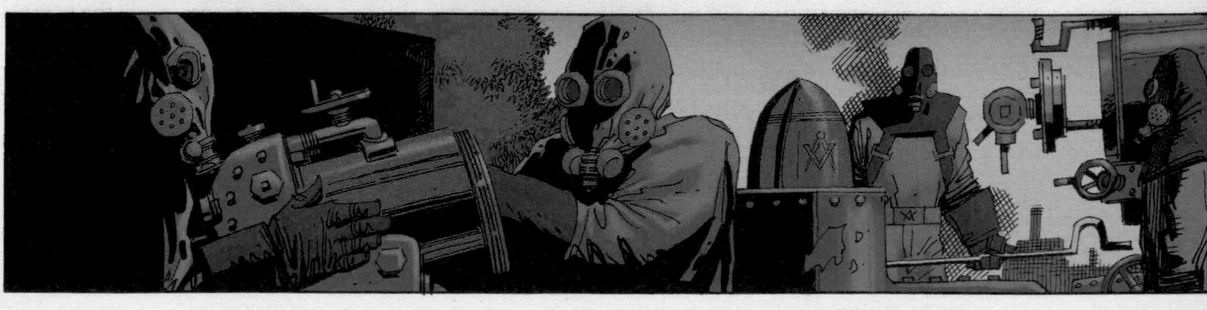

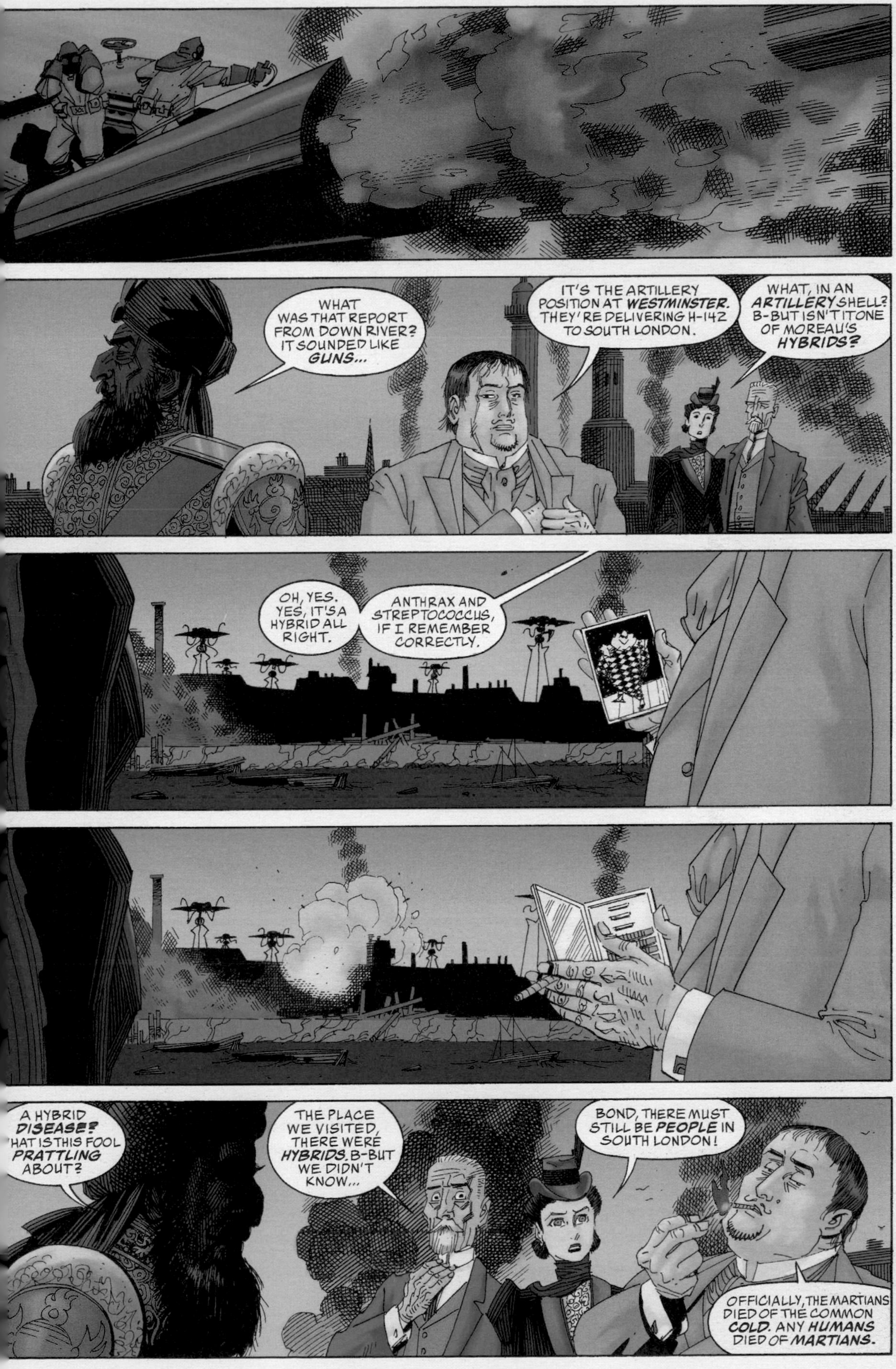
WHAT WAS THAT REPORT FROM DOWN RIVER? IT SOUNDED LIKE GUNS...
IT'S THE ARTILLERY POSITION AT WESTMINSTER. THEY'RE DELIVERING H-142 TO SOUTH LONDON.
WHAT, IN AN ARTILLERY SHELL? B-BUT ISN'T IT ONE OF MOREAU'S HYBRIDS?
OH, YES. YES, IT'S A HYBRID ALL RIGHT.
ANTHRAX AND STREPTOCOCCUS, IF I REMEMBER CORRECTLY.
A HYBRID DISEASE? WHAT IS THIS FOOL PRATTLING ABOUT?
THE PLACE WE VISITED, THERE WERE HYBRIDS. B-BUT WE DIDN'T KNOW...
BOND, THERE MUST STILL BE PEOPLE IN SOUTH LONDON!
OFFICIALLY, THE MARTIANS DIED OF THE COMMON COLD. ANY HUMANS DIED OF MARTIANS.

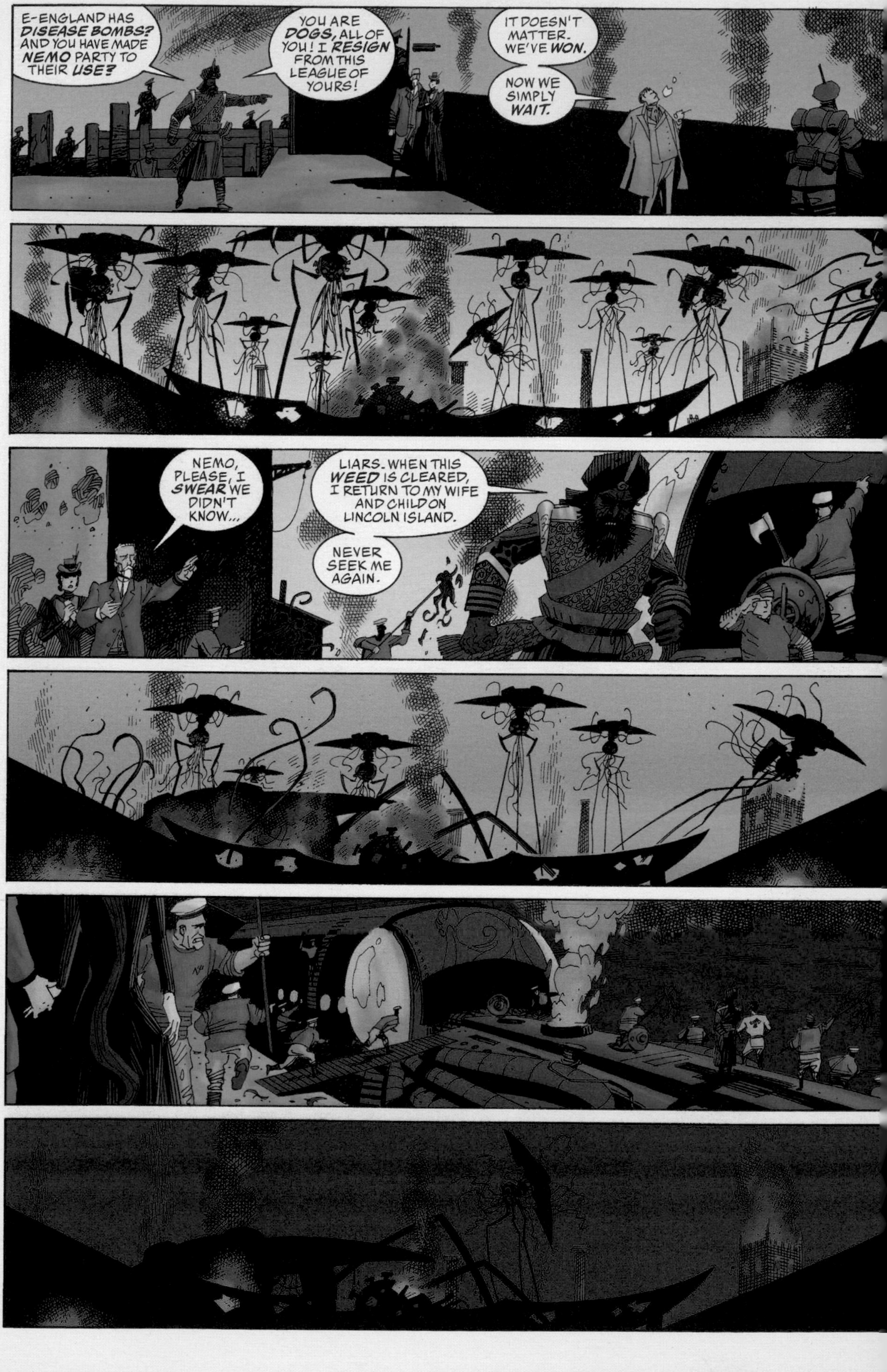
E-ENGLAND HAS DISEASE BOMBS? AND YOU HAVE MADE NEMO PARTY TO THEIR USE?
YOU ARE DOGS, ALL OF YOU! I RESIGN FROM THIS LEAGUE OF YOURS!
IT DOESN'T MATTER. WE'VE WON.
NOW WE SIMPLY WAIT.
NEMO, PLEASE, I SWEAR WE DIDN'T KNOW...
LIARS. WHEN THIS WEED IS CLEARED, I RETURN TO MY WIFE AND CHILD ON LINCOLN ISLAND.
NEVER SEEK ME AGAIN.

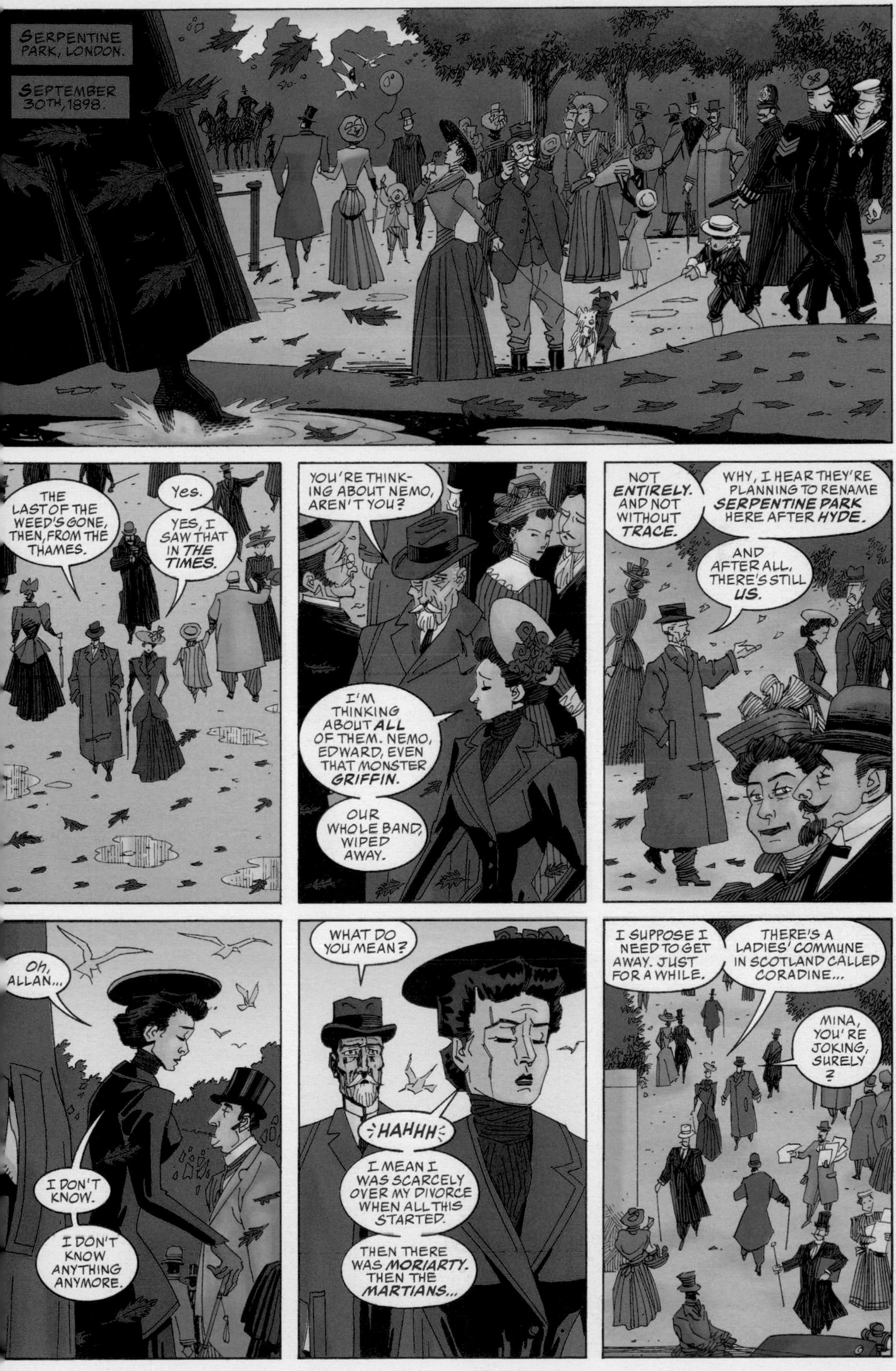
SERPENTINE PARK, LONDON.
SEPTEMBER 30TH, 1898.
THE LAST OF THE WEED'S GONE, THEN, FROM THE THAMES.
Yes.
YES, I SAW THAT IN THE TIMES.
YOU'RE THINKING ABOUT NEMO, AREN'T YOU?
I'M THINKING ABOUT ALL OF THEM. NEMO, EDWARD, EVEN THAT MONSTER GRIFFIN.
OUR WHOLE BAND, WIPED AWAY.
NOT ENTIRELY. AND NOT WITHOUT TRACE.
WHY, I HEAR THEY'RE PLANNING TO RENAME SERPENTINE PARK HERE AFTER HYDE.
AND AFTER ALL, THERE'S STILL US.
Oh, ALLAN...
I DON'T KNOW.
I DON'T KNOW ANYTHING ANYMORE.
WHAT DO YOU MEAN?
HAHHH
I MEAN I WAS SCARCELY OVER MY DIVORCE WHEN ALL THIS STARTED.
THEN THERE WAS MORIARTY. THEN THE MARTIANS...
I SUPPOSE I NEED TO GET AWAY. JUST FOR A WHILE.
THERE'S A LADIES' COMMUNE IN SCOTLAND CALLED CORADINE...
MINA, YOU'RE JOKING, SURELY?

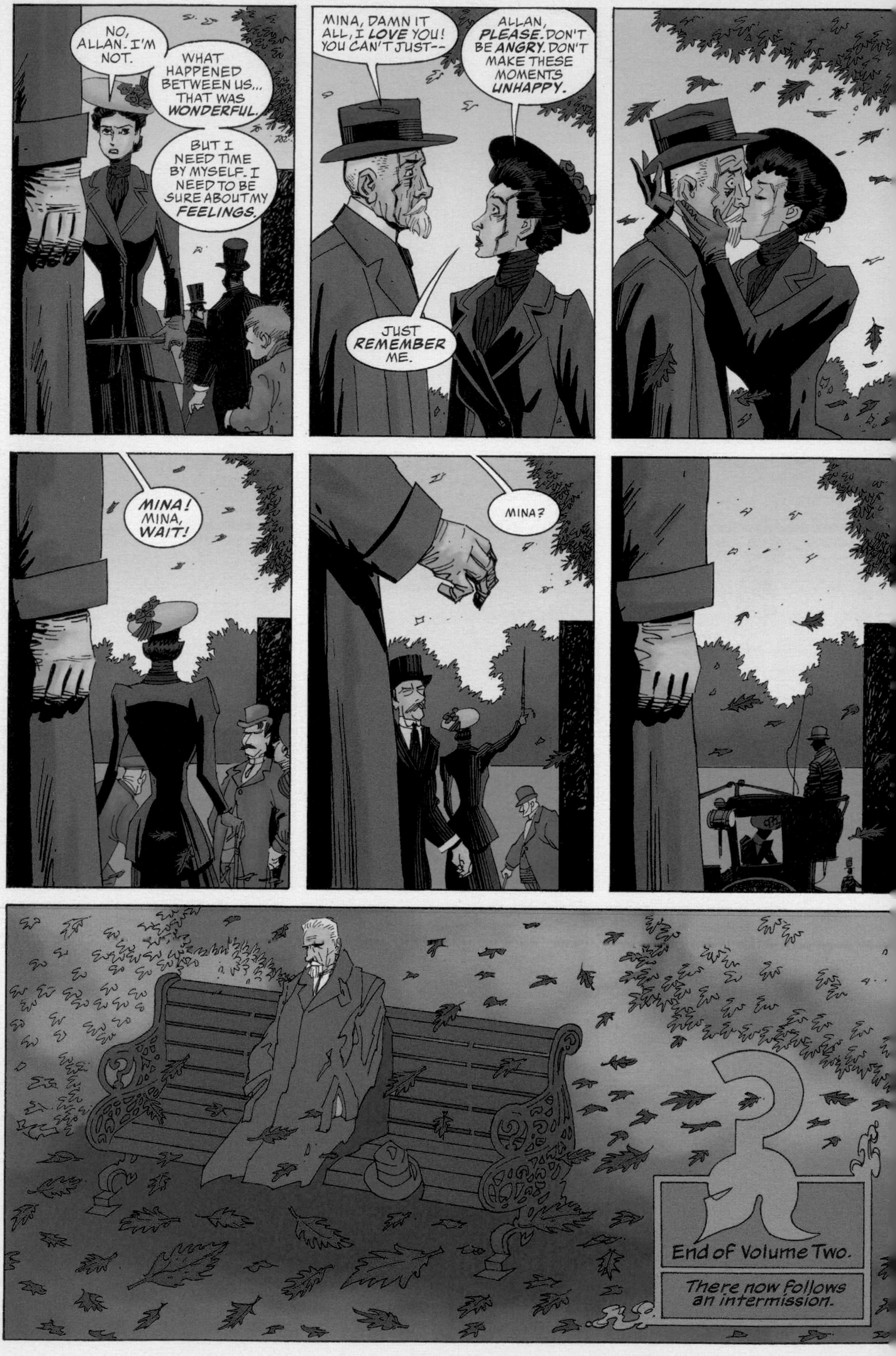
NO, ALLAN. I'M NOT.
WHAT HAPPENED BETWEEN US... THAT WAS WONDERFUL.
BUT I NEED TIME BY MYSELF. I NEED TO BE SURE ABOUT MY FEELINGS.
MINA, DAMN IT ALL, I LOVE YOU! YOU CAN'T JUST--
ALLAN, PLEASE. DON'T BE ANGRY. DON'T MAKE THESE MOMENTS UNHAPPY.
JUST REMEMBER ME.
MINA! MINA, WAIT!
MINA?
End of Volume Two.
There now follows an intermission.

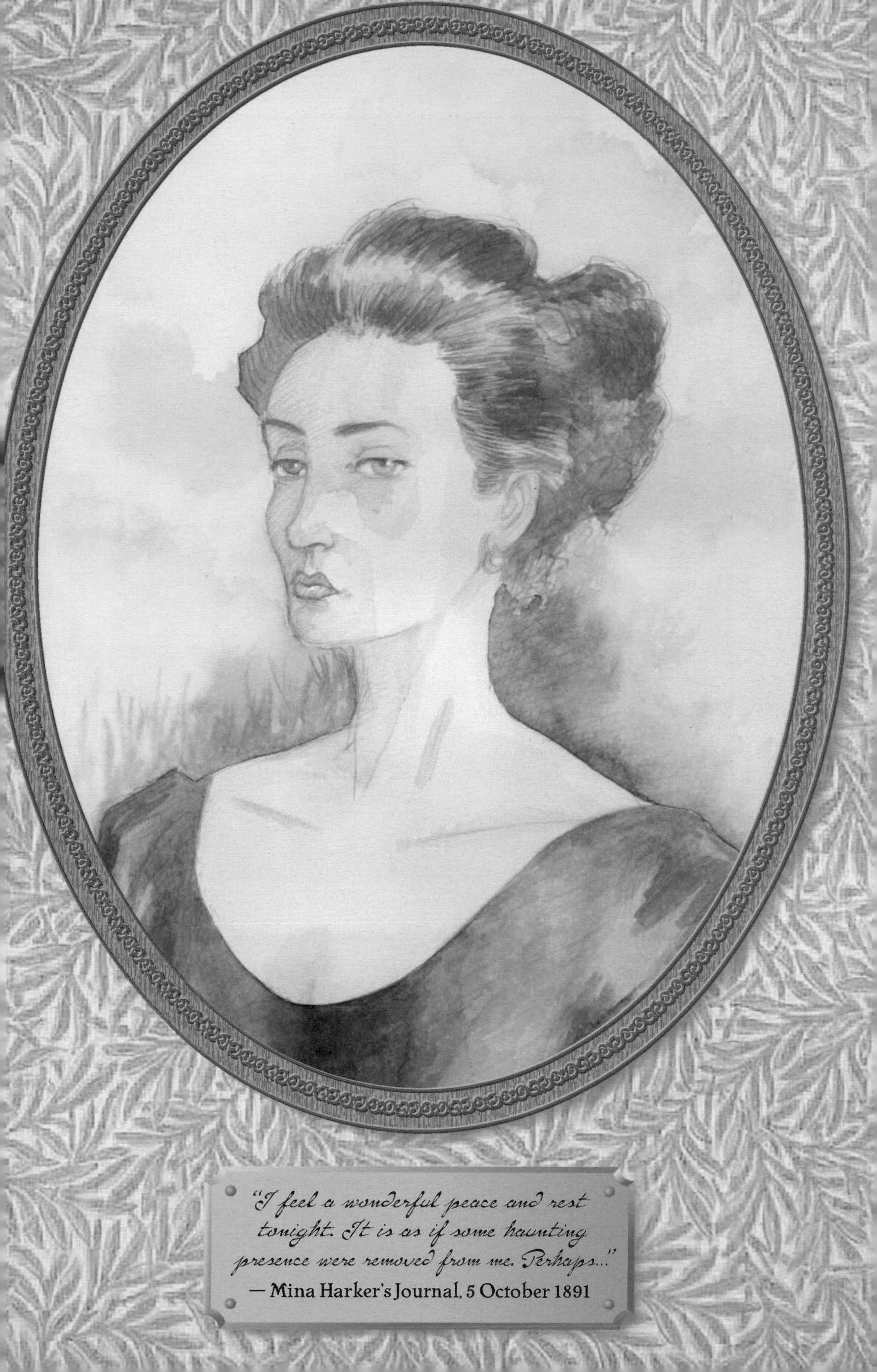

"I feel a wonderful peace and rest tonight. It is as if some haunting presence were removed from me. Perhaps..."

— Mina Harker's Journal, 5 October 1891

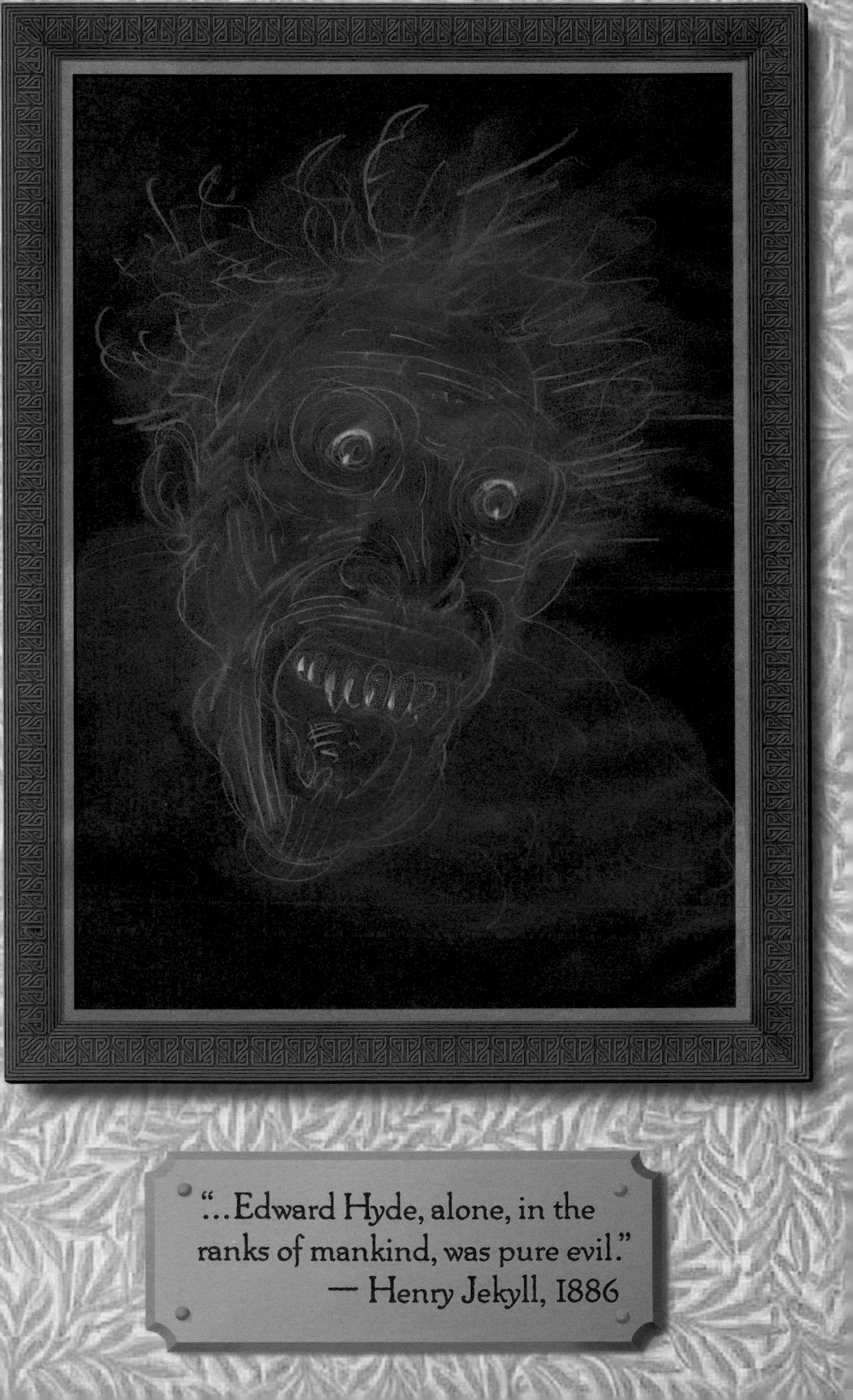

"...Edward Hyde, alone, in the ranks of mankind, was pure evil."
— Henry Jekyll, 1886

"This is day one of year one of the new epoch — the epoch of the Invisible Man. I am Invisible Man the First."
— Hawley Griffin, 1897

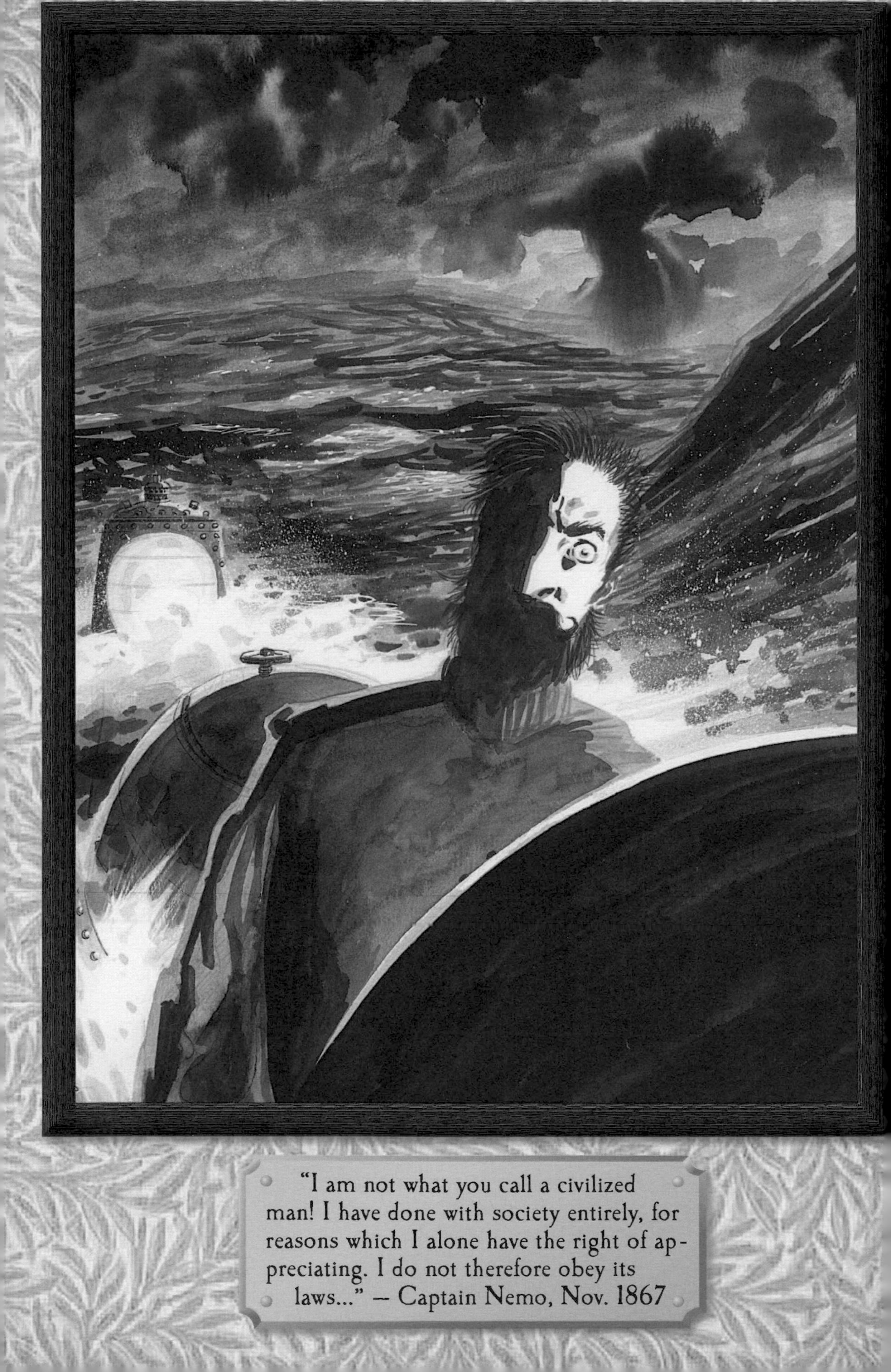

"I am not what you call a civilized man! I have done with society entirely, for reasons which I alone have the right of appreciating. I do not therefore obey its laws..." – Captain Nemo, Nov. 1867

"I've killed many men in my time, but I have never slain wantonly or stained my hand in innocent blood, only in self defence." — Allan Quatermain, 1880

CONTINENTAL STUDIES, CABINET PHOTOGRAPHS, &c., &c.—In Sealed Packets, 1s. 2d., 2s. 6d., 5s., 10s., and 20s.
35, Holywell Street, Strand, London, W.C.

FOOTLIGHT FAVORITES.

In Tights, Costume and Showing Bust.

PRICE, 6d EACH,

. . . . 5/ A DOZEN.

Sent by Mail, Postpaid, to any Address.

Sadie Stephens—tights
Vesta Tilley—tights
Kate Vaughan—costume

Ida Bell—tights
Lillie Welch—tights
Alice Anderson—costume
Miss Stuard—tights
Blanche Bell—bust
Annie Irish—bust
Ada Lewis—bust and cost
Emma Warde—tights
Mlle. Zucchi—tights
Jennie Cali—tights
Miss Bell—tights
Mrs. Leslie Carter—cos.
Helen Courtland—tights
Carrie Deane—tights
Mrs. Fitzherbert—costume
Helen Gilmore—tights
Jessa Hatcher—tights
Miss Joseph—tights
Mabel Love—bust
Mlle. Myrame—tights
Louise Llewellyn—tights
Carrie Perkins—tights
Miss Robinson—tights
Maggie Garrett—costume
Daisy Hughes—costume
Effie La Tour—tights
Mary Moore—costume
Anneta Phillipi—tights
Lillie Richardson—tights
Annie Sutherland—tights
Edith Wright—tights
Maggie Mitchell—bust
Mlle. Lefevre—bust
Nellie Handley—tights
Elsie Gray—tights

Send 1d Stamp for Complete List.

RICHARD K. FOX,

149, FLEET ST., LONDON, E. C.

SPICY BOOKS & CARDS.

ALL GENUINE. NO TRASH. GOOD VALUE. Revelations of Girlhood, 1s. 2d.; Fanny Hill, or the Career of a Woman of Pleasure, illus., 1s. 2d. cloth edn., 8 colored plates, 5s.; Maria Monk, or Awful Disclosures in a Nunnery, 40 illus., 1s. 6d.; Bride of the First Night, 1s. 3d.; Aristotle's Complete Works, 352 pages, colored plates, 2s. 6d.; All About the Girls, 1s. 2d.; Boccaccio's Decameron, 3s. 6d.; Moll Flanders, 2s. 3d.; Rosario, or the Female Monk, 2s. 6d.; Lady's Maid, illus., 1s. 2d. French Transparent Playing Cards, 52 in pack, 5s.; 16 positions of Matrimony, 1s. Photos—Life Studies, 25, 6d.; 50, 9d.; or 100, 1s. 3d. Illustrated Lists and Contents Sheet, 1 stamp. Address—
G. REID, West Green Road, London, N.

TO MARRIED LADIES.

TRY THE FRENCH REMEDY. Not a Dangerous Drug, but a wonderful Secret Invention. Never fails. Particulars free on receipt of stamped addressed envelope.—Apply, M.D., 217, Graham Road, London, N.E.

SEXUAL POWER

Positively and Permanently restored in 2 to 10 days, **effects in 24 hours;** almost immediate relief. No nauseating drugs, minerals, pills or poisons, but the **delicious MEXICAN CONFECTION,** composed of fruits, herbs and plants. The most **POWERFUL tonic known.** Restores the Vigor, Snap and Health of youth. Sealed book **free,** giving full particulars. Address SAN MATEO MED. CO., P.O. Box 481, St. Louis, Mo.

DON'T MARRY without consulting Dr. Anderson, Masonic Temple, P. 5. Chicago. He cures organic weakness by entirely new and scientific methods; state conditions and send for free book

$100 FORFEIT

If it does not cure the effects of Self-Abuse, Early Excesses, Emissions, Nervous Debility, Loss of Sexual Powers, Impotency, Varicocele, Pimples on the Face, etc. Enlargement Certain. I will send **FREE** the Recipe of a never failing cure. All letters in plain, sealed envelope. Address, with stamp, **C. K. TUPPAR,** Sportsmen's Goods, Marshall, Michigan.

NO NEED TO WEAR BLOOMERS

Use PETERSON'S BICYCLE SKIRT HOLDERS

Keeps the skirt from creeping and blowing up. Invisible and adjustable. Comfortable to wear. No need to detach from skirt when walking. For sale by cycle dealers or sent prepaid on receipt of 50 cents. **Agents Wanted.**

H. S. PETERSON & CO.
114 Clark St., Chicago, Ill.

PATENT CORSETS

SWANBILL CORSET, 14s. 6d.
French Corset, 31s. 6d.
Black Satin, 21s. and 31s. 6d.

ILLUSTRATED CATALOGUE POST FREE.

546, Oxford St., London, W.

ANTI-STIFF

To Strengthen the Muscles.

It has a particularly Warming, Comforting and Stimulating effect on all WEAK or STIFF Muscles; quick in action; clean and pleasant in use.

For Sale by Druggists and Dealers in Sporting Goods.

E. FOUGERA & CO., *Sole Agents,*
26-30 NORTH WILLIAM STREET, NEW YORK.

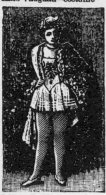

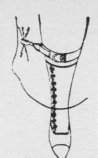

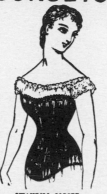

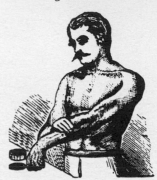

THE BATCHELOR'S FRIEND

YOUNG MEN! Whilst engrossed in monodextrous literature, have you endured **page-turner's torment?** Then do not delay in purchasing the hands-free **Bawdy Browsing Mechanism,** illustrated right, for it will surely be required when you peruse the scandalous displays in **THE LEAGUE OF EXTRAORDINARY GENTLEMEN VOLUME ONE,** available now in a soft edition for $14.95 U.S. dollars, $22.95 Canadian dollars, from **AMERICA'S BEST COMICS.**

LADIES secure a beautiful complexion by using the Bon-Ton Face Steamer, which removes tan, freckles, pimples and wrinkles. Any lady can steam her own face. Lady agents wanted in every city in the U. S. and Canada. Send $3 to the Bon-Ton Face Steamer Co., 2240 Glenwood Ave., Toledo, O., and we will send you prepaid, one Bon-Ton Steamer.

PAT: APPLED FOR.

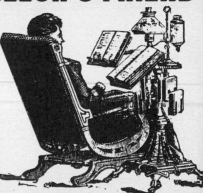

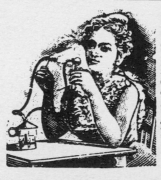

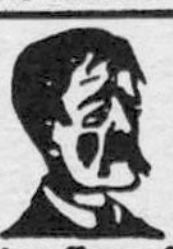

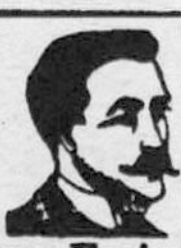

The New Traveller's
ALMANAC

H. M. STATIONERY OFFICE

British Library
DO NOT REMOVE

DISINFECTED BY INSP. No. 9123 NOBLE'S ISLAND

FANTIPPO EC 7 KOKO

KING KOR

EX LIBRIS
POISON

LAPUTA

ENTRY FORBIDDEN
SKULL ISLAND

Freeland

KLOPSTOKIA 124892 K

MANCHALOUR

ΞΙΡΟΣ

Ruritania
23.11.1930
ZENDA

FRAGRANT
Be in Love
Be Mysterious
• ISLAND •

LATE
WONDERLAND
LATE

PASSED BY
C*NS*R
NUMBER
1984
M

The New Traveller's

ALMANAC

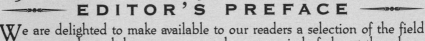

—▸◂— EDITOR'S PREFACE —▸◂—

We are delighted to make available to our readers a selection of the field reports and travel documents accrued over a period of almost three hundred years by those agents of British Intelligence whose activities are contained in a series of files and ledgers distinguished neither by name nor number, but merely by a solitary question-mark.

About the earliest such gathering of unique individuals in service to the Crown, little is known save that they were reputedly convened during the seventeenth century and were referred to unofficially as "Prospero's Men." Led, apparently, by a Duke of Milan with interests in the occult sciences, the other members of this first ensemble would seem to be shadowy and obscure personages with little evidence confirming their existence save for the material in these files. Two of the group were rumoured to be conjurings of sorcery rather than mortal beings, whilst a late addition to the company, the wide-eyed traveller called only "Christian," claimed that he had wandered into our world from some neighbouring etheric territory, to which he was, by various uncanny means, prevented from returning.

The existence and the implication of such other-worldly realms would come to be the source of an increased concern amongst the British secret service in the centuries that followed Christian's eventual disappearance, as the reader may discover in accounts below of expeditions to the marvellous archipelago known as The Blazing World, or of the fated and disastrous Bellman Expedition into the interior of a puzzling well or pit near Oxford in the 1870s.

The first team was disbanded in the 1690s, after Christian's disappearance. In the eighteenth century that followed there are documents and line engravings to suggest a second group was formed under the management of a seafaring surgeon and adventurer named Lemuel Gulliver. Other members of this new fraternity would seem to have eventually included a mild-mannered clergyman from Kent, a Mr. Bumppo from America, a married English couple called the Blakeneys and a Mistress Hill, who would appear to have been no more than a libertine.

The records of these earlier bands have been here edited together with those notes accumulated by Miss Wilhelmina Murray in the period from 1899 to 1912, when, as one of the two remaining members of the five-strong team assembled in the early months of 1898, she roamed the world extensively, adding considerably to the body of social, political and geographic information here contained. For the convenience of the reader we have here compiled the information found within the various documents into a single commentary that will proceed through various areas of the globe in turn, commencing with our British Isles, and, in our subsequent editions, moving on to deal with Europe, the Americas, Asia and Africa, and finally Earth's polar regions. We shall quote the diverse individuals who have contributed to these accounts in cases where we feel that this may be illuminating or appropriate. It is sincerely hoped the reader will enjoy the mental travels that these notes towards a new cartography allow, and be provided with fresh inspirations for forthcoming holidays and outings.   Most sincerely yours,   The Editors

Chapter One

The British Isles:
From The Streaming Kingdom to The Blazing World

The Streaming Kingdom, in the English Channel, while located closer to the coasts of France than those of England, is included here both as a south-most point from which we may commence our journey, and also due to an account penned in his ship's log by the notorious 18th century pirate, Captain Clegg. For reasons that remain unclear, this infamous and murderous buccaneer had seen fit to entrust the record of his voyages to a pious Kentish clergyman, the Reverend Dr. Syn, who was for reasons equally opaque affiliated to the group directed by Lemuel Gulliver. Clegg's log gives an account of a young pirate crewman drowned while off the coast of France, followed by a reported supernatural visitation:

"Woken at five bells by the mate, with great alarms. The fellow claimed that on his watch he'd seen our young friend lately drowned off Picardy, by some strange means returned to life, and changed so that he swam there in the water with new skin upon him, that would flicker with a hundred little lights of different colours, such as I have seen on cuttlefish and creatures of the like. From the mate's account, our greatly altered former shipmate spoke with him, and told him he was now a subject of The Streaming Kingdom, a domain of underwater gardens and fish-slaves maintained beneath our English Channel, ruled by a mighty regent whose name in our tongue was something not unlike 'His Royal Wetness,' or 'Imperial Liquidity,' or something foolish of that nature. Presuming this to be some manner of delirium or nutmeg-vision, had mate flogged before returning to my quarters."

Despite the captain's swiftly-reached assumption that his mate had seen this curiously-transformed aquatic human while in an intoxicated state, we note that there may be a confirmation of the mate's tale in accounts of the four-inch aquatic infants found within the submarine caves of St. Brendan's Isle off Ireland's western coast, concerning which more presently.

The South of England hides a wealth of curious and remarkable locations, both those of antiquity and of more recent times. Most famous are the ruins from the Arthurian period to be found in Cornwall, open to the general public and thus relatively widely known. Of less celebrity is the concealed cave in the cliffs just east of Helston, where it is believed that Arthur's mentor Merlin was incarcerated by his rival thaumaturge, the sorceress Nyneve. There are conflicting claims regarding the true nature of the cave: the French authorities claim to possess the mummified remains of Merlin, found inside an oak somewhere in Brittany, believed to be the prior location of Broceliande Forest. English experts on Arthurian period design have pointed to the cave's many peculiar features (the bronze door with its ivory and cedar bars, the perfectly round chamber with its grass-green marble floor, the carved rock-crystal bed that is the chamber's centrepiece), and have suggested that the cave is, rather than the tomb of Merlin, the retreat used by the famous lovers Tristan and Isolde when they were banished from the court of Cornwall by the jealous rage of Isolde's husband, Mark. If this is so, then possibly the relics found in Brittany are the remains of Merlin after all, unless the final resting place of the near-legendary magician lies in some other, as yet undiscovered, Cornish cavern.

From the ancient to the relatively modern, there are two experimental townships on or near England's south coast. Most well-known is Victoria, a small model community established in the 1840s at a cost of some four million pounds, not far from Bournemouth. Built conforming to a perfect square with sides each one mile long, the model town has broad and sweeping avenues designed to limit the secluded urban corners in which vice might thrive, Victoria having been conceived upon a stringent moral and religious basis with exclusion as the strictly enforced punishment for all infringements. For example, if marriage in Victoria should terminate with a divorce then both of the offending couple are immediately expelled, as is the minister who was presiding at their wedding and the congregation that were present at the same.

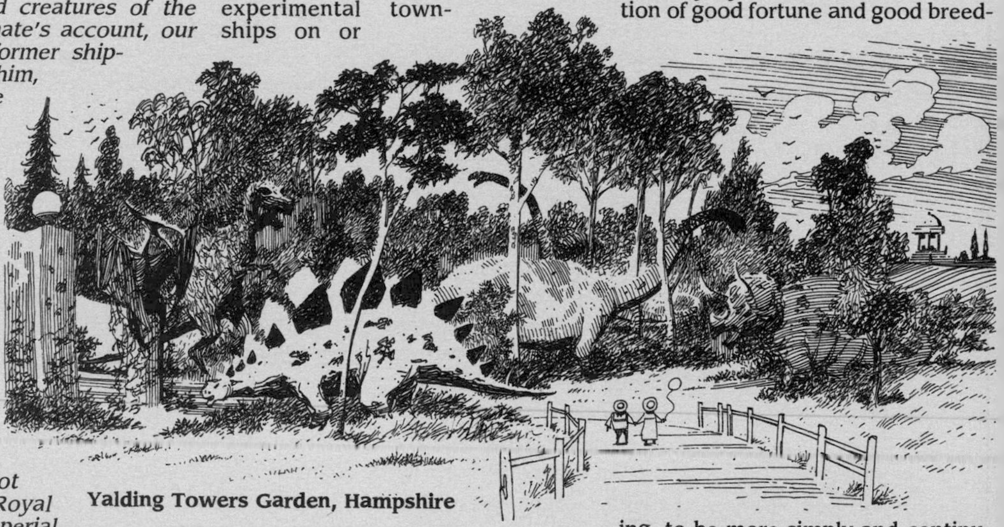

Yalding Towers Garden, Hampshire

While this may seem unduly strict to modern sensibilities, it may be useful to compare Victoria with the model town established further north as recently as 1899, in Avondale, not far from Warwick. The United Avondale Phalanstery, while founded on idealist and communal grounds for the improvement of humanity would, to this latter end, painlessly put to death all children born deformed or crippled in the province. Although officially these practices were halted by new laws imposed in late 1907, there is evidence that Avondale and other similar phalansteries continued culling less-than-satisfactory infants until 1912.

Much more accommodating and benevolent, if more difficult to find, is the delightful village known as Commutaria, established on the Portsmouth-Waterloo line just past Haslemere. Founded, allegedly, by a remote descendant of the aforementioned Cornish sorcerer Merlin, Commutaria has been described by various rail-passengers who've made unscheduled stops there as the very acme of conviviality. The village seems to have a micro-climate of its own, enjoying weather more predictable and pleasant than elsewhere in Britain. It is also said that life in Commutaria seems, presumably by some chance combination of good fortune and good breeding, to be more simply and continuously agreeable than life in other shires. Upon the breeze are constant scents of Sunday roasts or fresh-baked bread, and every hostelry rewards the seeker with whatever he or she desires: a roaring log fire, possibly, or an enthralling tome by Dornford-Yates one hasn't read yet. The only drawback to the place would seem to be its geographical uncertainty. As one wistful and disappointed former visitant has put it, "It isn't always there." This odd, elusive quality perhaps connects the village with more sinister evasive sites, like Abaton in Scotland, or even the mind-warping horrors of "Snark Island," both discussed below.

The South of England, obviously, is also famous for its many architectural curiosities and follies, its stately homes and legend-haunted cottages. From bleak, magnificent Baskerville Hall out in the wilds of Dartmoor, to Crotchet Castle there in the Thames Valley with its several dozen statues of the goddess Venus, every type of dwelling place is represented. At Yalding Towers, near Liddlesby in Hampshire, one may marvel at stone prehistoric animals concealed within the shrubbery, while at Ravenal's Tower outside Ivybridge in Kent is the perplexing tomb of Richard Ravenal (1720-1779), said to have been cursed so that he could be buried neither by earth nor sea. Ravenal's body thus resides in an octagonal room halfway up his tower. If one should choose to visit Ivybridge and Ravenal's resting place, then nearby Rochester will certainly reward a visit. On its outskirts stands an isolated cottage called "The White House," bordering a gravel pit where there have been reported sightings of a stalkeyed monster known to the locals as a Psammead, or sand-fairy.

Alternatively, travellers may gravitate to the more rural areas of Sussex. Wilhelmina Murray, in 1904, visited (for reasons best known to herself) an elderly bee-keeper who resided near the seaside cove of Fulworth. While in Sussex, it appears Miss Murray also made investigations that concerned folklore surrounding the "Wish House" at 14 Wadloes Road in Smalldene, where it was believed that spectral presences afforded opportunities for selfless folk to take upon themselves the sufferings of loved ones. Making her enquiries, Murray was referred to the Starkadder family farm, not far from Smalldene, where a Starkadder relative, Miss Ada Doom, was rumoured to have recently encountered some form of distressing apparition in a woodshed. We quote here from Wilhelmina's journal notes upon the subject:

"The farm was hideous, and its inhabitants quite clearly interbred or mad or both. I did my best to question Miss Doom and to ascertain if the phenomenon which she'd encountered in the shed could be related to the spectral footsteps evidently heard at Wadloes Road, but I could get no sense out of the woman, who in any case was wretchedly afflicted by the most impenetrable Sussex accent. All the cattle on the farm appeared to be diseased, and I am certain I saw cows with one or more legs simply fallen off. Made my excuses and departed with all haste. What all these dreadful rustic people need is someone sensible and well brought-up to come along and sort them out."

As we move northward up the

country, to the west the hills of Wales seem crammed with mysteries and marvels almost beyond counting. Many notable Arthurian-era sites are here, most splendid being the remarkable City of Legions in Glamorganshire, where parts of the city's two churches and its college of astronomy are still unusually intact, given their venerable age. One of the most peculiar Arthurian ruins to be found in Wales, at Archenfield, is Amr's Tomb, allegedly the resting place of Arthur's son, Amr, slain by the King for reasons no longer entirely clear. The most bewildering aspect to the tomb is in the mutability of its construction. In common with other peculiar struc-

Miss A. L., 1871

tures that we shall encounter elsewhere in the world (such as the so-called "Witch House" to be found on Pickman Street in Arkham, Massachusetts), the geometry and the dimensions of the tomb seem to be flexible, so that its length, when measured, has been known to vary between six and fifteen feet within a single twenty-four hour period. This varying of space and distance may have a connection with another Welsh phenomenon, the castle known as Yspaddaden Penkawr which appears to get further away the closer one approaches. Also worth a visit while in Archenfield is nearby Anchester, where one may shudder at the gloomy but imposing sight of Exham Priory, with its dismal history of ineffectual pest-control, as its dark bulk rears into view through the inevitable rain.

Travelling to the east coast out of Wales (perhaps taking a train from the small but friendly railway station found in Llaregyb, close to the River Dewi) one finds that there's comparatively little to remark upon in England's most easterly reaches save for the great national embarrassment, since its discovery in 1673 by Captain Robert Owemuch,

of the floating island Scoti Moria, alternatively known as Summer Island. Most usually located in the wide Thames-Isis gulf about a mile southeast of Clacton, Scoti Moria is noted only for its powers of mobility and for the shameful indolence and sloth displayed by its inhabitants. Referring to themselves as Naiads, these incorrigible wastrels have simply not bothered to discover agriculture or, indeed, any pursuit involving labour whatsoever. In its stead, their lives would seem entirely centred upon sprawling around smoking, interrupted only by frequent but unduly noisy games of ninepins.

It is in the middle of the country that we come across some of Great Britain's more enduring riddles. Not far from Bedegraine Forest lies the picturesque and world-famed English university town of Camford, which most recently achieved some notoriety due to the efforts of Professor Presbury who held the chair in the university's department of Comparative Anatomy, and was engaged in a much publicised attempt to manufacture a rejuvenating serum using biological materials obtained from monkeys. Also notable while passing through this charming town is Fergus Castle, raised on a small island in the River Cam. Allegedly, this was the site where Arthur's knight Sir Marhalt slew the giant Taulurd and the castle to this day remains a light and airy structure, unencumbered by the dour fortifications seen at other fortresses, these made unnecessary by the natural moat provided by the River Cam itself.

It is in nearby Oxford, though, that middle England's mysteries take on a darker hue. It was here, on the River Thames's banks somewhere between Godstow and Folly Bridge in 1865 that the presumed abduction of a little girl took place, plunging the Nation's newspapers into a morbid speculative frenzy and immersing Oxford in a pall of fearful gloom unrivalled till the much more frequent child abductions, rapes and murders of the twentieth century. The girl in question, sensitively known as "Miss A. L." to the contemporary press so as to spare the feelings of her relatives, had last been seen at play upon the riverbanks, where she was being minded by an elder sister. To her subsequent unending guilt and shame, the older girl drifted off to sleep, lulled by the warm and pleasant afternoon, awakening soon after to discover her young sister gone.

During the next four months, the riverbank and its surrounding area were searched with an increasing sense of hopelessness by the police and members of the public. Finally,

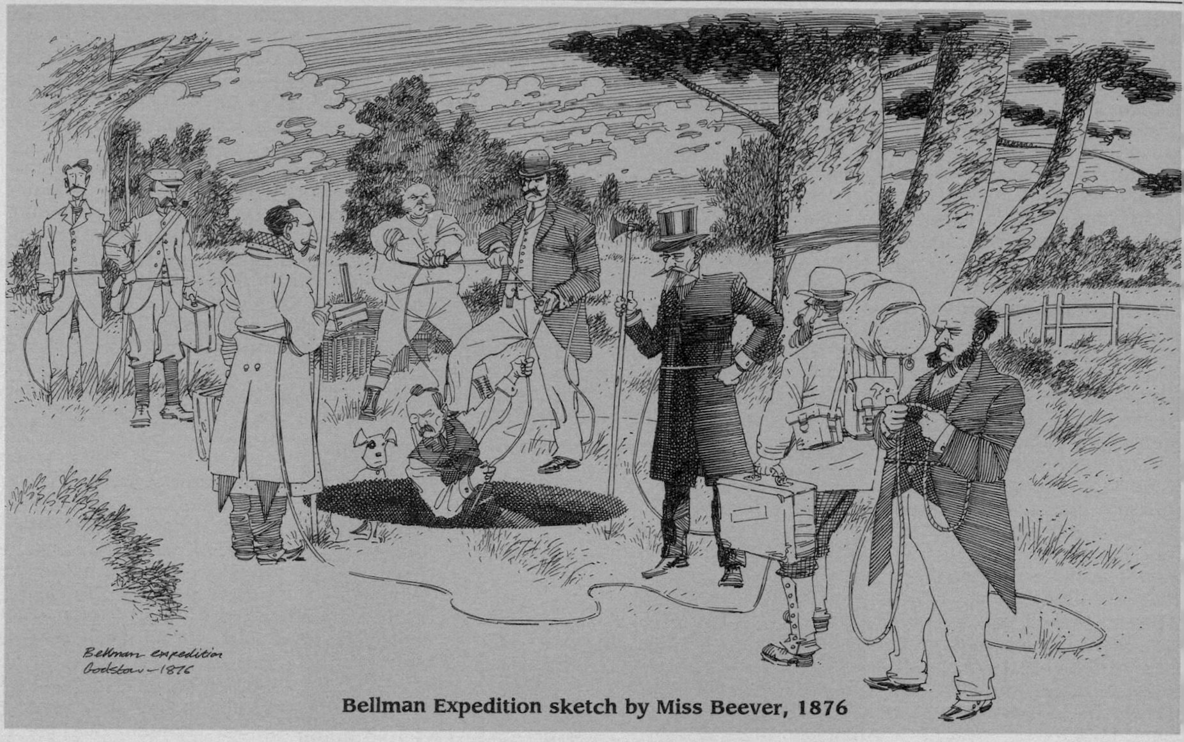
Bellman expedition
Godstow—1876

Bellman Expedition sketch by Miss Beever, 1876

in mid-October when the abductee's despairing family had begun funeral arrangements for their missing child, the girl was found alive, discovered soaking wet and barely conscious, suffering from exposure in the very meadow she had vanished from the previous summer. Questioned after her recovery, the girl recounted how she'd fallen down a puzzling "hole" that she'd found in the riverbank, only to find herself in a disorienting realm where many laws of physics, even laws of logic, were entirely different from those laws in our own world. Miss A. L. was most astonished to learn that some months had passed since she had vanished, having up until that point believed that her adventures had all taken place during a single timeless afternoon.

Although the child recovered, there were two less happily-concluded sequels to her exploits, the first taking place in 1871 when Miss A. L. was once more taken into the bewildering territory that she had discovered, this time during the occasion of a family visit to the Deanery of Christ Church College, Oxford. If we are to believe Miss A. L.'s account, the mirror set above the mantel in the Deanery began displaying properties not utterly dissimilar from those of the peculiar hole she'd stumbled into six years previous, allowing her to pass once more into the contra-rational underworld that she'd described. This time, although the time spent in the other world seemed to the child much longer in duration, little more than seven minutes had elapsed before she re-emerged from the strange portal flickering above the mantelpiece, which closed not long thereafter. However, in this instance there were complications. The child's hair-parting was now worn on the other side, and on examination it appeared that the positions of the organs in her body had been quite reversed. Apparently in consequence of this, Miss A. L. could no longer keep down or digest her normal food, and in late November of that year was weakened unto death by this disorder.

There was still, however, one more tragedy to come. In the five years that followed Miss A. L.'s demise, there was much shocked and disapproving talk in Oxford of the possibility that the original "hole" that claimed the luckless child might still be yawning open somewhere on the river's banks, waiting to waylay some other hapless infant. Finally, it was resolved by a committee of the town's professionals that this strange, fatal aperture should be located and explored, with the intention of then sealing it forever to protect the area's young. An Oxford clergyman named Dr. Eric Bellman led the group, accompanied by an assortment of locals including a banker, a lawyer, various shopkeepers (a butcher, and a lacemaker, Miss Beever, the expedition's only female member) and a shoeshine vendor who, while from the working classes, had some military experience and was thus considered useful to the team.

It was in April, 1876, that Bellman's group located the peculiar hole, perhaps a mile from Godstow, where the small girl had initially vanished from our world of rationality almost eleven years before. The "hole," described by Bellman in his notes and in the ink-and-pencil drawings of Miss Beever, was a *"darkly luminescent disk some five feet in diameter. It leads not down into the earth as one might readily suppose, but is a type of well-like space in which, much further down, it would seem various objects float suspended."* Bellman further notes that this bewildering aperture seemed to sometimes vanish for irregular periods of time, then reappear for stretches just as random and as unpredictable. On April 23rd, all roped together in the style of mountaineers, the party made their long-prepared descent into the chasm. Three hours after the commencement of the expedition, the strange portal vanished, leaving an unnaturally clean-cut end of rope that Bellman's group had fastened to a nearby cedar as an anchor. The explorers were not seen again for seven months, all save for one who was not seen again at all.

In October of that same year, most of Bellman's group were discovered semi-conscious, soaking wet and suffering from exposure in the same place that the missing child had been discovered, more than a decade before. All of them were hopelessly insane. One of them, more horribly, had suffered an incomprehensible metamorphosis, so that he seemed to be almost a photographic negative, relative to his previous appearance. His skin was now an eerie, unreflective black, while his formerly black hair and even the black fabric of his waistcoat had been turned a ghastly white. (Like Miss A. L., this individual could no longer digest our world's food, and died within a week of his return.) It seemed the group had kept a journal of their travels, but upon inspection this turned out to have been written in the form of cryptic nonsense poetry. Only infrequent references within this text suggest that the group had visited the same world as the twice-transported child, such as the mention of a form of local fauna called a "jub-jub" that is mentioned in both the accounts of Miss A. L. and Eric Bellman's hopelessly deranged adventurers.

The Oxford baker who'd accompanied the expedition was not with the group when they were found, nor was his body subsequently recovered. Reverend Bellman could not give a clear account of what had happened to the man, nor could his team's other surviving members. For some weeks there was hot debate as to whether the Reverend and his fellows should be tried for murder, but at last it was decided that their mental states made them unfit to plead and they were quietly incarcerated in a nearby mental institution. In 1901, Miss Wilhelmina Murray visited the institution, interviewing Eric Bellman who by then was the sole member of the expedition twenty-five years earlier that still remained alive, a frail man in his early eighties. Her recorded comments follow.

"Visited the Reverend Dr. Bellman at the hospital this evening. Most distressing. The poor man cannot complete a sentence without wandering off into disjointed wordplay or delirious flights of fancy. As I had been instructed by our chubby taskmaster, I questioned Bellman closely on his expedition to the place that his demented journal notes refer to as 'Snark Island.' It was useless. Asked how one might find this place, Bellman grew agitated and snatched up a page out of my notebook, claiming that it was a perfect map of how the island might be reached. The page in question, I should note, was yet unused and thus entirely blank.

"When I brought up the subject of the missing baker, Mr. Eric Bellman grew sombre and, it seemed to me, evasive. He would only say, 'The last word that he spoke was "boo."' I left the hospital a little under two hours later having managed to elicit no more information from this tragic, tortured individual. For reasons that are presently obscure to me, I kept the featureless blank 'map' that Bellman had torn from my notebook, and I find that I keep staring at it as I write these words. Why does it fill me with...unease? No. That is not the word. Dread. Why does this blank leaf fill me with dread?"

Marginalia and footnotes from the primary documents of which this compilation is comprised suggest that Military Intelligence Group Five placed great importance on the realm that Bellman's group and Miss A. L. had visited. One note suggests that there may be connections between this strange world and its bizarre inhabitants and certain tunnels found beneath an island in East Anglia, at Winton Pond. Other jottings, in a different hand, put forward the hypothesis that whatever exists beyond the Oxford hole is not some other-worldly plane, but is entirely a terrestrial phenomenon, perhaps a subterranean extension of

Coal City, Vril-ya Country or the Roman State, underworld kingdoms that we shall encounter further north.

Indeed, while there stands the occasional stately home with its surrounding legends (like Harthover Place in Yorkshire with its possible connection to the marine infant carcasses discovered at St. Brendan's Isle; or Nightmare Abbey on the edge of Lincolnshire, a place so cursed that its afflictions almost seem amusing), the majority of Northern England's sites of interest would seem to have a subterranean aspect. Alderly Edge, a windswept and remote location in the hills of Cheshire, is reputed to conceal the entrance to a massive cave containing scores of mediaeval knights in some state of suspended animation. Other underground inhabitants of a less reassuring nature are suggested by the yawning pit or bore-hole found amongst the ancient ruins of Diana's Grove in Staffordshire, not far from Mercy Farm and the nearby ancestral pile of Castra Regis, home to the illustrious Caswell family until the sad events of their annus horribilus in 1911, the details of which, widely reported at the time by the contemporary press, need no repeating here.

However, it is not until we come to Newcastle that the extent of the vast subterranean honeycomb that lies beneath our surface world becomes apparent. It was in Newcastle, in 1871, that an intended rescue mission into one of the proverbially coal-bearing area's many mines (exact location classified) stumbled upon a vast and otherworldly subterranean culture called the Vril-ya. Tall and winged, with red skin and black eyes, the Vril-ya are a socially enlightened race of great longevity. According to reports, they can heal wounds or cure an illness with the mere touch of their lips...quite literally "kissing it better"...and they have artificial servants, cleverly constructed from machinery, attending to their every whim. One puzzling margin-note appended to the documents relating to the Vril-ya is a comment on their language. In the Vril-ya tongue, words with the prefix Na denote all that is "bad" or antithetical to joy and wholesomeness. Thus "Nania" is a Vril-ya word denoting sin, or evil. This word is underlined in our source-documents, and a hand-written note refers the reader to an apple-tree currently being grown as a government project at Kew Gardens. Other than an obvious misspelling of the Vril-ya word as "Narnia?" scrawled in nearby, we have no clue as to the relevance, if any, of these cryptic jottings.

Bordering the lands of the Vril-ya (and thus also somewhere beneath the North of England), across one of their subterranean seas, there have been relics found pertaining to a settlement comprising a lost Roman legion and their numerous descendants. Of this so-called "Roman

State," little is known as of this writing, but it is suggested that it may be situated between the vast territories of the Vril-ya and the twilight structures of Coal City under Scotland, presently to be discussed.

Before we leave the North of England, though, and journey to the shores of Ireland, there is one location that we must take care not to exclude: up in Northumberland, upon the North Sea coast, stands Bamburgh Castle, a rectangular stone keep erected circa 1160 A.D. on the ruins of a pre-existing castle, a Dark Ages structure built around the year 500 A.D. From pieces of this earlier structure used when raising Bamburgh Castle during the great Norman castle-building era, we can deduce that it had, itself, been constructed utilising terracotta shards belonging to an earlier Roman-period domicile. This, then, was Joyeusegarde, the fortress raised directly after the Roman withdrawal from these shores in the fifth century, where Launcelot of Camelot lived in adultery with Arthur's wife Guinevere. After his King's death at Mordred's hands on Salisbury Plain, the guilt-plagued hero starved himself to death, requesting that his body be returned to Joyeusegarde, where it was placed in the sixth-century tomb erected on the grounds. Set thus apart from the main castle, it was spared the Norman renovations and still stands as of this present day, though in a state of grievous disrepair. Within our borrowed files are records of two separate visits to the tomb, and a comparison between the two may prove instructive.

The first was penned by Prospero, Duke of Milan, as his group worked their way up country on their expedition to The Blazing World in 1682. Calling at Joyeusegarde to see the tomb and pay respects to the Arthurian-era hero, the Duke records his great dismay at the dilapidation of the monument: "The ceiling gapes, collapsed, so that an oar of sunlight falls across this vault and stripes the carven form at rest on his sarcophagus. The elements and keepsake-hunters both have scoured its features with unkindness, so that little save a weathered granite knob remains to represent the nobel countenance, and many details of his armour and effects are likewise rendered indistinct. The dogs curled at his feet are mostly disappeared, with one a formless lump, the other nothing save a paw. Ah, ill-made knight, that thy unmaking should prove more ill yet, with all about thy funeral stones now tumbled into disrepair. The moss encroaches, and men's minds forget the eyes, the brow, his streaming beast-mane hair."

Compare this with the brief and clearly unimpressed account of Wilhelmina Murray when she visited the tomb in 1912: "All very nice, I must say. Launcelot is much as I imagined him, clean-cut and handsome, wearing mediaeval armour with three greyhounds sleeping at his feet. Other than that, it rained, we had another beastly row, and all in all I shall find our return to London an immense relief."

It's clear that in the intervening period between these two accounts, the tomb had been restored according to Romantic notions of the hero, rather than with a concern for authenticity. Thus it would seem that through misguided efforts to restore the past, the face of England's greatest champion has been all the more thoroughly lost to us, for all time.

Let us travel now to Ireland, before we progress to Scotland and parts north. It is in rural Ireland that we seem to find phenomena of a more whimsical, fantastic nature, such as Gort Na Cloca Mora, near Glyn Cagny, where a hollow tree apparently grants access to another subterranean kingdom, this one the abode of Leprechauns. In the nearby glen, Glyn Cagny, famed for two philosophers residing there in ancient times, there is a pool wherein dwell a peculiar breed of salmon said to be the most profound and learned creatures in all Ireland. Not far from the glen we find the hidden cave referred to locally as the domain of The Sleepers of Erinn, where Irish god-king Angus Og and his bride Caitlin are believed to now reside.

Also in rural Ireland, some way southeast of Glyn Cagny, we find the Lake of the Cauldron, named for the massive cauldron hauled from its depths by one of the giant race inhabiting that country in its prehistoric past. (Giant-era finds are much more rare in England, an exception being the peculiarly modern-seeming "Giant's Garden" that surrounds an outsized tower near Camford. Unbelievably, these ruins were not discovered until 1888. While their great scale marks them as having been a giant's habitat, historians are puzzled by the recent-seeming elements of the design which would appear to date the ruins from the fifteenth century, by which time giants were thought to have been long extinct.) The huge, corroded cauldron still stands on the lake's shore, and, it is alleged, still has the property of bringing back to life any dead man immersed within it. Strangely, persons in this way revived from death are also rendered mute and

thus unable to communicate concerning such experience as they may have of life beyond the grave.

Nearer to Dublin, we find Leixlip Castle, an enchanting site with numerous Grecian temples on its grounds. Despite its ease upon the eye, however, Leixlip nurses a dark history. Redmond Blaney was Leixlip's first baron-tenant, and it was his daughter Jane who seemingly fell foul of the strange castle's curse during the eighteenth century, when she disappeared at the conclusion of an idle stroll through Leixlip's terraced grounds. Jane Blaney is still seen, however, looking cold and famished, as an apparition sometimes glimpsed out of the corner of the eye by visitors when passing through the castle's kitchens.

In Dublin itself we find an unrelated case of haunting (besides that of the famous spectral seafood vendor, Miss Malone) that pertains to a demolished eighteenth century building in the centre of the city, once known as "The Red House" for the striking redness of the tiles that formed its roof. The building's owner, Mr. Harper, had his house demolished in the early 1860s when he grew disturbed by a peculiar disembodied hand that floated in the night outside his dwelling, seeking entrance. Though unverified, it is reported that the final straw came when the hand managed to invade a bedroom on the second floor, where Harper's wife is said to have been dreadfully mishandled by this floating, scrabbling horror.

As distressing as the apparition that disturbed the Harpers must have been, it pales beside the dark and lingering mysteries we encounter as we make our way through Ireland to its western reaches. On or near the western coast there stand two houses, each dissimilar to the other, linked only by the bewildering properties attributed to them. Forty miles east of Galway stands a house that presently belongs to a middle-aged gentleman, one Mr. Mathers. Local legends or tall tales suggest that Mathers' house may somehow form a gateway to a strangely different Ireland, where the laws of physics and of logic seem more similar to those reported in the realm that Miss A. L. and Eric Bellman vanished into, rather than to those in our own

world.

Even more alarming than the Mathers house are the unearthly ruins we discover on the windswept western coast of Ireland. These apparently once formed a house built on a wild crag jutting out above a chasm, where lived a half-mad recluse, alone save for his dog and for a silent, haunted-looking sister. Sodden, faded notebooks found amongst the ruins by travellers in the first decade of the twentieth century hint that the house was somehow situated on a borderland between our own world and another, but a world even more terrifying and apocalyptic than the realm to which the nearby Mathers house is said to provide entrance to.

Some way off Ireland's western coast we reach the island known as that of Saint Brendan the Blessed. An impressive sight, the island rears up from the North Atlantic on great pillars of black basalt streaked with serpentine or sandstone in a startling display of colours. While astonishing in its own right, the island is made more remarkable and worthy of attention by discoveries made in the 1860s of a strange form of marine life to be found within the massive caves beneath the isle. Explorers in the caves have been excited to discover the brine-pickled bodies of what seem to be some water-breathing form of tiny humanoid, all of the specimens thus far retrieved being four inches long or less, and in their colouring and appearance not at all unlike small human children that have been transformed to perfect miniatures by some fantastic method. Rumour, since the 1860s, links the island and its curious fauna with Harthover Place in Yorkshire, but the linkage, insufficiently investigated, still remains obscure.

Returning now to Scotland for the last stretch of our journey through the British Isles, we should first comment on Coal City, the remarkable underground world extending from the New Aberfoyle caverns, fifteen hundred feet beneath Earth's surface, sprawling under Stirling, Renfrew and Dumbarton and believed to link up with the cave-world of the Roman State a little to the south. Set up by miners in the middle of the nineteenth century, the architecture of the settlement has been justly described as "staggering," from its proud castellated entrance to its chapel of St. Giles that rears above Coal City's bordering subterranean loch. Heated and lit by electricity (used to provide Coal City with an artificial "day"), the miners' splendid commune has in recent years drawn as much revenue from tourists as it has from coal production. Would that all such sites of interest to be found in Scotland were as easy to locate. Whether we speak of Abaton, the moving town glimpsed somewhere on the

A peculiar breed of salmon, Glyn Cagny, Ireland

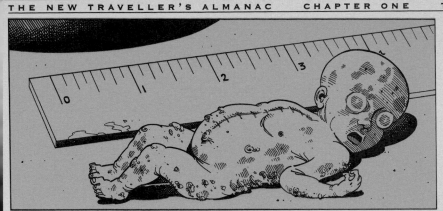

Tiny water-breathing humanoid form, reproduced by kind permission of The Lancet

road from Troon to Glasgow by Sir Thomas Bullfinch in the 1890s, or whether we refer to equally-elusive Brigadoon, a Highland village that seems to have disappeared from the maps on May 22nd, 1753, only to reappear for one day at a time at century-long intervals, we are forced to note the shifting and phantasmal nature that has come to typify the Scottish mystery-site.

True, there are places with a definite and fixed location, such as Airfowlness, on Scotland's western coast where what seem to be courts or parliaments of sea birds are held annually, or Coradine, the fascinating matriarchal settlement up to the north of Scotland so admired by Wilhelmina Murray on her visit there in 1899. Such places pale to insignificance, however, beside the more evasive settlements, such as the place known as The Glittering Plain, which also has a second, secret name, the speaking of which is forbidden, but which is, reputedly, "The Acre of the Undying." Hidden in a coastal Highland valley, entrance to the glen apparently transforms the traveller to an immortal, such as all who dwell within The Glittering Plain (see Wilhelmina Murray's journey to the City of Ayesha out in Africa during 1901), but thus transformed they may not ever leave the valley.

Oddly, there would seem to be connections that exist between The Glittering Plain and a remote isle to the North of Scotland, famous for its wreckers and its pirates, called the Isle of Ransom. The only building on the isle of any note, the Hall of Ravagers, contains a carven likeness that is said to be an image of The Glittering Plain's immortal king. During 1683, Prospero's group called briefly at the Isle of Ransom before passing further northward in their hired trawler on the fateful expedition to The Blazing World, which we must now address.

The Blazing World, psychically charted by the Duchess of Newcastle in the fateful year of 1666, is a great archipelago of islands stretching from the North Pole to the outskirts of the British Isles, linked by a great crystal stream bordered to either side by cities made of coral, marble, agate, amber or pale alabaster. The Duchess claimed these structures were inhabited by a variety of different races: bear-men, gruff and philosophical, or fox-men, sly and skilled in politics, along with ape-men, worm-men, lice-men, parrot-men and so on in a profusion that seemed near unending. When Prospero's band reached the archipelago in the harsh January of 1683, they found it had one property at least in common with the shifting and elusive kingdoms of the Scottish Highlands, in that it was not entirely there, in any ordinary sense. Prospero's notes convey the mounting apprehension of his crew as they sail out amongst these insubstantial islands in their rented ship.

"This place confounds my wits, if place it be and no mere sum of intimations, forms half-glimpsed and vistas plainer to Imagination's inner eye, as with the imps seen in a scrying-glass, than to the outer sight. Fantastic battlements of streaked and polished agate loom up vast and intricate upon the eye's peripheries, that turn to grey and endless waves of icy fog when gazed upon direct. Were it not for my conjurings, I should see nothing. Robert Owemuch, who we travel with, claims that he sees naught but the sea and our impending doom. He is anxious and deprived of sleep by the great bellowings of Caliban, who has retired below decks in a state of fearfulness and vows that he shall not emerge until we are brought once more to dry land. The sprite of air, of course, can see The Blazing World quite plainly as it darts excitedly ahead of our frail, wind-tossed craft, reporting to me all that it has viewed. Of all of us, the traveller Christian seems at once the least afraid and yet the most absorbed within himself. He stands and stares across the rail, whipped by the spray, as if he sees enchanted realms where I may not, though this be merest speculation since he speaks no word to me, or any man."

Christian, it will be remembered, had arrived in our world during the 1670s, claiming to come from a more perfect and, it seems, symbolic realm. According to the tireless journeyman's own words, he had been travelling from a city named Destruction when he came across a town founded upon material desires and worldly commerce that was called Vanity Fair. Becoming lost amongst its bawdy, brothel-haunted streets, Christian turned down an alleyway from which he stepped into the streets of London in the year of 1678, seemingly unable to return to his beloved shining country, and thus forced into a disagreeable alliance with the sorcerer Prospero, whose magic, diabolically inspired though it might have been, provided Christian's strongest chance of finding his way home. Whether this came to pass or not may be discovered in our final passage from the notes of Prospero, written upon the voyage's last day before the rented trawler turned once more for home.

"Christian has gone, and frightful mystery descends upon our storm-flung craft. It was at first light when I came upon him stood beside the rail and gazing out across the foam-crown'd breakers. When I asked if he did spy The Blazing World, he answered that he did, and though he knew not if it be a part of his misplaced, beloved country he did think that it may be in some means a companion to that glorious Land. Thus saying, he began to climb across the rail as if to fling himself into the towering waves, so that I sought to stay him, whereupon a fearful marvel did occur. Christian walked off from us, over the wave-tops, with his bundle-staff across his shoulder, seeming from his gait as if he strolled upon some level path and not the raging billows spread about him. Below decks, my brute sent up a monstrous howl of fear and anguish, and even my sprite seemed to dart nervously about the upper mast. Some way off from our craft, Christian turned back his head and waved before continuing away, at last to vanish in the dazzle from the waters, where the sun had broken through the fleece of cloud above, and since that time we have seen none of him. Good pilgrim, fare thee well upon thy bless'd and flint-strewn way, and think thee well alike on one thou once thought foe. Mayhap we'll meet again come that glad day when for thy realm I quit these fields of woe."

Prospero, long in mourning for his child Miranda, Queen of Naples, disappeared in 1695 as did his "brute" and "spirit of the air." It is not known whether this happened (as claimed by the Duke's sometime colleague, Captain Robert Owemuch) during a return trip to The Blazing World. Nor is it known if the magician managed, as had Christian, to step from this world into that weirdly immanent terrain, or if he vanished under the cruel fathoms of the Arctic Ocean, too far from The Streaming Kingdom to be born anew amongst its flooded, lantern-fish illuminated avenues.

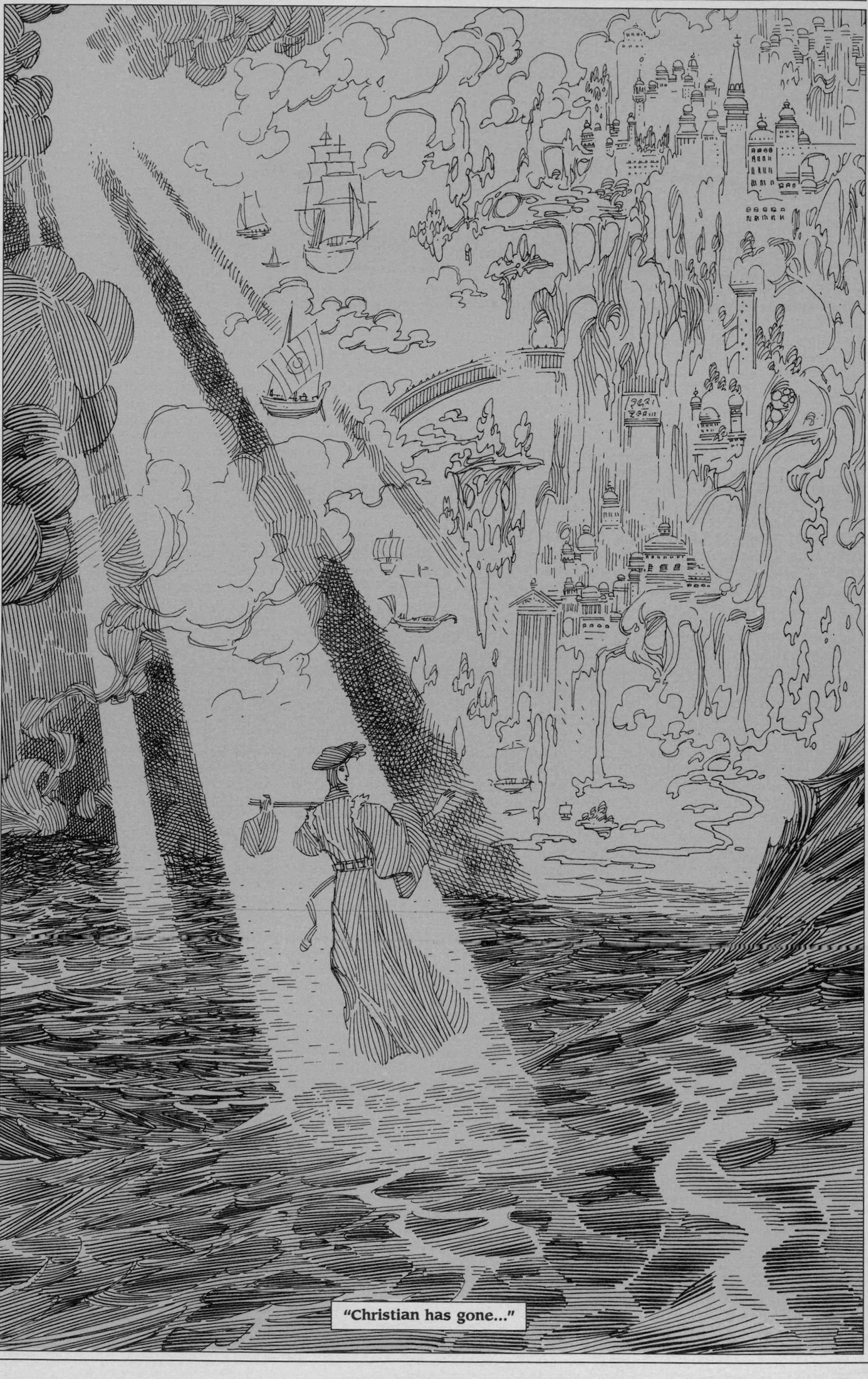
"Christian has gone..."

Chapter Two
Europe: From Aiolio to Zenda

The Imaginary Isle

In this installment of our guide for today's traveller, culled from the annals of our centuries-old league, we look at continental Europe, with its remote kingdoms, frequently unnerving customs, and its many sites of interest. Starting in the southwest, we refer to journal notes by Wilhelmina Murray, written on her travels undertaken at the 19th century's end. Africa-bound down the west coasts of Spain and Portugal, Miss Murray noted the variety of coastal islands passed en route.

"Tuesday. Landed in Philomela's kingdom, half a small island west of La Coruna on Spain's coast. King Philoponus gave this doleful kingdom to his daughter Philomela. When her funds ran out, she took to murdering and robbing guests, with some escaping to the nearby realm of Philoponus via a bridge protected by a stone colossus. This long-fallen statue's feet, on crumbling plinths of brick beside the bridge-mouth, are still visible. Crossing the bridge we visited the fort of Philoponus, where were lovely vases made from a peculiar soft glass, and also what remains of a perpetual motion engine, with its tiny dancing figures turned to shapeless lumps across the centuries. Predictably, its motion had turned out to be less than perpetual.

"Wednesday. We passed by the Capa Blanca Isles, where bullfighting occurs, a beastly sport which some animal-lover really should persuade them to abandon. Further south was Mayda, Island of the Seven Cities, just northeast of the Azores. The isle's seven cathedrals sounded fascinating; but we didn't call there, nor upon Nut Island, though we saw that island's fishermen, Nutanauts as they're called, in their nutshell canoes. These are remarkable, carved out of single shells up to fifteen feet long. I waved, but nobody waved back. East lay the coast of Coromandel, a small independent country on the edge of Portugal, where was raised the castle of a locally-famed nobleman, the Yonghi-Bonghi of Bo. I know one shouldn't laugh at foreigners and the preposterous names they give themselves, but, honestly, I ask you."

Various though the islands dotting Spain and Portugal's west coast appear to be, their strangeness pales beside that of the isles just east of Spain, in the Mediterranean. The Milanese magus Duke Prospero described these in his log while sailing for Gibraltar's straits in 1625.

"We found an Isle called Lanternland by some, where great Demosthenes burned midnight oil, and putting in to shore at my command upon its soil saw men to glowworms turned: each Lord and Lady dressed with glass and gem that caught the shine of wanton candleflame. Jewelled crest and diamond hem, blazing they pass, no two the same, their radiance near divine.

"Not far away an oracle is found; a bottle in a crypt upon an isle where did sweet Bacchus make a vineyard grow. The bottle speaketh with a cracking sound, and I did like its augurs not at all. We sailed south, past the Lotus-Eater's land of yellow sand and endless afternoon. A fellow there his care will soon forget in fragrant blooms, where hides worse slavery yet. Ogygia too we passed and left behind, where fair Calypso walked in violet meads, and so we came to find instead a place, a curious atoll by an island near. This ring-shaped land, that is called only 'Her,' surrounds a calm, clear pool, where fountains rise whose waters do not fall (which would disturb the silvered mirror still), but are instead upon the air there spread into a disc, twin of the lake below, each one reflected in the other's glass. Between them sits a lone white silent swan, that seldom moves but sometimes lifts its wings.

"The atoll's king, we were surprised to learn, a Cyclops is, one of that fearsome breed whereof Odysseus spake though sweeter far of disposition and inclined to treat the traveller with hospitality. His maids served us with sweets and the *pancire*, a native, justly-famed delicacy, while women danced provokingly, their skirts raised up like peacock tails thus to reveal their soft white under-things and curious shoes, strange Panic clogs, cleft at the sole and heel. The one-eyed regent wears about his head an iron contraption with two mirrors fixed before his eye, repelling natural light so that he can see nothing save that which be lighted by a purplish ray, its brightness of a colour that I may not name. Our host, he told us, to this kingdom came from the small island we had spied nearby which was, he said, the isle, the very same, where his ancestor and Odysseus met with such disastrous consequence and yet, we were assured, he harboured no ill will. Nevertheless, we made excuses soon, returning to our ship and sailing on, past the Imaginary Isle, so called, whereon are lovely forests and pearl-littered strands, soils rich with lapis lazuli and jade. Here singing mermaids live, white stags, pink deer, and unicorns, and other things beside. Men are forbidden, greyhounds rule as kings, and we passed on that could not there abide.

"Not far beyond we passed an isle as bleak as the Imaginary Isle seemed sweet and fair, a pois'nous land called the Great Garabagne where everywhere are monsters and despair. Next came we to Aiolio and saw its great bronze wall fired by the sunset's light, beyond where lived once the great King of Winds, Aiolos Hippotades who kept storms in oxskin sacks, and with his wife, six sons and his six daughters lived in luxury, also in incest, and impunity. We sailed on, through Gibraltar's yawning straits, with to our North the south-most tip of Spain where is the mountain Animas raised up near Soria, where once Knights Templar walked. On All Saints night, 'tis said, a great wild hunt is raised amongst the restless dead, who ride the mountainside, that wolves might howl for dread, and chase a spectral maid with scarf of blue.

"Beyond the straits verdant Anostus lay, with its twin rivers, Pleasure called, and Grief. The trees beside these streams two fruits provide, and should a man but eat of one then all desire will flee. Age will reverse and he will at last as a blissful infant crawl. Eat of the other fruit and, it appears, man's life is passed in misery and tears."

Compared to their surrounding islands, Spain and Portugal possess few sites of interest. Portugal has the republic of Andorra, confused often with the country of that name located in the Pyrenees. The Portuguese Andorra is a godly place that nonetheless displays violent antipathy to foreigners, especially to Jews. More interestingly, in Spain's La Mancha province, is the landbound island, Barataria, where twenty years before Prospero's voyage a squire named Sancho Panza ruled, albeit only for a week. Not far from Barataria we find a grotto, Montesinos' Cave, the sole account of which is that of Panza's master, Don Quixote, who Duke Prospero encountered in the early 1620s. The knight described the cave as having in it meadows where a crystal castle stood, enclosing the tomb of the hero Durandarte, enchanted by the sorcerer Merlin centuries before. As with many otherworldly kingdoms, Montesinos' Cave exists only sporadically, thus offering few opportunities for even the determined traveller, who should continue to the Pyrenees.

Within these mountains are a number of peculiar communities and ruins. Westward, hills enclose a desert valley where we find the willfully eccentric country Exopotomania, where the normal laws of physics obviously do not obtain. Sunrays are striped light and dark. A native yellow mollusc, if its shell is cracked, will leak a water droplet shaped like a transparent heart.

Further east is Andrographia, a bold social experiment in which each family is seen to be the state in microcosm. Nearby, perched on a rock above a precipice, we find the iron-clad castle of the 16th century sorcerer Atlante, thought to have been built by demons, with rusted walls that have a hellish glow if viewed by sunset.

Next comes a Pyrenean city that apparently cannot be named for reasons of what is puzzlingly described as "theological security." Its southern half contains a mansion, Triste-le-Roy, reached by committing murders at the three points of a mystic triangle, where travellers may learn the geometrically determined site of their own deaths. Continuing east, we pass the garrulous land of Auspasia to reach Bengodi, where presumably vast surpluses of produce have resulted in a mountain of grated parmesan cheese, the area smelling much like vomit as a consequence. However, there are also gemstones unique to Bengodi, including an invisibility-bestowing heliotrope used in the first experiments of Hawley Griffin.

Reaching the coast, close to the Balearic Islands is Trypheme, described by Marguerite Blakeney, visiting the country with her husband Percy and their fellow operative Miss Hill during the 18th century. "Trypheme is shameless, governed by but two decrees. Subjects must not disturb their neighbours, but may otherwise do anything that does not contravene rule one. Society thus governed seemingly allows for a content unspoiled by guilt, where citizens pursue, untroubled, their own pleasures. This thrills both Percy and dear Fanny,

which is quite exhausting. As is customary with the women here, Fanny and I wear only silver sandals and a kerchief, making Percy positively scarlet with embarrassment."

North, within French territory, is Papafiguiera, the inhabitants of which are famously obese. One governor was said to be so fat that, seated, his rear covered several square feet. Near Papafiguiera on the northern Costa Brava are a host of tiny islands, mentioned by Duke Prospero while headed for Gibraltar. These include Ptyx, Bran Isle and Clerkship, Laceland, Leaveheaven-alone and Breadlessday. Amorphous Island, made from viscous, protean coral and with trees like snail-horns, lies north, while Ruach, the "Windy Island" whose inhabitants were cured of flatulence by special wind from Aiolio, lies south. In between are Cyril Island (a self-propelled volcano that is currently the home of

Cyril
Island

Captain Kidd), the Fortunate Islands (which include the Isle of Butterflies, the wings of which are large enough to cut sails from), and Fragrant Island (where statues depict the deity between two nymphs, proclaiming his commandments, "Be in Love" and "Be Mysterious"), along with the pie-island Pastemolle, Thermometer Island where the inhabitants have various forms of non-human genitalia, and a stupefying plethora of others.

Let us now examine the French mainland. Southeast of Marseilles we find the flower-carpeted peninsula of Flora, murderously beset by witches during early 1830, though these were successfully repelled. North is Lubec, a town in south Provence founded by colonists from Thermometer Island, with all the genital peculiarities so common in that place. Thus, in Lubec, male genitalia are removable, stored in the Town Hall and hired out only for producing servants. North of Lubec stand two extraordinary castles: Trinquelage is a stone medieval fortress that is sometimes haunted by a great assembly of spectral nobles, while to the west is

Nameless Castle, where men speak a mix of truth and lies, and either sit but never stand or stand but never sit.

West of Provence are lands once belonging to the kingdom of Poictesme, guarded by the Fellows of the Silver Stallion. A like-named group exists in modern Nimes, built on Poictesme's ruins, but appears to be a lodge of local businessmen who have no notion of their order's antecedents. Further west, in what is now Auvergne, we have a medieval province that shared borders with Poictesme, known as Averoigne. Under these places there exists the subterranean Grande Euscarie, ruled by tool-using mammoths who took refuge there during the Ice Age, entering through caves in the Pyrenees. Some fossil centaurs have been found close to the underground land's outmost reaches, and it's thought that the cave-system might stretch to Fontainebleau near Paris, where the buried kingdoms of the Fatipuffs and Thinnifers are found.

Returning to the surface, close to Bergerac we find Baron Hugh's Castle, visited by envoys from the Devil in the 15th century. One of these, falling in love with a mortal, was with his betrothed turned to a statue. Though the statues are today eroded beyond recognition, visitors pressing their ears close to the statues' breasts will still report the audible beat of the lovers' hearts inside their mantles of worn stone.

West of the Dordogne in the Bay of Biscay is the modest and agrarian republic Calejava, founded by one Dr. Ava in the 1600s upon communitarian ideals, described by Mina Murray in her journal notes as "scrupulously fair; screamingly dull." Beneath the Bay of Biscay is the sunken city Belesbat, not far off from Saint Vincent, opulent till nearby villagers learned that this wealth was gained by murdering wayfarers and put the city's occupants to sword. Soon after, storms arose, submerging Belesbat, in which state it remains. In the late 19th century further sunken ruins were unearthed nearby, perhaps a separate sunken city (named by its discoverers as, simply, "Disappeared") or perhaps a mere suburb of Belesbat itself. Other theories link both sites with the Atlantean colony, Atlanteja, off the coast of Brittany, or hold that these locations are all outposts of the Streaming Kingdom as discussed in our first chapter.

Also off Brittany we find another group of islands that were passed through by Miss Murray on her way to Africa. "Near Brittany we passed above Le Douar, a strange, inverted, sunken island capsized in the 13th century, with mountains at the island's rim forming a seal that trapped an atmosphere beneath the upturned bowl. Le Douar's interior is still inhabited by people who've adapted to the sub-sea pressures, and sustain themselves on a unique variety of fungus. Also, they've tamed the power of Radium to light their otherwise dark ocean-bottom realm. Later, on our starboard bow we saw the Isle of Boredom, our captain's description of which I paid no attention to. Then, in the distance we saw Magic Maiden's Rock, where an enchantress born in Argos lured ships to their doom until a knight from Crete first won her heart then pushed her to her death, which sounds a rather rotten trick.

"Next day we passed Realism Island, where once stood a tower to honour God, with the world's animals, even the ugly ones, carved into its facade to represent the work of the divine Creator. Sadly, its designer suffered injuries to the head and could no longer recall why he'd built the thing, deciding that, in its appalling ugliness, it was a monument to Realism. Hence the island's name. We carried on past Cork (not Cork in Ireland, obviously) that Lucian described. The isle, now uninhabited, is made entirely out of cork, as were the feet of its unusual population, who as a result could walk on water, greatly aiding them with fishing and the like."

Nearby, on the mainland, are two former islands that have since attached themselves to the French coast. The first is Alca, where the native penguins were transformed to humans by the Angel Gabriel, though this legend may satirically refer to the plump, pear-shaped bodies of the island's close-bred population, or to their distinctive waddling gait. Near Alca is the former Isle of Asbefore, once part of an archipelago, with its fellow islands (Farapart, Jumptoit, Incognito) now seemingly sunken; Asbefore has known only one incident of interest, this being a successfully repelled invasion by a group of turkey hunters from the town of Bang-Bang-Turkey, which is close to Brest in Brittany. Also near Brest we find the mouth of the Atlantic tunnel linking Brittany with New York. Commenced quite recently in 1924, destroyed by sabotage in 1927, the tunnel will best be remembered for the chance discovery of Atlanteja, as discussed above, uncovered during the folly's construction.

Further inland is Broceliande forest where the oak believed by French historians to be the final resting place of Merlin is located. A hole in the trunk allows a glimpse into the dark interior where there indeed appears to be a pile of human bones. Next we reach Banoic, north of Rennes in what was western Gaul, ruled by King Ban, father of Launcelot. During the 18th century this area was subsumed in the Hurlubierean Empire, which collapsed in 1837 after the resumption of religious wars waged on an argument over the colour of the egg from

which the Divine Bat was hatched. Nothing today remains of the great glory that was once Hurlubiere. Just southeast of Banoic is the River Loire. On its north bank, not far from Blois, is the proposed site of the city Morphiopolis, whose people will exist in ageless slumber during which their vital processes will be suspended. Doctor Morpho, who invented during 1920 the vitality-suspension drug that, it's alleged, will make this possible, is also the proponent of this strange time-capsule city scheme.

Upon the south bank of the Loire is the eight-sided Abbey of Theleme, where the motto is "Do as you will" and where permission to grow rich and happy has replaced oaths of obedience, poverty and chastity. The Abbey was founded in 1534 by the giant Gargantua, who, amongst other things, provided Paris with its name during the 16th century, when he discharged the contents of his massive bladder. The luckless citizens were washed away or drowned by a great flood of urine that poured steaming from the much-relieved colossus, who, when he viewed the destruction his emission had provoked, could not contain his mirth. At this, those who'd survived the deluge angrily cried "Look! He's drowned us *par ris* (for a laugh)," with the unlucky city known as Paris ever after.

The museums of Paris contain many relics from much earlier times such as the Amran period, when France was Aquilonia and was ruled briefly by a Swedish warrior-king named Amra, though some suggest this was a nickname meaning "lion" or "lionheart." Relics also exist from earlier pre-Bronze-Age periods, dominated by the cruel Melnibonean empire, these remains including the corroded hilt of a black sword embossed with runes, perhaps Earth's earliest known written language.

Modern Paris also has its charms. Like most French cities, Paris has its own "Parthenion Town," bordello districts with permitted, regulated prostitution. This scheme, first adopted in the 18th century, has not been free of criticism but is agreed, even by Suffragettes like Wilhelmina Murray, to be far preferable to the alternative. Less graspable is Neverreachhereland, an achingly lovely landscape possibly connected with the metaphysical domains encountered in our own United Kingdom, that can't be visited but only fleetingly perceived in certain objects, such as infants' paintings, or one's own name in a childish hand carved on an ancient desk.

Beneath the city's Opera House exist the caves where in 1881 the deranged and hideous "Phantom" carried out his crimes. In 1913, Mina Murray and her second extraordinary league fought their French counterparts Les Hommes Mysterieux here, these being aeronaut Jean Robur, the frightening night-sighted Nyctalope and several others. Murray calls the cave "a dismal place, that echoed still with grief and rage. I thought the Nyctalope would kill me there, just prior to A.J. shooting him, and can't imagine a more dreadful place to die." Through sewers under Paris (notable for their disputed "Jean Valjean" graffiti) we travel from the Paris Opera to the Graveyard of Unwritten Books, in chambers under the Hotel de Sens, where are those manuscripts that either were suppressed, unfinished, or else never started. Passageways connect these silent galleries with the underground region of the Fattipuffs and Thinnifers beneath Fontainebleau forest, lit by floating neon-filled balloons.

Back on the surface, just outside of Paris lies Lofoten Cemetery, with its crows grown fat on human flesh and its reported spectres. Nearby there is Montmorency, where the scientist Martial Canterel maintains his villa, Locus Solus, with its many

Les Hommes
Mysterieux

wonderful inventions. Visitors must see the rain-prediction apparatus in the villa's gardens, and a huge flying beetle hung beneath, made from extracted human teeth.

Also near Paris is the city Fluorescente, built on avant-garde philosophies. Fruit is piled at every intersection, invisible dogs roam the streets, and nocturnal sounds are muffled by thin rubber sheets. Explaining Fluorescente, townsfolk usually quote the local motto: "Fluorescente is where a street singer puts darkness to a test of silence spread like a pool of red wine." Fluorescente borders Vincennes, east of Paris, under which is yet another subterranean site, this being the notorious Suicide City. This dismal refuge of the world's failed suicides was found during 1912 Police investigations of an underground rail line between Bastille and Vincennes, and was allegedly founded by survivors of London's notorious Suicide Club, disbanded 1882.

Moving from Paris to the coast we come to Etretat and Hollow Needle, cave-lair of Arsene Lupin. Amongst Les Hommes Mysterieux, encountered in 1913 by Mina Murray's reformed team, it is not certain if Lupin survived that episode. As with his rival Fantomas, remains were never found and both the master-thief and arch-fiend may have managed to escape. Further north is Quiquendone, on the Escaut in Flanders, where in 1870 a deranged engineer named Dr. Ox turned townsfolk into violent beasts with side effects from gas-lighting experiments. Dr. Ox, believed dead, was in fact admitted to a nearby township, Expiation City, built for purposes of ethical atonement and said to have aided the rehabilitation of various master villains.

Along the Belgian border are the forests of Ardennes, with their enchanted castles, four of which reared proud above the trees until 1913. North, the castle of the murderer Bluebeard stood, while further south was the retreat of the deformed French noble called "The Beast." Eastwards lie two demolished fortresses, one home to an inbred Royal family cursed by cataleptic fits, with lovely Princess Rosamund as the most famous sufferer. The other fort, Carabas Castle, had been previously called Ogre Castle until the ogre was provoked into transforming to a mouse and promptly eaten by a talking feline

dressed in striking footwear. Near these ruins stands a broken fountain, picked clean of the gold and alabaster once adorning it, alleged to have been made by Merlin for the great knight Tristan. Called the Fountain of Love, with a nearby dried-up stream known as the River of Love, both sites were destroyed along with the four castles by the shellfire of the Great War.

Moving on to Greece, in the Aegean we find more peculiar islands. Xiros, furthest east, is a notoriously haunting land, its shape indelibly imprinted on the mind of

**Example of
the extinct Siren Bird**

even distant viewers, who cannot forget the island's talcum sands or crystal waters. A mysterious phenomenon called zahir is believed to manifest here, having various forms, including tigers, astrolabes, and Argentinean coins, none of which once seen can be forgotten, even in one's sleep. Westward, Devil's Island was ruled by the giant Bandaguido, with his daughter Bandaguida and their child, until the dynasty was overthrown in the 3rd century AD. Nearby is Abdera, famous for its devotion to the horse, despite the horse revolt in the 5th century BC, when Abdera's well-educated horses overthrew the city's government, butchering men and mules and scandalizing women until Hercules himself quelled the revolt. Lemuel Gulliver's margin-

notes conjecture that the banished intellectual horses of Abdera may have sired the Houyhnhnms, talking horses the much-travelled Gulliver had previously encountered.

On the east coast of Greece itself we find the ruins of the morbid city Ptolemais, bordered by the Charonian Canal, while over Phlegra are the floating remnants of the avian citadel Cloudcuckooland, founded by Pesithetaerus in 400 BC. Today a sorry, decomposing spectacle, Cloudcuckooland has sailed too high for birds to still inhabit, and cannot be seen without recourse to a strong telescopic lens. Westwards are still more islands. Aiaia, Circe's island, is amongst the most well-known, along with Scylla and Charybdis (now without their monstrous dwellers) and the Wandering Rocks, a group of now-unmoving islands that were said once to have clashed together, as remarked on by the Captains Ulysses and Jason. Also popular is Siren Island, where are sold stuffed examples of the extinct Siren bird with its eerie approximation of a woman's face, developed over centuries to aid this flightless giant avian in attracting human prey. Not far off, the volcanic isle Pyrallis is the sole habitat outside Crete for dragonfly-winged reptiles called pyrotocones, which feed on flame.

Below Mediterranean waters we find the Arabian Tunnel leading to the Red Sea, its existence proved by Nemo, Sikh submariner, who released marked fish in the Gulf of Suez, these fish later turning up near Syria. The tunnel's length comes close to intersecting with another shaft, this being the Arcadian Tunnel linking Greece with Italy, once said to be the haunt of satyrs and reserved for bitterly unhappy lovers. On the Italian mainland at the tunnel's far end, we're near the Straits of Otranto and the castle of the same name, empty since the 18th century, when it was plagued by apparitions, which included a giant helmet covered with black plumage. Further north is Portiuncula, where people seek some quality or thing lost in their past, while under Italy we find Meloria Canal, employed in 1300 by privateer Luigi Gottardi of Genoa, using African slave labour, to facilitate an invasion of Venice. Across Italy rotted webs of string are found, complex and covering several acres, remnants of the mobile town Ersilia, whose populace connect their homes with different-coloured threads to mark the various relationships of the inhabitants. When this net hinders everyday affairs the town moves on, established elsewhere, leaving only decomposing lace to mark the fragile human bonds that once existed there.

In Torelore on Italy's west coast, men customarily entered confinement while their pregnant women were conscripted in the Torelorean army, with the country over-run during the 14th century as a result. Islands nearby include the one where Prospero, his daughter and his spirits dwelled in 1600.The wizard's hermitage still stands although its library of rare occult books has gone. Ennasin Island, close to Sicily, has red-painted people whose distinctive noses look exactly like the ace of clubs, while nearby lie the industrious Island of the Busy Bees and the Island of the Day Before, its waters swarming with Beelzebub fish and two-headed eels.

Back on the mainland, in the Apennines we find the ruined Abbey of the Rose, burned down in 1327, and the ill-famed Castle of Udolpho, with its dark history. Should these grim sites depress the traveller, they should seek amusement in the hilltop town of Pocapaglia, so steeply situated that its poultry wear small hammocks underneath their tails, preventing eggs from rolling off downhill. With spirits lifted, they may then pass on to Switzerland, and prosperous Goldenthal, famed for its honey. Once a slum known only for its poverty and low-life, the village was transformed by moral reform to a rich (and smug) communitarian Utopia. In the Swiss Alps exists the snow-swept realm of King Astralgus and his alpine spirits, famed for rescuing lost travellers, while south upon the Austrian border is the Balbrigian and Bouloulabassian United Republic, kingdoms united when former scullery-boy King Gauwain poisoned the water-cistern and the entire population of Balbrigia.

Moving from Austria into Bavaria we find perhaps the smallest and most socially retarded country in the world, the Duchy of Grand Fenwick, founded in the 17th century by Sir Roger Fenwick, his insufferable Englishness preserved in both the Duchy's language and its customs. European commentators, while surprised by Grand Fenwick's continuing survival, feel the Duchy will hang on as long as it doesn't do anything ridiculous such as declaring war on the United States. Grand Fenwick should not be confused with the nearby Grand Duchy, famous for its feline prodigy, Murr Cat (a relative of the boot-wearing cat who ruled Carabas Castle in Ardennes). The local sport is mimicry, so skilled that in the 18th century a dwarf named Zaches passed himself off as a Minister called Zinnober. Zaches came from the

alpine village Weng, a bleak place that can drive the unprepared insane. The dwarfish populace of Weng advise drinking and whoring as the remedy for this dementia.

More pleasant are the sites in west Bavaria visited by the Blakeneys and Miss Hill during the 1790s, as described by Marguerite Blakeney in her journal. "West of Munich lies delightful woodland where our coachman said a place known as 'The Wood Between the Worlds' was sometimes found if one possessed a certain ring made out of yellow dust. Nearby stood Runenberg, a mountain where lone travellers report encounters with a nearly-naked woman who gives them a precious casket which is gone when they awaken. Percy speculated that this woman might originate from our eventual destination, Horselburg, where we arrived shortly thereafter. Set down in the ornamental gardens at the base of Venusberg (as it's more generally known) we finally located in amongst the phallic topiaries an exquisite alabaster archway decorated with erotic figures, leading to a tunnel of enormous moths with wings as rich as oriental rugs. Finally we emerged into the kingdom underneath the hill ruled by Queen Venus (named, presumably, after the Goddess), who welcomed us most pleasantly. The things we saw in those next days! In our palace boudoir were depictions by a rogue named Dorat of a Marquis, his young mistress and her poodle that were simply filthy, however much Fanny admired them. I much preferred to witness how Queen Venus makes her unicorn Adolphe sing each morning, after which we shared her customary royal breakfast. Delicately flavoured, something like an almond custard, it apparently works wonders for the skin."

Just west of Venusberg on the Swiss border, we find the remarkable city of holes, Cittabella, and the nearby Nexdorea, where debutantes are reared to become Queens. Descriptive catalogues are circulated in nearby bachelor kingdoms, and Nexdorea subsequently provides Queens for most of Europe's small, obscure kingdoms and principalities. Northwest lies the deserted Palace of Prince Prospero, no relative to our Duke of Milan, with its seven different-coloured chambers, that was devastated by an outbreak of the Red Death in the 16th century. Continuing northwest we pass the troubling police-state of Meccania upon the Franco-German border and come to Micromona, where Marguerite Blakeney's narrative resumes.

"Males being barred from Micromona, Percy left us at the border and went on to nearby Silling Castle (owned by some nobles saved by Percy from the guillotine), where we would join him later. This was some weeks, so blissful was my time with Fanny there in Micromona, where girls are queens while boys

are slaves. The Micromonan ladies all believe that they are angels and refuse contamination by the male sex. Thus their friendships are with other women, and we did not want for sweet attentions. Offspring are reportedly produced by shaking branches on a tree 'that grew in Paradise,' but actually by a method of insemination such as farmers use with animals, this accomplished in a scented grove of saplings, with the shaking of the trees depending on the vigour of its application. The sight is truly heavenly.

"At last we bade farewell to Micromona, heading on to Silling. Percy, looking shaken, bags already packed, met us outside and told us we should journey on immediately rather than suffer the vile hospitalities within, cruel sexual games played by aristocrats over the 120 days between November 1st and February 28th. Sickened, he had regretted having saved his hosts from execution, and suggested we should head on to Cockaigne, sometimes known as Cuccagna. This was rather a mixed blessing. Idleness is thought a virtue, so we could stay in bed. However, since foods grow like flowers there, with homes made from confections, Fanny and I had trouble keeping trim, and thought we'd soon be ordering underthings from Papafiguiera. On our last day we visited a builders that exported houses made of food (cottages of gingerbread and such) to other parts of Germany. Terribly interesting."

Also in Germany is Mummelsee, a supernatural lake providing entrance to the subterranean realm of Centrum Terrae, miles beneath the surface. Or perhaps a trip to Nuremberg might be in order. Here, in Presidential antechambers, is a curious wardrobe granting access to the otherworldly "Kingdom of the Dolls." It was from this strange realm, or areas adjacent, that an apple pip was taken and used to grow the privately-kept tree within Kew Gardens mentioned in our last installment. Whether this tree will provide wood for a similar wardrobe is as yet uncertain.

In the Rhine Valley past Cologne, we find the subterranean haunt of vagrants known as Under River, and, nearby, a ruined mansion called the Black House, both locations famous only in the psychiatric history of a violet-eyed young derelict who turned up in 1907, out of nowhere. Alienists were fascinated by the detail of the man's delusions, which concerned a sprawling castle to which he was heir, its architecture and its rituals described so vividly that many still believe his "Castle Gormenghast" exists, although no trace was ever found. Northward lies Auenthal, home of author Maria Wuz, who wrote books with titles taken from more famous works, next suing those who'd written the originals for plagiarism. Pierre Menard, second to chronicle the history of Don Quixote, was influenced by Wuz, with Wuz's

Ruins of the Snow
Queen's Castle

Canterbury Tales amongst his favourites. Still further north is Berlin, near the Falun Fault, with hellish open-pit mines half a mile long that were until 1819 thought to be the entrance to a hidden kingdom. Travellers reported petrified monstrosities, visions of heaven, and metallic plants grown from transparent earth. However, in 1905, exhaustive tests revealed this paradise was caused by noxious gasses in the pit's depths.

Continuing northwest we pass the hollow willow leading to the underground realm of the Regentrude, a woman with the wearying responsibility of managing the rain. Next we reach Hamburg and the quarter called Sainte Beregonne, only accessible via a thin alleyway between two businesses on Mohlenstrasse. The timeless nature of Sainte Beregonne and its air of abandonment originate in a dimension called the Great Beyond, believed to own the quarter. Further east is Auersperg Castle, gothic home of the notorious 19th-century black magician Axel Auersperg, while off the Baltic coast are the Ear Islands, where live the Auriti, simple fishermen whose ears are large enough to cover their whole bodies, and sharp enough to hear fish shoaling far below the waves. Westward in Belgium, in a valley outside Brussels, are colonies collectively referred to as Harmonia, communitarian environments where all repression is forbidden, making the retreat a favourite of the Blakeneys and Miss Hill. Marguerite Blakeney's journal states, "Harmonia is the most tolerant place, although I wish the local children were not quite so unrestrained. In regiments known as 'Small Orders' they dress as hussars and ride about making a frightful row with bells and cymbals." On the

Dutch border is the independent land of Gynographia, where men dominate women and which Percy Blakeney described as "not as much fun as I'd hoped." Nearby in Holland is the sleepy hamlet of Vondervotteimittis, whose carpenters carve only clocks or cabbages. The area's one incident of interest occurred during 1845, when a mysterious stranger caused the village clock to strike thirteen, precipitating an uproarious sequence of events during which furniture became ambulatory while pets and livestock ran amok in the streets.

Just off the coast of Holland is the island Laiquihire, reportedly the home of unseen deities, but we must travel northward past the Mer-King's underwater realm near Denmark to the marvels found in Scandinavia and beyond. In northeast Greenland stand the hills known as the Devil's Teeth, reachable by a natural basalt bridge. Tunnels lead to a carved mammoth, beyond which lay Erikraudebyg, a Viking colony founded in the 10th century by Erik the Red, famed for anachronistic fauna such as a two-horned rhinoceros believed to have been extinct since the Pliocene. Leaving Greenland behind we come to Iceland and its neighbouring islands, which include Estotiland whose folk are skilled in every science save that of navigation, and Drogio, further south, where ritual cannibalism is still practiced in the confines of exquisitely jewelled temples. On the Icelandic mainland we discover the extinct volcano Hekla, with a chasm at its foot where ghosts of drowned men will traditionally appear upon their day of drowning. Other strange nearby phenomena include a form of fire that fails to ignite tinder, and a form of water that will burn like wood,

such stories circulated since the 16th century. Westward lies the extinct volcano Snaefells Jokull, which in 1863 was used by Hamburg's famed Professor Lidenbrock to enter the vast realm discovered by the 16th-century Icelandic scholar, Arne Saknussemm. Some of this underground land lies beneath the north of Scotland, and may be connected with Coal City, Roman State and Vril-ya country, mentioned in our previous installment.

East lies the Norwegian coast and Daland's Village, the only known port where the famous Flying Dutchman was allowed to land, one day each seven years. Nearby, in mountains outside Bergen, a crevasse leads to another tangle of sub-surface realms, such as Nazar, discovered by Norwegian traveller Nicholas Klim during the 1730s. He reported regions ruled by women, educated apes, or walking trees and even places where the populace were half musical instrument. Nazar has links with caves in central Norway's Dovre Fjell mountains, where trolls have been seen as recently as the late 19th century. Westwards, beneath the ocean between the United States and Norway, is the undersea realm Capillaria, inhabited by lovely women with translucent skin, known as Oihas. As with submarine worlds mentioned earlier, Capillaria may be an outpost of the Streaming Kingdom, far beneath the English Channel.

Passing on through Sweden, formerly Cimmeria, we reach northern Finland, where we find the stunning ruins of the Snow Queen's Castle, immense ice-halls looming empty and severe beneath the Northern Lights. Southwards, at Finland's tip, are friendlier places such as

Moominvalley, Daddy Jones' Kingdom and the Lonely Island, all inhabited by an unusually pacifistic breed of troll, perhaps a breakaway strain from the trolls of Dovre Fjell, retaining none of its Norwegian cousin's more alarming attributes. On Lonely Island there exists a breed of small and tube-like animal known as the Hattifattener, which, while mute and enigmatic, is reported to be very nourishing when boiled, much like a larger form of macaroni noodle. From the north we move to the last leg of our unusual European odyssey, being the dark lands of eastern Europe, visited by Wilhelmina Murray and a youthful male friend during 1912. Miss Murray and her paramour travelled by coach from Poland to the Balkans, though apparently in an extreme state of anxiety that caused her journal entries to be somewhat incomplete and hurried.

"We passed Klopstokia, a remarkable small country full of athletes on the eastern Polish border, and then circumnavigated hurriedly the tiny and yet somehow monstrous kingdom seized by the horrendous King Ubu the First in 1896. Just west of this we saw the distant outline of Klepsydra Sanatorium, where Dr. Gotard's time-reversal theories recently made news. A. thought that we should visit this to check for correspondences with the rejuvenating fountain in Ayesha's kingdom, but the sooner we are past this doleful countryside the better I shall feel. Our carriage took us through the City of the Happy Prince, where I had thought to find some cheer, but could have scarcely been more wrong. It is a run-down place with a neglected Jewish quarter, its sole monument an empty plinth in the town square where formerly there stood the statue of the Happy Prince himself. Its gems and gilt picked from it by a bird in the late 19th century, it looked so wretched that the City councillors had it removed. Apparently they have, as yet, found nothing more uplifting that might take its place.

"We crossed Czechoslovakia's border not long after midnight on our trip's third day. From Strelsau, capital of Ruritania (a kingdom seventy miles east of Dresden) we were sent west to the Ruritanian country town of Zenda, with its famous castle, where we found a coach-inn for the night. A. wanted to have marital relations, but I'm far too nervous about our eventual destination to relax and told him so, which led to moody silences the following morning heading south to Lutha, a small landlocked country nestling between the borderlines of Austria, Czechoslovakia and Hungary. Along the way we passed a frightening edifice known only as 'The Castle,' then through a nearby valley where there's said to be a penal settlement, although we didn't see it. Soon the valley led into Wolf's Glen, where local legend states that sportsmen may buy seven magic bullets, the

cost being naught but their immortal soul. Lutha, when we reached it, seemed a pleasant place, but there are local rumours that concern Prince Peter, Lutha's regent, who apparently declared the country's rightful royal heir Prince Leopold to be insane, incarcerating him within Blentz fortress, which we saw, and which looked absolutely horrid.

"From Lutha we drove west to Flavna on Czechoslovakia's eastern border, where I should have liked to visit the still-standing Tower of Suleiman. However, prior to reaching Flavna, the road bent due South, taking us through the independent countries of Sylvania and Freedonia and into northern Hungary. Dear

Lord, this appalling place. It all comes back to me with such tremendous force. I only hope that I do not break down, or at least not when A. is present. At last we reached the castle high in the Carpathians where He lived once, or carried out those functions which to Him were the equivalent of living. I still cannot bring myself to write His name, despite the fact that it all happened more than fifteen years ago. What a ridiculous, weak thing I am.

"We visited the ruins by daylight, A. insisting that we take revolvers, though I told him these would be no use at all, and that we'd best take sharpened walking-canes instead. The castle was a husk, its rotting

"The Castle," near Lutha

halls, once sumptuous, now the retreat of bats, ancestral portraits made anonymous by guano. In the crypt the stone sarcophagi were all in disarray, but empty. What was I expecting? Did I fear (or hope?) that He'd still be alive, or that His cold-fleshed concubines would still reside here, and have news of Him? He's dead. He died out on the ice, that dreadful, beautiful old man. He only pours like fog beneath the door-frame in your dreams, you stupid woman.

"The one disquieting thing that we discovered was a sheaf of mildewed letters written to the for-mer occupant by persons from a Transylvanian city east of Belgrade. These, I hope, were writ in rust-brown ink, though the content, with its cheerful reminiscences of awful acts performed on earlier visits, sug-gests otherwise. It struck me that although this castle's owner may be dead, his kind might still exist near-by, and thus we headed on for

Transylvania, to put my mind at rest. In Transylvania we passed the ruins of Castle Karpathenburg, profitably haunted by an operatic ghost until, if I remember the newspaper article correctly, this was exposed as an ingenious hoax in 1892, its perpe-trator blowing both his castle and himself to smithereens in what would seem to have been terrible chagrin.

"Continuing, we travelled onward through the most astonish-ingly dismal town I've ever seen, this being called the City of Dreadful Night. Surrounding mountains mean that sunlight never falls here, and indeed, though we passed through it during afternoon, it was pitch dark. The appropriately-named River of Suicides winds round the city, where the sleepless, tragic population shuffle soundlessly through ghastly lamp-lit streets. Above the town's main palace was the statue of a woman with spread wings and deep, grief-stricken eyes. Our driver told

us this was Melencolia, the city's patron goddess, and even a glimpse of her left us both thoroughly depressed. We travelled on until we reached the outskirts of the place named in the letters we'd discovered at the castle, the awful vampire city of Selene.

"The buildings, all exquisitely adorned with decorations that seemed Indian or Chinese, were immaculate but wreathed in a thick atmosphere of terror, which A. said that he felt also. Naturally, we made our visit by the light of morning and so found the eerie streets deserted, though not, I imagine, uninhabited. Almost every house-front bore the proud crest of some noble blood-imbibing lineage or other, with embossed in silver, gold or black, the family name. Bathory. Yorga. I even fancied I caught sight of the name Hapsburg, though in this I surely was mistaken.

"I'd been right. They were there in their hundreds, but what could we do? The two of us could hardly work our way around the city spearing monsters before nightfall, even if we'd had the nerve for it, which I am not sure that we did. The best we could resolve was to return here at some future date, preferably with weaponry and reinforcements, to eradicate the dreadful parody of life which we could smell (the same smell He had, but much worse) behind the decorated shutters of Selene.

"We left that silent and night-marish place behind us, some time before nightfall, and crossed into the Balkan territories, where next day we found a pleasant inn quite near Evarchia on the Black Sea. The sub-lime Evarchian 'gaudy bird' seems to be common hereabouts, and we were woken by its song upon the morning following. I am much calmed having put Transylvania behind us, and the two of us spent some few hours in bed before we rose.

"We were thus in a wholly better mood when we made an excursion to the coast, then hired a boat to carry us to Leuke, a small island that the God Poseidon was alleged to have created as a place to bury the great hero Achilles, whose temple is still standing. The shrine, unattend-ed save for huge white birds who mourn above the hero's grave and bathe his temple walls with water shaken from their wings, was beau-tiful by the light of the setting sun. This is the place, it's said, where Helen married Achilles while Thetis and Poseidon served as witnesses, and also where A. and myself were moved to conjugal activity, unwit-nessed save by the enormous sail-white shapes that circled keening overhead, like dumbstruck angels."

At this point we conclude our tour of Europe, but advise the read-er to refer to the next chapter of our New Traveller's Almanac, in which we focus our attentions upon the Americas and their surrounding islands.

The City of Dreadful Night

Chapter Three
The Americas: In the Rubble of Utopia

As we turn to the fabulous Americas, we are confronted by a territory so massive that one scarcely knows where to commence. Perhaps as good a spot as any is the sub-aquatic realm beneath the waters of Drake Passage, off the tip of South America, where the Atlantic and Pacific oceans meet. The science-pirate Captain Nemo, who kept a base at nearby Lincoln Island in the South Pacific, speculates about this underwater kingdom in his entry to the logbook of the Nautilus for July 15,1897.

"This morning, first mate Ishmael reported a fresh sighting of what we have come to call the ghost submersible, an vehicle much like *The Nautilus,* which I had thought to be unique. Broad Arrow Jack has recently returned from Tierra del Fuego, where he'd been put ashore to learn whatever might be known of this elusive craft, and served us up an interesting account of his discoveries; The locals tell tales of an English naval sergeant, one James Winston Pepper, lost at sea in 1870, supposedly dragged down by undertows through emerald waters and eventually washed up upon the shores of a subsurface paradise where harmony reigned everywhere. The realm, named Pepper's Land after the sergeant, is reputedly the source of the garishly-coloured phantom submarine we've sighted. It may also be the home of a malignant species of blue dwarf or troll (perhaps related to the Nordic kobolds) that turns up occasionally in Argentina, but of this Broad Arrow Jack could tell us nothing more."

The Lincoln Island pirate haven had been used by Nemo since the 1870s, and it was here that the Sikh mariner returned in the last months of 1898, venturing from the isle only infrequently thereafter until the occasion of his death in May, 1909. Our accounts of the surrounding islands have been mostly gleaned from either Nemo's records or from those of a Miss Diver, whose connection to the Captain is unclear but who made entries in the logbook of the Nautilus commencing in the later months of 1910. According to our notes, south-east of Nemo's base existed a great cluster of small islands called the Riallaro Archipelago, surrounded by a ring of fog, and thus remaining undiscovered by the outside world until the European steamship *Daydream* found its way there during 1900. Nemo's *Nautilus,* however, being unencumbered by the surface mists, lists Riallaro's islands in a logbook entry dated February 1881.

"Aleofane, or 'Gem of Truth,' is an island where fame is sold and traded, almost as a form of currency, and where communication seemingly depends entirely upon facial tics such as raised eyebrows. Fanattia is filled with wild-eyed reformers attempting to abolish each other, while Figlefia is populated utterly by libertines. Upon Spectralia and neighbouring Astralia they worship ghosts or astral bodies. Haciocram, an isle of prophets, declares that the true number of the Beast is '1999,' and on Kloriole, Broolyi, Swoonarie, Limanora and a dozen other islands, one may find beliefs and ways of life as varied and as ludicrous. Upon Coxuria, for example, there exists a race of pygmies who are confident that the creator of the Universe resembles them in shape and size. Altogether a strategically disastrous group of territories that avail me nothing in my plans to bring the British Empire to its knees."

Southeast of Riallaro we find Manouham, famed for its fascinating open-sided tombs, and nearby Letalispons with its fragile, airy towers and its inhabitants, the Cerebellites, who spend the first half of their 120-year-long lifespan growing older and the last half growing younger. Both these islands are near Juan Fernandez, not far off the coast of Chile, as is neighbouring Frivola, the Frivolous Island. Here beasts have claws as soft as velvet, horses collapse beneath the slightest weight as if made of straw, and all things from the easily-bent trees to the opinions of the population are entirely insubstantial. A stranger by his very nature to frivolity, Nemo, for the most part, seems to have restricted his Pacific explorations to locations north of Lincoln Island, in the coastal waters of Peru and Ecuador.

Amongst these are the delightful children-governed isle of Meipe, The Land of Parrots (named after a prince who had been magically transformed to such a bird), and the obscure immensity known as Mount Analogue. This mountain towers from the Pacific and is very possibly the tallest mountain on the Earth, yet its existence is, to the greater percentage of Earth's population, utterly unknown. This is because the space around Mount Analogue is strangely curved in such a way that even light-rays bend around the island, rendering it effectively invisible. Paradise Island, further north, is notable for its domesticated lions, while nearby Coral Island is famed for its glittering Diamond Cave, as mentioned by the three young Englishmen who, in the early 1850s, as the sole survivors of the shipwrecked *Arrow,* were cast up there.

Closest to Nemo's base at Lincoln is the pink island known as Rose, where in the 18th century, and therefore prior to Nemo's day, one Captain Clegg (affiliated in some way to the adventurers assembled by ship's surgeon Lemuel Gulliver) attended an important conference of leading pirates, his impressions given in his log. "We met by our

The Pirates' Conference, Rose Island

unanimous consent on *The Black Tiger,* owned by Slaughterboard, who is a good man and an enemy to none of us, though I like his yellow bunkmate not a bit. Blood was there, strutting and twirling his moustache while bragging of his endowments, and also John Silver, hopping around and cackling, though I have always found him a likeable-enough old rogue. Pugwash I cannot make up my mind about. He seems a rather soft and inoffensive little chap, not at all cut out for life on the high seas. Hook, on the other hand, while very capable, is an enigma, especially when pressed upon exactly where it is he hails from. Things proceeded amiably enough until we all had too much grog and Blood got in a foppish slapping-match with Pysse-Gummes, whereupon we disembarked and all found our own berths."

As we continue northwards we pass Orofena where, just prior to the Great War, another shipwrecked trio of Englishmen succeeded in waking the sleeping god Oro and his daughter Yva, with the Earth almost tipped off its axis by the irritable god as a result. Subsequent earthquakes have reduced what Orofenian statuary and architecture that still exist to a pitiable rubble amongst which the graceful native Orofenians maintain their deep and understandable mistrust of Europeans. Slightly further north (although apparently maintaining strong diplomatic connections with Meipe, above) is Maina, home of the irrepressibly creative Articole tribe whose most famous writer, Routchko, published the monumental, almost seventeen-thousand-page-long *Why I Cannot Write.* Venturing further northward still we sight the changing-coloured sands that bound Cook's Island, where a cook from London and her burglar husband have ruled since an incident involving a wish-granting flying carpet that occurred during the first years of the twentieth century. As we draw close to the equator, we encounter the vast Mardi Archipelago, containing numerous fascinating realms such as the island of maimed and one-legged gladiatorial enthusiasts, Diranda, and witch-isle Minda or Valapee, Isle of Yams, with its unusual currency of human teeth.

Heading northwest towards Colombia we pass by Hunchback Island, where non-hunchbacks are regarded as deformed, and come to one of the peculiar areas of the South Pacific that local islanders believe inspires men to communicate in song, such as the beauteous Bali Hai near Japan, or in this case, Zara's Kingdom, ruled by British-educated Princess Zara and a sextet of exemplary Englishmen, including

Captain Corcoran who'd previously served aboard Her Majesty's Ship *Pinafore.* One puzzling incident recorded by this Captain in his memoirs concerns Marsh's Island, close to Zara's Kingdom and named after Captain Obed Marsh of Innsmouth,

The Marvellous Islands

Massachusetts, who dropped anchor there in 1830. Islanders from Zara's land believe that Marsh's Island is the haunt of hideous fish-like humanoids called "Deep Ones," and to judge from Captain Corcoran's memoir this would seem to be the case. Corcoran tells of not only encountering a small group of these creatures, but, incredibly, of teaching them to sing (albeit only in thick, bubbling, inhuman voices) at a command performance held for Princess Zara. Just one of the songs written for this production has survived, and here it is reproduced in part:

" *When I was a boy an eldritch book informed me I'd inherited the Innsmouth Look.*

I'd gills and wide-spaced eyes, you see, and I frolicked at the bottom of the deep blue sea (He frolicked at the bottom of the deep blue sea).

I went into the ocean depths most willingly, and now I am a tentacled monstrosity (He went into the ocean depths most willingly, and now he is a tentacled monstrosity)."

Before turning our attentions to the islands in the South Atlantic off the eastern coast of South America, there is one final isle deserving of attention. This is Noble's island, close to Ecuador, where an English biologist (apparently employed by British Military Intelligence) performed experiments of a most confidential nature that we nonetheless believe to have involved hybridisation, during the late 19th century. This belief, we should add, is supported only by the testimony of the clearly half-demented hermit Edward Prendick, who Miss

Wilhelmina Murray and her colleague Allan Quatermain encountered on their trip to the South Downs during the terrible Martian incursion in the latter half of 1898.

The South Atlantic, starting from the waters off Tierra del Fuego, is as filled with fascinating isles as the Pacific, such as Hoste, an island republic ruined by a gold-rush during 1891, or Geometer's island, with its massive, soundless cities where the locals pass their lives drawing transient pictures in the sand. Not far away are Greedy Island, where the portly natives worship the obese god Baratrogulo, and the adjacent Doctor's Island, prosperous from treating stomach ailments. Nearby Foolyk ekes out a precarious existence having poetry as its sole export, while the natives of Philosopher's Island pass their time by weighing air or establishing the sex of angels. Heading northward up the coast of Argentina we next come to Rampole Island, sole habitat of the giant ground-sloth and reputedly the haunt of cannibals, just south of Villings, an attractive island purchased recently, in the late 1920s, by Morel, a scientist dedicated to the perfect reproduction of real human beings. A little west of Villings we find Brisevent, in an archipelago known as the Marvellous Islands, where lived centaurs, ape-men, amazons and the infrequent cyclops. Bordering this group of curiously-populated islands to the east is Houyhnhnms Land, where Lemuel Gulliver encountered talking horses (possibly related to the exiled horses of Abdera as discussed in our last chapter), while marooned here by a mutinous crew in 1711.

Moving North into the waters off Brazil we pass the fair, enlightened, pagan island of Eugea, inhospitable Nimatan with its exquisite lunatic asylums, the former Roman colony of Oceana, and the idealistic republic known as Spensonia, founded by a group of yet more shipwrecked Englishmen who washed up there in the last years of the eighteenth century. At last, only a few nautical miles beyond Spensonia we reach another, far more famed island republic, the acclaimed "perfect society" known as Utopia, named for its earliest known regent, King Utopos. Until its pitiful decline during the later sixteenth and early seventeenth centuries, Utopia was known throughout the world as the ideal state that mankind might socially aspire to. During the early sixteenth century, Utopia was ruled by the extraordinary giant Gargantua, and was indeed the birthplace of his son, the similarly-sized Pantagruel. Wars with neighbouring kingdoms in the later fifteen-hundreds so destabilised Utopia that, at this current time of writing (1931), the former perfect country is a dismal ruin on an island that is all but uninhabited, potential visitors deterred by an oppressive air of melancholy that surrounds Utopia's creeper-conquered rubble.

Travelling on past Spidermonkey Island, where a war between two tribes in 1839 was settled by a visiting English doctor whom the islanders have since referred to as "King Jong," we move westward around upper South America to reach the seas of the West Indies. Here we find Vendchurch's Island with its fierce, carnivorous sea-lions, and Fonesca that is ringed by such impenetrable cloud that it is often thought to vanish magically. Here too is Oroonoko Island where the reddish-yellow islanders will treat someone as dead if they have not appeared for dinner, and the quarrel-free Ferdinand's Island colonised by slaves in the mid-eighteenth century. Most interesting, however, are two islands separated by perhaps a mile of water and yet seemingly oblivious to each other's presence. One is the island of Speranza, sometimes called the Island of Despair, where one Rob Crusoe, late of York, spent many years of loneliness and hardship following his shipwreck there during the last days of September, 1659. Ironically, well within swimming distance of Speranza is an island known as Herland, populated by a race of lovely women who produce their daughters by means of parthenogenesis, and who had not so much as glimpsed a man since the fourth century AD. If only the beached mariner had owned some earlier edition of this almanac, his isolation might have been agreeably abated.

Further westward is the Caribbean, with its own array of islands, such as Tacarigua, called by poets "burning Tacarigua" for the irresistible delights to be encountered there, from lavish operas to the erotic *hodeidah* dance performed by the young native women. Cannibal Island, nearby, is unique in that its hunters favour suffocating smoke as their means of bagging game, while Chita is an island famous for its trees like giant lettuce and the brutal Chinese executioner who came to power there in the early twentieth century. The Isle of Birds, much more hospitable, is known for its variety of wildfowl and prodigiously-sized snakes, and boasts a small community of sweet bucolic innocence established by the shipwrecked Comte D'Uffai in the first decades of the eighteenth century. We also have the pirate island San Verrado, where they kidnapped Cuban women until the destruction of the island's fort by English warships during the late eighteenth century, and the feared Zaroff's Island, owned by an expatriate Russian Count whose pass-times include hunting human beings. Cacklo-gallinia is ruled by chickens that are

six feet tall and far from perfectly behaved, yet who reportedly were generous in their treatment of one Samuel Blunt, an Englishman with what would now appear to be customary British navigational abilities, who was marooned there in the early 1720s. The only other isle of note within the Caribbean is, bewilderingly, the isle belonging to the Milanese Duke and occultist Prospero, which we have already located between Italy and Africa. The sorcerer himself, asked how one island could exist in two remote locations at the same time, would only reply ambiguously, "In mine eye do all places coexist, may be at once in Tartary or France, just as we may the Seraphim enlist and bid them on a single pin-head dance."

Of course, the South American mainland itself is equally replete with wonder-drenched locations. Within the Patagonian region of south Argentina, we find Leonard's Land, established by a French philosopher who believed egalitari-

Speranza

an government to be intrinsically connected with the weather, erecting numerous lofty weathervanes across the area as an aid to settling legislative matters. Further north, not far from Buenos Aires, we find Babel, an imposing South American metropolis that should not be confused with its Biblical namesake. There are two important landmarks in the city, the first being the Palace of Justice, apparently constructed in admiring imitation of The Castle in Czechoslovakia, as mentioned in our previous installment. Here, those waiting for their cases to be heard will often pass the time by helping out with minor bureaucratic tasks, eventually promoted to become the Magistrate who'll find them guilty in absentia. The other major edifice of note in Babel is the city's spectacular library, sometimes

called "The Universe." This library, with its tiers of hexagonal galleries that are said to be infinite in number, contains every conceivable book that could ever be written, translated to every conceivable language. Somewhere within, therefore, exists a perfect catalogue of all the library's tomes (along with a potentially infinite number of false catalogues) with generations of librarians expended in the search for this master codex.

Further north, a country in its own right at the northern boundary of Argentina, we find Madragal, with its history of skirmishes with Parapagal, not far from Paraguay. While the origins of this historical hostility appear to be uncertain, its results may be best judged by the unusual number of glass eyeballs, hooks and wooden legs that one can't help but note amongst the mostly-crippled populace. Meanwhile, on the eastern border between Argentina and its neighbor Chile exists Cesares Republic, a Protestant settlement established by the Dutch during the 1600s, wherein Catholics are barred from holding Governmental office. Northeast of there, within the upper reaches of Chile itself, is Agzceaziguls, a desert country nestling on the Bolivian border, where desperately poor descendants of the Incas live amongst fantastic treasures such as the pink palaces of Gunda, with their jewel-crypts guarded by a score of golden idols that have emeralds for eyes. Not far from Agzceaziguls, within the south-most reaches of Peru, stands a solitary Pink Palace that may once have been a part of Gunda, but which stands in much better repair than Gunda's palaces, and which is still inhabited. Herein lives the Pink Child, an ageless and perfectly beautiful girl (possessing neither knees nor elbows, since these body parts are less than beautiful), who spends her days amidst exquisite loveliness and whose sole utterance is said to be "I pray thee, do not rise." Although she has once travelled widely, witnessing the filth and squalor of the world, this has not ruffled her deportment or serene refinement, and she still draws swans with one pink fingertip upon the scented air of the Pink Palace, murmuring, "I pray thee, do not rise."

Bolivia, as we continue north, is home to the immense lake (or small inland sea) known as Lost Time, beneath which a great multitude of succulent young turtles swim through terraces of underwater flowers. The waters, although generally choked with refuse, will, at random intervals across the centuries, spontaneously emit the sweet perfume of roses, upon which occasions life and commerce gradually return to the abandoned villages that mark the landlocked ocean's edge. Some distance east of Lost Time, between Paraguay, Brazil and Argentina is Roncandor, where in 1839 benign dictator "Dr. Olivero"

Goldfinger
Expedition,
1928

(actually an Englishman named Oliver) established himself by assassinating the previous incumbent. Oliver's regime, based on the ideas of Rousseau and Voltaire, ended when Oliver faked his own death and returned to England, with little trace remaining in Roncandor now of this brief golden age.

Indeed, for traces of a literally golden age we must return to the most northerly edge of Bolivia, where, between Peru and the Amazon basin, the English adventurer Sir Walter Raleigh located the fabled Incan kingdom known as El Dorado, where, as he described it, everything from cobblestones to cooking implements and weaponry was made from nothing but the purest gold. It need hardly be said that subsequent excursions to the region have been utterly unable to locate this glittering realm, including the most recent expedition, which was launched in the late 1920s by a young Swiss-German millionaire named Auric Goldfinger, who returned empty handed.

Before examining the riches of Brazil, there are a handful of intriguing sites throughout the rest of South America which merit our attention. In the Andean hills of Ecuador, as an example, there exists a valley in the shadow of Mount Parascotopetl where all of the populace are blind from birth, while high in the Colombian Andes we find Golden Lake, the streams that feed it being so gold-rich that one might readily suppose Sir Walter Raleigh to have slightly mislocated El Dorado. Heading east across Colombia itself we pass through the delightful almond-scented village of Macondo, with its constant music of bells,

chimes, and cuckoo clocks, established possibly as long ago as 1580 by one Jose Arcadio Buendia. Macondo would seem to have been governed since either by identically-named descendants or, incredibly, perhaps by the extraordinarily long-lived Buendia himself. Passing on into Venezuela we find (or, in fact, don't find) Ewaipanoma, the land around a tributary of the Orinoco whose inhabitants have eyes set in their shoulders and mouths in their breasts, described by the less-than-reliable Sir Walter Raleigh who, some commentators have suggested, may have simply made some of these places up.

Brazil, however, is repository to marvels of less doubtful provenance. On its south-western shore, just past ill-starred Nolandia we reach Happiland, a country free of civic strife due to an early monarch who imposed a limit upon the amount of gold a king might legally maintain within his treasury. While by no means a wealthy country, Happiland has long outlasted the nearby island republic of Utopia, once its superior. Aglaura, north of Happiland and some miles west of Rio de Janeiro, almost seems to be two cities somehow occupying the same space. One is drab and characterless, yet at times from its washed-out streets it's possible to glimpse a different city, rich with meaning, the import of which is sadly inexpressible. Further north, upon the coast, we come to Watkinsland, with an abandoned city on its high plateau and a variety of curious fauna, including the unpleasant man-sized and mostly bipedal hominid that has been referred to as a "rat-dog." Lemuel Gulliver, who was aware of

Watkinsland through second-hand accounts, believed these rat-dogs to be cousins of the Yahoos, an equally noxious species he'd encountered on the not-far-distant island of the Houyhnhnms. Not far from Watkinsland to the northwest is Quivera, a ruby-rich land that, incredibly, was settled by the Welsh during 1170. It is Brazil's interior, however, that is home to some of South America's more notable locations. Deep within the forests of the Amazon, for instance, is reputed to exist the ancient jungle kingdom known as Mu, quite possibly the same kingdom described by the great 18th century traveller Candide and his instructor Dr. Pangloss as "the Fabulous Land." In other sources Mu is sometimes known as "Yu," or "Yu Atlanchi," and it is near here that the world-famous "bird girl" Riolama or Rima was discovered in the last years of the nineteenth century. Jacob Epstein's statue of Riolama still stands next to the same artist's rendering of Edward Hyde in London's former Serpentine Park, renamed Hyde Park after the events of 1898.

The most astonishing of Brazil's mystery sites, which we have saved for last, is Maple White Land, a plateau in Amazonas State explored in 1912 by sometime League associate George Challenger. Here (as in Erikraudebyg, referred to in our previous instalment) there survive a multitude of species long since thought to be extinct, including the sabre-toothed tiger and many dinosaurs. A species of ape-man, again conceivably related to the "rat-dogs" or the Yahoos, once existed on the plateau before being ethnically purged by a local Indian tribe called the Accala, and some locations close to Maple White Land have shown signs of infestation by species that would seem to be pre-historic in their origin. Some few miles down the Amazon from the volcanic plateau, for example, there is a secluded lake known as the Black Lagoon by local Indian tribes, where monstrous amphibian bipeds have apparently been sighted. These may be some hitherto unknown Silurian throwbacks that have come downstream from Maple White Land, or might even be kin to the vocally-trainable sea-things found on Marsh's Island, far away in the Pacific.

As we move on to North America, let us first pay attention to its many islands, starting with those in the North Atlantic. Furthest north, off Canada's east coast, there is the miserable Island of Birds (not to be confused with the Isle of Birds found in the Caribbean) where the sole inhabitant, Amanachem the Ugly, forbids visitors, while some way south, just off Newfoundland, we have Waferdanos, where fur-covered Waferdanians go naked and enjoy a simple and idyllic lifestyle. Both these islands lie above the western end of the submarine country Capillaria, as discussed in our last chapter. The ruins of another previously mentioned underwater passage, namely the Atlantic Tunnel, similarly run beneath a number of the islands (once known as "The Wicked Archipelago") to be found further south, out in the North Atlantic off America's east coast. These include notoriously rain-swept Buyan Island, cheese-like Caseosa and the startling island Cabbalussa, where the cannibal women all have asses' hooves and mimic certain breeds of spider by first copulating with, then eating, their unwilling suitors. Neighbour-ing Dream Island, with its famous city gates of horn and ivory, shares characteristics with Yspaddaden Penkawr castle in Wales, in that it allegedly seems to get further away the more nearly one approaches. Idol Island and Winkfield's Island, on the other hand, seem to possess no supernatural properties, and are only remarkable for their conversion to Christianity during the eighteenth century by the oddly-named Miss Unca Eliza Winkfield and the priest who was her husband (and her cousin). Further south, however, on the island of Militia, we find mention of a man-mimicking variety of shrub known as a Simlax, which Miss Winkfield was apparently unable to convert. For some time it was thought the Simlax might have some connection with the mobile vegeta-tion on the nearby Island of Moving Trees, but this phenomenon was found to be illusion, caused by the branch-camouflaged barges belong-ing to the local fishermen.

When Prospero's occasional companion Captain Robert Owe-Much visited these waters with his ships the *Excuse*, the *Pay-Naught*

and the *Least-in-Sight* during the early 1670s, his logbooks gave a brief account of various islands found in the vicinity. "The Island of the Moving Trees, so called, we passed upon our starboard bow as we departed from Ursina and its neighbouring isle Vulpina, with the former well-known for its Zodiacal circus where are pitted rams and scorpions, goats and fishes, crabs and lions, all one against the other, and the latter famous for its mighty naval fleet. After a while, to port we sighted the Island of Fortune, where I am informed the sun is worshipped and all atheists are burned, which for the atheists seems less than for-tunate. Close to it we could see the Island of Chance, where all reputed-ly is chaos and misrule is king, so that a horse may well be born with human hands and rise to be a tailor, while a man or woman born with horsehooves will be set to graze out in the fields. Keeping these isles to port we caught a strong north wind and headed south, passing Philosophy Isle where all men are philosophers and thus cannot agree upon a single form of governance, and also passing an isle that is but recently risen from the sea, a mere outcrop of rock that as yet goes unnamed but which to me appears as though shaped like a fine York ham. This likeness may be caused by appetite, for I am long since sick

with salt beef. Sailing on, we are now headed for a place called the Island of the Palace of Joy, further south, where a very pretty gentle-man that I once met, by name Orlando, told me there were fair pavilions all of gold and crystal to be seen, though these were but illu-sions of the sorcerer Malagigi." This mention of a person named Orlando is far from unique in the League's annals, though as we shall see the gender of this person seems to vary, while accounts from different cen-turies, describing this Orlando as both young and beautiful, would indicate we may be talking about more than just one individual.

One island on America's east coast that Owe-Much does not name is Rossum's Island, only recently made famous by the noted physiologist Old Rossum, who's resided there since 1920 and has recently made claims that he is clos-er to his goal of making living proto-plasm, with which he intends to manufacture artificial human beings, or "robots" as he quaintly calls them. Of more serious interest to intelligent adults are those few islands off the western coast of Mexico and North America, com-mencing with Quarll Island in the south. Close to Mexico, Quarll Island has long held a reputation as a pirate haven, when in fact only one person ever lived there, this being

Scientific Expedition to The Black Lagoon, 1930. No survivors.

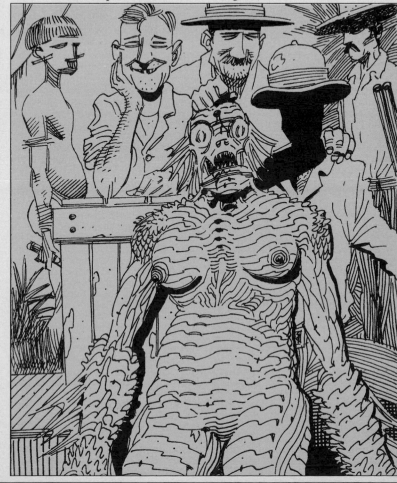

yet another shipwrecked English-man named Philip Quarll, who seems to have been cast away there during 1675. Perhaps Quarll Island's notoriety is gained from its proximi-ty to nearby Treasure Island, where the pirate captain Flint was said to have concealed his famous treasure in the mid 1750s.

Further north, far off the coast of California there are several islands that much-travelled Lemuel Gulliver recalled and contributed for inclusion in the records of the League, such as Glubbdubdrib, Balnibari and Laputa, but since these are closer to Japan we shall examine them along with Asia and the far Australias in Chapter Five. With these eliminated, only three islands remain, these being Captain Sparrow's Island, with its satyrs, blue pigs and gigantic birds called rukas; and the two islands sheltering beneath the western California out-cropping of Brobdingnag, both set-tled by shipwrecked mariners and called Great Mother's Island and Orphan Island. Great Mother's Island was first colonised by ship-wrecked women in the first years of the twentieth century, while Orphan Island had been colonised in 1855 by numerous orphans cast away while bound for California with their teacher, one Miss Charlotte Smith, who founded a society based on Victorian values, the remains of which may still be seen today.

Turning now to the mainland, we find the majority of North America's most interesting sites to be in the mid-west or on the eastern seaboard. This is not to say that there is nothing worthy of a visit to be found in either Canada or California, merely to observe the greater number of such places to be found towards the east. Up in the great northwest expanses of the Klondike region, for example, stands Thieves City, built above a boiling lake to spare it from the Arctic chill, where qualifying as a citizen requires one to have broken one or more laws in the country he origi-nated from, yet paradoxically per-mits no crime within its city limits. Not far south, in the east Yukon Territory, we find amongst the snows a tropical oasis known as Dead Man's Valley, which would seem to have as many prehistoric animals sheltering within it as does Maple White Land, and which may indeed provide the source for some reported prehistoric sightings that we shall encounter further south. Elsewhere in Canada, within Snow River country, exists another anom-alous and temperate valley, called the Valley of the Beasts, where an astonishing variety of animals appear to coexist quite peacefully together, while in the southeast, Lake Superior boasts islands that may be of interest to the enterpris-ing traveller. On Haunted Island, spectres of gigantic Indians are sometimes seen, perhaps dead members of the tribe who still today pay homage to the deities of the nearby Canadian Floating Isles, beautiful and idyllic islands that will vanish in concealing fog should any wonder-struck canoeist try to make an approach.

Working our way now down the west coast of America we must pass quickly through the frankly absurd area called Rootabaga Country,

Orlando

which lies somewhere between Canada and Washington State, and where the bib-wearing pigs may be related to the talking porcine crea-tures to be found cross country in upper New York State, which we shall presently discuss. Elsewhere in Washington State we discover Chisholm Prison, thought to be escape-proof until the ingenious professor Van Dusen did just that during the first years of the twenti-eth century, while travelling further south, just past the logging town of Twin Peaks, with its many interest-ing Indian legends, we find areas of dense forest sometimes called "The Deep, Deep Woods" by locals. Doll-like creatures have been seen here, thought by some to be escapees from the otherworldy realm we shall hear word of that exists beyond some spatial flaw above the fields of Kansas. Others have insisted that these sinister and smiling toy-things have their origins, along with vari-ous other extra-human creatures, in a supposedly-haunted dell within the Deep, Deep Woods called Glastonbury Grove, but this cannot be verified.

Moving through Oregon we pass by Cricket Creek (one of the places where there have been various reports of living dinosaurs, perhaps migrated south from Dead Man's Valley in the Yukon), and upon the nearby coast the city of Mahagonny, where trappers from the frozen north can rest within the comfort of one of the city's many brothels. Next we come to California where, near Mendocino, we find France-Ville, a magnificently-managed city founded in the 1870s by a French scientist called Sarrasin. Some dis-tance further down, near Monterey, at a number 5 Thallo Street in Pacific Grove, lives the intriguing although somewhat musty-smelling scientist Tyco M. Bass, while San Francisco is home to the Western American Explorer's Club, whose Professor William Waterman Sherman was involved in the myste-rious "21 Balloons" incident of 1883. Out in rural California, not far from Merced, is the long-established set-tlement called iDEATH, famed for its watermelons. Hardened sugar from these is used to make trout-hatch-eries, cabins, sculptures or indeed almost anything one might require. Continuing south, past a vast spread of rusted, obsolete machinery from the 19th century known locally as The Forgotten Works, we come eventually, just past Mexico's bor-der, to the charming villa of Don Diego de la Vega where the masked adventurer known as "The Fox" was sometimes sighted during the nine-teenth and even early twentieth cen-turies. Other than Brobdingnag, the peninsula of giants that juts from California into the Pacific (thought to be the birthplace of the fabled lumberjack Paul Bunyan and his cel-ebrated blue ox, Babe), we must look east in search of further memo-rable locations, save to mention that a crewman who had sailed with Robert Owe-Much from the isle of Scoti Moria, discussed in our first chapter, came with Owe-Much to America, eventually to settle near Los Angeles. The crewman, a fellow named Lebowsky, had been former-ly a member of the Naiad race of Scoti Moria, but it is not known if he continued the traditional Naiad habits of smoking and nine-pins once established in America, or indeed if he produced any subse-quent offspring of any note.

Moving east, the most souther-ly point we have on record is the ruined city of Tcha, a supposedly Atlantean colony on the Yucatan peninsula. While giving mention to Louisiana's marvelously atmospher-ic Yoknapatawpha County, the next place of interest that we encounter, heading north, is the New Mexico ranch home of the early 20th centu-ry gunfighter and balladeer Gene Autry. While the famous singing cowboy's home is not itself remark-able, beneath it sprawls the subter-ranean empire of Murania, an out-post of the massive underground land Atvatabar that runs beneath America from Canada to Ecuador, its entrance at the North Pole. Atvatabar is also connected to the similarly subterranean Etidorhpa's Country, entered through cave sys-tems in Kentucky, and the Inca Tunnel running from the same Kentucky caves towards Peru, but

Atvatabar's polar entrance makes it more suitable for inclusion in our closing chapter. As we travel up the centre of the country, to the east beyond the wildernesses of Drexara are the Appalachian hills where Silver John (a balladeer and possibly a colleague of Gene Autry) has commemorated in verse the existence of both the hillbilly settlement called Dogpatch, with its famously attractive females, and the nearby Valley of the Shmoon, where little edible food is grown, but where nobody goes hungry. Westwards, meanwhile, lies Oklahoma, another location that seems to inspire men to song and dance, at least to judge by the Nature Theatre of Oklahoma, which recruits performers from stadiums across the U.S. to appear as angels or devils (depending on gender) in the theatre's largely unwatched productions.

Northward, over Kansas, there would seem to be some massive flaw in space, as mentioned earlier, permitting access to extensive extra-worldly territories that British Military Intelligence came to believe were congruent with similar realms already encountered elsewhere, as in the disturbing cases close to Oxford mentioned in our opening chapter. Further north still, in Wyoming, we discover Lake La Metrie and its legendary talking monster, while eastwards in Montana is Red Gap, where displaced English butler Marmaduke Ruggles mentions in his memoirs having met the famous former Texas Ranger and masked vigilante John Reid, shortly prior to Reid's retirement to the coast to raise a family. Iowa has Rampart Junction, a rural town that seems somehow forbidding (although no outsider has ever alighted at its dusty railroad station to investigate), and up near North Dakota in the forgotten county of Apodidraskiana is the haunt of fugitives called Dotandcarryone Town, but more promising by far are the strange places found upon America's east coast.

In Florida, located in the depths of the Great Cypress Swamp near Gainesville, is the actual Fountain of Eternal Youth described by the explorer Ponce de Leon, a natural spring, which, while yet to have its revitalizing properties proven by science, would seem to still attract the elderly to Florida in search of it. Great Cypress Swamp is of more interest to us as the site of certain grim events, at a neighbouring graveyard, which involved a Mr. Randolph Carter of Massachusetts, whom we shall encounter shortly. Great Cypress Swamp also runs into Okeefenokee Swamp, upon the Georgia/Florida border, where yet more talking animals have been reported, though it is believed that these have no connection with the elder horrors found by Mr. Carter and his unfortunate colleague Mr. Harley Warren. Higher up the coast, in Carolina, it appears that youthful ingenuity is prized with both South

Carolina's Readestown and North Carolina's Wrightstown named for rival boy inventors, while neighbouring Bayport has found fame within the last few years as home to many mysteries requiring intervention by teen-aged youths for their solution.

In Virginia, various local authors (such as Musgrave, Kennaston and Townsend, all of Fairview, close to Lichfield) have referred to local legends that concern a hunting party of three men that set out from the Jamestown colony during January, 1610, of whom no trace was ever found, save for a journal which tells how the hunters stumbled on "a terrible Place" and concludes with the disturbing entry "Staires! We have found staires!" A little north, in Maryland, stands the spectacular estate of Arnheim, built in the 1840s by a millionaire named Ellison, although this has done little to reverse the area's slump in property prices, generally attributed to the

dismal ruins of the Usher property, jutting unappealingly out of a stagnant lake not far from Baltimore. More northward still, near Philadelphia, are the remains of Mettingen, a bleak estate with a gloomy temple, where a Mr. Mettingen of Saxony once studied puritanical religious notions in the eighteenth century. Mettingen's piety did not prevent his death from the results of an explosion, nor the later family-murder and subsequent suicide of his son Theodore.

New York and New York State are filled with wonders, from the eerily dilapidated summer-houses in the swamp called Gone-Away Lake, close to Creston, and the reported talking pigs and other animals of upstate Centerboro, to the river Island of the Fay found in the Catskills, and the allegedly-haunted town of Sleepy Hollow near to Greensburgh, on the Hudson. Not far from Greensburgh is the small Dutch settlement famed for its well-

Conversation with
Edward Framingham,
Lake La Metrie,
Wyoming

known case of genuine suspended animation, one Van Winkle, who slept through the War of Independence, while the nearby town of Hadleyburg, formerly famous for its decency, has only known shame since its much-deserved humiliation by a passing stranger during 1899. Close to New York City is Roadtown, a remarkable experiment constructed during 1893, resembling nothing so much as a several-hundred-mile-long sky-scraper set on its side, while in New York itself a basement of unknown location is believed to be the resting place of Flatland, an entirely flat environment in which live two-dimensional beings, discovered by a mathematician during 1884. Neighbouring Connecticut is unre-markable save for the proverbially pretty and agreeable womenfolk to be found in the small town of Stepford, and it is on the genuinely dreadful states of Maine and Massachusetts that we must now focus our attention. During 1899, Miss Wilhelmina Murray (who had been recuperating in the matriarchal settlement of Coradine in Scotland following the dire events of 1898) and Mr. Allan Quatermain were sent by Military Intelligence to Massa-chusetts, ordered to investigate reports that linked this state with the dream-like unearthly territories to be found in England, an increas-ing source of concern for Miss Murray's masters at that time. Her account follows.

"September 7th, 1899. I must write it all down. Write it, or dream about it endlessly for the remainder of my life. When Allan came to visit me in Coradine and told me that the fat men had a job for us, I think that I was pleased and looking forward to adventure, with the nightmare of the

Arkham

men from Mars now safely in the past. If only I'd known then what I know now. Our ship put in at a bleak seaport called New Bedford, which I think that I remember Nemo's first mate Ishmael mentioning to me once, and no sooner had we set foot on the quay than I was overcome by the most miserable foreboding and presentiment of evil. We arranged a carriage that would take us to the old colonial city of Arkham, where M. had informed us that a high num-ber of extra-normal events were centered, but our driver was a gar-rulous thickly-accented local of a type that I have since found to be common in the area, who regaled us with spine-chilling tales of 'sartin mysteries, as ye might say' that were attached to the region's many hideous locations. He spoke of the feared property in nearby Maine owned by a terrible munitions deal-er named (I think) Belasco, the area surrounding the town of Jerusalem's Lot that has developed an evil repu-tation, and even made a pretty-sounding village called Eastwick seem alarming when he claimed a Massachusetts lunatic, Whateley by name, had prophesied that Lucifer himself would one day 'set his cleft hoof' on the town. He babbled on about magical tokens to be found at a Victorian house on Walden Street in Concord, and spoke of 'sartin talking toad-things, like' that might be found at Whiton House on the South Shore. As we passed a lofty and forbidding residence in rural Massachusetts that our driver called Hill House, he told us of an awful-sounding lottery held in a nearby town, invariably resulting in the winner's murder, and in general made the whole region sound so ghastly that, when we passed Beaulieu, a walled town on the Miskatonic River leading into Arkham, I did not have need to ask the reason for its strong fortifica-tions.

"Arkham. I have never known a town to be at once so frightening and so picturesque. Our driver set us down in Church Street, where we had arranged rooms in what seems to be the city's sole hotel, a wretched, faded building where we sat and talked into the night about our mission. M. had passed on reports, mostly the testimonials of asylum inmates it would seem, which appeared to hint at a peculiar dream-territory accessible from cer-tain (or perhaps I should say 'sartin') places in or around Arkham, such as the architecturally peculiar 'Witch House' that stood no more than a block or so down Parsonage Street from our grim and lackluster hotel. We slept but fitfully, beset by hideous dreams that we could not recall upon awakening, and in the morning, after some discreet enquiries, were directed to the library of Arkham's Miskatonic University where we were told could frequently be found a scholar, a young man said to have some knowledge of this world of dreams,

named Randolph Carter. Allan seemed perplexed, saying he recog-nized the name from somewhere, and when we eventually encoun-tered the alarmingly young-looking Mr. Carter, he grew more perplexed still, claiming that he'd seen his face before, though he could not think where. Carter seemed flattered by our interest and professed himself to be an Anglophile, promising he would help us all he could. Admitting to a limited familiarity with this dream-landscape, he con-fessed to fears that some of its more monstrous inhabitants might have ventured into our own world, citing a talking cat that had been seen on Mulberry Street in nearby Spring-field, believed by Carter to hail from the dream-world town of Ulthar. He also mentioned a closer location, on the Aylesbury Pike between Arkham and nearby Dunwich, an abandoned house which he believed to be a form of gateway, and to which he agreed to take us. What followed seemed to happen with a frightening rapidity, and I have needed Allan to supply a number of the details.

"Carter took us to the ruined house, which he believed had once been used by one of Massa-chusetts's many diabolically-inclined and inbred families for their appalling rituals. Hearing what is best described as a much-amplified slithering sound from the adjacent woods, Allan and young Carter strode off manfully to make investi-gations, warning me that I should in no circumstances go into the ruin alone, although from what tran-spired it rather seems I must have done, although I have no memory of this. The next thing I recall, and which I hesitate to write down here, is finding myself standing in a state of undress (and, I am ashamed to say, of some arousal) staring as though drugged into what seemed to be a beautiful and shimmering land-scape, perhaps a painting by some ether-drinker, where a huge and lovely flower extended slender mauve-tinged petals out towards me. I was only roused from this delirium by a frightened yell from Allan, somewhere off behind me, which caused me to awaken and to comprehend the horror of my cir-cumstances: I stood almost naked in a derelict and filthy room where, on the walls, were grotesque symbols that I almost understood, scrawled in what seemed to be long-dried ordure. Coming in some fashion through the walls towards me were transparent tentacles, about to wrap themselves around my flesh when Allan pulled me back and, cursing dreadfully, removed me from the house, where he and Mr. Carter wrapped me in their jackets. Since then, I have suffered a dire fever and shall be, for once, glad to see London. Allan, shaken by the episode, says he feels old, and thinks a holiday in Africa might be the thing for us, but we shall see. I am so ill at present I can think of nowhere save for England."

Chapter Four
Africa and The Middle East: Lights of a Dark Continent

In 1899, returned from harrowing experiences in the Americas, Miss Wilhelmina Murray and her sole remaining partner in the league that she had founded a year earlier, Mr. Allan Quatermain, found themselves involved in Government investigations into the United Avondale Phalanstery, then but recently established, that would occupy them until the late months of 1900, whereupon they both resolved to make their postponed trip to Africa. Perhaps the most mysterious of the continents discussed within this almanac, such knowledge as we have of Africa from our accumulated logs and journals is gleaned for the most part from accounts originating either with Quatermain or with his former comrade Captain Nemo, although the ambiguous figure Orlando, seemingly affiliated to the Prospero, Gulliver and later Murray groups, has also made his or her contribution.

As is becoming clear from this ongoing exploration of our world and its locations, many of the most exotic sites would seem to be found upon curious, secluded islands, and in this Africa is no exception, with perhaps a third of all its mystery locales found situated upon isles within its coastal waters. Captain Nemo, in addition to the base that he maintained at Lincoln Island (as discussed in our last chapter), also made use of an underground port known as Nautilus Harbour, within an extinct volcano on one of the Canary Islands off the northwest coast of Africa. From here he travelled to and charted all the islands and, indeed, small continents found in the South Atlantic off Africa's western coasts. Upon the seabed east of his volcanic grotto, his log notes a great proliferation of stone ruins that Nemo thought to be the submerged townships of Atlantis, with his commentary also making mention of similar architectural relics found in the north-most extremes of the Sahara, such as the much feared and fabled Nameless City, which brings up the intriguing possibility that the lost continent may have included northern Africa, at one time, in its territories.

Wilhelmina Murray, travelling to Africa in 1900, in the last months of the nineteenth century, records the islands passed off the Moroccan coast, just after her reports of those isles found off Portugal, as mentioned in our opening chapter. "We sailed past bleak Mongaza Island, where with good eyes you can see the horrid idol raised beside the so-called Boiling Lake. A giant called Famongomadan apparently sacrificed young virgins to the idol in the early sixteenth century, by which time I thought science had assured us the giant race of Earth's prehistory was long extinct. Travelling on we passed Mogador, a walled island city with the most peculiar hollow dragons on its battlements, through which the wind keens hauntingly. I confess that when I heard the sound my eyes filled up, and I thought of our former comrade, Nemo, who I am informed once kept an island base near here, in a volcano. I wish things had not ended with him in the way they did. I became so melancholy that I barely noticed the Fixed Isle, separated from Morocco by the slenderest ocean channel, which if I recall my girlhood's history lessons properly was ruled by Amadis of Gaul at one time. We sailed on (I fancied that I spied at one point the volcanic isle in the Canaries that was Nemo's stronghold, but this no doubt was just wistful imagination) and at last, passing the isle of Lixus whereupon gold hornet-bees drone busily about the island's sole surviving gold-leafed tree, we put to shore near Nouakchott upon the western coast of Mauritania."

Nemo himself lists many of the islands south of here in records of a voyage made to the Cape of Good Hope during the July of 1890. "We avoid the islands known as the Harmattan Rocks where cormorants fish for pearls, surrounded as they are by dangerous spars and boulders that make navigation hazardous, and soon pass by the isle called No-Man's-Land, where I have heard a curious crocodilian creature may be found, possessing a giraffe-like neck and lengthy tail. We next enjoy perhaps a week of open sea; passing Liberia and the Cote D'Ivoire upon our port bow, coming at last in sight of Nacumera, the large island, now deserted, where we found the skeletons of strange dog-headed humans in full armour, dating from perhaps the fourteenth century, when last we journeyed here. On this occasion, sailing on we find a place that I have previously heard of, called the Island of the Blessed. This is a charming place, draped in what seems perpetual twilight, and with scented breezes blowing from the long-dry bed of what was once, I'm told, a river of perfume. Of the ethereal spirit-beings that once lived here, numinous forms dressed in purple shawls of spider-web, nothing is to be seen, and I suppose they are no more. We travel onward, passing by Wild Island where I am informed the local fauna have enlisted a live dragon in their service, though I am surprised in that one seldom hears of such things this far west, at least not these days. It may be that the dragon has its origins on Silha, further south, where live such venomous beasts beside a lake, said to be formed by tears from the first man and woman when they lived there after being cast from Paradise.

"Silha is the most northerly island of the Dondum Archipelago, where are the remains of many curious peoples to be found, most notably hermaphrodites, dwarves with mouths in the top of the their heads, and also a species of quadrupedal humans who would seem to have been covered in bright feathers. On Dondum itself I've seen the massive skulls of cyclopean giants and many other things besides, but in this instance cannot linger and so pass on south towards the minor continent Genotia, some miles off the coast of German Southwest Africa.

Nacumera

Skull Island

Piracy has a long tradition in Genotia and its surrounding isles, and I have always found that I am welcome here, even amongst the Mithras-worshippers found in Ximeque, Genotia's largest region. Gynopyrea, on Genotia's southern coast, is infamous for its effeminate behaviour and its men-girls. It is subsequently far too popular amongst a certain section of my crew, and we head on past Neopie Island, which perhaps goes too far to the opposite extreme in that, being once ruled by Amazons, women are by and large detested, with all foreign females put to death. Pandoclia, nearby, is similar in that its women are controlled more strictly than its men, as is quite proper, with a curfew that forbids them to go out during the evening. Nimpatan, a large island of silk-garbed and gold-worshipping scoundrels, lies further south, and I tell Ishmael to remind me we should plunder it on our way back from Cape Town, our eventual destination."

Though it would seem that Nemo travelled very little in the Indian Ocean, it is thanks to documents found amongst the effects of the great Sikh submariner after his death by one Miss Diver that we know so much about that area's islands. A collector of rare nautical exotica and memorabilia, Nemo had during the 1880s purchased an old parchment manuscript, in Arabic, later authenticated as one of the last surviving copies of the log kept by the famed seagoing Iraqi adventurer Sindbad. It is from this fragile document that we have gathered the majority of the accounts below relating to the islands found off Africa's east coast and in the more northerly climes of the Arabian Sea.

The most southerly of these islands is Canthahar, where the long-lived and agile inhabitants worshipped Monsky, the Sun, and Raka, the Moon, while nearby Cucumber Island, off the east coast of South Africa, is said by Sindbad to be famous for its tree-grown cucumbers and its ferocious windstorms. Three unnamed islands mentioned in the manuscript are probably those settled by the now-obligatory ship-wrecked Englishman, a sometime-associate of Lemuel Gulliver named Sir Charles Smith who was cast up there during 1740, and called by him New Britain. One of these, Rock Island, is still populated by devout religious nudists who engrave the Ten Commandments on each wall of every dwelling.

Further north, just south of Madagascar, is the isle of Bustrol, where Sindbad reports that the inhabitants have formed themselves into perfect square provinces. Upon the Madagascan mainland he describes the northern swamp-isle of Aepyornis, with its talking fourteen-foot-tall birds, which he supposes to be related to the giant avian Rocs that he had once encountered further north. He also notes that some way east of Madagascar is an island where the cliffs, viewed from the sea, resemble nothing so much as a massive human skull, where monstrously proportioned primates had allegedly been seen, along with dragons, Rocs and other creatures of that nature. Just north-east of Madagascar off the coast of Mozambique, although not mentioned by the legendary Iraqi sailor, there exists a mountainous island where in 1782 a stranded Englishwoman, Mrs. Hannah Hewit, built not only her own house of clay bricks but also a mechanical man as

a companion (and possibly, as certain sailors' stories have indecently suggested, as a paramour). Meillcourt, further north still, was in Sindbad's time the province of the peaceful Troglocites and Quacacites, and had not yet been named after the French explorer shipwrecked here during the early eighteenth century, while on nearby "Island of Iron" Marbotikin Dulda, he makes glowing mention of the temple called Miudia-blo, with its colossal statue of the deity built so that its twelve zodiac-sign heads rotate according to the phases of the moon.

From here, just off the coast of Kenya, up to the Arabian Sea itself extends a marvellous archipelago containing perhaps a score of islands, the majority of which were first explored by Sindbad or else his acquaintances. Rondule, the island furthest south, ruled by a hundred chieftains, is famed for the frequent laughter of its jovial people, while on Lamary the naked locals hold women in common and subsist, it's said, upon a diet of fattened children. A sub-group of islands nearby, the Waq archipelago, are said by Sindbad to be ruled by women and roamed by both genii and wild beasts, while of one of the otherwise unremarkable islands of Waq Sindbad makes the mystifying observation that it would make a bad place for a small group of schoolboys to be marooned. To the north, the isle where stands the Mihragian Kingdom is the one location in the world where the sea-stallions come ashore to mate, while King's Kingdom, on an adjacent island, is believed to be the burial site of Solomon, son of David. Sindbad also mentions fearsome serpents here, and mountain-sized fish found in the island's coastal waters. Meanwhile, off Somalia's Coast, is the Azanian Empire, where the cannibal Sakuyu tribe would sometimes trade anthropophagous recipes with cousins from far Lamary.

Double Island, which seems to both rise and submerge at will, lies to the east, while Camphor Island, known for its generous camphor trees and giant horned animal, the *karkadann*, lies further west, as does the island of the Diamond Mountains, where carnivorous jewels can strip the avaricious and unwary traveller down to a skeleton in seconds. Continuing north we pass Old Man of the Sea Island, with its terrible ancient inhabitant reputedly killed by Sindbad, though we only have the mariner's own word for this, and the island of The Mountain of Clouds, its peak only accessible to one wrapped in camel-hide and then carried aloft by a vulture. The nearby Island of Grey Amber, meanwhile, has its tide-lines strewn with so much cast-up treasure that it is to this day renowned as a beachcomber's paradise, whereas Bragman, the Land of Faith, was so devout and dull that Alexander couldn't be bothered to conquer it. The people of the Island of Connubial Sacrifice, at least as they're described by Sindbad, customarily entomb live partners with dead spouses, while a neighbouring tribe will drug visitors with a concoction of coconut milk and hallucinogens before serving them up, cooked or raw, at their banquets.

Manghalour, off the coastline of Saudi Arabia, is another colony established by a shipwrecked Frenchman in the eighteenth century by the simple expedient of overthrowing and then exiling the isle's existing Muslim leadership, and if we venture into the Red Sea we find both the linguistically extraordinary island known as Polyglot, and also Taerg Natib, whose twenty-foot-tall population are all strictly Protestant, and where Papists have thus been summarily burned since the early fifteenth century. In the Arabian Sea near the mouth of the Persian Gulf we have Calonack, not far from Pakistan, where people live within the gorgeous shells of giant molluscs and where every species of the world's fish may be found in staggering profusion off the island's coasts, while further west, Parthalia is inhabited by giants of great longevity, one of whom was said to have assisted in constructing Rome. Astounding though these many islands be, we must now focus our attentions on the mainland, and, commencing with the Middle East, work westward into Africa itself.

Furthest south, sharing borders with Pakistan, Afghanistan and Persia we have the mountainous country Ardistan and its surrounding territories, as described by League associates William Samson Senior and his son, also called William Samson, the feared (and currently famed) "Wolf of Kabul." Reports filed by the Samsons over a fifty year period from around 1880 to the present day describe a fascinating range of sites, not least of which is the immense and glorious palace of the Mir of Ardistan as found in Ard, the capital, reputedly constructed by giant craftsmen from nearby Parthalia. A triple-headed volcano called Djebbel Allah on the northern borders makes a hazard of the route to neighbouring El Hadd, home of the much-admired white lancers, while nearby lands such as Djinnistan, Djunubistan, Ussulistan, Tshobanistan and the giant-built isthmus known as the Chatar Defile have been characterised by the younger Mr. Samson as "pest-holes of tyrants and warlords who seem to find no higher purpose in life than destroying and maiming each other. I have a good mind to let Chung take his *Clicky-Ba* to the whole bloody lot of them." Forty years earlier, his father had made similar remarks concerning the adjacent warring lands of Farghestan and the old Christian kingdom of Orsenna: "If these people have got so much respect for God, then why are they always bloody showing him up in public? I had respect for our Mum, but if I'd gone and massacred half the kids next door she'd have been mortified. She'd never have set foot past our front step again."

The Garamanti tribe inhabiting the Rifei mountains in Afghanistan, with their fanatically observed laws (all offspring after a couple's third child put to death; worship of more than two gods at a time punishable by death; those inventing any new laws condemned to death) also come in for vivid criticism from both Samsons, but we shall pass on towards the west and Persia, where we find the mountain-ringed land of Tallstoria, which employs convict labourers on public services, in reasonable conditions, as a less costly and preferable alternative to prison. Moving westward into neighbouring Iraq, a visit to Samarah and its splendid palace Alkoremi is advised, with the five adjoining palaces (dedicated to the pleasures of each of the five senses) built by the notoriously-damned Caliph Vathek. Not far away, upon the desert borders of Iraq and Syria, stands the fabulously jewelled and mosaic-decorated City of Sand, inhabited since the Crusades by the Sheik of the Mountain and his followers, but this is best seen from a distance, as the city does not welcome tourists. Indeed, it tends to poison them, then turn them loose into the barren desert, there to perish.

In Saudi Arabia, on the Iraqi border at the end of beautiful Fakreddin Valley is the ruined palace Ishtakar, with its black marble terraces where nothing grows, nor lives, and no birds sing, as mentioned by both the notorious Lord Byron and his fellow poet William Ashbless. Underneath these terraces are rumoured to be chambers filled with evil genii, where the demon Eblis once held court in halls of marvellous treasures. It was for a glimpse of these that the doomed Caliph Vathek forfeited his soul, his heart bursting into eternal flame in consequence. From Ishtakar it's possible to see the jewel-like and almost unreachable city of Jannati Shah, at the foot of the dazzling Mountains of Gold, where in the first years of our current century a group of white men, mostly from America,

Parthalia

ventured to steal the Great Pearl Star, bequeathed by a dying Mohammed to his most-favoured wife Ayeshah (not related to the famously long-lived West African Queen Ayesha that we shall encounter later in this narrative, or at least not in so far as we are currently aware). To the southwest, in the vast deserts bordering Yemen, are the gemmed remains of Irem Zat El-Emad, or Irem with the Lofty Buildings, where the half-collapsed jewel-studded spires were built in imitation of Paradise by King Sheddad, who was destroyed with all his family and retainers by a wave of sound, perhaps from space, upon the eve of taking up his residency there. Northwest we pass Golden Mountain, where a sultan's treasure horde was once concealed, and skirt the Christian city Nova Solyma in Israel, where the citizens, despite their Christianity, believe the Universe to be a monstrous uterus, to come at last to Egypt and to continental Africa itself.

In Egypt, on the Red Sea coast we find the ruined palace-principality called Here or Ici, given recently by King Fuad of Egypt to the sole surviving daughter of Czar Nicholas the second, the Grand Duchess Olga. There have been rumours lately in the scandal-sheets to the effect that the Grand Duchess, having been believed killed with her family in 1917, intends to make the fortress a refuge for other famous people who'd prefer the world to think them dead, but this is merely vulgar speculation. Further north, the traveller may choose to take a barge-trip down the curious Brissonte River with its mouth near that of the more famous Nile, and view the freakish tribes inhabiting its various river-islands, including men whose feet point backwards and who thus have difficulty in determining if they are coming, or, indeed, are going. Not far from the Brissonte, upon the beaches close to Alexandria, is Monsters' Park. Here, great Alexander famously repelled frequent invasions of sea-monsters by the clever ruse of building numerous gigantic replicas of the creatures themselves along the coastline, scaring the marauding monsters

back into the ocean. These quite terrifying statues have survived the intervening ages well, commented on by both Orlando and, more recently, by Allan Quatermain. Further south is Heliopolis, a later Freemason-inspired "City of the Sun" that should not be confused with its more venerable namesake, while upon the border with Sudan exists the subterranean Sunless City, with its midnight galleries of guardian gods and monsters, not far from Khartoum.

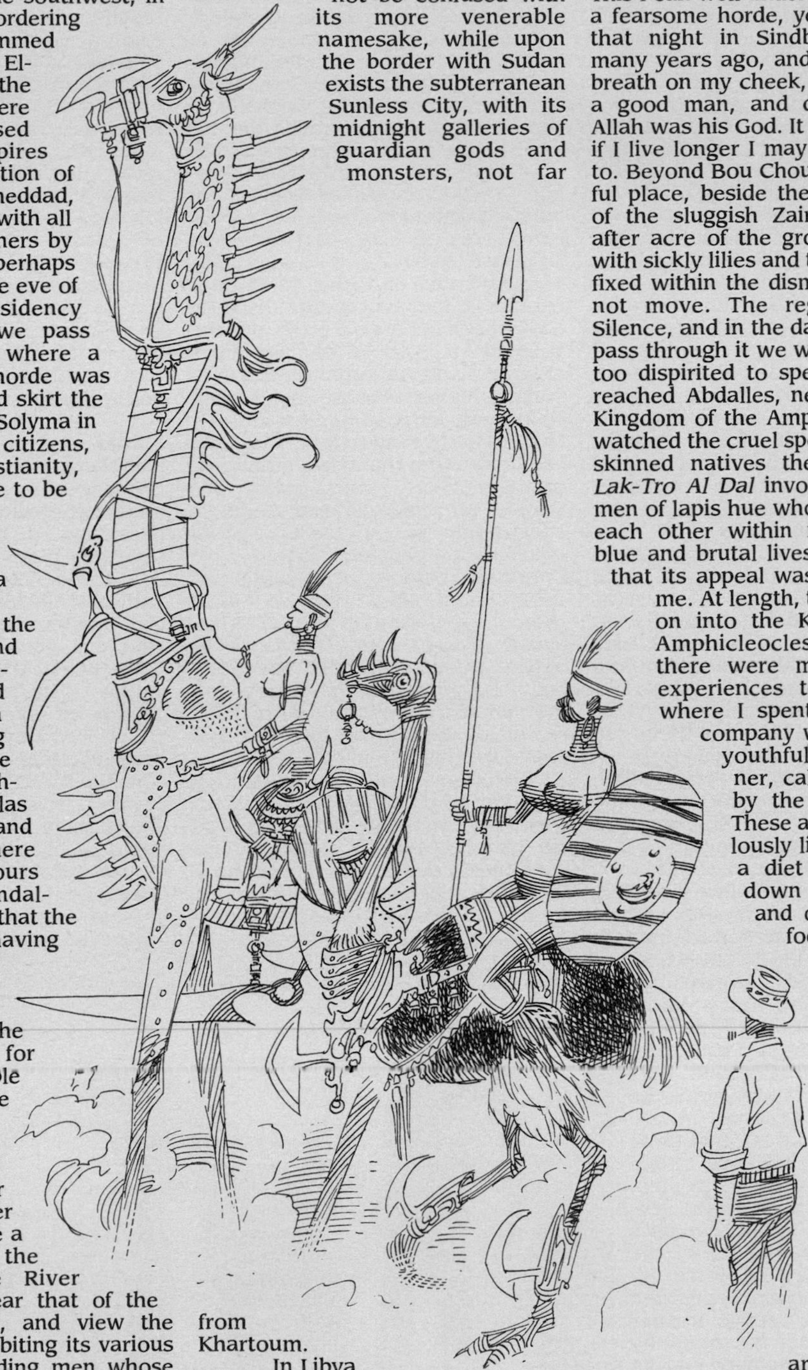

In Libya, to the west, we have locations mentioned by the ever-young and slender gallant named Orlando, who adventured in North Africa during the early sixteenth century, apparently a male during this part of his or her career. "I journeyed to the northwest with my bearers into Libya and therein sought the Kingdom of the Amphicleocles, where it is said the men are red as devils while the

women are as pale as alabaster, and methinks that both alike sound fair and sweet. We passed the ruined citadel of Bou Chougga and heard rumours of a Christian settlement beneath the earth; its founders fled there to escape the frightful influx of Mohammedans into the continent. This I can well understand. They are a fearsome horde, yet when I slept that night in Sindbad's arms so many years ago, and felt his spiced breath on my cheek, I knew he was a good man, and devout, though Allah was his God. It is a puzzle that if I live longer I may see an answer to. Beyond Bou Chougga is a dreadful place, beside the yellow waters of the sluggish Zaire, where acre after acre of the ground is choked with sickly lilies and the clouds hang fixed within the dismal sky, and do not move. The region is called Silence, and in the days it took us to pass through it we were all of us far too dispirited to speak. At last we reached Abdalles, neighbour to the Kingdom of the Amphicleocles, and watched the cruel sports of the blue-skinned natives there. The game *Lak-Tro Al Dal* involves five naked men of lapis hue who beat and whip each other within inches of their blue and brutal lives, and I confess that its appeal was largely lost to me. At length, then, we passed on into the Kingdom of the Amphicleocles itself, where there were many wondrous experiences to be had and where I spent some time in company with a beguiling youthful message-runner, called a *Foul-brac* by the peoples there. These are most marvellously light, existing on a diet of naught but down and cobwebs, and on insubstantial foodstuffs of this like, so make for splendid partners in a dance, or otherwise."

South of Libya, the Republic of Chad is described in part by Allan Quatermain, who visited the area during the course of what are surely his most famous exploits. "Heading into Chad we had the Mountains of the Moon behind us to the north and Umbopa fairly put the wind up Curtis, Good and I by telling us that we were now in Arimaspian Country, where the one-eyed natives wage continual war against the gryphon population. When he told us about Mermecolions (half lion, half ant, they can eat neither flesh nor grain and thus will always die for want of sustenance) we knew the rogue was joking with us. Then, a mile south, Curtis tripped upon a skeleton half buried in the undergrowth that looked like that of some enormous lion, yet had a beak, and now we don't know what to think." An unspecified time later, perhaps days or even weeks, Quatermain makes the following entry: "As we passed from Chad through Central Africa, we made camp in Albino Land, a region sparsely populated by albino Negroes, rather slight of build and with the finest, whitest hair I've ever touched. Their eyes are also quite remarkable, like those of birds. It is a strange effect that suits them well, especially the females. Whatever idle thoughts I had of these grew dim, however, when we moved south into Makalolo and I saw the women warriors there, tall Nubian beauties pledged to fight in service of a monarchy made up of Queen and Queen. We had the fortune to observe a military parade of these, spears glinting in the sun, all mounted upon armoured ostriches or else on towering war-giraffes, a spectacle I shall remember all my days.

"Continuing south, we made hard going of Zaire, thanks largely to our difficulties with the many local tribes such as the ferocious Bulanga and the utterly dreadful wife-trading cannibals of the M'tezo, who eat all their spare female relatives. We skirted round a hamlet called Ben Khatour's Village that's allegedly some sort of Arab colony, and then, crossing an arid plain into the densest and most lushly fertile jungle I have ever known, we came into the kingdom Pal-Ul-Don. Here, in A-lur, the well-named City of Lights, we almost thought that we had found the place our expedition is in search of, so astounding are the carven terraces of pallid limestone with their monster-heads in startling relief (these were not wholly unlike the supposed gryphon skeleton we thought we'd found in Arimaspian Country, but bigger, with a ruff of bone behind the head and two rhino-like horns grown from the beak). Passing on, however, on the south horizon we at last beheld the miles-high peaks called by the local people Saba's Breasts, which mark the plateau Kukuanaland whereon we hope to find our goal, the diamond-laden lost mines of King Solomon himself."

Returning the attentions of our Almanac to the southeast we come to Abyssinia and the neighbouring Kingdom of Ishmaelia, widely known today as a focus of European business interests, that unfortunately does not enjoy the usual subsequent prosperity. Before Ishmaelia came to prominence, however, Abyssinia itself was commented upon at length by League associate Orlando, visiting the area in the early sixteenth century. "How many years, I wonder, has it been, or centuries, since last I knew the pleasure of these sands between my toes?

Travelling without company I soon came to those dear, familiar ruins in the north, set on their stone plateau; those tumbled relics of a city that I still walk in my dreams of childhood, where my girlish fingertips still know each dent in each worn stone as though it were a long lost cousin. Tethering my horse I found my way through the familiar labyrinths and chambers, mounting finally the old iron ladder to our city's central courtyard, or at least its remnants. Some of my old fellows left their hole-like dwellings at the city's outskirts to come greet me, though the Troglodyte condition is much worse in them, and has advanced since last we met. I hardly could make out a word they spoke, though our discourse was amiable, and they seemed most amazed to find me now a man, insisting that I drop my britches and provide them evidence of this. I asked after my much-beloved old Greek friend, Mr. Cartaphilus, but from what I could make out of their reply have not seen him for some time, and think that he still roams the world disconsolately, seeking some eventual cure for what he views as our abiding curse.

"I left the city once more, and continued on to Nubia where perfumed Senapho is ruler, though I knew him when men called him Prester John. Along my way I saw again the places I remember from my youth, like lovely Saba (native name for Sheba who was consort to King Solomon). In the southwest, they say, are mountains named for Saba's breasts, close by bright diamond mines that the great King and sorcerer once owned. It is at Saba here in Abyssinia, though, that Solomon and Sheba's tomb is found, all made from gold and crystal and shot through with precious jewels. The tomb is somewhat overgrown, though I saw several of the natives as they worked to trim the rampant vegetation back. They were all men in middle life and thus their skin had stripes of black and yellow, for the Sabans are born with a hide of brilliant daffodil that turns as dark as night come their old age. I journeyed on, and rode a while beside the Marvellous River where I saw a unicorn and tiger, both asleep together on the further shore, and to the east I heard the music of sun-worshippers with gongs and cymbals, carried on a dusk breeze from the Temple of the Sun in Mezzorania, its distant spires and bridges blazing in the last lights of the day."

Elsewhere in the same documents Orlando makes mention of the City of the Apes, ransacked and pillaged nightly by ferocious simians, not far east in the southern reaches of Somaliland. All these areas are today, of course, part of the larger country known as Freeland, a vast independent state established in the 1880s by the International Free Society, extending down the continent past Kenya into Tanganyika and the Sultanate

of Zanzibar. Close by, on Tanganyika's coastline we find Jolliginki, where the Land of Monkeys is located. It was here that the great naturalist John Dolittle (a school-friend of George Edward Challenger, occasional consultant to Miss Murray's secondly-assembled League) discovered the purportedly two-headed animal that caused such an intense controversy amongst zoologists and scientists around the century's end, unequalled until the discovery of Piltdown Man in 1912. A little further south, upon the coast of Portuguese East Africa, there is Bong Tree Land, famed for its succulent ring-sporting pigs, while further south still, passing swiftly though Basilisk Country and avoiding both its manticores and the lethal gaze of its native serpents, we reach Butua in Bechuanaland. This cruel and bestial realm, notorious for the fearful treatment meted to its womenfolk, was said by Percy Blakeney to be an occasional resort for the depraved aristocrats of Silling castle, high in Germany's Black Forest, as referred to in our second chapter. North of here, in German Southwest Africa there stands the city of Beersheba, where the citizens believe in the existence of two more Beershebas, one infernal and the other one celestial, though reportedly they have some difficulty in establishing which one is which.

It is now time for us to turn our Almanac's attentions to the west of Africa, resuming Wilhelmina Murray's commentary from the point at which we left it in our opening paragraphs, with Murray and her escort Mr. Quatermain arriving in Nouakchott on the coast of Mauritania. "So this is Africa, and not at all what I'd anticipated, at least in so far as the feel of the place is concerned. It's as clean and as open as wind, and has an intangible *bigness* to it that is most like that experienced in certain music. The smells have all the texture and the intricacy of a painting. I'm not getting this across at all well, and had best abandon the attempt. After we'd docked and disembarked, Allan procured us cheap hotel accommodation in Nouakchott from which we could carry out all the more local of our explorations, with the first of these being a tour of Mauritania itself. On our first day, out walking in the hot, damp forests near the coast, we stumbled on a most peculiar site, being a long abandoned hut apparently untouched by either local folk or wildlife. You will think me mad, but there seemed something strangely English about this abode, with its clay cladding and its window grids of woven branches; its roof thatched after a style that I am sure I've seen in Devon. Inside was a quaint stone fireplace and rudimentary furnishings, and I had quite a nasty turn when I happened upon a baby's crib containing a small skeleton, though Allan reassured me that

the bones appeared to him to be those of an infant monkey, possibly some unfamiliar species of gorilla. This information, while more comforting than the alternatives, did little to dispel the melancholy strangeness of the place, and we elected to leave everything just as we found it, making our way back through the dark trees where great apes howled somewhere above us.

"In the next few weeks we travelled widely in the nearby regions, and I got the sense that Allan was not here to merely see the sights, but had some other purpose of his own, making enquiries of the local men in languages that he seemed fluent in but which I did not understand. I must admit, I entertained the notion that his old addictions had perhaps resurfaced and that he sought drugs (perhaps the substance called *taduki,* which he often mentions), though this turned out not to be the case.

"We journeyed into eastern Mauritania where, we were told, exist two isolated outposts of the Roman Empire, Castra Sanguinarius and Castrum Mare, though we had no luck in finding these and carried on towards Morocco and Algeria. In Morocco we rode through the marvellous oasis of Giphantia, so uniquely fertile that new species will arise, evolve and then become extinct within the space of a few weeks, and past the walled and dead City of Brass, long stripped of all its riches and its bottle-imps, as we made for Tangiers. Here, in a quarter of the city that tourists have named 'the Interwoven Zone,' Allan made his by-now furtive enquiries of a seedy-looking chap who had the sweet, medicinal aroma on his dusty clothing that I now associate with opium, and we were led through narrow streets to a stone house with cool, dark rooms where we were introduced to one of the most utterly repellent and unsettling individuals that it has been my misfortune to encounter.

"Squatting in a corner swathed in shapeless robes, with only one deformed hand visible, clutching the fuming mouthpiece of a hookah pipe, I would not even swear our host was human. A pretty but subdued young Arab boy lay curled up like a dog upon the rush mat where the creature sat, but had a frightened air to him and did not meet our eyes. Our host's voice, issuing from the darkened cave-mouth of his cowl, was guttural yet sounded somehow slippery. We were informed that we were in the presence of a...I believe the word was 'Mudwunk' or 'Mugwump' or something like that...and that this creature could provide us with whatever drugs or sexual activities we might desire. I was about to leave when Allan asked the monster if we could instead buy information. He desired to know where might be found the kingdom of a woman called Ayesha, the first time (but not the last) I was to hear the name. After a pause, the being shook the cowled, misshapen lump that was its head, and bade us leave. Outside, in some high dudgeon, I demanded Allan make some explanation of his secretive enquiries and a full account of this Ayesha woman that he seemed so willfully intent on finding. Seeming both abashed and hesitant, he told me that he had encountered this Ayesha many years ago, a deathless Queen sustaining herself through the centuries by immersion in a fountain or a 'Fire of Life,' some manner of volcanic phenomenon found in her kingdom, although Allan had no idea where this place might be. He told me that of late he has been feeling old (he is in his mid-seventies), most noticeably upon those occasions when we try to make love, and that his greatest desire was that he should be young again, for me. I was so moved by this, I swore to help him on the instant. Later on, when we made camp upon the desert outskirts of Algeria, fearing that this 'Fire of Life' may prove a disappointment, I endeavoured to convince him, with a demonstration, that he still possessed youth and vitality enough for me, wherein I fancy that I met with some success.

"Algeria was vast and beautiful, with something Biblical about the sky at night, although I don't know what I mean by that, exactly. The northern deserts, stretching east into Tunisia, have such grandeur that I felt alarmed by all the stories in the newspapers that I had read across the years on how the French intended to transform this area, with interlinked canals, to a 'Saharan Sea.' I hope this never comes to pass. Elsewhere within Algeria we passed through a reputed cannibal-and-sorcerer infested region called Crotalophoboi Land, although I am glad to report that we met neither of these dangers, nor did we encounter any locals, so that we could not investigate the rumour that their eyes are set into the bottom of their feet. Travelling further south we saw the prosperous kingdom of Macaria to the west of us and soon passed into Brodie's Land, apparently sometimes referred to as Mlch Country after its inhabitants, the Mlch. Having read the accounts by my great eighteenth-century predecessor Lemuel Gulliver of travels into Houyhnhnms Land, it strikes me that the Mlch are similar to the bestial Yahoos that he speaks of, only more peculiar still in that their memory appears to function in reverse, so that they are unable to recall events that took place only moments since, but will have vivid recollections of things that will happen in five minutes time. Leaving the ragged brutes behind us, throwing filth and shrieking in our wake, we headed into the more southern parts of French West Africa.

"Headed for Niamey, we first passed through the outskirts of the city known as Blackland, where surrounding desert has been turned to verdant fields and orchards by the rain-making device of the reputedly insane French scientist Marcel Camaret. Camaret's employer, and the ruler of this territory, is the wanted English murderer and kidnapper named William Ferney, more frequently referred to in the gutter press as 'Harry Killer.' Though I am sure our masters would be pleased were we to capture Mr. Ferney and return with him to England, the unholy reputation of his small militia of armed thugs (known sardonically as Ferney's 'Merry Fellows') led us to accept discretion as the better part of valour, and we kept as far away from Blackland as we could while we rode onto into Uziri Country, where we similarly tried our hardest to avoid the fierce Waziri tribe. The valley country Midian, where the people were converted to fanatically devoted Christians during the first century by Paul of Tarsus, proved as inhospitable, and I confess that I was rather glad as we passed by Niamey into Upper Volta. Here, heading northwest towards the French Sudan, we saw the legendary minarets of Opar glinting high above that citadel's impregnable and massive walls, which reared like smooth grey cliffs out from a quilt of green.

"In French Sudan we managed to pass through the Valley of the Sepulchre without becoming caught up in a theological dispute between the separate 12th century Crusader colonies of Nimmr, and its sister city at the valley's other end. Investigating rumours of a secret and forbidden city ruled by a fierce warrior queen, we next camped by the great volcano Tuen-Baka, in which we believed this Kingdom (called Ashair by local tribesmen) to be situated. The next morning we saw (from a distance, thankfully) the scuttling forms of a repulsive breed of lizard-men on the volcano's higher slopes, from which Allan concluded that whoever ruled in Ashair could have no connection to his Queen Ayesha, and suggested we move on. The deep, enormous footprint, possibly from some variety of dinosaur, that we discovered not far from the place that we had slept may also have exerted some degree of influence on my companion's eagerness to leave the area. We passed on through the outer reaches of the Great Thorn Forest where we had a startling encounter with the towering tribeswomen of Alali, harsh-eyed goddesses who stand some eight or nine feet tall and who would only speak to or acknowledge me, apparently regarding Allan as beneath contempt. They said that they knew nothing of Ayesha, but advised me to be out of the Thorn Forest before darkness fell, lest I should fall prey to their hated enemies, the tribesmen of nearby Minuni who, the women told me, would kill any giantesses that they came across. When I protested that I was no giantess as they were, they explained that the Minuni, being somewhere between ten and thirteen inches tall, would almost certainly see me as such and set about me anyway. The thought of tiny, armed men quite unnerved me when I read of something similar in Dr. Gulliver's notes from the eighteenth century, and so it was that I required no further urging to move on with Allan towards Dakar on the coast, from whence we thought to make our disappointed way back to our hotel base in Nouakchott."

This was not to be, however. Heading north along the coast from Dakar in the final days of 1900, Quatermain and Murray found a coastal kingdom that, despite the many wondrous things they'd seen thus far, still staggered them. "I cannot believe I am not dreaming. Riding into Fantippo, the first thing that I heard besides the distant screeches of macaws and monkeys was the sound of carol-singers, halfway through the final verse of *'Once in Royal David's City.'* They were celebrating Christmas, which I've only just remembered is tomorrow. Then we saw the bright red English pillar-box amongst a clump of palm trees, and our puzzlement became complete. A Negro in an English postman's uniform was emptying the contents of the post-box, envelopes with large and vivid

Fantippo

stamps, into his sack. He sweated copiously, the uniform's thick navy-blue material clearly unsuited for the West African sun." Making enquiries, Quatermain and Murray learned that Fantippo's King Koko, much impressed by what he'd heard of England's postal service, had decided he would emulate it back at home. Investigating further, the pair were delighted to discover that the land's Postmaster General owned a detailed map of Africa in which the continent had been divided neatly into postal districts. District EC7, corresponding roughly with the British Protectorate of Uganda, had Ayesha's city, Kor, listed amongst its prominent addresses. Much encouraged by their find, the couple celebrated Christmas in Fantippo, little knowing that it was to be their last together. Setting out once more for the interior in the first weeks of 1901, they headed for Uganda and the City of Ayesha, following which,

if we are to believe Miss Murray's uncharacteristically untidy notes upon the subject, the great veteran explorer met with his demise.

On the 8th of January, 1901, they trekked southeast, into Guinea, passing through the jungle region known as the Ape Kingdom by its natives, where the drumming of the simian hominids' famed "Dum-Dum" ceremony echoed on the wind above the forest canopy, and skirted by the secret lake called Junganyika which reputedly contains those waters that are left from Noah's flood. Travelling on through Sierra Leone, they passed the Kingdom of the One-Eyed, where the population will traditionally put out one of their eyes in solidarity with one-eyed monarchs, and went on into Liberia, founded by slaves from America during the early nineteenth century, before progressing to the Cote d'Ivoire. Here they saw the droppings-fouled great wall bounding the city of Xujan, where madmen worship parrots, before journeying on to the Gold Coast and Togo, passing through the Empire known as Ponukele-Drelchkaff (then embroiled in war between King Talou VII and King Yaour IX) upon their way. As they rode through the province of Dahomey to Nigeria, Murray insisted that they pay a visit to the famed Viceroyalty of Ouidah, where she wished to inspect both the Cathedral of the Immaculate Conception and the famed ancestral home of the Viceroy Francisco Manoel da Silva. Finding both of these locations "dingy, and in need of a good dusting," the pair journeyed on into Nigeria itself.

"Nigeria seems profoundly strange," observed Miss Murray in her journal, "or at least if we are to believe the stories told us by our guides and bearers. In the north, they say, is Sleepless City, where the natives never sleep themselves and thus will bury sleeping travellers, believing them to be deceased. If this happens to you, or indeed should you endure any variety of death, disfigurement or maiming, your companions would do well, apparently, to carry your remains to Fixit City on Nigeria's Bauchi Plateau, where the natives seemingly are able to mend anyone from nothing more than bones or hanks of hair. Dead's Town, deep in the Nigerian bush and dwelled in by the lately dead, sounded somewhere to be avoided, as did the cruel and insanely capricious more northerly town, Unreturnable-Heaven. We saw swamp-bound Wraith-Island

from a distance, and although its beautiful inhabitants are said to be the most hospitable of people, we thought we detected several monstrous forms wallowing in the shallows off its coast and so passed on through Cameroon towards the Congo. On our way we had the most delightful treat of falling in amongst a herd of the most civilised and gentle elephants that I have ever seen, one of whom I thought I saw wearing a small golden crown atop his head, although Allan insists that I must be mistaken. The charm of this encounter lasted until we passed by the horrid little hut, deep in the Congo and still ringed by decomposing heads on poles, where ivory-trader's agent Kurtz met his deserved demise, recounted in the papers published by a Mr. Marlow just a year or two ago. We hurried on through Belgian Congo, and into Uganda, where we saw the mountain-ringed plateau whereon lies Kor rise up from the surrounding landscape like some dreadful fortress from the Middle Ages."

It is here that Mina Murray's journal starts to become messy and erratic, though this is forgivable when we consider the tremendous upsets that she must have been enduring. She describes with great lucidity how she and Quatermain, bearers now fled, made their way through the mountains down the bed of a dried prehistoric canal, where they saw members of the Amahagger tribe, dressed in their antelope and leopard skins, dancing about fires made from burning mummies looted from the catacombs beneath the mountains. She tells how they eventually reached Kor itself, which they discovered to be now ruled by a native Amahagger woman posing as Ayesha (whom, they learned, was now believed to have been reincarnated somewhere off in Asia). This quite ordinary mortal woman, fearful that the duo would expose her as less than a god-

dess to her followers, informed them how they might reach the supposed "Fire of Life," which was a day's march east, within a meteoric crater. Murray next recounts the couple's journey to this place and their discovery of the strange and luminescent pool that spat and bubbled at the crater's centre.

"It was utterly unearthly, filled with neither fire nor liquid but a strange blue energy that glowed like flame but spurted up and fell in globules more like water. All around the edges of the pool a great variety of names had been patiently carved by idle hands into the ancient rock. We saw the name 'Orlando' and a word that I thought might have been the ancient Greek for 'Homer.' We undressed, me taking off even my scarf, and I elected to go first into the pool, which, neither hot nor cool, had the most eerie tingling sensation that accompanied its luminous cascade. I climbed out of its further side as Allan started to climb in behind me, and beheld myself in disappointment. I'd not changed at all. These hateful scars were still about my throat, and all my body was the same. I next heard Allan make a cry behind me, and..." At this point, Mina Murray's description becomes mostly unreadable. The next five pages following the above entry have all been crossed out so heavily as to be quite beyond recovery, and when the narrative resumes the pair have left Uganda and are in Anglo-Egyptian Sudan, headed north with Quatermain seemingly in ill health.

"Following our dreadful disappointment in Ayesha's kingdom when we learned the so-called Fire of Life had **no effect whatsoever,** Allan seemed to lose the will to live. We traveled north through Blemmyae Country, where we saw the preserved body of one of the region's earliest inhabitants, whose face was in his chest and had no head. Allan was so ill I feared he would not last until we reached his much-beloved lost land of Zuvendis,

beyond forests, hills and marshlands further north. With this achieved, however, I am sad to say that he did not last long. In the Zuvendian capital Milosis, where he'd once pretended to have died during the 1880s, Allan Quatermain expired and was interred next to the graves made for his friends Sir Henry Curtis and the giant Umslopogaas. Obviously, I was dreadfully upset. All is not doom and gloom however, for just prior to Allan's death we found out that a son of his he'd thought long dead (also called Allan) was in fact alive and living in Milosis.

"This younger Allan is one of the most attractive, firm-muscled young men I have ever had the fortune to encounter, and it would be fair to say that an attraction has been evident between us since the start of our acquaintance. We resolved that he should leave Zuvendis and that we should travel on together as companions, possibly paying a visit to the ruined city off in Abyssinia that we found a stone-etched map of by the crater-pool in Kor. I am certain it is what his father would have wished."

The callous and dismissive tone with which Miss Murray hurries through her sparse description of her lover's death, along with the indecent haste she shows in forming a romantic bond with Quatermain's young son have both contributed (along with her divorcee status) to an appraisal of Miss Murray as "promiscuous" in the personal files maintained by her superiors at Military Intelligence. These files also express great disappointment that the "Fire of Life," the source of immortality and endless youth (of some interest to England's ruling class), should have turned out to be a myth, and recommend that Murray's travels be curtailed in future. This did not prevent her and the younger Allan Quatermain, however, from embarking on a trip to China during late 1906, as we shall learn during our Almanac's next fascinating chapter, when we focus our attention upon Asia and the far Australias.

Chapter Five

Asia and the Australias: Visions of Cathay

When Mina Murray and her intimate companion Allan Quatermain the second (son of the original explorer, as discussed in our last chapter), following their African excursions journeyed back to England in the summer of 1901, they found a country fraught with the elations and anxieties of a new, unfamiliar century. The nation's difficulties in rebuilding London and returning to full military strength after the Martian landings during 1898 had clearly played their part in losing Britain the Boer War, and by 1901 the dreadful airship wars afflicting early twentieth century Europe were already underway. National pride, however, had been raised by the delayed and yet surprisingly successful British lunar expedition by Professor Selwyn Cavor, planned originally for 1900. There prevailed an atmosphere of jittery excitement and wild rumour, such as several unsubstantiated sightings of reputedly deceased detective Sherlock Holmes, which would not be confirmed until the following year.

Quatermain Jr. and Murray seem to have been occupied with relatively minor local matters and investigations for the next few years, confining themselves to the British Isles and largely looking into supernatural phenomena, related to the Government's increased concern at the idea of hostile, alien dimensions bordering our own. In the later months of 1901, for example, Wilhelmina Murray visited the Oxford mental institution where the sole survivor of an expedition into these alarming territories during the 1870s, this being the Reverend Dr. Eric Bellman, was confined. 1902 saw Quatermain and Murray visiting the shores of Ireland, possibly as part of a two-year investigation into "borderland" or "gateway' sites such as the Mathers house discussed in our first chapter, although journals from this period are either missing or suppressed. During 1904 they were investigating rural English mystery locations such as Winton Pond near Ipswich or Smalldene in Sussex, and it was not until 1906 that they came to travel overseas again. At this time England was preparing to embark upon an Anglo-Russian Convention covering Afghanistan, Tibet and Persia that would extend Britain's influence within the European power blocs. When it was suggested that Miss Murray, as the sole surviving member of the 19th-century League, should visit Asia with an eye to strengthening diplomatic links, she readily agreed provided that she be escorted by her paramour, the younger Quatermain.

Their journeys through Russia, Mongolia and China, during which they were to meet for the first time the sensuous and eternal ambiguity known as Orlando, have provided almost all the information in our logs and journals that pertains to Asia (saving only for those entries made by Lemuel Gulliver's group in the later eighteenth century), and therefore comprise the most substantial portion of our current narrative. We shall, then, save Miss Murray's Oriental travels and adventures until later, and commence instead with a consideration of more southerly extremes, south of Australia and New Zealand, at the very borders of the vast Antarctic wastes we shall discuss at length in our last chapter. Here, to Australia's southwest there is the island kingdom of

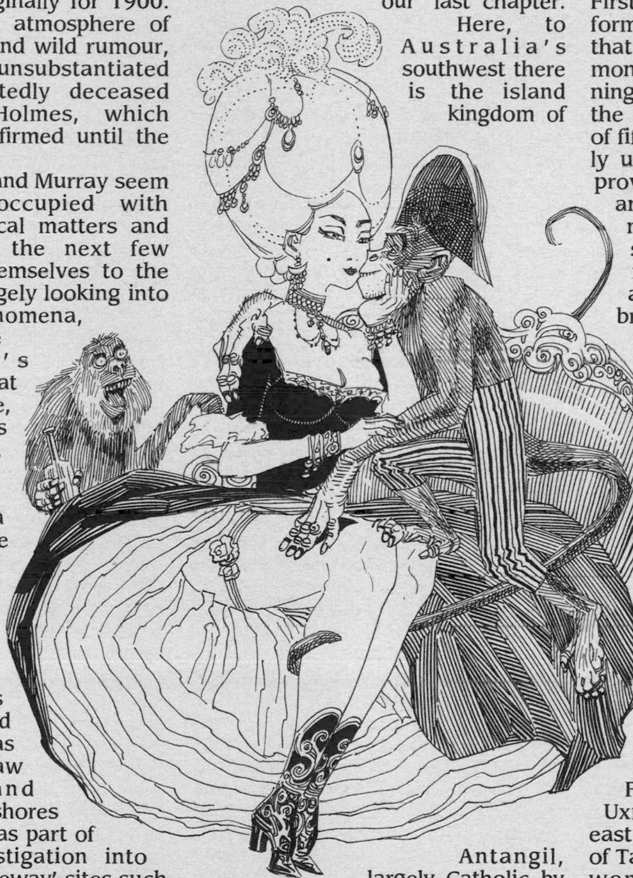

Antangil, largely Catholic by inclination, where the seasons seem to happen all at once and where a strange amphibious lion-faced creature thrived until the breed was hunted to extinction in the 18th century. Some distance east of Antangil we find a longer list of since-exterminated species (unicorns, winged horses, concave dromedaries with a hollow where the hump should be) upon the minor continent Terre Australe, where the hermaphrodite, bisexual natives live in pleasant harmony and yet regard Europeans as "sea monsters." Travelling further, to the southeast of New Zealand lie the weed and coral-crusted ruins of Standard Island, a huge artificial island-ship constructed in the 1890s with the backing of American financiers, called "The Pearl of the Pacific" and the world's ninth wonder before it was tragically destroyed by storms in 1895. Not far north from this looming hulk are the Jumelles, two islands best known for the vicious punishments awarded to adulterers, polygamists and such, while further east lie prehistoric Caspak and the nearby isle of Oo-Oh where the winged, malignant Wieroo people are believed by some to be degenerate cousins of the Vril-ya found beneath Newcastle in the north of England.

Meanwhile, in the southern reaches of Australia itself we come to what remains of Farandoulie, close to the largely-rebuilt city of Melbourne, which was itself almost destroyed by the ape-reared Farandoulien monarch Saturnin the First during the 1870s. Saturnin had formed his kingdom on the principle that man and ape should live harmoniously together, and was planning a campaign to similarly liberate the simians of India when his army of fifty thousand primates was fatally undermined by the British, who provided the monkeys with whisky and prostitutes. Moving further north, it is still possible to see small tribes of Erewhonians, a rustic but intensely beautiful and previously highly civilised branch of humanity who in the later nineteenth century still possessed a culture both enlightened and extensive. Sadly, by our current year of 1930, it appears that native Erewhonians are all but extinct on the Australian mainland, with the few remaining groups forced to eke out a marginal, precarious existence in the dusty ruins of their once magnificent and proud civilization.

North of Australia exists a massive spread of islands, ranging from the somewhat puritanical but brightly-dressed folk of Altruria in the far west, past the East Indies and New Guinea, on to savage Flotsam and the Mayan colony of Uxmal in the east. Westward, just east of Altruria there are the islands of Taprobane and New Gynia, where women rule. Forest-covered Taprobane hosts a serpent with one head at either end. Upon an isolated hill there stands the City of the Sun, discovered by a vessel from Genoa in the seventeenth century, where science and the liberal arts are venerated, where the colour black is frowned upon and where those who have been accused of sodomy must walk the city for two days in penance with a shoe hung round their neck. The founder of the eighteenth century group, ship's surgeon Lemuel Gulliver, made various comments in his log about this chain of islands when, as an old man, he

Bandelies

took his cadre of incredulous adventurers on a last voyage to those exotic islands that he claimed to have discovered in his youth:

"Soon wearying of solemn Taprobane, and New Gynia and its female tyranny, we raised our anchor and went east, so coming presently to Lilliput, just off Sumatra's southern tip. Putting to shore and making our way carefully inland so that we should not step upon a cultivated field nor trample some good farmer's herd, thus we arrived outside the capital, Mildendo, with its city walls that tower in height some thirty inches. This, as Mistress Hill remarked, is scarcely level with her garter, though she and my other colleagues marvelled greatly at the tiny native folk that milled upon the battlements, regarding us in panic. Lilliput, it seems, is altered much since last I put by in those parts. Its miniscule inhabitants, I fear, have swifter, briefer lives than we of greater stature, so that many generations may have passed within this score or so of years, and my first visit is forgotten or else naught but legend. It seemed plain that our arrival was the cause of much distress amongst the populace, and so we left and made instead for Java.

"This largest island of the Indonesian chain was misidentified as recently as 1753, called Bingfield's Island by one William Bingfield, late of England. Shipwrecked here and unaware that this was Java, he imagined he'd discovered it and named the island for himself. Here we put in and visited the kingdom of Melinde, being fortunate to journey there during a lull in its incessant slave-trade war with neighbouring Ganze, and going on from here came to Kronomo, a walled city-kingdom some five miles in its circumference to the isle's

south-east. Near here we searched in vain for some sight of the fierce and shaggy Dog-birds that once occupied this territory (which Mr. Bumppo hoped to shoot) but left without a glimpse, supposing that these fabulous meat-eating beasts must all be dead. Southeast of Java we came by the massive island of Australia and were much perplexed, since this was clearly not the much more famous landmass of that name. Investigating, we discovered that the island was divided as two separate countries, the most easterly known as Sporoumbia, with its capital city Sporoundia apparently inhabited entirely by those born deformed or monstrous. Neighbouring Sevarambia, to the west, was much more civilised and pleasing and we were delighted, after being disappointed by the Dog-bird, to encounter many species of the unique local fauna, notably the bandelies, a large, goatheaded deer, quite like a maneless horse but with fantastic horns of what seemed glass, which we at length persuaded Mr. Bumppo not to take as trophies.

"Journeying up around the eastmost tip of Java we passed first by Pathan, where trees grow honey, meal and wine, and where giant reeds with jewels clasped at their roots are used to build both homes and ships. Next we struck northward, past New Guinea on our starboard bow, while off to port we saw both Pala, where the potent moksha fungus may be found, and oil-rich neighbouring Rendang. North of New Guinea we passed through the Luquebaralideaux Islands, where pork-sausage creatures called andouilles are said to roam in strings, nourishing themselves by supping from the many mustardstreams which course there. Heading east we moored quite near Cuffycoat's Island, home of eloquent

orang-utans and barbarous cannibals, where in the night a shoal of local mermaids swam up alongside, to pester Mistress Hill and Mrs. Blakeney with incessant questions as to what the latest ladies' fashions were that might be found in Europe. In the morning we pressed onwards past the towering volcanic island of Manoba to the south, and also sighted off New Guinea's eastern coast the great island Bensalem, that once traded with Atlantis and where monkeys have been trained to sweep the streets by recourse to a brain-improvement process called suturization. Some way off Bensalem we could also see the lonely isle of Uffa, and a place that local seafarers have told us has been lately settled by the shipwrecked family of a Swiss pastor, named by them New Switzerland.

"We next went north, since it is my intent to take our fellowship as far as wondrous Balnibarbi and Laputa. On our way we skirted Yoka Island, with its shaven-headed samurai, and the extensive island commonwealth of Oceana, its rich culture a result of being frequently invaded by the Romans and the Teutons. Further on, we came at last to the familiar waters of Glubbdubdrib, Isle of Sorcerors, whereby we dropped our anchor and next went ashore to be most graciously received by the isle's governor (who may have been a son of the man holding this position when I last was in these parts, or else that eminence himself somehow kept young by magic. If it is this last, then I confess it for a talent I should not much mind myself). The governor is still empowered to command the spectral dead as servants, and still willing to oblige a favoured guest by summoning the spirit of his or her choice. Though I entreated my companions to refuse this generous offer, Mr. Blakeney was most adamant, insisting on the company of a revered and ancient ancestor from his own lineage. When conjured, this shade proved to be not wholly the aristocratic personage of Blakeney family legend, but instead the spirit of a one-eyed horse thief with a desperate mania for public self-pollution. Disheartened with the vision of his heritage provided by this squinting, pizzle-waving apparition, Mr. Blakeney fast succumbed to melancholia, insisting that we sail without delay on the next morning's tide.

"Thus we came to the larger isle of Luggnagg, further north, and though we did not visit long I took the opportunity to introduce my fellows to a doleful-looking Struldbrugg that we met upon the beach. He looked to be in middle life, as many Struldbruggs do, but as the coin-sized spot near his left brow had darkened to its deepest black he may well have been several hundred years in age. Despised and envied by Luggnagg's mortal inhabitants, the Struldbruggs lead a largely solitary existence, and the fellow we encountered seemed mistrustful of our questions. Asked about the origins of his deathless condition, he replied after consideration that he thought his immortality and brow-mark both traits he and his kind had inherited from some long-distant forebear, said in legend to have been a visitor to Luggnagg, come from distant Abyssinia, where our informant thought there might exist a city of undying folk like he. When I remarked I thought it likelier this Afric city of immortals be no more than wistful myth, our Struldbrugg friend became offended and stormed off along the surf-line, no more to be seen, whence we sailed on, passing Tracoda to the east, where the cave-dwelling natives speak in hisses like the serpents that provide their staple diet. East of Tracoda, I have heard, exist three islands named for their distinctly coloured sands, green, red, and black, where legend tells of monk-protected tunnels leading off to far Tibet, but these we had no leisure to investigate, and so with a good wind made north for Balnibarbi, which we reached the following afternoon.

"Balnibarbi, it distresses me to note, is every bit as hopeless and impoverished as when I saw it last, with the energies its population might quite reasonably be expected to expend in growing food or building decent houses for themselves instead diverted to their endless stream of 'projects.' I observed how one such project, that of trying to extract sunlight from cucumbers, which I'd remarked upon during my previous visit, had since grown to a thriving industry with great cucumber-patch plantations to provide for it. I could not tell quite how much sunlight was yet manufactured by this novel process since it rained without cease all the time we were in Balnibarbi, but it may be there is something to it. My companions were by this time asking rancorously why I'd fetched them to this dismal place, upon which I invited them to risk the rain by tilting back their heads and gazing upwards. Doing so, they gasped as one.

"Above us, half-masked by the stormy grey from which the pelting downpour fell there hung the dark mass of Laputa, flying island homestead of the science-and-learning preoccupied Tomtoddies, as I've sometimes heard Laputans called. I told my comrades of Laputa's many marvels, of its striking and flirtatious women and its foods served up in musical or else mathematical shapes, but with there being no way we might reach the island, I fear my descriptions fell well short of the adventure that my fellows had been promised. They were very good, and did not chaff me as we tramped back through the

Balnibarbi rain towards our ship, although when I suggested we sail on and try to spot the language-obsessed island called Locuta that a son of mine once told me he had found, they grew less amiable and threatened to maroon me if we did not sail at once for less obtuse and more inviting climes, to which I most reluctantly gave my assent, and we made south again, for Indonesia.

"We passed east of Zipang, or of Japan as it is these days called, and went south by way of Formosa, which possesses off its coast another smaller island of the same name, where the women and the men go naked save for plaques of gold and silver. Further on, northwest of Borneo, we saw the mountain Tushuo rising from the sea with the gigantic peach-tree at its peak where once two famed ghost-catchers lived, and heading on passed by the Island of the Roc, so called, that

is in fact not isle at all but rather a mere egg of those colossal fowl, its tip protruding from these China seas. Nearby we saw another, smaller island, situated opposite a river-mouth in nearby Borneo. Protected by a reef it seemed fecund and full of life, yet to my knowledge it has never been explored nor named. We sailed on past the Isle of Salmasse where some trees grow meal while others drip a fearful venom, as on Pathan near to Java, and came likewise by the islands Raso (where men will be hung if they fall ill) and strange Macumeran, where the hound-headed populace adore their ox-god with unfathomable rituals and barking, howling incantations. Finally we reached the gulf of Siam, mooring near the isle of Tilibet, a place that I myself had never visited yet which was recommended to me by my eldest son, John, who himself is something of a traveller, as with my various other children and

Laputa

descendants. Putting into shore, I think I speak for all of us when I say that our time amongst the short-lived Tilibetans was peculiarly moving. Whilst the company of the immortal Struldbruggs can ofttimes become dispiriting and lead the mind to a consideration of one's own mortality, the Tilibetans, who can talk when scarcely a day old, yet who die spent and ancient by the age of twenty, have an opposite effect, exciting the profoundest sympathy.

"We stayed perhaps a month there, long enough to witness babies grown to strong young children or to see a youthful beauty lose her bloom, then journeyed on round the Malay peninsula, through the Malacca straits into the Bay of Bengal. Here, in the northernmost expanses we discovered an enormous isle called India that clearly was not the more famed sub-continent known by that name, with nearby a strange island where the trees seemed merely balls of cotton-wool glued onto posts, inhabited by animals in human dress, of which I must confess our Mr. Bumppo bagged a couple. It transpired our island was in fact a Phoenix-governed Animal Republic, and it seemed expedient that we head on before the locals took exception to our

young friend's sportsmanship. Thus did we pass Mask Island, where the King of Spain some years ago exiled his sister and her husband, the Viceroy of Catalonia, both the lovers cruelly fitted with an irremovable iron mask, and likewise sailed on by Sri Lanka. Here, I'm told, exists the kingdom of Agartha, veiled divinely from the memory of man, the throne of which is decorated with the figures of two million gods, with its existence central to the very continuity of mankind and ... but I confess that I have quite forgot the point I sought to make, or why I ever thought this place important.

"Travelling on into the Indian Ocean, finally we put ashore on Feather Island, only recently discovered by the noted French balloonist and philosopher, the Chevalier D'Etoile. Here my companions were confronted by a veritable paradise, so that they did not make against me any more complaint. Why, even Mistress Hill and Lady Blakeney seemed transfixed by all the flowers and perfumed air and crystal streams, nor any less by the exquisite beauty of the local women, with the long and trailing feathered plumes they have grown from their scalps instead of hair. So perfect is this place, we are resolved to set aside the matter of our ultimate return to England for as long as possible."

At this point Lemuel Gulliver concludes his log, at least so far as it is relevant to present matters, and we must rely upon the

former Indian prince turned science-pirate, Captain Nemo, for our notions of the Indian subcontinent itself. In the first volume of his uncompleted memoirs, Nemo speaks of being taken by his father as a boy to visit Lomb, a city on the western coast of India near Mangalore, known for its pepper trade, its infant sacrifice, and the ox-worship that it has imported from Macumeran. He comments witheringly on this beast-worship practiced by his countrymen, with reference to Goatland, just northwest of Lomb, where the red-bearded billy-goat is venerated, but he reserves his deepest scorn for the religious manias of Mabaron, a ten-day journey north of Lomb, where numerous pilgrims kill or mutilate themselves before the monstrous jewelled and golden idol-god of the False Christians. Much more to the Captain's taste is Mancy, almost opposite to Mabaron on India's eastern coast, and he speaks warmly of its wealth, its culture and cuisine, especially of bignon, a fine wine produced in Cansay, Mancy's lagoon-built "City of Heaven." Nemo also comments favourably upon the Pygmy Kingdom on the Dalay River just northeast of Mancy, where he marvels at the craftsmanship of the both short and short-lived natives. Likewise meeting his approval we find Jundapur, in the northwest, with its magnificent Palladian palace and its local legend of a woman who fell fatally in love with the disguised god Krishna there. The Sikh submariner, however, speaks less fondly of the feared Black Jungle, on its island in the Ganges delta:

"I recall my father and perhaps a score of his light cavalry taking me on a dreadful expedition for the purposes of strengthening my character and furthering my learning, starting out in the Black Jungle, on the delta island Raymangal, south of Calcutta. In amidst the lightless vegetation here we saw the dauntingly immense granite pagoda-sanctuary of the Thugs, its corners marked with effigies of three-headed Trimurti and its dome crowned with a towering woman-headed serpent. Not far off, my father pointed out for me the banyan tree where is concealed the entrance to a deep cave of pink stone wherein are virgins strangled for the blessed goddess Kali. Rather hastily, I thought, we headed north from here and, passing by Calcutta, came upon the east shore of the Ganges to the more alluring and yet no less fearsome kingdom known as Gangaridia. Here, father said, were talking animals come from the nearby Animal Republic in the Bay of Bengal, who lived in harmony with local shepherds, peaceful people who did not eat flesh, but who in battle made ferocious warriors by virtue of their mounts, fierce talking unicorns that once impaled ten thousand of the King of India's war-elephants in the defence of their diamond-rich territory.

Feather Island

Great Sage

"We went on north from here and came after a time, by night, into the Sacred Valley, beyond the Great Rungit Valley, on the border. Making our way down into the valley by a most precarious path involving stone steps, tunnels, and a metal ladder, we walked for an hour and so came to the famed Temple of Kali with its moat of crocodiles, illuminated by vast flaming braziers set to each side of its massive doors. The valley and its many smaller temples were breathtaking in the moonlight, but yet we elected to pass on and not make camp until we'd gained its further side. Here, in the morning, looking north, we saw the River Physon in its devil-haunted valley that is said to be a way to Hell, and heard the distant yet incessant sound of fiendish drums and trumpets with which that dire valley ever rings. Beyond it, father told me, was a nameless isle whereon lived giants, each as tall as five like him, while further northward yet were women who had precious stones for eyes, that they might slay men as the basilisk doth. Off to the northwest, he said, there was the inland ocean bordering Cathay, wherein was found the island kingdom of Pentexoire, governed once by the immortal Prester John. More westward still, he told me, in the wilds of Bactria were many griffins, of which a few sparse although still fearsome flocks might yet be spotted as far south as Hyderabad during their great irregular migrations. Also he spoke of the Dream Kingdom, near to Bactria, its great wall keeping pure a culture based on dreams, with a cloudy capital where neither sun nor moon had ever shone. So it was, my mind alive with all these sights, that we struck out for home."

Nemo's account, with its brief reference to Pentexoire, leads us indirectly to the writings of ambiguous long-term League associate Orlando, who was him or herself colleague to Pentexoire's Prester John, and who was travelling in Asia during 1906:

"Can this really be the twentieth century already? I suppose it must be, for I found myself dressed in the most absurd silk skirt and hat, stepping carefully on my raised heels down the gangway of the massive, dirty steamer that had brought me here to Zipang, or Japan as I expect I must get used to calling it, arriving in the port of Nagasaki. On our way here from Formosa across the East China Sea we passed Alcina's Island, near to Japan's coast, where I once travelled some five hundred years ago. Our captain, whom I think was rather taken with me, said that some descendants of the sorceress Alcina's monster army...centaurs, dog-men and the like...could still be found there, roaming in the hills, albeit in a great state of degeneration.

"Putting in to Nagasaki, I'm relieved to say the place is still almost as beautiful as I recall. The rather pretty lady managing my rooming house sat up with me into the night regaling me with stories of the city's recent history, including the sad tale of a young local beauty, Cho-cho-san, with family still living in the nearby streets, who'd killed herself some few years after her desertion by the handsome U.S. Naval officer she'd married in the early 1890s. Very sad, I must say. My hostess and I were by now quite drunk from warmed rice wine, and I may have said something rather forward when, in an attempted compliment, I compared her more slender figure favourably with my own. She laughed delightfully and said that I was flirting with her, warning me that I should take care not to visit Titipu, a nearby town where the local Mikado had decreed that such flirtation was a crime that merited beheading. When I told her that my steamer sailed for China in the morning and that I should have no time to visit anywhere, much less be executed, she insisted I'd had too much *sake* and should be tucked up

in bed at once, which shortly later I suppose I was, after a fashion.

"The next day I said my farewells then put to sea once more, bound for Shanghai. On our way we passed by the minor continent Hsuan, where in 90 BC the Emperor Wu Ti revived the lately-dead by burning incense, and sailed on by those two enticing isles, Babilary, whereon women rule, and Women's Island, where there are no men at all. At length we reached Shanghai, and I set out to reacquaint myself with China, an old friend whose spiced perfume and beguiling ways I have not known for far too long. The first place that I went to was Albraca, near the Russian border in the far northeast, that once was the proud fortress-capital of Galafrone's kingdom. I stood there amongst the tall grass and the massive tumbled stones that are now all that remaining of those times, and let the wuthering breeze pluck at my yellow dress, my chestnut hair. I thought about Angelica, Galafrone's daughter, of the lips and breasts and thighs that drove me once to madness, as they did so many knights of Charlemagne. I killed the King of Tartary for her, back in the 1480s. Where have all those wars and passions gone that seemed then so important?

"To be honest, being in Albraca made me rather weepy, and it was with some relief that I struck south once more, shortly arriving in Peking, which, like Nagasaki, is refreshingly but little changed since last I saw it. It was to the city's newly built (at least to me) museum that I went however, eager for a sight of the peculiar exhibit that has been displayed there since the last years of the nineteenth century. This, in its very up-to-date glass case, is quite extraordinary: it appears to be a man-like monkey or perhaps an ape-like man, and has been thought by some of the distinguished scientists come from England to examine it to be one of the 'missing links' from Mr. Darwin's entertaining theory. This idea, to me, seemed quite preposterous. For one thing, it would seem that this unusual animal is stuffed, and is thus only some few hundred years of age at very best. If this alone did not sufficiently rule out a prehistoric origin for the exhibit, I should also point out that the monkey-man is dressed in what seemed to be the traditional Chinese costume of the eighteenth century, its colours faded and its gorgeous fabrics now distressed with age. A signboard placed within the cabinet identified this strangely noble beast, in Chinese characters, as 'Great Sage, Equal to Heaven,' though even after I'd painstakingly translated this, I was left none the wiser.

"Enquiries that I made amongst the local market-traders indicated that at least according to their great-grandparents, the ape-human was in fact a minor god of sorts, who had his origins upon an island in the nearby Yellow Sea, where he had reigned as Monkey King upon his Mountain of Flowers and Fruit. Asked about the isle's precise location, they could only tell me that it was not far from P'eng Lai, an enchanted vase-shaped island where it was alleged Taoist immortals lived, described to their immediate forebears by a famous wandering storyteller called Kai Lung during the nineteenth century. When asked about P'eng Lai, of course, all they would say was that it was close to the island where the Mount of Flowers and Fruit stood. They did, however, mention that the monkey-creature had at some remote point in the past transgressed against the gods so that they bound him for some several thousand years beneath a peak known as Five Element Mountain, some miles to the southwest of Peking, which I resolved to set out and investigate upon the following day.

"Upon my way there, I passed through a dreadful city called Perinthia, apparently built upon strict astrological precepts to mirror the heavens. By dint of maintaining their zodiacal isolation, however, the whole population is grossly inbred, with Perinthia peopled by monsters in direct result. If Perinthia genuinely reflects Heaven, then we must suppose that the gods there are three-headed hunchbacks with several club-feet. I travelled on, although Five Element Mountain, when I reached it, seemed rather an ordinary edifice, and I elected simply to meander on, as has so often been my way during this strange, ferocious, and amusing thus-far-endless life of mine. I went as far north as the border with Mongolia, where walking in the desert by the failing light of day I reached a place called Watcher's Corner where a monstrous and mournful creature paces back and forth, forever with one fretful eye on the horizon. When I asked the creature what it watched for, it began a long, depressing story that concerned a friendly camel with a burning candle set upon each hump, though I confess that I grew bored and stole away not halfway through the telling.

"Some distance further west I saw the mountain Waiting Wife, said to have once been a young woman watching for her husband gone away to war, turned finally to stone by all that waiting. I wondered idly if she had been petrified by her own tears, then headed south, passing the towering scaffold-city of Isaura with its pulleys and its buckets, raised above the thousand wells of its deep-buried lake, where the religion is divided between those who think divinity resides in the well-depths and those who think divinity, in fact, is in the ever-rising buckets. I continued south, and after some great while reached Gala, an agreeably appointed kingdom which, however, I must with considerable distaste report, collects funds from its populace without taxation by resorting to a public lottery. Perhaps this is a tax upon the credulous, in which case I suppose that I broadly agree with it. From Gala I went down and into Indo-China, where, amongst the jungles of Cambodia, I saw the tunnel-riddled but majestic city of Pnom Dhek, its neatly-tended gardens rising from the shrieking, growling greenery, and not far off saw also great Lodidhapura, Pnom Dhek's rival city, with its royal family cursed by leprosy. Tiring of jungle far more swiftly than you'd think, I soon struck north again through Burma, where near Mandalay I ventured in Gramblamble Land and visited the famous city Tosh, beside Lake Pipple-popple. Here, again, I demonstrated my perhaps allowable taste for museums by visiting the great Municipal Museum where the elders of the major animal clans once existing locally are kept preserved by brandy, vinegar and cayenne pepper in ridiculously huge glass bottles.

"From Gramblamble Land I ventured north across the Southwest Wilderness, where sugar canes are thicker than a man in girth and grow almost a thousand feet in height. I must stress that while camping in this wilderness I did *not* kill and eat a local form of rabbit called a 'lying-beast' or 'rumour' that spreads stories and, when its delicious somewhat-chicken-flavoured flesh is eaten, will compel the eater to tell lies. Once past these endless wastelands I continued to the northwest and so came at last upon the Himalayan foothills, which I knew marked the beginnings of Tibet. Although I did not know it then, they also marked the start of some six months of wild adventure in amongst those ancient, mystic hills. I had a dreadful time kept as a hostage at a monastery of sinister Bon sorcerers, a place called So Sa Ling, where young men were dissolved alive to make an ointment granting everlasting life, which the magicians then rubbed on. Since I am not a young man at this current time, I did not end up as an embrocation but was kept instead for other purposes which, whilst only slightly more pleasant, at least in the end afforded me an opportunity to make good my escape. After some days further travel I beheld Mount Tsintsin-Dagh, the lamasery of the Silent Brothers there atop its pinnacle. The mountain's waters, I have heard, contain a kind of radiant energy bestowing health and life, which made me think of that blue pool which made me as I am, away in what is now called the British Protectorate of Uganda. I did not visit Tsintsin-Dagh, however, but pressed on ahead.

"By this means I came firstly to True Lhassa, where the soil is rich in diamonds and the river almost slimy with gold sediment. Though I have heard the Buddhist holy city here is truly heavenly, with its enormous gold and purple palace of the current Dalai Lama, I have also heard that by the very virtue of True Lhassa's sacred nature, all outsiders will be put immediately to death, and so decided to continue onward and likewise continue in my current incarnation for a time, since in all honesty I've grown quite fond of it, particularly these near-violet nipples that I find myself at present sporting. For not unrelated reasons, I also avoided the mysterious cloudy valley just north of True Lhassa, where two rival cults of sorcerors (or perhaps more-than-human supernatural forces) called the White Lodge and the Black Lodge are believed to be at war, with human souls and freakish twilight entities both as their pawns. Thus it was that at last I came to the lovely valley in the shade of the blue mountain called Mount Karakal, where is the beautiful bronze-dragon-decorated lamasery of Shangri-La. Here I was welcomed by the long-lived holy men who seemed to see in me some form of kindred spirit, possibly due to my own longevity, although I was not of their faith.

"This does not mean, of course, that I might not at some point be persuaded to conversion. I was both surprised and pleased to note the healthy reverence which this form of Tibetan Buddhism affords the sexual act, and was some weeks into a most agreeable course of instruction with an elderly but virile lama when our idyll was disturbed by the arrival of new travellers in the area. This turned out to be a very handsome couple who, being dressed in clothing too warm for wear during the day and far too cold to wear at night, could be determined at first glance to both be English. With closer inspection, though, they both proved much more interesting. Both had that quality, a kind of inner radiance, that I have often been said to possess myself, and which I have come to associate with those like I who've found another lease of life within that far Ugandan crater. Stranger still, it turned out that by some coincidence they are affiliated to that League, in service to the British Crown, that I have found my destiny entwined with more than once across the centuries. The rather dashing gentleman, it seems, goes by the name of Allan, while his utterly enchanting young companion in her pretty scarf was introduced to me as Wilhelmina."

At this juncture, where the astute reader will have guessed the journal of Orlando to converge with the promised account of Quatermain and Murray's travels in the Orient, we should perhaps return to that pair, who, the reader will remember, were deployed to Russia by their masters during 1906 in an effort to affirm a diplomatic link prior to the Anglo-Russian pact relating to Afghanistan, Tibet and Persia. Mina Murray's journal tells the story of their travels after they arrived at the port of St. Petersburg, now Leningrad, in the late March of that eventful year.

"Going by coach out of St. Petersburg we rattled first through Dodon's kingdom, with the only bright spot in its shabby capital being the golden weathercock atop the city's highest steeple. This, we're told, was once alive, allowing Dodon's kingdom to thrive in peace and prosperity by warning them of any coming danger. When I said I thought that this was tosh, Allan replied that Tosh was actually a city in the heart of Burma. Much as I adore him he can be intensely irritating when he thinks he's being humorous. Heading on to Moscow we gave a wide berth to Pauk, a large place with a desperate atmosphere that's not unlike that of a dirty bathroom, where there is reported to reside a horrid spider bigger than a man, so ghastly that those brought to Pauk spend the remainder of their miserable lives clinging together as they weep in horror at the scampering of this vile apparition. Not, strictly speaking, quite my cup of tea, and so we carried on to Moscow where we were most courteously received by one of the Tsar's ministers and given generous accommodation in a fine hotel.

"Our intimate relations on that night, while I believe they seemed to both of us a little jaded, were at least conducted briskly and with a sufficient vigour to plunge both of us into a long, deep sleep, during which I endured a dreadful, muddled dream where I appeared to be in Moscow, although not the Moscow of our present day, but rather as it might be in, say, twenty years or so. There was some nonsense that concerned a large black talking cat, and a well-dressed man that according to the logic of the dream I knew to be the Devil. I awoke quite unrefreshed, and Allan and I went for breakfast with the minister who met us yesterday. He told us we may travel unrestrictedly in Russia and its neighbouring territories, which we told him was a journey we were both much looking forward to, intending to set out next day.

"With all of Russia to explore, we first agreed to visit those locations in this westernmost extreme of Russia, down the Black Sea's east coast to the Caspian. We headed south from Moscow, passing by the wretched remnants of the town of Gloupov, ruined by the ongoing historic imbecility of its inhabitants. (Gloupov means 'stupid,' so we are reliably informed.) Journeying on, we travelled through the large, apparently borderless town of Ibansk which, though its architecture is bewilderingly elaborate, seems as inane as Gloupov for the way in which it manages its day-to-day affairs, and also for the hit-and-miss, near catastrophic nature of its general history. In fact, one might quite justifiably remark that many of these western Russian towns are not distinguished save by their incredible stupidity. Take Paflagonia, for example, with its half-baked penal system where the guilty are somehow convinced to flagellate themselves; or nearby Blackstaff which is governed by a strange, capricious fairy that attends to children's christenings; or else Crim Tartary where the most senior families have names like Spinachi, Broccoli and Sauerkraut. Upon the other hand, however, I must say that our ride through the city Phyllis seemed to offer fascinating views at every turn, though I am told that should one stay within the city too long it becomes a dismal blur where one can barely bother to distinguish between light and shade.

"Just as intriguing was the city of Despina on the Black Sea's northern coast. Apparently, if it's approached by camel via the desert it looks very like a massive ship, while should it be approached by ship across the sea, it looks much like the hind end of a camel. Just east of Despina, in the Tartary Desert, we saw from far off the fortress Bastiani, but did not go close enough to get more than a faint impression of its size nor its impregnability. It stands upon the edge of Abcan, a wide territory in constant darkness due to Abcan's emperor persecuting Christians. Much smaller, and more to my taste, a little further south we found the sprawl of caverns, rocks and whirlpools wherein the poetic dreamer Alastor maintained his cave-retreat, and where his tomb still stands o'ergrown by ivy in a mountain recess. More southerly still we passed through the land of Gondour, where the Caliph rules a system in which, whilst even the lowest peasant has one vote, those of a greater social standing may have two, or fifty, or a hundred. Crossing to the Caspian ocean's eastern shore, we next spent some time travelling in Amazonia, or Feminy, a land of women which extends from here into the west of China, where men are still frowned upon, though not as much as they were by the fierce, one-breasted warrior women who were the initial founders of this territory.

"North of Feminy we passed through Ivanikha, where the peasantry are all named Ivan, and, crossing the boundless, junk-filled country known as 'X' (presumably because this run-down place could not afford more than one letter for its name) came finally into a province called the Land of Wonder. Here, amongst a friendly population of red-headed Jews, we saw the splendid palace, Faithstone, in the capital, and were delighted by the nightingales that sang at dusk from sag-

Shangri-La

ging branches in fruit-heavy trees. We next went east, passing the half-constructed city Thekla, where the builders, who are using the star-spattered heavens as their blueprint, are apparently delaying the completion of their city so as to further put off the start of its destruction. Similarly half-done was the nearby city Moriana, which seemed at first sight all made from glass and crystal and translucent alabaster, with the sun's last rays at play in a sublime aquarium dapple on its coral columns and its massive chandeliers. The city is completely without depth, however, something like a stage flat or facade, and passing on its far side one sees only creaking wooden struts and filthy sheets of corrugated tin. Eudoxia, a little further east, conversely, first appeared to be a senseless maze of streets and passages, but when we were shown the carpet (possibly of divine origin) in which all Eudoxia is represented in the swirls and arabesques, we saw a near-celestial order to the place which made us almost sad to leave. Nearby Zemrude was more ambiguous: I was myself in quite a decent mood as we passed through, and, looking upward, only saw the airy balconies, the saffron curtains billowing. Allan, however, rather in a sulk about the rut our sexual passions would seem to have fallen into, only saw the fish-heads in the gutters, the cracked pavements and the choked-up drains.

"Octavia, in the northeast, is a fragile cobweb-city of rope walkways strung across a chasm, while further on Valdrada, built above a lake, seemed no more real than its perfect reflection, hung eternally inverted in the waters at the city's base. From here we headed south to Vladivostok, passing through the Land of the Goat Worshippers, goatskin-clad savages who loan their wives to strangers, and saw fabled Xanadu, wild vegetation bursting upwards through the holes in its long-ruined pleasure dome. Here we turned back and travelled west through southeast Russia, past the high-piled platform city of Zenobia, through daily-replaced Leonia with massive waste-heaps on its outskirts, and amongst the ringed canals of Anastasia, city of unlimited desire. We went through Urnland, famed for horsemanship and for its language that has only one word, *undr*, mean-

ing 'wonder,' before moving on into Mongolia itself. We saw Mount Poyang, with its dog-flesh eating deity, and travelled over buried Argia, where soil replaces air and empty space replaces solid things, so coming into China. We went southwards through Eusapia, which has a subterranean double of itself built underneath it where the fragile dead are housed in buried versions of their homes, and crossed into Tibet where after some time we came to a glorious blue mountain with a valley spread beyond it. Here we found the exquisite lamasery called Shangri-La, arriving to discover one aged lama in flagrante with the loveliest girl I've ever seen. She is, I think, an Englishwoman, at least currently. Her name's Orlando.

"That first night, the three of us drank wine and talked and talked. Some of the things she told me I cannot repeat, but let us say that we three found we had a great affinity between us, having travelled to a lot of the same places, such as central southern Africa, for instance. Furthermore, we learned that she was not entirely unfamiliar with our currently-depleted League and had indeed, by means which I may not explain, known at least two groups of our predecessors. Our talk turned in general to longevity, and we discussed both Prester John, who had a kingdom to the west of here and whom Orlando knew, apparently, and also Queen Ayesha, believed by Orlando to be at present incarnated in the land of Kaloon, also to the west. A little drunk, we vowed to visit both these places with her, then discussed the wider moral and aesthetic issues of a greatly increased lifespan. She smiled, a little wickedly, and said that one's perspectives change, perhaps, across the centuries. As she said, *'It becomes a question not of whether one will ever try a thing, but when.'* We sat a while in pleasurable and intoxicated silence after this, and then Orlando gave first Allan then myself the sweetest goodnight kisses, and then, shortly after, we retired.

"Next day, in the most elevated spirits, we set out from Shangri-La with our new more-than-friend, and headed west towards the vast land of Kaloon. Here we viewed the Khan's Palace, dominating Kaloon city since the time of Alexander, and were shown the way to Mount K'un Lun,

sometimes called Hes or Fire Mountain, further west. Here there resides, apparently, either the incarnated goddess Isis, or alternately (according to Mount K'un Lun's Chinese neighbours), Hsi Wang Mu, the Royal Mother of the West, who gained her immortality, allegedly, by fornicating some three thousand youths to death. Orlando spoke quite wistfully about a gathering of immortals said to happen every three thousand years or so atop the mountain's peak, where the undying meet to eat the peaches of eternal life, but said that she had never witnessed this. She also said that she believed Isis or Hsi Wang Mu to be instead another incarnation of Ayesha, though she thought it best that we did not investigate since K'un Lun was believed to be protected by a human-headed tiger named Lu Wo.

"We travelled on instead west from Kaloon through Chitor. Here we saw the Victory Tower, where an insubstantial creature known as the A Bao A Qu will follow the ascendants, gathering form and visibility with each completed step. Only if the climber has reached spiritual perfection will the creature gain the topmost step and full embodiment, however, and Orlando said that this had only happened once. We went on with her through the lovely Kingdoms of Radiant Array and Joyous Groves, north of the Himalayas, thus avoiding the ill-favoured Kingdom of Myriad Lights, and came, past China's western border, to that glittering inland ocean said to flow from Paradise, with its magnetic rocks of adamand, where the island Pentexoire is located. Here, Orlando said, lived Prester John before he went to Nubia and called himself Senapho. She showed us, in the poignant ruins of his kingdom, Trees of Sun and Moon that spoke with Alexander once, foretelling his demise, and we three lounged delightfully beneath them, gorging on their fruit, said to provide five hundred years of life. All three of us ate dozens, laughing as we wiped juice from each other's chins."

Here Mina's log concludes, and with it this Asian chapter of our Almanac. Be sure to reserve your copy of our final issue, wherein, with an exploration of Earth's polar regions, we conclude our mapping of the whole fantastic globe in its entirety.

Xanadu

Chapter Six
The Polar Regions:
To The Ends Of The Earth

In this final chapter of our guide for the contemporary wayfarer we transfer our attentions to those most remote extremities of our fantastical domain, the polar icecaps. The North Pole and environs were researched during 1907 by the Orlando-Murray-Quatermain triumvirate on their return from Asia to the British Isles, a journey upon which, under instruction from their Vauxhall masters, they were forced to undertake an Arctic crossing. As for the Antarctic region, this was circumnavigated by the *Nautilus* in 1894, during exploratory ventures launched from Lincoln Island by an ageing, jaded Captain Nemo who, during that period, longed to recapture the excitement of his youth, as evidenced by his acceptance four years later of Miss Wilhelmina Murray's offer to enlist within her fledgling League. Logbooks loaned to the current editors by a Miss Diver tell, in the great Sikh submariner's own hand, of what he found while on his eight-month polar expedition.

"Sailed from Lincoln with the morning tide, and heavy heart. I am discouraged by the fact that my young wife has lately given birth not to a son and heir, as I had been convinced the gods would surely grant me, but a daughter that she has named Janni, for her mother. Though she often brings the child to me and tries to make me love her, I cannot, so great has been my disappointment. Thus I take my men, my *Nautilus*, and leave mother and babe both wailing on the beach, bound for Antarctica, where I may find a cold that is a match for the bleak iciness within my bosom now.

"Passing the tip of South America we sailed amongst the islands of an archipelago called Megapatagonia, where on the various shorelines we perceived mirage-like structures that would flicker in and out of view as if they were but half-substantial. Populating these near-phantom towns and houses we saw a bewildering variety of human-like inhabitants, all in a similarly shimmering and ghostly state, here in one instant and then gone the next. It seemed to us that there were apemen, bear-men, otter-men and a great profusion of like monsters, with each species dwelling on its separate isle. I was reminded of a tale that I once heard of an almost identical archipelago that ran not from Tierra del Fuego to Earth's southern pole, as was the case with Megapatagonia, but instead stretched from the Orkney Islands in the north of Britain to the planet's arctic reaches, called the Blazing World. Here too, some said, were flickering townships kept by diverse strains of beast-men, and I thought to put in at one of the more southerly islands in the chain, there to investigate this seeming symmetry

of two ethereal strings of land, each reaching to a pole and each inhabited by such a wide menagerie of spectral, cross-bred animals and humans.

"Our landing, near what seemed either a gracefully appointed harbour or a strip of barren shoreline from one moment to another, was a curious affair which raised more questions than it had set out to put at rest. We walked amongst the strangely fox-like people of the island as their figures stuttered in and out of being, noting in the moments that they co-existed in the same world as ourselves that we could even hear brief snatches of their conversation. This, to our endless mystification, we at last identified as French, albeit spoken backwards in oddly disturbing reversed voices. They even spoke of a capital city called 'Sirap.' Along with my men, I came to feel as though we trespassed at the borders of a wholly other realm and so, returning to my *Nautilus*, pressed southward on my voyage, passing around the Antarctic peninsula, circling the shining island of fire-elementals called Pyrandia, and then coming at last into McMurdo Sound, where, in an area called by some the Academic Sea, we discovered the Leap Islands and three-sided Caphar Salama.

"The Leap Islands appeared at first almost a more solid and real continuation of the wraith-islands of

Megapatagonia

Megapatagonia, being both archi-pelagos and home to what seemed animals in human form, but putting into Aggregation Harbour on the isle of Leaphigh we found a society that was less eerie and unnerving than that backwards-speaking half-world we had lately quit. The folk of the Leap Islands are not mere degraded humans, but are rather monkey-men called Monikins who have attained a state of great advancement and a culture that is likewise eminently civilised. Though it is not their native language, they speak French for the convenience of visitors, and took great pride in showing us their Palais des Arts et des Sciences, along with their Academy of Latent Sympathies. We stayed amongst this simian people for some time, while I confess I tried to think of ways by which their island kingdom might be plundered, my old habits dying hard, but in the end was thwarted by the fact that Monikins have naught but promises (which by their very nature none can steal or capture) in the stead of currency. Denied our loot, we skirted the nearby triangular island Caphar Salama where is the wealthy, pious city Christianopolis that I would have gladly sacked were it not fortified in so impreg-nable a fashion, and so we sailed on and came by Victoria Land's penin-sula, where some few miles inland we could make out a skyline near-identical to that of Paris, marking the capital of a place I've heard tell of that is called Antarctic France. Although there are intriguing rumours of immortals that survive the centuries encased in the pre-serving ice, we all elected to head on, with the Antarctic coast on our port side for some few months till finally we came in sight of a lone island, close to what I knew to be Enderby Land.

"The island is called Tsalal, and I knew it to be where the schooner *Jane Guy*, come from Liverpool, was wrecked in 1828, its crew and pas-sengers reportedly all massacred by the fierce, sturdy blackamoors that are this curious isle's inhabitants. I feel this is a cursed place, where the laws of nature seem as readily sus-pended as amongst the apparition-haunted isles of Megapatagonia. The blackish-looking waters that sur-round the island, on examination, prove to be divided into viscous, slopping strata of unmixed and sep-arate colours, most unnaturally it seems to me. Then there is the great aversion of the natives to the colour white, which seems to be connected with some awful figure from the island's ancient folklore, their great dread for which is conveyed by a stream of frantic, chattered syllables that sound like 'Te-ke-li-li.'

"Knowing Tsalal to have con-nections with a place called Present Land a great distance inland, and furthermore deciding to resolve the many mysteries that I have heard of that concern these territories, I took a party of twelve men and several sleds ashore not far from Mawson,

off the Amery ice-shelf, leaving my first mate to take the *Nautilus* around the continent and meet us on the coast of Palmer Land, beside the Weddell Sea. As we struck out upon our bitter trek across the ice, after some days, far to the south we could make out by the bright rays of early afternoon a kind of golden glinting in the atmosphere, which I informed my men was caused by the sun's rays reflecting from the mostly gold interior of the chasm that pro-vided entrance to the underground Empire of the Alsondons. I under-stand there are connections between the Alsondons' Empire and Antarctic France, and entertained my men with tales of how they tell time in the Empire, with a young bare-breasted maiden stood upon a pedestal in the town square while a young man stands with his hand placed on her bosom and calls out the seconds by the beating of her heart. This account excited much good-natured ribaldry amongst my crew and warmed us as we carried on across the trackless white towards the South Polar plateau and Present Land that lay ahead.

"After perhaps a week or more we drew close to the ring of icy peaks, the so-called Iron Mountains that surround the plateau, where we found a crude inscription carved in the rock commemorating the arrival at this spot of the survivors from the shipwrecked whaler *Mercury* during November in 1906. Noting that the climate grew considerably warmer as we neared the pole (and thus the travelling less difficult) we pushed on through the sere and towering hills, and so we came upon our first breathtaking glimpse of Present Land, a phosphorescent blue and white plateau, beautifully scarred by wandering canals and streams that stretched away towards the misty, jagged spikes that marked the mountain-ring's far side. So taken were we with this vista that we only narrowly avoided falling into a vast hole, apparently quite bottomless, that only later did I think might be the mythic aperture which leads to the vast subterranean world called Pluto, which, if stories are to be believed, possesses an identical entrance-hole situated at the world's North Pole and guarded by a ring of Iron Mountains said to be the twin of these. Making our way with caution round this chasm, we con-tinued into Present Land, at which point I discovered that my timepiece had quite simply stopped, all moments here being subsumed within the present.

"Possibly because of this strange temporal effect, my memories of our time spent in that land would seem to have no sequence to them, and present themselves to me in nothing but a confused jumble of impres-sions and strange images that all seem to be happening at once: I fleetingly recall a number of the very palest people I have ever seen, their flesh like white, translucent alabaster, and there is the vaguest

recollection of a cavern all in gold that rang with feverish voices chant-ing in their nonsense language 'Te-ke-li-li.' I have disturbing intima-tions of a tall white shape, much larger than a man, that coincide with memories of one of my crew screaming, and half-glimpses of a kind of sphinx, but fashioned all from ice; although this last may have been naught but a symbolic dream while lost in that peculiar place. All I may know with certainty is that when we at last arrived on the far side of that ringed range, close to a group of peaks that I've since named the Mounts of Madness, we discovered that there were now only eight of us, five of our company being apparently no more, though none of us could clearly recollect what had become of them.

"My timepiece having once more started ticking, I assumed that we were out of Present Land and there-fore out of danger. Under this quite false assumption we moved on between those massive, snow-swept spires of rock that loomed oppres-sively about us, and it was in their frozen, desolated valleys that we found the ruins, yet ruins of what I cannot say. It seemed the long-abandoned and half-buried relic of some citadel, though there existed some outlandish quality within its architecture, within its geometries, that made me think it was not built by human hands, if it was built by anything that could be called a hand at all. Huge passages etched with unsettlingly worn and weathered hieroglyphics led at a deceptively slight incline down into the passage-ways and chambers there beneath the empty, snowbound city, and I curse myself for ordering all my remaining men to follow me in my investigation of those ancient icicle-hung catacombs. I do not wish to pain myself with the detailed recounting of what happened in those hellish tunnels, save to say that we encountered something that might best be characterized as intel-lectually precocious slime or froth. Something that piped the Hellish incantation we had heard once in Tsalal and then again in Present Land. Something that claimed my men so that it was myself alone, wild eyed and maddened, that met with the *Nautilus* upon the coastline of the Weddell Sea at Palmer Land. I had crossed above the subterranean land known as Kosekin Country without realizing it, although I had encountered several of the small black natives of that place, who fled from my repetitive, demented cry of 'Te-ke-li-1i! Te-ke-li-li!,' not without good cause.

"Why, so distraught was I, I bare-ly recognised the *Nautilus*, nor my own crewmen come to bear me home to Lincoln Island, and fought with my fellows as they carried me aboard. Some days later, when I was recovered, none dare ask me what had happened to their shipmates, and for my part I was not inclined to

Mounts of Madness

the ocean's lowest reaches, utterly without emotion but with bulging lamps of intellect grown from their foreheads. When I finally met his famous brother...only some two years ago now, though it seems another life entirely...I found him perhaps more likeable and warm than our remote, impassive Mr. M, but sensed that this was more a case of the detective having greater mastery of social niceties than his more pompous sibling, rather than an indication of true human feeling. Two intimidating mental monsters, it is clear that they are both from the same pod, although one pea, it must be said, is somewhat fatter and more ripened than the other.

"Having received instructions to commence this pointless polar trek while Allan and Orlando and myself were otherwise quite pleasantly disported in the comfy suite of our Moscow Hotel, we had no choice but to set out for Tiksi, although I am very glad to say that our new sometime lady-friend elected to come with us, saying she would like to see how London was adapting to this still-new and uncertain century. On our seemingly interminable coach-trek to the northern seaport, during which time Christmas came and went, we found a place not far east of Igarka on the River Yenisey, where our inn-keeper told us that nearby were said to exist caverns representing one of the few entrances outside the northern polar waste itself to a fantastic subterranean realm named Pluto (or by some accounts Plutonia), but we were all anxious to arrive at Tiksi and commence our arduous journey, otherwise we might have passed more time there and investigated these outlandish stories further.

"Reaching Tiksi some time later, we were able to enlist the services of an old Czechoslovakian ex-naval man named Rudolf Svejk along with those of the corroded, filthy icebreaker he owned, a vessel named *The Josef*, seemingly named for a son that the decrepit seafarer has not seen now for some few years. Yesterday morning we set out upon the iron-grey Lapev tide and passed the New Siberian Islands, heading northeast up towards the Chukchi Sea, where we arrived mid-afternoon today. Beyond the isle Vrangelya, Allan pointed out the briefly-famed Elisee Reclus Island, where to one end of it we saw the glittering dome, reportedly constructed upon lava columns by a former glassblower, of Cristallopolis, a geyser-heated colony of France established in the early 1890s. Near the island's further shore we also made out Maurel City, a near-simultaneously established colony, this time American, of characteristically outsized igloos clustered by a mountain range. Allan informed us that a gold seam was discovered there some years ago, which probably explains why the two nations still maintain their colonies upon this otherwise unsightly outcrop.

raise the matter."

Although British Intelligence were not aware during 1906 of Nemo's Antarctic discoveries, they were increasingly alarmed, as we have seen, by the bizarre transphysical dimensions that appeared to border our own world. Surviving records which have been declassified suggest that during 1905, one of the half-dozen faintly sinister reformed "mad" scientists employed by Britain's Government made the suggestion that these other realms might be connected in some fashion to the Earth's magnetic poles. They had noticed the peculiar symmetry, remarked upon above by Captain Nemo, that existed between Megapatagonia (visited briefly by Lemuel Gulliver's team in the last years of the eighteenth century) and Britain's Blazing World (which Prospero's men explored almost a hundred years before, in 1683). Reasoning that this apparent mirroring might hold the key to the phe-

nomena obsessing them, it seems that during late 1906 British Intelligence were made aware of the scant information they possessed concerning Earth's North Pole, and thus elected to send a communication to their agents Murray and the younger Quatermain, instructing them to make their way from Russia back to Britain by means of an arctic crossing. Mina Murray's journals for the period make her reaction to these orders witheringly clear:

"December 28th, 1906. How warming to think of Messrs. Holmes and Bond squeezing their rival bellies in beside the cosy hearth of some prestigious London Gentleman's club as we succeed in chartering a rusted old icebreaker out of Tiksi, by the delta of the River Lena, and set out amongst the icefloes of the Lapev Sea. I hope the pair of them are choked on their aperitifs. Bond is a weasel while Holmes is more like one of those monstrous armoured fish that haunt

"January 3rd, 1907. We now head west, progressing through the loose-packed floes that mark the edges of the polar icecap. By our captain's reckoning, we are now somewhere in the region of Franz Josef Land, though none of us as yet have spotted this confetti of small islands. When we put towards the cap itself some days ago, we left Elisee Reclus Island in our wake and headed on past Vichebolk Land, an impoverished island kingdom where the natives have been led into their current, wretched state by their insistent worship of Vietso, a relentlessly communitarian god whose cult, I think I am correct in saying, came originally from nearby Russia. I believe I read a mention of the island in the records of our presently-reduced League's eighteenth century predecessors, where that odd ensemble's venerable senior member Lemuel Gulliver claimed he'd discovered Vichebolk Land in 1721, but then, of course, he claimed a lot of frankly absurd things when he'd a mind to.

"We sailed on towards the west, keeping the pack ice on our starboard bow, and two days since saw the most unexpected and extraordinary sight: we saw, wading along the icecap's coastline, two gigantic and bipedal reptiles such as we are currently assured inhabited the furthest reaches of Earth's past. These dino-saurian monsters, as I think they're termed, appeared however to be casually engaged in thoughtful conversation with each other as they strolled along the icy shore, rather than bloody and primordial battle, and we noted that both wore what seemed for all the world to be a kind of sealskin cover-all. Orlando said (I think in jest, although I rather wonder) that many years ago, as a young man, she'd been an amorous acquaintance of the legendary sailor from Iraq named Captain Sinbad or 'Sinned-Bad' as she insisted on pronouncing it. The seafarer had spoken of a land he'd once heard tell of under Earth's North Polar region, called the North Pole Kingdom, where enormous cultured lizards had for many centuries maintained a large, advanced civilization, and we all supposed that the two creatures we had seen were from that place, perhaps come up to take the air and sun when tiring of their world of artificial electro-magnetically created heat and light. We headed on without event, though rather slowly, and at sunset yesterday we glimpsed what proved to be the claw-carved ice caves that comprise the region called Polar Bear Kingdom, where we were intrigued to find the gentle yet ferocious-looking ursine natives quite conversant with the English language and entirely unsurprised by our arrival in the frigid coastal waters of their realm.

"As they showed us the stores of ice-bound frozen dino-saurians they use as food (some of them dressed in sealskin and, I fear, come from the North Pole Kingdom further east), they told us how they had been lately visited by representatives of an American who manufactured phosphate drinks and was most anxious in securing the pictorial rights to any suitably appealing bear activity, for purposes of advertising. They said also that the representatives had next struck further north in hope of finding an elusive polar witch-doctor with whom they sought to make a similar agreement. As of yet, the men had not returned, and our hosts gloomily supposed that they had perhaps stumbled through the mountain-door of nearby subterranean Mandai Country, just a little further north, becoming lost in that strange land of naked blonde men who had fur as white as polar bears themselves. The towering, softly-spoken beasts of the Polar Bear Kingdom said that daily they anticipated the arrival of replacement representatives come from the phosphate soda company to deal with them, and had indeed hoped we ourselves might be such persons. They seemed somewhat disappointed when they led us back towards our ship and waved farewell with their great paws as we sailed on, with Norway's Svalbard islands visible to our port side.

"January 8th, 1907. We have come ashore now, if these partly melted clots of ice and snow may be described as shore, and we are finding these new territories most strange. The morning after we had bidden farewell to the polar bears we came in sight of Gaster's Island, sometimes called the island of the Belly-Worshippers, and even saw one of the isle's processions as it wound along the shore, holding a hideous idol-figure of the island's ravenous god Manduce aloft. Thinking it wiser to avoid the place we headed on, and soon found ourselves grinding to a halt amidst the ice-bound waters of the most astounding ocean I have ever seen or heard of. It appeared to be a veritable sea of frozen words, all of the world's sounds turned to ice and gathered there in great miles-wide deposits. In the Spring, so Captain Svejk assured us, there would be a thaw, upon which these enormous drifts of syllables and vowels and consonants would all melt back to insubstantial noises once again, but that was still some months away. The crystallized words spread about us, an immense variety of different languages, of different scales and colours. Looming up to one side of our ice-locked vessel was the German word 'Volk' carved in capitals some fifty yards high, made from ice that was a vivid and translucent scarlet, all shot through with onyx veins of glittering black. Other similarly massive words in different tongues and hues rose from the baffling landscape here or there, while scattered in heaped, gleaming piles between them there were smaller words, quite evidently of a lesser stature although no less radiant nor prismatic. Allan and Orlando both competed, climbing down onto the curlicued italic frozen wave-tops of that vast verbal morain, in finding me the prettiest word to wear as jewelry in my hair. Allan found me the word 'optative' (which we believe may be connected with Greek grammar), just three inches long and made from ice of olive green with little flecks of gold. Orlando took the prize however by retrieving for me the delicious-looking word 'Vulpecula,' apparently a constellation, fashioned out of crystals that were beautifully mottled in two shades of brilliant blue. I wore it and it looked most fetching until yesterday, when suddenly it melted, leaving me with wet hair and a fleeting whisper of the word 'Vulpecula,' as in the voice of an old man, close to my ear.

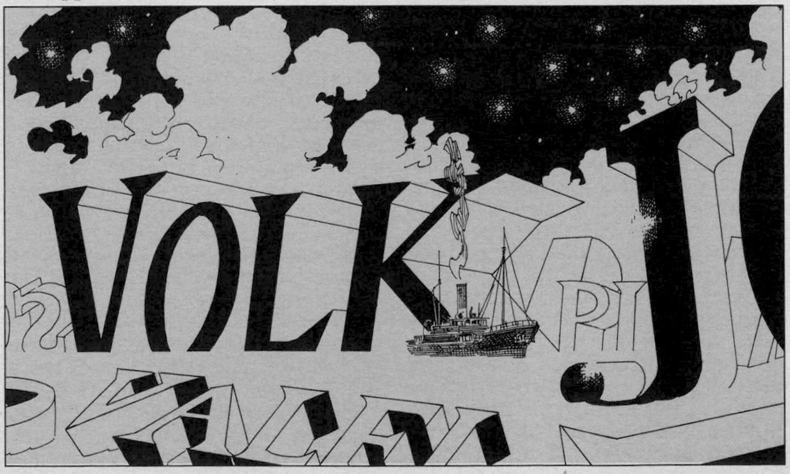
VOLK

"We pressed on through the tight-packed adjectives and in amongst some almost berg-like nouns and saw off to our starboard bow the stark volcanic rock known as Queen Island, as discovered by the most unfortunate Captain John Hatteras in 1861. Through our binoculars we could make out the tattered British flag that Hatteras, prior to his subsequent descent into insanity, had planted there at the volcano's summit. It seemed quite a sorry thing, and did not flutter, being frozen stiff. Continuing, we came at last in sight of those great islands in their seas of ice that led like massive stepping stones towards the icecap proper: giant Thule, and fabulous Hyperborea. Thule, with its demon-worshipping and hide-clad savages the Scritifines, we did not wish to visit, though Hyperborea seemed more verdant and hospitable. However, as it was, we were prevented by the ice from going further and were forced to put in to the polar icecap, just a little south of where Hyperborea was at present temporarily connected to the arctic 'mainland' by a glistening bridge of frost. Here, in the freakishly warm territory called The Back of the North Wind, my hair-slide melted.

"This was yesterday. We slept aboard *The Josef* last night (which I have the feeling is a good ship that attempts to do its best, but nonetheless has brought us to catastrophe), and earlier this morning Allan and Orlando and myself, leaving the captain with his vessel, set out to explore the land that we find ourselves stranded in. The Back of the North Wind, as noted earlier, seems ever bathed in springtime warmth, so that we walk on grass where nothing but the gentlest breeze has ever stirred, and everything is filled with inner light by some means I cannot describe. We have already met one of the somewhat wistful-looking folk that live here, who explained that this land was the realm of the North Wind himself, an elemental and titanic figure, seldom wholly visible save when in belting rain or snow, who sat at some kind of portal near the ice-bridge that we'd seen, joining Hyperborea with the polar icecap. We bade *adieu* to this rather forlorn and sorry chap (in old and faded naval uniform, if I recall correctly) and went on some way across this balmy and delightful landscape, coming just a while ago to the small orchard where I sit amongst the falling apple-blossom as I write these words. We had a picnic with the rations we had brought, and now both Allan and Orlando are laughing as they play the fool in the long grass, calling for me to join them. It is so very warm, I may as well take off my...I have just seen something. Something small seems to be moving through the swaying grass towards us. I glimpsed brilliant yellow for a moment and I seemed to hear a bell.

"I'd better finish here and warn the other two that there is somethi—

* * * * * *

"March 19th, or thereabouts, 1907. So much to tell about, not least the sudden jump in date. We are some distance past the Back of the North Wind at present, and have learned that while to us it seemed we spent perhaps three days within that land, to judge from the position of the stars almost two months have passed. But oh, what we have seen and heard. The picnic I had started to describe above was interrupted when we were surrounded by a group of most insistent...well, I dare say one would have to call them toys, since they were none of them a living being in the strict sense of that phrase, though they possessed both animation and intelligence. Bursting from out the undergrowth to ring us round came hordes of what appeared to be diminutive stuffed bears, their glass eyes glinting with an eerie, keen intelligence. Commanding them from his bright yellow vehicle was what looked for all the world to be a small boy made from painted wood, his conical blue hat tipped with the tiny bell of silver that had first alerted me. We were all so startled when we realised that these clearly manufactured things could talk that we allowed them to accompany us to their settlement without resistance. (I suppose we could have just trampled on the soft or fragile-looking little things, but somehow not a one of us possessed the heart.)

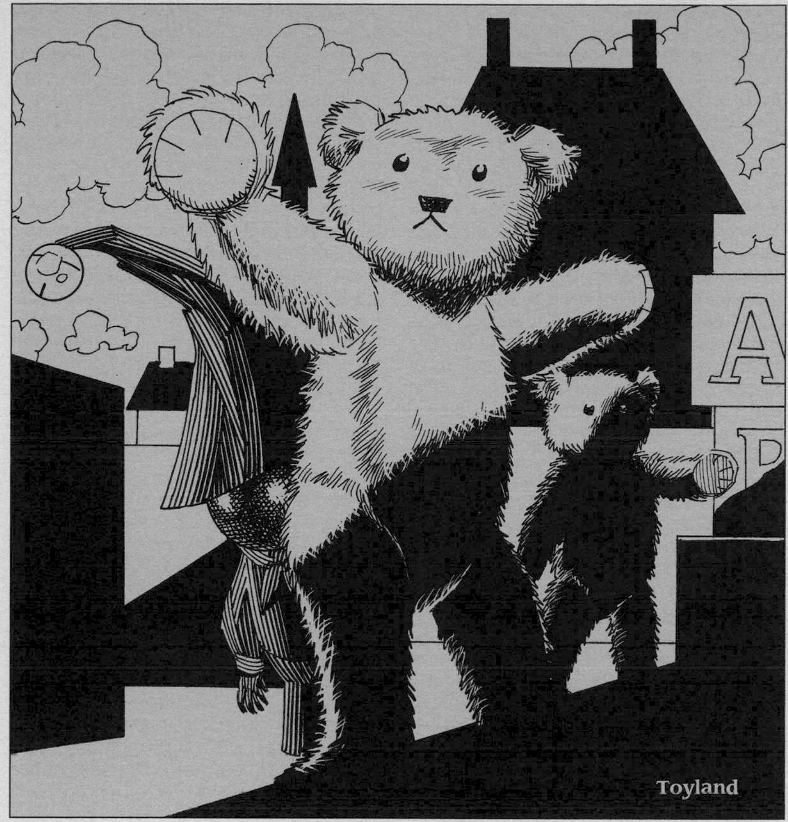
A
P
Toyland

"Their realm, the quaintest little town, with houses that seem made from building-blocks, is Toyland. How it came to be here, or indeed exist at all, entails a truly fascinating story that I will endeavour to pass on as I was told it by the talking toys. Apparently, sometime around 1815, an inventor by the name of Spalanzani had enlisted the assistance of a manufacturer of spectacles, a doctor named Coppelius, to help with the construction of a mechanism so ingenious in its workings that it might be said almost to think and live, or at least in so far as we are able to assess such things. The beautiful doll-woman that resulted from this partnership was named Olympia, and after several exploits and misadventures with Coppelius, the doctor came to feel that his creation might be happier if she might somehow be amongst her own kind, which is to say self-aware and animated toys. Venturing to the arctic so that he might work in solitude, Coppelius had stumbled on the green and pleasant Back of the North Wind by accident, as had we also, and elected to construct his tiny kingdom of self-sensible automatons there in that realm. Within some years he had not only built a score or so of like machines to serve as subjects of his Queen Olympia, but he had also taught these living toys the secret of their own design and manufacture, so that with the doctor's death they might continue to expand as a vital community.

"We met with Queen Olympia, who seemed so personable and quick witted that had it not been for the artificial doll-like flawlessness of her great pulchritude we might have thought her human. She seemed fascinated by our tales, and we with hers, no more so than when she introduced to us her consort, who, although he might be honestly described as artificial or constructed life, was not by any means a toy. For one thing, it appeared that he was fashioned out of human flesh, his musculature rather frighteningly pronounced, as with an anatomical exhibit. We learned that this at once horrific and yet somehow noble individual was the creation of a young, ambitious, European doctor who had known Doctor Coppelius and, two years after the creation of Olympia, had sought to emulate the elder man's achievement by constructing his own artificial being, this time from the fragments of dead men and galvanised by an electric current. Following a series of quite tragic turns of fortune, this accursed creation with its terrifying near-gelatinous visage found its way to the arctic where it wandered in grim solitude for many years. At last by chance its wanderings led it here into Hyperborea (seemingly the same realm as The Back of the North Wind, so I assume the ice-bridge that we saw was permanent), where it was both bemused and gratified to find that the mechanical inhabitants did not respond to its appearance with alarm. On meeting with the beautiful Olympia and learning of their creators' acquaintance, the tall, wild-haired monster realized that here he'd found the bride that he had always sought, and so the two of them had married and had ruled as King and Queen of Toyland ever since, in matrimonial bliss.

"While we were in their land—however long that may in truth have been—they did their best to educate us as regards the icecap's other regions and inhabitants. Some distance further north, they said, near the North Pole itself, there stood a ring of high peaks said to have a twin at Earth's South Pole and called the Iron Mountains. These protect the cavern-entrance to an underground realm of vast size called Pluto or Pellucidar by some, Atvatabar or else Ruffal by others, though this last is thought to be a tiny suburb of the greater subterranean kingdoms. We were told to steer well clear of Evileye Land, a dire surface region where the females had two pupils in one eye and in their other eye the image of a horse, these women capable of killing with a single glance. After a pleasant while of further such instructive conversation, our delightful though alarming hosts suggested that the three of us perhaps should travel on, out of their land towards the icecap's rim, explaining that as time itself would sometimes pass at different rates within their realm, we may find that we'd stayed there longer than we'd thought, so that our Captain and our transport both could be long gone. We found this thought alarming, and resolved to head back to the frozen coast without delay, although before we left Olympia ventured us two further pieces of advice. She told us to avoid the territory of a powerful and ferocious arctic 'sha-man' or witch-doctor who dwelled slightly further to the north, and also said that Toyland was occasionally visited by someone she described as a 'bold, fearless black balloonist,' an explorer that she thought we might well be advised to meet. She said that she would tell this person of our band when next he came there, though if ought will come of this I do not know. And so at last we quit that place, the three of us, and found ourselves beneath the two-month-shifted stars, where I now write these words by lamplight in our tent (the snows and arctic cold resumed the moment we left Toyland). What tomorrow holds, none of us have the first idea.

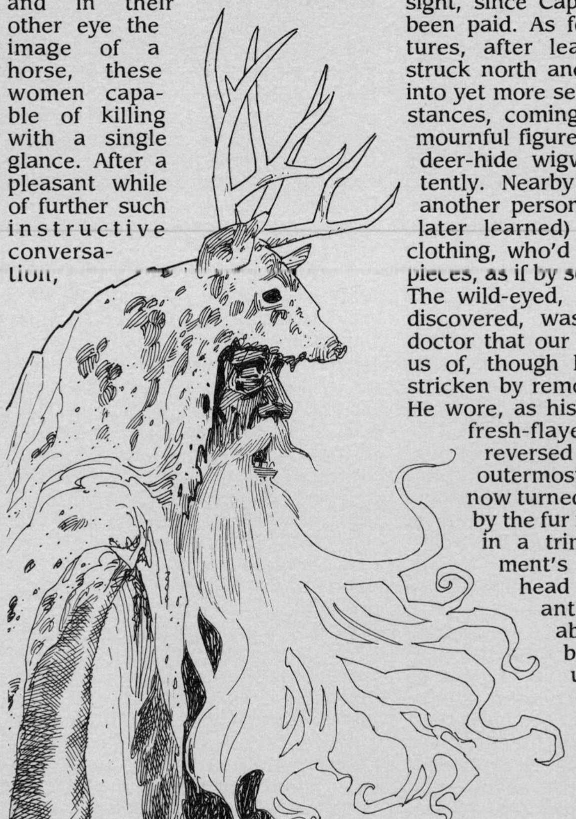

"March 25th, 1907—the true date. I've checked it with our captain for we are now safely back aboard *The Josef,* which had been conveniently delayed until the Spring's first thaw, and then had headed northward up the icecap's edge to see if we were anywhere in sight, since Captain Svejk had not been paid. As for our own adventures, after leaving Toyland, we struck north and shortly blundered into yet more sense-defying circumstances, coming on a strange and mournful figure crouched before a deer-hide wigwam howling penitently. Nearby was the body of another person (an American, we later learned) in modern arctic clothing, who'd been partly torn to pieces, as if by some form of animal. The wild-eyed, bearded fellow, we discovered, was the same witch-doctor that our friends had warned us of, though he seemed far too stricken by remorse to do us harm. He wore, as his magician's robe, a fresh-flayed reindeer hide reversed so that the skin was outermost, its bloody red by now turned almost black, lined by the fur inside that stuck out in a trim around the garment's edge. The beast's head formed a cowl, the antlers jutting there above his lined, grey-bearded face. He told us between moans of anguish that he was the 'sha-man' of the North Pole, charged at the mid-winter solstice with delivering the gift of cheer to all the homes on Earth, his disembodied soul darting around the globe born by his flying spirit animals while all the time his body lies here in his wigwam, raving mad and stained with vomit from the mind-affecting spotted mushrooms that he must take to achieve his trance. Apparently, this Christmas past, his trance was interrupted by two rash Americans who represented the same phosphate-drink concern the polar bears had told us of. This breach of the magician's most important yearly ritual was met by the witch-doctor's fierce invisible familiars, or 'little helpers' as he called them, who had torn one of the representatives into the shreds we saw a short way off. The other fled, but only after reassuring the frantically-apologizing witch-man that his actions did not constitute a reason to break off their hoped-for future business dealings.

"We left him weeping there and went on to the icecap's coast, where with some luck we found *The Josef* and our captain (mostly by the trail of rust and oil his ship had left there in the previously gem-clear polar waters). Since then we have sailed south past the meteoric aggregate some call 'The Real North Pole,' with its immense ice-column and its vast circular lake, and crossed the Sea of Giants, where the scattered islands were once haunted by both troll and cyclops, coming into Peacepool by Jan Mayen's Land. Peacepool itself, where there is said to live an enigmatic and benign old woman known as Mother Carey, was hidden from us by a ring of ice-white cliffs, but we saw one or two of the odd-shaped and curiously-coloured creatures that the crone apparently constructs from seawater, swimming beside our boat.

"We now head back for Britain through the ghostly archipelago that I have read of in the journals of my League's 17th-century predecessors, called the Blazing World. It is quite wonderful. Orlando, Allan and myself stand awestruck at the prow and watch the spectral alabaster quaysides with their human-animal inhabitants glide slowly past, below a rippling Aurora Borealis. It was here the traveller Christian and his sometime colleague Prospero, Duke of Milan, both vanished without trace on separate occasions. We all hope that we'll come back here some day, if only to join them. I can think of no more splendid place in which to be lost for eternity."

Here end Miss Murray's notes, and with them we conclude also our Almanac. We hope that the intrepid youngster of today will find it useful in their global circumnavigations, and who knows? It may be that some travellers thus inspired will bring back with them fresh accounts of new and marvellous lands beyond the seas, perhaps to be included in future revisions of our present gazetteer. It only remains for us to wish the reader good luck and a most hearty bon voyage!

THIS BOOK IS AVAILABLE BY SUBSCRIPTION ONLY AND IS NOT SOLD AT GENERAL BOOK-STORES. FURTHER COPIES MAY BE PURCHASED FOR 5/- FROM H.M. STATIONERY OFFICE, DEPT. D5, VAUXHALL CROSS, LONDON.

DIVISION 5 FIVE

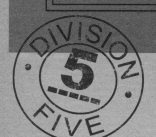

DESTRUCTION — NOTICE —

ACT IMMEDIATELY

By order of H.M. Office of Bowdlerisation. READERS SHOULD DETACH AND DESTROY ALL SCENES OF AN UNSAVOURY NATURE.

Failure to comply will lead to a Custodial Sentence.

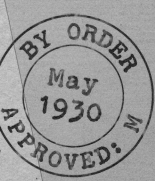

DESTROY
AUTHORISATION
H.M. PRINTING OFFICE
BY DIRECTION,
ACT IMMEDIATELY

BY ORDER
May
1930
APPROVED: M

THE GAME OF EXTRAORDINARY GENTLEMEN

Welcome, dear readers, to a smashing diversion for those wet afternoons in late January, when the blight is heavy upon the wisteria and Father hangs creaking from a rafter in the west wing. Taking the role of your favourite staunch adventurer, you may progress around our board according to the throw of a single die, following the instructions upon each square as you do so, until at last you reach Ayesha's fabled Fountain of Eternal Life and quaff the heady balm of immortality. **NOTE:** Players must provide their own counters and dice. A small wager does no harm, and may prove educational. — Mr. Moore and Mr. O'Neill, creators

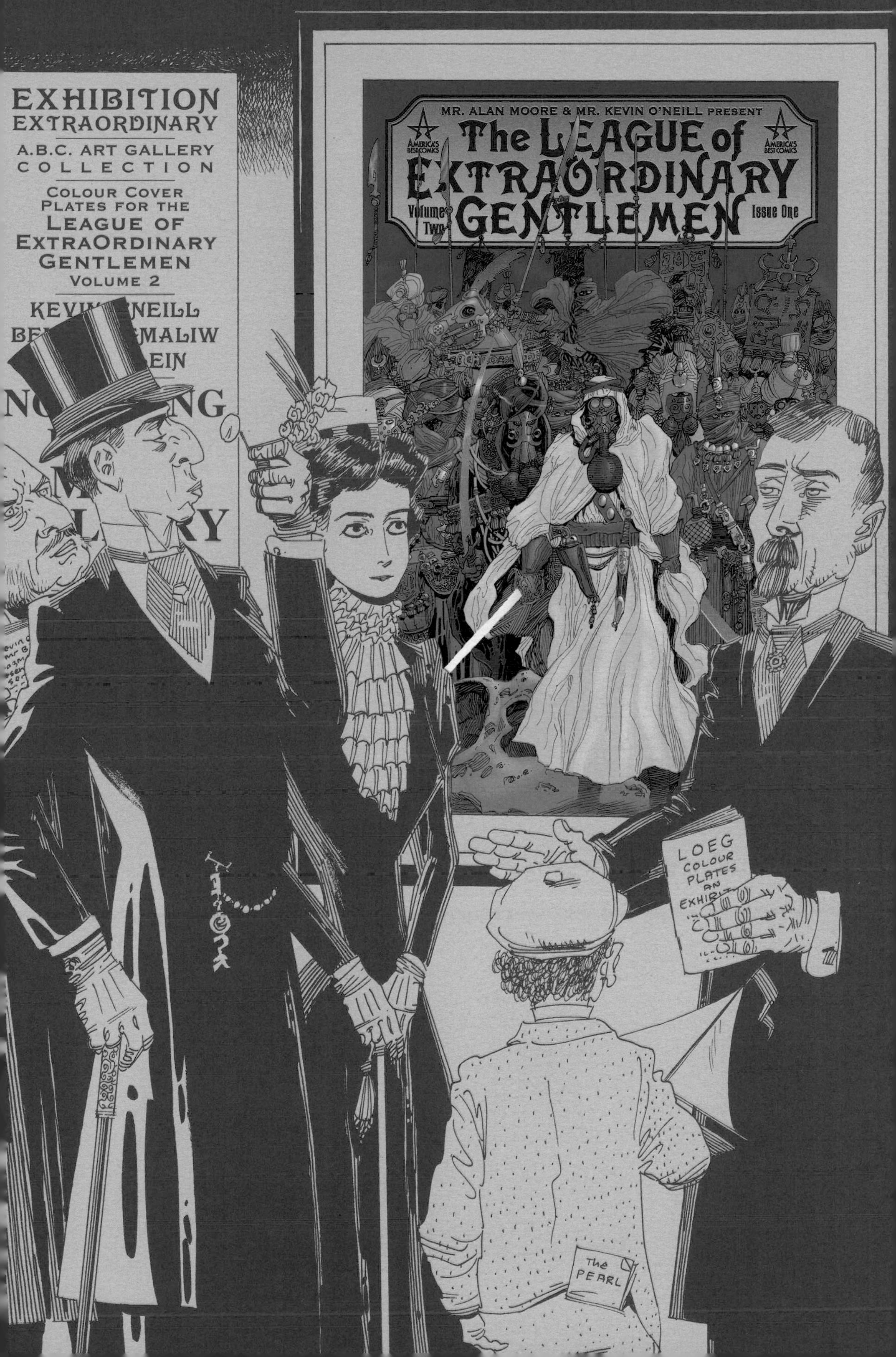

EXHIBITION EXTRAORDINARY
A.B.C. ART GALLERY COLLECTION
COLOUR COVER PLATES FOR THE LEAGUE OF EXTRAORDINARY GENTLEMEN VOLUME 2
MR. ALAN MOORE & MR. KEVIN O'NEILL PRESENT
The LEAGUE of EXTRAORDINARY GENTLEMEN
Volume Two
Issue One
AMERICA'S BEST COMICS
LOEG COLOUR PLATES AN EXHIBIT
The PEARL

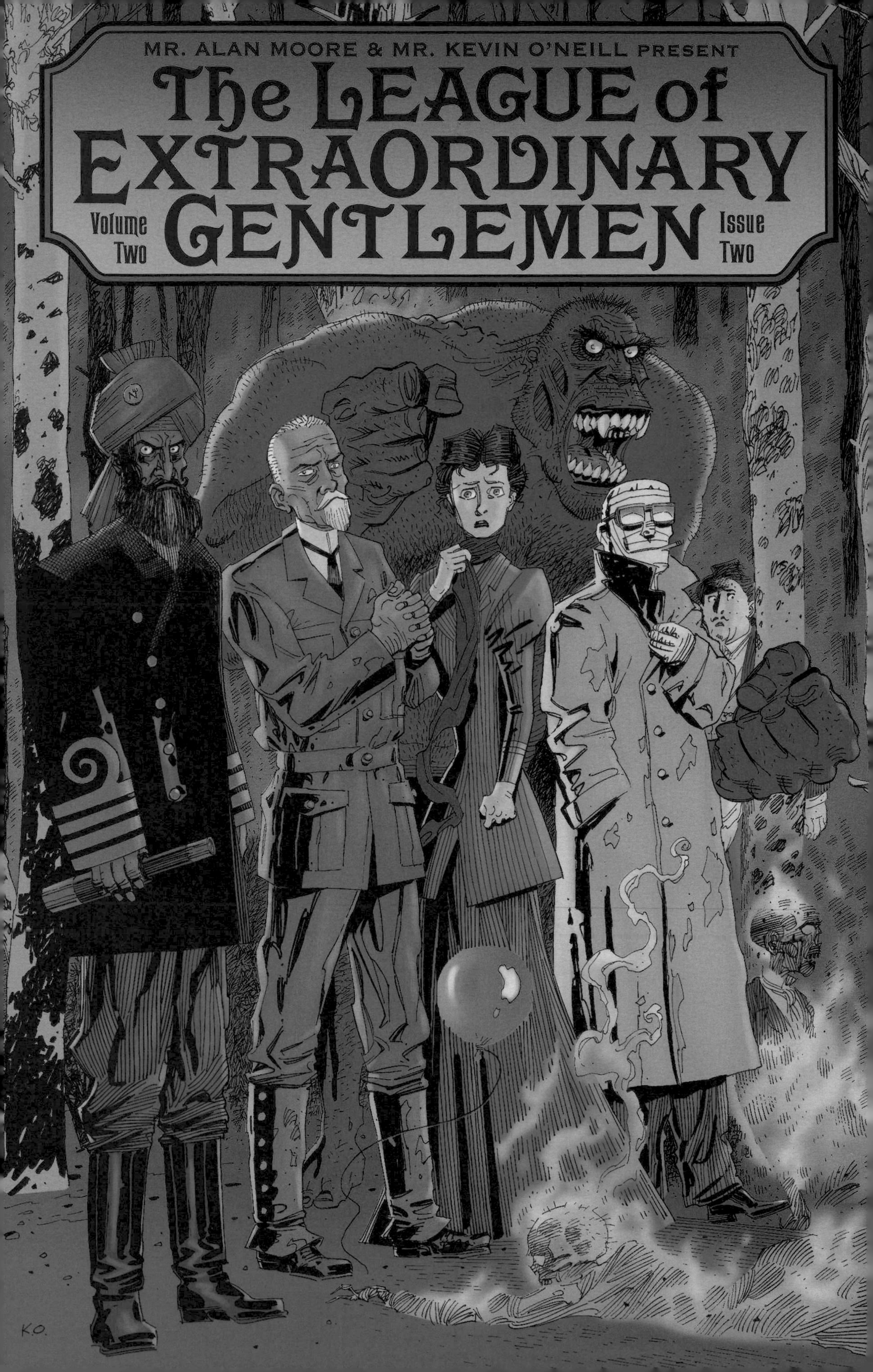
MR. ALAN MOORE & MR. KEVIN O'NEILL PRESENT
The LEAGUE of EXTRAORDINARY GENTLEMEN
Volume Two
Issue Two
K.O.

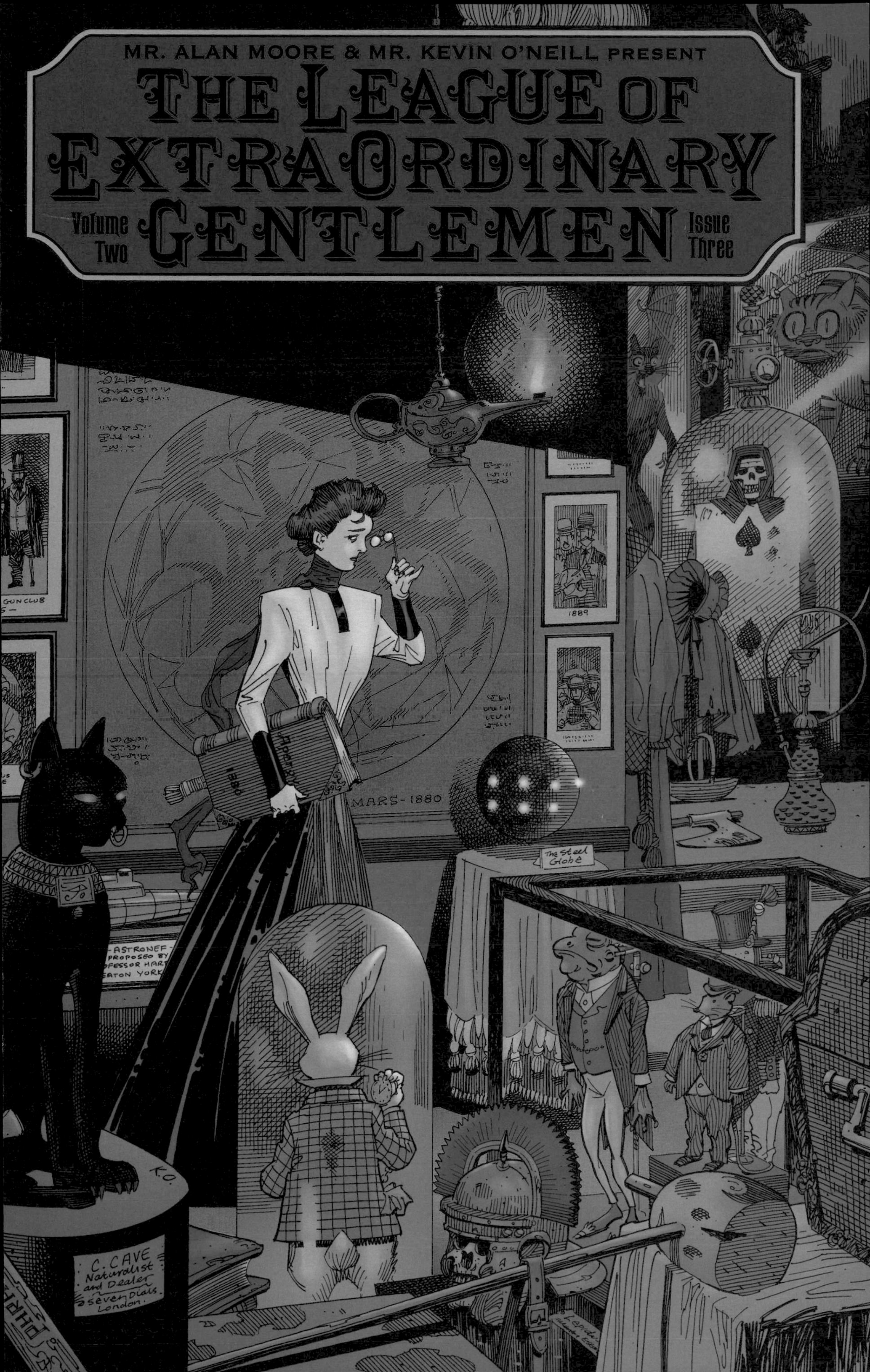
MR. ALAN MOORE & MR. KEVIN O'NEILL PRESENT
THE LEAGUE OF EXTRAORDINARY GENTLEMEN
Volume Two
Issue Three
GUN CLUB
1889
MARS-1880
The Steel Globe
K.O.
C. CAVE
Naturalist
and Dealer
2 Seven Dials
London.

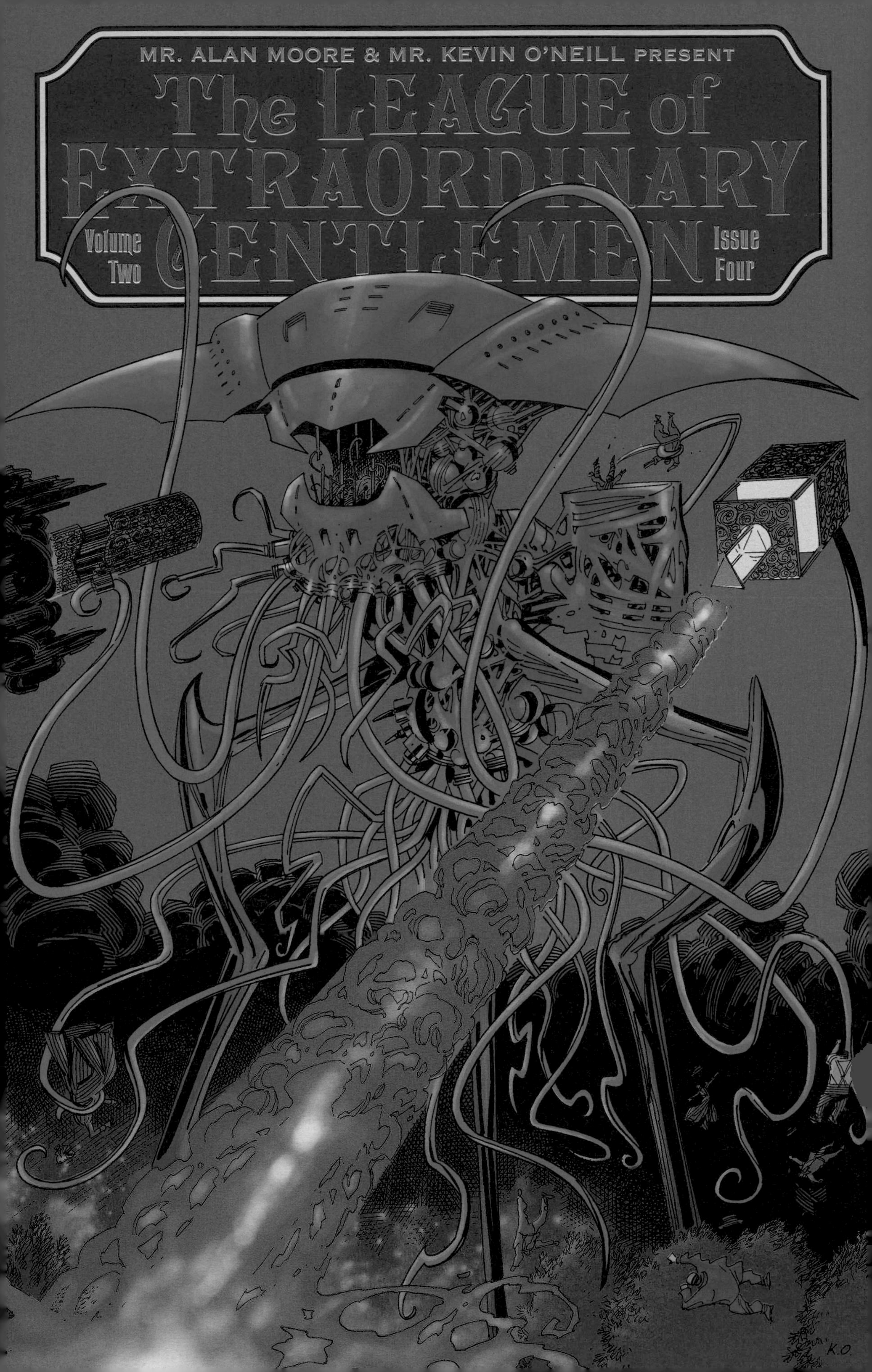
MR. ALAN MOORE & MR. KEVIN O'NEILL PRESENT
The LEAGUE of EXTRAORDINARY GENTLEMEN
Volume Two
Issue Four
K.O.

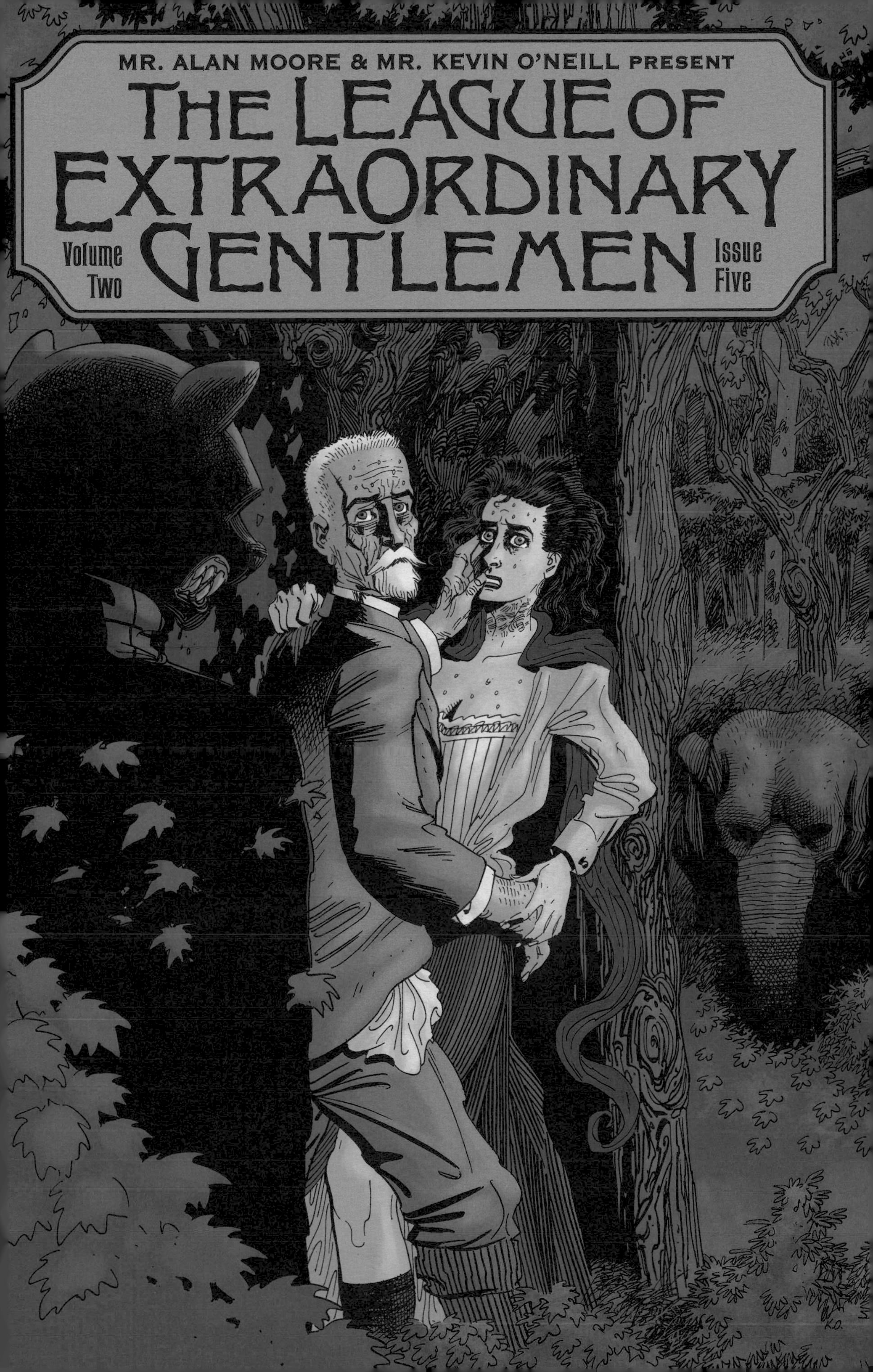
MR. ALAN MOORE & MR. KEVIN O'NEILL PRESENT
THE LEAGUE OF EXTRAORDINARY GENTLEMEN
Volume Two
Issue Five
K.O.

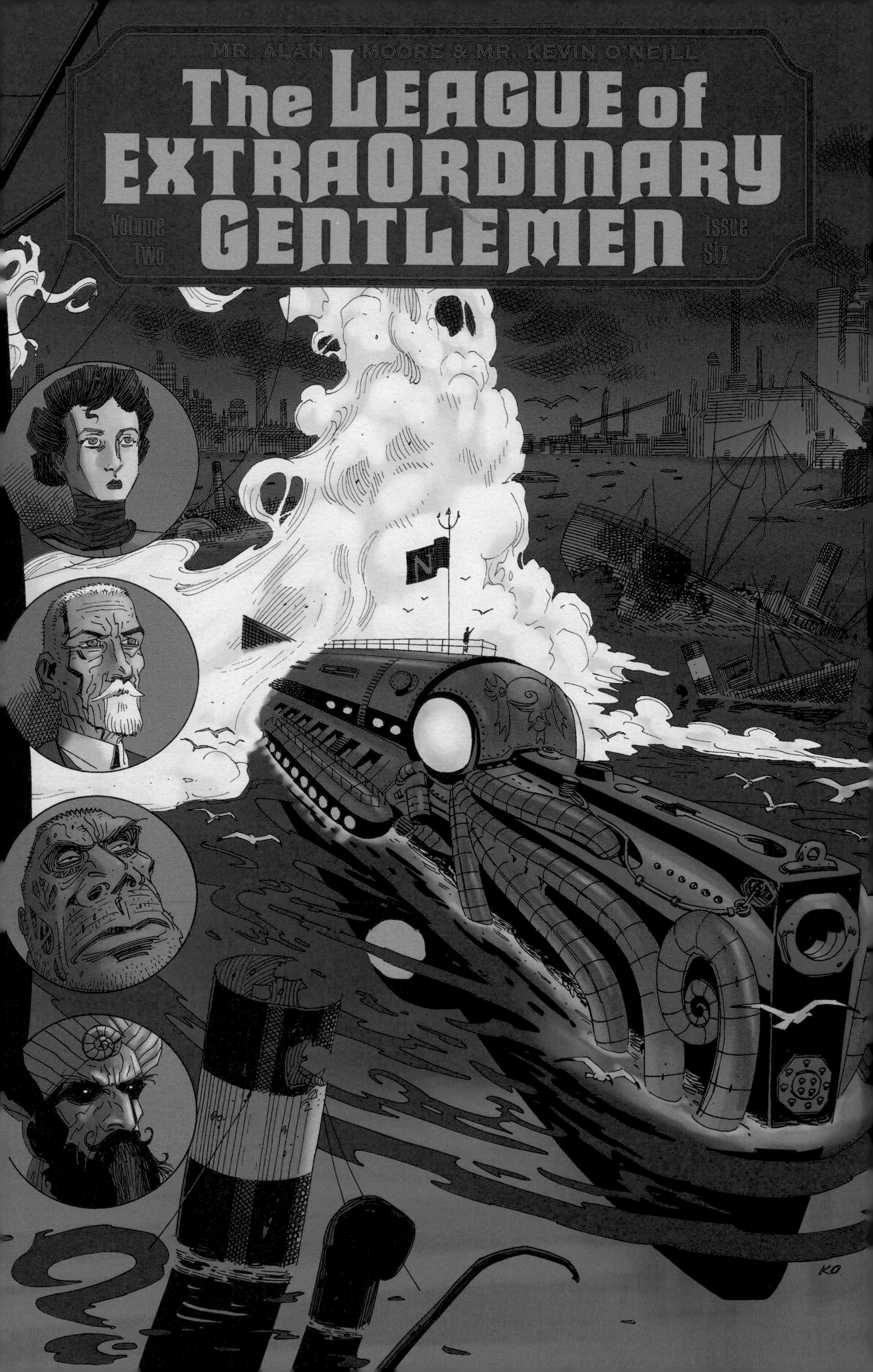
MR. ALAN MOORE & MR. KEVIN O'NEILL
The LEAGUE of EXTRAORDINARY GENTLEMEN
Volume Two
Issue Six
KO.

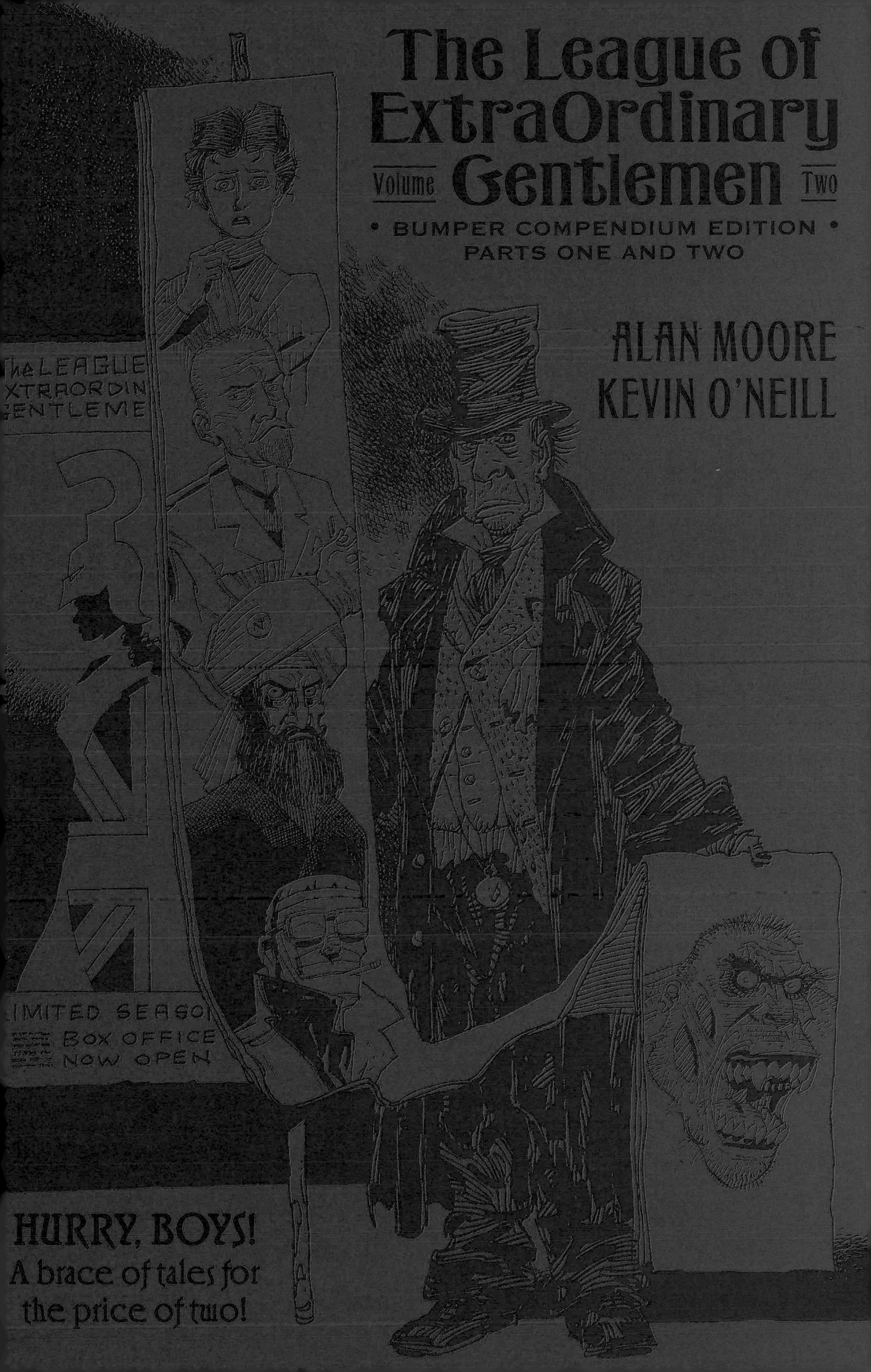

The League of ExtraOrdinary Gentlemen
Volume Two
• BUMPER COMPENDIUM EDITION •
PARTS ONE AND TWO
ALAN MOORE
KEVIN O'NEILL
The LEAGUE
XTRAORDIN
ENTLEME
IMITED SEASO
BOX OFFICE
NOW OPEN
HURRY, BOYS!
A brace of tales for
the price of two!

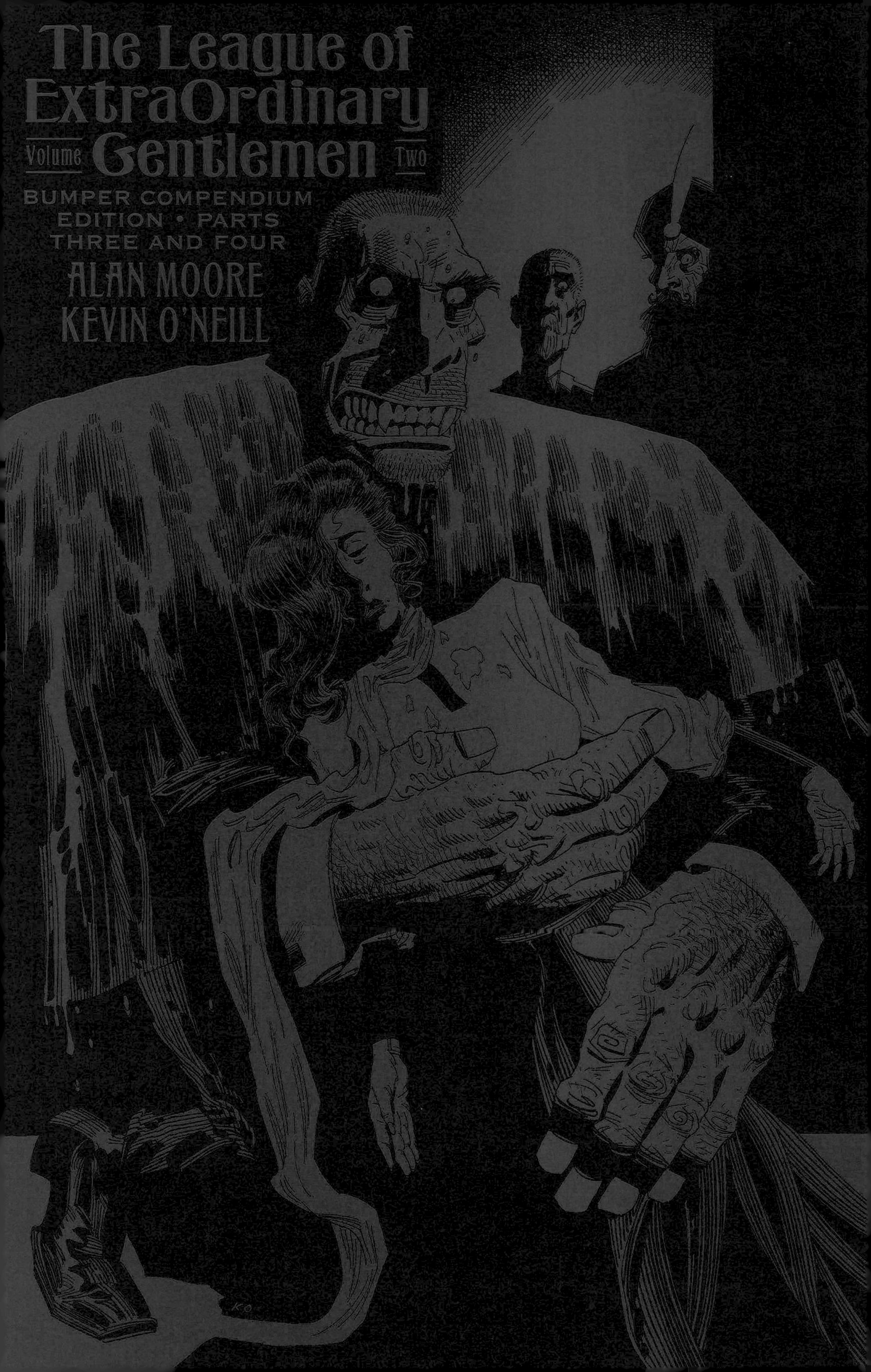
The League of ExtraOrdinary Gentlemen
Volume Two
BUMPER COMPENDIUM EDITION • PARTS THREE AND FOUR
ALAN MOORE
KEVIN O'NEILL

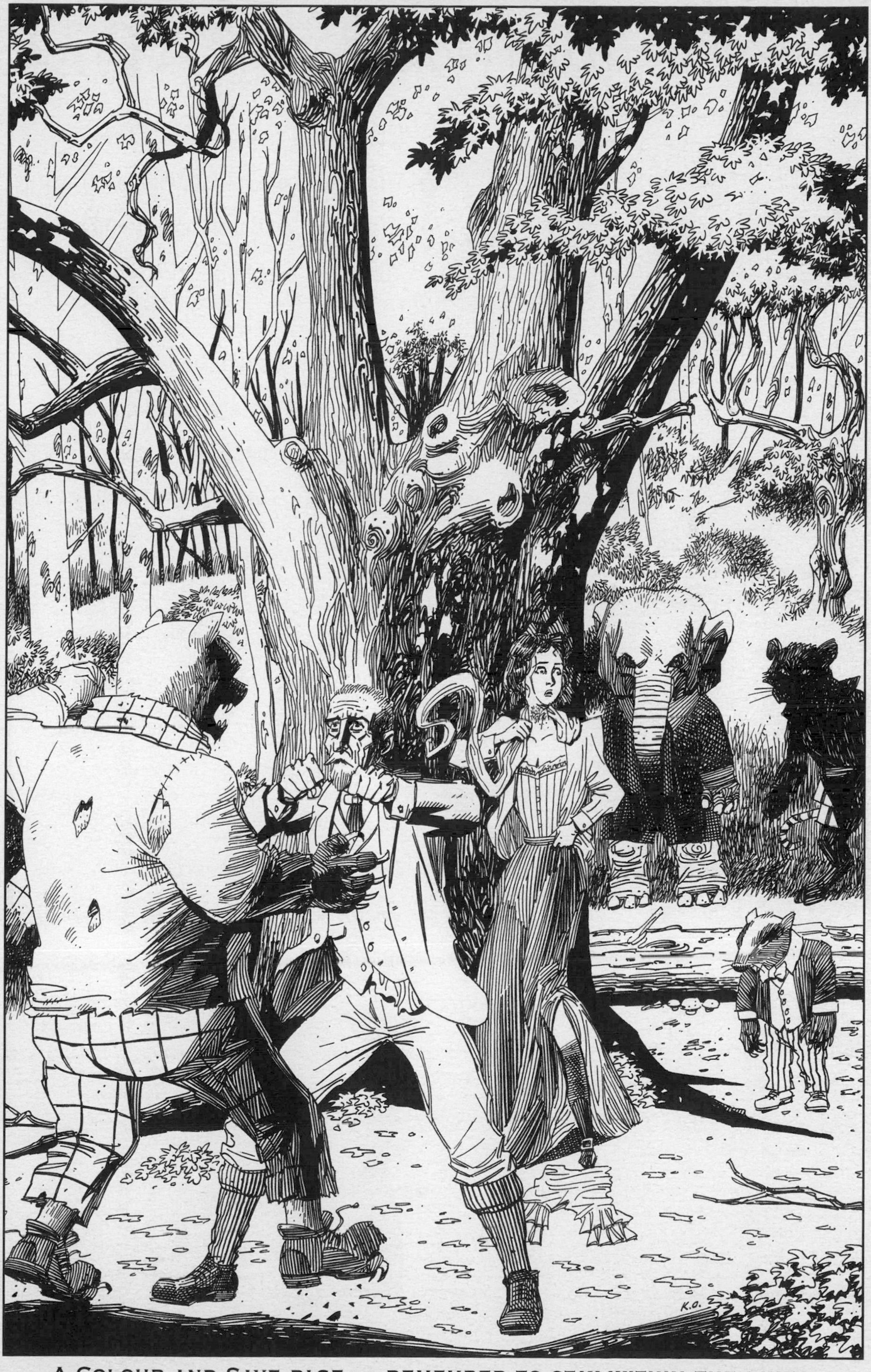

A Colour and Save page — remember to stay within the lines.

A CAUTIONARY FABLE

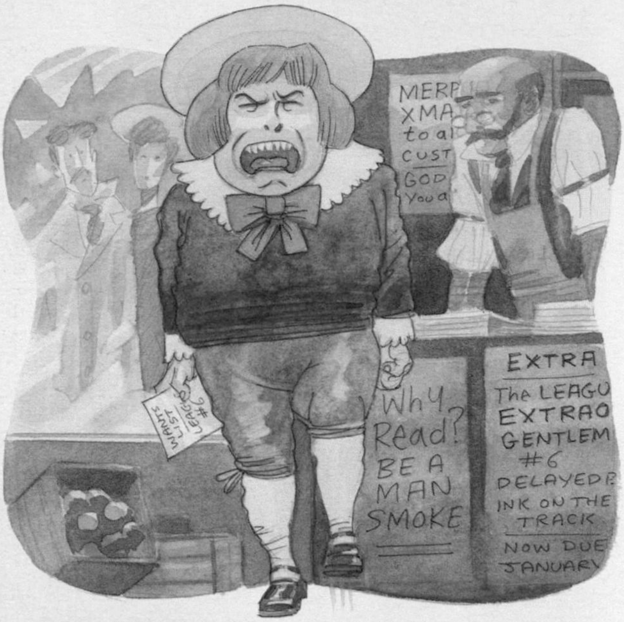
Why Read? BE A MAN SMOKE
EXTRA
NOW DUE JANUARY

This is the tale of Teddy Teague
who could not wait to read his "League."
With each new month he would complain
"Where's issue six? It's late again!"

Vexed and frustrated he would write
disgruntled letters filled with spite
That called the authors work-shy fops
and threatened them with riding crops.

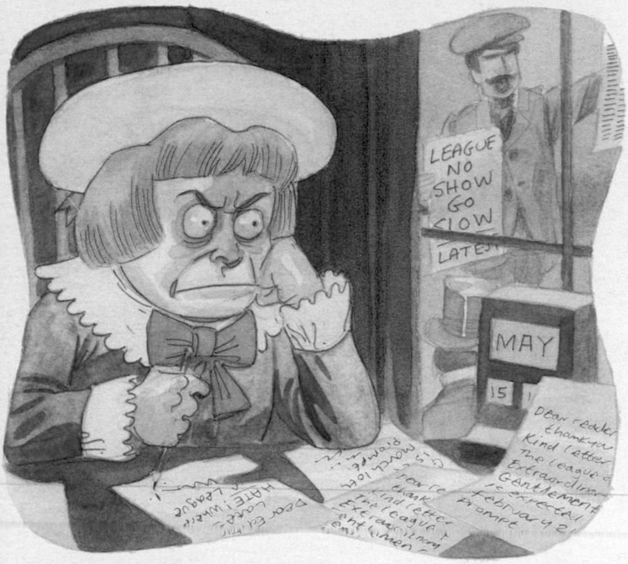
LEAGUE NO SHOW GO SLOW
MAY
15

Grown vain on cash from Tinsel Town,
the pair won't take this lying down
And, finding out where Teddy lives,
go round and do him in with shivs.

In summary, our tale makes clear
that Patience is a virtue dear.
So, gentle reader, know your place,
and don't get on our ****ing case.

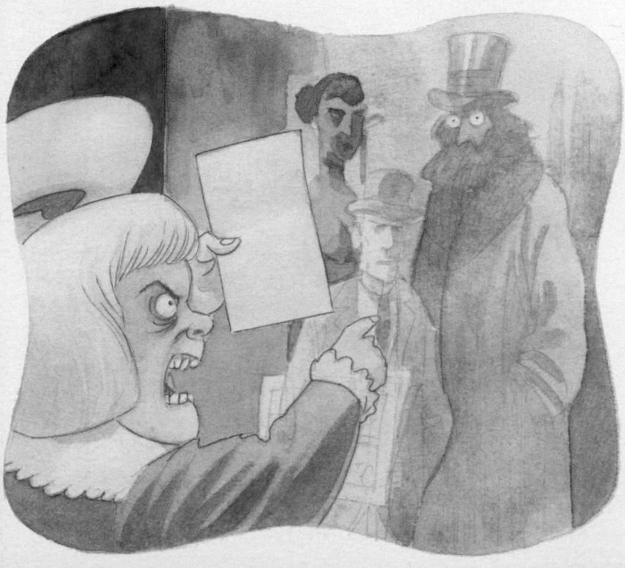

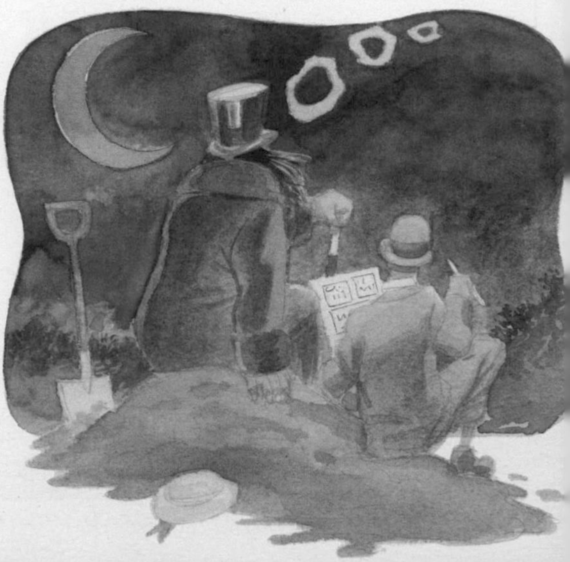

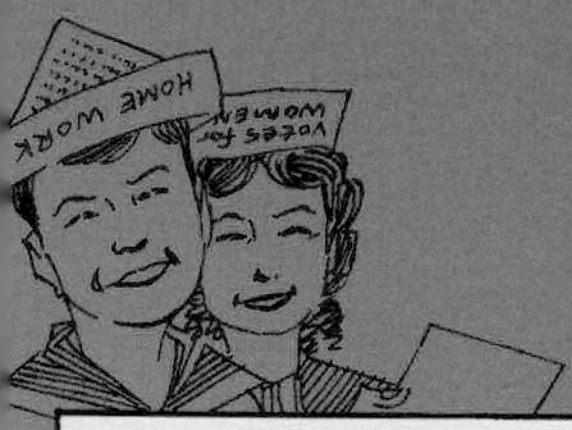

How To Make Nemo's Nautilus

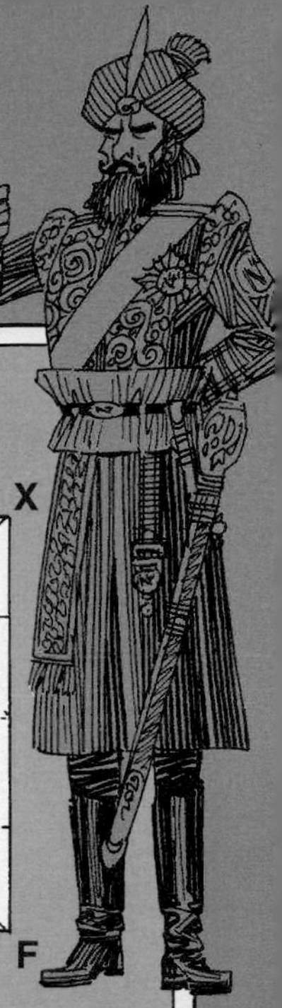

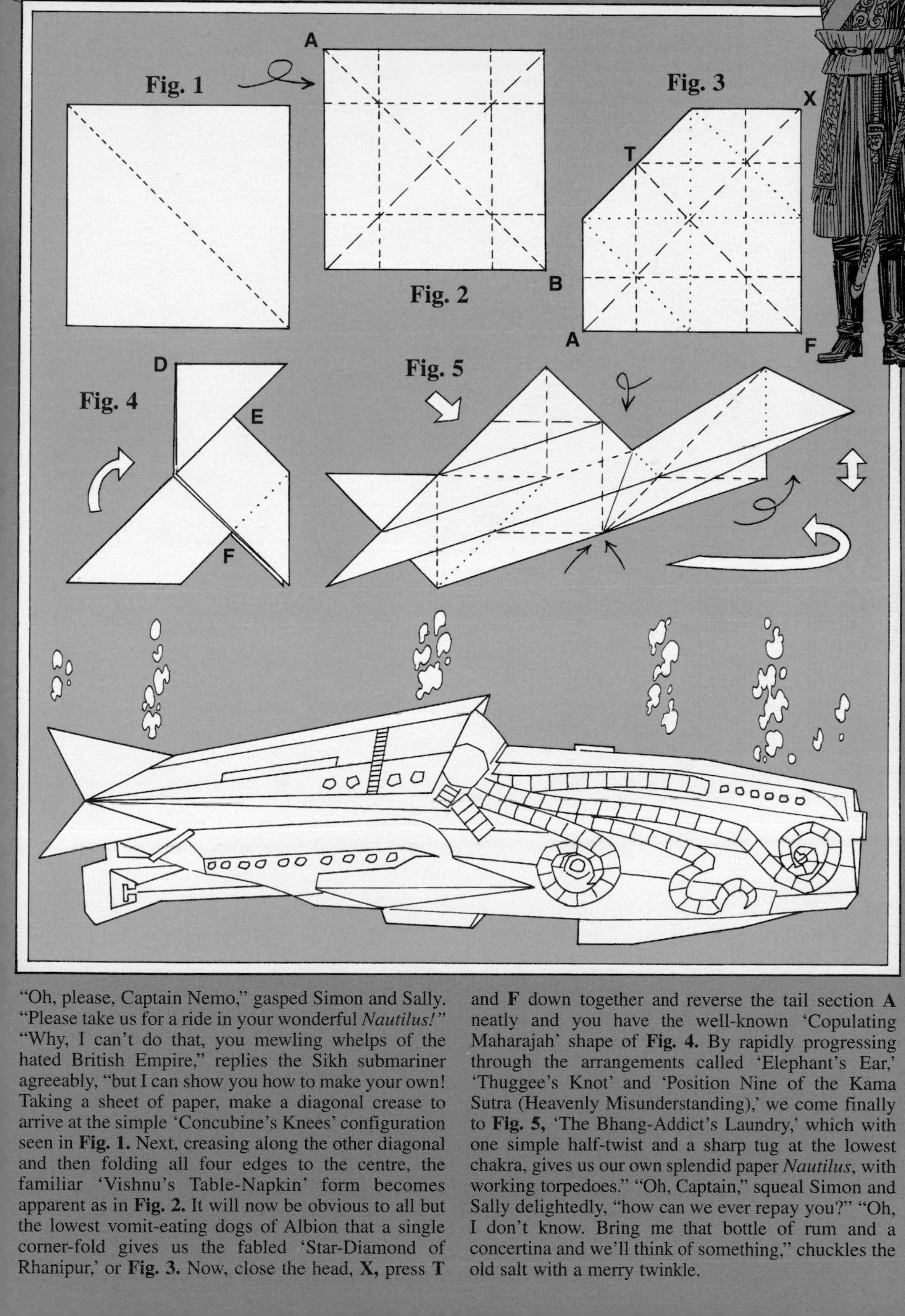

Fig. 1
A
Fig. 2
B
Fig. 3
X
T
A
F
D
Fig. 4
E
F
Fig. 5

"Oh, please, Captain Nemo," gasped Simon and Sally. "Please take us for a ride in your wonderful *Nautilus!*" "Why, I can't do that, you mewling whelps of the hated British Empire," replies the Sikh submariner agreeably, "but I can show you how to make your own! Taking a sheet of paper, make a diagonal crease to arrive at the simple 'Concubine's Knees' configuration seen in **Fig. 1.** Next, creasing along the other diagonal and then folding all four edges to the centre, the familiar 'Vishnu's Table-Napkin' form becomes apparent as in **Fig. 2.** It will now be obvious to all but the lowest vomit-eating dogs of Albion that a single corner-fold gives us the fabled 'Star-Diamond of Rhanipur,' or **Fig. 3.** Now, close the head, **X,** press **T** and **F** down together and reverse the tail section **A** neatly and you have the well-known 'Copulating Maharajah' shape of **Fig. 4.** By rapidly progressing through the arrangements called 'Elephant's Ear,' 'Thuggee's Knot' and 'Position Nine of the Kama Sutra (Heavenly Misunderstanding),' we come finally to **Fig. 5,** 'The Bhang-Addict's Laundry,' which with one simple half-twist and a sharp tug at the lowest chakra, gives us our own splendid paper *Nautilus*, with working torpedoes." "Oh, Captain," squeal Simon and Sally delightedly, "how can we ever repay you?" "Oh, I don't know. Bring me that bottle of rum and a concertina and we'll think of something," chuckles the old salt with a merry twinkle.

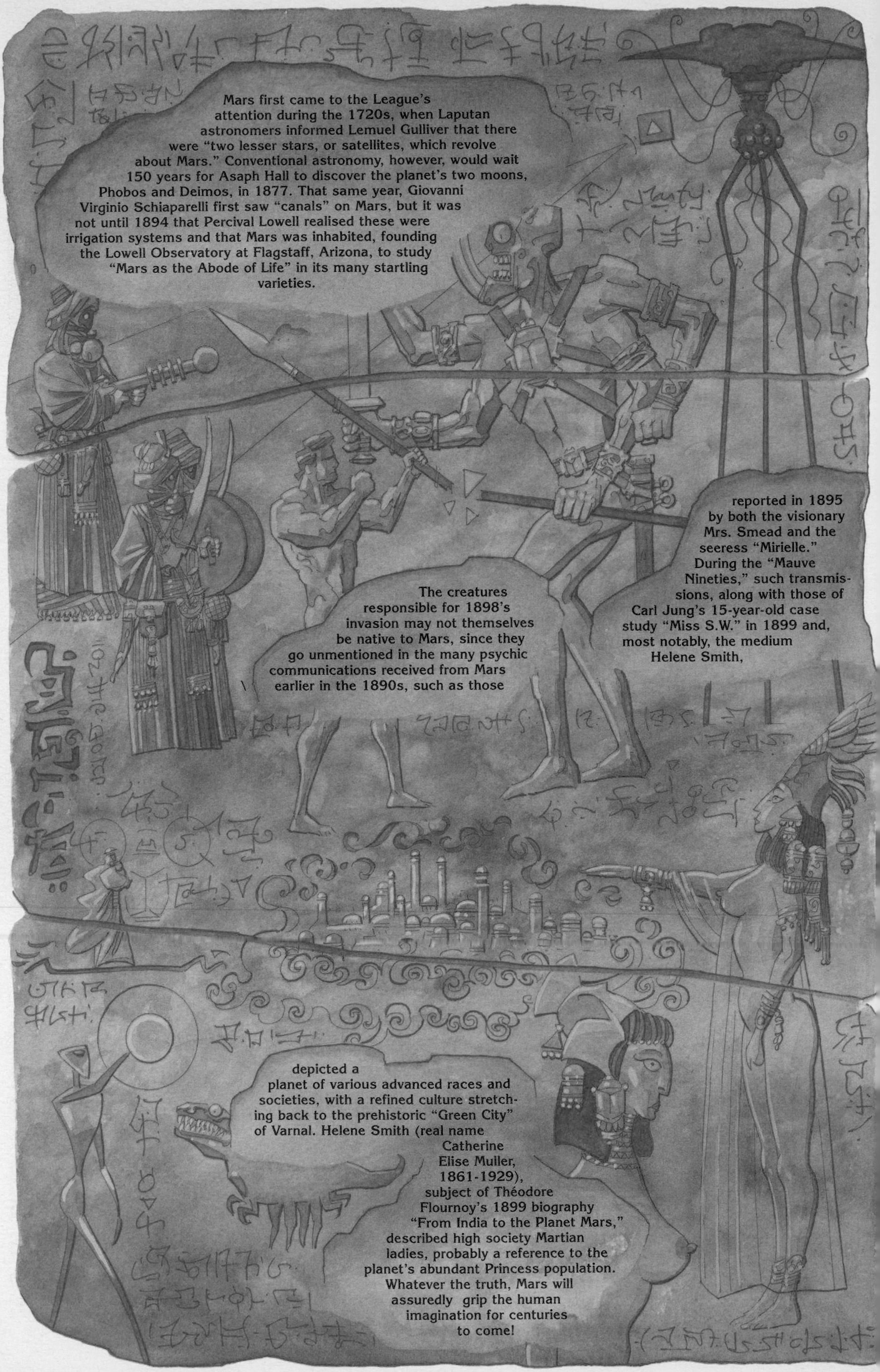
Mars first came to the League's attention during the 1720s, when Laputan astronomers informed Lemuel Gulliver that there were "two lesser stars, or satellites, which revolve about Mars." Conventional astronomy, however, would wait 150 years for Asaph Hall to discover the planet's two moons, Phobos and Deimos, in 1877. That same year, Giovanni Virginio Schiaparelli first saw "canals" on Mars, but it was not until 1894 that Percival Lowell realised these were irrigation systems and that Mars was inhabited, founding the Lowell Observatory at Flagstaff, Arizona, to study "Mars as the Abode of Life" in its many startling varieties.
The creatures responsible for 1898's invasion may not themselves be native to Mars, since they go unmentioned in the many psychic communications received from Mars earlier in the 1890s, such as those
reported in 1895 by both the visionary Mrs. Smead and the seeress "Mirielle." During the "Mauve Nineties," such transmissions, along with those of Carl Jung's 15-year-old case study "Miss S.W." in 1899 and, most notably, the medium Helene Smith,
depicted a planet of various advanced races and societies, with a refined culture stretching back to the prehistoric "Green City" of Varnal. Helene Smith (real name Catherine Elise Muller, 1861-1929), subject of Théodore Flournoy's 1899 biography "From India to the Planet Mars," described high society Martian ladies, probably a reference to the planet's abundant Princess population. Whatever the truth, Mars will assuredly grip the human imagination for centuries to come!

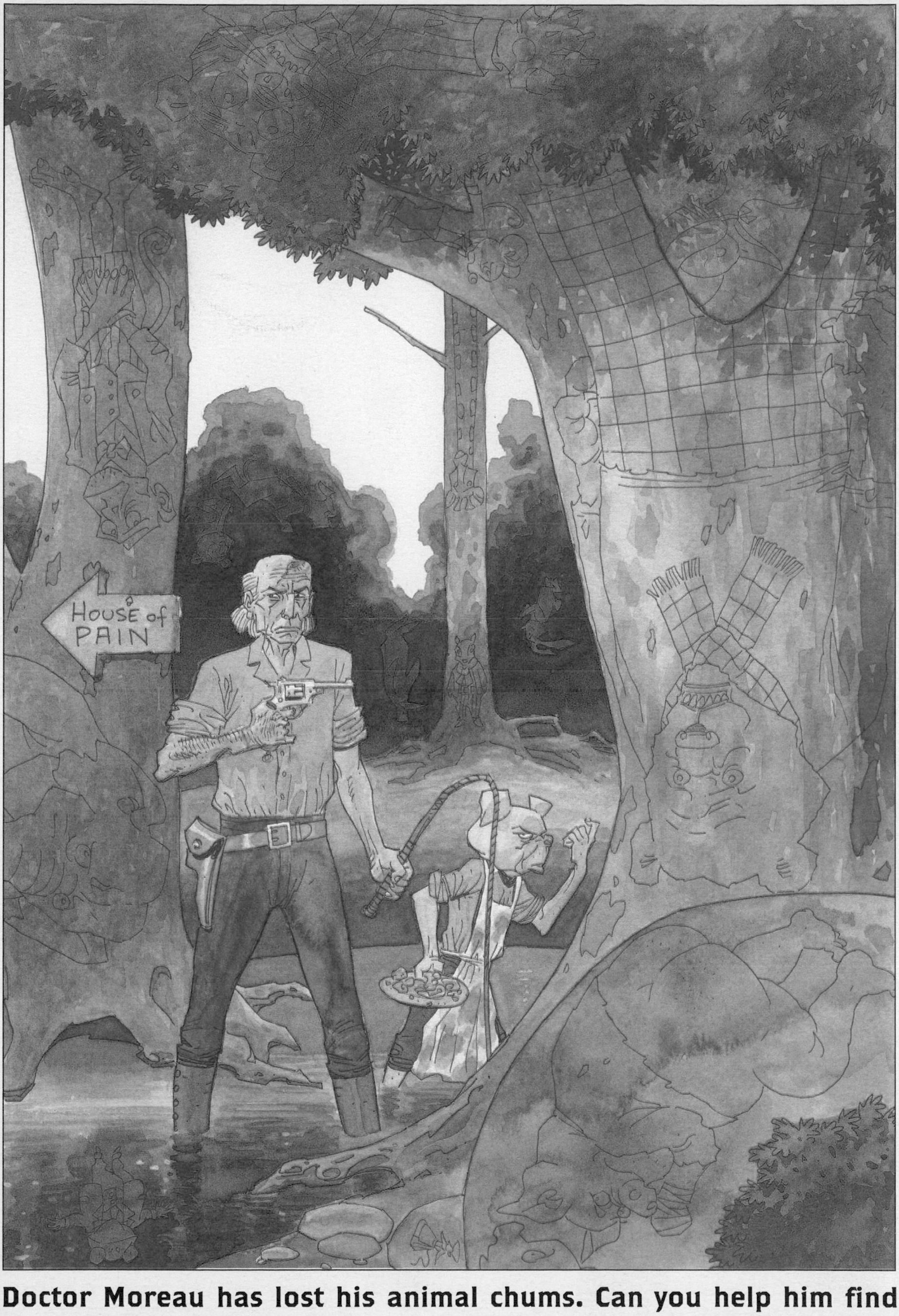
HOUSE of
PAIN

Doctor Moreau has lost his animal chums. Can you help him find them? H-11 is at a loss. They are quite close. Can you see them? Turn the picture all sorts of ways, and look in all the corners, and see if you can find them. Have you found them yet?

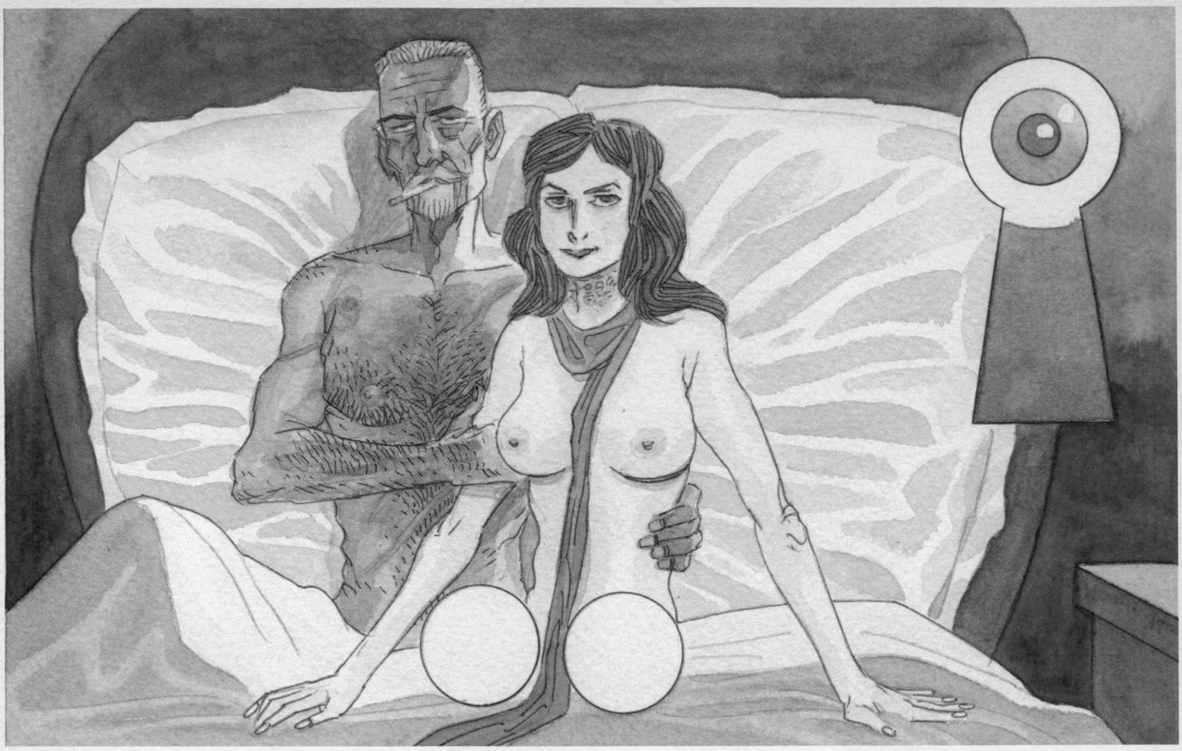

Above we reproduce one of the more respectable saucy "Art" postcards depicting members of the League that enjoyed under-the-counter circulation during the early years of the twentieth century. Simply cut out the two holes above, poke your first two fingers through and watch in delight as Miss Murray dances a vigorous Can-Can. Alternately, you may do as I myself did and construct miniature net stockings with tiny leather boots to fit over your fingertips, enabling a rapid descent into licentious delirium by kissing and licking one's own knuckles. (You may wish to ask Mother if she will help you with the scissors.)

CAMPION BOND'S MORAL MAZE

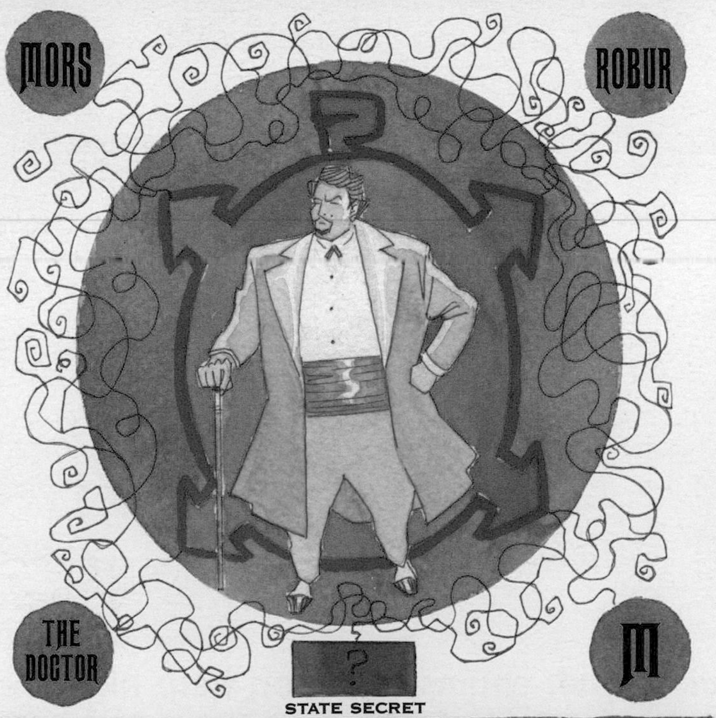
MORS
ROBUR
THE DOCTOR
M
?
STATE SECRET

Campion Bond wishes to leak a state secret. One path leads to wealth and status, the others to being found dead in the woods. If you lack moral fibre but fancy a punt, choose carefully then set off, you young rascal! Remember, one choice only!

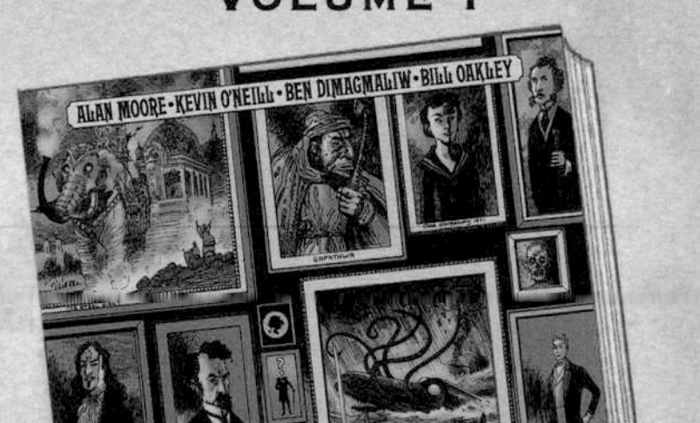
ALAN MOORE • KEVIN O'NEILL • BEN DIMAGMALIW • BILL OAKLEY
VOLUME ONE
THE LEAGUE OF EXTRAORDINARY GENTLEMEN

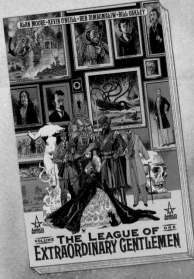

The Season's Greetings to our readers! For those of you too miserly (or perhaps too impoverished after paying the exorbitant cover price on the present volume) to buy a Christmas card for your neglected elderly parent this year, simply cut out the unfathomable absinthe-doodle by Mr. O'Neill below, and watch their slack, wrinkled faces animated by surprise, bafflement, genuine fear, and many other expressions that you had believed them long incapable of.

Ho ho ho! Merry Christmas!

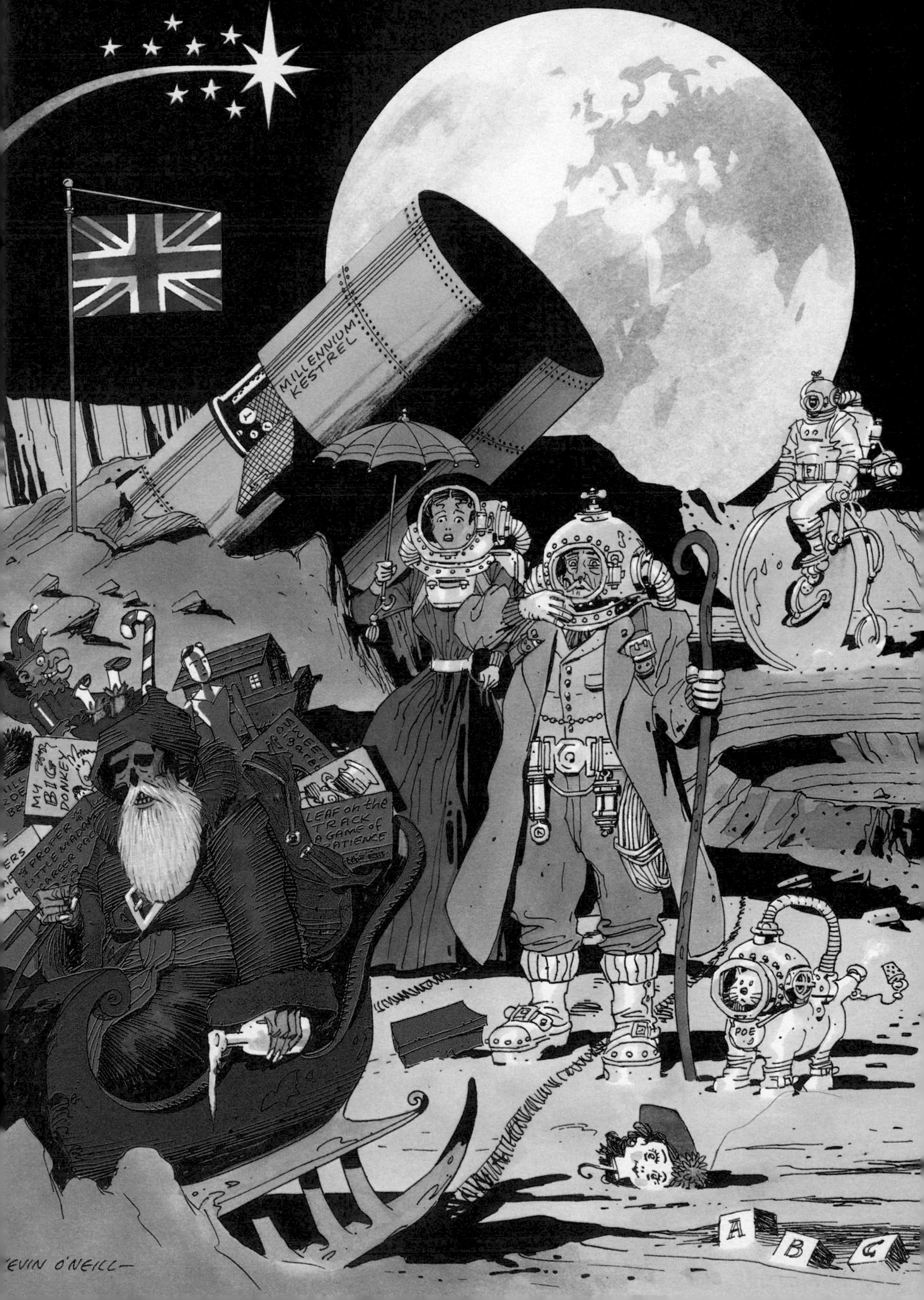
MILLENNIUM KESTREL
MY BIG DONKEY
LEAF on the TRACK A GAME of PATIENCE
POE
A
B
C
EVIN O'NEILL—

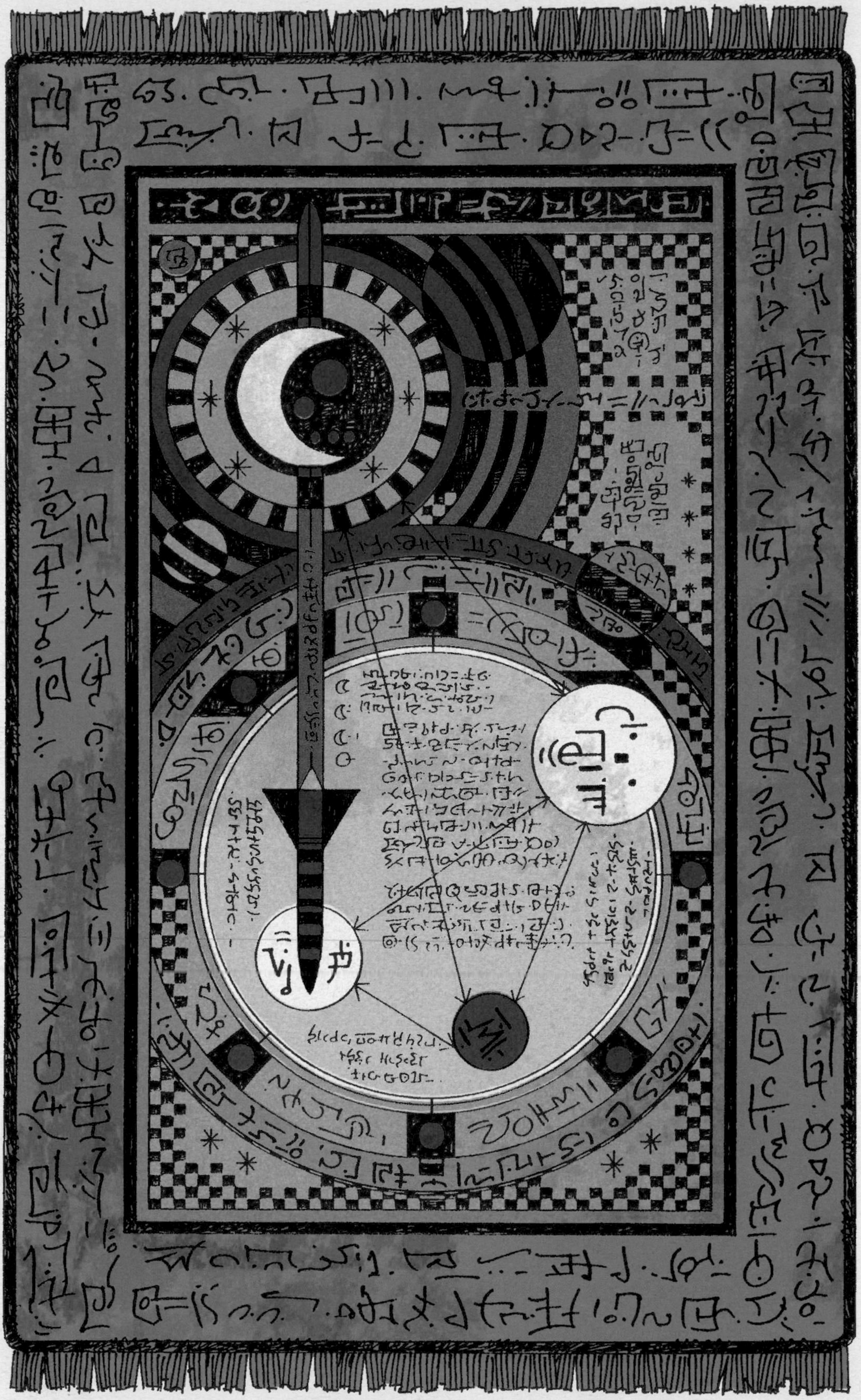